"Be prepared because most skeptical Bible scholars are seeking to feed your doubts not your faith" – Edward D. Andrews

EDWARD D. ANDREWS

THE NEW TESTAMENT DOCUMENTS

CAN THEY BE TRUSTED?

THE NEW TESTAMENT DOCUMENTS

Can They Be Trusted?

Edward D. Andrews

Christian Publishing House
Cambridge, Ohio

Copyright © 2020 Edward D. Andrews

All rights reserved. Except for brief quotations in articles, other publications, book reviews, and blogs, no part of this book may be reproduced in any manner without prior written permission from the publishers. For information, write, support@christianpublishers.org

Unless otherwise stated, Scripture quotations are from Updated American Standard Version (UASV) Copyright © 2022 by Christian Publishing House

THE NEW TESTAMENT DOCUMENTS: Can They Be Trusted? by Edward D. Andrews

- **ISBN-10** : 194958609X
- **ISBN-13** : 978-1949586091

Table of Contents

Book Description 16

Preface 17

Introduction 18

    The Scroll or Roll Book 22

    Indications of Universality 24

    The Making of a Codex 28

    The Craft of the Scribe 28

    Study of Ancient Handwriting 29

    Majuscule Hand 31

    Publishing Industry of the Ancient World 32

    Importance of Textual Criticism 38

    Distribution of Greek New Testament Manuscripts 38

    The Range of Textual Criticism 40

CHAPTER 2 The New Testament Secretaries and Their Materials 43

    Textual Criticism Defined 43

    Papyrus or Parchment? 47

CHAPTER 3 The Book Writing Process of the New Testament: Authors and Early Christian Scribes 53

    The Place of Writing 53

    The Scribe of the New Testament Writer 54

    Inspiration and Inerrancy in the Writing Process 60

    Chicago Statement on Biblical Inerrancy ICBI 60

    Inerrancy of Scripture 61

    Questions to Consider 64

    World-Renowned Bible Scholars Define Inspiration 64

    The Publishing, Copying, and Distributing Process 67

    Why Would the Holy Spirit Miraculously Inspire 66 Fully Inerrant Texts and Then Allow Variant Errors in the Copies? 73

    Distribution of Greek New Testament Manuscripts 75

    The Range of Textual Criticism 77

How did God inspire the Bible Authors? How Were They Moved Along by the Holy Spirit? How Did Jesus Bring Remembrance to the Apostles? 80

CHAPTER 4 The Formation of the New Testament: An Insight into the Process 85

    Understanding the Origins of the Greek New Testament Manuscripts 85

    Understanding Publication: From Ancient Times to Today 86

    The Original Documents 88

    Characteristics of the Original Manuscripts 92

    Handwriting Style of the Original Manuscripts 92

    Distinct Handwritings in the Original Manuscripts 94

    The Autographs Endings May Have Been Shorter 95

    No Inscriptions or Subscriptions 96

    The Presence of Nomina Sacra 96

    Handwriting of the Archetypes 96

    The Publishing of the Greek New Testament Books 97

    Dissemination of the Epistles, Revelation, and Acts 100

    The Multiplication of Manuscript Copies 101

    The Diverse Roles of Scribes in Biblical Times 102

    Scriptoria and Christian Writing Centers in the Early Church 106

    The Emergence of the Early Christian Codex 110

CHAPTER 5 Unveiling the Transmission of the Text: A Journey Through Time 118

    Introduction: The Importance of Textual Transmission 118

    From Oral Tradition to Written Word 120

    The Role of Scribes in Early Transmission 122

    Papyrus, Parchment, and Paper: The Materials of Transmission 123

    The Art of Copying: Understanding Ancient Scribal Practices 124

    The Septuagint and the Old Testament Transmission 125

    Early Christian Scribal Practices and New Testament Transmission 127

    Textual Variations: Causes and Implications 129

    The Emergence of Textual Families: Alexandrian, Western, Byzantine, and Caesarean 130

The Role of Patristic Citations in Textual Transmission 134
From Manuscript to Printed Text: The Gutenberg Revolution 136
Critical Texts and Their Influence: Textus Receptus, Westcott and Hort, and Others 137
Modern Textual Criticism: Methods and Goals 138
The Quest for the Original Text: Challenges and Advances 139
The Impact of Archaeology: the Chester Beatty Papyri and the Bodmer Papyri 141
The Future of Textual Transmission: Digital Age and Beyond 142

CHAPTER 6 The Formation of the Canon: Criteria and Controversies 144

Understanding the Concept of Canon 144
The Canon in Historical Context 145
Criteria for Canonization: The Factors Considered 147
The Apostolic Connection: A Primary Criterion 148
Orthodoxy and Antiquity: Criteria Based on Content and Age 148
The Role of Universality and Standardization in the Manuscripts of Early Christianity in Canon Formation 149
The Process of Canonization: A Gradual Formation 151
Key Figures and Councils in Canon Formation 152
The Muratorian Fragment: A Glimpse into Early Canon 153
Controversies and Disputes in Canon Formation 155
Apocryphal and Pseudepigraphal Writings: Books That Didn't Make the Cut 156
The Impact of Canon Formation on Christianity 157
The Canon Today: A Reflection on Its Relevance and Authority 158

CHAPTER 7 What Are Bible Difficulties and How Should We Approach Them? 160

Inerrancy: Can the Bible Be trusted? 165
Inerrancy: Practical Principles to Overcoming Bible Difficulties 169
Inerrancy: Are There Contradictions? 180
Inerrancy: Are There Mistakes? 185
Inerrancy: Are There Scientific Errors? 188
Procedures for Handling Biblical Difficulties 191

CHAPTER 8 The Jesus-Paul Connection: An Examination of Their Relationship 193

    Introduction: The Intriguing Question of Jesus-Paul Connection 193

    Jesus and Paul: A Brief Overview of Their Lives 194

    Paul's Conversion: The Road to Damascus Experience 195

    Paul's Understanding of Jesus: An Analysis of His Epistles 196

    The Influence of Jesus' Teachings on Paul's Writings 198

    Paul's Interpretation of Jesus' Death and Resurrection 199

    Jesus and Paul: Comparing Their Views on the Kingdom of God 200

    Jesus' Ethical Teachings and Paul's Moral Instructions 201

    The Role of the Holy Spirit in Jesus' and Paul's Teachings 202

    Jesus, Paul, and the Law: Similarities and Differences 203

    The Concept of Love in the Teachings of Jesus and Paul 204

    Christology: Paul's Perception of Jesus as the Christ 206

    Paul's Role in the Early Church: An Extension of Jesus' Mission 207

    Debates and Controversies Surrounding the Jesus-Paul Relationship 208

    Paul's Influence on Christianity: A Jesus-Paul Synergy 210

CHAPTER 9 Pauline Forgeries: Myth or Reality? 212

    The Epistle of Paul to the Ephesians 212

    The Epistle of Paul to the Colossians 215

    The Second Epistle of Paul to the Thessalonians 219

    The First Epistle of Paul to Timothy 222

    The Second Epistle of Paul to Timothy 226

    The Epistle of Paul to Titus 228

    The Epistle of Paul to the Hebrews 230

CHAPTER 10 Beyond the Canonical: A Look at Other Pseudo-Gospels 235

    Introduction: Exploring Beyond the Canonical Gospels 235

    The Emergence of Other Gospels: Historical Context 236

    The Gospel of Thomas: A False Collection of Jesus' Sayings 237

    The Gospel of Peter: An Apocryphal False Passion Narrative 238

    The Gospel of Mary: A Gnostic Text 239

The Infancy Gospels: False Narratives of Jesus' Early Life 240

Gnostic Gospels: An Overview and Their Influence 240

The Nag Hammadi Library: A Garbage Heap Trove of Gnostic Texts 241

The Dating and Authorship of Non-Canonical Gospels 242

Examining the Theological Differences: Orthodoxy vs Gnosticism 243

Assessing Historical Reliability: Canonical vs Non-Canonical Gospels 244

The Criteria for Canonicity: Why Four Gospels? 245

Answering Objections: Why Not More Gospels? 246

The Significance of the Canonical Gospels in Christian Faith 247

CHAPTER 11 Miracles in the New Testament: Fact or Fiction? 249

The Miracles—Did They Really Happen? 249

Why Some Do Not Believe 250

Is it a Violation of Natural Laws? 250

What About Counterfeit Miracles? 251

Miracles Are Not a Contemporary Occurrence 252

The Question of Veracity: Can We Be Certain? 252

The Most Evidenced Miracle 253

The Empty Tomb 253

The Verdict of Luke, the Doctor 254

Witnesses of the Resurrected Jesus 255

Miracles Really Happen 256

CHAPTER 12 Historical Corroborations of the New Testament: Unveiling the Evidence 258

Introduction: The Importance of Historical Corroboration 258

The New Testament and Its Historical Context 259

Historical Evidence from Within the New Testament 261

The Role of Archaeology in Corroborating the New Testament 262

Corroborations from Ancient Manuscripts and Inscriptions 263

The Witness of Ancient Historians: Christianity's First to Third Centuries Non-Christian Witnesses for the Historicity of Jesus Christ 264

The New Testament and Jewish Sources: The Talmud and Midrash 271

The Crucifixion of Jesus: Historical Evidence 272

Corroborations for the Apostolic Actions and Early Christian Persecution.273

Paul and His Missionary Journeys: Archaeological and Historical Evidence 274

Geographical and Topographical Accuracy in the New Testament 275

Linguistic and Cultural Consistencies in the New Testament..........................276

The Historicity of Jesus: A Case Study in New Testament Corroboration ...277

The Resurrection of Jesus: Examining the Historical Evidence......................278

The Historical Reliability of Acts: A Case Study 279

Objections and Responses: Addressing Skeptical Claims................................279

Conclusion: The Trustworthiness of the New Testament in Light of Historical Evidence 281

CHAPTER 13 Assessing the Trustworthiness of the New Testament: A Balanced Evaluation 282

Introduction: The Quest for Trustworthiness 282

Understanding the Nature of the New Testament Documents 283

The Importance of Authorship: Apostolic Connections and Early Dates 284

Historical Accuracy: Corroborations and Consistencies..................................285

The Transmission of the New Testament Texts: Fidelity Over Centuries....286

The Canon of the New Testament: Criteria and Formation...........................286

Assessing Alleged Contradictions: Contextual Interpretation and Harmonization..293

The Jesus of the Gospels: Consistency of Character and Message 295

Pauline Authorship: Responding to Claims of Forgeries.................................296

The Role of Miracles: Supernatural Events within a Historical Framework.297

The Resurrection: The Foundation of New Testament Reliability.................301

The New Testament and Archaeology: Unearthing Historical Support 302

Non-Canonical Gospels: Understanding Their Place and Purpose................303

The Impact of the New Testament: Its Transformative Power as Evidence 304

The Testimony of Early Church Fathers: Affirmation of New Testament Texts 305

Dealing with Difficult Passages: Trustworthiness Amidst Complexity..........306

Responding to Modern Criticisms: An Apologetic Approach........................307

Conclusion: The Trustworthiness of the New Testament—A Balanced Evaluation..308

CHAPTER 14 Overcoming Modern Skepticism: A Response to Contemporary Challenges 310

Introduction: The Rise of Modern Skepticism 310

Identifying the Common Objections: A Catalogue of Contemporary Challenges 311

The Problem of Miracles: Responding to Philosophical Naturalism 312

Alleged Contradictions: A Closer Look at the Text 313

Questioning the Historical Jesus: An Apologetic Response 314

The Trustworthiness of the Gospels: Overcoming the Myth Theory 315

The Resurrection: Addressing Skepticism About the Central Event 316

The Reliability of Paul's Letters: Countering Claims of Pseudepigraphy 317

The Formation of the Canon: Responding to Claims of Arbitrary Selection 318

Non-Canonical Gospels: Why They Don't Threaten the Canonical Four 319

The Role of the Early Church: Countering the Conspiracy Theory 321

The Challenge of Science and Faith: Compatibility, Not Conflict 322

The Problem of Evil: A Christian Response 323

Ethical Objections: Slavery, Women's Roles, and Homosexuality in the New Testament 324

The Exclusivity of Salvation: Responding to Religious Pluralism 327

Biblical Prophecy: An Antidote to Skepticism 327

The Power of Testimony: Personal Experiences and the Case for Faith 328

Equipping for Engagement: Tools for Effective Apologetics 329

CHAPTER 15 The New Testament and Archaeology: Digging into Historical Context 331

Introduction: The Interplay of Archaeology and the New Testament 331

The Nature and Role of Biblical Archaeology 332

Archaeological Evidence for New Testament Cities: Jerusalem, Capernaum, and More 333

The World of Jesus: Archaeology and the Gospels 334

Archaeological Insights into the Life and Times of Jesus 335

Pontius Pilate and the Trial of Jesus: Archaeological Corroboration 336

The Crucifixion and the Tomb of Jesus: Archaeology and the Easter Story 337

The Book of Acts in the Light of Archaeology 338

Unearthing Evidence for Paul's Missionary Journeys 339

The Seven Churches of Revelation: What Archaeology Reveals 341

Archaeology and the Persecution of the Early Church 342

Archaeological Discoveries and the Reliability of New Testament Texts 343

Responding to Skepticism: Archaeology as an Apologetic Tool 345

The Limits and Strengths of Archaeology in New Testament Study 346

Archaeology, Faith, and the New Testament: An Integrated Approach 347

CHAPTER 16 New Testament Textual Criticism: The Quest for the Original Text 349

Introduction: The Purpose and Importance of Textual Criticism 349

The Transmission of the New Testament Text: From Original to Copies ...350

Understanding the Manuscript Evidence: Papyri, Uncials, Minuscules, and Lectionaries 352

The Multitude of Manuscripts: An Embarrassment of Riches 353

The Early Translations and the Church Fathers: Additional Witnesses to the Text 354

The Variants in the Text: Nature, Types, and Significance 355

The Science and Art of Textual Criticism: Principles and Methods 360

Major Textual Issues in the New Testament: Case Studies 361

The Role of Conjectural Emendation in Textual Criticism 362

Addressing Allegations of Corruption and Conspiracy 363

The Reliability of the Text: Comparisons with Other Ancient Documents .. 363

The Implications of Textual Variants for Doctrinal Integrity 364

Textual Criticism and Bible Translation: An Interconnected Process 365

Modern Developments in Textual Criticism: The Role of Technology 367

Responding to Skepticism about Textual Integrity 368

CHAPTER 17 Understanding the New Testament Authors: Their Lives and Times 370

Introduction: Unraveling the Lives Behind the Words 370

The Apostles: Witnesses to the Life of Jesus 371

Matthew: A Tax Collector Turned Gospel Writer 373

Mark: The Interpreter of Peter 373

Luke: The Physician and Detailed Historian and Companion of Paul 375

John: The Beloved Disciple and His Unique Perspective 376

Paul: From Persecutor to Proclaimer of the Gospel and Author of Fourteen Letters 377

James: The Brother of Jesus and Leader of the Jerusalem Church 378

Peter: Passionate Fisherman Turned Apostle 379

Jude: A Servant of Jesus Christ and Brother of James 380

The Social, Political, and Religious Context of the New Testament Authors 381

The Writings of the New Testament That Touched on Jewish and Greco-Roman Culture 382

Understanding the Language, Genre, and Style of the New Testament Authors 383

Responding to Claims of Pseudonymity and Forgery in New Testament Writings 384

Conclusion: The New Testament Authors and the Message They Proclaimed 385

CHAPTER 18 The New Testament's Impact: How Trustworthy Texts Shaped History 386

Introduction: The New Testament's Profound Influence on History 386

The Early Church: The Formation and Growth of Christianity 387

The Persecution of Christians and the Triumph of the Faith 388

The Development of Christian Doctrine: Creeds, Councils, and Controversies 389

The Role of the New Testament in Shaping Christian Worship and Liturgy 389

The New Testament's Impact on Art, Architecture, and Music 390

The Bible and the Founding of Educational Institutions: From Monasteries to Universities 391

The New Testament and the Moral Transformation of Society 392

The Reformation: Sola Scriptura and the Return to the New Testament 393

The Missionary Movement: Taking the Gospel to the Ends of the Earth 394

The New Testament's Influence on Social Reforms and Human Rights Movements 395

The Role of the New Testament in Shaping Political Thought and Government 396

The New Testament and the Development of Modern Science 397

The New Testament's Impact on Language, Literature, and Popular Culture 398

Responding to Criticisms and Misconceptions about the New Testament's Influence 399

Conclusion: The Trustworthiness of the New Testament and Its Lasting Legacy 400

APPENDIX A What Are Textual Variants and How Many Are There? . 401

Miscounting Textual Variants 404

Variant Reading and Variation Unit 409

Number of Variants, Significant and Insignificant Variants vs. Level of Certainty 411

Level of Certainty 411

The Certainty of the Original Words of the Original Authors 419

APPENDIX B Papyrus 52 (P52) - A Small Fragment of John 18:31–33, 18:37–38, Dating from Around 100-150 CE 423

APPENDIX C Papyrus 66 (P66) - A Manuscript of John 1:1–6:11, 6:35b–14:26, 29–30; 15:2–26; 16:2–4, 6–7; 16:10–20:20, 22–23; 20:25–21:9, 12, 17, Dating from Around 100-150 CE 432

APPENDIX D v Papyrus 75 (P75) - A Manuscript of Luke 3:18–24:53; John 1–15, Dating from Around 175-225 CE 434

APPENDIX E Papyrus 104 (P104) - A Manuscript of Matt. 21:34–37, 43, 45(?), Dating from Around 100-150 CE 436

APPENDIX F Papyrus 45 (P45) - A Manuscript of the Gospels and Acts, Dating from Around 175-225 CE 438

APPENDIX G Papyrus 90 (P90) - A Manuscript of John 18:36–19:7, Dating from Around 100-150 CE 440

APPENDIX H Papyrus 115 (P115) - A Manuscript of Rev. 2-3; 5-6; 8-15; Dating from Around 225-275 CE 442

APPENDIX I Papyrus 46 (P46) - A Manuscript of the Pauline Epistles, Dating from Around 100-150 CE 444

APPENDIX J Papyrus 47 (P47) - A Manuscript of Revelation 9:10-17:2, Dating from Around 200-225 CE 446

APPENDIX K Papyrus 72 (P72) - A Manuscript of Jude, 1 Peter, 2 Peter, Dating from Around 200-250 CE 448

APPENDIX L Papyrus 137 (P137) The Earliest Fragment of Mark 1:7-9; 1:16-18, Dating from Around 100-125 CE 450

APPENDIX M Codex Vaticanus (B or 03): Dating from 300-330 CE ... 452

APPENDIX N Codex Sinaiticus (ℵ or 01): Dating from 330-360 CE..... 454

APPENDIX P Codex Alexandrinus (A or 02): A 5th-century manuscript 456

APPENDIX P Codex Ephraemi Rescriptus (C or 04): A 5th-century Greek manuscript of the Bible 458

APPENDIX Q Codex Bezae (D or 05): A 5th-century manuscript containing most of the four Gospels and Acts, and a small part of III John in Greek and Latin texts 460

APPENDIX R Codex Washingtonianus (W or 032): A 4th or 5th-century manuscript of the Gospels 462

APPENDIX T Codex Claromontanus (D or 06): A 5th or 6th-century Greek and Latin diglot manuscript of the Pauline Epistles 464

APPENDIX U Codex Basilensis (E or 07): A 8th-century Greek manuscript of the Gospels 466

APPENDIX V Codex Seidelianus I (H or 013): A 9th-century Greek uncial manuscript containing the text of the four Gospels...................................... 468

APPENDIX W Codex Regius (L or 019): An 8th-century uncial manuscript containing the text of the four Gospels 470

Bibliography 472

Edward D. Andrews

Book Description

In an era where skepticism towards religious texts is on the rise, "The New Testament Documents: Can They Be Trusted?" offers a comprehensive and thoughtful examination of the credibility of the New Testament. Edward D. Andrews, drawing on years of meticulous research, tackles the major objections to the historicity of these foundational Christian texts in one detailed volume.

The book embarks on a journey, starting with the formation of the Gospels, exploring the process and people involved. It delves into the transmission of the text, illustrating how these sacred writings have been preserved over centuries. The exploration continues with an investigation into the formation of the canon and a thorough analysis of alleged contradictions.

Andrews presents an insightful examination of the intricate relationship between Jesus and Paul and addresses the contentious issue of supposed Pauline forgeries. He also provides a balanced look at other Gospels that have come to light over time. The book does not shy away from the topic of miracles, offering a rational and scholarly perspective on these supernatural events as presented in the New Testament.

Throughout the book, Andrews underscores his analysis with historical corroborations from all parts of the New Testament. The reader is presented with a wealth of evidence supporting the credibility of these ancient documents.

"The New Testament Documents: Can They Be Trusted?" utilizes the latest scholarship to respond to New Testament objections yet remains accessible to non-specialists. This book serves as a robust resource for anyone seeking to deepen their understanding of the New Testament and its reliability. Whether you're a scholar, a student, a Christian seeking to fortify your faith, or a skeptic searching for answers, this book offers a well-reasoned, informative, and engaging exploration of the trustworthiness of the New Testament documents.

Preface

The New Testament stands at the heart of Christianity, its messages forming the bedrock of Christian faith and practice. The writings it encompasses have been revered, studied, and debated for centuries. Yet, in our modern era, questions about its reliability and historicity are increasingly raised, not only within scholarly circles but also in popular media. These questions, these doubts, are what led me to write "The New Testament Documents: Can They Be Trusted?"

In my decades of research, I have seen the need for a comprehensive, accessible work that addresses the objections raised against the New Testament. A work that neither dismisses the skeptics outright nor glosses over the complexities inherent in studying ancient texts. This book is my response to that need.

We begin our exploration with the formation of the Gospels, delving into the process and people behind these foundational documents. We then journey through time, tracing the transmission of the text and scrutinizing the process of canon formation. Every alleged contradiction is examined, and contentious issues, such as the relationship between Jesus and Paul and the claims of Pauline forgeries, are addressed head-on.

We step beyond the boundaries of the canonical to look at other gospels that have emerged over the years. We also delve into the supernatural - the miracles as recorded in the New Testament, considering their credibility and significance.

Throughout the book, I have drawn on historical corroborations to provide additional evidence supporting the reliability of the New Testament. I firmly believe that when we approach these texts with both open minds and critical thinking, we find a wealth of evidence affirming their trustworthiness.

This book is not merely an academic exercise. It is a journey of discovery, a quest for truth, and an invitation to engage with the New Testament in a deeper and more informed manner. Whether you are a believer, a skeptic, a scholar, or a curious reader, I hope that this book will encourage thoughtful reflection, foster understanding, and perhaps even ignite a renewed appreciation for the rich and complex tapestry that is the New Testament.

Welcome to "The New Testament Documents: Can They Be Trusted?" Let's embark on this journey together.

Edward D. Andrews

Chief Translator of the Updated American Standard Version

Edward D. Andrews

Introduction

At the intersection of faith, history, and scholarship lies the New Testament, a collection of writings that has not only shaped religious beliefs for centuries but has also left an indelible imprint on the course of human history. The reliability of these documents, however, is not universally accepted, with critics pointing to a variety of factors that they believe undermine the credibility of these texts.

In "The New Testament Documents: Can They Be Trusted?", we delve into these criticisms head-on, not to dismiss them outright, but to engage with them in a thoughtful, systematic manner. Our quest is not to win an argument, but to seek understanding, to shed light on the questions that have been raised, and to explore the richness of the New Testament from a perspective grounded in extensive research.

This book is organized in a way that invites you to journey with me, starting from the origins of the Gospels, the transmission of texts, and the formation of the canon. We will examine alleged contradictions, explore the relationship between Jesus and Paul, and investigate the claims about supposed Pauline forgeries. The narrative expands beyond the canonical to consider other gospels, and we will also grapple with the supernatural, examining the miracles described in the New Testament.

Each chapter builds on the previous ones, deepening our understanding and providing an increasingly nuanced view of the New Testament. As we journey together, we will draw on historical corroborations that provide additional insights into the text, its context, and its reliability.

This book is for everyone who has ever wondered about the New Testament. For the believers who want to deepen their understanding of these sacred texts. For the skeptics who question their reliability. For the scholars who dedicate their lives to these ancient texts. And for the curious readers who are simply interested in learning more about the New Testament.

So, whether you are a seasoned scholar, a student of theology, a skeptic seeking answers, or a curious reader interested in the New Testament, I invite you to join me on this journey of exploration and discovery. Together, let's seek to answer the question: Can the New Testament Documents Be Trusted?

Let the journey begin.

CHAPTER 1 The Making of New Testament Books

As Luke, Paul, Peter, Matthew, James, or Jude handed their authorized text off to be copied by others, i.e., published, what would it have looked like? What is the process that the New Testament writers would have followed to get their book ready to be published, copied by others? Once they were prepared for publication, how would they be copied throughout the centuries, up until the time of the printing press of 1455 C.E.?[1] As we open our Bible to the Gospel of Matthew, or the letter to the Romans, or any of the 27 books of the New Testament, how can we have confidence that what we are reading is a reflection of the original in our language? If we were to bring home from a bookstore a copy of the KJV, ASV, RSV, ESV, CSB, LEB, NASB, NLT, NIV, NRSV, UASV, or any of the other one hundred and fifty plus English translations, could we have confidence that what we are reading is, in fact, the Word of God? Some translations have footnotes throughout that say, "Other ancient MSS[2] read …. What exactly does that mean, and which is the Word of God: the words in the main text of our Bible, or the others below in the footnote?

The science and art of textual criticism have answered these questions and more. It is a science because there are rules and principles and a method or process that is to be followed if the textual scholar is to get back to the original reading.[3] It is an art because the human agent needs to be balanced with those rules and principles. It is

---

[1] B.C.E. means "before the Common Era," which is more accurate than B.C. ("before Christ"). C.E. denotes "Common Era," often called A.D., for *anno Domini,* meaning "in the year of our Lord."

[2] Manuscripts, MS would be singular manuscript, while MSS will refer to more than one.

[3] When we use the term "original" reading or "original" text in this publication, it is a reference to the exemplar manuscript by the New Testament author (e.g. Paul) and his secretary, if he used one (e.g. Tertius), from which other copies were made for publication and distribution to the Christian communities.

like driving a car. The driver needs to follow all driving rules as he stays between the lines of his side of the road to reach his destination. So too, the textual scholar needs to stay within the rules to reach his destination of establishing the original words of the original texts. However, the designers of the roads were not rigid to the point of making those two lines so narrow that there was no room for the driver to miss obstructions, which might be in his path. This extra room would help the driver to avoid objects that could result in a crash. The same holds true for the textual scholar having room within the lines of his field to prevent a wreck, causing him not to reach his desired destination, i.e., the original reading.

From ancient times until 1455 C.E., anything that was authored was done literally, by hand. A "manuscript" is a handwritten text. It did not matter if it were a poem, letter, receipt, book, or marriage certificate; it would still have been produced and copied by hand. In addition, it would mostly have been done one copy at a time in the early decades of Christianity. In the second century C.E., it may have been copied in a scriptorium, i.e., a room in a monastery for storing, copying, illustrating, or reading manuscripts. In the scriptorium, there would have been a lector (reader) who would have read aloud slowly as multiple scribes or copyists took down what he was saying.

The modern-day young person is far removed from the 1920s to the 1980s where people actually used physical paper, pens, pencils, and envelopes to write letters. The same material was used for homework in school. Today, everything is digital: Microsoft Word Docx, PDFs, laptops, tablets, social media, and smartphones. A twenty-year-old today would likely find it challenging to write a letter with merely pen and paper. He would find it tedious and physically taxing. His lack of practice in writing would make it more difficult to be proficient in making the letters, and it would not be aesthetically pleasing. The hand, wrist, and forearm would get very tired to the point where he would need to take a break.

In early Christianity, manually copying a Bible text would be far more arduous than what was just described. There would be many different physical and mental tasks involved in the process of Tertius copying the book of Romans as the apostle Paul dictated to him, which would have been laborious and strenuous. The same would be even more true of the copyists who would then use Romans' original copy to make other copies. He would not have had the luxury of having the words dictated, and he would have to look at the exemplar back and forth thousands of times as he made his copy that contained 7,000+ words. Imagine if he were copying the entire Greek New Testament of 138,162 words.

Additionally, far more was involved than simply reading the exemplar and writing a word or phrase in the copy. The material that was being written on was papyrus or parchment. Papyrus was a material prepared in ancient Egypt from the pithy stem of a water plant, used in sheets throughout the ancient Mediterranean world for writing. Parchment was a stiff, flat, thin material made from the prepared skin of an animal and used as a durable writing surface in ancient and medieval times. More on this later.

When the materials used and the working environment are understood, we will fully appreciate why ancient people hired secretaries (scribes). The scribe would lay out a layer of strips that he had cut from the papyrus plant. The pithy juices of the plant would be put in the strips. Another layer would have been placed at right angles over top of the first layer. Something flat and heavy would be placed on the papyrus sheet so the two could be bonded by pressure, which would have produced what we would consider a sheet of papyrus paper. It was no easy task writing on the surface of this papyrus sheet, as the material was rough and fibrous.

The scribe could be seen sitting on the ground with his legs crossed, a board laying over his knees. He would be hunched over, holding the exemplar sheet of papyrus with the fingers of, say, his left hand and his thumb of the same hand resting on the papyrus sheet he was using to make his copy. Or, if a professional scribe, he would pin his sheets of papyrus down. To the other corner of the board would be a small container of ink that he had personally made from a mixture of soot and gum. If this scribe were not experienced at making documents, or he was using below-average level materials, his calamus, or reed pen, could very well snag and tear the papyrus, or the writing could be unreadable. To the right of this scribe, we would see a sharp knife, which would have been used to sharpen his reed pen, and a damp sponge that would be used to erase any errors he might make. Since he is copying a New Testament book, he would likely be doing his level best to write every letter with the greatest of care, meaning he would be writing slowly, all of this bringing with it some difficulty. Imagine the constant sharpening of his pen with his knife and the continuous replenishing it with ink to keep the strokes even.

Working as a scribe or copyist for long hours each day can cause back, neck, and shoulder pains, headache, eyestrain, and overuse injuries of the arms and hands. When the scribe constantly bends his head forward, the muscles in his neck, chest, and **back become almost stiffened in that position**, giving him rounded shoulders and making it more challenging for him to stand upright. Bad posture from the life of a copyist can lead to bad balance. The average human head weighs almost 12 pounds (5.44 kg). This is equal to a bowling ball! When the copyist has his neck bent to 45 degrees, his head exerts nearly 50 pounds (ca. 23 kg) of force on his neck. The weight and pressure affect his breathing and mood, aside from straining joints and muscles in his neck and shoulders.

As we can mentally picture, this scribe was carrying out many simultaneous tedious tasks as he went about copying a book of the New Testament. If he had some experience or a professional in making documents and copying literature, he would have had to consider the page before him to calculate the proper word division. He would be using stichoi notations at the end of the copying process, that is, notes on how many lines were copied to get paid, which means that he had to keep track of his lines. The scribe would always have to be conscious of an imaginary upper and lower line that he sought to keep his text between. Unlike our notebooks today, papyrus and parchment sheets did not come with ruled lines. The scribe would use an unsharpened instrument to draw 25-30 pressure lines on his page to receive the text. Before he even began the above, he would have to have the ability to estimate just how many sheets would be needed for the project. This would change if he were making a copy of an individual gospel or a codex of all four gospels, or the gospels and Acts, or a copy of Paul's epistles, or even one of Paul's epistles such as Romans. He would have to determine how he would construct the codex: was it to be one gather or multiple gathers. If it were multiple gatherings, how many sheets would he need in each gathering? To estimate these things, he would have to determine the size of the letters, how many letters to a line, how big were the margins. These are just some fundamental difficulties involved as early scribes made copies of our New Testament books.

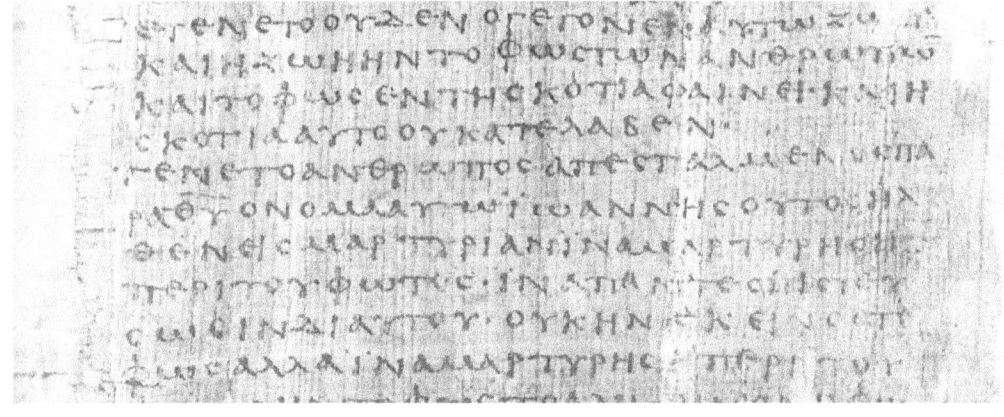

One of the Earliest New Testament Manuscripts: P[66] Papyrus

The Scroll or Roll Book

A scroll is a roll of papyrus, parchment, or other material, used for a written document. Even though it was continuous, the scroll was generally divided into pages by gluing separate sheets at the edges. Usually, the reader or lector and the writer unrolled the scroll one page at a time, leaving it rolled up on both sides of the current page that was showing. The scroll is unrolled from side to side, with the text being written or read, from top to bottom. For example, if it were Hebrew, it would be written from right to left, and one would open that scroll by rolling to the right. On the other hand, if it were Greek, it would be written from left to right, or even in an alternating direction with other languages. Boustrophedon is an ancient method of inscribing and writing in which lines are written alternately from right to left and from left to right. Usually, professional scribes would justify both sides of the pages, aligned with both left and right margins. On the papyrus scroll, Harold Greenlee writes,

> Papyrus scrolls are mentioned several times in the New Testament; references are usually translated as "book." Luke 4:17 speaks of the scroll (*biblion*) of the prophet Isaiah. John uses the same word to refer to his gospel in John 20:30. The "books" or "scrolls" mentioned in 2 Tim 4:13 may be either parchment scrolls or leather scrolls of the Old Testament. Rev 6:14 describes the sky as vanishing like "a scroll when it is rolled up."[4]

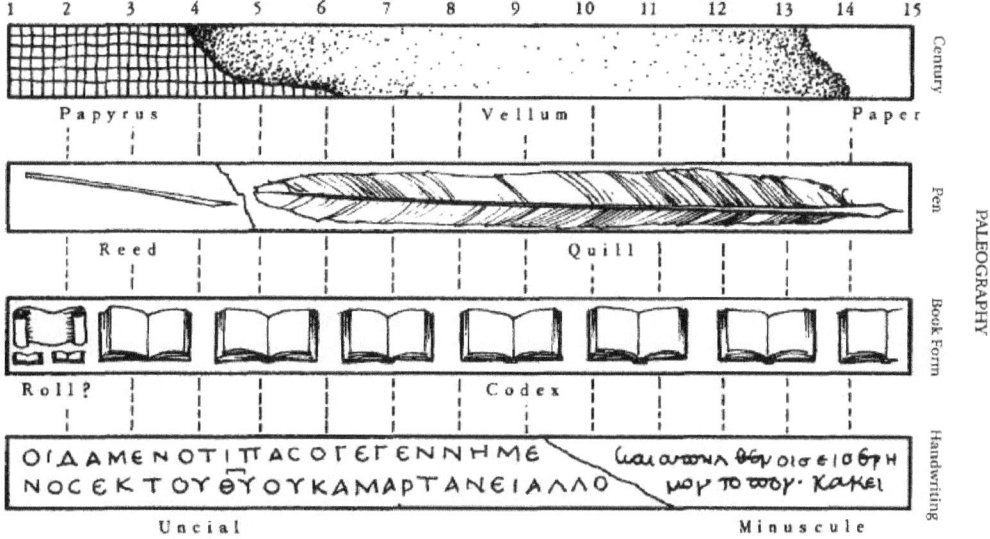

Harold Greenlee, Introduction to New Testament Textual Criticism, (p. 23)

The parchment scroll used by Moses to pen the first five books of the Old Testament; goes back to about the late sixteenth-century B.C.E. The scroll was the first form to receive writing, which was in a format that could be edited by the author or scribe and was used in the Eastern Mediterranean ancient Egyptian civilizations. The codex (bound book) got its start from Latin authors in the first-century C.E. (widely used in the second-century), some 1,500 years after the scroll. The early Christians popularized the codex in the second-century C.E. Some would even argue that the Christians invented it. However, it appears that Christians mainly began using the roll, or scroll, at least until about the end of the first century C.E. Nevertheless, from the close of the first to the third century C.E., there was a struggle between those who encouraged the use of the codex and those preferring scrolls. Traditionalists, familiar and comfortable with using the scroll, were unwilling to give up deep-rooted conventions and traditions. Nevertheless, the popularization of the codex played a

---

[4] J. Harold Greenlee, *Text of the New Testament, From the Manuscript to Modern Edition* (Grand Rapids, MI: Baker Publishing, 2008), 13-14.

significant role in the displacement of the scroll. Therefore, the scroll continued to be used for centuries.

Scrolls were used for literary works. Continuous rolls were twenty or thirty feet long and nine to ten inches high. (Psa. 40:7) The text was written in columns, which formed the pages. (Jer. 36:23) Our English word "volume" literally means *something rolled up*. Imagine being in the synagogue of Nazareth when Jesus was handed the scroll of the prophet Isaiah, where he skillfully unrolled with one hand while simultaneously rolling it up with the other hand until he reached the place he wanted to read. (Lu 4:16-17; Isa. 61:1-2) The ink used on the surface of the scrolls had to withstand being rolled and unrolled, so special ink was developed. In addition, the Jews would discard any scroll that had too many letters missing from wear and tear. It was not until about the fifth-century C.E. that the codex finally outnumbered the scroll by a ten to one margin in Egypt. When we consider the surviving examples, we also see that the scroll had almost vanished by the sixth-century C.E.

The Codex Book

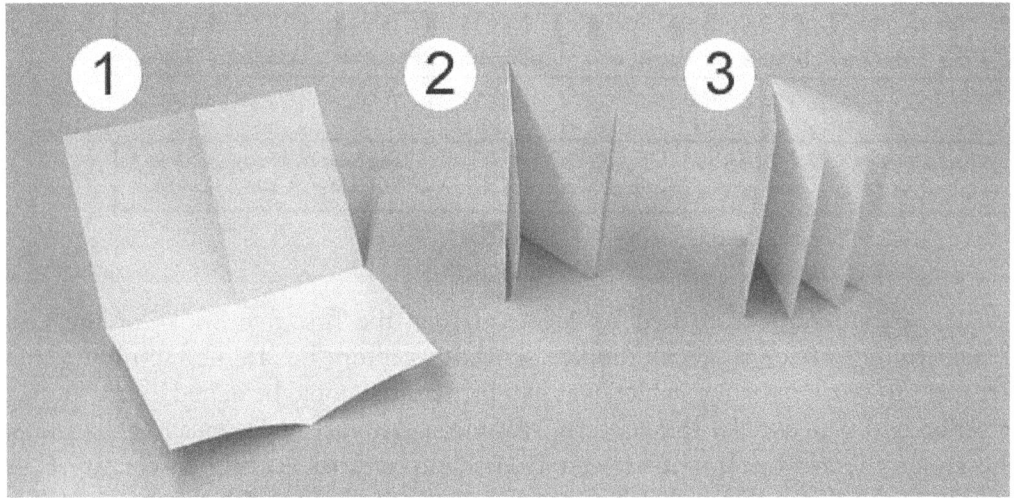

A typical four-leaf quire can be formed from a single sheet of papyrus, parchment, or paper by folding and then cutting the sheet

A codex is a collection of ancient manuscript texts, especially of the Biblical Scriptures, in book form.[5] It is made up of papyrus sheets or parchment inscribed with handwritten material, which is created by folding a single sheet of standard-sized pages, giving the scribe two leaves or four pages.

Indications of Universality

- All of the early papyrus was **in codex (book) form.** (125-400 C.E.)

---

[5] Late 16th century: < Latin, "block of wood, book, set of statutes"

- The standardization of **the nominal sacra (sacred names)** very early on: God Θεός ΘΣ; Lord Κύριος ΚΣ; Jesus Ἰησοῦς ΙΣ; Christ Χριστός ΧΣ; Spirit Πνεῦμα ΠΝΑ, being in a contracted format and with a horizontal line above the letters. Eventually, it would be 15 sacred names. The following second-century manuscripts that clearly show these nomina sacra are as follows: vP4+P64+P67 dates to (150-175 C.E.), P32 dates to (150-200 C.E.), P46 dates to 150 C.E.), P66 dates to about (150 C.E.), P75 dates to about (175 C.E.), and P90 dates to (150-200 C.E.). This means that the nomina sacra for Lord, Jesus, Christ, God, and Spirit are standard by 150 C.E.
- Initially, there were some inconsistencies in the application, but universally it was soon decided to use the nomina sacra regardless of whether the referent, meaning, or context was mundane or sacred in its use.
- By the late first century, New Testament books were being collected in codex form: the Gospels or the Gospels and Acts. The early second century saw the collection of the apostle Paul's letters, which included Hebrews.
- There was the standardization of the codex size for the Gospels, like our 8.5 x 11 inches today. The standard size in the second/third centuries was 11.5-14 cm (4.5-5.5 inches) **Width** x 14.5-17 cm (5.7-6.7) **Length**. A new standard size began to develop in the third century. Just the fact that they had a standard size for the Gospels is unusual because this is not the case for Paul's letter or any other books.

The first codices were made with waxed-coated wooden tablets. The people of Greece and Rome used waxed tablets before the Christian era. Schoolboys were sometimes given waxed tablets on which the teacher had written letters in model script with a stylus. Today, we have the blackboard (UK) or chalkboard (US), initially made of smooth, thin sheets of black or dark gray slate stone. In the early part of the 20th century, schoolchildren even had smaller slate tablets. They had a reusable writing surface on which text or drawings could be made with sticks of calcium carbonate, i.e., chalk.

Roman wax tablet and stylus

To make the waxed tablets of Jesus' day, one would slightly hollow out a flat piece of wood and fill that void with wax. These tablets were also used for temporary writing like modern chalkboards. They were also commonly used for corresponding with others. Greenlee writes, "They were also used at times for legal documents, in which case two tablets would be placed face to face with the writing inside and fastened together with leather thongs run through holes at the edges of the tablets. In one of his writings, St. Augustine mentions some tablets he owned, although his were made of ivory instead of wood."⁶ An example of temporary (short-term, momentary) writing is found in the Gospel of his ability to speak, was asked what name he wanted his son to have. Luke 1:63 reports, "And he asked for a writing tablet and wrote, 'His name is John.'"

Polyptychs [**pol·yp·tych** ˈpälipˌtik] is an arrangement of three or more panels with a painting or carving on each, usually hinged together. Some were discovered at Herculaneum, an ancient Roman town near modern Naples that was destroyed along with Pompeii by the eruption of Mount Vesuvius in 79 C.E.

In time, sheets of foldable material replaced rigid tablets. The codex has been viewed as the most significant advancement in the development of the book, aside from the printing press.⁷ Some of the earliest surviving codices were made of papyrus, being preserved in the dry sands of Egypt.

When we consider the thought of unrolling and using a scroll instead of the codex, we can likely think of many advantages of one over the other. The codex can contain far more written material; it is much easier to carry and more convenient. Some in the early days of the codex even mentioned these advantages. Nevertheless, some were slow to move away from the scroll's prolonged use. Again, the Christians played a significant part in the eventual death of the scroll. Their evangelism would have been far more cumbersome without the codex.

The Codex Gigas, 13th century, Bohemia.

---

⁶ J. Harold Greenlee, *Introduction to New Testament Textual Criticism* (Grand Rapids, MI: Baker Academic, 1995), 8-9.

⁷ Colin H. Roberts; T. C. Skeat, *The Birth of the Codex*, (London, Oxford University Press, 1983), 1.

Compared to the scroll, the codex was also far more affordable because both sides of the pages could be written on, getting more value for one's money. Moreover, instead of having one book with each scroll, one could have the whole of the old or New Testament. The fact that one could find Bible passages far more accessible and faster, this, too, added to the codex's success. This preference for the codex was not only true for Christians but also lawyers and the like. When we think of the early Christians, we are reminded that they evangelized to the point of going from 120 disciples in the upper room on Pentecost 33 C.E. to more than one million Christians spread throughout the Roman Empire at the beginning of the second century C.E. In addition, early Christians were evangelists, who used pre-evangelism, i.e., apologetics. They could have what we now call proof texts, easily located, to make their arguments to pagans and Jews alike. Then, the fact that the codex book had a wooden cover made it more durable than the scroll, adding to its advantages. Codices were useful, sensible, and likely practical for personal reading. The Christians of the third century C.E. had parchment pocket Gospels.

Larry Hurtado, in his blog (*The Codex and Early Christians: Clarification & Corrections*), writes,

> Bagnall offered figures (pp. 72-74) comparing the number of non-Christian and Christian codices from Egypt datable to the early centuries, also giving the percentages of Christian codices of the total. His own data show, e.g., that Christian codices amount to somewhere between 22-34% of the total for the 2nd-3rd centuries CE. Yet Christian books overall amount to only ca. 2% of the total number of books (codices and rolls) of these centuries. Of course, there are more non-Christian codices, but the first point to note is that Christian codices comprise a vastly disproportionate percentage of the total number of codices in this period.
>
> The very data provided by Bagnall clearly show that Christians invested in the codex far more than is reflected in the larger book-culture of the time. That is, the early Christian *preference* for the codex is undeniable, and this preference is quite distinctive in that period. Bagnall actually reached the same judgment, stating, "Christian books in these centuries ($2^{nd}/3^{rd}$) are far more likely to be codices than rolls, quite the reverse of what we find with classical literature." (p. 74)
>
> My second point also stands and is supported by Bagnall: the early Christian preference for the codex seems to have been especially keen when it came to making copies of texts used as scripture (i.e., read in corporate worship). For example, 95+% of Christian copies of OT writings are in codex form. As for the writings that came to form the NT, they're all in codex form except for a very few instances of NT writings copied on the back of a re-used roll (which were likely informal and personal copies made by/for readers who couldn't afford a copy on unused writing material). Here

again, Bagnall grants the same conclusion, judging that, although they were ready to copy "the Christians adopted the codex as the normative format of deliberately produced public copies of scriptural texts" (p. 78), but were ready to use rolls for other texts (76).[8]

The Making of a Codex

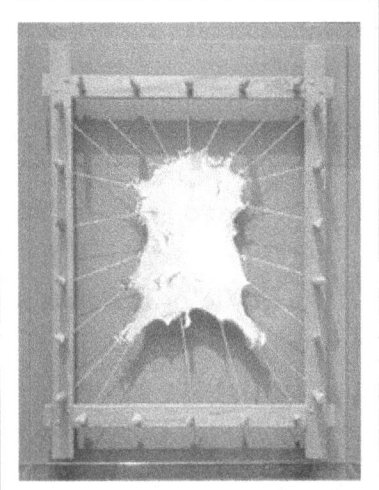

Skin of a stillborn goat on a stretcher (modern) – The J. Paul Getty Museum

Making a codex began with a dried and treated sheepskin, goatskin, or another animal hide. "The pelts were first soaked in a lime solution to loosen the fur, which was then removed. While wet on a stretcher, the skin was scraped using a knife with a curved blade. As the skin dried, the parchment maker would adjust the tension so that the skin remained taut. This cycle of scraping and stretching was repeated over several days until the desired thinness had been achieved. Here, the skin of a stillborn goat, prized for its smoothness, is stretched on a modern frame to illustrate the parchment making process."[9] The first step for preparing the pages to receive writing was setting up the quires, i.e., a bundle of parchment sheets folded together for binding into a book, especially a four-sheet bundle folded once to make eight leaves or sixteen pages. Raymond Clemens and Timothy Graham point out that "the quire was the scribe's basic writing unit throughout the Middle Ages."[10]

The Craft of the Scribe

The *recto* is the front side of a papyrus sheet or parchment sheet, while the *verso* is the back of a page. If the scribe were writing on a papyrus sheet, he would write his script on the horizontal lines of the fibers on the recto side of his sheet. If the scribe were using a parchment sheet, the manuscript had pinpricks placed in it to be ruled with lines to accommodate writing better. In some of the documents, we can still see faintly visible lines. It was similar to modern-day tablet paper, with horizontal lines running across the page to receive text, and vertical lines, which served to mark the

---

[8] Retrieved Thursday January 17, 2019, The Codex and Early Christians: Clarification & Corrections, https://larryhurtado.wordpress.com/2014/09/16/the-codex-and-early-christians-clarification-corrections/

[9] Retrieved Monday September 15, 2014 "*The Making of a Medieval Book*" The J. Paul Getty Trust. http://www.getty.edu/art/exhibitions/making/

[10] Raymond Clemens, Timothy Graham. *Introduction to Manuscript Studies*. Ithaca: Cornell University Press, 2008, 14.

boundaries, justify both sides. The scribal schools had different techniques for ruling manuscripts. Sometimes, a textual scholar can identify a particular manuscript's school, based on how it was ruled, giving us the place of its origin. The parchment's hair side was darker than that of the flesh side, so scribes placed the quires so that the hair side faced the hair side of the corresponding page, making it more reader-friendly.

Study of Ancient Handwriting

The study of ancient handwriting and manuscripts is an essential skill for paleographers, but also for the textual scholar as well. The style of the characters that make up an alphabet change every fifty years or so; thus, it is essential to know the eras of different styles. Moreover, scribes use abbreviations and contractions for various reasons. Therefore, the student of ancient handwriting must know how to interpret them. For example, several contractions and abbreviations are found in our earliest manuscripts of the Christian Greek New Testament.[11] We briefly mentioned this earlier.

The abbreviations that are most relevant to this discussion are what have become known as the sacred names, or nomina sacra (nomen sacrum, singular), such as Lord ($\overline{KC}$),[12] Jesus ($\overline{IH}$, $\overline{IHC}$), Christ ($\overline{XP}$, $\overline{XC}$, $\overline{XPC}$), God ($\overline{\Theta C}$), and Spirit ($\overline{\Pi NA}$). These sacred names are abbreviated or contracted by keeping the first letter or two and the last letter. Another essential feature is the horizontal bar placed over these letters to help readers recognize that they are encountering a contraction. The early Christian writers had three different ways that they would pen a sacred name: **(1)** suspension, **(2)** contraction, and **(3)** longer contraction. The suspension was accomplished by writing only the first two letters of "Jesus," for example (ιησους = ιη), and suspending the remaining letters (σους). The contraction was accomplished by writing only the first and last letter of Jesus (ιησους = ις) and removing the remaining letters (ησου).

The longer contraction would simply keep the first two letters and the last letter (ιης). After penning the suspension or contraction, the scribe would place a bar over the $\overline{name}$. This practice of placing a bar over the name was likely carried over from the typical way of scribes putting bars above contractions, especially numbers, which were represented by letters, e.g., $\overline{IA}$ = eleven.

---

[11] It should be noted that the early manuscripts were written in what we consider all uppercase letters, known as majuscule, the large rounded letters used in ancient manuscripts. Moreover, there were no breaks between the letters, so a phrase like GODISNOWHERE could be divided as GOD IS NO WHERE or GOD IS NOW HERE.

[12] In the fourth and third centuries B.C.E., the sigma form of Σ was simplified into a C-like shape in koinē Greek.

When students of ancient handwriting know these individual letterforms, ligatures,[13] punctuation, and abbreviations, they can read and understand the text. Of course, textual scholars must learn the language of the manuscripts they are studying; in our case, Greek. They need to be an expert in the forms of the language, the various handwriting styles, writing customs, and able to identify different hands within the same manuscript and scribal notes and abbreviations. They also need to study the language development over the years and its history to better analyze the texts. As we have discussed, students of ancient handwriting must know the writing materials, which will enable them to better identify the period in which a document was copied.[14] One of the primary goals of paleographers is to ascertain the text's date and its place of origin. For these reasons alone, they must consider the style and formation of a manuscript and the style of handwriting used therein.

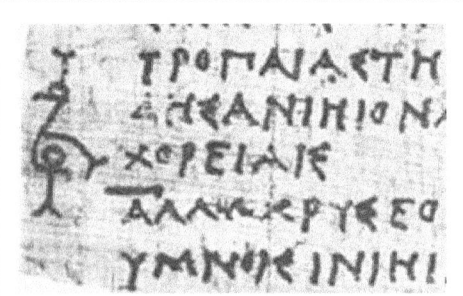

Detail of the Berlin Papyrus 9875 showing the 5th column of Timotheus' Persae, with a coronis symbol, to mark the end.

For example, with the majuscule hand, we have what is known as the **Ptolemaic Book Hand**, and how it developed is difficult to say because we have so few examples, which are not datable. It is not until we reach the third century B.C.E. that we can have confidence in the Ptolemaic bookhand era. This period's hands are stiff, awkward, and sharply defined (e.g., **Ε, Σ,** and **Ω**). Moreover, the letters evidenced no consistency in size. At times, there was a fineness, and pleasing subtlety attained. When we arrive at the second century B.C.E., we find the letters becoming more rounded and more uniform in size. However, one can detect a loss of unity in the first century. On this, Comfort writes, "Paleographers date the emergence of the Roman Uncial as coming on the heels of the Ptolemaic period, which ended in 30 BC. Thus, early Roman Uncial begins around 30 BC, and the Roman Uncial hand can be seen throughout the first two to three centuries of the Christian era. The Roman Uncial script, generally speaking, shares the characteristics of literary manuscripts in the Roman period (as distinct from the Ptolemaic period) in that these manuscripts show a greater roundness and smoothness in the forms of letters and are somewhat larger than what was penned in the Ptolemaic period. Furthermore, the Roman Uncial typically displays decorative serifs in several letters,

---

[13] A ligature is a character that consists of two or more letters joined together, e.g. "æ". We do not normally find ligatures in majuscule manuscripts. In the minuscule manuscripts, it can be difficult to determine a ligature due to the fact it is a manuscript with a running hand.

[14] Robert P. Gwinn, "Paleography" in the Encyclopaedia Britannica, Micropædia, Vol. IX, 1986, p. 78.

but not all. (By contrast, the Decorated Rounded style aims at making the decorations rounded and replete.)"[15]

Majuscule Hand

During the Byzantine period (300-650 C.E.), the dominant type of book-hand became known as the biblical hand. It had its earliest beginnings toward the end of the second-century C.E., being used by all, not necessarily having any connection to Christian literature. In addition, manuscripts from Egypt, of vellum or papyrus dating to around the fourth century C.E., contained other forms of script, i.e., a sloping somewhat unpolished rough hand resulting from the literary hand, which continued until about the fifth century C.E. The three early great codices, Vaticanus and Sinaiticus of the fourth century C.E. and Alexandrinus of the fifth century C.E., were penned in majuscules of the biblical hand. The hand that produced Vaticanus is the least demonstrated. The letters are characteristic of the biblical hand but do not possess the later manuscripts' heavy look, with a greater roundness to them. Sinaiticus, which was copied shortly after that, has larger, heavier letters. In Alexandrinus, we notice a development in the form, a definite distinction between thick and thin strokes.

Vaticanus, From Page Matthew 1:22-2:18

Sinaiticus, From Page Matthew 2:5-3:7

Codex Alexandrinus of the fifth century, The Center for the Study of New Testament Manuscripts

---

[15] Philip Comfort, *Encountering the Manuscripts: An Introduction to New Testament Paleography & Textual Criticism* (Nashville, TN: Broadman & Holman, 2005), 110.

Once we enter the sixth century C.E., we notice in the manuscripts, vellum or papyrus, that the heavier hand became the standard but still possessed an attractive appearance. However, there was a steady decline in the centuries to come, as the writing appears to be done artificially, i.e., as a matter of duty or custom, without thought, attention. The thick strokes became heavier; the cross strokes of **T** and **Θ** and the bottom of **Δ** were equipped with sagging spurs. This era of an unpleasant hand followed in sequence, morphing from sloping to upright.

Publishing Industry of the Ancient World

Today, most people would not imagine the ancient world's having a large publishing industry, yet this was the case. The ancient writings of famous authors were great pieces of literature that were highly sought after from the moment they were penned, much as today. Thus, there was a need for the scriptorium[16] to fill orders for both pagan and civil literature and the Bible books. There was a need for hundreds of copies, and as Christianity displaced paganism, the demand would grow exponentially.

The **Autograph** ("self-written") was the text written by a New Testament author or the author and scribe as the author dictated to him. If the scribe was taking down dictation (Rom. 16:22; 1 Pet. 5:12), he might have done so in shorthand.[17] Whether by shorthand or longhand, we can assume that both the scribe and the author would check the scribe's work. The author would have authority over all corrections since the Holy Spirit did not inspire the scribe. The finished product would be the autograph if the inspired author wrote everything down as the Spirit moved him. This text is also often referred to as the **Original**. Hence, the terms *autograph* and *original* are often used interchangeably. Sometimes textual scholars prefer to distinguish, using "original" as a general reference to the text that is correctly attributed to a biblical author. This designation does not focus on the process of how a book or letter was written.

---

[16] A scriptorium was a room for storing, copying, illustrating, or reading manuscripts.

[17] "The usual procedure for a dictated epistle was for the amanuensis (secretary) to take down the speaker's words (often in shorthand) and then produce a transcript, which the author could then review, edit, and sign in his own handwriting. Two New Testament epistles provide the name of the amanuensis: Tertius for (Romans 16:22) and Silvanus (another name for Silas) for 1 Peter 5:12." Philip Comfort, *Encountering the Manuscripts: An Introduction to New Testament Paleography & Textual Criticism* (Nashville, TN: Broadman & Holman, 2005), 06.

Andrews qualifies what Comfort had to say about shorthand. There is the **slight possibility** of Tertius or other Bible author's scribes taking it down in shorthand and after that making out a full draft, which would have been reviewed by both Paul and Tertius. This is only the case if it is comparable to what a modern-day court reporter does. In some sense, they are taking down whoever is speaking down in shorthand. Imagine a courtroom where you have a witness talking fast, the prosecution interrupts, the defense jumps in with his rebuttal and the judge snaps his ruling, and the witness resumes his or her account of things. All of that is taken down explicitly word for word in shorthand, and if ever turned into longhand, it would be exactly what was said, down to the uh and um common in speech. So, if the shorthand of the day had that kind of capability; then, it is conceivable. We must remember these are the Bible author's dictated words to the scribe based on their inspiration, not the word choice or writing style of the scribe.

The *original* can also be referred to as the first **Authorized Text** (**Archetypal Manuscript**), i.e., the text first used to make other copies. We should also point out that some textual scholars debate whether the original or autograph of any given book was actually the first text used to make copies. And they prefer to call the latter the **Initial Text** instead, not requiring that it actually be the autograph. Conservative scholars would maintain that they are the same. Neither term should be confused with what is known as an ordinary **exemplar**, which is any authorized text of the book from which other copies were made. The original text necessarily was the first exemplar used to make copies, but additional copies of high quality were used as exemplars. We will frequently use exemplar to refer to any document that serves as a standard that a scribe employed as his text for making another copy. Usually, a scribe would have a main or primary exemplar from which he makes most of his copies and one or more secondary exemplars to compare what he found in his primary exemplar. Scribes sometimes substituted text from other exemplars for what they have in their main exemplars.

We have mentioned the **Scriptorium**, a room where multiple scribes or even one scribe worked to produce the manuscript(s). A lector would read aloud from the exemplar, and the scribe(s) would write down his words. The **Corrector** was the one who checked the manuscripts for needed corrections. Corrections could be by three primary persons: **(1)** the copyist himself, **(2)** the official corrector of the scriptorium, or **(3)** a person who had purchased the copy. While those correctors were contemporaneous with the original scribe(s), others could have corrected the text centuries later. When textual scholars speak of the **Hand**, this primarily refers to a person who is making the copy, distinguishing his level of training. Paleographers have set out four basic levels of handwriting. First, there was the *common hand* of a person who was untrained in making copies. Second, there was the *documentary hand* of an individual who was trained in preparing documents. The third level was the *reformed documentary* hand of a copyist who was experienced in preparing documents and copying literature. The fourth was the *professional hand*, the scribe experienced in producing literature.[18]

We must keep in mind that we are dealing with an oral society. Therefore, the apostles, who had spent three and a half years with Jesus, first published the Good News orally. The teachers within the newly founded Christian congregations would repeat this information until it was memorized. After that, those who had heard this gospel would, in turn, share it with others (Acts 2:42, Gal 6:6). In time, they were moved by the Holy Spirit to see the need for a written record, so Matthew, Mark, Luke, and John would pen the Gospels, and other types of New Testament books would be written by Paul, James, Peter, and Jude. From the first four verses of Luke, we can see

---

[18] Philip Comfort, *Encountering the Manuscripts: An Introduction to New Testament Paleography & Textual Criticism* (Nashville, TN: Broadman & Holman, 2005), 17-20.

that Theophilus[19] was being given a written record of what he had already been taught orally. In verse 4, Luke says to Theophilus, "[My purpose is] that you may know the exact truth about the things you have been taught."

When the Son of God on Golgotha, outside of Jerusalem on Friday, Nisan 14 33 C.E. about 3:00 p.m., gave his life, Matthew, Mark, Luke, and John did not write their Gospels immediately. Matthew first wrote his Gospel in Hebrew some 12-17 years after Jesus' ascension, 45-50 C.E. Shortly after that, he translated it into Greek. Luke followed with his Gospel about 56–58 C.E. Then, Mark and his Gospel were written about 60–65 C.E. Finally, John's Gospel was written some 65 years after Jesus death in about 98 C.E. One thing few biblical scholars in the seminaries address today is how these apostles Matthew, John, and the disciples Mark and Luke were able to record the life, ministry, and death of Jesus Christ with such unerring accuracy.

The appearance of the written record did not mean the end of the oral publication. Both the oral and the written records would be used together. Many did not read the written documents themselves, as they could hear them read in the congregational meetings by the lector. This would apply to those who could read because they may not have been able to afford to have copies made for themselves. Paul and his letters came to be used in the same way as he traveled extensively but was just one man and could only be in one place at a time. It was not long before he took advantage that he could be in one place and dispatch letters to other locations through his traveling companions. These traveling companions would not only deliver the letters but also know the issues well enough to address questions that might be asked by the congregation leaders to which they had been dispatched.

In summary, the first century saw the life and ministry of Jesus Christ, the Son of God, and his death, resurrection, and ascension. After that, his disciples spread this gospel orally for at least 12-17 years before Matthew penned his gospel. The written record was used in conjunction with the oral message.

In the first-century C.E., the Bible books were being copied individually. In the late first century or the beginning of the second century, they began being copied in groups. At first, it was the four gospels and then the book of Acts with the four gospels and shortly after that a collection of the Apostle Paul's writings. Each of the individual books of the New Testament was penned, edited, and published between 45 and 98 C.E. A group of the apostle Paul's letters and the gospels were copied and published

---

[19] Theophilus means "friend of God," was the person to whom the books of Luke and Acts were written (Lu 1:3; Ac 1:1). Theophilus was called "most excellent," which may suggest some position of high rank. On the other hand, it simply may be Luke offering an expression of respect. Theophilus had initially been orally taught about Jesus Christ and his ministry. Thereafter, it seems that the book of Acts, also by Luke, confirms that he did become a Christian. The Gospel of Luke was partially written to offer Theophilus assurances of the certainty of what he had already learned by word of mouth.

between 90 to 125 C.E. The entire 27 books of the New Testament were not published as a whole until about 290 to 340 C.E.

Thus, we have the 27 books of the New Testament that were penned individually in the second half of the first century. Each of these would have been copied and recopied throughout the first century. The copies of these copies would, of course, be made as well. Some of the earliest manuscripts that we now have indicate that a professional scribe copied them. Many of the other papyri provide evidence that a semi-professional hand-copied them, while most of these early papyri give proof of being made by a copyist who was literate and experienced at making documents. Therefore, either literate or semi-professional copyists produced most of our early papyri, with some being made by professionals.

Sadly, we do not have the autographs. Even if we did, we would have no way to authenticate them. We do, however, have copies of New Testament manuscripts that go back to the second and third centuries C.E. Over the centuries, this copying of copies continued. The authors were inspired so that the originals were error-free. However, this is not the case with those who made copies; they were not under the Holy Spirit's influence while making their copies. Therefore, these copies must have contained unintentional mistakes, as well as intentional changes, differing from the originals and each other. However, this is not as problematic or alarming as it may first sound. By far, most of the copyist errors are trivial, such as differences in spelling, word order, and such.

It is true that other copyist errors, a tiny portion, are noteworthy (significant), arising from the copyist's desire to correct something in the text that he perceived as erroneous or problematic. In an even smaller number of cases, the scribe made changes to strengthen orthodox doctrine. However, these changes have little to no effect on doctrines because other passages addressing the same beliefs provide the means to analyze and correct the copyist's "corrections." Moreover, they are easily analyzed and corrected so that we know what the original contained. Furthermore, we have enough textual evidence to know what words were in the original.

In the language of textual criticism, changes to the original text introduced by copyists are called "variant readings." A variant reading is a different reading in the extant [existing] manuscripts for any given portion of the text. The process of textual criticism is examining variant readings in various ancient manuscripts to reconstruct the original wording of a written text. These variants in our copies of the New Testament manuscripts are primarily the reason for the rise of the science of textual criticism in the 16th century. After that, we have had hundreds of scholars working extremely hard over the following five centuries to restore the New Testament text to its original state. Keep in mind that textual criticism is not just performed on the Old and New Testament texts, but in all other ancient literature as well: Plato (428/427–348/347 B.C.E.), Herodotus (c. 484–c. 425 B.C.E.), Homer (Ninth or Eighth Century B.C.E.), Livy (64or 59 B.C.E.–17 C.E.), Cicero (106–43 B.C.E.), and Virgil (70–19

B.C.E.). However, as the Bible is the greatest work of all time, directly influencing countless Christians' lives (billions), it is the most crucial field.

Here, we should also expound more on the "criticism" portion of the term textual criticism. It may be helpful if, for a moment, we address biblical criticism in general, which is divided into two branches: lower criticism and higher criticism. Lower criticism, also known as textual criticism, is an investigation of manuscripts by those who are known as textual scholars, seeking to establish the original reading, which is available in the thousands of extant copies. Higher criticism, also known as literary criticism, investigates the restored text to identify any sources that may lie behind it. Therefore, we can say the following:

LOWER CRITICISM (i.e., textual criticism) has been the bedrock of scholarship over the last 500 years. It has given us a master text, i.e., a critical text, reflecting the original published Greek New Testament. It had contributed to the furtherance of Bible scholarship, removing interpolations, correcting scribal errors, and giving us a restored text, allowing us to produce better translations of the New Testament. However, of late, the dissecting higher criticism mindset of the 19th and 20th centuries has seeped into the field of New Testament Textual Studies.

HIGHER CRITICISM (i.e., literary criticism, biblical criticism) has taught that much of the Bible was composed of legend and myth. It claims that Moses did not write the first five books of the Bible, 8th century B.C.E. Isaiah did not write Isaiah, there were three authors of Isaiah, 6th century B.C.E. Daniel did not write Daniel, it was penned in the 2nd century BCE. Higher critics have taught that Jesus did not say all that the Gospels have him saying in his Sermon on the Mount and that Jesus did not condemn the Pharisees in Matthew 23, as this was Matthew because he hated the Jews. These are just the highlights, for there are thousands of tweaks that have undermined the word of God as being inspired and fully inerrant. Higher critics have dissected the Word of God until it has become the word of man and a very jumbled word at that. Higher criticism is still taught in almost all the seminaries. It is common to hear so-called Evangelical Bible scholars vehemently deny that large sections of the Bible are fully inerrant, authentic, accurate, and trustworthy. Biblical higher criticism is speculative and tentative in the extreme.

Constantine Von Tischendorf was a world-leading textual scholar and a renowned Bible scholar. Tischendorf was educated in Greek at the University of Leipzig. During his university studies, he was troubled by higher criticism of the Bible, as taught by famous German theologians, who sought to prove that the Greek New Testament was not authentic. He rejected higher criticism, which led to his noteworthy success in defending the authenticity of the Bible text. NT Textual scholar Harold Greenlee writes, "This 'higher criticism' has often been applied to the Bible in a destructive way, and it has come to be looked down on by many evangelical Christians."[20] The sad situation is that modern-day textual scholarship as a whole is unwittingly or knowingly moving the goalposts for some unknown reason. It is now the earliest knowable text in textual criticism, the sociohistorical approach to New Testament Textual Studies, and the newest trend to redate our earliest NT papyri to later dates.[21]

The New Testament in the Original Greek is a Greek-language version of the New Testament published in 1881. It is also known as the **Westcott and Hort** text, after its editors Brooke Foss Westcott (1825–1901) and Fenton John Anthony Hort (1828–1892). (Textual scholars use the abbreviation "**WH**") It is a critical text (Master Greek text of the NT seeking to ascertain the original wording of the original documents), compiled from some of the oldest New Testament fragments and texts discovered at the time. The two editors worked together for 28 years.

The Nestle Greek New Testament (first published in 1898) is a critical edition of the New Testament in its original Koine Greek, now in its 28th edition, forming the basis of most modern Bible translations and biblical criticism. It is now known as the Nestle-Aland edition after its most influential editors, Eberhard Nestle and Kurt Aland. Textual scholars use the abbreviation "**NA**." The NA is now in its 28th edition (2012), which is abbreviated NA^{28}. Throughout the 130 years since 1881, there have been hundreds of manuscript discoveries, especially the early papyri that date within decades of the originals. One might expect significant changes been the WH text of 1881 and the 2012 NA^{28} text. However, The NA^{28} is 99.5% the same as the 1881 WH Greek New Testament.

In contrast, **higher criticism** (i.e., literary criticism) has attempted to provide rational explanations for the composition of Bible books, ignoring the supernatural element and often eliminating the traditional authorship of the books. Late dating of the copy of Bible books is widespread, and the historicity of biblical accounts is called into question. It would not be an overstatement to say that the effect has often challenged and undermined the Christian's confidence in the New Testament. Fortunately, some conservative scholars[22] have rightly criticized higher critics for their illogical or unreasonable approaches in dissecting God's Word.

---

[20] Greenlee, J. Harold. *The Text of the New Testament: From Manuscript to Modern Edition* (p. 2). Baker Publishing Group.

[21] For defense against this redating, see THE P52 PROJECT: Is P52 Really the Earliest Greek New Testament Manuscript? Christian Publishing House (May 26, 2020) ISBN-13: 978-1949586107

[22] Such Bible scholars as the late R. A. Torrey, Robert L. Thomas, Norman L. Geisler, Gleason L. Archer Jr., and current scholars such as F. David Farnell, as well as many others have fought for decades to educate readers about the dangers of higher criticism.

Importance of Textual Criticism

Christian Bible students need to be familiar with Old and New Testament textual criticism as essential foundational studies. Why? If we fail to establish what was originally authored with reasonable certainty, how can we translate or even interpret what we think is the actual Word of God? We are fortunate that there are far more existing New Testament manuscripts today than any other book from ancient history. Some ancient Greek and Latin classics are based on one existing manuscript, while with others, there are just a handful and a few exceptions that have a few hundred available. However, over 5,898[23] Greek New Testament manuscripts have been cataloged for the New Testament,[24] 10,000 Latin manuscripts, and an additional 9,300 other manuscripts in such languages as Syriac, Slavic, Gothic, and Ethiopic Coptic, and Armenian. This gives New Testament textual scholars vastly more to work within establishing the original words of the text.

The other difference between the New Testament manuscripts and those of the classics is that the existing copies of the New Testament date much closer to the originals. Some of the manuscripts are dated to about a thousand years after the author had penned the book in the Greek classics. Some of the Latin classics are dated from three to seven hundred years after the author wrote the book. When we look at the Greek copies of the New Testament books, some portions are within decades of the original author's book. One hundred and thirty-nine Greek NT papyri and five majuscules[25] date from 110 C.E. to 390 C.E.

Distribution of Greek New Testament Manuscripts

- The **Papyrus** is a copy of a portion of the New Testament made on papyrus. At present, we have 147 cataloged New Testament papyri, many dating between 110-350 C.E., but some as late as the 6th century C.E.

---

[23] While at present here in 2020, there are 5,898 manuscripts. There are **140 listed Papyrus** manuscripts, 323 Majuscule manuscripts, 2,951 Minuscule manuscripts, and 2,484 Lectionary manuscripts, bringing the total cataloged manuscripts to 5,898 manuscripts. However, you cannot simply total the number of cataloged manuscripts because, for example, $P^{11/14}$ are the same manuscript but with different catalog numbers. The same is true of $P^{33/5}$, $P^{4/64/67}$, $P^{49/65}$ and $P^{77/103}$. Now this alone would bring our 140 listed papyrus manuscripts down to 134. 'Then, we turn to one example from our majuscule manuscripts where clear 0110, 0124, 0178, 0179, 0180, 0190, 0191, 0193, 0194, and 0202 are said to be part of 070. A minuscule manuscript was listed with five separate catalog numbers for 2306, which then have the letters a through e. Thus, we have the following GA numbers: 2306 for 2306a, and 2831- 2834 for 2306b-2306e.' – (Hixon 2019, 53-4) The problem is much worse when we consider that there are 323 Majuscule manuscripts and then far worse still with a listed 2,951 Minuscule and 2,484 Lectionaries. Nevertheless, those who estimate a total of 5,300 (Jacob W. Peterson, Myths and Mistakes, p. 63) 5,500 manuscripts (Dr. Ed Gravely / ehrmanproject.com/), 5,800 manuscripts (Porter 2013, 23), it is still a truckload of evidence far and above the dismal number of ancient secular author books.

[24] As of January 2016

[25] Large lettering, often called "capital" or uncial, in which all the letters are usually the same height.

- The **Majuscule** or **Uncial** is a script of large letters commonly used in Greek and Latin manuscripts written between the 3rd and 9th centuries C.E. that resembles a modern capital letter but is more rounded. At present, we have 323 cataloged New Testament Majuscule manuscripts.

- The **Minuscule** is a small cursive style of writing used in manuscripts from the 9th to the 16th centuries, now having 2,951 Minuscule manuscripts cataloged.

- The **Lectionary** is a schedule of readings from the Bible for Christian church services during the year, in both majuscules and minuscules, dating from the 4th to the 16th centuries C.E., now having 2,484 Lectionary manuscripts cataloged.

We should clarify that of the approximate 24,000 total manuscripts of the New Testament, not all are complete books. There are fragmented manuscripts with just a few verses, but manuscripts contain an entire book, others that include numerous books, and some that have the whole New Testament, or nearly so. This is expected since the oldest manuscripts we have were copied in an era when reproducing the entire New Testament was not the norm. Instead, it was far more common to copy a single book or a group of books (i.e., the Gospels or Paul's letters). This still does not negate the vast riches of manuscripts that we possess.

What can we conclude from this short introduction to textual criticism? There is some irony here: secular scholars have no problem accepting classic authors' wording with their minuscule amount of evidence. However, they discount the treasure trove of evidence that is available to the New Testament textual scholar. Still, this should not surprise us as the New Testament has always been under-appreciated and attacked somehow, shape, or form over the past 2,000 years.

On the contrary, in comparison to classical works, we are overwhelmed by the quantity and quality of existing New Testament manuscripts. We should also keep in mind that about seventy-five percent[26] of the New Testament does not even require the help of textual criticism because that much of the text is unanimous, and thus, we know what it says. Of the other twenty-five percent, about twenty percent make up trivial scribal mistakes that are easily corrected. Therefore, textual criticism focuses mainly on a small portion of the New Testament text. The facts are clear: the Christian, who reads the New Testament, is fortunate to have so many manuscripts, with so many dating so close to the originals, with 500 hundred years of hundreds of textual scholars who have established the text with a level of certainty unimaginable for ancient secular works.

---

[26] The numbers in this paragraph are rounded for simplicity purposes.

After discussing the amount of New Testament manuscripts available, Atheist commentator Bob Seidensticker writes, "The first problem is that more manuscripts at best increase our confidence that we have the original version. That does not mean the original copy was history ...."[27] That is, Seidensticker is forced to acknowledge the reliability of the New Testament text as we have it today and can only try to deny what it says. He also tells us of the New Testament, "Compare that with 2000 copies of the Iliad, the second-best represented manuscript."[28] Of those 1,757 copies of the Iliad, how far removed are they from the alleged originals? The Iliad is dated to about 800 B.C.E. There are several fragments of the Iliad that date to the second century B.C.E. and one to the third century B.C.E., with the rest dating to the ninth century C.E. or later. That would make this handful of fragmented manuscripts 500 years removed and the rest about 1,700 years removed from their original.

The Range of Textual Criticism

The Importance and scope of New Testament textual studies can be summed up in the few words used by J. Harold Greenlee; it is "the basic biblical study, a prerequisite to all other biblical and theological work. Interpretation, systematization, and application of the teachings of the NT cannot be accomplished until textual criticism has done at least some of its work. It is, therefore, deserving of the acquaintance and attention of every serious student of the Bible."[29]

It is only reasonable to assume that the original 27 books written first-hand by the New Testament authors have not survived. Instead, we only have what we must consider being imperfect copies. **Why the Holy Spirit would miraculously inspire 27 fully inerrant texts and then allow human imperfection into the documents** is not explained for us in Scripture. (More on this later) Why didn't God inspire the copyists? We do know that imperfect humans have tended to worship relics that traditions hold to have been touched by the miraculous powers of God or to have been in direct contact with one of his special servants of old. Ultimately, though, all we know is that God had his reasons for allowing the New Testament autographs to be worn out by repeated use. From time to time, we hear of the discovery of a fragment possibly dated to the first century, but even if such a fragment is eventually verified, the dating alone can never serve as proof of an autograph; it will still be a copy in all likelihood.

---

[27] 25,000 New Testament Manuscripts? Big Deal. - Patheos,

http://www.patheos.com/blogs/crossexamined/2013/11/25000-new-testament-manuscrip (accessed November 28, 2015).

[28] Ibid

[29] J. Harold Greenlee, *Introduction to New Testament Textual Criticism* (Grand Rapids, MI: Baker Academic, 1995), 8-9.

If we ask why didn't God inspire copyists, then it will have to follow, why didn't God inspire translators, why didn't God inspire Bible scholars that author commentaries on the Bible, and so on? Suppose God's initial purpose was to give us a fully inerrant, authoritative, authentic, and accurate Word. Why not adequately protect the Scriptures in all facets of transmission from error: copy, translate, and interpret? If God did this, and people were moved along by the Holy Spirit, it would soon become noticeable that when people copy the texts, they would be unable to make an error or mistake or even willfully change something.

Where would it stop? Would this being moved along by the Holy Spirit apply to anyone who decided to make themselves a copy, testing to see if they too would be inspired? In time, this would prove to be actual evidence for God. This would negate the reasons why God has allowed sin, human imperfection to enter humanity in the first place, to teach them an **object lesson**, man cannot walk on his own without his Creator. God created perfect humans, giving them a perfect start, and through the abuse of free will, they rejected his sovereignty. He did not just keep creating perfect humans again and again, as though he got something wrong. God gave us his perfect Word and has again chosen to allow us to continue in our human imperfection, learning our **object lesson**. God has stepped into humanity many hundreds of times in the Bible record, maybe tens of thousands of times unbeknownst to us over the past 6,000+ years, to tweak things to get the desired outcome of his will and purposes. However, there is no aspect of life where his stepping in on any particular point was to be continuous until the return of the Son. Maybe God gave us a perfect copy of sixty-six books. Then like everything else, he placed the responsibility of copying, translating, and interpreting on us, just as he gave us the Great Commission of proclaiming that Word, explaining that Word, to make disciples. – Matthew 24:14;28-19-20; Acts 1:8.

As for errors in all the copies we have, we can say that the vast majority of the Greek text is not affected by errors. The errors occur in variant readings, i.e., portions of the text where different manuscripts disagree. Of the **small amount** of the text affected by variant readings, the vast majority of these are minor slips of the pen, misspelled words, etc., or intentional but quickly analyzed changes. We are certain what the original reading is in these places. A **far smaller number** of changes present challenges to establishing the original reading. It has always been said and remains true that no central doctrine is affected by a textual problem. Only rarely does a textual issue change the meaning of a verse.[30] Still, establishing the original text wherever there are variant readings is vitally important. Every word matters!

It is true that the Jewish copyists and the later Christian copyists were not led along by the Holy Spirit, and, therefore, their manuscripts were not inerrant, infallible.

---

[30] Leading textual scholar Daniel Wallace tells us, after looking at all of the evidence, that the percentage of instances where the reading is uncertain and a well-attested alternative reading could change the meaning of the verse is a quarter of one percent, i.e., 0.0025%

Errors (textual variants) crept into the documents unintentionally and intentionally. However, the vast majority of the Hebrew Old Testament and Greek New Testament has not been infected with textual errors. For the portions impacted with textual mistakes, we can be grateful for the tens of thousands of copies that we have to help us weed out the errors. How? Well, not every copyist made the same textual errors. Hence, by comparing the work of different copyists and manuscripts, textual scholars can identify the textual variants (errors) and remove those, leaving us with the original content.

Yes, it would be **the most significant discovery** of all time if we found the original five books penned by Moses himself, Genesis through Deuteronomy, or the original Gospels of Matthew, Mark, Luke, and John. However, first, there would be no way of establishing that they were the originals. Second, truth be told, we do not need the originals. **Yes, you heard me**. We do not need those original documents. What is so important about the documents? Nothing, it is the content on the original documents that we are after. And truly, miraculously, we have more copies than needed to do just that. **We do not need miraculous preservation** because we have miraculous restoration. We now know beyond a reasonable doubt that the Hebrew Old Testament and the Greek New Testament critical texts are about a 99.99% reflection of the content that was in those ancient original manuscripts.

CHAPTER 2 The New Testament Secretaries and Their Materials

One of the greatest tragedies in the modern-day history of Christianity [1880 - present] is that churchgoers have not been educated about the history of the New Testament text. They are so misinformed that many do not even realize that the Hebrew text lies behind our English Old Testament, and the Greek text lies behind our English New Testament. Sadly, many seminaries that train the pastors of today's churches have also required little or no studies in the history of the Old or New Testament texts.

Textual Criticism Defined

Again, New Testament textual criticism is the study of families of manuscripts, especially the Greek New Testament, as well as versions,[31] lectionaries,[32] and patristic quotations,[33] along with internal evidence, in order to determine which reading is the original. Comparing any two copies of a document even a few pages long will reveal variant readings. "A textual variant is simply any difference from a standard text (e.g., a printed text, a particular manuscript, etc.) that involves spelling, word order, omission, addition, substitution, or a total rewrite of the text."

Again, it needs to be repeated; when we use the term "textual *criticism*," we are not referring to something negative. In this instance, "criticism" refers to a careful,

---

[31] A version is a translation of the New Testament into another language, such as Latin, Syriac, Coptic, Armenian, Georgian, and so on.

[32] A Lectionary is a book containing readings from the Bible for Christian church services during the course of the year.

[33] Patristic quotations are New Testament quotations from early Christian writers, such as the Apostolic Fathers, including Clement of Rome, Ignatius of Antioch, Polycarp of Smyrna, Hermas, and Papias. There were also the Apologists: Justin Martyr, Theophilus of Antioch, Clement of Alexandria, and Tertullian, to name a few. After them came the Church Fathers, e.g. St. Augustine or St. Ambrose whose works have helped to shape the Christian Church.

measured, or painstaking study and analysis of the internal and external evidence for producing our New Testament Greek text generally called a "critical text." Today, the goal of many New Testament textual scholars is to recover the earliest text *possible*, while the objective of the remaining few, such as the author of this book, is to get back to the *ipsissima verba* ("the very words") of the original author.[34]

Variant readings occur only in about 5 percent of the Greek NT text, and so all the manuscripts agree about 95 percent of the time. Only about 2,100 variant readings may be considered "significant" and in no instance is any point of Christian doctrine challenged or questioned by a variant reading. Only about 1.67 percent of the entire Greek NT text still is questioned at all. We may be confident that our current eclectic, or critical, Greek NT text (an eclectic, or critical text is one based on the study of as many manuscripts as possible), is far beyond 99 percent established. In fact, there is more variation among some English translations of the Bible than there is among the manuscripts of the Greek NT. God's Word is infallible and inerrant in its original copies (autographs), all of which have perished. Textual critics of the Greek NT will continue their work until, if possible, the original of every questioned reading is firmly established.[35]

An investigation of the enormous supply of Greek manuscripts and the ancient versions in other languages shows that they have preserved for us the very Word of God.

Throughout the first five books of the Bible being penned by Moses (beginning in the late sixteenth century B.C.E.), and down to the time of the printing press (1455 C.E.)–almost 3,000 years–many forms of material have been used to receive writing. Material such as bricks, papyrus sheets, animal skin, broken pottery, metal, wooden tablets with or without wax, and much more have been used to pen or copy God's Word. The following are some of the tools and materials.

 **Stylus**: The stylus was used to write on a waxed codex tablet. The stylus could be made of bone, metal, or ivory. It would be sharpened at one end for the purpose of writing and have a rounded knob on the other for making corrections. The stylus could also be used to write on soft metal or clay.

---

[34] Dr. Don Wilkins writes. "This goal, which will be mentioned in passing throughout the book, is a philosophical difference with some implications for TC practice. Both groups of critics will arrive at what they consider the earliest form of the text, but the authors take this to be the autograph as a matter of faith. One of the implications for practice is that conjectures are not considered viable options for variant readings. Another is that every word of the autograph can be found in some extant Greek NT manuscript."

[35] Charles W. Draper, "Textual Criticism, New Testament," ed. Chad Brand et al., *Holman Illustrated Bible Dictionary* (Nashville, TN: Holman Bible Publishers, 2003), 1574.

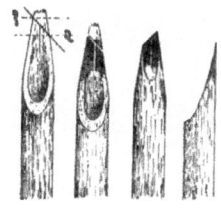

Reed Pen: The reed pen was used with ink to write on papyrus or parchment manuscripts. Καλαμος (kalamos) is the Greek word for "pen." (2 John 12; 3 John 13) There is no doubt that all the early extant papyrus manuscripts were copied with a reed pen, producing an impressive and pleasing script.

Quill Pen: The quill[36] pen came into use long after the reed pen. Quill would have been unsatisfactory for writing on papyrus, but parchment would have been an excellent surface for receiving writing from a quill pen. Of course, history shows that as parchment more fully displaced papyrus, the quill pen likewise replaced the reed pen. The quill was sharpened for use much like the reed, by having the tip sharpened and slit.

The first page of papyrus 66, showing John 1:1-13 and the opening words of v.14

Papyrus: Papyrus was the writing material used by the ancient Egyptians, Greeks, and Romans made from the pith of the stem of a water plant. It was cut into strips, with one layer laid out horizontally and the other vertically. Sometimes it was covered with a cloth and then beaten with a mallet. Scholarship has also suggested that paste may have been used between layers, and then a large stone would be placed on top until the materials were dry. Typically, a sheet of papyrus would be between 6–9 inches in width and 12–15 inches long. These sheets were then glued end to end until scribes had enough length to copy the book they were working on. The writing was done only on the horizontal side, and it was rolled so that the writing would be on the inside. If one were to attempt to write across the vertical side, it would be difficult because of the direction of the papyrus fibers. The scribe or copyist would have used a reed pen to write on the papyrus sheets (cf. 3 John 13). Papyrus was the primary material used for writing until about 300 C.E. It was used with a *roll* or *scroll* (a document that is rolled up into itself), as well as the *codex* (book) form.

Writing on the papyrus sheet, even the correct side, was no easy task by any means because the surface was rough and fibrous. "Defects sometimes occurred in the making through retention of moisture between the layers or through the use of spongy strips which could cause the ink to run; such flaws necessitated the remaking of the sheet."[37] The back pain from long periods of sitting cross-legged on the ground bent over a papyrus sheet on a board made writing letters unappealing. The dealing

---

[36] The quill pen was the principal writing instrument in the Western world from the 6th to the 19th centuries C.E.

[37] Nabia Abbot, *STUDIES IN ANCIENT ORIENTAL CIVILIZATIONS* (Chicago, IL: The University of Chicago Press, 1938), 11.

with running ink, the reed pen possibly snagging and tearing the papyrus sheet, having to erase illegible characters were all deterrents from personally writing a letter.

Early papyrus manuscripts, such as $P^{4/64/67}$ P^{32} P^{46} P^{52} P^{66} P^{75} $P^{77/103}$ P^{101} P^{87} P^{90} P^{98} P^{104} P^{109} P^{118} P^{137}, which date 100-150/175 C.E. Then we have P^{1} P^{5} P^{13} P^{20} P^{23} P^{27} P^{29} P^{30} P^{35} P^{38} P^{39} P^{40} P^{45} P^{47} P^{48} $P^{49/65}$ P^{69} P^{71} P^{72} P^{82} P^{85} P^{95} P^{100} P^{106} P^{107} P^{108} P^{111} P^{110} P^{113} P^{115} P^{121} P^{125} P^{126} P^{133} P^{136}, which date 175-250 C.E., to mention only a few. Then, the renowned Codex Vaticanus (300-325 C.E.) and Codex Sinaiticus (325-350 C.E.) were written on parchment: creamy or yellowish material made from dried and treated sheepskin, goatskin, or other animal hides.

Papyri copy - Greek Manuscript

One may wonder why more New Testament manuscripts have not survived. It must be remembered that the Christians suffered intense persecution during intervals in the first 300 years from Pentecost 33 C.E. With this persecution from the Roman Empire came many orders to destroy Christian texts. In addition, these texts were not stored in such a way as to secure their preservation. They were actively used by the Christians in the congregation and were subject to wear and tear. Furthermore, moisture is the enemy of papyrus, and it causes them to disintegrate over time. This is why, as we will discover, the papyrus manuscripts that have survived have come from the dry sands of Egypt. Moreover, it seems not to have entered the minds of the early Christians to preserve their documents because their solution to the loss of manuscripts was simply to make more copies. Fortunately, making copies transitioned to the more durable animal skins, which would last much longer. Those that have survived, especially from the fourth century C.E. and earlier, are the path to restoring the original Greek New Testament.[38]

Animal Skin: About the fourth century C.E., Bible manuscripts made of papyrus began to be superseded by the use of vellum, a high-quality parchment made from calfskin, kidskin, or lambskin. Manuscripts such as the famous Codex Sinaiticus (01) and Codex Vaticanus (03, also known as B) of the fourth century C.E. are parchment, vellum, codices. This use of parchment as the leading writing material continued for almost a thousand years until it was replaced by paper. The advantages of parchment over papyrus were many, such as (1) it was much easier to write on smooth parchment, (2) one could write on both sides, (3) parchment lasted much longer, and (4) when desired, old writing could be scraped off and the parchment reused.

---

[38] Cf. J. H. Greenlee, *Introduction to New Testament Textual Criticism* (Peabody: Hendrickson, 1995), 11.

A 2,000-year-old Dead Sea Isaiah Scroll. It matches closely the Masoretic text and what is in the Bible today

Papyrus or Parchment?

The Hebrew Old Testament that would have been available to the early Christians was written on the processed hide of animals after the hair was removed, and the hide was smoothed out with a pumice stone.[39] Leather scrolls were sent to Alexandria, Egypt, in about 280 B.C.E., to make what we now know as the Greek Septuagint.[40] Most of the Dead Sea scrolls discovered between 1947 and 1956 are made of leather, and it is almost certain that the scroll of Isaiah that Jesus read from in the synagogue was as well. Luke 4:17 says, "And the scroll of the prophet Isaiah was given to him. He unrolled the scroll and found the place where it was written."

The Dead Sea Scroll of Isaiah (1QIsa) dates to the end of the second century B.C.E., written on 17 sheets of parchment, one of the seven Dead Sea Scrolls that were first recovered by Bedouin shepherds in 1947. The Nash Papyrus is a collection of four papyrus fragments acquired in Egypt in 1898 by W. L. Nash, dating to about 150 B.C.E. It contains parts of the Ten Commandments from Exodus chapter 20 and some verses from Deuteronomy chapters 5 and 6. It is by far one of the oldest Hebrew manuscript fragments.

Vellum is a high-quality parchment made from calfskin, kidskin, or lambskin. After the skin was removed, it would be soaked in limewater, after which the hair would be scraped off, the skin then being scraped and dried, and rubbed afterward with chalk and pumice stone, creating an exceptionally smooth writing material. Both

---

[39] A very light porous rock formed from solidified lava, used in solid form as an abrasive and in powdered form as a polish.

[40] A Greek translation of the Hebrew Bible started in about 280 and completed about 150 B.C.E. to meet the needs of Greek-speaking Jews outside Palestine.

leather and papyrus were used before the first-century Christians. During the first three hundred years of Christianity, the secular world viewed parchment as being inferior to papyrus. It was relegated to notebooks, rough drafts, and other non-literary purposes.

A couple of myths should be dispelled before continuing. It is often remarked that papyrus is not a durable material. Both papyrus and parchment are durable under normal circumstances. This is not negating the fact that parchment is more durable than papyrus. Another often-repeated thought is that papyrus was fragile and brittle, making it an unlikely candidate to be used for a codex, which would have to be folded in half. Another issue that should be sidelined is whether it was more expensive to produce papyrus or parchment. Presently there is no data to aid in that evaluation. We know that papyrus was used for all of the Christian codex manuscripts up to the fourth century, at which time we find the two great parchment codices, the Sinaiticus and Vaticanus manuscripts. Parchment of good quality has been called "the finest writing material ever devised by man." (Roberts and Skeat, The Birth of the Codex 1987, 8) Why then did parchment take so long to replace papyrus? This may be answered by R. Reed, in *Ancient Skins, Parchments, and Leathers:*

> It is perhaps the extraordinary high durability of the product, produced by so simple a method, which has prevented most people from suspecting that many subtle points are involved…. The essence of the parchment process, which subjects the system of pelt to the simultaneous action of stretching and drying, is to bring about peculiar changes quite different from those applying when making leather. These are (1) reorganization of the dermal fibre network by stretching, and (2) permanently setting this new and highly stretched form of fibre network by drying the pelt fluid to a hard, glue-like consistency. In other words, the pelt fibres are fixed in a stretched condition so that they cannot revert to their original relaxed state. (Reed 1973, 119-20)

> Where the medieval parchment makers were greatly superior to their modern counterparts was in the control and modification of the ground substance in the pelt, before the latter was stretched and dried …. The major point, however, which modern parchment manufacturers have not appreciated, is what might be termed the integral or collective nature of the parchment process. The bases of many different effects need to be provided for simultaneously, in one and the same operation. The properties required in the final parchment must be catered for at the wet pelt stage, for due to the peculiar nature of the parchment process, once the system has been dried, and after-treatments to modify the material produced are greatly restricted. (Reed 1973, 124)

> This method, which follows those used in medieval times for making parchment of the highest quality, is preferable for it allows the grain surface of the drying pelt to be "slicked" and freed from residual fine hairs while

stretching upon the frame. At the same time, any process for cleaning and smoothing the flesh side, or for controlling the thickness of the final parchment may be undertaken by working the flesh side with sharp knives which are semi-lunar in form.... To carry out such manual operations on wet stretched pelt demands great skill, speed of working, and concentrated physical effort. (Reed 1973, 138-9)

Enough has been said to suggest that behind the apparently simple instructions contained in the early medieval recipes there is a wealth of complex process detail which we are still far from understanding. Hence it remains true that parchment-making is perhaps more of an art than a science.[41]

Scroll or Roll: The scroll dominated until the beginning of the second century C.E., at which time the papyrus codex was replacing it. Papyrus enjoyed another two centuries of use until it was replaced with animal skin (vellum), which proved to be a far better writing material.

The writing on a scroll was done in 2- to 3-inch columns, which allowed the reader to have it opened, or unrolled, only partially. Although movies and television have portrayed the scroll as being opened while holding it vertically, this was not the case; scrolls were opened horizontally. It would be rolled to the left for the Greek or Latin reader as those languages were written left to right. The Jewish reader would roll it to the right as Hebrew was written right to left.

The difficulty of using a scroll should be apparent. If one had a long book (such as Isaiah) and attempted to locate a particular passage, it would not be user-friendly. An ancient saying was, "A great book, a great evil." The account in the book of Luke tells us:

Luke 4:16–21 Updated American Standard Version (UASV)

[16] And he [Jesus] came to Nazareth, where he had been brought up; and as was his custom, he went to the synagogue on the Sabbath day, and he stood up to read. [17] And the scroll[42] of the prophet Isaiah was given to him. And he unrolled the scroll[43] and found the place where it was written,

[18] "The Spirit of the Lord is upon me,
because he has anointed me
to proclaim good news[44] to the poor.

---

[41] R. Reed, *Ancient skins, parchments and leathers* (Studies in Archaeological Science) Cambridge, MA: Seminar Press, 1973, 172.
[42] Or a *roll*
[43] Or *roll*
[44] Or *the gospel*

He has sent me to proclaim release to the captives
   and recovering of sight to the blind,
   to set free those who are oppressed,
¹⁹ to proclaim the favorable year of the Lord."

²⁰ And he rolled up the scroll⁴⁵ and gave it back to the attendant and sat down; and the eyes of all in the synagogue were fixed on him. ²¹ And he began to say to them, "Today this Scripture has been fulfilled in your hearing."

Codex: The trunk of a tree that bears leaves only at its apex was called a *caudex* in Latin. This name was modified to *codex* and applied to a wooden tablet with raised edges, with a coat of wax placed within those raised edges. The dried wax would then be used to receive writing with a stylus. We might compare it to the schoolchild's slate, such as seen in some Hollywood Western movies. Around the fifth century B.C.E., some of these were being used and attached by strings that were run through the edges. It is because these bound tablets resembled a tree trunk that they were to take on the name "codex."

Codex Vaticanus ("Book from the Vatican"), Facsimile, Fourth century. It is one of the earliest manuscripts of the Bible, which includes the Greek translation of the bulk of the Hebrew Scriptures as well as most of the Christian Greek Scriptures

As we can imagine, this bulky item also was not user-friendly! Sometime later, the Romans would develop a lighter, more flexible material, the parchment notebook, which would fill the need before the development of the later book-form codex. The Latin word *membranae* (skins) is the name given to such notebooks of parchment. In fact, at 2 Timothy 4:13, the apostle Paul requested of Timothy that he "bring the cloak that I left with Carpus at Troas, also the books [scrolls], and above all the parchments [*membranas*, Greek spelling]." One might ask why Paul used a Latin word (transliterated in Greek)? Undoubtedly, it was because there was no Greek word that would serve as an equivalent to what he was requesting. It was only later that the translated "codex" was brought into the Greek language to reference what we would know as a book.

---

⁴⁵ Or *roll*

The ink of ancient manuscripts was usually one of two kinds. There was ink made of a mixture of soot and gum. These were sold in the form of a bar. It was dissolved in water in an inkwell and produced a very black ink. There was also ink made out of nutgalls, which resulted in a rusty-brown color. Aside from these materials, the scribe would have had a knife to sharpen his reed pen, as well as a sponge to erase errors. With the semi-professional and professional scribe, each character was written with care. Thus, writing was a slow, tedious, and often difficult task.

'I, Tertius, Greet You in the Lord'

Tertius is among the many greetings that we find at the end of the letter of Paul to the Romans, wherein he writes, "I am greeting you, I, Tertius, the one having written this letter, in the Lord." (Rom. 16:22) Of Paul's fourteen letters, this is the only occurrence where we find a clear reference to one of his secretaries.

Little is known of Tertius, who must have been a faithful Christian, based on the greeting "in the Lord." He may have been a member of the Corinthian congregation who likely knew many Christians in Rome, which is suggested because his name is Latin for "third." Quartus for "fourth" is one of the other two who added their greetings: "Erastus the city treasurer greets you, and Quartus the brother, i.e., a member of the Corinthian congregation. (16:23b) Some scholars have suggested that Quartus could have been the younger brother of Tertius.[46] Others have suggested that Tertius was a slave or a freedman.[47] This is also suggested by his Latin name and that slaves were commonly involved in the scribal activity. From this, we could conjecture that Tertius likely had experience as a professional scribe, who became a fellow-worker with the apostle Paul, helping compile the longest of Paul's letters. It was common for Bible authors to use a scribe, as, for example, Jeremiah similarly used Baruch, just as Peter used Silvanus (Jer. 36:4; 1 Pet. 5:12). Of Paul's fourteen letters, six certainly involved the use of a secretary: Romans (16:22), 1 Corinthians (16:21), Galatians (6:11), Colossians (4:18), 2 Thessalonians (3:17), and Philemon (19).

---

[46] Chad Brand et al., eds., "Tertius," *Holman Illustrated Bible Dictionary* (Nashville, TN: Holman Bible Publishers, 2003), 1573.

[47] When the Roman Empire was in power, one who was released from slavery was called a "freedman" (Gr *apeleutheros*), while a "freeman" (Gr *eleutheros*) was free from birth, having full citizenship rights, as was the case with the apostle Paul – Ac 22:28 (Balz and Schneider 1978, Vol. 1, P 121).

Penning the Book of Romans

The letter of Paul to the Romans was written while he was on his third missionary journey as a guest of Gaius in Corinth, about 55-56 C.E. (Ac 20:1-3; Rom. 16:23). We know for a certainty that Paul used Tertius as his secretary to author the book of Romans. However, we cannot say with absolute certainty how he was used. Some have argued, "from evidence outside of the New Testament that it was common practice for authors to dictate their letters to an amanuensis or secretary."[48] Did the secretary take that dictation down in shorthand[49] and then compose the letter, even contributing content, with the New Testament author giving the final approval? Alternatively, was the secretary used in a more limited fashion, such as editing spelling, grammar, and syntax? Otto Roller points out that for an author to dictate a letter to a scribe verbatim would require the author to speak very slowly, i.e., syllable by syllable.[50] There will be more on this later. For now, whatever method was used, the work of a secretary was no easy job. What we do know is that the sixty-six books of the Bible were "inspired by God," and "men spoke from God as they were carried along by the Holy Spirit." – 2 Timothy 3:16; 2 Peter 1:21.

---

[48] See Gordon J. Bahr, "*Paul and Letter Writing in the First Century*," Catholic Biblical Quarterly 28 (1966): 465-77.

See also, John McRay, Paul: His Life and Teaching (Grand Rapids, MI: Baker Academics, 2003), 270.

[49] Again, there is the **slight possibility** of Tertius or other Bible author's scribes taking it down in shorthand and after that making out a full draft, which would have been reviewed by both Paul and Tertius. This is only the case if it is comparable to what a modern-day court reporter does. In some sense, they are taking down whoever is speaking down in shorthand. Imagine a courtroom where you have a witness talking fast, the prosecution interrupts, the defense jumps in with his rebuttal and the judge snaps his ruling, and the witness resumes his or her account of things. All of that is taken down explicitly word for word in shorthand, and if ever turned into longhand, it would be exactly what was said, down to the uh and um common in speech. So, if the shorthand of the day had that kind of capability; then, it is conceivable. We must remember these are the Bible author's dictated words to the scribe based on their inspiration, not the word choice or writing style of the scribe.

[50] Otto Roller, *Das Formular der Paulinischen Briefe: Ein Beitrag zur Lehre vom antiken Briefe* (Stuttgart: W. Kohlhammer, 1933), p. 333.

CHAPTER 3 The Book Writing Process of the New Testament: Authors and Early Christian Scribes

The Place of Writing

When we think of the apostle Paul penning his books that would make up most of the New Testament, some have had the anachronistic tendency to impose their modern way of thinking about him, such as presupposing where he would have written it. As I am writing this page, I am tucked away in my home office, seeking privacy from the hustle and bustle of our modern world. This was not the case in the ancient world, where Paul lived and traveled. People of that time favored a group setting, not isolation. The apostle Paul probably would have been of this mindset. Paul would not have necessarily sought a quiet place to author his letters, to escape the noise of those around him. As for myself, I struggle to get back on track if I am interrupted for more than a couple of minutes.

Most during Paul's day would have been surprised by this way of thinking, i.e., seeking quiet and solitude to focus all of one's energy on the task of writing. Those of Paul's day, including himself, would not have even noticed people talking around them, nor would they have been troubled by what we perceive as interruptions, such as others' discussions, which were neither relevant nor applicable to the subject of their letter writing.

The Scribe of the New Testament Writer

Philip W. Comfort informs us that an **amanuensis** is a "scribe or secretary. In ancient times a written document was first produced by an author who usually dictated the material to an amanuensis. The author would then read the text and make the final editorial adjustments before the document was sent or published. Paul used the writing services of Tertius to write the epistle to the Romans (Rom. 16:22), and Peter was assisted by Silvanus in writing his first Epistle (see 1 Pet. 5:12)."[51]

Dr. Don Wilkins, a Senior Translator for the NASB, also tells us that amanuensis is a "Latin term for a scribe or clerk (plural 'amanuenses'). When used in the context of textual criticism, it refers specifically to a person who served as a secretary to record first-hand the words of a New Testament book if the author chose to use a secretary rather than write down the words himself. Tertius (Rom. 16:22) is our example. The degree to which an amanuensis may have contributed to the content of any particular book of the Bible is a matter of speculation and controversy. At one end of the spectrum is the amanuensis, who merely took dictation (the position preferred here). At the other is the possibility that a New Testament author may have told his amanuensis what he wished to communicate in general terms, leaving it to the amanuensis to actually compose the book." This author would wholeheartedly disagree with the latter view, as the New Testament authors alone were inspired to give us the words of God, and the scribe was merely the vehicle for doing so.

The ancient Greco-Roman society employed secretaries or scribes for various reasons. Of course, the government employed some scribes working for chief administrators. Then, there were the scribes who were used in the private sector. These latter scribes (often slaves) usually were employed by the wealthy. However, even high-ranking slaves and freed slaves employed scribes. Many times, one would find scribes who would write letters for their friends. According to E. Randolph Richards, the skills of these unofficial secretaries "could range from a minimal competency with the language or the mechanics of writing to the highest proficiency at rapidly producing an accurate, proper, and charming letter."[52] Scribes carried out a wide range of administrative, secretarial, and literary tasks, including administrative bookkeeping (keeping records of a business or person), shorthand and taking dictation, letter-writing, and copying literary texts.

The most prominent ways that a scribe would have been used in the first century C.E. would have been as (1) a recorder, (2) an editor, and (3) a secretary for an author. At the very bottom of the writing tasks, he would be used to record information, i.e.,

---

[51] Philip Comfort, *Encountering the Manuscripts: An Introduction to New Testament Paleography & Textual Criticism* (Nashville, TN: Broadman & Holman, 2005), 379.

[52] E. Randolph Richards, The Secretary in the Letters of Paul (Heidelberg, Germany: Mohr Siebeck, 1991, 11

as a record keeper. When they were needed or desired, the New Testament scribes were being used as secretaries, writing down letters by dictation. Tertius took down the book of Romans as Paul dictated to him, which was some 7,000+ words. He would have simply written out the very words that the apostle Paul spoke. Some have argued that longhand in dictation was not feasible in ancient times because the author would have to slow down to the point of speaking syllable-by-syllable. They usually cite Cicero as evidence for this argument because of his writings' numerous references to dictation. Cicero stated in a letter to his friend Varro that he had to slow down his dictation to the point of "syllable by syllable" for the sake of the scribe. However, the scribe he was using at that time was inexperienced, not his regular scribe. Of course, it would be challenging to retain one's line of thought in such a dictation process. It should be noted that Cicero had experienced scribes who could take down dictation at an average pace of speaking, even rapid speech.[53] There is evidence that scribes in those days were skilled enough to take down dictation at the average speech rate. Therefore, we should not assume that the apostles would not have had access to such scribes in the persons of Tertius, Silvanus, or even Timothy.

In fact, Marcus Fabius Quintilianus (b. 35 C.E. d. 100 C.E.) complained that a scribe who could write at the speed of everyday speech can make the speaker feel rushed, to the point of not being able to have time to ponder his thoughts, "On the other hand, there is a fault which is precisely the opposite of this, into which those fall who insist on first making a rapid draft of their subject with the utmost speed of which their pen is capable, and write in the heat and impulse of the moment. They call this their rough copy. They then revise what they have written, and arrange their hasty outpourings. But while the words and the rhythm may be corrected, the matter is still marked by the superficiality resulting from the speed with which it was thrown together. The more correct method is, therefore, to exercise care from the very beginning, and to form the work from the outset in such a manner that it merely requires being chiseled into shape, not fashioned anew. Sometimes, however, we must follow the stream of our emotions since their warmth will give us more than any diligence can secure. The condemnation which I have passed on such carelessness in writing will make it pretty clear what my views are on the luxury of dictation which is now so fashionable. For, when we write, however great our speed, the fact that the hand cannot follow the rapidity of our thoughts gives us time to think, whereas the presence of our amanuensis hurries us on, and at times we feel ashamed to hesitate or pause, or make some alteration, as though we were afraid to display such weakness before a witness. As a result, our language tends not merely to be haphazard and formless, but in our desire to produce a continuous flow we let slip positive improprieties of diction, which show neither the precision of the writer nor the

---

[53] E. Randolph Richards, PAUL AND FIRST-CENTURY LETTER WRITING: Secretaries, Composition and Collection (Downers Grove, IL: IVP Academic, 2004), 29-30; Murphy-O'Connor, *Paul the Letter-Writer*, 9–11; Shorthand references Plutarch, *Cato Minor*, 23.3–5; Caesar, 7.4–5; Seneca, *Epistles*, 14.208.

impetuosity of the speaker. Again, if the amanuensis is a slow writer or lacking in intelligence, he becomes a stumbling-block, our speed is checked, and the thread of our ideas is interrupted by the delay or even perhaps by the loss of temper to which it gives rise."[54]

Therefore, again, we have evidence that some scribes were capable, skilled to the point of writing at the average speed of speech. While Richards says that this is by way of shorthand, saying it was more widespread than initially thought, where the secretary uses symbols in place of words, forming a rough draft that would be written out fully later,[55] this need not be the case. True, there is some evidence that shorthand existed a hundred years before Christ. However, it was still rare, with few scribes having the ability. Whether this was true of the scribes that assisted our New Testament authors is an unknown. It is improbable but not necessarily impossible.

Who in the days of the New Testament authors would use the services of scribes? Foremost would be those who did not know how to read and write. Within ancient contracts and business letters, one can find a note by the scribe (illiteracy statement), who penned it, stating he had done so because his employer could not read or write. For example, an ancient letter concludes with, "Eumelus, son of Herma, has written for him because he does not know letters."[56] It may be that they were able to read but struggled with writing. Then again, it may simply be that they wrote slowly and were unwilling to spend the time improving their skills. An ancient letter from Thebes, Egypt, penned for a certain Asklepiades, concludes, "Written for him hath Eumelus the son of Herma …, being desired so to do for that he writeth somewhat slowly."[57]

On the other hand, whether one knew how to read and write was not always the decisive issue in the use of a secretary. John L. McKenzie writes, "Even people who could read and write did not think of submitting their readers to unprofessional penmanship. It was probably not even a concern for legibility, but rather a concern for beauty, or at least for neatness," (McKenzie 1975, 14) which moved the ancients to turn to the services of a secretary. Although the educated could read and write, some likely felt that writing was tedious, trying, tiring, and frustrating, especially where lengthy and elaborate texts were concerned. It seems that if one could avoid the tremendous task of penning a lengthy letter, entrusting it to a scribe, so much the better.

---

[54] Retrieved Tuesday, February 12, 2019 (Institutio Oratoria, 10.3.17–21) http://bit.ly/2Zazw2X

[55] E. Randolph Richards, PAUL AND FIRST-CENTURY LETTER WRITING: Secretaries, Composition and Collection (Downers Grove, IL: IVP Academic, 2004), 72.

[56] See examples in Francis Exler, *The Form of the Ancient Greek Letter: A Study In Greek Epistolography* (Washington D.C.: Catholic University of America, 1922), pp. 126-7

[57] Adolf Deissmann, *LIGHT FROM THE ANCIENT EAST: The New Testament Illustrated by Recently Discovered Texts of the Graeco-Roman World* (New York and London. 1910). 166-7.

The apostle Paul had over 100 traveling companions, like Aristarchus, Luke, and Timothy, who served by the apostle's side for many years. Then, there are others such as Asyncritus, Hermas, Julia, or Philologus, of whom we barely know more than their names. Many of Paul's friends traveled for the sake of the gospel, such as Achaicus, Fortunatus, Stephanas, Artemas, and Tychicus. We know that Tychicus was used by Paul to carry at least three letters now included in the Bible canon: the epistles to the Ephesians, the Colossians, and Philemon. Tychicus was not simply some mail carrier. He was a well-trusted carrier for the apostle, Paul. The final greeting from Paul to the Colossians reads,

Colossians 4:7-8 Updated American Standard Version (UASV)

7 All my affairs Tychicus, my beloved brother and faithful minister and fellow slave in the Lord, will make known to you. 8 I have sent him to you for this very purpose, that you may know how we are and that he may encourage your hearts,

Richards offers the following about a letter carrier, saying he "was often a personal link between the author and the recipients in addition to the written link. . . . [One purpose] for needing a trustworthy carrier was, he often carried additional information. A letter may describe a situation briefly, frequently with the author's assessment, but the carrier is expected to elaborate for the recipient all the details."[58] Many of Paul's letters deal with teachings and one crisis after another; the carrier was expected to be aware of these on a much deeper level so that he could orally explain and answer any questions. Therefore, he needed to be a highly trusted messenger who was literate.

As was mentioned, Tertius was the scribe Paul used to pen his letter to the Romans. We cannot assume that all of Paul's companions were proficient readers and writers. However, we can infer that Paul would task coworkers, who were able to carry and read letters and understand the condition of the people or congregation where they were being sent or stationed. Yes, at a minimum, these would have been proficient readers. In addition, the scribes whom Paul used, such as Tertius, would very likely have been semi-professional or professional. It would have been simply senseless to entrust the secretarial work of taking down the monumental words of the book of Romans, for example, to an inexperienced scribe. What skills would Tertius need to carry out the task of penning the book of Romans?

The ordinary coworker of Paul would likely have been able to read proficiently but likely possessed minimum writing skills. Paul would have chosen workers whose skills would have equipped them to carry out their assignments. Again, Tertius would have been the exception to the rule; most likely, he would have been a professional scribe. He would have been able to glue the sheets together if it was to be a roll or stitch the pages together if a codex. He would need to know the appropriate mixture of soot and gum to make ink and to be able to use his knife to make his own reed pen.

---

[58] E. Randolph Richards, The Secretary in the Letters of Paul (Heidelberg, Germany: Mohr Siebeck, 1991, 7.

Richards writes that a professional scribe would also "draw lines on the paper. Small holes were often pricked down each side, and then a straight edge and a lead disk were used to lightly draw evenly spaced lines across the sheet."[59] If Tertius had not been trained as a copyist of documents, he would have made many minor errors because his attention would have been on the sense of what he was penning, as opposed to the exact words, as is typical of the unconscious mind.

Porter writes, "Textual criticism has also recognized that even original authors may have **revised their work**, and these works have **gone through editions**." Stanley E. Porter (p. 35) *How We Got the New Testament*

Comfort writes, "When I speak of the original text, I am referring to the 'published' text— that is, the text in its **final edited form** as released for circulation in the Christian community."[60]

HOW do you edit the Holy Spirit? If the author was moved along by the Holy Spirit and all original Scripture is inspired, **why the need for editing?**

Some might say, "We believe that the NT authors themselves penned or dictated a one-time, single, and only version of their texts, unedited and uncorrected under the inspiration of the Holy Spirit."

However, I would pause to ponder Paul dictating the book of Romans to Tertius. Tertius was **not** inspired, so is he capable of going without making one single scribal error for 7,000+ words in his human imperfection? Are we removing the Holy Spirit in any way if Paul scratches out a few words that Tertius got wrong and wrote the correct word above it? Or is it the slippery slope to consider this possibility? If we hold fast to "I believe that the NT authors themselves penned or dictated a one-time, single and only version of their texts, unedited and uncorrected under the inspiration of the Holy Spirit," then we have to answer those kinds of questions. We have to raise them ourselves by writing, "some might ask, how is it ..." Peter said, "always being ready to make a defense to everyone who asks you to give an account." – 1 Peter 3:15.

We need to be willing to modify (or clarify) what we said above to include our qualification that Paul would edit the letter to the Romans as was described, as the amanuensis (i.e., Tertius) was not inspired. Paul would **not** change his original dictation in the process, and the outcome would be a single document, corrected, as necessary. We would also say that Paul might not make the actual corrections but might direct the amanuensis to do that as Paul watched. We do not go beyond this, i.e., postulating a fresh copy made from the original before publication, etc.

---

[59] E. Randolph Richards, PAUL AND FIRST-CENTURY LETTER WRITING: Secretaries, Composition and Collection (Downers Grove, IL: IVP Academic, 2004), 29.

[60] Philip W. Comfort (p. 19), The Quest for the Original Text of the New Testament (Grand Rapids: Baker Academic, 1992)

Did Tertius take Paul's exact dictation, word for word?

Robert H. Mounce writes,

> The only legitimate question about authorship relates to the role of Tertius, who in 16:22 writes, "I Tertius, who wrote down this letter, greet you in the Lord." We know that at that time in history an amanuensis [scribe], that is, one hired to write from dictation, could serve at several levels. In some cases he would receive dictation and write it down immediately in longhand. At other times he might use a form of shorthand (tachygraphy [ancient shorthand]) to take down a letter and then later write it out in longhand. In some cases an amanuensis would simply get the gist of what a person wanted to say and then be left on his own to formulate the ideas into a letter.[61]

It might seem quite the task for Tertius to take down Paul's words in longhand. However, this is not to say that it was impossible, just difficult. Paul might have had to speak in a slow to normal speech rate, **but not** syllable-by-syllable. Tertius would indeed have been writing on a papyrus sheet with a reed pen, intending to be legible; however, he would have been very skilled in his trade. Then again, there is the **slight possibility** of Tertius taking it down in shorthand and after that making out a complete draft, which would have been reviewed by both Paul and Tertius. This is only the case if it is comparable to what a modern-day court reporter does. In some sense, they are taking down whoever is speaking down in shorthand. Imagine a courtroom where you have a witness talking fast, the prosecution interrupts, the defense jumps in with his rebuttal, and the judge snaps his ruling, and the witness resumes their account of things. All of that is taken down explicitly word for word in shorthand, and if ever turned into longhand, it would be precisely what was said, down to the uh and um common in speech. So, if the shorthand of the day had that kind of capability; then, it is conceivable. We must remember these are the Bible author's dictated words to the scribe based on their inspiration, not the scribe's word choice or writing style.

The last option by Mounce in the above is contrary to the attitudes that both the scribes and the New Testament authors would have had. Paul and Tertius knew that Paul's words were Spirit-inspired, that is, God's words. God chose to convey a message through Matthew, Mark, Luke, John, Peter, Jude, James, and Paul, not Tertius and Silvanus, Timothy, or others. We cannot say with any certainty whether Tertius or Silvanus took their authors' words down in shorthand or longhand. However, we can say that the human author was dictating the Word of God to the scribe, and in no way was it composed by the scribe. Yes, it is true that the Spirit-inspired author, who is

---

[61] Robert H. Mounce, *Romans*, vol. 27, The New American Commentary (Nashville: Broadman & Holman Publishers, 1995), 22.

literally moved along by the Holy Spirit, retained their style of expressing the message but not the scribe. Mark's writing style is concise, even abrupt at times. His Gospel contains rapid changes of thought. The style of writing of First and Second Timothy is the same as Titus, which adds authenticity to the letter to Titus.

Inspiration and Inerrancy in the Writing Process

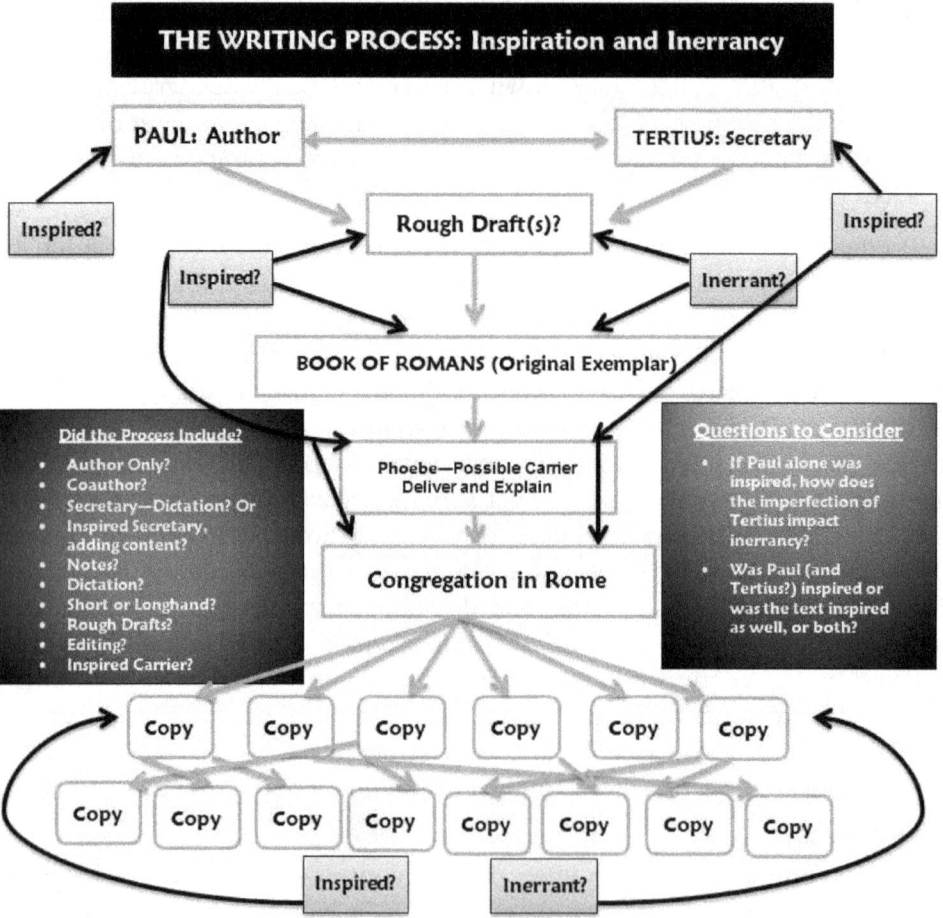

All Scripture is Inspired by God

In this context, inspiration is **the state** of a human being moved by the Holy Spirit, which results in an inspired, fully inerrant written Word of God.

Chicago Statement on Biblical Inerrancy ICBI

Article VII

We affirm that **inspiration** was the work in which God by His Spirit, through human writers, gave us His Word. The origin of Scripture is divine. The mode of divine **inspiration** remains largely a mystery to us. We deny that **inspiration** can be reduced to human insight, or to heightened states of consciousness of any kind.

Article VIII

We affirm that God in His Work of **inspiration** utilized the distinctive personalities and literary styles of the writers whom He had chosen and prepared. We deny that God, in causing these writers to use the very words that He chose, overrode their personalities. ["I would argue that if by human imperfection an author was going to choose an inappropriate word that would fail to communicate the meaning intended by God that the Holy Spirit would then override that word choice." – Edward D. Andrews]

Article IX

We affirm that **inspiration**, though not conferring omniscience, guaranteed true and trustworthy utterance on all matters of which the Biblical authors were moved to speak and write. We deny that the finitude or fallenness of these writers, by necessity or otherwise, introduced distortion or falsehood into God's Word.

Article X

We affirm that **inspiration**, strictly speaking, applies only to the autographic text of Scripture, which in the providence of God can be ascertained from available manuscripts with great accuracy. We further affirm that copies and translations of Scripture are the Word of God to the extent that they faithfully represent the original. We deny that any essential element of the Christian faith is affected by the absence of the autographs. We further deny that this absence renders the assertion of Biblical **inerrancy** invalid or irrelevant. [There is no miracle of preservation, but rather, it is preservation by restoration. Today, what we have, thanks to hundreds of textual scholars over a few hundred years, is a 99.99% restored original language text. – Edward D. Andrews]

Article XI

We affirm that Scripture, having been given by divine inspiration, is infallible, so that, far from misleading us, it is true and reliable in all the matters it addresses. We deny that it is possible for the Bible to be at the same time infallible and errant in its assertions. Infallibility and inerrancy may be distinguished, but not separated.

Inerrancy of Scripture

Inerrancy of Scripture is **the result** of the state of a human being moved by the Holy Spirit from God, which results in an inspired, fully inerrant written Word of God.

Article XII

We affirm that Scripture in its entirety is **inerrant**, being free from all falsehood, fraud, or deceit. We deny that Biblical infallibility and **inerrancy** are limited to spiritual, religious, or redemptive themes, exclusive of assertions in the fields of history and science. We further deny that scientific hypotheses about earth history may properly be used to overturn the teaching of Scripture on creation and the flood.

Article XIII

We affirm the propriety of using **inerrancy** as a theological term with reference to the complete truthfulness of Scripture. We deny that it is proper to evaluate Scripture according to standards of truth and error that are alien to its usage or purpose. We further deny that **inerrancy** is negated by Biblical phenomena such as a lack of modern technical precision, irregularities of grammar or spelling, observational descriptions of nature, the reporting of falsehoods, the use of hyperbole and round numbers, the topical arrangement of material, variant selections of material in parallel accounts, or the use of free citations.

Article XV

We affirm that the doctrine of **inerrancy** is grounded in the teaching of the Bible about **inspiration**. We deny that Jesus' teaching about Scripture may be dismissed by appeals to accommodation or to any natural limitation of His humanity.

Article XVI

We affirm that the doctrine of **inerrancy** has been integral to the Church's faith throughout its history. We deny that inerrancy is a doctrine invented by Scholastic Protestantism, or is a reactionary position postulated in response to negative higher criticism.

Authoritative Word of God

The **authoritative** aspect of Scripture is that God by way of inspiration gives the words the authors chose to use power and authority, so that the outcome (i.e., originals) is the very Word of God, as though God were speaking to us himself.

Article I

We affirm that the Holy Scriptures are to be received as the **authoritative** Word of God. We deny that the Scriptures receive their authority from the Church, tradition, or any other human source.

2 Timothy 3:16-17 Updated American Standard Version (UASV)

[16] All Scripture is inspired by God and profitable for teaching, for reproof, for correction, for training in righteousness; [17] so that the man of God may be fully competent, equipped for every good work.

What does this mean? The phrase "inspired by God" (Gr., *theopneustos*) literally means, "Breathed out by God." A related Greek word, *pneuma*, means "wind," "breath," life, "Spirit." Since *pneuma* can also mean "breath," the process of "breathing out" can rightly be said to be the work of the Holy Spirit inspiring the Scriptures. The result is that the originals were accurate, fully inerrant, and authoritative. Thus, the Holy Spirit moved human writers so that the result can truthfully be called the Word of *God*, not the word of man.

2 Peter 1:21 Updated American Standard Version (UASV)

²¹ for no prophecy was ever produced by the will of man, but men carried along by the Holy Spirit spoke from God.

The Greek word here translated "men carried along by," "men moved by" (NASB)," (φέρω pherō), is used in another form at Acts 27:15, 17, which describes a ship that was driven along by the wind. So, the Holy Spirit, by analogy, 'navigated the course' of the Bible writers. While the Spirit did not give them each word by dictation,[62] it certainly kept the writers from inserting any information that did not convey the will and purpose of God.

The heart of what the International Council on Biblical Inerrancy (ICBI) stood for is apparent in "A Short Statement," produced at the Chicago conference in 1978:

A SHORT STATEMENT

1. God, who is Himself Truth and speaks truth only, has inspired Holy Scripture in order thereby to reveal Himself to lost mankind through Jesus Christ as Creator and Lord, Redeemer and Judge. Holy Scripture is God's witness to Himself.

2. Holy Scripture, being God's own Word, written by men prepared and superintended by His Spirit, is of infallible divine authority in all matters upon which it touches: it is to be believed, as God's instruction, in all that it affirms, obeyed, as God's command, in all that it requires; embraced, as God's pledge, in all that it promises.

3. The Holy Spirit, Scripture's divine Author, both authenticates it to us by His inward witness and opens our minds to understand its meaning.

4. Being wholly and verbally God-given, Scripture is without error or fault in all its teaching, no less in what it states about God's acts in creation, about the events of world history, and about its own literary origins under God, than in its witness to God's saving grace in individual lives.

---

[62] Dr. Don Wilkins, Senior Translator of the NASB writes, "Exactly how the Spirit guided the writers is a mystery, and the words "thus says the Lord" in prophecy most likely do introduce a dictated message. However, those familiar with Greek can easily see stylistic differences between the NT writers which seem to reflect different personalities and rule out verbatim dictation from a single source."

5. The **authority of Scripture** is inescapably impaired if this total divine **inerrancy** is in any way limited or disregarded or made relative to a view of truth contrary to the Bible's own; and such lapses bring serious loss to both the individual and the Church.

Questions to Consider

We have been using the book of Romans as our example, so we will continue with it. We know that Paul was the author who gave us the inspired content of Romans, Tertius was the secretary who recorded Romans, and Phoebe was likely the one who carried the letter to Rome or else accompanied the one who did. Thus, we have at least three persons: the author, the secretary (amanuensis; scribe), and the carrier.

What is inspiration?

Inspiration is a "theological concept encompassing phenomena in which human action, skill, or utterance is immediately and extraordinarily supplied by the Spirit of God. Although various terms are employed in the Bible, the basic meaning is best served by Gk. *theopneustos* "God-breathed." (2 Tim. 3:16) This means "breathed forth by God" rather than "breathed into by God" (Warfield)." (Myers 1987, 524) **Verbal plenary inspiration** holds that "every word of Scripture was God-breathed." Human writers played a significant role. Their individual backgrounds, personal traits, and literary styles were authentically theirs but had been providentially prepared by God for use as his instrument in producing Scripture. "The Scriptures had not been dictated, but the result was as if they had been (A. A. Hodge, B. B. Warfield)."[63]

World-Renowned Bible Scholars Define Inspiration

Benjamin B. Warfield: "Inspiration is, therefore, usually defined as a supernatural influence exerted on the sacred writers by the Spirit of God, by virtue of which their writings are given Divine trustworthiness."[64]

Edward J. Young: "Inspiration is a superintendence of God the Holy Spirit over the writers of the Scriptures, as a result of which these Scriptures possess Divine authority and trustworthiness and, possessing such Divine authority and trustworthiness, are free from error."[65]

---

[63] Allen C. Myers, *The Eerdmans Bible Dictionary* (Grand Rapids, MI: Eerdmans, 1987), 525.

[64] B. B. Warfield, *The Inspiration and Authority of the Bible* (Philadelphia, PA: Presbyterian and Reformed Pub. Co., 1948), p. 131.

[65] Edward J. Young, *Thy Word Is Truth* (Grand Rapids: Eerdmans, 1957), p. 27.

Charles C. Ryrie: "Inspiration is ... God's superintendence of the human authors so that, using their own individual personalities, they composed and recorded without error His revelation to man in the words of the original autographs."[66]

Paul P. Enns: "There are several important elements that belong in a proper definition of inspiration: (1) the divine element–God the Holy Spirit superintended the writers, ensuring the accuracy of the writing; (2) the human element—human authors wrote according to their individual styles and personalities; (3) the result of the divine-human authorship is the recording of God's truth without error; (4) inspiration extends to the selection of words by the writers; (5) inspiration relates to the original manuscripts."[67]

Were both Paul and Tertius inspired, or just Paul?

Only Paul and other Old and New Testament authors were inspired. First, as was stated above, **Verbal plenary inspiration** holds that "every word of Scripture was God-breathed." However, God **did not**, generally speaking, dictate the books of the Bible word by word to the Bible authors as if they were dictating machines.

As the apostle Paul states, God spoke "in many ways" to his servants before the arrival of Jesus Christ. (Heb. 1:1-2) We do have one specific circumstance: The Ten Commandments, wherein the information was divinely provided in written form. Therefore, a scribe would only have to copy them into the scrolls created by Moses. (Ex. 31:18; Deut. 10:1-5) At other times, information was communicated by verbal dictation, literally word for word. When introducing the large number of laws and statutes of the covenant with Israel, "Jehovah said to Moses: 'Write these words, for in accordance with these words I have made a covenant with you and with Israel.'" (Ex. 34:27) And on other occasions, the prophets also were frequently given precise messages that were to be delivered. These were then recorded after that, which then became part of the inspired, fully inerrant Scriptures. – 1 Kings 22:14; Jeremiah 1:7; 2:1; 11:1-5; Ezekiel 3:4; 11:5.

2 Thessalonians 3:17 Updated American Standard Version (UASV)

[17] The greeting is by my hand, Paul's,[68] which is a sign in every letter; this is the way I write.

An appended note to every letter with his signature "distinguishing mark" is like a boss signing a letter that he dictated to a secretary. It is unthinkable that Paul would sign or make a distinguishing mark on anything without reading through it and, after that, making any necessary corrections or having Tertius makes the corrections. This supposes that Paul looked over all of his letters, which would also suppose that the scribe could not have been inspired because if he were, then there would have been

---

[66] Charles C. Ryrie, *A Survey of Bible Doctrine* (Chicago: Moody, 1972), p. 38.
[67] Paul P. Enns, *The Moody Handbook of Theology* (Chicago: Moody Press, 1989), p. 161.
[68] Lit *the greeting by my hand of Paul*

no mistakes in the document, which means it would not have been needed to be looked over let alone corrected. So again, there would have been no need for Paul to check the work of an inspired secretary. Again, more plainly, if Tertius had been inspired, Paul would have had no need to look the text over the moment he set the pen down. There is no need to read into silence and suggest that the secretary was inspired. While Tertius was likely a professional scribe and indeed engaged in his work, they were also coworkers and traveling companions. As was stated earlier, in a small percentage of cases, information was transmitted by verbal dictation, word for word from God by way of the Holy Spirit to the author. For example, when God delivered the large body of laws and statutes of his covenant with Israel, Jehovah instructed Moses: "Write for yourself these words." (Ex 34:27) In another example, the prophets were often given specific messages to deliver. (1 Ki 22:14; Jer. 1:7; 2:1; 11:1-5; Eze. 3:4; 11:5) Additionally, the Bible authors did dictate word for word what they received under inspiration to their secretaries, i.e., amanuenses/scribes. In other words, any word choices or writing styles belonged to the Bible author.

Jeremiah 36:4 Updated American Standard Version (UASV)

⁴Then Jeremiah called Baruch the son of Neriah, and Baruch wrote on a scroll at the **dictation of Jeremiah** all the words of Jehovah that he had spoken to him. (Bold mine)

If Paul alone was inspired, how does the imperfection of Tertius affect inerrancy?

First, we should state that just because Paul used Tertius, Peter used Silvanus, or Jeremiah used Baruch to pen the Word of God, they did not thereby detract from or weaken the authority of God's Word or the inerrancy of Scripture. The dictation that Paul gave Tertius was the result of divine inspiration as he, Paul, was moved along by the Holy Spirit. Tertius merely recorded Paul's dictation, word by word. Whether Tertius was a professional scribe[69] or had the skills of a semi-professional scribe, he must have made at least a few slips of the pen, as the epistle to the Romans was some 7,000 words, and writing conditions were challenging. Afterward, however, Paul would have reviewed the document with Tertius, correcting any errors before publishing the official, authoritative text.

What about Phoebe? What role did the carrier have in the process?

Those used by New Testament authors to deliver the Word of God to people or congregations would have been some of Paul's most trusted, competent coworkers. Paul had over one hundred of these. Indeed, in the case of congregations contacting Paul with questions and concerns, Paul responded with an inspired letter, the carrier would be made aware of those questions and concerns. Paul would have spoken to the carrier at length about these matters, going over what he meant by the words he

---

[69] In the strictest sense, a professional scribe is one who was specifically trained in that vocation and was paid for his services.

had used. This would have provided the carrier sufficient knowledge; if the person or congregation had any question(s) that the carrier could address. This process is not indicated within the Scriptures. Are we to believe God and Paul, for that matter, would send a simple carrier who was left in the dark as to what he was carrying? And that no congregational leader would have follow-up questions, which God would have foreseen? Hardly.

The Publishing, Copying, and Distributing Process

In the above, we spoke of the initial aspect of the publishing process, i.e., the moment Paul decided to pen a letter to a congregation like the Romans, the Ephesians, the Colossians, or a person such as Philemon. We discussed the process that Paul went through with his secretary (e.g., Tertius), to the carrier (e.g., Phoebe, Tychicus), and the recipients (e.g., Roman congregation). Now we turn to the circulation aspect, i.e., getting the book out to more readers. Harry Y. Gamble says the following in *The Publication and Early Dissemination of Early Christian Books*:

> The letters of Paul to his communities, the earliest extant Christian texts, were dictated to scribal associates (presumably Christian), carried to their destinations by a traveling Christian, and read aloud to the congregations.[70] But Paul also envisioned the circulation of some of his letters beyond a single Christian group (cf. Gal. 1: 2, 'to the churches of Galatia', Rom. 1:7 'to all God's beloved in Rome'—dispersed among numerous discrete house churches, Rom. 16: 5, 10, 11, 14, 15), and the author of Colossians, if not Paul, gives instruction for the exchange of Paul's letters between different communities (Col. 4: 16), which must indeed have taken place also soon after Paul's time.[71] The gospel literature of early Christianity offers only meager hints of intentions or means of its publication and circulation. The prologue to Luke/Acts (Luke 1: 1–4) provides a dedication to 'Theophilus', who (whether or not a fictive figure) by that convention is implicitly made responsible for the dissemination of the work by encouraging and permitting copies to be made. The last chapter of the Gospel of John, an epilogue added by others after the original conclusion of the Gospel (20: 30–1), aims at least in part (21: 24–5) to insure appreciation of the book and to promote its use beyond its community of origin. To take another case, the Apocalypse, addressed to seven churches in western Asia Minor, was almost surely sent in separate copy to each. Even so, the author anticipated its wider copying and dissemination beyond those original

---

[70] On the dictation of Paul's letters to a scribe, see E. R. Richards, The Secretary in the Letters of Paul (WUNT 42; Tubingen: Mohr, 1991), 169–98; for couriers see Rom. 16: 1, 1 Cor. 16: 10, Eph. 6: 21, Col. 4: 7, cf. 2 Cor. 8: 16–17. Reference to their carriers is common in other early Christian letters (e.g., 1 Pet. 5: 12, 1 Clem. 65: 1, Ignatius, Phil. 11.2, Smyr. 12.1, Polycarp, Phil. 14.1). For the general practice see E. Epp, 'New Testament Papyrus Manuscripts and Letter Carrying in Greco-Roman Times', in B. A. Pearson (ed.), The Future of Early Christianity (Minneapolis: Fortress, 1991), 35–56. Reading a letter aloud to the community, which seems to be presupposed by all the letters, is stipulated only in 1 Thess. 5: 27.

[71] This is shown for an early time by the generalization of the original particular addresses of some of Paul's letters (Rom. 1: 7, 15; 1 Cor. 1: 2; cf. Eph. 1: 1).

recipients, and so warned subsequent copyists to preserve the integrity of the book, neither adding nor subtracting, for fear of religious penalty (Rev. 22:18–19). The private Christian copying and circulation that is presumed in these early writings continued to be the means for the publication and dissemination of Christian literature in the second and third centuries. It can be seen, for example, in the explicit notice in The Shepherd of Hermas (Vis. 2.4.3) that the book was to be published or released in two final copies, one for local use in Rome, the other for the transcription of further copies to be sent to Christian communities in 'cities abroad'. It can also be seen when Polycarp, bishop of Smyrna, had the letters of Ignatius copied and sent to the Christian community in Philippi, and had copies of letters from them and other churches in Asia Minor sent to Syrian Antioch (Phil. 13). It is evident too in the scribal colophons of the Martyrdom of Polycarp (22.2–4), and must be assumed also in connection with the letters of Dionysius, bishop of Corinth (fl. 170 ce; Eusebius, H.E. 4.23.1–12).

From another angle, the physical remains of early Christian books show that they were produced and disseminated privately within and between Christian communities. Early Christian texts, especially those of a scriptural sort, were almost always written in codices or leaf books—an informal, economical, and handy format—rather than on rolls, which were the traditional and standard vehicle of all other books. This was a sharp departure from convention, and particularly characteristic of Christians. Also distinctive to Christian books was the pervasive use of nomina sacra, divine names written in abbreviated forms, which was clearly an in-house practice of Christian scribes. Further, the preponderance in early Christian papyrus manuscripts of an informal quasi-documentary script rather than a professional bookhand also suggests that Christian writings were privately transcribed with a view to intramural circulation and use.[72]

If Christian books were disseminated in roughly the same way as other books, that is, by private seriatim copying, we might surmise that they spread slowly and gradually in ever-widening circles, first in proximity to their places of origin, then regionally, and then transregionally, and for some books this was doubtless the case. But it deserves notice that some early Christian texts appear to have enjoyed surprisingly rapid and wide circulation. Already by the early decades of the second century Papias of Hierapolis in western Asia Minor was acquainted at least with the Gospels of Mark and Matthew (Eusebius, H.E. 3.39.15–16); Clement of Rome, Ignatius of Antioch, and Polycarp of Smyrna were all acquainted with collections of Paul's letters; and papyrus copies of various early Christian texts were current in Egypt.[73] The Shepherd of Hermas, written in Rome near the mid-second century, was current and popular in Egypt not long after.[74] Equally interesting, Irenaeus' Adversus haereses, written about 180 in Gaul, is shown by papyrus fragments to

---

[72] On these features see H. Gamble, Books and Readers in the Early Church (New Haven: Yale University Press, 1995), 66–81, and L. Hurtado, The Earliest Christian Artifacts (Grand Rapids: Eerdmans, 2006).

[73] For Clement, Ignatius, and Polycarp, see A. F. Gregory and C. M. Tuckett, eds., The Reception of the New Testament in the Apostolic Fathers (Oxford: OUP, 2005), 142–53, 162–72, 201–18, 226–7. For early Christian papyri in Egypt see Hurtado, Earliest Christian Artifacts, appendix 1 (209–29). The most notable case is P52 (a fragment of the Gospel of John, customarily dated to the early 2nd cent.).

[74] Some papyrus fragments of Hermas are 2nd cent. (P.Oxy. 4706 and 3528, P.Mich. 130, P.Iand. 1.4).

have found its way to Egypt by the end of the second century, and indeed also to Carthage, where it was used by Tertullian.[75]

The brisk and broad dissemination of Christian books presumes not only a lively interest in texts among Christian communities but also efficient means for their reproduction and distribution. Such interest and means may be unexpected, given that the rate of literacy within Christianity was low, on average no greater than in the empire at large, namely in the range of 10–15 percent.[76] Yet there were some literate members in almost all Christian communities, and as long as texts could be read aloud by some, they were accessible and useful to the illiterate majority. Christian congregations were not reading communities in the same sense as elite literary or scholarly circles, but books were nevertheless important to them virtually from the beginning, for even before Christians began to compose their own texts, books of Jewish scripture played an indispensable role in their worship, teaching, and missionary preaching. Indeed, Judaism and Christianity were the only religious communities in Greco-Roman antiquity in which texts had any considerable importance, and in this, as in some other respects, Christian groups bore a greater resemblance to philosophical circles than to other religious traditions.[77]

If smaller, provincial Christian congregations were not well-equipped or well-situated for the tasks of copying and disseminating texts, larger Christian centers must have had some scriptorial capacity: already in the second century: Polycarp's handling of Ignatius' letters and letters from other churches shows its presence in Smyrna; the instruction about the publication of Hermas' The Shepherd suggests it for Rome; and it can hardly be doubted for Alexandria, since even in a provincial city like Oxyrhynchus many manuscripts of Christian texts were available.[78] The early third-century Alexandrian scriptorium devised for the production and distribution of the works of Origen (Eusebius, H.E. 6.23.2), though unique in its sponsorship by a private patron and its service to an individual writer, surely had precursors, more modest and yet efficient, in other Christian communities. It also had important successors, not the least of which was the library and scriptorium that flourished in Caesarea in the second half of the third century under the auspices of Pamphilus.[79]

---

[75] For the A.H. in Egypt: P.Oxy. 405; for Tertullian's use of A.H. in Carthage, see T. D. Barnes, Tertullian (Oxford: Clarendon, 1971), 127–8, 220–1.

[76] The fundamental study of literacy in antiquity is still W. V. Harris, Ancient Literacy (Cambridge, Mass.: Harvard University Press, 1989); see now also the essays in J. H. Humphrey, ed., Literacy in the Roman World (Journal of Roman Archaeology, suppl. ser. 3; Ann Arbor: University of Michigan, 1991), and in W. A. Johnson and H. N. Parker, eds., Ancient Literacies (Oxford: OUP, 2009).

[77] M. Beard, 'Writing and Religion: Ancient Religion and the Function of the Written Word in Roman Religion', in Humphrey, Literacy in the Roman World, 353–8, argues that texts played a relatively large role in Greco-Roman religions, yet characterizes that role as 'symbolic rather than utilitarian', which was clearly not the case in early Christianity. The kind of careful reading, interpretation, and exposition of texts that we see in early Christianity and in early Judaism (whether in worship or school settings) provides, mutatis mutandis, an interesting analogy to the activity of elite literary circles.

[78] On the question of early Christian scriptoria (the term may be variously construed), see Gamble, Books and Readers, 121–6. Hurtado, Earliest Christian Artifacts, 185–9, rightly calls attention to corrections by contemporary hands in early Christian papyri as pointing to at least limited activity of a scriptorial kind.

[79] The role of Pamphilus and the Caesarean library/scriptorium in the private production and dissemination of early Christian literature, esp. of scriptural materials, was highlighted by Eusebius in his Life of Pamphilus, as quoted by Jerome in his Apology against Rufinus (1.9).

> Absent such reliable intra-Christian means for the production of books, the range of texts known and used by Christian communities across the Mediterranean basin by the end of the second century would be without explanation.[80]

When we think of publishing a book today, there are some similarities to the ancient process, but it was not the same for Christian communities in the ancient world of the Roman Empire. Paul dispatched Tychicus as a carrier with a letter to the Ephesians, the Colossians, and Philemon and a potential fourth letter to the Laodiceans. Tychicus was competent, trusted, and a skilled coworker who delivered these letters hundreds of miles from an imprisoned Paul, with enough information to bring God's Word to the first-century Christian congregations. However, in the letter to the Colossians, Paul said, "When this letter has been read among you, have it also read in the church of the Laodiceans; and see that you also read the letter from Laodicea." (Col. 4:16) In other words, it was to be a circuit letter. Paul had also stated to the Thessalonians in a letter to them, "I put you under oath before the Lord to have this letter read to all the brothers." (1 Thess. 5:27) Paul encouraged the distribution of his letters.

Remember the process from the above; the book would be shared with friends of similar interests, and then the circles grew wider and wider to friends of friends and others. First, Paul's primary level of friends would be his more than one hundred traveling companions and fellow workers, some being the carriers who delivered the books. Second, the friends in the Christian congregation would have the letter read to them, who would then share it with other fellow congregations. In the secular (non-Christian) circle of friends, interested readers who wished to have a copy would have their slaves (i.e., scribes) make a copy or copies of a book. The same would have been valid within the Christian congregation. When the Laodiceans read the letter that Paul had sent to the Colossians, they would have had one of their wealthy members use his literate and trained scribe to make a copy for their congregation and maybe even a few copies for other members. The same would hold true when the Colossians received the letter written to the Laodiceans. Eventually, Paul's letters would have been gathered in one codex to circulate as a group, such as P^{46}. Papyrus 46 is an early Greek New Testament manuscript written on papyrus. Its most probable date between 100 and 150 C.E. Michael Marlowe says that P^{46} contains (in order) "the last eight chapters of Romans; all of Hebrews; virtually all of 1–2 Corinthians; all of Ephesians, Galatians,

---

[80] Charles E. Hill; Michael J. Kruger, *THE EARLY TEXT OF THE NEW TESTAMENT* (Oxford, United Kingdom: Oxford University Press, 2012), 32-35.

Beyond the uses of Christian texts in congregational settings, there were already in the 2nd cent. some Christian circles that pursued specialized and technical engagements with texts, usually in the service of theological arguments and exegetical agendas. The 'school-settings' of teachers such as Valentinus and Justin, and a little later of Theodotus, Clement, and Origen, were Christian approximations to the kinds of literary activity associated with 'elite' reading communities in the early empire.

Philippians, Colossians; and two chapters of 1 Thessalonians. All of the leaves have lost some lines at the bottom through deterioration."

The scriptorium was a room for copying manuscripts, where a lector would read aloud from his exemplar, with a room full of copyists taking down his dictation. Recent scholarship has suggested that we remove the concept of the scriptorium in the time of Jesus and the apostles of the first century C.E. because this was not a practice until the fourth century C.E. Harry Y. Gamble addresses this effectively when he writes,

> It is difficult to determine just when Christian scriptoria came into existence. The problem is partly of definition, partly of evidence. If we think of the scriptorium as simply a writing center where texts were copied by more than a single scribe, then any of the larger Christian communities, such as Antioch or Rome, may have already had scriptoria in the early second century, and in view of Polycarp's activity something of the kind can be imagined for Smyrna. If we think instead of a scriptorium as being more structured, operating, for example, in a specially designed and designated location; employing particular methods of transcription; producing certain types of manuscripts; or multiplying copies on a significant scale, then it becomes more difficult to imagine that such institutions developed at an early date.[81]

Gamble goes on to inform us that Origen's scriptorium of about 230 C.E. was an exception. Just a few short years later, the scriptorium of Cyprian was a more official version of what we think of when picturing scriptoria. Then, there is the scriptorium that was attached to the Christian library in Caesarea, which we know was commissioned to produce fifty New Testament manuscripts in short order. It may even have been added in the third century when Pamphilus (latter half of the 3rd century–309 C.E.) built the library. A more official type of scriptorium could likely be found in this period at other Christian epicenters, such as Rome, Jerusalem, and Alexandria. Comfort tells us that "church history and certain manuscript discoveries from other parts in Egypt suggest that Alexandria had a Christian scriptorium or writing center."[82] Gamble adds, "It was only during the fourth and fifth centuries that the scriptoria on monastic communities came into their own, also in association with monastic libraries."[83]

While it is challenging, if not impossible, to identify a specific Alexandrian scriptorium for our early manuscripts of the second century, or even if they were

---

[81] Henry Y. Gamble, *Books and Readers in the Early Church: A History of Early Christian Texts* (New Haven, CT, New Haven University Press, 1995), 121.

[82] Philip Comfort, *Encountering the Manuscripts: An Introduction to New Testament Paleography & Textual Criticism* (Nashville, TN: Broadman & Holman, 2005), 22.

[83] Henry Y. Gamble, *Books and Readers in the Early Church: A History of Early Christian Texts* (New Haven, CT, New Haven University Press, 1995), 121-2.

produced in a scriptorium at all, we do know that professional scribes produced them. There are many possibilities: (1) the professional scribe could have produced them in a Christian scriptorium. On the other hand, (2) the professional scribe could have been a Christian who worked for a scriptorium, who then used his skills to produce copies. Then again, (3) it could have been that the scribe formerly worked in a scriptorium but now was the private scribe of a wealthy Christian who used his skills to make copies. We know that about a million Christians spread throughout the Roman Empire at the beginning of the second century (c. 130 C.E.). Therefore, the copying of manuscripts could very well have been within the Christian community, i.e., from the Christian congregation to the Christian congregation and wealthy Christians acquiring personal copies for themselves.

We have several early manuscripts that evidence that they were very likely produced in a scriptorium, even if it was simply a room attached to a Christian library, which had a handful of copyists. For example, a professional scribe undoubtedly did P46 (100-150 C.E.) because it contained stichoi marks, which are notes at the end of sections, stating how many lines were copied. This was a means of calculating how much a scribe should be paid. It is likely that an employee of the scriptorium numbered the pages, indicating the stichoi marks. Moreover, this same scribe made corrections as he went. Another example would be P^{66} (also c. 100-150 C.E.) according to Comfort:

> It is also fairly certain that P^{66} was the product of a scriptorium or writing center. The first copyist of this manuscript had his work thoroughly checked by a diorthotes [corrector], according to a different exemplar—just the way it would happen in a scriptorium. Of course, it can be argued that an individual who purchased the manuscript made all the corrections, which was a common practice in ancient times. But the extent of corrections in P^{66} and the fact that the paginator (a different scribe) made many of the corrections speaks against this (see description of P^{66} in chap. 2). It was more the exception than the rule in ancient times that a manuscript would be fully checked by a diorthotes. P^{66} has other markings of being professionally produced. The extant manuscript still shows the pinpricks in the corners of each leaf of the papyri; these served as a guide for left hand justification and right hand. The manuscript also exhibits a consistent set of marginal and interlinear correction signs. Another sign of professionally produced manuscript is the use of the diple (>) in the margin, which was used to signal a correction in the text and/or the need for a correction in the text. There are very few of these in the extant New Testament manuscripts.[84]

---

[84] Philip W. Comfort, *New Testament Text and Translation Commentary: Commentary on the Variant Readings of the Ancient New Testament Manuscripts and How They Relate to the Major English Translations* (Carol Stream, IL: Tyndale House Publishers, Inc., 2008), 26.

The production and distribution of New Testament manuscripts were carried out at the congregation and individual Christian levels in the early days of Christianity.

Moreover, this process did not negate the use of professional scribes. Just as Paul would not have used an inexperienced scribe to produce the epistle to the Romans. Congregations and wealthy Christians would have likely used professional scribes to make copies. Of course, there are exceptions to the rule, and some congregations may not have had access to a professional scribe, so they would have to have chosen to use the best person available to them. Nevertheless, if a congregation had access to a person experienced at making documents or a semi-professional or professional scribe, they would have lacked good sense or practicality not to take advantage of such a person. Think of anything we want to have done in our Christian congregation today: would we not seek a professional if we had access to one as a member, be it plumbing, wiring, teaching, or computer technology? We naturally look to the most skilled person that we can find, even if we have a clogged-up commode. Would we do any less if we were in the first century and had just received a letter from the apostle Paul, who was imprisoned hundreds of miles away in Rome?

Why Would the Holy Spirit Miraculously Inspire 66 Fully Inerrant Texts and Then Allow Variant Errors in the Copies?

Agnostic New Testament textual and early Christianity scholar Dr. Bart D. Ehrman states, "For the only reason (I came to think) for God to inspire the Bible would be so that his people would have his actual words; but if he really wanted people to have his actual words, surely, he would have miraculously preserved those words, just as he had miraculously inspired them in the first place. Given the circumstance that he didn't preserve the words, the conclusion seemed inescapable to me that he hadn't gone to the trouble of inspiring them."[85]

New Testament textual scholar Dr. Dirk Jongkind offers a brief response, "God chose not to give us exhaustive knowledge of every detail of the text, though he could have done so. Still, he has given us abundant access to his words. In other words, to say that God inspired the words of the New Testament does not mean that God is therefore under an obligation to preserve for us each and every detail."[86]

Why didn't God inspire the copyists? Some have become anxious because this question has plagued them, or some Bible critic has challenged them. Therefore, they are looking for the silver bullet to quench their personal concern or have a ready, quick response for the Bible critic. Draw comfort in that there are hundreds, if not

---

[85] Misquoting Jesus: The Story Behind Who Changed the Bible and Why (San Francisco: HarperSanFrancisco, 2005), 211.

[86] An Introduction to the Greek New Testament, Produced at Tyndale House, Cambridge, Crossway.

thousands, of great responses to attacks from Bible critics that will cause them to move onto another victim in their quest to stumble God's people. However, there are good reasons, rational responses to some questions that will not be fully answered until the second coming of Jesus Christ. What lies below is the latter. Before delving into the rational, reasonable reasons why God would inspire the authors but not the copyists, let's talk a little about what we do have.

Some people have unreceptive hearts and minds. They are Pharisaical because they are not interested in an answer, and the Word of God, reason, and logic will not get through their callused hearts. Suppose I have only taught one thing in my 32 years. In that case, it is this, identify these people fast, or you will waste much of your life, giving reasonable, rational responses to then have the person reject it out of hand and move onto something else as though they never brought it up. Mind you, an angry person, a person with doubts, is not necessarily a Pharisaical person. There are reasons for some to doubt. There are reasons for some to be angry. If the person is treating you with disdain, mocking, talking down to you, these and other things are indications of a Pharisaical attitude.

Christian Bible students need to be familiar with Old and New Testament textual studies as the two are essential foundational studies. Why? If we fail to establish what was originally authored with reasonable certainty, how are we to translate or even interpret what we think is God's actual Word? We are fortunate that there are far more existing New Testament manuscripts today than any other book from ancient history. Some ancient Greek and Latin classics are based on one existing manuscript, while with others, there are just a handful and a few exceptions that have a few hundred available. However, the New Testament has over 5,898 Greek New Testament manuscripts that have been cataloged (As of January 2021),[87] 10,000 Latin manuscripts, and an additional 9,300 other manuscripts in such languages as Syriac, Slavic, Gothic, Ethiopic, Coptic, and Armenian. This gives New Testament textual scholars vastly more to work within establishing the original words of the text.

The other difference between the New Testament manuscripts and those of the classics is that the existing copies of the New Testament date much closer to the

---

[87] While at present here in 2020, there are 5,898 manuscripts. There are **140 listed Papyrus** manuscripts, 323 Majuscule manuscripts, 2,951 Minuscule manuscripts, and 2,484 Lectionary manuscripts, bringing the total cataloged manuscripts to 5,898 manuscripts. However, you cannot simply total the number of cataloged manuscripts because, for example, $P^{11/14}$ are the same manuscript but with different catalog numbers. The same is true of $P^{33/5}$, $P^{4/64/67}$, $P^{49/65}$ and $P^{77/103}$. Now this alone would bring our 140 listed papyrus manuscripts down to 134. 'Then, we turn to one example from our majuscule manuscripts where clear 0110, 0124, 0178, 0179, 0180, 0190, 0191, 0193, 0194, and 0202 are said to be part of 070. A minuscule manuscript was listed with five separate catalog numbers for 2306, which then have the letters a through e. Thus, we have the following GA numbers: 2306 for 2306a, and 2831- 2834 for 2306b-2306e.' – (Hixon 2019, 53-4) The problem is much worse when we consider that there are 323 Majuscule manuscripts and then far worse still with a listed 2,951 Minuscule and 2,484 Lectionaries. Nevertheless, those who estimate a total of 5,300 (Jacob W. Peterson, Myths and Mistakes, p. 63) 5,500 manuscripts (Dr. Ed Gravely / ehrmanproject.com/), 5,800 manuscripts (Porter 2013, 23), it is still a truckload of evidence far and above the dismal number of ancient secular author books.

originals. In the case of the Greek classics, some of the manuscripts are dated about a thousand years after the author had penned the book. Some of the Latin classics are dated from three to seven hundred years after the time the author wrote the book. When we look at the Greek copies of the New Testament books, some portions are within decades of the original author's book. Seventy-nine Greek papyri, along with five majuscules,[88] date from 110 C.E. to 300 C.E.

Distribution of Greek New Testament Manuscripts

- The **Papyrus** is a copy of a portion of the New Testament made on papyrus. At present, we have 141 cataloged New Testament papyri, many dating between 110-350 C.E., but some as late as the 6th century C.E.

- The **Majuscule** or **Uncial** is a script of large letters commonly used in Greek and Latin manuscripts written between the 3rd and 9th centuries C.E. that resembles a modern capital letter but is more rounded. At present, we have 323 cataloged New Testament Majuscule manuscripts.

- The **Minuscule** is a small cursive style of writing used in manuscripts from the 9th to the 16th centuries, now having 2,951 Minuscule manuscripts cataloged.

- The **Lectionary** is a schedule of readings from the Bible for Christian church services during the year, in both majuscules and minuscules, dating from the 4th to the 16th centuries C.E., now having 2,484 Lectionary manuscripts cataloged.

	Distribution of Papyri by Century and Type			
DATE	ALEX	WEST	CAES	BYZ
100-150/175 C.E.	7Q4? 7Q5? $P^{4/64/67}$ P^{32} P^{46} P^{52} P^{66} P^{75} $P^{77/103}$ P^{87} P^{90} P^{98} (bad shape, differences) P^{101} P^{109} (too small) P^{118} (too small) P^{137} 0189 P. Oxyrhynchus 405 P. Egerton 2	P^{104}	0	0
175-250 C.E.	P^1 P^5 P^{13} P^{20} P^{23} P^{27} P^{30} P^{35} P^{39} P^{40} P^{45} P^{47} $P^{49/65}$ P^{71} P^{72}	P^{29} (Metzger Western & Aland Free; too small to	0	0

---

[88] Large lettering, often called "capital" or uncial, in which all the letters are usually the same height.

	P⁸² P⁸⁵ P⁹⁵ P¹⁰⁰ P¹⁰⁶ P¹⁰⁸ P¹¹⁰ P¹¹¹ P¹¹³ P¹¹⁵ P¹²¹ (too small) P¹²⁵ P¹²⁶ (too small) P¹³³ P¹³⁶ P¹⁴¹ 0220 0232 P. Oxyrhynchus 406 P. Egerton 3	be certain) P³⁸ P⁴⁸ P⁶⁹ 0171 0212 (mixed) P¹⁰⁷ (Independent)		
250-300 C.E.	P⁸ P⁹ P¹² P¹⁵ P¹⁶ P¹⁷ P¹⁸ P¹⁹ P²⁴ P²⁸ P⁵⁰ P⁵¹ P⁵³ P⁷⁰ P⁷⁸ P⁸⁰ P⁸⁶ P⁸⁸ P⁸⁹ (too small) P⁹¹ P⁹² P¹¹⁴ P¹¹⁹ P¹²⁰ P¹²⁹ (too small) P¹³¹ P¹³² too small) P¹³⁴ 0162 0207 0231 P. Antinoopolis 54	P³⁷ (Free, mostly Western)	0	0
290-390 C.E.	P³ P⁶ P⁷ P¹⁰ P²¹ P⁵⁴ P⁶² P⁸¹ P⁹³ P⁹⁴ P¹⁰² (too small) P¹¹⁷ (too small) P¹²² (too small) P¹²³ P¹³⁰ (too small) P¹³⁹ (too small) 057 058 059 / 0215 071 0160 0163 0165 0169 0172 0173 0175 0176 0181 0182 0185 0188 0206 0214 0217 0218 0219 0221 0226 0227 0228 0230 0242 0264 0308 0312 P. Oxyrhynchus 4010 P. Oxyrhynchus 5073	P²¹ (mixed) P²⁵ (independent) P¹¹² (independent) P¹²⁷ (independent; like no other)	0	0
4ᵗʰ / 5ᵗʰ Century C.E.	P¹¹ P¹⁴ P³³/P⁵⁸ P⁵⁶ P⁵⁷ P⁶³ P¹⁰⁵ (too small) P¹²⁴ 0254			069 P. Oxyrhynchus 1077?

We should clarify that of the approximate 24,000 total manuscripts of the New Testament, not all are complete books. There are fragmented manuscripts with just a few verses, manuscripts containing an entire book, others that include numerous books, and some that have the whole New Testament, or nearly so. This is expected since the oldest manuscripts we have were copied in an era when reproducing the entire New Testament was not the norm, but rather a single book or a group of books (i.e., the Gospels or Paul's letters). This still does not negate the vast riches of manuscripts that we possess.

What can we conclude from this short introduction to New Testament textual studies? There is some irony here: secular scholars have no problem accepting classic authors' wording with their minuscule amount of evidence. However, they discount the treasure trove of evidence that is available to the New Testament textual scholar. Still, this should not surprise us, as the New Testament has always been under-appreciated and attacked in some way, shape, or form over the past 2,000 years.

On the contrary, in comparison to classical works, we are overwhelmed by the quantity and quality of existing New Testament manuscripts. We should also keep in mind that seventy-five percent[89] of the New Testament does not require textual scholars' help because that much of the text is unanimous, and thus, we know what it says. Of the other twenty-five percent, about twenty percent make up trivial scribal mistakes that are easily corrected. Therefore, textual criticism focuses mainly on a small portion of the New Testament text. The facts are clear: the Christian, who reads the New Testament, is fortunate to have so many manuscripts, with so many dating so close to the originals, with 500 hundred years of hundreds of textual scholars who have established the text with a level of certainty unimaginable for ancient secular works.

After discussing the amount of New Testament manuscripts available, Atheist commentator Bob Seidensticker, writes, "The first problem is that more manuscripts at best increase our confidence that we have the original version. That does not mean the original copy was history …."[90] That is, Seidensticker is forced to acknowledge the reliability of the New Testament text as we have it today and can only try to deny what it says. He also tells us of the New Testament, "Compare that with 2000 copies of the Iliad, the second-best represented manuscript."[91] Of those 2,000 copies of the Iliad, how far removed are they from the alleged originals? The Iliad is dated to about 1260–1180 B.C.E. The most notable Iliad manuscripts are from the 9th, 10th, and 11th centuries C.E. That would make these manuscripts over 2,000 years removed from their original.

The Range of Textual Criticism

The Importance and scope of New Testament textual criticism could be summed up in the few words used by J. Harold Greenlee; it is "the basic biblical study, a prerequisite to all other biblical and theological work. Interpretation, systemization, and application of the teachings of the NT cannot be done until textual criticism has

---

[89] The numbers in this paragraph are rounded for simplicity purposes.
[90] 25,000 New Testament Manuscripts? Big Deal. – Patheos,
http://www.patheos.com/blogs/crossexamined/2013/11/25000-new-testament-manuscrip (Retrieved Monday, August 10, 2020).
[91] Ibid

done at least some of its work. It is, therefore, deserving of the acquaintance and attention of every serious student of the Bible."[92]

It is only reasonable to assume that the Old Testament's original 39 books and the 27 books written first-hand by the New Testament authors have not survived. Instead, we only have what we must consider being imperfect copies. **Why the Holy Spirit would miraculously inspire 66 fully inerrant texts and then allow human imperfection into the copies.** This is not explained for us in Scripture. We do know that imperfect humans have tended to worship relics where traditions hold to have been touched by the miraculous powers of God or to have been in direct contact with one of his special servants of old. Ultimately, though, all we know is that God had his reasons for allowing the Old and New Testament autographs to be worn out by repeated use. From time to time, we hear of the discovery of a fragment possibly dated to the first century, but even if such a fragment is eventually verified, the dating alone can never serve as proof of an autograph; it will still be a copy in all likelihood.

Pondering: If we ask why didn't God inspire copyists, then it will have to follow, why didn't God inspire translators, why didn't God inspire Bible scholars that author commentaries on the Bible, and so on? Suppose God's initial purpose was to give us a fully inerrant, authoritative, authentic and accurate Word. Why not adequately protect the Scriptures in all facets of transmission from error: copy, translate, and interpret? If God did this, and people were moved along by the Holy Spirit, it would soon become noticeable that when people copy the texts, they would be unable to make an error or mistake or even willfully change something.

Where would it stop? Would this being moved along by the Holy Spirit apply to anyone who decided to make themselves a copy, testing to see if they too would be inspired? In time, this would prove to be actual evidence for God. This would negate the reasons why God has allowed sin, human imperfection to enter into humanity in the first place, to teach them an **object lesson**, man cannot walk on his own without his Creator. God created perfect humans, giving them a perfect start, and through the abuse of free will, they rejected his sovereignty. He did not just keep creating perfect humans again and again, as though he got something wrong. God gave us his perfect Word and has again chosen to allow us to continue in our human imperfection, learning our **object lesson**. God has stepped into humanity many hundreds of times in the Bible record, maybe tens of thousands of times unbeknownst to us over the past 6,000+ years, to tweak things to get the desired outcome of his will and purposes. However, there is no aspect of life where his stepping in for any particular point was to be continuous until the return of the Son. Maybe God gave us a perfect copy of sixty-six books. Then like everything else, he placed the responsibility of copying, translating, and interpreting on us, just as he gave us the Great Commission of

---

[92] J. Harold Greenlee, Introduction to New Testament Textual Criticism (Grand Rapids, MI: Baker Academic, 1995), 8-9.

proclaiming that Word, explaining that Word, to make disciples. – Matthew 24:14;28-19-20; Acts 1:8.

Reflecting: Some Bible critics seem, to begin with, the belief that if God inspired the originals and fully inerrant, the subsequent copies must continue to be inerrant for the inerrancy of the originals to have value. They seem to be asking, "If only the originals were inspired, and the copies were not inspired, and we do not have the originals, how are we to be certain of any passage in Scripture?" In other words, God would never allow the inspired, inerrant Word to suffer copying errors. Why would he perform the miracle of inspiring the message to be fully inerrant and not continue with the miracle of inspiring the copyists throughout the centuries to keep it inerrant? First, we must acknowledge that God has not given us the specifics of every decision he has made about humans. If we begin asking, "Why did God not do this or do that," where would it end? For example, why didn't God just produce the books himself and miraculously deliver them to people as he gave the commandments to Moses? Why not use angelic messengers to pen the message or produce the message miraculously instead of using humans? God has chosen not to tell us why he did not move the copyists along by the Holy Spirit to have perfect copies, and it remains an unknown. However, I would note that if we can restore the text to its original wording through the art and science of textual criticism, i.e., to an exact representation thereof, we have, in essence, the originals. This is the preservation of Scripture through the restoration of Scripture.

As for errors in all the copies that we have, however, we can say that the vast majority of the Greek text is not affected by errors. The errors occur in variant readings, i.e., portions of the text where different manuscripts disagree. Of the **small amount** of the text affected by variant readings, the vast majority of these are minor slips of the pen, misspelled words, etc., or intentional but quickly analyzed changes, and we are certain what the original reading is in these places. A **far smaller number** of changes present challenges to establishing the original reading. It has always been said and remains true that no central doctrine is affected by a textual problem. Only rarely does a textual issue change the meaning of a verse.[93] Still, establishing the original text wherever there are variant readings is vitally important. Every word matters!

It is true that the Jewish copyists and the later Christian copyists were not led along by the Holy Spirit, and therefore their manuscripts were not inerrant, infallible. Errors (textual variants) crept into the documents unintentionally and intentionally. However, the vast majority of the Hebrew Old Testament and Greek New Testament has not been infected with textual errors. The portions impacted by textual errors are the many tens of thousands of copies that we have to help us weed out the errors.

---

[93] Leading textual scholar Daniel Wallace tells us, after looking at all of the evidence, that the percentage of instances where the reading is uncertain and a well-attested alternative reading could change the meaning of the verse is a quarter of one percent, i.e., 0.0025%

How? Well, not every copyist made the same textual errors. Hence, by comparing the work of different copyists and manuscripts, textual scholars can identify the textual variants (errors) and remove those, leaving us with the original content.

Yes, it would be the most significant discovery of all time if we found the original five books penned by Moses himself, Genesis through Deuteronomy, or the original Gospels of Matthew, Mark, Luke, and John. However, first, there would be no way of establishing that they were the originals. Second, we do not need the originals. Third, we do not need those original documents. What is so important about the documents? It is the content on the original documents that we are after. And truly, miraculously, we have more copies than needed to do just that. We do not need miraculous preservation because we have miraculous restoration. We now know beyond a reasonable doubt that the Hebrew Old Testament and the Greek New Testament critical texts are a 99% reflection of the content in those ancient original manuscripts.

How did God inspire the Bible Authors? How Were They Moved Along by the Holy Spirit? How Did Jesus Bring Remembrance to the Apostles?

Biblical inspiration is the quality or state of being moved along or by or under the Holy Spirit's direction from God.

2 Timothy 3:16 Updated American Standard Version (UASV)	**2 Peter 1:21** Updated American Standard Version (UASV)	**John 14:26** Updated American Standard Version (UASV)
16 All Scripture is **inspired by** God and profitable for teaching, for reproof, for correction, for training in righteousness;	21 for no prophecy was ever produced by the will of man, but men **carried along by** the Holy Spirit spoke from God.	26 But the Helper,[94] the Holy Spirit, whom the Father will send in my name, that one will teach you all things and **bring to your remembrance** all that I have said to you.

How Were the Bible Authors Inspired By God, That Is, Given Divine Direction?

Inspired By θεόπνευστος (theopneustos)

The Greek phrase "inspired by God" translates the compound Greek word θεόπνευστος (theopneustos), which literally means, literally, "God-breathed" or "breathed by God." The Greek phrase here needs to be nuanced so at not to be less than what was meant or go beyond what was meant. The Bible author was under God's influence, to the extent that he was guided or directed by God but not to the extent of

---

[94] Or, *Advocate*. Or, *Comforter*. Gr., *ho ... parakletos,* masc.

dictation. To a lesser extent, Christians are guided by the inspired Word of God if they have an accurate understanding and apply it correctly in their lives. The Bible author was allowed to convey God's Word within their own writing style but would be controlled or guided to the point that he would not choose words, phrases, sentences that would miscommunicate the wrong message.

Carried Along By φερόμενοι (pheromenoi)

The Greek word φερόμενοι (pheromenoi) literally means to **cause** the Bible author to be carried along or moved along by the Holy Spirit. It means to guide, direct, lead.

Bring to Remembrance ὑπομνήσει (hupomnēsei)

The Greek word ὑπομνήσει (*hupomnēsei*) literally means to God put in the mind of the Gospel authors. God **caused** the Gospel authors (Matthew and John, Mark by way of Peter, Luke by Peter, research, and others) to recall in detail what they had formerly experienced.

The apostle Paul says that God spoke "in many ways" to his servants in Old Testament times before Christ coming. (Heb 1:1-2) The Ten Commandments were divinely provided in written form. Scribes, thereafter, would have had to merely copy it into the scrolls used by Moses. (Ex. 31:18; Deut. 10:1-5) In some very special cases, the words put into Scripture by a Bible author inspired by God, moved along by the Holy Spirit, would have been transmitted by verbal dictation, literally word for word. This would have likely been the case in situations such as the Mosaic Law given to Israel. Jehovah commanded Moses: "**Write these words**, for in accordance with these words I have made a covenant with you and with Israel." (Ex 34:27) The prophets who would author Bible books were also frequently given precise messages from God that they were to deliver, and then God put these same words in the mind of the prophetic authors. God **caused** the prophet (Isaiah, Jeremiah, Ezekiel, Daniel, and others) to recall in detail what they had formerly delivered to others, now becoming Scriptures. – 1 Kings 22:14; Jeremiah 1:7; 2:1; 11:1-5; Ezekiel 3:4; 11:5.

There are other ways that the Bible authors, such as dreams and visions. We are told, "Then the mystery was revealed to Daniel in a **vision of the night**. Then Daniel blessed the God of heaven." (Dan. 2:19) "In the first year of Belshazzar king of Babylon, Daniel saw a **dream and visions** of his head as he lay in his bed. Then he wrote down the dream and told the sum of the matter." (Dan. 7:1) Readers might not know that Bible authors were more often given visions while they were awake, fully conscious, giving the author the thoughts of God directly to his mind. "In the thirtieth year, in the fourth month, on the fifth day of the month, as I was among the exiles by the Chebar canal, the heavens were opened, and **I saw visions** of God." (Eze 1:1) "In the third year of the reign of King Belshazzar **a vision appeared to me**, Daniel, after that which appeared to me at the first." (Dan. 8:1) "And this is how I saw the horses in **my vision** and those who rode them: they wore breastplates the color of fire and of sapphire and of sulfur, and the heads of the horses were like lions' heads, and fire and smoke and sulfur came out of their mouths." (Rev. 9:17) Other visions were given to the Bible author when he was in a trance. Even though the author was clearly awake and conscious, he was extremely, deeply absorbed by what he saw, blocking out all else around him. – Ac 10:9-17; 11:5-10; 22:17-21.

Another way Bible authors received the Word of God was through angelic messengers. "For if the word spoken through angels proved reliably certain, and every transgression and disobedience received a just penalty." (Heb 2:2) "You who received the law as delivered **by angels** and did not keep it." (Ac 7:53) "Why, then, the Law? It was added because of transgressions, until the seed should arrive to whom the promise had been made; and it was **transmitted through angels** by the hand of a mediator." (Gal. 3:19) The angelic representatives spoke in God's name. Therefore, the message they delivered could therefore correctly be called "the word of Jehovah." – Gen 22:11-12, 15-18; Zech. 1:7, 9.

Regardless of how the Bible author received the Word of God, be it, dictation, God directly putting words in the minds of the author, perfect recall, dreams, visions, angelic representatives, being led along by the Holy Spirit, it was all inspired by God or "God-breathed."

Authors evidenced individuality that is still compatible with the Bible's being inspired by God.

The Bible authors were not merely robots who put down dictated words, literally word for word. "The revelation of Jesus Christ, which God gave him to show to his servants the things that must soon take place. He made it known by sending his angel to his servant John, who bore witness to the word of God and to the testimony of Jesus Christ, even to all that he saw." (Rev. 1:1-2) The "God-breathed" revelation was given to him through an angel, which John then conveyed in his own words. Like many things, God allowed humans to use their God's given minds, and in the case of His Word, in choosing words and expressions (Hab. 2:2), he allowed them to use their own style, but he always maintained adequate control and guided them so that the Bible book would be accurate and true. In addition, it would also be according to God's will and purposes. (Prov. 30:5-6) This concept is even conveyed in Scripture itself. "Besides being wise, the Preacher also taught the people knowledge, weighing and studying and arranging many proverbs with great care. The Preacher sought to find words of delight, and uprightly he wrote words of truth." – See also Lu 1:1-4.

This is why every Bible commentary volume explains to its reader the style of that particular author and the background of the individual author. The ones chosen to be Bible authors were not only qualified to do so but had qualities and characteristics that moved God to choose them. In some cases, God likely got them ready before having to serve this particular purpose of being a Bible author. Matthew was a tax collector before being chosen as a disciple, so we note that he makes many particular references to numbers and money amounts. (Matt. 17:27; 26:15; 27:3) On the other hand, Luke was a "physician" (Col 4:14), so we find him using unique expressions that show that he had a medical background. – Lu 4:38; 5:12; 16:20.

In many cases where the Bible speaks about the Bible author receiving "the word of Jehovah" (UASV) or things that were said, it is likely that this was given, not word for word, but rather the author was given an image in his mind of God's purpose. After that, the author would put it in his own words. This can be inferred by the author's sating he 'saw' things rather than his 'hearing' what God said or "the word of Jehovah." – Isaiah 13:1; Micah 1:1; Habakkuk 1:1; 2:1-2.

The authors of God's Word express it that "God has given me the tongue of those who are taught, that I may know how to sustain with a word him who is weary. Morning by morning he awakens; he awakens my ear to hear as those who are taught. Jehovah God has opened my ear, and I was not rebellious; I turned not backward." (Isa 50:4-5) These authors were ready and submissive to being guided by God. Isaiah was eager to do God's will and sought to be led. "My soul yearns for you in the night; my spirit within me earnestly seeks you. For when your judgments are in the earth, the inhabitants of the world learn righteousness." (Isa 26:9) In the case of Luke, he had specific objectives that he sought to carry out. (Lu 1:1-4) In many cases, Paul was writing to fill a need. (1 Cor. 1:10-11; 5:1; 7:1) God guided these authors so that their words in their style went along with his purpose. (Prov. 16:9) These men were chosen because their hearts and minds were already in harmony with God's will and purposes. In fact, they already 'had the mind of Christ.' They were not interested in human wisdom nor in "speak[ing] visions of their own minds," as was the case with the false prophets, "who follow their own spirit." – 1 Corinthians 2:13-16; Jeremiah 23:16; Eze 13:2-3, 17.

As to the being led along by the Holy Spirit, "there are varieties of activities" that would come upon these Bible authors. (1 Cor 12:6) Much information was already at the fingertips of the authors. In other words, it already existed in manuscript evidence, such as genealogies and specific historical accounts. (Lu 1:3; 3:23-38; Num. 21:14, 15; 1 Kings 14:19, 29; 2 Kings 15:31; 24:5) In the case of using historical records, the Holy Spirit would serve as a protection against inaccurate information being part of the Bible author's book. Not everything said by other persons that would end up in the Word of God was inspired by God, but the Holy Spirit guided the author to make it part of the Scriptures and record it accurately. (Gen. 3:4-5; Job 42:3; Matt. 16:21-23) We end up with clear evidence of why it is good to heed God's Word and apply it correctly in our lives. Doing or saying what we think, feel, or believe, ignoring God's Word, or being ignorant of God and his message leads to much heartache.

Then, again, there is information in the Bible that is far beyond human abilities to acquire. We can consider what happened before the creation of the heavens and the earth, as well as man. (Gen. 1:1-26) Humans are also oblivious to what happens in the spiritual heavens as well. (Job 1:6-12, etc.) Then, we have prophecies that foretell events that are to take place decades, centuries, or millenniums after the prophets penned them. We also have revelations as to what God's will and purposes are for humanity. When we think of Solomon's wise sayings, he certainly had much life experience to share. Others had vast knowledge of the Scriptures themselves, not to mention their experience at living by God's Word. They still needed to be moved along by the Holy Spirit, so that the information that they conveyed would be "living and active and sharper than any two-edged sword and piercing as far as the division of soul and spirit, of both joints and marrow, and able to judge the thoughts and intentions of the heart." – Hebrews 4:12.

There are times that Paul said things that were not taken from anything that Jesus had taught. "To the rest, I say (**I, not the Lord**) that if any brother has a wife who is an unbeliever, and she consents to live with him, he should not divorce her." (1 Corinthians 7:12-15) The first thing to notice is Paul saying, God inspires me, so I can say this and the Lord (Jesus), did not touch on this, but I am. Let us take a look at the context and historical setting. Paul says, "Now concerning virgins I do not have a command from the Lord, but I am giving an opinion as one shown mercy by the Lord to be trustworthy." (1 Cor. 7:25) "But in my opinion she is happier if she remains as she is, and I think that I too have the Spirit of God." (1 Cor. 7:40) Paul's point is clear; he, too, is inspired and moved along by the Holy Spirit. Paul's direction was "God-breathed" and so was Scripture, having the same authority as the rest of those Scriptures. – 2 Peter 3:15-16.

CHAPTER 4 The Formation of the New Testament: An Insight into the Process

Understanding the Origins of the Greek New Testament Manuscripts

As we dive into the study of the trustworthiness of the New Testament documents, it's crucial to first comprehend the background of how these manuscripts were produced and distributed during the early days of the church. This understanding forms the bedrock of our exploration of how the New Testament was shared with the earliest Christians.

In this chapter, we'll delve into how the New Testament was circulated via the creation of manuscripts. We'll analyze the surviving New Testament manuscripts, along with other manuscripts of Christian writings. This will allow us to glean insights into the publication process of the Greek New Testament during the early church era.

We'll start with the initial publications, then proceed to examine the attributes of the earliest manuscripts, attempting to piece together the history of New Testament publication. As 2 Timothy 3:16-17 states, "All Scripture is God-breathed and is useful for teaching, rebuking, correcting and training in righteousness, so that the servant of God may be thoroughly equipped for every good work." Therefore, understanding the origins and authenticity of these manuscripts is of utmost importance.

The creation of manuscripts was the pivotal method for spreading the New Testament writings. This very production process, however, resulted in the emergence of textual variations in subsequent manuscripts, which led to the need for textual criticism. As 1 Peter 3:15 reminds us, "But in your hearts revere Christ as Lord. Always be prepared to give an answer to everyone who asks you to give the reason for the hope that you have. But do this with gentleness and respect," reinforcing the importance of our study.

Understanding Publication: From Ancient Times to Today

When we think of "publication" in our modern times, we often associate it with written materials such as books, newspapers, and magazines. However, in ancient times, publication encompassed both oral and written dissemination. To publish something, be it a poem or a political decree, meant broadcasting it to a group of people through oral presentation or written proclamation. In most cases, a written record served as a means for oral proclamation, as many people of that era were illiterate and relied on oral communication to receive information.

For instance, renowned poets of ancient times, such as Homer, would publish their works by reciting them orally. Their poems, like the Iliad and the Odyssey, were later written down by others. The famous Greek philosopher, Socrates, also shared his ideas orally, with his student Plato documenting them for posterity. As Romans 10:17 says, "So faith comes from hearing, and hearing through the word of Christ."

Following this tradition, Jesus, the prophetic poet, disseminated His teachings orally. As far as we know, Jesus did not write down His teachings. He propagated the good news through oral proclamation, often using poetic styles akin to Old Testament prophecies, facilitating memorization. As Proverbs 22:17-18 encourages, "Incline your ear, and hear the words of the wise, and apply your heart to my knowledge, for it will be pleasant if you keep them within you, if all of them are ready on your lips."

Jesus was also a master storyteller, using parables that were simple, unique, and memorable. His method of traveling throughout Galilee and Judea, proclaiming the good news of the Kingdom, reached and impacted thousands. In those times, oral publication was more effective than written publication, as books were costly to produce and many could not read. Most people relied on oral proclamation and listening to receive messages.

In line with this, Jesus taught His disciples orally, and they committed His teachings to memory. When the time came for these teachings to be written down, they were aided by the Holy Spirit, who reminded them of all that Jesus had taught (John 14:26). Following Jesus' death and resurrection, His disciples continued His publishing work, known as the kerygma, the Greek term for "proclamation".

In ancient times, a king would disseminate his decrees throughout his realm through a kerux, a town crier or herald. Each New Testament disciple saw themselves as a kerux, a herald, and publisher of the Good News. Paul referred to himself as "a herald and an apostle" (1 Tim. 2:7; 2 Tim. 1:11), as it was his role as an apostle to be a herald.

The apostles shared a common proclamation or kerygma, the "publishing" of the death, resurrection, and exaltation of Jesus. Initially, this publishing was oral, via preaching in various cities throughout the Greco-Roman world. Gradually, it became both oral and written, through the apostles' writings, proclaimed in churches worldwide.

The fundamental message always centered on Jesus' resurrection, the divine act in history that validates the words and works of Jesus and forms the basis for the Christian hope of immortality. Without the resurrection, the church would be a mere gathering of well-intentioned, religious individuals who placed their faith in the superior philosophical and ethical teachings of an unusually gifted man. The resurrection is the solid proof that Jesus is who He claimed to be. Therefore, the kerygma is a declaration that Christ has risen from the dead, and by this great act, God has brought salvation.

The early apostles propagated this kerygma to all believers while also recounting the deeds and words of Jesus. Thus, the first-century Christians initially received an oral presentation of the gospel from the apostles who had been with Jesus (see Acts 2:42) and then written documents that preserved the oral and perpetuated the apostolic tradition (see Luke 1:1–4).

This oral proclamation served as a form of catechetical instruction, a method commonly used during Hellenistic times where a teacher would recite Jesus' words and deeds, and the congregation would orally repeat what was taught and commit it to memory. According to Galatians 6:6, the teachers in the early church were considered the catechists, the oral proclaimers of the word (see also 1 Cor. 14:19).

Luke, in the preface to his Gospel (1:1–4), expressed his intention to affirm, via the written word, what Theophilus had already been taught by catechism—i.e., oral recitation. Thus, the written word in Luke's Gospel was an inscribed replication of the oral proclamation.

This practice shows the interconnectedness between the oral and written forms of publication in the early Christian era. It highlights the importance of preserving and passing on the teachings and deeds of Jesus through both forms, ensuring that future generations would have access to the Good News. The written texts provided an invaluable resource that could be revisited and studied, offering an enduring testimony to the life and teachings of Jesus Christ.

Following the passing of the apostles and their immediate coworkers, the significance of the written text grew. Christians of subsequent generations were likely first introduced to the gospel through the written Gospels. Yet, most of these believers wouldn't have read the Gospel themselves; instead, it would have been orally delivered to them during church gatherings by trained readers, known as lectors. In this way, the kerygma continued to be disseminated orally, supported by written documents.

Of all the apostles, Paul was possibly the most successful in announcing and disseminating the kerygma. His numerous apostolic journeys took him to hundreds of towns and villages where he proclaimed the news of Jesus' resurrection and salvation. Over time, Paul recognized the geographic and temporal constraints of his missionary work—he could only be in one place at a time. As a result, he broadened his missionary work by dispatching coworkers with the gospel and by writing circular letters that these coworkers would read to various churches. Papyrus and pen became another, quicker method for disseminating Paul's revelations about Christ and the church. (We'll delve into this more below.)

The apostles Peter and John also utilized the written word to record their experiences of Jesus' life and teachings, as well as their instructions on Christian living. Like Paul, their initial proclamation of the kerygma was oral. But later in life, they documented their accounts of Jesus' ministry to provide an accurate, apostolic presentation of the kerygma—one that would endure past their lifetimes. Tradition holds that Peter's Gospel came to us through Mark's writing, and John penned a Gospel in his later years. Both apostles also wrote letters recounting their personal interactions with Jesus Christ (see 2 Pet. 1:12–21; 1 John 1:1–4), their proclamations of apostolic truth, and their encouragement for effective Christian living.

The key takeaway from this introductory look at the publishing process is that the New Testament's good news initially came as oral proclamation, then was written down—primarily to preserve and continue the original proclamation as delivered by the apostles chosen by Jesus. If the apostles hadn't recorded the kerygma, and it had continued solely as oral tradition, the gospel would have evolved over time, shaped by the whims of whoever proclaimed it. Ultimately, the gospel might have become entirely different from its original form. Therefore, the written documents safeguard the integrity of apostolic truth as conveyed by Jesus' first followers. Generations of Christians have relied on the authenticity of these published documents for their faith and lives.

The Original Documents

To better comprehend the early evolution of the written text of the New Testament books, it is beneficial to use terminology from the publishing sphere. In both ancient and modern times, books were "published," although the volume of copies produced was significantly less in antiquity. Nonetheless, the processes share many similarities.

In contemporary times, an author first drafts their work using pen and paper, a typewriter, or a computer. The first written draft is the "original" or the "autograph." It is possible that the author will be content with this initial draft and make no further revisions, though this is uncommon. More often, the author will make subsequent edits to enhance the work before publication. This iterative process may involve several drafts. A contemporary author may also employ a professional "ghost writer" or a secretary (scribe) to transcribe dictated material, which the author then reviews and revises. Once the author is satisfied with the final draft, the manuscript is sent to a publisher. The publisher, in collaboration with the author, edits the text and then publishes the first approved version. This "authorized" text is the archetype from which all copies in the first printing are made. The author's initial text, stashed in a drawer somewhere, is likely to be quite different from the final, archetypal published text. Regardless, the final published work is attributed to the author and becomes the standard text (or archetypal manuscript) from which all future copies should be made.

Some believe that the situation for the New Testament writings parallels this publishing process. An author, such as John or Paul, first writes a book or dictates an epistle. These are the autographs. We know several New Testament books (particularly the epistles) were dictated to an amanuensis (a secretary), while others were written by the author themselves. The standard process for a dictated epistle involved the amanuensis transcribing the speaker's words (often in shorthand) and then producing a manuscript for the author to review, edit, and sign in their own handwriting. Two New Testament epistles mention the amanuensis by name: Tertius for Romans (Romans 16:22) and Silvanus (another name for Silas) for 1 Peter (1 Peter 5:12). Paul must have dictated other epistles since he specifically mentioned that he wrote the closing salutation in his own handwriting: 1 Corinthians (16:21), Galatians (6:11), Colossians (4:18), and 2 Thessalonians (3:17). He stated that he did this in all his epistles to authenticate them and protect them against forgery. The words in 2 Thessalonians 3:17 are particularly interesting, where Paul signed off the epistle in his own hand, verifying his bona fide signature. This was a common practice in ancient letter writing—where the writer served as an amanuensis and the author signed off.

Silas (also known as Silvanus) assisted Peter in writing his first epistle (1 Peter 5:12). This implies that Silas either served as an amanuensis for Peter, translated Peter's letter (from Aramaic to Greek) as Peter dictated it, or wrote a letter based on Peter's ideas. This practice was common in ancient times and is still prevalent today. Some people, not adept at writing, delegate that task to another, who transcribes the author's thoughts in words (a "ghost writer" in modern terminology). This ancient practice could explain the stylistic disparity between Peter's two epistles (1 Peter and 2 Peter). Essentially, Peter used two different writers. Therefore, 2 Peter comprises Peter's final thoughts, written by another, potentially Jude, due to the striking similarities between

Jude's own letter and 2 Peter. This practice of having another writer help document one's thoughts was not uncommon in ancient times, and it offers a plausible explanation for the stylistic differences between 1 Peter and 2 Peter. Consequently, it can be inferred that Peter utilized different writers for each of his letters. This understanding further supports the idea that the Gospel of Mark, closely associated with Peter, is a shared authorship, with Peter supplying the Gospel history and narrative, while Mark provided the literary presentation.

Silvanus (or Silas) could potentially be considered one of the earliest Christian scribes. He was involved in composing the letter from the Jerusalem Council to Antioch (Acts 15:22). Subsequently, he appears as a close collaborator of both Paul and Peter. His name is mentioned in the introduction of both 1 and 2 Thessalonians (as a co-writer with Paul), and then at the conclusion of 1 Peter (5:12). Some scholars observe similarities among 1 and 2 Thessalonians, the decree of Acts 15, and 1 Peter. Silas and/or other significant Christian scribes may have been instrumental in assembling the published version of various New Testament books.

For some New Testament books, there may be a minor difference between the autograph and the original published text. This is particularly true for the shorter letters written by the author themselves, as there would have been little reason for editing. This is the case for 2 John (v. 12), 3 John (v. 13), and Philemon (v. 3), and likely other occasional epistles (i.e., letters written primarily to address specific situations). However, other books appear to have undergone two stages: initial writing, followed by editing for publication. The "published" works include the four Gospels (initially published separately), Acts, Romans, Ephesians, Hebrews, 1 Peter, and Revelation. Each of these books, from their inception, were intended for an audience beyond a single locality. By the end of the first century, it is highly probable that there were additional publications of the Gospels as a collection, as well as a collection of Pauline Epistles. These collections could be considered "authorized" as they were produced under the supervision of a coworker of the apostles, such as Silvanus.

The Role of the New Testament Scribe

Previously, we discussed Tertius, Paul's scribe, who transcribed his letter to the Romans. It's important to realize that not all of Paul's associates would have been skilled readers and writers. Nevertheless, we can surmise that Paul would have assigned duties to those who could transport and read letters, and who could also comprehend the conditions of the people or congregations they were being dispatched to or stationed with. Indeed, these individuals would have, at the very least, been proficient readers. Furthermore, Paul's scribes, such as Tertius, would likely have been semi-professional or professional. Entrusting the transcription of the profound contents of a book like Romans to an unskilled scribe would have been unwise. What competencies would Tertius have needed to successfully pen the book of Romans?

A typical associate of Paul's would likely have been a proficient reader but would only have basic writing skills. Paul would have selected individuals whose abilities would have allowed them to complete their tasks. Tertius, however, would likely have been an exception; he was probably a professional scribe. He would need to know how to bind the sheets together if creating a scroll or sew the pages together if producing a codex. He would need to understand the correct mixture of soot and gum to create ink and how to craft his own reed pen. As Richards notes, a professional scribe would also "draw lines on the paper. Small holes were often pricked down each side, and then a straight edge and a lead disk were used to lightly draw evenly spaced lines across the sheet." If Tertius wasn't trained as a document copyist, he would have likely made several minor mistakes, as his focus would have been on the meaning of what he was transcribing, rather than the precise words, a common characteristic of the subconscious mind.

Stanley E. Porter notes, "Textual criticism has also recognized that even original authors may have revised their work, and these works have gone through editions." (p. 35) *How We Got the New Testament*. Comfort writes, "When I speak of the original text, I am referring to the 'published' text— that is, the text in its **final edited form** as released for circulation in the Christian community."[95] So how does one edit the Holy Spirit? If the author was guided by the Holy Spirit and all original Scripture is inspired, why the need for editing?

Some might argue that the New Testament authors themselves wrote or dictated a single, one-time version of their texts, unedited and uncorrected, under the inspiration of the Holy Spirit. However, let's consider Paul dictating the book of Romans to Tertius. Tertius was not inspired, so could he, in his human imperfection, go without making a single scribal error for 7,000+ words? Does correcting Tertius' errors detract from the Holy Spirit's inspiration in any way? Or does it open up a slippery slope to consider this possibility? As Peter said, we should always be prepared to defend our beliefs to anyone who asks us to explain them (1 Peter 3:15).

We should be willing to adjust (or clarify) our previous statement to include our belief that Paul would correct the letter to the Romans, as the scribe (Tertius) was not inspired. In this process, Paul wouldn't change his original dictation, and the final document would be a single, corrected version. We might also propose that Paul might not have made the corrections himself but might have instructed the scribe to do so under his supervision. However, we won't speculate beyond this, for instance, suggesting a fresh copy was made from the original before publication, etc.

Did Tertius transcribe Paul's exact dictation, word for word? Robert H. Mounce asks this very question, noting that a scribe could serve at several levels, from writing

---

[95] Philip W. Comfort (p. 19), The Quest for the Original Text of the New Testament (Grand Rapids: Baker Academic, 1992)

down dictated words in longhand, using a form of shorthand (tachygraphy), to simply capturing the essence of a message and then independently composing it into a letter.[96]

It may seem like a formidable task for Tertius to transcribe Paul's words in longhand. While not impossible, it would indeed have been challenging. Paul would likely have had to speak at a slow to moderate pace, but not syllable-by-syllable. Tertius, writing on a papyrus sheet with a reed pen, would aim to be legible. Given his professional expertise, he would have been quite skilled at this. Another possibility is that Tertius might have first used shorthand to record Paul's dictation, then later produced a full draft, which both he and Paul would review. This would be similar to the method used by modern court reporters, who use shorthand to record rapid and overlapping speech in a courtroom setting. If the shorthand of the day had a similar capability, then this scenario is plausible. But we must remember that these are the Bible author's dictated words to the scribe, inspired by divine guidance, not the word choice or writing style of the scribe.

Mounce's last option, that an amanuensis (scribe) might independently formulate the ideas into a letter, seems to be at odds with both the attitudes of the scribes and the New Testament authors toward the task of transcription. God chose to convey his message through Matthew, Mark, Luke, John, Peter, Jude, James, and Paul, not through Tertius, Silvanus, Timothy, or others. While we cannot definitively state whether Tertius or Silvanus transcribed their authors' words in shorthand or longhand, we can assert that the human author was dictating the Word of God to the scribe, and it was not composed by the scribe.

Characteristics of the Original Manuscripts

As it stands, no original manuscripts (autographs) or prototype texts of any book of the New Testament survive today. Consequently, we cannot definitively say what they looked like. However, we can infer some potential characteristics based on existing documents from the first century and a bit of imaginative reasoning. It's plausible that the original New Testament writings might have had several of the following features.

Handwriting Style of the Original Manuscripts

The original manuscripts could have been written in any type of handwriting, likely not polished, as these texts could have undergone editing. In other words, the original could resemble what we consider a draft today. If we had the opportunity to examine a first draft of an original manuscript, we might find editorial corrections inserted between lines or in the margins, potentially made by the author, a scribe

---

[96] Robert H. Mounce, *Romans*, vol. 27, The New American Commentary (Nashville: Broadman & Holman Publishers, 1995), 22.

(amanuensis), or both. One notable characteristic of a first draft could be substantial corrections written in the same hand as the main text. P. Oxyrhynchus 2070, an anti-Jewish dialogue presumably penned by a Christian, serves as a great example of such an "original manuscript" due to its many corrections in the same handwriting as the text.

It's plausible that authors like Luke and the writer of Hebrews would have edited their own texts before publication. In contrast, some New Testament writers, such as Paul, appear to have allowed their works to be published without extensive editing. Paul's writings, for instance, often retain anacolutha—grammatical inconsistencies indicative of uncorrected dictation (see Ephesians 3:18 as an example). Similarly, John's Revelation seems to have been recorded and published without correcting several grammatical errors (see Revelation 1:4, 15; 10:7; 11:1; 14:19; 16:4).

Worldwide museums and libraries house hundreds, if not thousands, of first-century manuscripts written in what we might call a "documentary" hand. These manuscripts demonstrate the wide array of handwriting styles that existed during that time. To gain a better understanding, I recommend consulting books that provide photographs and descriptions of manuscripts from this era. Some initial suggestions include *Greek Literary Hands* by C. H. Roberts, *Greek Manuscripts of the Ancient World* by E. G. Turner, and *La Papirologia* by Orsolina Montevecchi. Specifically, the following manuscripts could provide a general sense of what a New Testament original manuscript might have looked like:

- P. London 2078 (81–96 CE)
- P. Fayum 110 (94 CE) (see *Greek Literary Hands* 11b)
- P. Oxyrhynchus 270 (94 CE)
- P. Oxyrhynchus 3057, thought to be the earliest Christian letter (late first/early second century)[97]

These manuscripts showcase a readable handwriting style, written relatively quickly. They are certainly not polished works, not the kind of material one would expect to see in a first "published" text—if the author aimed to make a favorable impression. Another manuscript, P52 (a papyrus manuscript of John dated around 110-150 CE), also provides insight into what an original manuscript might have resembled. The handwriting is legible, written somewhat swiftly, in a relaxed style that mirrors that found in P. Fayum 110.

---

[97] Philip Comfort, *Encountering the Manuscripts: An Introduction to New Testament Paleography & Textual Criticism* (Nashville, TN: Broadman & Holman, 2005), 7.

Distinct Handwritings in the Original Manuscripts

If we were searching for an original manuscript, we could expect to see two different handwritings in the text: that of the scribe (amanuensis) and that of the author. In Hellenistic times, it was customary for the author of a letter or official document to dictate the content to their amanuensis and then sign it off in their own handwriting, usually in a cursive style to establish a personal signature. Numerous examples of this practice exist in extant papyri containing letters and documents. For reference, consider these examples: P. Fayum 110 (110 CE); P. London II, 308 (146 CE); P. Oxyrhynchus 246 (66 CE); P. Oxyrhynchus 286 (82 CE); P. Oxyrhynchus 3057 (around 100 CE, possibly the earliest Christian letter). Another interesting example is P. Oxyrhynchus 2192, a letter about sending books between Alexandria and Oxyrhynchus, which shows the main body of the letter in one handwriting, followed by three short notes in three different hands.

Three of Paul's letters explicitly mention the practice of the author signing off in their own handwriting (1 Corinthians 16:21; Colossians 4:18; 2 Thessalonians 3:17–18). In 2 Thessalonians 3:17–18, Paul stated, "I, Paul, write this greeting with my own hand, which is my signature in every letter—this is the way I write it." Here, Paul ended the epistle with his distinctive signature, likely in cursive. In two other letters (Galatians 6:11–18; Philemon 19–25), Paul took over the writing and penned in his own hand, probably continuing until the end of the letter. In Galatians 6:11, he mentioned how he wrote in large script—bigger than the script of his amanuensis. (A textual variant in Galatians 6:11 suggests that he wrote in a "different" hand.) In Philemon, he took the pen from the amanuensis and wrote in his own hand, "I, Paul, will repay." These are the only explicit references to Paul writing in his own hand. However, it can be inferred that all of Paul's final greetings of grace and peace were written in his own hand, including Romans 15:33; 1 Corinthians 16:21–24; 2 Corinthians 13:13; Galatians 6:11–18; Ephesians 6:23–24; Philippians 4:21–23; Colossians 4:18; 1 Thessalonians 5:26–28; 2 Thessalonians 3:17–18; 1 Timothy 6:21b; 2 Timothy 4:22; Titus 3:15; and Philemon 19–25.

By extension, this distinction of handwriting could also be present in the other New Testament letters. This includes the final greetings and blessings in Hebrews 13:24–25; 1 Peter 5:12–14; 2 John 13; 3 John 14; and Revelation 22:21. If the author also wrote the concluding doxologies, this would include Romans 16:25–27 (which appears at the end of chapter 14 in some manuscripts and at the end of chapter 15 in P46); 2 Peter 3:18; and Jude 24–25—assuming, of course, these were part of the original writings.

This would mean that only two New Testament epistles would lack any special handwriting at the end—namely, James and 1 John. I suspect that 2 John and 3 John were written from start to finish by the same hand—that of the author's, as suggested by 2 John 12 and 3 John 13.

Regarding John chapter 21 specifically, some scholars have suggested that it may have been added later than the rest of the Gospel. The majority of scholars believe that John chapter 21 was not added later but is an original part of the Gospel of John. One of the main reasons for this belief is that John chapter 21 fits well with the themes and style of the rest of the Gospel. The chapter includes elements such as the appearance of Jesus to his disciples after his resurrection, the miraculous catch of fish, and the reinstatement of Peter, which are consistent with other accounts in the Gospel. In addition, early church fathers such as Irenaeus and Hippolytus of Rome, who lived in the second and third centuries, quoted from John chapter 21 in their writings, which suggests that the chapter was part of the original Gospel.

This author believes that the entire Bible, including the book of John, is inspired by God and therefore should be accepted as part of the canon of Scripture. I, as a conservative Christian scholar, would argue that John chapter 21 was not added later but is an original part of the Gospel of John. I am committed to the inerrancy and authority of Scripture, and I would view the Gospel of John, including chapter 21, as being inspired by God and without error. There is no convincing evidence to support the idea that John chapter 21 was added later. I would point to the internal coherence of the Gospel of John and the absence of any manuscript evidence to suggest that chapter 21 was a later addition.

The Autographs Endings May Have Been Shorter

The original manuscripts, or "autographs," of the New Testament likely featured endings that were shorter than those we see in later manuscripts. If one were to find the autograph of the Gospel of Mark, it would end at Mark 16:8, as is the case in the Sinaiticus and Vaticanus manuscripts. Also, several of the concluding doxologies and blessings in the New Testament epistles might be shorter or altogether absent compared to later manuscripts. Textual variations in nearly all the concluding verses and shorter texts in many of the early manuscripts strongly suggest that the original endings to most of the epistles were concise. For instance, the word "amen" was likely added for oral, liturgical presentation, as it is appended to the end of each Gospel, Acts, and all but three epistles (Romans, Galatians, Jude) in later manuscripts.

Upon examining the other features of the concluding verses—the final greetings, blessings of grace and peace, and some doxologies—it becomes apparent that these were expanded over the course of textual transmission. This can be seen in the textual variants for verses such as Philippians 4:23; 2 Timothy 4:22; Titus 3:15; 1 Peter 5:14; 2 Peter 3:18; and Jude 25. For example, the second-century papyrus P87 ends Philemon with a simple "Grace be with you," instead of the longer "The grace of the Lord Jesus Christ be with your spirit." Similarly, the third-century papyrus P72 ends 1 Peter with "Greet one another with the kiss of love," without the addition of "Peace be to all the ones in Christ," as is found in all other manuscripts. These shorter endings might offer us a closer look at what the original autographs looked like.

No Inscriptions or Subscriptions

The original New Testament writings, whether autographs or published archetypes, wouldn't have included inscriptions (titles) or subscriptions, as these were all added later. The four Gospels wouldn't have been referred to as "Gospels" (euaggelion), as this term was a second-century descriptor. For example, the title "Gospel according to John" (euaggelion kata Ioannen) could have been added to the original codex of P66 by a later hand. Neither would the book of Acts have been titled as such by Luke, nor would John have named his apocalypse "Revelation." The Epistles, by their nature, wouldn't have included titles. Some, like Ephesians, didn't even name the city in their opening address, as evidenced by the lack of the words "in Ephesus" (Eph. 1:1) in the three earliest manuscripts (P46 א B).

The Presence of Nomina Sacra

The autographs might have incorporated primary nomina sacra (sacred names) for Kurios (Lord), Christos (Christ), Iesous (Jesus), and Theos (God) in their earliest forms. No New Testament or Christian Greek Old Testament manuscripts discovered thus far have used these divine titles in any form other than nomina sacra. These date back to the late first century and early second century, suggesting that nomina sacra could have been included in the original writings or at least the earliest publications.

Handwriting of the Archetypes

The handwriting of the archetypes, being published texts, would likely be more refined than the autographs. This script might be what's known as "bookhand" or "reformed documentary" script. If a professional scribe was employed for the archetype, it could have had a calligraphic appearance. If the author penned the archetype, it would be less polished, unless the author was a skilled penman.

Speculating creatively, the script of many New Testament archetypes might have resembled that of the Greek Minor Prophet Scrolls from Nahal Hever (8Hev XIIgr), dated to the early first century AD. These manuscripts likely bear the closest resemblance to the earliest New Testament manuscripts, as Jewish scribes could have carried over their practices. The late first-century and early second-century Greek Old Testament manuscripts produced by Christians might provide some parallels, like the Chester Beatty VI (Numbers and Deuteronomy) with its good Roman hand, or P. Yale 1 (Genesis) and P. Baden 4.56 (Exodus and Deuteronomy).

Non-biblical manuscripts from the mid-first century, the period when most New Testament books were written, might also provide comparisons. Some of these include P. Oxyrhynchus 2555 (after 46 CE), P. Oxyrhynchus 3700 (before 48–49 CE), P. Oxyrhynchus 2471 (ca. 50 CE), P. Med. 70.01 (55 CE), and P. Oxyrhynchus 246 (AD 66).

If professional scribes familiar with creating literary texts produced the earliest publications, they would have a "book hand" look, as seen in P. Fayum 6 (early first century), P. Fayum 7 (early first century), and P. Oxyrhynchus 2987 (ca. 78–79 CE).

However, it's worth noting that none of the extant New Testament manuscripts have a mid-first-century look. A few, such as P52 and P104, bear resemblances to hands of the late first century or early second century.

Please note that this is largely speculative, aiming to provide some insight into what the autographs and archetypes of the individual books of the New Testament may have looked like. The goal here is to give students an idea of how the original writings could have appeared, while acknowledging that we can only base our assumptions on the available evidence and educated conjecture. It is important to approach these ideas with a healthy dose of skepticism and an open mind for new discoveries and insights that could further our understanding of the New Testament's origins and development.

The Publishing of the Greek New Testament Books

The process of publishing the New Testament writings unfolded in several stages, providing a roadmap for understanding the early stages of the transmission of the New Testament text.

Firstly, individual writings were produced between 50 and 98 CE. These standalone pieces formed the foundational building blocks of what would eventually become the New Testament. Passages like the Gospel of Matthew, the Epistle to the Romans, or the Revelation of John, were each crafted in their own right during this period.

The second stage involved the collation of these separate writings into collections. For instance, the four Gospels and Paul's major Epistles were gathered into distinct volumes. This phase likely occurred around 100–125 CE. During this time, it is conceivable that Paul himself may have overseen the collection of his major letters, or at least advocated for their assemblage.

Lastly, the entire New Testament – encompassing all 27 canonical books – was consolidated into a single unit. This did not occur until the early fourth century, and even then, it was combined with the Greek Old Testament into one codex, as exemplified by Codex Vaticanus and Codex Sinaiticus.

It's crucial to note that the focus of this discussion is on the initial two phases of publication, in which the writings were first developed and then gathered into collections. This contrasts with the perspective of scholars like David Trobisch, who in "The First Edition of the New Testament," concentrates on what he labels a "Canonical Edition" of the New Testament. While he doesn't provide a specific date for this edition, it's clear that it couldn't have been created earlier than the third century. Thus, his examination addresses a much later phase of publishing than the one being discussed here.

The Story of Jesus: From Oral Tradition to Written Gospels

The Gospels serve as the accounts of Jesus' life and teachings, penned by those who witnessed his ministry first-hand. Much like the way we learn about Socrates through the writings of his disciples, Plato and Xenophon, our knowledge of Jesus is shaped by the narratives of his followers. It's important to note that their accounts held credibility due to the presence of other disciples who could dispute any inaccuracies or fabrications. There were not only the Twelve Apostles but also seventy-two additional disciples (Luke 10:1) and even more followers who witnessed the risen Christ (1 Corinthians 15:6). Any falsehoods in the narratives about Jesus would have been exposed by this large group of witnesses.

The early Christian community relied heavily on the apostles' oral transmission of Jesus' life and teachings (Acts 2:42). These spoken accounts, along with the Septuagint, nourished the spiritual lives of the early church.

Luke referred to early written accounts about Jesus as "narratives" (Luke 1:1). It wasn't until the mid-second century that these accounts were termed "gospels" (euaggelion). Luke wrote his Gospel to affirm and provide certainty to Theophilus about what he had been taught orally. The written Gospel, therefore, was not meant to replace or revise the oral teachings but to affirm and extend them. This transition from oral to written accounts is seen in Mark's Gospel, which is based on Peter's spoken messages, and potentially in John's Gospel, where the content may have been preached before being written.

These Gospels were eventually published, with Luke's two-volume work (Luke and Acts) likely funded by Theophilus, to whom it was dedicated. Early Christian history recorded by Eusebius reveals that both Mark and Luke "published" their Gospels, indicating they created master copies for further distribution. Similarly, John's Gospel was "published" while he was living in Ephesus.

The motivation to write these Gospel accounts likely came from the impending death of the apostles, who wished to leave a lasting, written testament to Jesus' life and teachings. Both Matthew and John, two of the Gospel writers and apostles, provide us with these valuable accounts. John asserts eyewitness authenticity in his Gospel, while Matthew's Gospel is accepted as an eyewitness account based on early church history.

The Gospels: Memoirs and Biographical Sketches

Papias of Hierapolis, a historian who compiled oral and written traditions about Jesus, defined the Gospel of Mark as apomenmoneumata (memoirs or reminiscences) based on Peter's sayings (chreiai); (refer to Eusebius, Church History 3.39.15). Justin Martyr, a Christian philosopher, similarly used the term apomenmoneumata to describe the Gospels. Apomenmoneumata, or memoirs, was a recognized literary form, often expanded chreiai (sayings/actions about specific individuals), set in a narrative framework and transmitted reliably by memory.

The Gospels fit well into the apomenmoneumata description, but they differ from full-fledged modern biographies. Only Luke provides a comprehensive account of Jesus Christ's life, but the focus remains on what Jesus did and said rather than an all-inclusive biography. Luke clarified his intent to Theophilus, stating, "In my former book, Theophilus, I wrote about all that Jesus began to do and to teach until the day he was taken up to heaven" (Acts 1:1–2). Similarly, the Gospel of John ends by emphasizing the miracles of Jesus and their purpose: "Jesus performed many other signs in the presence of his disciples, which are not recorded in this book. But these are written that you may believe that Jesus is the Messiah, the Son of God" (John 20:30–31).

While not exhaustive biographies, the Gospels likely resembled biographical works familiar to Hellenistic readers. Some scholars draw parallels between Xenophon's Memorabilia and the Synoptic Gospels or Plato's Dialogues and the Fourth Gospel. The Gospels could be grouped with other biographies of the time, such as the Life of Aesop, the Life of Homer, the Jewish Lives of the Prophets, and the life of Secundus the Silent Philosopher, based on structure and style. Burridge's comparative study indicates that the Gospels closely align with ancient biographics in terms of literary and semantic evidence.

Like popular biographies, the Gospels are structured around a chronological framework of a person's life, interspersed with anecdotes, maxims, speeches, and documents. They often serve a didactic purpose, presenting Jesus as a model of virtue. A similar structure can be found in Plutarch's Lives, a highly popular work in the Greco-Roman world. However, the Gospels are more than chronological displays; they are crafted narratives designed to be literary works. The authors—Matthew, Mark, Luke, and John—applied different literary techniques to present Jesus Christ in distinct ways.

What sets the Gospels apart from other memoirs or biographies is their subject: Jesus Christ, who claimed to be the Son of God. His life story is unparalleled: born of a virgin, Jesus preached salvation and eternal life for those who accepted him as Messiah and Son of God, was crucified, resurrected, appeared to his disciples, and ascended to heaven. The Gospel writers were inspired by these events and guided by the Spirit, as promised by Jesus himself: "But the Advocate, the Holy Spirit, whom the Father will send in my name, will teach you all things and will remind you of everything I have said to you" (John 14:26). This promise ensured that the disciples would remember and accurately record the life and teachings of Jesus.

Dissemination of the Epistles, Revelation, and Acts

Delving into the publication of the Epistles, we begin with Paul's letters. Paul composed several personal missives (to Timothy, Titus, and Philemon) and numerous epistles. Adolf Deissman distinguishes between a letter and an epistle. A letter, he says, is personal communication between two individuals, not intended for wider audience. An epistle, on the other hand, is a stylized literary piece that seems personally addressed to one or more individuals but is designed to reach a broader audience. Paul's epistles largely adhere to this description. Two of Paul's epistles, Romans and Ephesians, were clearly intended to be encyclical treatises—to be read by all churches. Only three of Paul's nonpastoral epistles are exclusively authored by Paul—Romans, Galatians, and Ephesians. Each holds a unique significance. Romans is Paul's magnum opus on the Christian life, Ephesians on the church, and Galatians presents a personal defense.

Paul had a strategic plan for disseminating his message. Initially, he aimed to travel extensively, proclaiming the gospel to as many people as possible, even aspiring to reach Spain, the westernmost edge of the known world (Rom. 15:18–24). However, he soon realized the limitations of this oral method—constrained by his capacity to travel. Thus, like Jesus, he sent out others to spread the gospel. He understood that his writings, delivered to various churches by his colleagues, could more effectively disseminate the gospel revealed to him. Paul's writings would enhance and prolong his mission. As time passed, Paul became renowned for his "epistles," characterized as "weighty and strong" (2 Cor. 10:10). Interestingly, his epistles were considered superior to his spoken messages, suggesting that Paul invested considerable effort into his writings, recognizing the lasting value of the written word.

Paul understood the authority behind apostolic letters, as demonstrated by the letter from the first Jerusalem church council. This first epistle from the church leaders assembled in Jerusalem set the precedent for subsequent epistles (see Acts 15). It was authoritative because it was apostolic, and it was accepted as God's word. Paul desired the churches to receive his words as God's word. He explicitly states this in 1

Thessalonians (2:13), insisting that his epistle be read to all church members (5:27). In the Second Epistle to the Thessalonians, Paul equates the authority of his epistles with his preaching (2:15). He told his audience that by reading his writings, they would understand the mystery of Christ revealed to him (Eph. 3:1–6). Thus, he encouraged other churches to read his epistles, promoting the circulation of his writings (Col. 4:16).

Peter and John also had dissemination strategies. Peter's first epistle, written to a dispersed Christian audience (the Christian diaspora in Pontus, Galatia, Cappadocia, Asia, Bithynia—1 Pet. 1:1), was intended to be widely read and must have been initially produced in several copies. John's first epistle was similarly published and circulated—likely to all churches in the Roman province of Asia Minor. Like Romans and Ephesians, First John is a comprehensive explanation of Christian life and doctrine, serving as a model for all orthodox believers. The book of Revelation starts with seven letters to seven churches in the same province, suggesting it was initially published in seven copies, each circulated by one of the seven "messengers" (Greek anggeloi—not "angels" in this context), as the book moved from one location to another.

On the other hand, the personal letters (Philemon, 1 and 2 Timothy, Titus, 2 John, 3 John) were not originally "published" and therefore, their circulation was limited. The same applies to Second Peter, which was not widely circulated in the early days of the church. However, the book of Hebrews seemed to have been disseminated broadly, aided by the assumption among Eastern Christians that it was Paul's work and thus, included in Pauline collections.

The book of Acts, penned by Luke as a sequel to his Gospel (see Acts 1:1–2), was also published originally. However, over time, this book became detached from Luke when the Gospel of Luke was grouped with the other Gospels in single-volume codices. This shift in arrangement somewhat obscured the intended continuity between Luke's Gospel and the book of Acts.

The Multiplication of Manuscript Copies

The spread of a published book relied heavily on the creation of multiple copies. Given the absence of efficient printing technology, these copies were manually produced by scribes, one at a time. The only method to expedite the process involved a master scribe slowly reading a text aloud while multiple scribes transcribed the spoken words. This method was typically reserved for high-demand texts like Homer's Iliad or Odyssey. Most other texts were copied individually— a single scribe using a single exemplar to create one copy.

In the early years of the church, copies of New Testament books were likely produced in this one-by-one manner. Many of the scribes tasked with this job were literate and had training, of varying degrees, in Alexandrian scribal practices or Jewish scriptural practices. Some scribes were skilled in making copies for libraries or book trade, others were adept at producing documents, while some possessed only basic

Greek writing skills without any formal training in book production. The quality of a manuscript often reflected the skill level of the scribe who produced it. A beautifully calligraphed, textually accurate manuscript indicated a diligent and skilled scribe, whereas a manuscript full of uncorrected errors and scrawled Greek suggested an untrained and generally incompetent scribe.

In ancient times, there were institutions dedicated to training scribes. Learning to write on clay or craft elegant majuscule letters probably required as much time as it currently takes students to learn to read and write. Aspiring scribes could either attend a formal school or train under a private teacher, with the latter being the more common route. These schools were affiliated with temples or scriptoria and were scattered widely. Trained scribes willing to teach could be found in even the smallest towns. Typically, each scribe had at least one apprentice who was treated like a family member during the learning process. This hands-on education was usually sufficient to prepare young scribes for routine commercial writing tasks, such as drafting legal and business documents or transcribing private correspondence. There are Assyrian reliefs depicting scribes transcribing dictations from an Assyrian monarch.

For more advanced study and training, attending a formal school was necessary. Schools attached to temples offered the resources required to teach sciences (including mathematics) and literature, which were essential for advanced scribes. In these schools, a promising scribe could even study to become a priest or a "scientist." Archaeological finds from ancient city ruins include "textbooks" used by students and schoolrooms with benches for students. Some of the unearthed ancient Near Eastern texts are simply schoolboy exercises or student copies of original documents, usually less elegant or legible than the originals penned by master scribes.

A variety of texts were available for student assignments in the temple schools. Elementary tasks might involve practicing writing a list of cuneiform signs, similar to our learning the alphabet—except there were about six hundred signs. Another simple task could be to copy dictionaries listing stones, cities, animals, and gods. After such preliminary exercises, students could graduate to literary texts and accurately copy portions of grand epics, hymns, or prayers. Thus, through rigorous study and a long-term program of instruction and practice, a gifted student could qualify for scribal service in virtually any field. Regrettably, the general population did not have access to develop reading, writing, and professional skills.

The Diverse Roles of Scribes in Biblical Times

In the era of the Bible, scribes performed a wide range of writing tasks. They often sat at the city gates or in open areas, assisting illiterate citizens with various writing tasks, such as correspondence, receipts, and contracts. In a more formal capacity, they maintained records and wrote annals. Some scribes, specifically religious scribes, were responsible for copying Scriptures. We see several of these individuals mentioned in the Old Testament, including Shebna (2 Kings 18:18, 37), Shaphan (2 Kings 22:8–12), Ezra (Ezra 7:6, 11; Nehemiah 8:1, 9, 13; 12:26, 36), Baruch (Jeremiah 36:26, 32), and Jonathan (Jeremiah 37:15, 20). In the time of Jesus, scribes were highly trained in writing and in understanding the Law. Jesus and his disciples had frequent interactions with scribes, as well as their associates, the priests and Pharisees (Matthew 2:4; 5:20; 7:29; 8:19; 9:3; 12:38; Mark 1:22; 2:6, 16; 3:22; 7:1, 5; 11:18; Luke 5:21, 30; 6:7; 9:22; 11:53; Acts 4:5; 6:12, 23:9).

When the early New Testament papyri were discovered in the early 1900s, scholars initially believed they were not the work of professionally trained scribes. Some even suggested they were the product of illiterate individuals with little concern for accurately copying the New Testament. Kenyon, for instance, argued that the earliest Christians, who were often poor, scattered, and illiterate, were unlikely to meticulously focus on transcription accuracy or to religiously preserve their books for future generations. Some early manuscripts indeed exhibit this lack of concern. For instance, we see a schoolboy practicing his lettering using the book of Romans (P10), a barely literate individual writing in Greek (P9), and scrawled amulets (like P78). We also see manuscripts prone to paraphrasing (as in P45), those heavily influenced by the "Western" expansions in the book of Acts (as in P38, P48, P112), or those with significant textual and calligraphic errors (as in P72).

However, as more papyri were discovered after Kenyon's time, it became clear that not all copies were poorly produced. In fact, upon editing the Chester Beatty papyri, Kenyon himself revised his views. The entire collection of early New Testament papyri reveals a wide range of scribal skills. Papyrologists like Grenfell, Hunt, Roberts, Wilcken, Hunger, Skeat, Cavallo, Seider, and Turner have noted that the handwriting of the early New Testament manuscripts can be categorized into four groups: professional (bookhand), reformed documentary, documentary, and common.

Professional scribes crafted pages with carefully formed letters, consistent letter spacing in scriptio continua (continuous writing without spaces between words), minimal abbreviations of numerals, and punctuation and spacing at the end of sections. These literary hands aimed at beauty and legibility. Other manuscripts, typically called "reformed documentary" or simply "documentary," demonstrate the skills of scribes trained in creating quality documents. These scribes worked more quickly, allowing for swiftly stroked letters, occasional ligatures, and abbreviations of numbers. These documentary-style scribes were often accustomed to producing legal documents or writing correspondence for individuals.

In the first three centuries of the Christian era, professional scribes were employed in library scriptoria, by book dealers, or by individuals requiring secretarial services. A scribe's role could be multifaceted, with the ability to work across these various fields. Therefore, a manuscript displaying a reformed documentary hand could have been executed by a professional scribe just as easily as a manuscript displaying a bookhand. In fact, some of the New Testament manuscripts that appear to be "reformed documentary" may have been the work of a professional scribe working at a faster pace.

Most of the early New Testament manuscripts from the second and third centuries exhibit a documentary or reformed documentary appearance. A few other manuscripts display a "common" hand, indicating that they may have been the work of an individual with basic Greek writing skills. This diverse range of handwriting styles reflects the varying degrees of literacy and scribal training among the early Christian community. Despite these variations, the painstaking work of these scribes played a crucial role in preserving the New Testament texts for future generations.

The Professional Bookhand

Several early New Testament manuscripts were evidently crafted by professional scribes skilled in the production of literary texts. Among these, the Gospel codex known as P4+64+67 stands out with its finely executed calligraphy, paragraph markings, double-columns, and punctuation. Noted papyrologist C. H. Roberts highlighted the professionalism of this manuscript, pointing out its text divisions follow a system also found in P75 and some significant fourth-century manuscripts (like Codex Sinaiticus (ℵ) and Codex Vaticanus (B)). This system, he noted, was not the creation of the scribe, implying it was a wider practice not limited to Egypt.

Other manuscripts that display a professional bookhand include P30, which exhibits clear Biblical Uncial; P39, a stunning specimen of early Biblical Uncial; P46, which presents stichoi notations, typical of paid scribes; P66, which is likely the product of a scriptorium; P75, the work of an extremely skilled scribe; P77+P103, showcasing finely crafted calligraphy, standard paragraph markings, and punctuation; P95, which contains a small portion of the Gospel of John; and P104, a treasure among the early papyri.

Based on the evidence from the existing papyri dated before 300 CE, at least nine professionally created manuscripts stand out for their remarkable bookhand calligraphy: P4+64+67, P39, P46, P66, P75, P77, P95, P103, and P104. Each of these manuscripts is explored in more detail in the following chapter.

Reformed Documentary

Many of the early New Testament papyri were composed in what is known as the "reformed documentary hand." This refers to a style where the scribe recognized that the work they were creating was not merely a legal document, but a piece of literary work. In "The Birth of the Codex," Roberts and Skeat observe:

"Christian manuscripts of the second century, although not meeting the highest standards of calligraphy, usually showcase a proficient style of writing referred to as 'reformed documentary.' This is likely the work of seasoned scribes, whether they were

Christian or not. Therefore, it's a reasonable assumption that these Christian text scribes received compensation for their efforts."

According to this interpretation, manuscripts showing a "reformed documentary" hand could have been created by a scribe who typically produced documents for individuals. When it came to crafting New Testament manuscripts, they might have been hired to make copies for individual Christians or they might have offered their services to a Christian congregation. In my estimation, there are at least fifteen "reformed documentary" New Testament manuscripts among the extant papyri predating 300 CE. These are P1, P30, P32, P35, P38, P45, P52, P69, P87, P90, P100, P102, P108, P109, and P110.

Documentary

Most of the earliest manuscripts seem not to have been produced by professional book-makers but by communities whose members included business individuals and lower-ranking officials accustomed to creating documents. A manuscript written in a "documentary" hand will not be as uniformly presented as those made by professional scribes. The lettering will not aim for bilinearity—that is, maintaining an even top and bottom line across each line of letters. The first letter on each line will often be larger than the rest, as can be seen in a documentary text like P. Bremer 5 (117 CE). This enlarged initial letter is a characteristic of documentary texts and Jewish Greek manuscripts, specifically those found at Nahal Hever.

In documentary texts, punctuation is not consistent, and the text typically features numerical abbreviations common in document writing. Two Revelation texts, P47 and P98, are good examples of this. Moreover, a documentary hand will often leave spaces between words or groups of words, as frequently done in legal contracts. This was not a practice of scribes creating literary texts.

The majority of the extant early New Testament manuscripts are either documentary or reformed documentary, crafted by church members who were trained in document writing and applied this skill to creating copies of Scripture. These copies were made for specific individuals who hired their services or for their congregations. As Gamble suggests, many of these scribes were likely the church lectors, whose responsibilities included maintaining and creating new copies of Scripture as needed, as well as preparing the text for reading to the congregation. According to my research, nearly half (27) of the early New Testament papyri are of the "documentary" type. These include: P5, P13, P15+P16, P17, P20, P23, P27, P28, P29, P37, P47, P48, P49+65, P50, P53, P70, P80, P91, P92, P101, P106, P107, P108, P111, P113, and P114.

Common

Sometimes, it can be challenging to distinguish between a poorly crafted "documentary" hand and a "common" hand. However, a common hand typically displays the work of someone with minimal proficiency in writing Greek. For example, P10, as previously mentioned, demonstrates the work of a novice Greek writer and serves as a good example of what might be termed a "common" hand. P9, which contains a portion of 1 John, also undeniably exhibits a "common" hand, as does P78, an amulet.

Interestingly, many of the manuscripts of Revelation show a common hand. This is the case for P18 and P24, and even more so for P98. Other papyri with Revelation are documentary, particularly P47. This could either be a mere coincidence of archaeology, or it could suggest that Revelation was not commonly read in churches and thus not frequently copied by trained scribes.

Scriptoria and Christian Writing Centers in the Early Church

Before the era of Constantine, did the early church have any scriptoria or writing centers producing Christian texts — including those of the Old and New Testaments and other Christian writings? If so, where? Several scholars have proposed major cities such as Alexandria, Caesarea, Antioch, Jerusalem, and Rome. The town of Oxyrhynchus, Egypt, can also be added to this list. Regrettably, there is no direct archaeological evidence of Christian scholars producing copies of Old and New Testament books in these cities except for Oxyrhynchus. It would be desirable to discover archaeological evidence from Alexandria, Egypt, particularly because it was the site of the great library, scriptoria, and an early Christian intellectual hub. However, nothing has been found in Alexandria due to two main reasons: (1) the great library was destroyed twice, consuming any biblical texts in the fires, and (2) Alexandria's location on the humid Mediterranean led to the destruction of any manuscripts. Nevertheless, church history and certain manuscript discoveries from other parts of Egypt suggest that Alexandria had a Christian scriptorium or writing center.

Christianity arrived in Alexandria sometime during the first century, and many Jews also resided in this city. Two centuries earlier, Hellenistic Jews in Alexandria had created the Septuagint (a Greek version of the Hebrew Bible) for the great Alexandrian library. Christians adopted this text and used it to validate Jesus' claim to being the Messiah. As Christians began to interpret the Septuagint, Jews abandoned it in favor of new translations of the Hebrew text. Christians in the Alexandrian church continued to use the Septuagint for apologetics and exposition, while also utilizing various New Testament books for instruction. Shortly after Christianity arrived in Alexandria, the local Christians established a catechetical school, the Didaskelion.

Eusebius, in his Ecclesiastical History, implies that this school began well before Pantaenus took charge (160–180 CE). Some scholars believe that Pantaenus may have started a scriptorium and possibly engaged in New Testament textual criticism, though there is no direct evidence for this.

Origen, Pantaenus' successor, employed numerous secretaries and scribes in both Alexandria and Caesarea. Eusebius stated, "As [Origen] dictated, there were ready at hand more than seven shorthand-writers, who relieved each other at fixed intervals, and as many copyists, as well as girls trained for beautiful writing" (Ecclesiastical History 6.23). Origen needed these secretaries and scribes for the vast amount of original writing he produced. We do not know whether he used their services (or those of other scribes) to make copies of the New Testament.

Another potential Christian writing center or scriptorium was Oxyrhynchus, an Egyptian city with close ties to Alexandria. C. H. Roberts, a papyrologist, posited that Oxyrhynchus was likely a center for Christianity in rural Egypt, suggested by the presence of an autograph manuscript of an anti-Jewish dialogue (P. Oxyrhynchus 2070), dated in the third century, and the number of Christian manuscripts discovered there. Roberts thus proposed the existence of a Christian scriptorium in Oxyrhynchus as early as the late second century. However, can this be conclusively determined from the existing documents?

Among the manuscripts unearthed in Oxyrhynchus, many are non-literary texts (such as letters, legal documents, business transactions), written by ordinary people — "tradesmen, farmers, minor government officials for whom knowledge of and writing in Greek was an essential skill, but who had little or no literary interests." Other manuscripts were literary — works of Homer, Pindar, and Philo, often created by professionals or those familiar with professional scriptorial practices.

Moreover, Oxyrhynchus has provided hundreds of biblical texts and Christian writings. To date, there are 140+ papyrus manuscripts of the New Testament; 43 of these are from Oxyrhynchus. This means nearly half of the existing New Testament papyrus manuscripts originated from this ancient Egyptian city. Almost all of the Oxyrhynchus manuscripts date between 200 and 400 CE, and a few have been dated in the second century: P32, P52, P77, P90, and P104.

There is evidence that some of these manuscripts were created by the same scribes (P15 and P16; P20 and P27; P77 and P103), but there are no other common textual features suggesting these manuscripts were created in a single local scriptorium. Instead, most of these manuscripts seem to be the work of individual scribes writing in a documentary or reformed documentary hand. We can suggest, at most, that Oxyrhynchus may have had a writing center where one or two scribes worked on producing copies of literary and biblical texts.

Another possibility is that the biblical writings found at Oxyrhynchus were initially created in Alexandria. We know that intellectuals at Oxyrhychus sourced most of their books from Alexandria. Oxyrhynchus had many significant connections with Alexandria, particularly in scholarship and scriptorial practices. According to paleographer E. G. Turner, several Alexandrians who owned property in Oxyrhynchus were professors at the famous Alexandrian Museum. Some of these professors, while living in Oxyrhynchus, coordinated with Alexandrians to obtain copies of various works of literature. These copies would have been made by the Alexandrian scriptorium and then sent to Oxyrhynchus. Therefore, certain manuscripts found in Oxyrhynchus likely originated in Alexandria. However, we cannot confirm if this included any biblical manuscripts.

A final possibility of linking some New Testament manuscripts to Alexandria involves the Bodmer Gospel papyri, P66 and P75, which originated from Jabal Abu Manna and probably once belonged to a Christian monastery established by Pachomius in the early fourth century. In the 1950s, several early biblical manuscripts were discovered near this monastery, known as the Dishna Papers or the Bodmer biblical papyri. Martin Bodmer purchased these from a dealer in Cairo in the 1950s and 1960s, but the dealer never revealed their origin.

James Robinson, an expert in Nag Hammadi manuscripts, determined the discovery site while investigating the origins of the Nag Hammadi manuscripts. The Bodmer biblical papyri were found in Jabal Abu Manna, located just north of the Dishna plain, twelve kilometers east of Jabal al-Tarif. Robinson suggests that these manuscripts likely belonged to a library in a Pachomian monastery.

Monasticism was introduced to this area around 320 CE by Pachomius, and by the time of his death, thousands of monks were residing in eleven monasteries within a sixty-mile radius along the Nile River. A century later, the monk population had increased to nearly fifty thousand. These monks read and memorized the Scriptures, especially the New Testament and Psalms, as part of their daily routine. Pachomius himself was actively involved in this practice as he read the Scriptures aloud to his congregation. Given that Pachomius and other monks in his monasteries were literate in both Coptic and Greek, it's plausible that they engaged with the Scriptures in both languages. However, over time, especially starting from the fifth century, almost all of them read only in Coptic.

The library in the Pachomian monastery was established after 320 CE, meaning all earlier manuscripts, particularly the New Testament papyri, must have been created in other scriptoria and later added to the library. The manuscripts from the fourth and fifth centuries vary in quality - some are poorly crafted while others display professional workmanship. This suggests that the monks may have produced some of their own rudimentary books while also receiving professionally made manuscripts from an external scriptorium. The latter were likely from Alexandria, considering that Athanasius from Alexandria frequently visited Pachomius's monastery.

While the direct connection between certain New Testament manuscripts and an Alexandrian scriptorium can't be definitively proven, there's no doubt that several New Testament manuscripts from the 2nd century were crafted by professional scribes. These scribes might have been operating in a Christian or secular scriptorium, applying their skills to reproduce New Testament books. Alternatively, they could have been working in what Gamble describes as "a writing center," where more than a single scribe would be involved in copying texts.

Two manuscripts, P46 and P66, stand out as the most plausible candidates to have been produced in a scriptorium due to their professional-looking nature. The scribe who crafted P46 was undoubtedly a professional, as evidenced by stichoi notations at the end of several books. Stichoi were used by professionals to denote the number of lines copied for appropriate compensation. It's highly likely that a scriptorium employee paginated the codex and indicated the stichoi. The scribe themselves made a few corrections while working, and several other readers made additional corrections.

P66 also seems likely to have originated from a scriptorium or writing center. The first copyist of this manuscript had their work meticulously checked by a diorthotes, following a different exemplar – a process consistent with scriptorium practices. Although it's possible that an individual who purchased the manuscript made all the corrections, a common practice in ancient times, the number of corrections in P66 and the fact that many were made by the paginator (a different scribe) suggest otherwise.

In addition to these marks of professional work, P66 shows pinpricks in the corners of each leaf of the papyri, serving as guides for text alignment. The manuscript also features a consistent set of correction signs both in the margins and interlinearly. Another tell-tale sign of a professionally produced manuscript is the use of the diple (>) in the margin, which signalled a correction in the text or the need for one. These signs are rare in the surviving New Testament manuscripts. The scribe of P48 used a diple to note a correction in Acts 23:27.

Another early manuscript, P. Oxyrhynchus 405, has diple markings. This manuscript contains Matthew's account of Jesus' baptism in a portion of Irenaeus's Against Heresies 3.9, which quotes Matthew 3:16–17. Each line of the quotation begins with a diple (>), suggesting that the wording in this quote required correction or verification, according to standard scriptoral practices. Although the text is fragmented, a careful transcriptional reconstruction suggests that this manuscript likely agrees with ℵ and B (in excluding αυτω) and the definite articles before πνευμα and θεου in Matt. 3:16.

Common Characteristics in Jewish and Christian Manuscripts

Before wrapping up this section on Christian scriptoria and writing centers, it's worth exploring the possibility that early Christian manuscripts could display influences from Jewish scriptoral practices. If this connection can be proven, it implies that the initial Christian writing centers might have been extensions of Jewish scriptoria to some extent.

When examining Greek Old Testament manuscripts and Christian Old Testament (as well as New Testament) manuscripts, several shared features become evident. For instance, both types of manuscripts often showcase an enlarged letter at the start of each line. This could suggest Jewish influence rather than a purely documentary style, as is often assumed. This insight comes from Peter Parsons, who compared some features of the Minor Prophet Scrolls from Nahal Hever with early Christian manuscripts. He noted the enlarged initials at line beginnings, and new sections marked out in the margin, giving the manuscript a documentary appearance. Early Christian books display the same characteristic, unlike copies of Greek classics. This leads to the speculation that the early Church texts were more aligned with business-world practices, reflecting the social environment where these texts circulated and their perceived value. The presence of the same characteristic in a pre-Christian Jewish manuscript might indicate that Christians adopted rather than originated this practice.

C. H. Roberts shared this viewpoint, stating that "documentary practice may not have been the only influence on Christian scribes." Roberts elaborated that the Minor Prophets scrolls exhibit "an enlarged letter, preceded by a small blank space, marking the beginning of a new phrase, while verses are marked off by larger spaces."

Regarding Christian Old Testament manuscripts, the characteristic of an enlarged letter at the line's start is visible in several Chester Beatty Greek Old Testament manuscripts: V (Gen.), VI (Num.-Deut.), VII (Isa.), VIII (Jer.), X (Dan.). When Philip W. Comfort reviewed the early New Testament manuscripts, he noticed this feature in the following papyri: P13 (to some extent), P23, P32, P46 (to a degree), P53, P70, P72, P78, P90, and P109.

The second physical feature in New Testament manuscripts potentially influenced by Jewish Greek Old Testament manuscripts is the use of the nomen sacrum for kurios (Lord). Philips argues that the most plausible explanation for this invention is that Christians creating copies of the Septuagint devised an alternative way to represent the sacred title, JHVH. Rather than including the Hebrew Tetragrammaton in a Greek text, they devised a Greek nomen sacrum, $\overline{KC}$, to represent "LORD."

The Emergence of the Early Christian Codex

Presently, printed books are so entrenched in our society that it's easy to forget that a mere two thousand years ago, they were virtually non-existent. Instead, scrolls were the primary medium for literary works—continuous rolls spanning twenty to thirty feet long and around nine to ten inches high. Skins or papyrus sheets were joined to form this "roll of the book" (Ps. 40:7), with the text inscribed in columns to form the pages (Jer. 36:23). The term "volume" itself derives from the act of rolling or revolving, as upon rollers. This gives us an image of Jesus in the synagogue of Nazareth, skillfully unrolling the scroll of the prophet Isaiah handed to him by the hazan, or attendant, until he found the appropriate passage (Luke 4:16, 17).

Then a shift took place. The codex emerged from humble beginnings to almost surpass the roll. But what exactly is a codex? The word "caudex" referred to a tree's stem, and it was applied to wooden tablets with raised rims, often coated with wax and used for writing with a stylus, akin to a school slate (Isa. 8:1). By the fifth century B.C.E., multi-leaf tablets were in use, bound together with strings threaded through holes. These assembled tablets resembled a tree trunk, hence the name codex.

Imagine lugging around these heavy, unwieldy wooden tablets! Unsurprisingly, there was a search for a lighter, more flexible material. The Romans devised the parchment notebook, bridging the gap between the tablet and the later book-form codex. As the style and material of the original tablet evolved, naming the new format became a challenge. In Latin usage, "membranae" was adopted to distinguish the parchment notebook. This term was used by Paul when he asked for "the scrolls, especially the parchments [membranas]" (2 Tim. 4:13). Paul's use of a Latin term—and even in a Latin sense—was likely due to the absence of a Greek equivalent to describe what he requested. Eventually, the term "codex" was incorporated into the Greek language to denote the book.

The Codex and its Adoption by Early Christians

Considering the evidence compiled so far, where does the development of the codex stand? As early as 1898, F. G. Kenyon, assistant keeper of manuscripts in the British Museum, proposed that the emergence of the codex was linked with the rise of vellum, particularly in the fourth century CE, and suggested that the papyrus codex was merely an unsuccessful experiment. At that time, very few papyrus manuscripts of the Bible had been discovered, leaving a three-century gap in the textual history of the Bible. Papyrus can only endure the test of time and weather in extremely dry climates, which is why those in search of papyrus must turn to regions where these conditions exist, such as around the Dead Sea and in Egypt.

Today, the scenario is markedly different, thanks to the dry sands of Egypt. In the past one hundred and ten years, a plethora of evidence has been unearthed, particularly from the ancient rubbish dumps of Oxyrhynchus and the Fayum, effectively closing the three-century gap and providing a clearer understanding of the role of the papyrus codex.

One striking observation is that nearly all discovered Bible manuscripts from the Christian era on papyrus are in codex form. This has led to the intriguing conclusion that while classical texts continued to be circulated in rolls for a considerable time, the codex appeared to be particularly suitable for Christian writings. A review of pagan literature revealed a mere 2.4 percent of codices to rolls for the second century CE (11 codices and 465 rolls). However, all Biblical manuscripts attributed to the second century are codices, and there's only one later manuscript of the Psalms certainly of Christian origin found in roll form. Currently, there are more than a hundred Bible codices on papyrus (some merely fragments), written before the end of the fourth century, spread across museums and collections worldwide. It's evident that early Christians quickly abandoned the roll form.

Dating Second-Century Bible Manuscripts

So, how can we determine that a manuscript hails from the second century CE? Do we find a date clearly marked on the first leaf? Few ancient manuscripts have survived with their dates intact, and when they do appear, they are not always reliable. Even modern books often only provide the date of publication on the title page. If this page is lost, the precise dating might be difficult; however, in this regard, manuscripts can have an edge over printed books.

The solution lies in the realm of paleography. This discipline involves meticulous investigation of the writing, its form, and style. Just as our modern languages are subtly molded by changes over time, so was the case in the early centuries. By comparing dozens of tiny features, a manuscript can be dated within a range of forty or fifty years. The introduction of slight spaces between words, limited punctuation, and various abbreviations have all aided in defining specific periods. Tables of characteristic letters have been compiled from non-literary papyri, like receipts, letters, petitions, and leases, which do provide exact dates, and these serve as a solid foundation for comparison. For instance, in the fragment of John's Gospel known as P52, the scribe added a small hook or flourish to some strokes, omitted certain marks, used a unique type of cross-stroke, and rounded specific letters—all recognized habits of early second-century writers.

While not all experts concur, most assign a dozen papyrus codices to the second century CE. These manuscripts are significant due to their early date and codex form and are listed below. Bible manuscripts are assigned internationally recognized numbers. The list of Christian Greek Scripture papyri is known as the Gregory-von Dobschütz list, and that for the Septuagint Greek version of the Hebrew Scriptures as the Rahlfs list, named after the most prominent scholars who maintained them. Furthermore, each manuscript carries a collection name and number to identify its origin or ownership.

Creating a Codex

When studying codices, several intriguing characteristics emerge. One early practice appeared to involve constructing a codex in a single massive quire. This was accomplished by stacking all the sheets on top of each other and then making one fold. A fragment known as P5, consisting of just one pair of leaves, contains part of

John 1 on one leaf and John 20 on the other. Therefore, to include all the chapters in between, this codex would comprise a single quire of around fifty leaves. The Isaiah codex from the Chester Beatty collection originally constituted a single quire of about 112 leaves. These types of codices often had their center leaves trimmed to stop them from protruding like a wedge when closed. This resulted in narrower columns of writing compared to the wider outer leaves.

In contrast, other early codices were composed of single-sheet quires only, meaning all sheets were folded first and then stacked for stitching. However, neither of these two extremes proved to be the most efficient. Quires of four or five sheets (eight to ten leaves) seemed to be the most convenient. However, some codices exhibit a mixture, as seen in the Bodmer John P66. Out of five existing quires, three have five sheets each, one has four, and the last one has eight sheets. The missing part of chapter six was a unique single-sheet quire.

The various ways sheets were laid down possibly reflect individual preferences. Each sheet consists of two layers of papyrus fiber glued together crosswise, so the side displaying the horizontal layer is known as the 'recto' and the side showing the vertical layer of fibers is the 'verso'. The method of laying down the sheets would change the appearance when the codex was opened. A recto page might face a verso page, but some might prefer to have recto facing recto and verso facing verso.

Some early codices, with two narrow columns of writing per page, were likely copied from scrolls with minimal disruption of the original layout. On the other hand, when an old scroll containing an epitome of Livy was repurposed by a frugal Christian, he copied from a Hebrew codex and even included the page numbers. Such a repurposed scroll is termed an opisthograph.

The Advantages of the Codex

What were the reasons for the preference of the codex over the widely used and familiar scrolls? Initially, codices were not available for purchase from booksellers. Some codices, which appear to have been created from cut-up scrolls, required specific motivations for these early amateur endeavors. The ability to combine the four Gospels into one codex was a significant advantage, as they would not conveniently fit onto a scroll. The Gospels of Matthew, Mark, Luke, and John would require 104 feet of scroll in total. A codex made it much easier and quicker to locate specific texts than a scroll, a feature that was crucial to early Christians who actively referred to their Scriptures. Pocket-sized codices have even been discovered, the smallest of which (P. Literary London 204, 3rd century CE, Psalm 2) had a page size of about three inches by two, containing twelve lines of writing. The practicality of a convenient reference form was quickly recognized. Lastly, the codex was more economical because both sides of the papyrus sheet were utilized.

The codex also played an important role in safeguarding the inspired books of Scripture. Today, the codex continues to provide evidence of the Biblical canon. When we discover nine of Paul's epistles bound into one codex (Chester Beatty P46), including the Epistle to the Hebrews, it affirms that this letter was esteemed at the same level as the other epistles. The codex formed a connection between the various inspired writings, making it harder for unrecognized work to be inserted into the collection. The rapid transition of the Septuagint version of the Hebrew Scriptures from scroll to codex indicates its frequent use and equal regard to the new writings.

The widespread use of the codex in Christian circles during the second century, even for the Septuagint, suggests that its adoption traces back to the first century CE. This could more easily explain the loss of the ending of Mark's Gospel, as it would be possible for the last leaf to be misplaced. Conversely, a scroll would typically be rolled with the ending inside, leading to more damage at the beginning. This is reflected in the greater number of scroll ends that have survived compared to beginnings.

Can we imagine the scene as the Christian Greek Scriptures began to form? What about Matthew, the tax collector turned Gospel writer? One account of the Gospels' growth asks: "Can it be supposed that when he left his business for what he saw to be a far higher interest, his habit of writing would be dropped?" His initial notes may have been made in a parchment notebook, and upon completion, his Gospel would likely circulate in a codex form. As demand for copies grew, the convenience of the codex would be fully exploited, making it possible for traveling ministers like Paul, Timothy, and Titus to carry pocket codices. When these ministers revisited the congregations, they would likely commend the brothers for their progress in using their newly received codices while encouraging those still using scrolls.

The second-century codex significantly demonstrates three points. It affirms the authenticity of God's Word, nearly bridging the gap between the apostolic era and the oldest existing manuscripts. It reveals the early Christians' eagerness to widely disseminate the Scriptures, reducing the high cost of books so that all could access these vital words of life. It helps us understand their frequent reference to their copies and their desire for quick and easy location of passages. May we emulate those ardent early Christians and diligently study our Bibles, like the Bereans of old, to affirm our faith. (Acts 17:11)

Ancient Codices of the New Testament

According to the timeline set by the Alands for the New Testament manuscripts, only three documents are dated to the second century: P52, P90, and P104. P98 is also listed as a second-century document, but with a degree of uncertainty. Three other papyri, namely P32, P46, and P66, are assigned to around 200 CE. However, some paleographers argue that these dates are overly conservative. Recent paleographic studies have attributed a greater number of papyri to the second century. These manuscripts include:

1. P4+P64+P67 (Suppl. Gr. 1120 + Gr. 17 + P. Barceloa 1), containing parts of Matthew and Luke. This manuscript is ascribed to the third quarter of the second century by T. C. Skeat and others.

2. P32 (P. Rylands 5), containing Titus. This manuscript is dated to the second century by T. C. Skeat and others.

3. P46 (Chester Beatty II), featuring Paul's major epistles (excluding the Pastoral Letters). This manuscript, typically dated around 200 CE, is considered earlier by paleographers like Wilckens, Kim, and me.

4. P52 (P. Rylands 457), containing John 18. Many paleographers such as Roberts, Bell, Turner, Cavallo regard this manuscript as the earliest existing piece of the New Testament (circa 115–125 CE).

5. P66 (P. Bodmer II), containing John. This manuscript, typically dated around 200 CE, is assigned to the mid-second century by paleographers like Hunger, Cavallo, and Seider.

6. P77 (P. Oxy. 2683 + P. Oxy. 4405), containing Matthew 23. This manuscript was dated to the late second century by Roberts, the editor of the original edition.

7. P90 (P. Oxy. 3523), featuring John 18–19. T. C. Skeat, the editor of the original edition, dated this manuscript to the late second century.

8. P98 (P. IFAO inv. 237b), containing Revelation 1. Wagner, the editor of the original edition, dated this manuscript to the late second century.

9. P103 (P. Oxy. 4403). Thomas, the editor of the original edition, dated this manuscript to the late second century. The manuscript may be part of the same codex as P77. If not, it certainly seems to be the work of the same scribe.

10. P104 (P. Oxy. 4404). Thomas, the editor of the original edition, dated this manuscript to the late second century.

Other Christian Codices from the Second Century

1. P. Egerton 2, Unknown Gospel. This gospel was likely written around 120–130 CE, but the discovered copy could not be later than 150 CE. It bears a striking resemblance to P52.

2. P. Oxyrhynchus 1, Gospel of Thomas. Grenfell and Hunt dated it to the second or third century. H. I. Bell suggested that the earlier date is quite probable. C. H. Roberts placed it in the second century.

3. P. Geneva 253, Christian Homily. This is a Christian homily from the late second century, containing parts of Matthew 10:11–13, 29–31 (or Luke 10:5–6; 12:6–7).

4. P. Oxyrhynchus 406, Theological Treatise? This codex, dated around 200 CE, preserves either a part of a theological treatise or an unknown New Testament epistle.

These collections of Christian Old Testament codices, New Testament codices, and other Christian codices provide evidence that Christians were utilizing the codex format as early as the second century, and likely even earlier. Only one Christian manuscript (P. Oxyrhynchus 405) has been discovered to be produced in scroll form (excluding those manuscripts written on the back of scrolls). This suggests that Christians consciously and universally transitioned from the Jewish form of the book—the scroll. It also indicates that there was a form of standardization in Christian bookmaking, thereby implying that individual efforts were not isolated.

In Summary

The Christian copyists of the early centuries were highly skilled and practical individuals. They were not only able to produce accurate copies of the original autograph rolls, but they also made significant advancements in the form of the written work itself. In fact, they were ahead of their pagan professional contemporaries in their use of the codex, which was a written work consisting of separate sheets bound together, typically with a wooden cover.

This innovation had many advantages over the traditional roll form. The codex was less expensive to produce, as the sheets could be bound together without the need for gluing them end to end. Additionally, the codex could contain far more content than a roll, allowing multiple works to be combined in one volume. For example, instead of having separate rolls for each of the Gospels, early Christians combined all four Gospels into a single codex, and likewise combined the letters of Paul into one volume. The Vatican Manuscript No. 1209 is a famous example of a codex that contains a significant amount of biblical text.

Moreover, the codex was much more convenient for readers. To find a specific passage, one only needed to turn to the last page of the book rather than unroll dozens of feet of manuscript. The early Christian copyists recognized the benefits of the codex and quickly adopted it as their preferred form for written works, if not the inventors of it themselves.

The Bible, as we have it today, owes much to these early Christian copyists who were dedicated to preserving the Scriptures accurately and efficiently. Their efforts helped ensure that the Word of God was transmitted faithfully from generation to generation.

CHAPTER 5 Unveiling the Transmission of the Text: A Journey Through Time

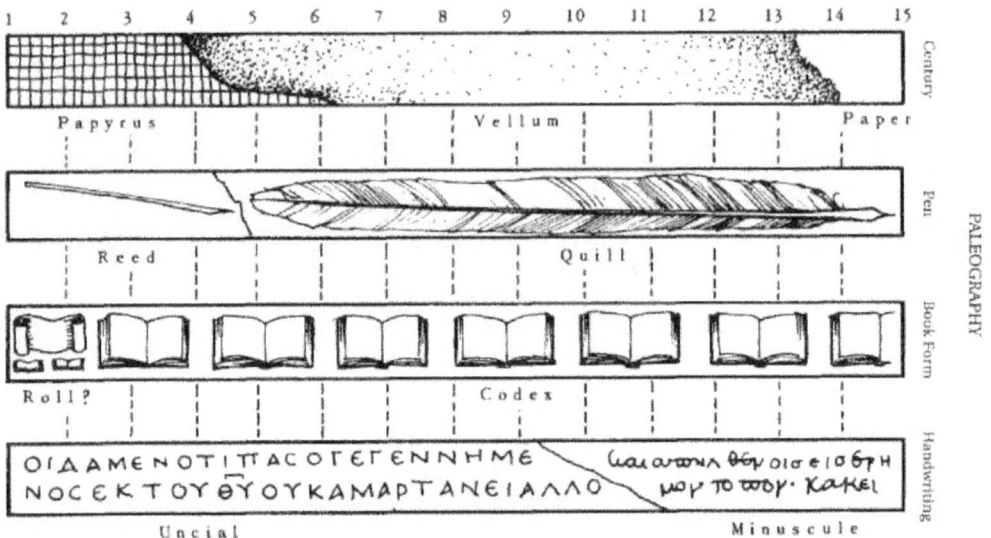

Introduction: The Importance of Textual Transmission

Textual transmission refers to the process through which the text of the Bible was copied, preserved, and passed down from generation to generation. This process is critical because the original manuscripts, or autographs, of the biblical books have not survived. Therefore, our understanding of the Bible depends on the accuracy of the copies we possess.

1. **Original Manuscripts and Their Loss**

The original manuscripts of the Bible were written on perishable materials such as papyrus and parchment. Over time, these materials degraded and the original manuscripts were lost. Additionally, the use of these texts, particularly in liturgical contexts, would have contributed to their wear and tear.

2. **The Process of Copying**

Given the inevitable decay of the original materials, the process of textual transmission began very early. Scribes were trained to meticulously copy the text. They had a deep respect for the sacred text and strove for extreme accuracy. However, like all humans, they were not immune to making mistakes. Errors could include misspellings, repetitions, omissions, or alterations, whether intentional or unintentional. This reality underscores the importance of having a multitude of manuscripts to compare and contrast, allowing scholars to discern the most likely original reading.

A verse that illustrates the copying process is Jeremiah 36:32, "Then Jeremiah took another scroll and gave it to the scribe Baruch son of Neriah, who wrote on it at the dictation of Jeremiah all the words of the scroll that Jehoiakim king of Judah had burned in the fire. And many similar words were added to them."

3. **The Multiplication of Manuscripts**

The Christian community spread rapidly throughout the Roman Empire and beyond, and with it, the need for copies of the Scriptures also grew. The early Christians copied and disseminated the Scriptures widely, resulting in a vast number of manuscripts in various languages. These copies, known as manuscripts, became the basis for the Bibles we have today.

4. **Textual Variants and Their Resolution**

Variations among the manuscripts are known as textual variants. These can be as simple as a single letter or as complex as an entire verse. Most variants are minor and do not affect the meaning of the text. However, some are more significant and require careful analysis to determine the original reading.

This is where the discipline of textual criticism comes into play. Textual critics examine the manuscripts, consider the nature of the variants, the context, the tendencies of the scribes, and other factors. They then make an informed decision about what the original text likely said. This process helps ensure that the Bible translations we have today are as close to the originals as possible.

A famous example of a textual variant is the ending of Mark's Gospel. Some ancient manuscripts end at Mark 16:8, while others include verses 9-20, which describe post-resurrection appearances of Jesus. Scholars continue to debate which ending is original.

5. **Preservation of the Text**

Despite the loss of the original manuscripts and the existence of textual variants, the overall integrity of the biblical text has been remarkably preserved over the centuries. The sheer number of existing manuscripts, their agreement with each other, and their correlation with citations from early Christian writers, all provide strong evidence for the reliability of the biblical text.

In Isaiah 40:8, it is written, "The grass withers, the flower fades, but the word of our God will stand forever." This verse speaks to the enduring nature of God's Word, which is reflected in the preservation of the biblical text through the process of textual transmission.

From Oral Tradition to Written Word

The transmission of the biblical text is a fascinating journey that spans thousands of years. Before the advent of writing, oral tradition was the primary method of preserving and conveying stories, laws, history, and other important cultural information. Even after writing was developed, oral tradition continued to play a significant role in the transmission of the text.

1. **Oral Tradition**

Oral tradition involves the verbal passing of stories, beliefs, and customs from one generation to the next. It was the primary means of preserving cultural narratives prior to the invention of writing. This was likely the case for many of the stories in the Bible, especially those in the Old Testament.

An example of the importance of oral tradition in the Bible is found in Deuteronomy 6:6-7, which reads: "These commandments that I give you today are to be on your hearts. Impress them on your children. Talk about them when you sit at home and when you walk along the road, when you lie down and when you get up." Here, the Israelites are instructed to teach God's laws to their children, underscoring the oral tradition's role in passing down religious teachings.

2. **From Oral to Written**

While the exact timeline is uncertain, at some point, these oral traditions began to be written down. The reasons for this transition are multiple: the need for consistency, the desire for widespread dissemination, the development of writing technologies, and the importance of preserving these narratives for future generations.

Exodus 24:4 provides an example of this transition: "Moses then wrote down everything the LORD had said." Here, Moses is writing down the laws given to him by God, illustrating the move from a spoken command to a written record.

3. **Early Writing Materials and Techniques**

The earliest biblical texts were likely written on scrolls made from papyrus or animal skins. The writing was done with a reed pen dipped in ink. Writing was a skilled craft, usually undertaken by scribes who had undergone extensive training.

Jeremiah 36:18 provides a glimpse into this process: "Baruch answered them, 'He dictated all these words to me, while I wrote them with ink on the scroll.'" In this passage, the prophet Jeremiah is dictating his prophecies to his scribe, Baruch, who then writes them down.

4. **The Canonization of the Text**

Over time, certain texts became recognized as authoritative and were included in the canon of Scripture. This process was not straightforward and involved many debates and decisions over the centuries. However, the result was the formation of the Bible as we know it today.

An example of a canonical text is found in 2 Timothy 3:16: "All Scripture is God-breathed and is useful for teaching, rebuking, correcting and training in righteousness." In this passage, the apostle Paul is affirming the divine authority of the Scriptures.

5. **Preservation and Transmission**

Once the biblical texts were written down and canonized, they needed to be copied and disseminated to ensure their survival and accessibility. Despite the challenges of this process, such as the decay of materials and human error, the biblical text has been remarkably well preserved over thousands of years.

One testament to the enduring nature of God's word is found in Isaiah 40:8: "The grass withers and the flowers fall, but the word of our God endures forever."

In conclusion, the transmission of the biblical text from oral tradition to the written word is a complex and fascinating journey. It involves the faithful retelling of stories, the painstaking work of scribes, the debates over canonicity, and the diligent preservation of texts across millennia. This process has resulted in the Bible we have today, a remarkable testament to the enduring power of God's Word. This sacred text has not only survived but also thrived, influencing countless generations with its teachings, stories, and wisdom.

6. **The Role of Communities**

The communities that held these stories, teachings, and laws were integral to their preservation. They valued these texts as sacred and used them for teaching, worship, and guidance. In the process, they meticulously copied, cared for, and transmitted these texts down the generations.

For example, in Acts 2:42, it's written: "They devoted themselves to the apostles' teaching and to fellowship, to the breaking of bread and to prayer." This highlights the role of the early Christian community in preserving and living out the teachings of the apostles.

7. **Translation into Various Languages**

As Christianity spread, the Bible was translated into many languages, starting with the Septuagint, a Greek translation of the Hebrew Scriptures, in the 3rd century BCE. Later, the Bible was translated into Latin (the Vulgate), Coptic, Syriac, and many other languages. Each translation required careful work to convey the original meanings accurately and was another step in the transmission of the biblical text.

Paul's letters to different communities, like the one in Romans 1:7, "To all in Rome who are loved by God and called to be his holy people," show that the message of the Bible was intended for diverse audiences, necessitating translations.

8. From Manuscripts to Printed Text

The invention of the printing press in the 15th century marked a significant turning point in the transmission of the Bible. This technology made it possible to produce copies of the Bible more quickly and accurately, leading to wider distribution and accessibility.

In conclusion, the transmission of the biblical text from oral tradition to written word is a testament to the enduring power and influence of these sacred texts. Through the dedication of countless individuals and communities, the teachings and stories of the Bible have been preserved and continue to inspire and guide people around the world today.

The Role of Scribes in Early Transmission

Scribes played a pivotal role in the early transmission of biblical texts. In a time before printing presses, it was their task to meticulously copy the scriptures by hand, preserving the word for future generations.

1. **Precision in Transcription**

The process of transcription required a high level of skill and precision. The scribes were tasked with copying every letter and word accurately, without adding or omitting anything. In fact, the Jewish scribes, or Soferim, developed complex systems to ensure the accuracy of their work, including counting the number of times each letter appeared in a book and noting the middle letter of the Pentateuch (Torah) and the Old Testament.

The level of precision expected of scribes is echoed in passages such as Deuteronomy 4:2: "Do not add to what I command you and do not subtract from it, but keep the commands of the LORD your God that I give you."

2. **Respect for the Sacred Texts**

Scribes held a deep reverence for the texts they were copying. Their work was not just a job; it was a sacred duty. They believed that they were handling the very words of God, and this belief guided their meticulous efforts.

This respect for the word of God is evident in Psalm 119:89: "Your word, LORD, is eternal; it stands firm in the heavens."

3. **Transmission of the Texts**

Once transcribed, these texts were used in public readings, religious services, and personal study, effectively transmitting the teachings and stories to a wider audience.

Scribes would also sometimes travel, bringing the sacred texts with them and spreading the teachings further.

Paul's letter to Timothy (2 Timothy 3:14-15) illustrates the importance of these scriptures in teaching and learning: "But as for you, continue in what you have learned and have become convinced of, because you know those from whom you learned it, and how from infancy you have known the Holy Scriptures, which are able to make you wise for salvation through faith in Christ Jesus."

4. **Preservation of the Texts**

Beyond their role in copying and spreading the texts, scribes also contributed to the preservation of the scriptures. They stored the scrolls in dry, safe places, protecting them from elements that could cause damage. Their efforts have resulted in the survival of numerous ancient biblical manuscripts, some of which are among the oldest extant pieces of literature in the world.

The role of scribes in the early transmission of biblical texts was monumental. Through their careful work and dedication, they ensured that the word of God was preserved, spread, and accessible to generations far beyond their own.

Papyrus, Parchment, and Paper: The Materials of Transmission

The transmission of biblical texts over centuries has involved a variety of materials, each chosen for its availability, durability, and usability. The main materials used include papyrus, parchment, and, more recently, paper.

1. **Papyrus**

Papyrus, an early form of paper, was made from the pith of the papyrus plant, a reed that was abundant along the Nile River in Egypt. The process involved cutting the pith into thin strips, arranging them in two layers at right angles, and pressing and drying them to form a sheet. These sheets could then be glued together to form a scroll, which was the typical form of book in the ancient world.

The use of papyrus is reflected in the Bible itself. For example, 2 John 1:12 reads, "I have much to write to you, but I do not want to use paper and ink. Instead, I hope to visit you and talk with you face to face, so that our joy may be complete." The term "paper" here is thought to refer to papyrus.

2. **Parchment**

Parchment, also known as vellum when made from calfskin, was another important material in the transmission of the Bible. Parchment was more durable than papyrus, making it a good choice for books that were expected to last. It was made by scraping and drying animal skins, usually from sheep or goats.

Parchment was the primary material used for the Dead Sea Scrolls, a collection of Jewish texts that include some of the oldest known copies of the Hebrew Bible.

3. **Paper**

Paper, as we know it today, was invented in China and spread to the Islamic world before reaching Europe. Paper was cheaper and easier to produce than parchment, leading to its eventual dominance.

With the invention of the printing press in the 15th century, paper became the standard material for book production, including Bibles. The ability to mass-produce Bibles using paper and print technology revolutionized the accessibility of the scriptures, allowing more people to own and read the Bible.

These three materials—papyrus, parchment, and paper—have each played a crucial role in the transmission of the biblical text over time. Through the careful work of countless scribes and the use of these materials, the Bible has been preserved and disseminated throughout the world.

The Art of Copying: Understanding Ancient Scribal Practices

The copying of biblical texts in ancient times was a meticulous and labor-intensive process. Scribes, who were professional copyists, played a crucial role in the preservation and transmission of these texts.

1. **The Scribe's Role and Training**

Scribes were usually educated men trained specifically for the task of copying texts. This training often involved memorizing large portions of text and learning the precise conventions of writing, including letter forms, spelling, and punctuation. The importance of scribes is highlighted in several biblical passages. For instance, in Jeremiah 36:4, it is mentioned that Baruch the son of Neriah acted as a scribe for the prophet Jeremiah.

2. **The Scribal Process**

Copying a text began with the preparation of the writing material, whether papyrus, parchment, or later, paper. The scribe would then carefully copy the text from an existing manuscript. Every effort was made to ensure accuracy. It was not just about copying the words, but also about maintaining the layout, including line breaks and spaces between words.

In Jewish tradition, especially for the copying of Torah scrolls, there were stringent rules that the scribes had to follow. They had to say each word aloud before writing it, they could not write from memory, and every finished scroll had to be checked against the original. Any scroll with mistakes had to be destroyed or corrected within 30 days.

3. **Corrections and Variations**

Despite the scribes' careful efforts, mistakes could and did occur. These could be simple errors, such as skipping a line or repeating a word, but they could also involve more substantive changes. In some cases, scribes made corrections, either erasing and rewriting or adding marginal notes, known as glosses. Over time, these glosses could be incorporated into the text, leading to variations between manuscripts.

In addition, scribes sometimes made intentional changes. These could be done to update the language or spelling, to harmonize passages, or to clarify the meaning of a text. For example, in Mark 1:2, some early manuscripts refer to "the prophet Isaiah," while others say, "the prophets." This is likely a scribal change to correct what was seen as a mistake (since the quotation is from both Isaiah and Malachi), but it shows how scribes could influence the text.

The practices of ancient scribes have a significant impact on our understanding of the Bible today. Scholars studying biblical manuscripts must consider not only the text itself, but also the scribes who copied it and the practices they used. This helps us to understand the history of the text and to reconstruct, as closely as possible, the original words of the biblical authors.

The Septuagint and the Old Testament Transmission

The Septuagint, also known as the LXX, plays a crucial role in the transmission of the Old Testament. It is the earliest known Greek translation of the Hebrew Scriptures, purportedly created by seventy-two Jewish scholars in the third century BCE, hence the name "Septuagint" (from the Latin "septuaginta," meaning "seventy"). This translation was initiated due to the widespread use of Greek in the Hellenistic world, particularly in Alexandria, Egypt, where there was a large Jewish diaspora.

The Septuagint was widely used during the time of Jesus and the apostles and is frequently quoted in the New Testament. For instance, the quote from Isaiah 7:14 in Matthew 1:23 ("Behold, a virgin shall conceive, and bear a son, and shall call his name Immanuel.") follows the Septuagint wording.

The significance of the Septuagint in the textual transmission of the Old Testament lies in several areas:

1. **Ancient Witness**: The Septuagint provides us with one of the oldest existing copies of the Old Testament, predating the Masoretic Text by about a thousand years.

2. **Variant Readings**: The Septuagint sometimes offers different readings of biblical texts compared to the Hebrew Masoretic Text. These variant readings can provide valuable insight into alternative textual traditions and the interpretation of difficult passages.

3. **Language Transition**: The Septuagint represents a significant stage in the transmission of the biblical text when the primary language of the text shifted from Hebrew to Greek. This transition reflected the influence of Hellenistic culture on the Jewish diaspora and eventually on the early Christian Church, which used the Septuagint extensively.

4. **Canonical Issues**: The Septuagint includes several books not found in the Hebrew Bible, known as the Apocrypha. These books are accepted as canonical by some Christian traditions (such as the Roman Catholic and Eastern Orthodox churches) but not by others (such as most Protestant denominations and Judaism). The inclusion of these books in the Septuagint raises important questions about the formation and boundaries of the biblical canon.

The primary weight of external evidence generally goes to the original language manuscripts, and the **Codex Leningrad B 19A** and the **Aleppo Codex** are almost always preferred. In Old Testament Textual Criticism, the Masoretic text is our starting point and should only be abandoned as a last resort. While it is true that the Masoretic Text is not perfect, there needs to be a heavy burden of proof in we are to go with an alternative reading. All of the evidence needs to be examined before concluding that a reading in the Masoretic Text is corrupt. The Septuagint continues to be very much important today and is used by textual scholars to help uncover copyists' errors that **might have** crept into the Hebrew manuscripts either intentionally or unintentionally. However, it cannot do it alone without the support of other sources. There are a number of times when you might have the Syriac, Septuagint, Dead Sea Scrolls, Aramaic Targums, and the Vulgate that are at odds with the Masoretic Text the preferred choice should not be the MT.

Initially, the Septuagint (LXX) was viewed by the Jews as inspired by God, equal to the Hebrew Scriptures. However, in the first century C.E. the Christians adopted the Septuagint in their churches. It was used by the Christians in their evangelism to make disciples and to debate the Jews on Jesus being the long-awaited Messiah. Soon, the Jews began to look at the Septuagint with suspicion. This resulted in the Jews of the second century C.E. abandoning the Septuagint and returning to the Hebrew Scriptures. This has proved to be beneficial for the textual scholar and translator. In the second century C.E., other Greek translations of the Septuagint were produced. We have, for example, **LXX**^{Aq} Aquila, **LXX**^{Sym} Symmachus, and **LXX**Th Theodotion. The consonantal text of the Hebrew Scriptures became the standard text between the first and second centuries C.E. However, textual variants still continued until the Masoretes and the Masoretic text. However, scribes taking liberties by altering the text was no longer the case, as was true of the previous period of the Sopherim. The scribes who copied the Hebrew Scriptures from the time of Ezra down to the time of Jesus were called Sopherim, i.e., scribes.

From the 6th century C.E. to the 10th century C.E. we have the Masoretes, groups of extraordinary Jewish scribe-scholars. The Masoretes were very much concerned with the accurate transmission of each word, even each letter, of the text they were copying. Accuracy was of supreme importance; therefore, the Masoretes use the side margins of each page to inform others of deliberate or inadvertent changes in the text by past copyists. The Masoretes also use these marginal notes for other reasons as well, such as unusual word forms and combinations. They even marked how frequent they occurred within a book or even the whole Hebrew Old Testament. Of course, marginal spaces were very limited, so they used abbreviated code. They also formed a cross-checking tool where they would mark the middle word and letter of certain books. Their push for accuracy moved them to go so far as to count every letter of the Hebrew Old Testament.

In the Masoretic text, we find notes in the side margins, which are known as the Small Masora. There are also notes in the top margin, which are referred to as the Large Masora. Any other notes placed elsewhere within the text are called the Final Masora. The Masoretes used the notes in the top and bottom margins to record more extensive notes, comments concerning the abbreviated notes in the side margins. This enabled them to be able to cross-check their work. We must remember that there were no numbered verses at this time, and they had no Bible concordances. Well, one might wonder how the Masoretes could refer to different parts of the Hebrew text to have an effective cross-checking system. They would list part of a parallel verse in the top and bottom margins to remind them of where the word(s) indicated were found. Because they were dealing with limited space, they often could only list one word to remind them where each parallel verse could be found. To have an effective cross-reference system by way of these marginal notes, the Masoretes would literally have to have memorized the entire Hebrew Bible.

In conclusion, the Septuagint is a significant factor in the transmission of the Old Testament, providing an ancient witness to the text, an example of language transition, a source of variant readings, and raising important canonical issues. It continues to be a valuable resource for biblical scholars and theologians studying the development and interpretation of the biblical text.

Early Christian Scribal Practices and New Testament Transmission

Early Christian scribal practices played an integral part in the transmission of the New Testament. Understanding these practices is crucial for comprehending how we have received the New Testament in its present form.

Scribes and Copying Techniques

The New Testament was written primarily in Koine Greek, the common language of the Eastern Mediterranean during the first century CE. Christian scribes, often not professional but rather literate believers dedicated to the task, meticulously copied these texts by hand.

The scribes would copy letter by letter, line by line, from the source manuscript to the new copy. Their techniques were designed to ensure accuracy and preserve the integrity of the scriptures. However, human error was inevitable, leading to minor variations such as spelling mistakes, accidental omissions, or duplications. These minor variations are known as "textual variants." In some instances, marginal notes made by one scribe might be incorporated into the body of the text by a subsequent scribe, leading to further variations.

Codices and Papyrus

Early Christians adopted the codex format (precursor to the modern book) instead of scrolls, which were commonly used for Jewish and pagan texts. Codices were more portable, easier to reference, and could contain more text, making them ideal for disseminating Christian writings.

Papyrus, a writing material made from the papyrus plant, was commonly used for these early codices. However, papyrus is not highly durable and, as a result, few early papyri have survived. Eventually, parchment (prepared animal skin) was adopted, which proved to be more durable.

Circulation and Preservation

The early Christian community was spread out and highly interconnected. Letters and writings from church leaders were circulated among these communities (Colossians 4:16), leading to the need for multiple copies. The wide circulation and frequent use of these texts likely contributed to their preservation, as worn-out copies would be replaced with new ones.

Canonical Formation

The process of determining which texts were authoritative and should be included in the New Testament canon was gradual and largely driven by consensus within the early Christian community. The four Gospels (Matthew, Mark, Luke, and John), the Acts of the Apostles, the Pauline epistles, and other letters gradually came to be accepted universally. Some books, like Revelation, took longer to gain acceptance.

In conclusion, early Christian scribal practices played a vital role in the transmission of the New Testament. Despite the challenges of manual copying and the passage of time, these texts have been remarkably well preserved, testifying to the dedication of the scribes and the resilience of the early Christian communities.

Textual Variations: Causes and Implications

The transmission of the Bible text over millennia has involved countless scribes copying the text by hand, introducing inevitable variations. Understanding the causes and implications of these variations is critical to the field of textual criticism, which seeks to reconstruct the original text of the Bible as closely as possible.

Causes of Textual Variations

Textual variations, also known as textual variants, arise from a range of causes:

1. **Accidental errors:** As scribes manually copied the text, they could accidentally skip words or lines (parablepsis), write a word or phrase twice (dittography), or make simple mistakes in spelling or transcription.

2. **Intentional changes:** Sometimes, scribes made conscious alterations to the text. These could be grammatical improvements, harmonizations (making passages more consistent with each other), explanatory additions, or doctrinal adjustments.

3. **Marginal notes:** Scribes often added notes in the margins of a manuscript for clarification or commentary. Later scribes might mistake these notes for part of the original text and incorporate them into the main body of the text.

Implications of Textual Variations

1. **Reconstructing the original text:** Textual criticism uses the variations among manuscripts to help reconstruct the original text. Techniques include comparing the ages of manuscripts, the geographical spread of a variant, and the tendencies of specific scribes or scriptoria.

2. **Understanding of the text:** Variations can offer insights into how different communities understood and interpreted the Bible. For example, a variant might reflect a local doctrinal emphasis or the influence of contemporary events.

3. **Reliability of the text:** Despite the presence of variations, the vast majority are minor and do not affect the overall message or doctrine of the Bible. The sheer number of surviving manuscripts and their consistency attest to the text's general reliability. As Paul expressed in 2 Timothy 3:16, "All Scripture is God-breathed and is useful for teaching, rebuking, correcting and training in righteousness."

4. **Historical context:** Variations can provide valuable historical information, such as changes in language and writing styles, development of theological ideas, and interactions between different Christian communities.

In conclusion, while textual variations might initially seem like a challenge to the reliability of the Bible, they are a normal part of the transmission process and, when properly understood, can actually contribute to our understanding of the Bible and its historical context. For a very detailed discussion of the number of variants, see APPENDIX What Are Textual Variants and How Many Are There?

The Emergence of Textual Families: Alexandrian, Western, Byzantine, and Caesarean

During the formative days of the Christian church, apostolic letters were dispatched to individuals or congregations, and gospels were penned to serve certain readerships. To amplify the impact and broaden the beneficiaries, these documents were duplicated. As these copies were manually produced, discrepancies in wording relative to the original were inevitable, ranging from minor to significant. Many of these disparities emanated from accidental causes such as misreading similar-looking words or letters. Homoeoarcton or homoeoteleuton errors would occur if the scribe's gaze jumped from one similar set of letters to another, resulting in textual omissions. Conversely, dittography would occur if the scribe inadvertently repeated a word or group of words. Itacism was a common error, where letters that sounded alike were miswritten. These inadvertent errors were almost certain when extensive passages were transcribed manually, and particularly if the scribe was visually impaired, interrupted, fatigued, or less attentive.

Other discrepancies surfaced from deliberate attempts to alleviate grammatical or stylistic discordance, or to clarify perceived ambiguities in the text. Copyists occasionally altered or added words that seemed more fitting, possibly sourced from a comparable passage, a process known as harmonization or assimilation. As a result, within the years following the creation of the documents that would eventually comprise the New Testament, countless variant readings emerged.

Further types of discrepancies arose when New Testament documents were translated from Greek into other languages. As Christianity spread to regions like Syria, North Africa, Italy, and different parts of Egypt in the second and third centuries, congregations and individuals naturally yearned for Scriptures in their native tongues. This prompted the creation of Syriac, Latin, and various Coptic dialect versions, followed by Armenian, Georgian, Ethiopic, Arabic, and Nubian versions in the East, and Gothic, Old Church Slavonic, and Anglo-Saxon versions in the West during the fourth and subsequent centuries.

The precision of these translations was contingent upon two factors: the translator's proficiency in both Greek and the target language, and the meticulousness applied to the translation process. Significant discrepancies arose in early versions when various translations were made from slightly different Greek texts and subsequently transcribed by scribes who adjusted the new copies to align with their preferred wording.

During the nascent centuries of Christian church expansion, "local texts" of the New Testament gradually evolved. Newly formed congregations around prominent cities like Alexandria, Antioch, Constantinople, Carthage, and Rome were supplied with Scripture copies reflecting the prevalent text form in those regions. As additional copies were made, unique readings and renderings were both preserved and somewhat expanded, resulting in a distinctive text type for each region. Today, by comparing these characteristic readings with quotations in the works of Church Fathers from these major ecclesiastical centers, it's possible to identify the type of text preserved in New Testament manuscripts.

However, local text distinctiveness tended to blend with other text types over time. For instance, a manuscript of the Gospel of Mark, copied in Alexandria and later brought to Rome, would inevitably influence the text form of Mark prevalent in Rome to some extent. Nevertheless, during the earliest centuries, the trend of developing and maintaining a specific text type prevailed over text mixing. Consequently, multiple distinctive New Testament text types emerged, with the most significant being **the Alexandrian text**. Often referred to as the Neutral text by Westcott and Hort (a term that presumes its superiority), the Alexandrian text is typically considered the best and closest to the original. The Alexandrian text is characterized by brevity and austerity, meaning it is usually shorter and lacks the grammatical and stylistic refinements seen in other text types, such as the Byzantine. Up until recently, the primary sources of the Alexandrian text were the codex Vaticanus (B) and the codex Sinaiticus (א), which are parchment manuscripts dating back to the mid-fourth century. However, with the acquisition of the Bodmer Papyri, particularly P66 and P75, both transcribed around the late second or early third century, it's now evident that the Alexandrian type of text can be traced back to an archetype that likely existed in the early second century. The Sahidic and Bohairic versions often contain typically Alexandrian readings, further supporting its widespread adoption and influence.

The "Western" text, widely disseminated in regions such as Italy, Gaul, North Africa, and even Egypt, traces its roots back to the second century. It was utilized by Marcion, Tatian, Irenaeus, Tertullian, and Cyprian. Its presence in Egypt is evidenced by P38 (circa 300 CE) and P48 (late third century). The primary Greek manuscripts showcasing a Western text type include codex Bezae (D) from the fifth century (comprising the Gospels and Acts), codex Claromontanus (D) from the sixth century (consisting of the Pauline epistles), and codex Washingtonianus (W) from the fifth century for Mark 1:1 to 5:30. Notably, the Old Latin versions offer significant testimony to the Western text type, with three primary groups: the African, Italian, and Hispanic forms of Old Latin texts.

The Western readings are characterized by a preference for paraphrase, with words, clauses, and even entire sentences freely modified, omitted, or inserted. Sometimes, this appears motivated by harmonization, while at other times it is to enrich the narrative with traditional or apocryphal material. Some alterations seem trivial with no discernable reason. A curious feature of the generally longer Western text is that it omits words and passages in certain places, like the end of Luke, which are present in other text types, including the Alexandrian. While earlier scholars, such as Westcott and Hort, viewed these shorter readings as original ("Western non-interpolations"), recent findings from the Bodmer Papyri have led many modern scholars to consider them as deviant readings.

The text of Acts presents a particular conundrum with the Western text as it is almost ten percent longer than the form generally accepted as the original text. Consequently, this volume allocates a higher proportion of space to variant readings in Acts than in any other New Testament book, accompanied by a unique introduction to the textual phenomena in Acts.

An Eastern text type, previously dubbed the Caesarean text, is partly preserved in several Greek manuscripts (including Θ, 565, 700), as well as the Armenian and Georgian versions. This text is characterized by a blend of Western and Alexandrian readings. Despite recent research challenging the existence of a distinct Caesarean text type, the individual manuscripts previously thought to be part of this group remain critical in their own right.

Another Eastern text type, prevalent in and around Antioch, is primarily preserved in Old Syriac manuscripts, namely the Sinaitic and Curetonian versions of the Gospels, and in the scriptural quotations found in the works of Aphraates and Ephraem.

The Byzantine text, also known as the Syrian text (according to Westcott and Hort), the Koine text (von Soden's term), the Ecclesiastical text (Lake's designation), and the Antiochian text (as per Ropes), is generally the latest of the distinct New Testament text types. It is primarily marked by clarity and completeness. The creators of this text aimed to eliminate any harsh language, merge two or more differing readings into a single expanded reading (a process known as conflation) and harmonize varying parallel passages. This combined text, possibly produced in Antioch, Syria, was transported to Constantinople and widely disseminated throughout the Byzantine Empire. Today, it is best represented by the codex Alexandrinus (for the Gospels; but not for Acts, the Epistles, or Revelation), later uncial manuscripts, and a large number of minuscule manuscripts. Therefore, from roughly the sixth or seventh century until the invention of movable type printing (1450-56 CE), the Byzantine text was widely recognized as the authoritative text and most commonly circulated.

With Gutenberg's press enabling faster and cheaper book production than manual copying, the debased Byzantine text became the standard New Testament form in printed editions. This was predictable, as the Greek New Testament manuscripts most accessible to early editors and printers were those containing the corrupt Byzantine text.

Desiderius Erasmus, the Dutch humanist scholar, prepared the first printed edition of the Greek Testament, published in Basel in 1516. Erasmus used multiple manuscripts for the various New Testament sections, as no single manuscript contained the entire Greek Testament. The majority of his text relied on two relatively inferior manuscripts from the twelfth century, housed in Basel's university library, one of the Gospels and one of Acts and Epistles. Erasmus compared them with two or three others, annotating occasional corrections in the printer's copy margins or between lines. For the book of Revelation, he had a single manuscript, borrowed from his friend Reuchlin. As this copy lacked the final leaf containing the last six verses, Erasmus relied on Jerome's Latin Vulgate, translating these verses into Greek. As expected, Erasmus's reconstructed verses contained several readings not found in any Greek manuscript—readings still present in today's printings of the so-called Textus Receptus of the Greek New Testament (see comment on Rev. 22.19). Elsewhere in the New Testament, Erasmus occasionally introduced material from the Latin Vulgate's current form into his Greek text (see comment on Acts 9.5-6).

Erasmus's Greek Testament was in such high demand that the first edition quickly sold out, prompting a second edition. The 1519 second edition, which corrected some (but not all) of the first edition's typographical errors, served as the basis for Martin Luther's and William Tyndale's New Testament translations into German (1522) and English (1525).

Subsequent years saw various editors and printers release numerous Greek Testament editions, all of which reproduced the later Byzantine manuscripts' text type. Even when an editor had access to older manuscripts—as when Theodore Beza, Calvin's friend and successor at Geneva, acquired the fifth-century manuscript known by his name today, as well as the sixth-century codex Claromontanus—he made relatively little use of them as they deviated too far from the later copies' standard text form.

Important Early Editions of The Greek New Testament

Among the significant early editions of the Greek New Testament are two published by Robert Etienne, better known by the Latin form of his name, Stephanus. A renowned Parisian printer, Stephanus eventually moved to Geneva, aligning himself with the city's Protestants. In 1550, he published his third edition, the editio Regia, in Paris. This grand folio edition was the first printed Greek Testament to contain a critical apparatus. He recorded variant readings from fourteen Greek manuscripts, as well as readings from another printed edition, the Complutensian Polyglot, on the inner margins of the pages. Stephanus's fourth edition (Geneva, 1551), which includes two Latin versions (the Vulgate and Erasmus's version), is significant as the first time the New Testament text was divided into numbered verses.

Theodore Beza, between 1565 and 1604, published no fewer than nine editions of the Greek Testament, with a tenth edition appearing posthumously in 1611. Beza's work is important due to its role in popularizing and standardizing what became known as the Textus Receptus. The Authorized or King James Bible translators of 1611 heavily utilized Beza's 1588-89 and 1598 editions.

The term Textus Receptus, applied to the New Testament text, originated from an expression used by Bonaventura and Abraham Elzevir (Elzevier), printers in Leiden. Their second edition of the Greek Testament (1633) prefaced the sentence: "Textum ergo habes, nunc ab omnibus receptum, in quo nihil immutatum aut corruptum damus" ("Therefore, you [dear reader] have the text now received by all, in which we give nothing changed or corrupted"). In a sense, this confident claim on behalf of their edition seemed justified, for their edition was, in most aspects, indistinguishable from approximately 160 other Greek Testament printed editions since Erasmus's first published edition in 1516. However, more accurately, the Byzantine form of the Greek text, reproduced in all early printed editions, was marred by countless scribal changes over the centuries, some minor, others of significant consequence.

The corrupt Byzantine text formed the basis for almost all New Testament translations into modern languages until the nineteenth century. During the eighteenth century, scholars gathered extensive information from many Greek manuscripts, as well as versional and patristic witnesses. But apart from three or four editors who cautiously corrected some of the Textus Receptus's more blatant errors, this debased New Testament text form was reprinted in edition after edition. It wasn't until the early nineteenth century (1831) that a German classical scholar, Karl Lachmann, dared to apply the criteria he used in editing classic texts to the New Testament. Later, other critical editions emerged, including those prepared by Constantin von Tischendorf, whose eighth edition (1869-72) remains a monumental compilation of variant readings, and the influential edition prepared by two Cambridge scholars, B. F. Westcott and F. J. A. Hort (1881). The latter edition served as the basis for the current United Bible Societies' edition. During the twentieth century, the discovery of several New Testament manuscripts much older than any previously available made it possible to produce New Testament editions that more closely approximate the original documents' wording.

The Role of Patristic Citations in Textual Transmission

The writings of the early church fathers, often referred to as "Patristic literature," offer an invaluable resource for the study of textual transmission. These church fathers frequently quoted or alluded to biblical passages in their works, providing us with thousands of snippets of the biblical text as it was known in their time and place.

Patristic Citations and Textual Transmission

Patristic citations play several significant roles in textual transmission:

1. **Preservation of Textual Readings:** In many cases, the writings of the church fathers preserve textual readings that may not be present in any extant manuscript. This can assist in reconstructing the text, particularly for periods or regions where manuscripts are scarce.

2. **Witness to Variants:** Patristic citations can provide evidence of variant readings and their geographical and temporal distribution. For instance, if a church father from North Africa in the 3rd century quotes a biblical verse differently than our extant manuscripts, it may indicate that a different reading was prevalent in that region and time.

3. **Understanding of the Text:** The way the church fathers interpreted and applied scripture can provide valuable insights into how early Christian communities understood the biblical text. This can help in clarifying ambiguous passages or identifying shifts in interpretation over time.

4. **Historical Context:** Patristic citations often come embedded in larger discussions of theology, Christian practice, or contemporary events. This context can provide a rich historical backdrop to the biblical text, illuminating its original meaning and ongoing reception.

Caveats in Using Patristic Citations

While patristic citations are a valuable resource, they must be used with care. Church fathers were not scribes; their primary aim was not to copy the text accurately but to expound on its meaning. Therefore, they often paraphrased or adapted biblical passages to fit their arguments. Also, the writings of the church fathers themselves underwent copying and transmission, introducing potential errors or alterations.

Biblical Verses

Scriptures underscore the importance of faithfully transmitting the Word. For example, Proverbs 30:5-6 says, "Every word of God is flawless; He is a shield to those who take refuge in Him. Do not add to His words, or He will rebuke you and prove you a liar." Yet, the human component in the transmission process, reflected in the variations found in patristic citations, highlights the task of discernment required in handling the scriptures.

In conclusion, the role of patristic citations in textual transmission is multifaceted. They serve as an essential witness to the text's early form and its interpretation, shedding light on the biblical text's journey through time.

From Manuscript to Printed Text: The Gutenberg Revolution

The Gutenberg Revolution refers to the advent of movable type printing in Europe, a development credited to Johannes Gutenberg in the mid-15th century. This innovation had a profound impact on the transmission of the biblical text, moving it from the exclusive domain of hand-copying scribes to the wide-scale production possible with the printing press.

The Gutenberg Revolution and Bible Transmission

1. **Mass Production:** Prior to the Gutenberg press, Bibles were copied by hand, a labor-intensive process that made them rare and costly. The Gutenberg press allowed for the mass production of Bibles, making them more accessible and affordable. This also meant that the text was standardized to a degree never before possible, reducing the risk of errors introduced through manual copying.

2. **The Gutenberg Bible:** Gutenberg's most famous work, often referred to as the 42-line Bible or the Mazarin Bible, was the first major book printed using movable type. This marked the transition of the Bible from a manuscript culture to a print culture.

3. **Spread of Literacy:** The availability of affordable printed material played a significant role in the spread of literacy. More people learning to read created more demand for books, and the Bible, as a foundational text of European culture, was at the forefront.

4. **Reformation and Translation:** The advent of the printing press coincided with the Reformation, a period of significant religious change. Key figures like Martin Luther translated the Bible into the vernacular and used the press to disseminate these translations widely, fundamentally changing the relationship between the common people and the Scriptures.

Biblical Verses

The Gutenberg Revolution might be seen in the light of passages like Isaiah 40:8, "The grass withers, the flower fades, but the word of our God will stand forever." Despite changes in technology, the enduring power and relevance of the biblical message remain.

Moreover, the democratization of access to the Scriptures aligns with the spirit of passages like Deuteronomy 31:11-12, where Moses commands the people to gather and hear the words of the law, "that they may learn to fear the LORD your God and be careful to do all the words of this law."

Conclusion

The Gutenberg Revolution marked a pivotal moment in the transmission of the biblical text, dramatically expanding access to the Scriptures and setting the stage for profound shifts in religious culture and practice. From handwritten manuscripts to printed text, the journey of the Bible reflects both the changes in human technology and the enduring significance of its message.

Critical Texts and Their Influence: Textus Receptus, Westcott and Hort, and Others

The transmission of the biblical text over time has been influenced by a variety of critical texts, each of which has played a significant role in shaping our understanding of the Bible. Among these, the Textus Receptus, Westcott and Hort's Greek New Testament, and others are key examples.

Textus Receptus

The Textus Receptus, or "Received Text," is a Greek text of the New Testament. Compiled by Erasmus in the 16th century, it was based on a handful of late Medieval manuscripts. The Textus Receptus was the basis for the New Testament of the King James Version and other early Protestant Bibles. The term "Received Text" comes from its preface: "What you have here is the text which is now received by all, in which we give nothing changed or corrupted." However, because it was based on relatively late manuscripts, later scholars have found it to contain numerous errors and it is not the primary basis for most modern translations.

Westcott and Hort

In the 19th century, Brooke Foss Westcott and Fenton John Anthony Hort compiled a critical edition of the Greek New Testament, using a wider array of manuscripts, including the then newly-discovered Codex Sinaiticus and Codex Vaticanus, which are older and more reliable than those used by Erasmus. Westcott and Hort used principles of textual criticism to create a text that, in their view, was closer to the original writings. Their work has had a significant influence on subsequent editions of the Greek New Testament and modern Bible translations.

Other Critical Texts

Besides the Textus Receptus and Westcott and Hort's New Testament, there are other important critical texts. The Novum Testamentum Graece, often referred to as the Nestle-Aland text, is currently in its 28th edition and is the standard scholarly text of the Greek New Testament. The United Bible Societies' Greek New Testament, currently in its 5th edition, is similar to the Nestle-Aland text and includes more detailed information about manuscript variants.

Biblical Verses

The importance of reliable biblical texts is underscored by verses such as Proverbs 30:5, "Every word of God proves true." The goal of all these critical texts is to ascertain, as accurately as possible, the original words of the biblical authors.

In 2 Timothy 3:16, it is written that "All Scripture is breathed out by God and profitable for teaching, for reproof, for correction, and for training in righteousness." This underscores the importance of having the most accurate and reliable text possible.

Conclusion

The transmission of the biblical text is a complex process involving many different manuscripts and editions. Critical texts like the Textus Receptus, Westcott and Hort's New Testament, and others play a crucial role in this process, helping us to better understand the original writings and their meaning. Through careful study and comparison of these texts, scholars continue to work towards a more complete and accurate understanding of the Bible.

Modern Textual Criticism: Methods and Goals

The field of modern textual criticism seeks to recover the original form of a text - in this case, the biblical text - by studying the copies made over centuries. This is a necessary endeavor because we don't have the original manuscripts (known as "autographs") of any biblical book. Textual critics examine the evidence from thousands of ancient manuscripts to determine the most likely reading.

Methods of Modern Textual Criticism

Textual criticism involves two primary methods: external evidence and internal evidence.

1. **External Evidence:** This method examines the manuscripts themselves - their age, their geographical distribution, and the textual families they belong to. Older manuscripts are generally considered more reliable because they've had less chance to accrue changes over time. Manuscripts are grouped into "families" based on shared characteristics, and these families can provide clues about the history of the text's transmission.

2. **Internal Evidence:** This method involves looking at the types of changes that may have occurred. Scribes might unintentionally introduce changes through simple human error, such as skipping a line or misreading a word. They might also make intentional changes, such as correcting what they perceive as a grammatical error or smoothing out an awkward phrase. By understanding these common types of changes, textual critics can often determine what the original reading most likely was.

Goals of Modern Textual Criticism

The ultimate goal of textual criticism is to get as close as possible to the original text. This is based on the belief that the original words are the most authoritative and thus the most important for understanding the message of the Bible. The more we can recover of the original text, the more accurately we can interpret its meaning.

Another goal is to understand the history of the text's transmission. By studying the changes that have occurred over time, we can learn about the scribes who copied the text, the communities that read it, and the various interpretations and understandings that have shaped its reading over time.

Biblical Verses

Several Bible verses speak to the importance of preserving the integrity of God's word. For example, Deuteronomy 4:2 cautions not to add or subtract from the commandments: "You shall not add to the word which I command you, nor take from it, that you may keep the commandments of the Lord your God which I command you." Similarly, Revelation 22:18-19 says, " I warn everyone who hears the words of the prophecy of this book: if anyone adds to them, God will add to him the plagues described in this book, and if anyone takes away from the words of the book of this prophecy, God will take away his share in the tree of life and in the holy city, which are described in this book." Verse 18 warns that if anyone adds to the words of the prophecy in Revelation, God will add to that person the plagues described throughout the book. This is a clear warning against attempting to augment or embellish the prophecies in Revelation. In verse 19, the warning is given about taking away from the words of the prophecy. If someone takes away from these words, their share in the tree of life and the holy city will be taken away. In the context of the Bible, the "tree of life" is a symbol of eternal life and the "holy city" refers to the New Jerusalem, a place of peace, joy, and worship of God. This is a warning against minimizing, omitting, or otherwise altering the words of the prophecy.

Conclusion

Modern textual criticism is a critical tool for studying the Bible. By examining the wealth of manuscript evidence and applying these methodologies, scholars can work toward a clearer understanding of the original biblical text and its subsequent transmission and interpretation. While the field is complex and involves a degree of uncertainty, it is guided by a deep respect for the text and a commitment to discerning its most authentic form.

The Quest for the Original Text: Challenges and Advances

The quest for the original text of the Bible is both exciting and challenging. It involves sifting through thousands of ancient manuscripts, each with its own unique set of variations. Despite the many obstacles, the field of textual criticism has made significant strides in clarifying the text's history and working toward a more accurate representation of the original.

Challenges in the Quest for the Original Text

1. **Absence of Autographs:** The original manuscripts of the Bible, penned by the original authors, are no longer in existence. This absence means that scholars must rely on copies of these originals, which were made over the centuries and are prone to scribal errors and changes.

2. **Manuscript Variations:** There are thousands of extant biblical manuscripts, and no two are exactly alike. These variations range from minor differences in spelling and punctuation to more significant discrepancies, such as different words, phrases, or even entire verses.

3. **Determining the "Best" Reading:** With so many manuscript variations, deciding on the "best" or most original reading can be challenging. Scholars must consider both the external evidence (the age and reliability of the manuscript) and internal evidence (the context and likely authorial intent).

Advances in the Quest for the Original Text

Despite these challenges, the field of textual criticism has made significant progress:

1. **Cataloging and Comparing Manuscripts:** Scholars have developed systems for cataloging the vast number of manuscripts and for comparing their various readings. This systematic approach has significantly streamlined the process of comparing textual variations.

2. **Understanding Scribal Practices:** By studying the common mistakes and intentional changes that scribes made, scholars can better understand the types of variations they encounter in the manuscripts. This understanding helps them determine which readings are likely to be original and which are probably the result of scribal alterations.

3. **Utilizing Technology:** Modern technology, such as digital imaging and computer algorithms, has revolutionized the field of textual criticism. These tools allow for more accurate transcriptions and comparisons of manuscripts, as well as the ability to decipher previously unreadable texts.

Biblical Verses

The Bible itself attests to the importance of accurately transmitting God's word. For example, a little repetition for emphasis, Deuteronomy 12:32 says, "See that you do all I command you; do not add to it or take away from it." This verse underscores the importance that the biblical authors placed on preserving the integrity of God's commands.

Conclusion

The quest for the original text of the Bible is a challenging but essential endeavor. Despite the obstacles, the field of textual criticism has made impressive strides in understanding the history of the biblical text and working toward a more accurate and authentic representation of the original. While the task is far from complete, the advances made thus far have greatly enhanced our understanding of the Bible and its transmission over time.

The Impact of Archaeology: the Chester Beatty Papyri and the Bodmer Papyri

Archaeology has significantly contributed to our understanding of the text of the Bible. Among the most important discoveries are the Chester Beatty Papyri and the Bodmer Papyri, which contain some of the earliest and most valuable copies of the New Testament.

Chester Beatty Papyri

The Chester Beatty Papyri, discovered in the 1930s, are a collection of early papyrus codices that have greatly enriched our knowledge of the biblical text. They are named after Sir Alfred Chester Beatty, an American mining magnate and philanthropist who acquired them. These manuscripts are dated from the second to the fourth century CE, and they contain portions of the Old and New Testaments, as well as other early Christian literature.

The most significant of these manuscripts, known as P46, is one of the oldest extant copies of the Pauline Epistles, dated to 100-150 CE. These epistles are integral to Christian doctrine, and the discovery of such an early copy was a monumental event in biblical scholarship.

Bodmer Papyri

The Bodmer Papyri, named after Martin Bodmer, who bought them in the 1950s and 1960s, are another significant collection of early Christian texts. Among these, P66 and P75 are particularly noteworthy.

P66, dating to around 100-150 CE, contains a large portion of the Gospel of John. This manuscript provides significant insights into the text of John's Gospel at a very early stage in its transmission.

P75, dating to around the late second or early third century (175-225 CE), contains most of Luke and John's Gospels. This manuscript is especially significant because its text closely aligns with the Codex Vaticanus, a fourth-century biblical manuscript. This close alignment suggests a well-controlled process of copying in the early centuries, contradicting the idea of a "wild" or uncontrolled text in early Christian times.

Biblical Verses

These discoveries have significant implications for understanding the reliability of the New Testament. They reinforce the claim made in 2 Timothy 3:16-17, "All Scripture is God-breathed and is useful for teaching, rebuking, correcting and training in righteousness, so that the servant of God may be thoroughly equipped for every good work." The preservation of these texts over centuries aligns with the biblical concept of the enduring word of God, as stated in Isaiah 40:8, "The grass withers and the flowers fall, but the word of our God endures forever."

Conclusion

The Chester Beatty Papyri and the Bodmer Papyri, among other archaeological finds, have greatly contributed to our understanding of the text of the Bible. These discoveries offer strong evidence for the integrity and reliability of the New Testament text, providing us with early and valuable witnesses to the biblical books.

The Future of Textual Transmission: Digital Age and Beyond

The digital age has revolutionized the study and transmission of the biblical text. Technological advancements have improved access to biblical manuscripts and enhanced the tools and techniques used in textual criticism.

Digitization of Manuscripts

One major development is the digitization of biblical manuscripts. Libraries and institutions worldwide are increasingly making digital copies of their manuscript collections available online. This has vastly improved access to primary sources, allowing researchers from around the globe to examine these texts without needing to physically travel to the manuscript's location. This digitization process has been instrumental in democratizing the study of biblical texts.

For instance, the Codex Sinaiticus, one of the most important books in the world, has been digitized and is freely available online. This provides an invaluable resource for scholars and laypeople alike, fulfilling the biblical admonition in 2 Timothy 2:15, "Do your best to present yourself to God as one approved, a worker who has no need to be ashamed, rightly handling the word of truth."

Digital Tools and Techniques

Technological advancements have also led to the development of sophisticated digital tools and techniques. For example, multi-spectral imaging technology has enabled scholars to read previously illegible or invisible texts on damaged manuscripts or palimpsests (manuscripts where the original writing has been scraped off and overwritten).

Furthermore, computer algorithms have been developed to assist in comparing textual variants across thousands of manuscripts, a task that would be impossible manually. These techniques are aiding scholars in their quest for the original text, reminiscent of Proverbs 25:2, "It is the glory of God to conceal things, but the glory of kings is to search things out."

Bible Software and Online Platforms

The digital age has also seen the rise of Bible software and online platforms that provide powerful tools for biblical study. Resources that once required a large library and hours of research can now be accessed with a few clicks. This has made in-depth study of the Bible more accessible to the public, echoing the sentiment in Deuteronomy 6:6-7, "And these words that I command you today shall be on your heart. You shall teach them diligently to your children and shall talk of them when you sit in your house, and when you walk by the way, and when you lie down, and when you rise."

Future Directions

Looking forward, we can expect continued advancements in technology to further revolutionize the study and transmission of the biblical text. As we move into an increasingly digital future, the enduring relevance of the Bible, reflected in Isaiah 40:8, "The grass withers, the flower fades, but the word of our God will stand forever," remains a testament to its timeless message. It is our responsibility to preserve, study, and disseminate this message in the most effective and accurate ways possible.

CHAPTER 6 The Formation of the Canon: Criteria and Controversies

Understanding the Concept of Canon

The concept of canon refers to a collection of sacred texts considered authoritative and divinely inspired by a religious community. In the context of the Bible, the canon represents the list of books acknowledged as Holy Scripture by Jewish and Christian communities. The process of canon formation was complex, involving various criteria and often marked by controversies over which texts should be included or excluded.

The idea of a canon is rooted in the recognition that certain texts hold spiritual authority and importance. In the case of the Hebrew Bible (the Old Testament), the canon developed over several centuries, eventually comprising three main sections: the Torah (the Law), the Nevi'im (the Prophets), and the Ketuvim (the Writings). As stated in Luke 24:44, Jesus acknowledged the significance of these divisions, saying, "These are my words that I spoke to you while I was still with you, that everything written about me in the Law of Moses and the Prophets and the Psalms must be fulfilled."

For the New Testament, the canon formation process took place over several centuries as well. The early Christian communities recognized the spiritual authority of the texts that eventually formed the New Testament canon. These texts were considered inspired by God and were consistent with the teachings of Jesus and the apostles, as suggested by 2 Timothy 3:16-17, "All Scripture is breathed out by God and profitable for teaching, for reproof, for correction, and for training in righteousness, that the man of God may be complete, equipped for every good work."

Several criteria were used in the formation of the biblical canon:

1. **Apostolic Authority**: A text needed to have a connection to an apostle or someone closely associated with an apostle. For instance, the Gospel of Matthew was believed to be written by the apostle Matthew, while the Gospel of Mark was thought to be based on the teachings of Peter, an apostle.

2. **Consistency**: The content of a text had to be consistent with the established doctrines and teachings of the early church. A text that contradicted these teachings or presented a different understanding of Jesus would not be considered for inclusion in the canon.

3. **Acceptance**: A text needed to be widely accepted and used by the early Christian communities. Books that were read, copied, and circulated among churches were more likely to be considered for inclusion in the canon.

4. **Divine Inspiration**: A text was required to be divinely inspired, meaning it was believed to be a revelation from God or a direct result of the Holy Spirit's guidance. This criterion is crucial for a text's authority and authenticity as scripture.

The process of canon formation was not without controversy, as some texts were debated, and others were excluded. The debates around the inclusion or exclusion of certain texts highlight the complexity and human aspect of this process. However, the formation of the biblical canon ultimately reflects the belief in the divine inspiration and authority of the chosen texts, as well as their significance for the spiritual growth and understanding of the religious community.

The Canon in Historical Context

The formation of the biblical canon was a complex and historical process that took place over several centuries. This process involved an array of religious, cultural, and historical factors that influenced the acceptance and rejection of various texts.

The Hebrew Bible, also known as the Old Testament, was the first part of the Christian canon to be formed. The process began as early as the Babylonian Exile in the 6th century BCE, with the Torah (the first five books of the Bible) widely accepted as canonical by the 5th century BCE. The Prophets, another section of the Hebrew Bible, were recognized as canonical by the 3rd century BCE. The Writings, the third and final section, was accepted by the 2nd century CE. The recognition of these texts as canon is suggested in Luke 24:44 where Jesus refers to the Law, the Prophets, and the Psalms (part of the Writings).

The New Testament canon, on the other hand, was formed over the first four centuries CE. Early Christian communities recognized the authority of the writings of the apostles and their close associates, which eventually led to the formation of the New Testament canon. The four Gospels (Matthew, Mark, Luke, and John) and the letters of Paul, for instance, were widely accepted by the end of the 2nd century CE. Other texts, such as the Catholic Epistles and the Revelation of John, were more debated and took longer to gain universal acceptance.

The process was largely organic and not regulated by a central authority. However, several regional church councils played important roles in affirming the canon. The Council of Hippo in 393 CE and the Council of Carthage in 397 CE, for instance, both affirmed the 27 books of the New Testament that are recognized today. While the Roman Catholic Church has claimed responsibility for deciding which books should be included in the Bible canon, the truth is that the canon, including the Christian Greek Scriptures, was already settled by the direction of God's Holy Spirit. This happened before the Council of Carthage in 397 CE, which only confirmed what had already been decided. Later noninspired catalogers can be valuable in acknowledging the Bible canon, but only because it was already authorized by God's Spirit. As Christians, we can trust and rely on the guidance of the Holy Spirit in understanding and interpreting the Scriptures.

In the historical context, the canonization process was influenced by several factors. The spread of Christianity throughout the Roman Empire, the rise of heretical movements, the need for a unified set of teachings, and the development of a liturgy are all factors that contributed to the formation of the New Testament canon. For instance, Marcion, a 2nd century Christian leader, proposed a drastically reduced canon that rejected the Old Testament and included only a portion of the New Testament. This sparked controversy and prompted church leaders to more clearly define the canon.

It's important to remember that the canon was not a random selection of texts but represented those writings that were widely recognized and used by Christian communities because they were believed to carry apostolic authority and were consistent with the teachings of Jesus. As stated in 2 Peter 3:16, the writings of the apostles were regarded as Scripture: "He (Paul) writes the same way in all his letters...which ignorant and unstable people distort, as they do the other Scriptures, to their own destruction."

Overall, the formation of the biblical canon was a historically rooted process that reflected the religious, cultural, and historical context of the Jewish and Christian communities. It reflects both the divine inspiration believed to be inherent in these texts and the human processes that recognized and preserved these texts as authoritative and sacred.

Criteria for Canonization: The Factors Considered

The formation of the biblical canon was guided by several criteria that were considered by early Christian communities and church leaders. These criteria helped to determine which texts were regarded as authoritative and inspired, and ultimately, which texts became part of the canon. Some of the key factors include:

Apostolic authority: Early Christian communities placed great importance on the connection between the texts and the apostles, who were the closest followers of Jesus. A text was more likely to be considered canonical if it was believed to be written by an apostle or someone closely associated with them. For example, the Gospel of Mark was accepted because it was believed to be based on the teachings of Peter, one of Jesus' apostles. Similarly, the Gospel of Luke was accepted because it was attributed to Luke, who was closely associated with the apostle Paul (Colossians 4:14, 2 Timothy 4:11, Philemon 1:24).

Consistency with the rule of faith: The texts that were included in the canon needed to align with the core beliefs and teachings of the Christian faith. The rule of faith served as a basic summary of Christian doctrine and helped to assess the orthodoxy of various texts. For instance, 1 Corinthians 15:3-4 emphasizes the centrality of Jesus' death, burial, and resurrection as key components of the Christian faith.

Widespread acceptance and usage: The texts that were considered for the canon were those that had been widely accepted and used by Christian communities throughout the Roman Empire. This broad acceptance was an indication of the texts' spiritual and theological value. For example, the four Gospels (Matthew, Mark, Luke, and John) were universally accepted by the Christian communities by the end of the 2nd century CE.

Inspiration: The texts included in the canon were believed to be inspired by God and to carry divine authority. As stated in 2 Timothy 3:16, "All Scripture is God-breathed and is useful for teaching, rebuking, correcting, and training in righteousness." The concept of divine inspiration helped to differentiate the canonical texts from other religious writings that were not considered to be of the same spiritual caliber.

Antiquity: The age of the texts played a crucial role in their consideration for the canon. Early Christian communities and church leaders tended to favor older texts that were written closer to the time of Jesus and the apostles. The belief was that these texts were more likely to be accurate and reliable, as they were closer to the original events and teachings.

These criteria helped early Christian communities and church leaders to determine which texts were considered canonical. It is important to remember that the process of canonization was not a rigid or strictly regulated process, but rather an organic development that was influenced by various religious, cultural, and historical factors. The criteria for canonization provided a framework for evaluating and discerning the texts that were ultimately accepted as part of the biblical canon.

The Apostolic Connection: A Primary Criterion

The Apostolic Connection was indeed a primary criterion for the inclusion of texts in the New Testament canon. This refers to the association of a text with one of Jesus Christ's original apostles. The apostles were the closest followers of Jesus, and their teachings and writings held a great deal of weight in early Christian communities. Therefore, a text that was believed to have been written by an apostle or by someone closely associated with an apostle was given strong consideration for inclusion in the canon.

This criterion is clearly evident in the New Testament itself. For example, many of the epistles in the New Testament are attributed to the apostle Paul. These letters were written to various Christian communities and individuals, providing teachings, admonishments, and encouragement. Because Paul was an apostle, his writings were highly valued and were quickly accepted as authoritative by the early Christian communities. This is evident in 2 Peter 3:15-16, where Peter refers to Paul's letters as Scripture: "Bear in mind that our Lord's patience means salvation, just as our dear brother Paul also wrote you with the wisdom that God gave him... His letters contain some things that are hard to understand, which ignorant and unstable people distort, as they do the other Scriptures, to their own destruction."

The Gospels, though not all directly written by apostles, were also considered to have an apostolic connection. The Gospel of Matthew is traditionally attributed to Matthew, one of the twelve apostles. The Gospel of John is traditionally linked to John, another of the apostles. The Gospels of Mark and Luke, while not written by apostles, were associated with apostolic figures. Mark was believed to be a disciple of Peter, and Luke was a companion of Paul, as indicated in Philemon 1:24 and 2 Timothy 4:11.

The apostolic connection was seen as a guarantee of the truth and reliability of a text. Because the apostles were considered eyewitnesses to the life, teachings, death, and resurrection of Jesus, their writings (or those closely associated with them) were given special authority. This authority was crucial in the formation of the New Testament canon.

Orthodoxy and Antiquity: Criteria Based on Content and Age

Orthodoxy and antiquity were additional key criteria in the formation of the canon of the New Testament.

Orthodoxy refers to the adherence of a text to the accepted teachings and doctrines of the Christian faith. A text that was in agreement with the core beliefs of Christianity, as understood by the early Church, was considered orthodox. A text that deviated from these teachings was viewed as heretical and was not included in the canon. The importance of orthodoxy is highlighted in the New Testament itself. For example, in 1 Timothy 6:3-4, the Apostle Paul warns Timothy about anyone who teaches false doctrines and does not agree with the sound instruction of our Lord Jesus Christ and to godly teaching.

Antiquity refers to the age of the text. The early church preferred older texts, which were closer in time to the life of Jesus and the apostles. It was generally believed that the older a text, the more likely it was to accurately preserve the teachings of Jesus and the apostles. This principle is seen in the New Testament, where the writings of the apostles and their immediate followers, who were closest in time to Jesus, were given the highest authority. For instance, in 2 Peter 3:2, Peter urges his readers to remember the words spoken in the past by the holy prophets and the command given by our Lord and Savior through your apostles.

The book of Hebrews (which tradition ascribes to Paul, although the author is technically unknown) provides an example of a text that met both criteria. Its content aligns with orthodox Christian beliefs, and its authorship dates to the first century, giving it the necessary antiquity.

In essence, these criteria ensured that the canon of the New Testament consisted of texts that were faithful to the teachings of Jesus as understood by the early Church, and that had a strong historical connection to the original apostolic community.

The Role of Universality and Standardization in the Manuscripts of Early Christianity in Canon Formation

The concept of universality and standardization in the manuscripts of early Christianity played a crucial role in the formation of the canon. These elements offer compelling evidence that there was a concerted effort to create uniformity in the transmission and interpretation of Christian texts. For example the use of the codex, the standardization of the nomina sacra, collections of New Testament books, and codex size – all point to the existence of a degree of organization and uniformity within the early Christian communities.

1. **Use of the Codex**: The transition from the scroll to the codex format is significant. The codex, with its book-like form, was more portable, durable, and easier to navigate than scrolls. This made it an ideal format for the dissemination of Christian texts, facilitating their widespread use and acceptance.

2. **Standardization of the Nomina Sacra**: The nomina sacra, or sacred names, are abbreviations of certain key terms found in early Christian manuscripts. The standardization of these abbreviations indicates a level of coordination and agreement among the scribes who copied these texts. This shared system of abbreviations shows a conscious effort to maintain consistency in the written representation of sacred names, strengthening the sense of a shared and uniform religious identity.

3. **Collections of New Testament Books**: The assembling of certain books into collections, such as the four Gospels, or the Gospels and Acts, or Paul's letters (including Hebrews), also illustrates an effort to standardize the Christian message. By grouping these books together, early Christians were shaping the way future generations would understand and interpret the Christian faith.

4. **Standardization of Codex Size**: The standardization of the codex size, particularly for the Gospels, is another indication of organized planning. By agreeing on a standard size for these texts, early Christians were not only facilitating their production and distribution but also reinforcing the unity of the Christian message contained within them.

5. **Explicit Requirements for Baptism**: The establishment of specific requirements for baptism, including education in basic doctrinal beliefs, praying, fasting, and a commitment to a moral life, shows the early Christian community's drive for uniformity in practice and belief.

As you've pointed out, the evidence of these practices indicates a high degree of organization and planning within the early Christian communities. This doesn't mean that all Christian communities were identical in their practices or beliefs, but it does show that there was a shared understanding of the core tenets of Christianity and a concerted effort to maintain these standards over time and across different regions.

These practices, in turn, influenced the formation of the Christian canon. The canon needed to reflect the beliefs and practices that were universally accepted and standardized across the diverse Christian communities. The texts that met these criteria were more likely to be included in the canon, while those that didn't were excluded.

This level of organization and standardization also shows the dedication of the early Christian community to preserving and transmitting the teachings of the faith. Despite facing significant challenges, they succeeded in ensuring the survival and spread of their texts, a testament to their commitment to their faith. This has ultimately led to the Bible as we know it today, a document that has maintained its integrity and relevance over the centuries.

The Process of Canonization: A Gradual Formation

The canonization of the Bible was a gradual process that spanned several centuries. The term "canon" comes from the Greek "kanon," meaning "rule" or "standard." In the context of the Bible, the canon refers to the collection of books that are accepted as authoritative Scripture by the Christian church.

The formation of the Old Testament canon began in ancient Israel, long before the birth of Jesus. By the time of Jesus, the Law (Torah), the Prophets (Nevi'im), and the Writings (Ketuvim) had been widely accepted as authoritative, although the specific books included in the latter two sections may not have been finally determined. This is evidenced by Jesus' reference to the Law and the Prophets in Luke 24:44: "Everything must be fulfilled that is written about me in the Law of Moses, the Prophets and the Psalms."

The process of New Testament canonization took place over a longer period. The earliest Christian communities relied primarily on oral tradition and the Septuagint, the Greek translation of the Hebrew Scriptures. However, as letters and accounts of Jesus' life began to circulate, some of these texts started to be recognized as authoritative.

The letters of Paul, for example, were among the first New Testament writings to be widely recognized as authoritative. In 2 Peter 3:15-16, the author refers to Paul's letters as Scripture: "Bear in mind that our Lord's patience means salvation, just as our dear brother Paul also wrote you with the wisdom that God gave him. He writes the same way in all his letters, speaking in them of these matters. His letters contain some things that are hard to understand, which ignorant and unstable people distort, as they do the other Scriptures, to their own destruction."

The four Gospels – Matthew, Mark, Luke, and John – were also accepted early on as authoritative accounts of Jesus' life, as evidenced by their widespread use in the early church and quotations by early Church Fathers.

However, not all books were accepted into the canon immediately or without controversy. Some books, such as Hebrews, James, 2 Peter, 2 and 3 John, Jude, and Revelation, were disputed for various reasons, including questions about their authorship, their theological content, and their general acceptance among the churches.

The final canon of the New Testament as we know it today was gradually recognized over several centuries. Significant milestones in this process include the Muratorian Canon (late 2nd century), which lists most of the New Testament books; the Easter Letter of Athanasius (367 CE), which lists the current 27 books; and the councils of Hippo (393 CE) and Carthage (397 CE), which affirmed the current New Testament canon.

It's important to remember that the church didn't create the canon, but recognized and affirmed the books that were already being used and accepted as authoritative. The Holy Spirit guided this process, ensuring that the books included in the canon were those that God intended to be part of His written revelation to humanity.

Key Figures and Councils in Canon Formation

The formation of the biblical canon was a complex process that involved numerous individuals, communities, and councils over the course of several centuries. Here are a few key figures and councils that played a significant role in the canonization process:

Marcion of Sinope (c. 85–160): Marcion was an early Christian theologian who proposed a drastically reduced version of the New Testament that included only a portion of Luke's Gospel and ten of Paul's letters. His rejection of the Old Testament and his perceived editing of the New Testament were seen as heretical by mainstream Christianity. However, his actions played a significant role in prompting the early Church to consider and define an authoritative list of texts.

Irenaeus of Lyon (c. 130–202): Irenaeus, a bishop of Lyon, was a significant figure in the early Church. He argued against various heretical groups and emphasized the importance of apostolic tradition. He recognized the four Gospels (Matthew, Mark, Luke, and John) and several other New Testament writings as authoritative.

Athanasius of Alexandria (c. 296–373): Athanasius was a significant figure in the early Church who played a key role in the Council of Nicaea. In his 39th Festal Letter written in 367 AD, he lists the 27 books of the New Testament exactly as we know them today. This is the first known list that matches the current New Testament canon.

Councils of Hippo (393) and Carthage (397): These North African councils, attended by Augustine among others, ratified the current 27-book New Testament canon. They affirmed the list that Athanasius had recognized in his Festal Letter.

Jerome (c. 347–420): Jerome, a Christian priest and theologian, was commissioned by Pope Damasus I in 382 to make a revision of the old Latin translations of the Bible. This revision became known as the Vulgate, which was widely accepted in the Western Church and became the standard Bible of the Western Church for centuries.

Council of Trent (1545–1563): In response to the Protestant Reformation, the Roman Catholic Church convened the Council of Trent, which reaffirmed the canon of Scripture as it had been recognized by the councils of Hippo and Carthage. This included the Deuterocanonical books, which the Protestant Reformers had rejected or designated as "Apocrypha".

Remember, while these figures and councils played important roles in the canonization process, the ultimate authority of these books comes from their divine inspiration. The role of these individuals and councils was not to decide what was Scripture, but to recognize and affirm the books that God had inspired.

The Muratorian Fragment: A Glimpse into Early Canon

A remarkable early catalog of biblical books is the fragment found by L.A. Muratori in the Ambrosian Library in Milan, Italy, and published by him in 1740. Although the beginning of the document is missing, its reference to Luke as the third Gospel suggests that Matthew and Mark were listed first. This Latin document, known as the Muratorian Fragment, dates back to the late 2nd century C.E. The following is a somewhat simplified translation of a portion of the fragment:

"The third book of the Gospel is by Luke, the well-known physician, who wrote it under his own name. The fourth Gospel is by John, one of the disciples. Despite differences in the individual Gospel books, there is no disagreement among believers, as all books under one guiding Spirit depict his birth, passion, resurrection, conversations with his disciples, and his two comings. The first coming was in humility and contempt, which has already happened, and the second will be in the glory of royal power, which is yet to come.

John consistently refers to these events in his letters, claiming to be not only a witness but also a narrator of all the Lord's wonderful deeds. The acts of all the apostles are recorded in one book by Luke, written for Theophilus.

Paul's letters, their purpose, and their origins are clear for those who seek to understand. Firstly, he wrote extensively to the Corinthians to prevent heresy, then to the Galatians against circumcision, and to the Romans about the order of the Scriptures, with Christ being their main subject. Paul, like John, wrote to only seven churches by name: Corinthians, Ephesians, Philippians, Colossians, Galatians, Thessalonians, and Romans. Even though he wrote twice to the Corinthians and Thessalonians for correction, it's shown that there's one church spread throughout the whole world.

John, in the Apocalypse, also writes to seven churches but addresses all. Paul wrote out of affection and love to Philemon, Titus, and twice to Timothy; these letters are held sacred in the honorable esteem of the Church.

Furthermore, an epistle of Jude and two bearing the name of John are recognized. We only accept the apocalypses of John and Peter, the latter of which some of us do not wish to be read in church." -The New Schaff-Herzog Encyclopedia of Religious Knowledge, 1956, Vol. VIII, page 56.

The Muratorian Fragment references just two epistles of John towards its end. However, as the above-mentioned encyclopedia page 55 notes, these two letters can only be the second and third, whose author merely calls himself 'the elder.' As for the apparent omission of Peter's first letter, it's thought that a few words, perhaps a line, in which I Peter and the Apocalypse of John were named as received might have been lost. Consequently, according to the Muratorian Fragment, this encyclopedia concludes: "The New Testament is regarded as definitely made up of the four Gospels, the Acts, thirteen epistles of Paul, the Apocalypse of John, probably three epistles of his, Jude, and probably I Peter, while the opposition to another of Peter's writings was not yet silenced."

The Muratorian Fragment is an important historical document that provides a glimpse into the formation of the New Testament canon in the late second century. Named after its discoverer, the Italian historian Ludovico Antonio Muratori, who found it in the Ambrosian Library in Milan in the 18th century, the Muratorian Fragment is a copy of perhaps the oldest known list of the books of the New Testament.

The fragment itself is a portion of a larger document and is in Latin, although most scholars believe the original was in Greek. Unfortunately, the beginning of the list is missing, and the fragment starts in a description of the Gospel of Luke, which it notes as being the third Gospel. The Gospel of John is mentioned as the fourth. This suggests that the Gospels of Matthew and Mark were likely included in the missing portion.

The document lists a number of other books: Acts, 1 Corinthians, 2 Corinthians, Ephesians, Philippians, Colossians, Galatians, 1 Thessalonians, 2 Thessalonians, Romans, Philemon, Titus, 1 Timothy, 2 Timothy, and the book of Jude. The Book of Revelation is also mentioned, but it seems to distinguish between the Revelation of John and a Revelation of Peter, accepting the first and rejecting the second.

Interestingly, the fragment also mentions the Wisdom of Solomon, a deuterocanonical book in the Catholic and Orthodox traditions but not accepted in the Protestant canon. The document rejects several other writings as illegitimate, such as the Shepherd of Hermas, although it suggests it can be read privately.

Although the fragment does not include a complete list of the current New Testament books due to its fragmentary nature, it provides an important snapshot of the canon formation process in the late second century. It shows a high degree of consistency with the later established canon, demonstrating that the central texts of Christianity were widely agreed upon relatively early in the history of the Church.

Controversies and Disputes in Canon Formation

The process of canon formation was not without its controversies and disputes. Early Christians did not immediately agree on which texts should be included in the canon, leading to debates over the status of certain texts.

One of the primary debates was over the concept of apostolicity, or whether a text was written by an apostle or someone closely associated with an apostle. For example, the Epistle of Hebrews was traditionally attributed to Paul, but its authorship has been a topic of debate since the early church due to its stylistic differences from Paul's other letters. Despite this controversy, the book's high theological value led to its acceptance in the canon.

The Book of Revelation also faced opposition. Its apocalyptic nature and symbolic imagery led some early Christian communities, especially in the East, to question its place in the canon. Despite the hesitations, it was eventually accepted, largely due to the tradition that connected it to the apostle John.

Another category of disputed texts included the "Antilegomena," or "spoken against" books, which faced opposition from some quarters of the early Church. This category includes books like 2 Peter, 2 and 3 John, James, and Jude. These books were eventually accepted into the canon, but not without debate.

The issue of pseudepigrapha, or falsely attributed works, also caused controversy. This category includes books like the Gospel of Peter and the Gospel of Thomas, which claimed apostolic authorship but were not accepted into the canon. These books often contained teachings that were inconsistent with the accepted body of Christian doctrine, which contributed to their exclusion.

On the other hand, the "Apocrypha," a collection of Jewish texts written in the last two centuries BCE and the first century CE, were included in the Septuagint (the Greek Old Testament) and accepted as canonical by some early Christians, especially in the East. However, these books were disputed by others, especially by those in the West and by Jewish communities. This led to their inclusion in the Roman Catholic and Eastern Orthodox Bibles, but their exclusion from the Protestant Bible.

Thus, the process of canon formation was complex and multifaceted, involving a mixture of theological, historical, and practical considerations. Despite the disagreements and controversies, a broad consensus gradually emerged over the course of several centuries, leading to the establishment of the Christian canon as we know it today.

Apocryphal and Pseudepigraphal Writings: Books That Didn't Make the Cut

Throughout the early centuries of Christianity, many writings were produced that were associated with various Christian communities but were not eventually included in the canon of the New Testament. These are commonly referred to as the apocryphal and pseudepigraphal writings.

The term "apocryphal" comes from the Greek word "apokryphos," which means "hidden" or "secret." In a Christian context, it often refers to religious texts that are not part of the canonized Bible. Similarly, "pseudepigraphal" comes from Greek words meaning "falsely attributed" and refers to works that have been attributed to authors who did not actually write them.

There are several reasons why these texts didn't make the canonical "cut."

1. Lack of Apostolic Authority: Many of these texts lack the apostolic authority that was seen as a crucial criterion for inclusion in the canon. They were not written by apostles or those closely associated with apostles, which cast doubt on their authenticity and authority.

2. Late Composition: Most of these writings were composed much later than the canonical New Testament books. Many of the apocryphal and pseudepigraphal texts date from the second century CE or later, while all the books of the New Testament were completed by the end of the first century CE.

3. Theological Discrepancies: Many of these texts contain teachings that were inconsistent with the doctrinal consensus of the early church. Some promoted ideas associated with Gnosticism, a theological movement that was considered heretical by mainstream Christianity.

4. Lack of Widespread Acceptance: These writings were not universally recognized or used by the early Christian communities. Unlike the canonical books, which were read and circulated widely, many of these texts had a more limited audience.

Some of the more well-known apocryphal and pseudepigraphal writings include the Gospel of Thomas, the Gospel of Peter, the Gospel of Judas, the Acts of Paul and Thecla, and the Apocalypse of Peter. These texts provide valuable insights into the diversity of early Christian thought and practice, even though they were not included in the canon.

While these writings were not included in the Bible, they have been preserved and studied for their historical and theological insights. They offer a window into various strands of early Christian thought that existed alongside and often in conversation with what would become orthodox Christianity. However, their lack of apostolic authority, late dating, theological discrepancies, and lack of widespread acceptance among the early Christian communities led to their exclusion from the canon.

Note the following statements by scholars on these noncanonical books:

"There is no question of any one's having excluded them from the New Testament: they have done that for themselves."—M. R. James, *The Apocryphal New Testament*, pages xi, xii.

"We have only to compare our New Testament books as a whole with other literature of the kind to realize how wide is the gulf which separates them from it. The uncanonical gospels, it is often said, are in reality the best evidence for the canonical."—G. Milligan, *The New Testament Documents*, page 228.

"It cannot be said of a single writing preserved to us from the early period of the Church outside the New Testament that it could properly be added to-day to the Canon."—K. Aland, *The Problem of the New Testament Canon*, page 24.

The Impact of Canon Formation on Christianity

The formation of the canon had a profound impact on the development of Christianity.

1. **Unity and Orthodoxy:** The process of canonization helped to establish a core set of beliefs and teachings, providing a basis for unity and orthodoxy among diverse Christian communities. The canon provided a benchmark against which other doctrines could be tested, and it became a vital tool in combating heretical movements. The Apostle Paul emphasized the importance of sound doctrine in his letters, such as in 2 Timothy 4:3, "For the time is coming when people will not endure sound teaching, but having itching ears they will accumulate for themselves teachers to suit their own passions."

2. **Authority of Scripture:** The canonization process reinforced the authority of Scripture within the Christian tradition. By recognizing certain texts as inspired and authoritative, the Church affirmed the significance of the Bible for teaching, rebuking, correcting, and training in righteousness, as stated in 2 Timothy 3:16: "All Scripture is breathed out by God and profitable for teaching, for reproof, for correction, and for training in righteousness."

3. **Scriptural Interpretation and Theology:** The formation of the canon also influenced the interpretation of Scripture and the development of theology. The canonization process involved a degree of interpretation, as the early Church fathers and councils had to discern which books were in line with the Christian faith. The resulting canon then served as the basis for further theological reflection and doctrinal development.

4. **Christian Identity and Practice:** The canon played a crucial role in shaping Christian identity and practice. The canonical books were not only considered authoritative but also served as models of faith and conduct. They provided narratives, teachings, and ethical guidelines that shaped the beliefs and behavior of Christian communities.

5. **Preservation and Transmission of Christian Texts:** The canonization process also had a practical impact on the preservation and transmission of Christian texts. Books that were recognized as canonical were copied and distributed more widely and were more likely to survive than non-canonical texts. This ensured that these texts would be available to future generations of Christians.

6. **Ecumenical Dialogue and Interfaith Understanding:** The establishment of a canon also provided a basis for dialogue and understanding between different Christian denominations and between Christianity and other religions. By defining a set of shared scriptures, the canon provided a common ground for discussion and exploration of differences in interpretation and belief.

In sum, the impact of canon formation on Christianity was multifaceted, affecting theological, ecclesial, practical, and interfaith dimensions of the Christian tradition. The canon served as a cornerstone for Christian faith and practice, helping to shape the identity and beliefs of Christian communities throughout history.

The Canon Today: A Reflection on Its Relevance and Authority

The canon of the Bible, as it is recognized today, continues to hold immense relevance and authority for Christians around the world, across denominational lines. The canon serves as the foundational text of Christianity, providing a basis for faith, worship, ethics, and theology.

1. **Basis for Faith and Worship:** The Bible serves as the basis for Christian faith and worship. It offers narratives about the life, death, and resurrection of Jesus Christ, as well as teachings and parables that guide Christians in their understanding of God and their relationship with Him. As Hebrews 4:12 says, "For the word of God is alive and active. Sharper than any double-edged sword, it penetrates even to dividing soul and spirit, joints and marrow; it judges the thoughts and attitudes of the heart."

2. **Guidance for Ethical Living:** The canon provides guidance for ethical living. The teachings of Jesus, particularly the Sermon on the Mount (Matthew 5-7), as well as the ethical instructions in the Epistles, provide a moral framework for Christians. For instance, in Galatians 5:22-23, Paul lists the fruits of the

Spirit—love, joy, peace, forbearance, kindness, goodness, faithfulness, gentleness and self-control—as virtues to cultivate.

3. **Foundation for Theology:** The canon serves as the foundation for Christian theology. The doctrines of the Trinity, the Incarnation, the Atonement, the Resurrection, and the Second Coming, among others, are all grounded in the biblical text. For example, the doctrine of the Trinity, while not explicitly stated in the Bible, is inferred from passages such as Matthew 28:19, "Therefore go and make disciples of all nations, baptizing them in the name of the Father and of the Son and of the Holy Spirit."

4. **Authority in Christian Practice:** The canon carries authority in Christian practice. It is used in liturgy, in the administration of sacraments, and in pastoral counseling. It also guides individual and communal prayer and devotion. As Paul writes in 2 Timothy 3:16-17, "All Scripture is God-breathed and is useful for teaching, rebuking, correcting and training in righteousness, so that the servant of God may be thoroughly equipped for every good work."

5. **Inspiration for Art and Culture:** The canon has also inspired centuries of art, literature, music, and culture, attesting to its enduring influence and relevance.

6. **Interpretive Challenges and the Role of Tradition:** It's worth noting that while the canon is authoritative, its interpretation can be challenging, given the cultural, historical, and linguistic distance between the original context of the biblical texts and today's readers. This is where the role of tradition, including the teachings of the Church Fathers, church councils, and ongoing theological reflection, comes into play in helping to interpret and understand the canon.

The canon of the Bible, therefore, continues to hold a central place in Christian life and thought. Despite the challenges of interpretation and the diversity of beliefs within Christianity, the canon remains a common ground and a shared source of authority for Christians worldwide.

CHAPTER 7 What Are Bible Difficulties and How Should We Approach Them?

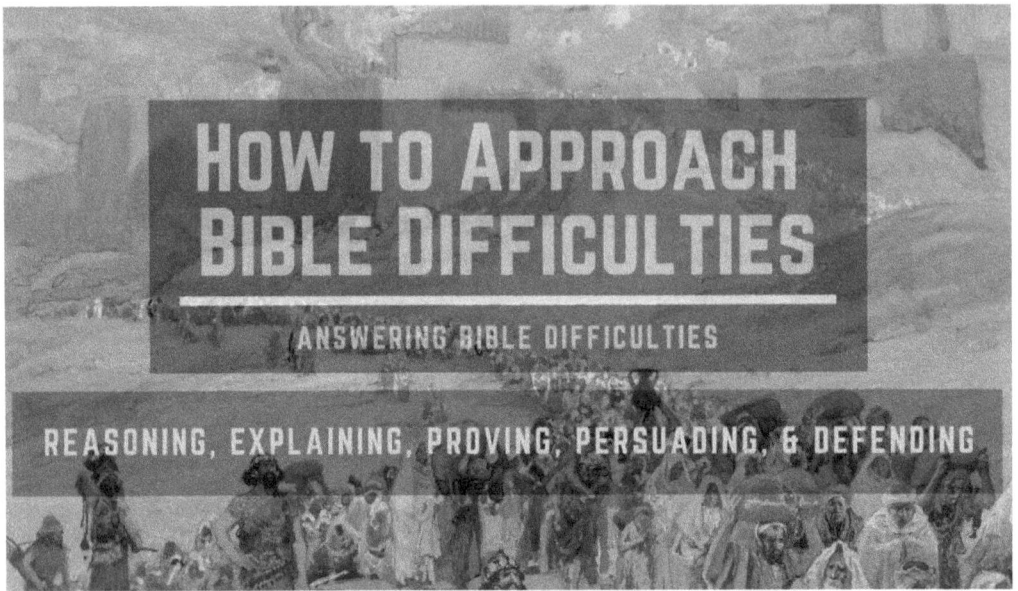

IT SEEMS THAT the charge that the Bible contradicts itself has been made more and more in the last 20 years. Generally, those making such claims are merely repeating what they have heard because most have not even read the Bible, let alone done an in-depth study of it. I do not wish, however, to set aside all concerns as though they have no merit. There are many who raise legitimate questions that seem, on the surface anyway, to be about well-founded contradiction. Sadly, these issues have caused many to lose their faith in God's Word, the Bible. The purpose of this chapter is, to help its readers to be able to defend the Bible against Bible critics (1 Pet. 3:15), to contend for the faith (Jude 1:3), and help those, who have begun to doubt. – Jude 1:22-23.

Before we begin explaining things, let us jump right in, getting our feet wet, and deal with two major Bible difficulties, so we can see that there are reasonable, logical answers. After that, we will delve deeper into explaining Bible difficulties.

Is God permitting Human Sacrifice?

Judges 11:29-34, 37-40? Updated American Standard Version (UASV)

²⁹ Then the Spirit of the Lord was upon Jephthah, and he passed through Gilead and Manasseh; and passed on to Mizpah of Gilead, and from Mizpah of Gilead he passed on to the sons of Ammon. ³⁰ And Jephthah **made a <u>vow</u>** to Jehovah and said,

"If You will indeed give the sons of Ammon into my hand, ³¹ then it shall be that **whatever** comes out of the doors of my house to meet me when I return in peace from the sons of Ammon, it shall be Jehovah's, and I will offer it up as a burnt offering." ³² So Jephthah crossed over to the sons of Ammon to fight against them; and Jehovah gave them into his hand. ³³ He struck them with a very great slaughter from Aroer as far as Minnith, twenty cities, and as far as Abel-keramim. So the sons of Ammon were subdued before the sons of Israel.

³⁴ When Jephthah came to his house at Mizpah, behold, **his daughter was coming out to meet him** with tambourines and with dancing. Now she was his one and only child; besides her he had no son or daughter.

³⁷ And she said to her father, "Let this thing be done for me: leave me alone two months, that I may go up and down on the mountains and weep because of my virginity, I and my companions." ³⁸ And he said, "Go." So he sent her away for two months; and **she left with her companions, and wept on the mountains because of her virginity.** ³⁹ At the end of two months she returned to her father, who **did to her according to the vow that he had made**; and she never known a man.⁹⁸ Thus it became a custom in Israel, ⁴⁰ that the daughters of Israel went year by year **to commemorate**⁹⁹ **the daughter** of Jephthah the Gileadite four days in the year.

It is true; to infer that having the idea of an animal sacrifice would really have not been an impressive vow, which the context requires. Human sacrifice will be repugnant if we are talking about taking a life. Jephthah had no sons, so he likely knew it was the daughter, who would come to greet him.

First, the text does not say he killed his daughter. The idea of some that he did kill her is concluded only by inference. While it is not good policy to interpret backward, using Paul on Judges, he does say humans are to be **"as a living sacrifice."** Therefore, Jephthah could have offered his daughter at the temple, "as a living sacrifice" in service, like Samuel.

This is not to be taken dismissively, because, under Jewish backgrounds, it is no small thing to offer a **perpetual virginity** as a sacrifice. This would mean Jephthah's lineage would not be carried on, the family name, was no more.

Second, the context says she went out to weep for two months, not mourn her death. It says, "she left with her companions, and **wept on the mountains because of her virginity."**

If she was facing imminent death, she could have married, and spent that last two months as a married woman. There would be absolutely no reason for her to mourn her virginity if she were not facing perpetual virginity. – Exodus 38:8; 1 Samuel 2:22

---

⁹⁸ I.e., *never had relations with a man*

⁹⁹ Or *lament*

Third, it was completely forbidden to offer a human sacrifice. – Leviticus 18:21; 20:2-5; Deuteronomy 12:31; 18:10

Imagine an Israelite believing that he could please God with a human sacrifice that was intended to offer up a human life. To do so would have been a rejection of Jehovah's Sovereignty (the very person you are asking for help), and a rejection of the Law that made them a special people. Worse still, this interpretation would have us believe that Jehovah knew this was coming, allowed the vow, and then aided this type of man to succeed over his enemies.

The last point is simple enough. If such a man as one who would make such a vow, in gross violation of the law, and then carry it out; there is no way he would be mentioned by Paul in Hebrews chapter 11 among the most faithful men and women in Israelite history.

In review, there is no way God would have granted and helped in Jephthah's initial success knowing the vow that was coming because both Jehovah and Jephthah would be as bad as the Canaanites. There is no way that God would accept such a vow and then go on to help Jephthah with his enemies yet again. Then, to allow such a vow to be carried out, to then put Jephthah on the wall of star witnesses for God in Hebrews chapter 11.

Does Isaiah 45:7 mean that God Is the Author of Evil?

Isaiah 45:7 King James Version (KJV)
⁷ I form the light, and create darkness: I make peace, and **create evil**: I the Lord do all these things.
	Isaiah 45:7 English Standard Version (ESV)
	⁷ I form light and create darkness,
	    I make well-being and **create calamity**,
	    I am the Lord, who does all these things.[100]

Encarta Dictionary: (Evil) (1) morally bad: profoundly immoral or wrong (2) deliberately causing great harm, pain, or upset

QUESTION: Is this view of evil always the case? No, as you will see below.

Some apologetic authors try to say, 'we do not understand Isaiah 45:7 correctly, because there are other verses that say God is not evil (1 John 1:5), cannot look approvingly on evil (Hab. 1:13), and cannot be tempted by evil. (James 1:13)' Well, while all of these things are Scripturally true, the question at hand is not: Is God evil, can God approvingly look on evil, or can God be tempted with evil? Those questions are not relevant to the one at hand, as God cannot be those things, and at the same time, he can be the yes to our question. The question is, is God the author, the creator of evil?

We would hardly argue that God was **not just** in his bringing "calamity" or "evil" down on Adam and Eve. Thus, we have Isaiah 45:7 saying that God is the creator of "calamity" or "evil."

Let us begin simple, without trying to be philosophical. When God removed Adam and Eve from the Garden of Eden, he sentenced them and humanity to sickness, old age, and death. (Rom. 5:8; i.e., enforce penalty for sin), which was to bring "calamity" or "evil" upon humankind. Therefore, as we can see "evil" does not always mean wrongdoing. Other examples of God bringing "calamity" or "evil" are Noah and the flood, the Ten Plagues of Egypt, and the destruction of the Canaanites. These acts of evil were not acts of wrongdoing. Rather, they were righteous and just, because God, the Creator of all things, was administering justice to wrongdoers, to sinners. He warned the perfect first couple what the penalty was for sin. He warned the people for a hundred years by Noah's preaching. He warned the Canaanites centuries before.

Nevertheless, there are times, when God extends mercy, refraining from the execution of his righteous judgment to one worthy of calamity. For example, he warned Nineveh, the city of blood, and they repented, so he pardoned them. (Jonah

---

[100] See Jeremiah 18:11, Lamentations 3:18, and Amos 3:6

3:10) God has made it a practice to warn persons of the results of sin, giving them undeservedly many opportunities to change their ways. – Ezekiel 33:11.

God cannot sin; it is impossible for him to do so. So, when did he create evil? Without getting into the eternity of his knowing what he was going to do, and when, let us just say, evil did not exist when he was the only person in existence. We might say the idea of evil existed because he knew what he was going to do. However, the moment he created creatures (spirit and human), the potential for evil came into existence because both have free will to sin (fall short of perfection). Evil became a reality the moment Satan entertained the idea of causing Adam to sin, to get humanity for himself, and then acted on it.

God has the right and is just to bring the *calamity of* or *evil* down on anyone that is an unrepentant sinner. God did not even have to give us the underserved kindness of offering us his Son. God is the author or agent of evil regardless of the source books that claim otherwise. If he had never created free will beings, evil would have never gone from the idea of evil to the potential of evil, to the existence of evil. However, God felt that it was better to get the sinful state out of angel and human existence, recover, and then any who would sin thereafter; he would be justified in handing out evil or calamity to only that person or angel alone.

Who among us would argue that he should have created humans and angels like robots, automatons with no free will? The moment he chose the free will, he moved evil from an idea to a potential, and Satan moved it to reality. God has a moral nature that does not bring about evil and sin when he is the only person in existence. However, the moment he created beings in his image, which had the potential to sin, he brought about evil. The moment we have a moral code of good and evil that is placed upon one's with free will; then, we have evil as a potential.

In English, the very comprehensive Hebrew word ra' is variously translated as "bad," "downcast (sad, NASB)," "ugly," "evil," "grievous (distressing, NASB)," "sore," "selfish (stingy, HCSB)," and "envious," depending upon the context. (Gen 2:9; 40:7; 41:3; Ex 33:4; Deut. 6:22; 28:35; Pro 23:6; 28:22)

Evil as an adjective **describes** the **quality of** a class of people, places, or things, or of a specific person, place, or thing

Evil as a noun, **defines** the **nature** of a class of people, places, or things, or of a specific person, place, or thing (e.g., the evil one, evil eye).

We can agree that "evil" is a thing. Create means to bring something into existence, be it people, places, or things, as well something abstract, for lack of a better word at the moment. We would agree that when God was alone evil was not a reality; it did not exist? We would agree that the moment that God created free will creatures (angels and humans), creating humans in his image, with his moral nature, he also brought the potential for evil into existence, and it was realized by Satan?

Inerrancy: Can the Bible Be trusted?

If the Bible is the Word of God, it should be in complete agreement throughout; there should be no contradictions. Yet, the rational mind must ask, why is it that some passages appear to be contradictions when compared with others? For example, Numbers 25:9 tells us that 24,000 died from the scourge, whereas at 1 Corinthians 10:8, the apostle Paul says it was 23,000. This would seem to be a clear error. Before addressing such matters, let us first look at some background information.

Full inerrancy in this book means that the original writings are fully without error in all that they state, as are the words. The words were not dictated (automaton), but the intended meaning is inspired, as are the words that convey that meaning. The Author allowed the writer to use his style of writing, yet controlled the meaning to the extent of not allowing the writer to choose a wrong word, which would not convey the intended meaning. Other more liberal-minded persons hold with *partial inerrancy*, which claims that as far as faith is concerned, this portion of God's Word is without error, but that there are historical, geographical, and scientific errors.

There are several different levels of inerrancy. *Absolute Inerrancy* is the belief that the Bible is fully true and exact in every way; including not only relationships and doctrine, but also science and history. In other words, all information is completely exact. *Full Inerrancy* is the belief that the Bible was not written as a science or historical textbook, but is phenomenological, in that it is written from the human perspective. In other words, speaking of such things as the sun rising, the four corners of the earth or the rounding off of number approximations are all from a human perspective. *Limited Inerrancy* is the belief that the Bible is meant only as a reflection of God's purposes and will, so the science and history is the understanding of the author's day, and is limited. Thus, the Bible is susceptible to errors in these areas. *Inerrancy of Purpose* is the belief that it is only inerrant in the purpose of bringing its readers to a saving faith. The Bible is not about facts, but about persons and relationships, thus, it is subject to error. *Inspired: Not Inerrant* is the belief that its authors are human and thus subject to human error. It should be noted that this author holds the position of full inerrancy.

For many today, the Bible is nothing more than a book written by men. The Bible critic believes the Bible to be full of myths and legends, contradictions, and geographical, historical, and scientific errors. University professor Gerald A. Larue had this to say, "The views of the writers as expressed in the Bible reflect the ideas, beliefs, and concepts current in their own times and are limited by the extent of knowledge in those times."[101] On the other hand, the Bible's authors claim that their writings were inspired of God, as Holy Spirit moved them along. We will discover shortly that the Bible critics have much to say, but it is inflated or empty.

---

[101] Gerald Larue, "The Bible as a Political Weapon," *Free Inquiry* (Summer 1983): 39.

2 Timothy 3:16-17 Updated American Standard Version (UASV)

¹⁶ All Scripture is inspired by God and profitable for teaching, for reproof, for correction, for training in righteousness; ¹⁷ so that the man of God may be fully competent, equipped for every good work.

2 Peter 1:21 Updated American Standard Version (UASV)

²¹ for no prophecy was ever produced by the will of man, but men carried along by the Holy Spirit spoke from God.

The question remains as to whether the Bible is a book written by imperfect men and full of errors, or is written by imperfect men, but inspired by God. If the Bible is just another book by imperfect man, there is no hope for humankind. If it is inspired by God and without error, although penned by imperfect men, we have the hope of everything that it offers: a rich, happy life now by applying counsel that lies within and the real life that is to come, everlasting life. This author contends that the Bible is inspired of God and free of human error, although written by imperfect humans.

Before we take on the critics who seem to sift the Scriptures looking for problematic verses, let us take a moment to reflect on how we should approach these alleged problem texts. The critic's argument goes something like this: 'If God does not err and the Bible is the Word of God, then the Bible should not have one single error or contradiction, yet it is full of errors and contradictions.' If the Bible is riddled with nothing but contradictions and errors as the critics would have us believe, why, out of 31,173 verses in the Bible, should there be only 2-3 thousand Bible difficulties that are called into question, this being less than ten percent of the whole?

First, let it be said that it is every Christian's obligation to get a deeper understanding of God's Word, just as the apostle Paul told Timothy:

1 Timothy 4:15-16 Updated American Standard Version (UASV)

¹⁵ Practice these things, be absorbed in them, so that your progress will be evident to all. ¹⁶ Pay close attention to yourself and to your teaching; persevere in these things, for as you do this you will ensure salvation both for yourself and for those who hear you.

Paul also told the Corinthians:

2 Corinthians 10:4-5 Updated American Standard Version (UASV)

⁴ For the weapons of our warfare are not of the flesh[102] but powerful to God for destroying strongholds.[103] ⁵ We are destroying speculations and every lofty thing raised up against the knowledge of God, and we are taking every thought captive to the obedience of Christ,

---

[102] That is *merely human*
[103] That is *tearing down false arguments*

Paul also told the Philippians:

Philippians 1:7 Updated American Standard Version (UASV)

⁷It is right for me to feel thus about you all, because I hold you in my heart, for you are all partakers with me of grace, both in my imprisonment and in the defense and confirmation of the gospel.

In being able to defend against the modern-day critic, one has to be able to reason from the Scriptures and overturn the critic's argument(s) with mildness. If someone were to approach us about an alleged error or contradiction, what should we do? We should be frank and honest. If we do not have an answer, we should admit such. If the text in question gives the appearance of difficulty, we should admit this as well. If we are unsure as to how we should answer, we can simply say that we will look into it and get back to them, returning with a reasonable answer.

However, we do not want to express disbelief and doubt to our critics, because they will be emboldened in their disbelief. It will put them on the offense and us on the defense. With great confidence, we can express that there is an answer. The Bible has withstood the test of 2,000 years of persecution and interrogation and yet it is the most printed book of all time, currently being translated into 2,287 languages. If these critical questions were so threatening, the Bible would not be the book that it is.

When we are pursuing the text in question, be unwavering in purpose, or resolved to find an answer. In some cases, it may take hours of digging to find the solution. Consider this: as we resolve these difficulties, we are also building our faith that God's Word is inerrant. Moreover, we will want to do preventative maintenance in our personal study. As we are doing our Bible reading, take note of these surface discrepancies and resolve them as we work our way through the Bible. We need to make this part of our prayers as well. I recommend the following program. Below are several books that deal with difficult passages. As we daily read and study our Bible from Genesis to Revelation, do not attempt it in one year; make it a four-year program. Use a good exegetical commentary like *The Holman Old/New Testament Commentary* (HOTC/HNTC) or *The New American Commentary* set, and *The Big Book of Bible Difficulties* by Norman L. Geisler, as well as *The Encyclopedia of Bible Difficulties* by Gleason Archer.

We should be aware that men under inspiration penned the originally written books. In fact, we do not have those originals, what textual scholars call autographs, but we do have thousands of copies. The copyists, however, were not inspired; therefore, as one might expect, throughout the first 1,400 years of copying, thousands of errors were transmitted into the texts that were being copied by imperfect hands that were not under inspiration when copying. Yet, the next 450 years saw a restoration of the text by textual scholars from around the world. Therefore, while many of our best literal translations today may not be inspired, they are a mirror-like reflection of the autographs by way of textual criticism.[104] Therefore, the fallacy could be with the copyist error that has simply not been weeded out. In addition, we must keep in mind that God's Word is without error, but our interpretation and understanding of that Word is not.

It should be noted that the Bible is made up of 66 smaller books that were handwritten over a period of 1,600 years, having some 40 writers of various trades such as shepherd, king, priest, tax collector, governor, physician, copyist, fisherman, and a tentmaker. Therefore, it should not surprise us that some difficulties are encountered as we casually read the Bible. Yet, if one were to take a deeper look, one would find that these difficulties are easily explained. Let us take a few pages to examine some passages that have been under attack.

This chapter's objective is not to be exhaustive, not even close. What we are looking to do is cover a few alleged contradictions and a couple of alleged mistakes. This is to give us a small sampling of the reasonable answers that we will find in the above recommended books. Remember, our Bible is a sword that we must use both offensively and defensively. One must wonder how long a warrior of ancient times would last who was not expertly trained in the use of his weapon. Let us look at a few scriptures that support our need to learn our Bible well so will be able to defend what we believe to be true.

When "false apostles, deceitful workmen, disguising themselves as apostles of Christ" were causing trouble in the congregation in Corinth, the apostle Paul wrote that under such circumstances, we are to *tear down their arguments* and *take every thought captive*. (2 Corinthians 10:4, 5; 11:13–15) All who present critical arguments against God's Word, or contrary to it, can have their arguments overturned by the Christian, who is able and ready to defend that Word in mildness. – 2 Timothy 2:24–26.

1 Peter 3:15 Updated American Standard Version (UASV)

¹⁵ but sanctify Christ as Lord in your hearts, always being prepared to make a defense[105] to anyone who asks you for a reason for the hope that is in you; yet do it with gentleness and respect;

Peter says that we need to be prepared to make a *defense*. The Greek word behind the English 'defense' is *apologia*, which is actually a legal term that refers to the defense of a defendant in court. Our English apologetics is just what Peter spoke of, having the ability to give a reason to any who may challenge us, or to answer those who are not challenging us but who have honest questions that deserve to be answered.

---

[104] Textual criticism is the study of copies of any written work of which the autograph (original) is unknown, with the purpose of ascertaining the original text. Harold J. Green, Introduction to New Testament Textual Criticism (Peabody, MA: Hendrickson, 1995), 1.

[105] Or *argument*, or *explanation*

2 Timothy 2:24-25 Updated American Standard Version (UASV)

²⁴ For a slave of the Lord does not need to fight, but needs to be kind to all, qualified to teach, showing restraint when wronged ²⁵ with gentleness correcting those who are in opposition, if perhaps God may grant them repentance leading to accurate knowledge[106] of the truth,

Look at the Greek word (*epignosis*) behind the English "knowledge" in the above. "It is more intensive than *gnosis* (1108), knowledge because it expresses a more thorough participation in the acquiring of knowledge on the part of the learner."[107] The requirement of all of the Lord's servants is that they be able to teach, but not in a quarrelsome way, and in a way to correct his opponents with mildness. Why? Because the purpose of it all is that by God, and through the Christian teacher, one may come to repentance and begin taking in an accurate knowledge of the truth.

Inerrancy: Practical Principles to Overcoming Bible Difficulties

Below are several ways of looking at the Bible that enable the reader to see he is not dealing with an error or contradiction, but rather a Bible difficulty.

Different Points of View

At times, you may have two different writers who are writing from two different points of view.

Numbers 35:14 Updated American Standard Version (UASV)

¹⁴ You shall give three cities across the Jordan and three cities you shall give in the land of Canaan; they will be cities of refuge.

Joshua 22:4 Updated American Standard Version (UASV)

⁴ And now Jehovah your God has given rest to your brothers, as he spoke to them; therefore turn now and go to your tents, to the land of your possession, which Moses the servant of Jehovah gave you beyond the Jordan. [on the other side of the Jordan, ESV]

Here we see that Moses is speaking about the east side of the Jordan when he says "on this side of the Jordan." Joshua, on the other hand, is also speaking about the east side of the Jordan when he says "on the other side of the Jordan." So, who is correct? Both are. When Moses was penning Numbers the Israelites had not yet crossed the Jordan River, so the east side was "this side," the side he was on. On the other hand,

---

[106] *Epignosis* is a strengthened or intensified form of *gnosis* (*epi*, meaning "additional"), meaning, "true," "real," "full," "complete" or "accurate," depending upon the context. Paul and Peter alone use *epignosis*.

[107] Spiros Zodhiates, *The Complete Word Study Dictionary: New Testament*, Electronic ed. (Chattanooga, TN: AMG Publishers, 2000, c1992, c1993), S. G1922.

when Joshua penned his book, the Israelites had crossed the Jordan, so the east side was just as he had said, "on the other side of the Jordan." Thus, we should not assume that two different writers are writing from the same perspective.

A Careful Reading

At times, it may simply be a case of needing to slow down and carefully read the account, considering exactly what is being said.

Joshua 18:28 Updated American Standard Version (UASV)

28 and Zelah, Haeleph and the Jebusite (that is, Jerusalem), Gibeah, Kiriath; fourteen cities with their villages. This is the inheritance of the sons of Benjamin according to their families.

Judges 1:21 Updated American Standard Version (UASV)

21 But the sons of Benjamin did not drive out the Jebusites who lived in Jerusalem; so the Jebusites have lived with the sons of Benjamin in Jerusalem to this day.

Joshua 15:63 Updated American Standard Version (UASV)

63 But as for the Jebusites, the inhabitants of Jerusalem, the sons of Judah could not drive them out; so the Jebusites live with the sons of Judah at Jerusalem until this day.

Judges 1:8-9 Updated American Standard Version (UASV)

8 And then the sons of Judah fought against Jerusalem and captured it and struck it with the edge of the sword and set the city on fire. 9 And afterward the sons of Judah went down to fight against the Canaanites living in the hill country and in the Negev[108] and in the Shephelah.[109]

2 Samuel 5:5-9 Updated American Standard Version (UASV)

5 At Hebron he reigned over Judah seven years and six months, and in Jerusalem he reigned thirty-three years over all Israel and Judah.

6 And the king and his men went to Jerusalem against the Jebusites, the inhabitants of the land, and they said to David, "You shall not come in here, but the blind and lame will turn you away"; thinking, "David cannot come in here." 7 Nevertheless, David captured the stronghold of Zion, that is the city of David. 8 And David said on that day, "Whoever would strike the Jebusites, let him get up the water shaft to attack 'the lame and the blind,' who are hated by David's soul." Therefore it is said, "The

---

[108] I.e. *South*
[109] I.e., lowland

blind and the lame shall not come into the house." ⁹ And David lived in the stronghold and called it the city of David. And David built all around from the Millo and inward.

There is no doubt that even the advanced Bible reader of many years can come away confused because the above accounts seem to be contradictory. In Joshua 18:28 and Judges 1:21, we see that Jerusalem was an inheritance of the tribe of Benjamin, yet the Benjamites were unable to conquer Jerusalem. However, in Joshua 15:63 we see that the tribe of Judah could not conquer them either, with the reading giving the impression that it was a part of their inheritance. In Judges 1:8, however, Judah was eventually able to conquer Jerusalem and burn it with fire. Yet, to add even more to the confusion, we find at 2 Samuel 5:5–8 that David is said to have conquered Jerusalem hundreds of years later.

Now that we have the particulars let us look at it more clearly. The boundary between Benjamin's inheritances ran right through the middle of Jerusalem. Joshua 8:28 is correct, in that what would later be called the "city of David" was in the territory of Benjamin, but it also in part crossed over the line into the territory of Judah, causing both tribes to go to war against this Jebusite city. It is also true that the tribe of Benjamin was unable to conquer the city and that the tribe of Judah eventually did. However, if you look at Judges 1:9 again, you will see that Judah did not finish the job entirely and moved on to conquer other areas. This allowed the remaining ones to regroup and form a resistance that neither Benjamin nor Judah could overcome, so these Jebusites remained until the time of David, hundreds of years later.

Intended Meaning of Writer

First, the Bible student needs to understand the level that the Bible intends to be exact in what is written. If Jim told a friend that 650 graduated with him from high school in 1984, it is not challenged, because it is all too clear that he is using rounded numbers and is not meaning to be exactly precise. This is how God's Word operates as well. Sometimes it means to be exact, at other times, it is simply rounding numbers, in other cases, the intention of the writer is a general reference, to give readers of that time and succeeding generations some perspective. Did Samuel, the author of Judges, intend to pen a book on the chronology of Judges, or was his focus on the falling away, oppression, and the rescue by a judge, repeatedly. Now, it would seem that Jeremiah, the author of 1 Kings was more interested in giving his readers an exact number of years.

Acts 2:41 Updated American Standard Version (UASV)

⁴¹ So those who received his word were baptized, and there were added that day about three thousand souls.

As you can see here, numbers within the Bible are often used with approximations. This is a frequent practice even today, in both written works and verbal conversation.

Acts 7:2-3 Updated American Standard Version (UASV)

² And Stephen said:

"Brothers and fathers, hear me. The God of glory appeared to our father Abraham when he was in Mesopotamia, before he lived in Haran, ³ and said to him, 'Go out from your land and from your kindred and go into the land that I will show you.'

If you were to check the Hebrew Scriptures at Genesis 12:1, you would find that what is claimed to have been said by God to Abraham is not quoted word-for-word; it is simply a paraphrase. This is a normal practice within Scripture and in writing in general.

Numbers 34:15 Updated American Standard Version (UASV)

¹⁵ The two and a half tribes have received their inheritance beyond the Jordan opposite Jericho, eastward toward the sunrising."

Just as you would read in today's local newspaper, the Bible writer has written from the human standpoint, how it appeared to him. The Bible also speaks of "to the end of the earth" (Psalm 46:9), "from the four corners of the earth" (Isa 11:12), and "the four winds of the earth" (Revelation 7:1). These phrases are still used today.

Unexplained Does Not mean Unexplainable

Considering that there are 31,173 verses in the Bible, encompassing 66 books written by about 40 writers, ranging from shepherds to kings, an army general, fishermen, tax collector, a physician and on and on, and being penned over a 1,600 year period, one does find a few hundred Bible difficulties (about one percent). However, 99 percent of those are explainable. Yet no one wants to be so arrogant to say that he can explain them all. It has nothing to do with the inadequacy of God's Word but is based on human understanding. In many cases, science or archaeology and the field of custom and culture of ancient peoples has helped explain difficulties in hundreds of passages. Therefore, there may be less than one percent left to be answered, yet our knowledge of God's Word continues to grow.

Guilty Until Proven Innocent

This is exactly the perception that the critic has of God's Word. The legal principle of being "innocent until proven guilty" afforded mankind in courts of justice is withheld from the very Word of God. What is ironic here is that this policy has contributed to these Bible critics looking foolish over and over again when something comes to light that vindicates the portion of Scripture they are challenging.

Daniel 5:1 Updated American Standard Version (UASV)

¹ Belshazzar the king made[110] a great feast for a thousand of his nobles, and he was drinking wine in the presence of the thousand.

Bible critics had long claimed that Belshazzar was not known outside of the book Daniel; therefore, they argue that Daniel was mistaken. Yet it hardly seems prudent to argue error from absence of outside evidence. Just because archaeology had not discovered such a person did not mean that Daniel was wrong, or that such a person did not exist. In 1854, some small clay cylinders were discovered in modern-day southern Iraq, which would have been the city of Ur in ancient Babylonia. The cuneiform documents were a prayer of King Nabonidus for "Bel-sar-ussur, my eldest son." These tablets also showed that this "Bel-sar-ussur" had secretaries as well as a household staff. Other tablets were discovered a short time later that showed that the kingship was entrusted to this eldest son as a coregent while his father was away.

He entrusted the 'Camp' to his oldest (son), the firstborn [Belshazzar], the troops everywhere in the country he ordered under his (command). He let (everything) go, entrusted the kingship to him and, himself, he [Nabonidus] started out for a long journey, the (military) forces of Akkad marching with him; he turned towards Tema (deep) in the west."[111]

Ignoring Literary Styles

The Bible is a diverse book when it comes to literary styles: narrative, poetic, prophetic, and apocalyptic; also containing parables, metaphors, similes, hyperbole, and other figures of speech. Too often, these alleged errors are the result of a reader taking a figure of speech as literal, or reading a parable as though it is a narrative.

Matthew 24:35 Updated American Standard Version (UASV)

³⁵ Heaven and earth will pass away, but my words will not pass away.

If some do not recognize that they are dealing with a figure of speech, they are bound to come away with the wrong meaning. Some have concluded from Matthew 24:35 that Jesus was speaking of an eventual destruction of the earth. This is hardly the case, as his listeners would not have understood it that way based on their understanding of the Old Testament. They would have understood that he was simply being emphatic about the words he spoke, using hyperbole. What he was conveying is that his words are more enduring than heaven and earth, and with heaven and earth

---

[110] I.e., held

[111] J. Pritchard, ed., *Ancient Near Eastern Texts* (1974), 313.

being understood as eternal, this merely conveyed even more so that Jesus' words could be trusted.

Two Accounts of the Same Incident

If you were to speak to officers that take accident reports for their police department, you would find that there is cohesion in the accounts, but each person has merely witnessed aspects that have stood out to them. We will see that this is the case as well with the examples below, which is the same account in two different gospels:

Matthew 8:5 Updated American Standard Version (UASV)

⁵ When he[112] had entered Capernaum, a centurion came forward to him, imploring him,

Luke 7:2-3 Updated American Standard Version (UASV)

² And a centurion's[113] slave, who was highly regarded[114] by him, was sick and about to die. ³ When he heard about Jesus, he sent some older men of the Jews[115] asking him to come and bring his slave safely through.[116]

Immediately we see the problem of whether the centurion or the elders of the Jews spoke with Jesus. The solution is not really hidden from us. Which of the two accounts is the most detailed account? You are correct if you said, Luke. The centurion sent the elders of the Jews to represent him to Jesus, so; that whatever response Jesus might give, it would be as though he were addressing the centurion; therefore, Matthew gave his readers the basic thought, not seeing the need of mentioning the elders of the Jews aspect. This is how a representative was viewed in the first century, just as some countries see ambassadors today as being the very person they represent. Therefore, both Matthew and Luke are correct.

Man's Fallible Interpretations

Inspiration by God is infallible, without error. Imperfect man and his interpretations over the centuries, as bad as many of them have been, should not cast a shadow over God's inspired Word. The entire Word of God has one meaning and one meaning only for every penned word, which is what God willed to be conveyed by the human writer he chose to use.

---

[112] That is *Jesus*
[113] I.e., army officer over a hundred solderiers
[114] Lit *to whom he was honorable*
[115] Or *Jewish elders*
[116] I.e., *save the life of his slave*

The Autograph Alone Is Inspired and Inerrant

It has been argued by conservative scholars that only the autograph manuscripts were inspired and inerrant, not the copying of those manuscripts over the next 3,000 years for the Old Testament and 1,500 years for the New Testament. While I would agree with this position as well, it should be noted that we do not possess the autographs, so to argue that they are inerrant is to speak of nonexistent documents. However, it should be further understood that through the science of textual criticism, we can establish a mirror reflection of the autograph manuscripts. B. F. Westcott, F. J. A. Hort, F. F. Bruce, and many other textual scholars would agree with Norman L Geisler's assessment: "The New Testament, then, has not only survived in more manuscripts than any other book from antiquity, but it has survived in a purer form than any other great book—*a form that is 99.5 percent pure.*"[117]

An example of a copyist error can be found in Luke's genealogy of Jesus at Luke 3:35–37. In verse 37 you will find a Cainan, and in verse 36 you will find a second Cainan between Arphaxad (Arpachshad) and Shelah. As one can see from most footnotes in different study Bibles, the Cainan in verse 36 is seen as a scribal error, and is not found in the Hebrew Old Testament, the Samaritan Pentateuch, or the Aramaic Targums, but is found in the Greek Septuagint. (Genesis 10:24; 11:12, 13; 1 Chronicles 1:18, but not 1 Chronicles 1:24) It seems quite unlikely that it was in the earlier copies of the Septuagint, because the first-century Jewish historian Josephus lists Shelah next as the son of Arphaxad, and Josephus normally followed the Septuagint.[118] So one might ask why this second Cainan is found in the translations at all if this is the case? The manuscripts that do contain this second Cainan are some of the best manuscripts that are used in establishing the original text: 01 B L A^1 33 (Kainam); A 038 044 0102 A^{13} (Kainan).

The Bible Was Miraculously Restored, not Miraculously Preserved

The Hebrew text was like the Greek NT; it had accumulated copyist errors, a few intentional, a good number accidental, between the Malachi days of 440 BCE and Rabbi Judah ha-Nasi (135 to 217 CE). The same thing happened to the Greek New Testament from about 400 CE to 1550 CE, a period of copyist errors. The good news is for the NT is fourfold: (1) the 144 NT papyri discovered in the early part of the 20th century, (2) a number of them dated within decades of the originals, and the great Codex Vaticanus (300-330 CE) and Codex Sinaiticus (330-360 CE), (3) that we have 5,898 Greek NT MSS; (4) then, there was the era of many dozens of textual scholars, from 1550 to the present who restored the text to its original words.

---

[117] Norman L. Geisler and William E. Nix: *A General Introduction to the Bible* (Chicago, Moody Press, 1980), 367. (Emphasis is mine.)

[118] *Jewish Antiquities*, I, 146 [vi, 4].

So, the Hebrew OT corruption ran in earnest between 440 BCE to 220 CE. At that time, the Greek Septuagint, a translation of the Hebrew Scriptures, was produced between 280 – 150 BCE, which became favored by the Jews to the point that they claimed it was inspired. However, the fact that the lingua franca of the Roman Empire ran from 330 BCE to 330 CE, the Christians in the first century CE wisely used the Greek Septuagint to evangelize, to show that Jesus Christ was the long-awaited Messiah. Then, Jerusalem was destroyed by General Titus and the Roman army in 70 CE, killing one million one hundred thousand Jews and carrying another seventy thousand back to Rome as slaves. No temple led to the creation of the Mishnah, an authoritative collection of exegetical material embodying the oral tradition of Jewish law and forming the first part of the Talmud. During the 150 years in the wake of the temple's destruction in Jerusalem in 70 CE, rabbinic sages throughout Israel at once were quick to seek out a new source for preserving Jewish practice. They debated and combined various traditions of their oral law. Growing this foundation, they set new constraints, boundaries, and requirements for Judaism. This gave the Jewish people direction for their day-to-day life of holiness, even though they lacked a temple. This new spiritual structure was summarized in the Mishnah, which Judah ha-Nasi compiled by about 200-217 CE.

In addition, the Jewish scholars set about creating a corrected text of the Hebrew Old Testament because they realized it had some textual variants from the sopherim (scribes). But it was the greatest textual scholars who have ever lived, the Masoretes, who made corrected copies from 500 to 900 CE. Below is an article about them. The beauty is that they did not erase the manuscripts with the errors; they kept them, then simply put the corrections in the margin, called the Masorah. So, the Hebrew text was corrected just as the Greek text was. And then, in 1947, we found the Dead Sea Scrolls, which dated as early as the 3rd century BCE and validated the Masoretic text. And ironically at this same time, many of the **best** NT papyri were coming to light that validated the work of Johann Jakob Wettstein [1693-1754 CE], Karl Lachmann [1793-1851], Samuel Prideaux Tregelles [1813-1875], Friedrich Constantin von Tischendorf [1815-1874], and especially Westcott and Hort of 1881.

MIRACULOUS RESTORATION, NOT MIRACULOUS PRESERVATION

OLD TESTAMENT
Transmission: 1500 BCE – 440 BCE
Corruption: 440 BCE – 220 CE
Restoration: 500 – 900 CE – Present
Corroboration MSS (Dead Sea Scrolls): 1947

NEW TESTAMENT
Transmission: 45 CE – 98 CE
Corruption: 440 CE -1550 CE

Restoration: 1550 CE – Present
Corroboration MSS (NT Papyri): 1900s-1960s-Present

A Lack of <u>Preservation</u> Does Not Mean a Lack of <u>Inspiration</u>

- The Bible **was miraculously inspired** as men were moved along by the Holy Spirit (*Absolute Inerrancy*)

- The Bible **was not miraculously preserved** as men's human imperfection gave us corruption (*Limited Inerrancy*)

- The Bible **was restored** through tens of millions of hours by many hundreds of (men) textual scholars from the 16th to the 21st centuries. (*Absolute Inerrancy Restored*)

The **men who restored the text** are no more perfect than the **men who** intentionally and unintentionally **corrupted the text**. However, even hundreds of **imperfect men**, through dozens of lifetimes of sweat and toil, arrived at **a perfect text** that was lost but now is found. With the copyists, you have tens of thousands of men **focusing on their work as an individual** in reproducing a copy; with the textual scholars, it is teams of hundreds of men focusing on all of the manuscripts to ascertain the original words of the original texts.

Many of the above scholars gave their entire lives to God and the Hebrew and Greek text.[119] Each of these could have an entire book devoted to them and their work alone. The amount of work they accomplished before the era of computers is nothing short of astonishing. Rightly, the preceding history should serve to strengthen our faith in the authenticity and general integrity of the Hebrew Scriptures and the Greek New Testament. Unlike Bart D. Ehrman, men like Sir Frederic Kenyon have been moved to say that the books of the Greek New Testament have "come down to us substantially as they were written." And all this is especially true of the critical scholarship of the almost two hundred years since the days of Karl Lachmann. All today can feel confident that what they hold in their hands is a mirror reflection of the Word of God that was penned in twenty-seven books, some two thousand years ago.

It is true that the Jewish copyists and the later Christian copyists were not led along by the Holy Spirit, and therefore their manuscripts were not inerrant, infallible. Errors (textual variants) crept into the manuscripts unintentionally and intentionally. However, the vast majority of the Hebrew Old Testament and Greek New Testament has not been infected with textual errors. For the portions impacted with textual errors, it is the many tens of thousands of copies that we have to help us to weed out the errors. How? Well, not every copyist made the same textual errors. Hence, by comparing the work of different copyists and different manuscripts, textual scholars

---

[119] **The Climax of the Restored Text**

can identify the textual variants (errors) and remove those, leaving us with the original content.

Yes, it would be the greatest discovery of all time if we found the actual original five books that were penned by Moses himself, Genesis through Deuteronomy. However, there would be no way of establishing that they were the originals. The fact is, we do not need the originals. We do not need those original documents. What is so important about the documents? The documents are not important; it is the content on the original documents that we are after. And truly, miraculously, we have more copies than needed to do just that. We do not need miraculous preservation because we have miraculous restoration. We now know beyond a reasonable doubt that the Hebrew Old Testament and the Greek New Testament critical texts are a 99.99% reflection of the content that was in those ancient original manuscripts. Some textual scholars might say that I am exaggerating with the 99.99%. An example of how that is not so can be found in the 1881 Westcott and Hort critical Greek NT, which is 99.5% the same as the 2012 28th edition of the critical Greek NT. The discovery of the NT papyri from the 1900s to the 1960s and up to the present has validated Westcott and Hort's Greek NT and let us know that the 2012 Nestle-Aland Greek NT is a mirror-like reflection of the original. To be frank, there are about 100+ textual variants where Westcott and Hort were correct, and the Nestle-Aland text is likely not correct. This is because they took the textual eclecticism method of determining the original, which was to focus on both external and internal evidence. Still, they leaned heavily on internal evidence, which is a bit more subjective. Regardless, we have the apparatus in the 28th edition of the Nestle-Aland that gives the translator the variants, allowing him to make an objective determination. Therefore, the 100+ textual variants can be decided on a case-by-case basis. So, yes, what we have is 99.99% reflective of the original.

The critical text of Westcott and Hort of 1881 [(FENTON JOHN ANTHONY HORT (1828 – 1892) and BROOKE FOSS WESTCOTT (1825 – 1901)] has been commended by leading textual scholars over the last one hundred and forty years, and still stands as the standard. Numerous additional critical editions of the Greek text came after Westcott and Hort: Richard F. Weymouth (1886), Bernhard Weiss (1894–1900); the British and Foreign Bible Society (1904, 1958), Alexander Souter (1910), Hermann von Soden (1911–1913); and Eberhard Nestle's Greek text, *Novum Testamentum Graece*, published in 1898 by the Württemberg Bible Society, Stuttgart, Germany. The Nestle in twelve editions (1898–1923) to subsequently be taken over by his son, Erwin Nestle (13th–20th editions, 1927–1950), followed by Kurt Aland (21st–25th editions, 1952–1963), and lastly, it was coedited by Kurt Aland and Barbara Aland (26th–28th editions, 1979, 1993, 2012).

Look at the Context

Many alleged inconsistencies disappear by simply looking at the context. Taking words out of context can distort their meaning. *Merriam-Webster's Collegiate Dictionary* defines context as "the parts of a discourse that surround a word or passage and can throw light on its meaning."[120] Context can also be "the circumstances or events that form the environment within which something exists or takes place." If we were to look in a thesaurus for a synonym, we would find "background" for this second meaning. At 2 Timothy 2:15, the apostle Paul brings home the point of why context is so important: "Do your best to present yourself to God as one approved, a worker who has no need to be ashamed, rightly handling the word of truth."

Ephesians 2:8-9 Updated American Standard Version (UASV)

⁸ For by grace you have been saved through faith; and that not of yourselves, it is the gift of God; ⁹ not from works, so that no man may boast.

James 2:26 Updated American Standard Version (UASV)

²⁶ For as the body apart from the spirit[121] is dead, so also faith apart from works is dead.

So, which is it? Is salvation possible by faith alone as Paul wrote to the Ephesians, or is faith dead without works as James wrote to his readers? As our subtitle brings out, let us look at the context. In the letter to the Ephesians, the apostle Paul is speaking to the Jewish Christians who were looking to the works of the Mosaic Law as a means to salvation, a righteous standing before God. Paul was telling these legalistic Jewish Christians that this is not so. In fact, this would invalidate Christ's ransom because there would have been no need for it if one could achieve salvation by meticulously keeping the Mosaic Law. (Rom. 5:18) But James was writing to those in a congregation who were concerned with their status before other men, who were looking for prominent positions within the congregation, and not taking care of those that were in need. (Jam. 2:14–17) So, James is merely addressing those who call themselves Christian, but in name only. No person could truly be a Christian and not possess some good works, such as feeding the poor, helping the elderly. This type of work was an evident demonstration of one's Christian personality. Paul was in perfect harmony with James on this. – Romans 10:10; 1 Corinthians 15:58; Ephesians 5:15, 21–33; 6:15; 1 Timothy 4:16; 2 Timothy 4:5; Hebrews 10:23-25.

---

[120] Merriam-Webster, Inc: *Merriam-Webster's Collegiate Dictionary*. Eleventh ed. (Springfield, Mass.: Merriam-Webster, Inc. 2003).

[121] Or *breath*

Inerrancy: Are There Contradictions?

Below I will follow this pattern. I will list the critic's argument first, followed by the text of difficulty, and conclude with an answer to the critic. What should be kept at the forefront of our mind is this: one is simply looking for the best answer, not absoluteness. If there is a reasonable answer to a Bible difficulty, why are the critics able to set them aside with ease? Because they start with the premise that this is not the Word of God, but only a book by imperfect men and full of contradictions; thus, the bias toward errors has blinded their judgment.

Critic: The critic would argue that there was an Adam and Eve, and an Abel who was now dead, so, where did Cain get his wife? This is one of the most common questions by Bible critics.

Genesis 4:17 Updated American Standard Version (UASV)

^{17} Cain had sexual relations[122] with his wife and she conceived, and gave birth to Enoch; and he built a city, and called the name of the city Enoch, after the name of his son, Enoch.

Answer: If one were to read a little further along, they would come to the realization that Adam had a son named Seth; it further adds that Adam "became father to sons *and daughters.*" (Genesis 5:4) Adam lived for a total of 800 years after fathering Seth, giving him ample opportunity to father many more sons and daughters. So it could be that Cain married one of his sisters. If he waited until one of his brothers and sisters had a daughter, he could have married one of his nieces once she was old enough. In the beginning, humans were closer to perfection; this explains why they lived longer and why at that time there was little health risk of genetic defects in the case of children born to closely related parents, in contrast to how it is today. As time passed, genetic defects increased and life spans decreased. Adam lived to see 930 years. Yet Shem, who lived after the Flood, died at 600 years, while Shem's son Arpachshad only lived 438 years, dying before his father died. Abraham saw an even greater decrease in that he only lived 175 years while his grandson Jacob was 147 years when he died. Thus, due to increasing imperfection, God prohibited the marriage of closely related people under the Mosaic Law because of the likelihood of genetic defects.—Leviticus 18:9.

Critic: If God is here hardening Pharaoh's heart, what exactly makes Pharaoh responsible for the decisions he makes?

Exodus 4:21 Updated American Standard Version (UASV)

^{21} Jehovah said to Moses, "When you go and return to Egypt see that you perform before Pharaoh all the wonders which I have put in your hand; but I will harden his heart so that he will not let the people go.

---

[122] Lit *knew*

Answer: This is actually a prophecy. God knew that what he was about to do would contribute to a stubborn and obstinate Pharaoh, who was going to be unwilling to change or give up the Israelites so they could go off to worship their God. Therefore, this is not stating what God is going to do; it is prophesying that Pharaoh's heart will harden because of the actions of God. The fact is, Pharaoh allowed his own heart to harden because he was determined not to agree with Moses' wishes or accept Jehovah's request to let the people go. Moses tells us at Exodus 7:13 (ESV) that "Pharaoh's heart was hardened, and he would not listen to them, as the Lord had said." Again, at 8:15 we read, "When Pharaoh saw that there was a respite, he hardened his heart and would not listen to them, as the Lord had said."

Critic: The Israelites had just received the Ten Commandments, with one commandment being: "You shall not make for yourself a carved image or any likeness of anything that is in heaven above, or that is in the earth beneath, or that is in the water under the earth." Therefore, how is the bronze serpent not a violation of this commandment?

Numbers 21:9 Updated American Standard Version (UASV)

⁹ And Moses made a bronze serpent and set it on the standard;[123] and it came about, that if a serpent bit any man, when he looked to the bronze serpent, he lived.

Answer: First, an idol is "a representation or symbol of an object of worship; *broadly*: a false god."[124] Second, it should be noted that not all images are idols. The bronze serpent was not made for the purpose of worship, or for some passionate devotion or veneration. There were times, however, when images were created with absolutely no intention of it receiving devotion, veneration, or worship, yet were later made into objects of veneration. That is exactly what happened with the copper serpent that Moses had formed in the wilderness. Many centuries later, "in the third year of Hoshea son of Elah, king of Israel, Hezekiah the son of Ahaz, king of Judah, began to reign. He removed the high places and broke the pillars and cut down the Asherah. And he broke in pieces the bronze serpent that Moses had made; for until those days the people of Israel had made offerings to it (it was called Nehushtan)."—2 Kings 18:1, 4.

Critic: Deuteronomy 15:11 (NET) says: "*There will never cease to be some poor people in the land;* therefore, I am commanding you to make sure you open your hand to your fellow Israelites who are needy and poor in your land." Is this not a contradiction of Deuteronomy 15:4? Will there be no poor among the Israelites, or will there be poor among them? Which is it?

---

[123] I.e., *pole*

[124] Merriam-Webster, Inc: *Merriam-Webster's Collegiate Dictionary*. Eleventh ed. (Springfield, Mass.: Merriam-Webster, Inc., 2003).

Deuteronomy 15:4 Updated American Standard Version (UASV)

⁴ However, there will be no poor among you, since Jehovah will surely bless you in the land which Jehovah your God is giving you as an inheritance to possess,

Answer: If you look at the context, Deuteronomy 15:4 is stating that if the Israelites obey Jehovah's command to take care of the poor, "there should not be any poor among" them. Thus, for every poor person, there will be one to take care of that need. If an Israelite fell on hard times, there was to be a fellow Israelite ready to step in to help him through those hard times. Verse 11 stresses the truth of the imperfect world since the rebellion of Adam and inherited sin: there will always be poor among mankind, the Israelites being no different. However, the difference with God's people is that those who were well off financially were to offset conditions for those who fell on difficult times. This is not to be confused with the socialistic welfare systems in the world today. Those Jews were hard-working men, who labored from sunup to sundown to take care of their families. But if disease overtook their herd or unseasonal weather brought about failed crops, an Israelite could sell himself into the service of a fellow Israelite for a period of time; thereafter, he would be back on his feet. And many years down the road, he may very well do the same for another Israelite, who fell on difficult times.

Critic: Joshua 11:23 says that Joshua took the land according to what God had spoken to Moses and handed it on to the nation of Israel as planned. However, in Joshua 13:1, God is telling Joshua that he has grown old and much of the Promised Land has yet to be taken possession of. How can both be true? Is this not a contradiction?

Joshua 11:23 Updated American Standard Version (UASV)

²³ So Joshua took the whole land, according to all that Jehovah had spoken to Moses, and Joshua gave it for an inheritance to Israel according to their divisions by their tribes, and the land had rest from war.

Joshua 13:1 Updated American Standard Version (UASV)

13 Now Joshua was old and advanced in years, and Jehovah said to him, "You are old and advanced in years, and there remains yet very much land to possess.

Answer: No, it is not a contradiction. When the Israelites were to take the land, it was to take place in two different stages: the nation as a whole was to go to war and defeat the 31 kings of this land; thereafter, each Israelite tribe was to take their part of the land based on their individual actions. (Joshua 17:14–18; 18:3) Joshua fulfilled his role, which is expressed in 11:23 while the individual tribes did not complete their campaigns, which is expressed in 13:1. Even though the individual tribes failed to live up to taking their portion, the remaining Canaanites posed no real threat. Joshua 21:44, *ASV*, reads: "Jehovah gave them rest round about."

Critic: The critic would point out that John 1:18 clearly says that *"no one has ever seen God,"* while Exodus 24:10 explicitly states that Moses and Aaron, Nadab and Abihu, and seventy of the elders of Israel *"saw the God of Israel."* Worse still, God informs them in Exodus 33:20: "You cannot see my face, for man shall not see me and live." The critic with his knowing smile says, 'This is a blatant contradiction.'

John 1:18 Updated American Standard Version (UASV)

^{18} No one has seen God at any time; the only begotten god^{125} who is in the bosom of the Father,^{126} that one has made him fully known.

Exodus 24:10 Updated American Standard Version (UASV)

^{10} and they saw the God of Israel; and under his feet was what seemed like a sapphire pavement, as clear as the sky itself.

Exodus 33:20 Updated American Standard Version (UASV)

^{20} But he [God] said, "You cannot see my face, for no man can see me and live!"

Answer: Exodus 33:20 is one-hundred percent correct: No human could see Jehovah God and live. The apostle Paul at Colossians 1:15 tell us that Christ is the image of the invisible God, and the writer informs us at Hebrews 1:3 that Jesus is the "exact representation of His nature." Yet if you were to read the account of Saul of Tarsus (the apostle Paul), you would see that a mere partial manifestation of Christ's glory blinded Saul – Acts 9:1–18.

When the Bible says that Moses and others have seen God, it is not speaking of *literally* seeing him, because first of all He is an invisible spirit person. It is a *manifestation* of his glory, which is an act of showing or demonstrating his presence, making himself perceptible to the human mind. In fact, it is generally an angelic representative that stands in his place and not him personally. Exodus 24:16 informs us that "the glory of the Lord dwelt on Mount Sinai," not the Lord himself personally. When texts such as Exodus 24:10 explicitly state that Moses and Aaron, Nadab and Abihu, and seventy of the elders of Israel *"saw the God of Israel,"* it is this "glory of the Lord," an angelic representative. This is shown to be the case at Luke 2:9, which reads: "And *an angel of the Lord* appeared to them, and *the glory of the Lord shone around them* [the shepherds], and they were filled with fear."

Many Bible difficulties are cleared up elsewhere in Scripture; for example, in the New Testament, you will find a text clarifying a difficulty from the Old Testament, such as Acts 7:53, which refers to those "who received the law *as delivered by angels* and did not keep it." Support comes from Paul at Galatians 3:19: "Why then the law? It was added because of transgressions until the offspring should come to whom the

---

[125] Jn 1:18: "only-begotten god", P^{66}ℵ*BC*Lsyr^{hmg,p}; **[V1]** "the only-begotten god," P^{75}33ℵcop^{bo}; **[V2]** "the only-begotten Son." AC^{3}(W^{s})QYf1,13 MajVgSyr^{c}

[126] Or *at the Father's side*

promise had been made, and it was put in place through angels by an intermediary." The writer of Hebrews chimes in at 2:2 with "For since the message *declared by angels* proved to be reliable, and every transgression or disobedience received a just retribution. . . ." As we travel back to Exodus again, to 19:19 specifically, we find support that it was not God's own voice, which Moses heard; no, it was an angelic representative, for it reads: "Moses was speaking, and God was answering him with a voice." Exodus 33:22–23 also helps us to appreciate that it was the back of these angelic representatives of Jehovah that Moses saw: "While my glory passes by . . . Then I will take away my hand, and you shall see my back, but my face shall not be seen."

Exodus 3:4 states: "God called to him out of the bush, 'Moses, Moses!' And he said, 'Here I am.'" Verse 6 informs us: "I am the God of your father, the God of Abraham, the God of Isaac, and the God of Jacob." Yet, in verse 2 we read: "And the angel of the Lord appeared to him in a flame of fire out of the midst of a bush." Here is another example of using God's Word to clear up what seems to be unclear or difficult to understand at first glance. Thus, while it speaks of the Lord making a direct appearance, it is really an angelic representative. Even today, we hear such comments, as 'the president of the United States is to visit the Middle East later this week.' However, later in the article it is made clear that he is not going personally, but it is one of his high-ranking representatives. Let us close with two examples, starting with,

Genesis 32:24-30 Updated American Standard Version (UASV)

²⁴ And Jacob was left alone, and a man wrestled with him until daybreak. ²⁵ When he saw that he had not prevailed against him, he touched the socket of his thigh; so the socket of Jacob's thigh was dislocated as he wrestled with him. ²⁶ Then he said, "Let me go, for the dawn is breaking." But he said, "I will not let you go unless you bless me." ²⁷ And he said to him, "What is your name?" And he said, "Jacob." ²⁸ And he said, "Your name shall no longer be called Jacob, but Israel,[127] for you have struggled with God and with men and have prevailed." ²⁹ Then Jacob asked him and said, "Please tell me your name." But he said, "Why is it that you ask my name?" And he blessed him there. ³⁰ So Jacob named the place Peniel,[128] for he said, "I have seen God face to face, yet my soul has been preserved."

It is all too obvious here that this man is simply a materialized angel in the form of a man, another angelic representative of Jehovah God. Moreover, the reader of this book should have taken in that the Israelites as a whole saw these angelic representatives and spoke of them as though they were dealing directly with Jehovah God himself.

This proved to be the case in the second example found in the book of Judges where an angelic representative visited Manoah and his wife. Like the above mentioned

---

[127] Meaning *he contends with God*
[128] Meaning *face of God*

account, Manoah and his wife treated this angelic representative as if he were Jehovah God himself: "And Manoah said to the angel of the Lord, 'What is your name, so that, when your words come true, we may honor you?' And the angel of the Lord said to him, 'Why do you ask my name, seeing it is wonderful?' Then Manoah knew that he was the angel of the Lord. And Manoah said to his wife, "We shall surely die, *for we have seen God.*" – Judges 13:3–22.

Inerrancy: Are There Mistakes?

I have addressed the alleged contradictions, so it would seem that our job is done here, right? Not hardly. Yes, there are just as many who claim that the Bible is full of mistakes.

Critic: Matthew 27:5 states that Judas hanged himself, whereas Acts 1:18 says, "Falling headlong, he burst open in the middle and all his intestines gushed out."

Matthew 27:5 Updated American Standard Version (UASV)

⁵ And he threw the pieces of silver into the temple and departed; and he went away and hanged himself.

Acts 1:18 Updated American Standard Version (UASV)

¹⁸ (Now this man acquired a field with the price of his wickedness, and falling headlong, he burst open in the middle and all his intestines gushed out.

Answer: Neither Matthew nor Luke made a mistake. What you have is Matthew giving the reader the manner in which Judas committed suicide. On the other hand, Luke is giving the reader of Acts, the result of that suicide. Therefore, instead of a mistake, we have two texts that complement each other, really giving the reader the full picture. Judas came to a tree alongside a cliff that had rocks below. He tied the rope to a branch and the other end around his neck and jumped over the edge of the cliff in an attempt at hanging himself. One of two things could have happened: (1) the limb broke plunging him to the rocks below, or (2) the rope broke with the same result, and he burst open onto the rocks below.

Critic: The apostle Paul made a mistake when he quotes how many people died.

Numbers 25:9 Updated American Standard Version (UASV)

⁹ The ones who died in the plague were twenty-four thousand.

1 Corinthians 10:8 Updated American Standard Version (UASV)

⁸ Neither let us commit sexual immorality, as some of them committed sexual immorality, only to fall, twenty-three thousand of them in one day.

Answer: We must keep in mind the above principle that we spoke of, the *Intended Meaning of the Writer*. We live in a far more precise age today, where specificity is highly important. However, we round large numbers off (even estimate) all the time: "there were 237,000 people in Time Square last night." The simplest answer is that the number of people slain was in between 23,000 and 24,000, and both writers rounded the number off. However, there is even another possibility, because the book of Numbers specifically speaks of "all the chiefs of the people" (25:4-5), which could account for the extra 1,000, which is mentioned in Numbers 24,000. Thus, you have the people killing the chiefs of the people and the plague killing the people. Therefore, both books are correct.

Critic: After 215 years in Egypt, the descendants of Jacob arrived at the Promised Land. As you recall they sinned against God and were sentenced to forty years in the wilderness. But once they entered the Promised Land, they buried Joseph's bones "at Shechem, in the piece of land that *Jacob bought* from the sons of Hamor the father of Shechem," as stated at Joshua 24:32. Yet, when Stephen had to defend himself before the Jewish religious leaders, he said that Joseph was buried "in the tomb that *Abraham had bought* for a sum of silver from the sons of Hamor." Therefore, at once it appears that we have a mistake on the part of Stephen.

Acts 7:15-16 Updated American Standard Version (UASV)

¹⁵ And Jacob went down to Egypt and died, he and our fathers. ¹⁶ And they were brought back to Shechem and buried in the tomb that Abraham had bought for a sum of silver from the sons of Hamor in Shechem.

Genesis 23:17-18 Updated American Standard Version (UASV)

¹⁷ So Ephron's field, which was in Machpelah, which faced Mamre, the field and cave which was in it, and all the trees which were in the field, that were in all its border around, were made over ¹⁸ to Abraham for a possession in the presence of the sons of Heth, before all who went in at the gate of his city.

Genesis 33:19 Updated American Standard Version (UASV)

¹⁹ And he bought the piece of land where he had pitched his tent from the hand of the sons of Hamor, Shechem's father, for one hundred qesitahs.[129]

Joshua 24:32 Updated American Standard Version (UASV)

³² As for the bones of Joseph, which the sons of Israel brought up from Egypt, they buried them at Shechem, in the piece of land that Jacob bought from the sons of Hamor the father of Shechem for one hundred qesitahs.[130] It became an inheritance of the sons of Joseph.

Answer: If we look back to Genesis 12:6-7, we will find that Abraham's first stop after entering Canaan from Haran was Shechem. It is here that Jehovah told Abraham: "To your offspring I will give this land." At this point Abraham built an altar to Jehovah. It seems reasonable that Abraham would need to purchase this land that had not yet been given to his offspring. While it is true that the Old Testament does not

---

[129] Or *pieces of money*; money of unknown value
[130] Or *pieces of money*; money of unknown value

mention this purchase, it is likely that Stephen would be aware of such by way of oral tradition. As Acts chapter seven demonstrates, Stephen had a wide-ranging knowledge of Old Testament history.

Later, Jacob would have had difficulty laying claim to the tract of land that his grandfather Abraham had purchased, because there would have been a new generation of inhabitants of Shechem. This would have been many years after Abraham moved further south and Isaac moved to Beersheba, and including Jacob's twenty years in Paddan-aram (Gen 28:6, 7). The simplest answer is that this land was not in use for about 120 years because of Abraham's extensive travels and Isaac's having moved away, leaving it unused; likely it was put to use by others. So, Jacob simply repurchased what Abraham had bought over a hundred years earlier. This is very similar to the time Isaac had to repurchase the well at Beersheba that Abraham had already purchased earlier. – Genesis 21:27–30; 26:26–32.

Genesis 33:18–20 tells us that 'Jacob bought this land for a hundred pieces of money, from the sons of Hamor.' This same transaction is also mentioned at Joshua 24:32, in reference to transporting Joseph's bones from Egypt, to be buried in Shechem.

We should also address the cave of Machpelah that Abraham had purchased in Hebron from Ephron the Hittite. The word "tomb" is not mentioned until Joshua 24:32, and is in reference to the tract of land in Shechem. Nowhere in the Old Testament does it say that Abraham bought a "tomb." The cave of Machpelah obtained by Abraham would eventually become a family tomb, receiving Sarah's body and, eventually, his own, and those of Isaac, Rebekah, Jacob, and Leah. (Genesis 23:14–19; 25:9; 49:30, 31; 50:13) Gleason L. Archer, Jr., concludes this Bible difficulty, saying:

> The reference to a *mnema* ("tomb") in connection with Shechem must either have been proleptic [to anticipate] for the later use of that shechemite tract for Joseph's tomb (i.e., 'the tomb that Abraham bought' was intended to imply 'the tomb location that Abraham bought'); or else conceivably the dative relative pronoun *ho* was intended elliptically [omission] for *en to topo ho onesato Abraam* ("in the place that Abraham bought") as describing the location of the *mnema* near the Oak of Morch right outside Shechem. Normally Greek would have used the relative-locative adverb *hou* to express 'in which' or 'where'; but this would have left o*nesato* ("bought") without an object in its own clause, and so *ho* was much more suitable in this context. (Archer 1982, 379–81)

Another solution could be that Jacob is being viewed as a representative of Abraham, for he is the grandson of Abraham. This was quite appropriate in Biblical times, to attribute the purchase to Abraham as the Patriarchal family head.

Critic: 2 Samuel 24:1 says that God moved David to count the Israelites, while 1 Chronicles 21:1 Satan, or a resister did. This would seem to be a clear mistake on the part of one of these authors.

2 Samuel 24:1 Updated American Standard Version (UASV)

¹ Now again the anger of Jehovah burned against Israel, and it incited David against them to say, "Go, number Israel and Judah."

1 Chronicles 21:1 Updated American Standard Version (UASV)

¹ Then Satan stood up against Israel and moved David to number Israel.

Answer: In this period of David's reign, Jehovah was very displeased with Israel, and therefore he did not prevent Satan from bringing this sin on them. Often in Scripture, it is spoken of as though God did something when he allowed an event to take place. For example, it is said that God 'hardened Pharaoh's heart' (Exodus 4:21), when he actually allowed the Pharaoh's heart to harden.

Inerrancy: Are There Scientific Errors?

Many truths about God are beyond the scope of science. Science and the Bible are not at odds. In fact, we can thank modern day science as it has helped us to better under the creation of God, from our solar system to the universes, to the human body and mind. What we find is a level of order, precision, design, and sophistication, which points to a Designer, the eyes of many Christians, to an Almighty God, with infinite intelligence and power. The apostle Paul makes this all too clear, when he writes, "For his invisible attributes, namely, his eternal power and divine nature, have been clearly perceived, ever since the creation of the world, in the things that have been made. So they are without excuse." – Romans 1:20.

Back in the seventeenth century, the world-renowned scientist Galileo proved beyond any doubt that the earth was not the center of the universe, nor did the sun orbit the earth. In fact, he proved it to be the other way around (no pun intended), with the earth revolving around the sun. However, he was brought up on charges of heresy by the Catholic Church and ordered to recant his position. Why? From the viewpoint of the Catholic Church, Galileo was contradicting God's Word, the Bible. As it turned out, Galileo and science were correct, and the Church was wrong, for which it issued a formal apology in 1992. However, the point we wish to make here is that in all the controversy, the Bible was never in the wrong. It was a misinterpretation on the part of the Catholic Church and not a fault with the Bible. One will find no place in the Bible that claims the sun orbits the earth. So where would the Church get such an idea? The Church got such an idea from Ptolemy (b. about 85 C.E.), an ancient astronomer, who argued for such an idea.

As it usually turns out, the so-called contradiction between science and God's Word lies at the feet of those who are interpreting Scripture incorrectly. To repeat the sentiments of Galileo when writing to a pupil–Galileo expressed the same sentiments: "Even though Scripture cannot err, its interpreters and expositors can, in various ways. One of these, very serious and very frequent, would be when they always want to stop at the purely literal sense."[131] I believe that today's scholars, in hindsight, would have no problem agreeing.

While the Bible is not a science textbook, it is scientifically accurate when it touches on matters of science.

The Circle of the Earth Hangs on Nothing

Isaiah 40:22 Updated American Standard Version (UASV)

^{22} It is he who sits above **the circle of the earth**,
  and its inhabitants are like grasshoppers;
who stretches out the heavens like a curtain,
  and spreads them like a tent to dwell in.

More than 2,500 years ago, the prophet Isaiah wrote that the earth is a circle or sphere. First, how would it be possible for Isaiah to know the earth is a circle or sphere, if not from inspiration? Scientific America writes, "As countless photos from space can attest, Earth is round–the "Blue Marble," as astronauts have affectionately dubbed it. Appearances, however, can be deceiving. Planet Earth is not, in fact, perfectly round."[132] Scientifically speaking, the sun is not perfectly, absolutely 100 percent round but in everyday speech, this verse is both acceptable and accurate, when we keep in mind it is written from a human perspective, not from a scientific perspective. Moreover, Isaiah was not discussing astronomy; he was simply making an inspired observation that man came to realize once he was in space, looking back at the earth, it is round. See the section about title, "Intended Meaning of Writer."

Job 26:7 Updated American Standard Version (UASV)

^{7} "He stretches out the north over empty space
and hangs the earth on nothing.

Here the author describes the earth as hanging upon nothing. Many have never heard of the Greek mathematician and astronomer Eratosthenes. He was born in about 276 B.C.E. and received some of his education in Athens, Greece. In 240 B.C., the "Greek astronomer, geographer, mathematician and librarian Eratosthenes

---

[131] Letter from Galileo to Benedetto Castelli, December 21, 1613.
[132] Charles Q. Choi (April 12, 2007). Scientific America. Strange but True: Earth Is Not Round. Retrieved Monday, August 03, 2015.
  http://www.scientificamerican.com/article/earth-is-not-round/

calculates the Earth's circumference. His data was rough, but he wasn't far off."[133] While man very early on used their God given intelligence to arrive at some outstanding conclusion that was actually very accurate, we learn two points here. Eratosthenes was a very astute scientist, while Isaiah, who wrote some 500 years earlier, was no scientist at all. Moreover, Moses, who wrote the book of Job over 1,230 years before Eratosthenes, knew that the earth hung upon nothing.

How Is the Sun Standing Still Possible?

Joshua 10:13 Updated American Standard Version (UASV)

¹³ And the sun stood still, and the moon stopped,
 until the nation avenged themselves of their enemies.

Is this not written in the Book of Jashar? The sun stopped in the midst of heaven and did not hurry to set for about a whole day.

The Canaanites had besieged the Gibeonites, a group of people that gained Jehovah God's backing because they had faith in Him. In this battle, Jehovah helped the Israelites continue their attack by causing "the sun [to stand] still, and the moon stopped, until the nation took vengeance on their enemies." (Jos 10:1-14) Those who accept God as the creator of the universe and life can accept that he would know a way of stopping the earth from rotating. However, there are other ways of understanding this account. We must keep in mind that the Bible speaks from an earthly observer point of view, so it need not be that he stopped the rotation. It could have been a refraction of solar and lunar light rays, which would have produced the same effect.

Psalm 136:6 Updated American Standard Version (UASV)

⁶ to him who spread out the earth above the waters,
 for his lovingkindness is everlasting;

Hebrews 3:4 Updated American Standard Version (UASV)

⁴ For every house is built by someone, but the builder of all things is God.

2 Kings 20:8-11 Updated American Standard Version (UASV)

⁸ And Hezekiah said to Isaiah, "What shall be the sign that Jehovah will heal me, and that I shall go up to the house of Jehovah on the third day?" ⁹ And Isaiah said, "This shall be the sign to you from Jehovah, that Jehovah will do the thing that he has spoken: shall the shadow go forward ten steps or go back ten steps?" ¹⁰ And Hezekiah answered, "It is an easy thing for the shadow to decline ten steps; no, but let the shadow turn backward ten steps." ¹¹ And Isaiah the prophet cried to Jehovah, and he

---

[133] Alfred, Randy (June 19, 2008). "June 19, 240 B.C.E: The Earth Is Round, and It's This Big". Wired. Retrieved Monday, August 03, 2015.

brought the shadow on the steps back ten steps, by which it had gone down on the steps of Ahaz.

How is it that the stars fought on behalf of Barak?

Judges 5:20 Updated American Standard Version (UASV)

[20] From heaven the stars fought, from their courses they fought against Sisera.

Judges 4:15 Updated American Standard Version (UASV)

[15] And Jehovah routed Sisera and all his chariots and all his army with the edge of the sword before Barak; and Sisera alighted from his chariot and fled away on foot.

In the Bible, you have Biblical prose, and Biblical poetry.

Prose: language that is not poetry: (1) writing or speech in its normal continuous form, without the rhythmic or visual line structure of poetry **(2)** ordinary style of expression: writing or speech that is ordinary or matter-of-fact, without embellishment.

Poetry: literature in verse: (1) literary works written in verse, in particular verse writing of high quality, great beauty, emotional sincerity or intensity, or profound insight **(2) beauty or grace:** something that resembles poetry in its beauty, rhythmic grace, or imaginative, elevated, or decorative style.

We have a beautiful example of both of these forms of writing communication in chapters four and five of the book of Judges. Judges, Chapter 4 is a prose account of Deborah and Barak, while Judges Chapter 5 is a poetic account. As we have learned from the above, poetry is less concerned with accuracy than evoking emotions. Poetry has a license to say things like what we find in of 5:20, which is in the poetry chapter: "from heaven the stars fought." This can be said, and the reader is expected not to take the language literally. What we can surmise from it though, is that God was acting against Sisera in some way, there was divine intervention.

Procedures for Handling Biblical Difficulties

1. You need to be completely convinced a reason or understanding exists.

2. You need to have total trust and conviction in the inerrancy of the Scripture as originally written down.

3. You need to study the context and framework of the verse carefully, to establish what the author meant by the words he used. In other words, find the beginning and the end of the context that your passage falls within.

4. You need to understand exegesis: find the historical setting, determine author intent, study key words, and note parallel passages. You need to slow down and carefully read the account, considering exactly what is being said

5. You need to find a reasonable harmonization of parallel passages.

6. You need to consider a variety of trusted Bible commentaries, dictionaries, lexical sources, encyclopedias, as well as books on Bible difficulties.

7. You should investigate as to whether the difficulty is a transmission error in the original text.

8. You must always keep in mind that the historical accuracy of the biblical text is unmatched; that thousands of extant manuscripts some of which date back to the second century B.C. support the transmitted text of Scripture.

9. We must keep in mind that the Bible is a diverse book when it comes to literary styles: narrative, poetic, prophetic, and apocalyptic; also containing parables, metaphors, similes, hyperbole, and other figures of speech. Too often, these alleged errors are the result of a reader taking a figure of speech as literal or reading a parable as though it is a narrative.

10. The Bible student needs to understand what level that the Bible intends to be exact in what is written. If Jim told a friend that 650 graduated with him from high school in 1984, it is not challenged, because it is all too clear that he is using rounded numbers and is not meaning to be precise.

CHAPTER 8 The Jesus-Paul Connection: An Examination of Their Relationship

Introduction: The Intriguing Question of Jesus-Paul Connection

The relationship between Jesus and Paul is a fascinating area of study, often raising the question of the degree to which Paul's teachings align with those of Jesus, and how Paul came to be such a prominent figure in the establishment of Christian doctrine and practice. This relationship can be explored from several perspectives, including the historical context, their teachings, and the role of revelation.

1. **Historical Context:** Paul, originally known as Saul, was a Jewish Pharisee who initially was a zealous persecutor of the early Christian movement (Acts 8:1-3). His conversion to Christianity following a visionary encounter with Jesus on the road to Damascus (Acts 9:3-6) led to a dramatic shift in his life. After his conversion, Paul became one of the most influential apostles, spreading the teachings of Jesus throughout the Mediterranean world.

2. **Teachings of Jesus and Paul:** When examining the teachings of Jesus (primarily found in the four Gospels) and those of Paul (found in his Epistles), we see both similarities and differences. Both focused on the Kingdom of God, the importance of love and grace, and the transformative power of faith.

Jesus' teachings often utilized parables and were rooted in the Jewish tradition, while Paul's writings, though also grounded in Judaism, were more directed at explaining the significance of Jesus' life, death, and resurrection to a largely Gentile audience. Paul's letters also dealt with practical issues and disputes in the early Christian communities.

3. **Role of Revelation:** Paul's connection to Jesus is significantly defined by his claim of receiving revelations from the risen Christ. In Galatians 1:11-12, Paul asserts, "For I would have you know, brothers, that the gospel that was preached by me is not man's gospel. For I did not receive it from any man, nor was I taught it, but I received it through a revelation of Jesus Christ." This claim undergirds Paul's authority and shapes his role as an apostle.

4. **Paul's Role in Early Christianity:** While Jesus is the central figure of Christianity, Paul played a crucial role in the development of Christian doctrine and the spread of Christianity beyond the Jewish community. Through his missionary journeys and his letters, Paul helped establish Christian communities across the Roman Empire and articulated key Christian doctrines.

In summary, the Jesus-Paul connection is a complex and fascinating topic. While they had no direct interaction during Jesus' earthly ministry, Paul's encounter with the risen Christ and his understanding of Jesus' teachings had a profound impact on his life and work, shaping the course of Christian history.

Jesus and Paul: A Brief Overview of Their Lives

Jesus and Paul are two of the most influential figures in Christianity. Their lives, though separate in time, have had significant and lasting impact on the faith and its followers. Here is a brief overview of their lives:

Jesus of Nazareth:

Jesus' life is primarily documented in the New Testament of the Bible, particularly in the four Gospels (Matthew, Mark, Luke, and John). He was born in Bethlehem, Judea, to Mary, a virgin, as foretold by angelic messages. His birth is celebrated as Christmas in Christianity.

Jesus began his public ministry around the age of 30, which included teaching, healing, and performing miracles. His teachings focused on love, forgiveness, faith, and the Kingdom of God. He gathered a group of disciples, who followed him and learned from his teachings.

Jesus' teachings and actions often challenged the religious authorities of his time, leading to his arrest, trial, and crucifixion under Pontius Pilate, the Roman governor. Christians believe that Jesus was resurrected three days after his death, appeared to many of his followers, and then ascended to heaven. His life, death, and resurrection are central to Christian beliefs about salvation and eternal life.

Paul of Tarsus:

Paul, originally known as Saul, was a Jewish Pharisee from the city of Tarsus in modern-day Turkey. His life is documented in the New Testament, particularly in the Acts of the Apostles and his own letters (the Pauline Epistles).

Paul initially persecuted the followers of Jesus, considering the Christian movement a heretical sect within Judaism. However, on a journey to Damascus to arrest Christians, he experienced a dramatic conversion. According to Acts 9:3-6, a bright light from heaven flashed around him, and he heard the voice of Jesus asking why Paul was persecuting him. Following this event, Paul became a devoted follower of Jesus.

Paul then embarked on several missionary journeys across the Roman Empire, spreading the teachings of Jesus and establishing Christian communities. He also wrote letters to these communities, providing guidance and resolving disputes. These letters form a significant part of the New Testament and provide insight into early Christian beliefs and practices.

Paul was arrested by Roman authorities for his Christian preaching and was eventually taken to Rome for trial. According to tradition, he was martyred in Rome by beheading.

In summary, while Jesus and Paul never met during Jesus' earthly life, Paul's conversion and subsequent work played a crucial role in the expansion and development of Christianity. His understanding and interpretation of Jesus' teachings have significantly shaped Christian theology.

Paul's Conversion: The Road to Damascus Experience

Paul's conversion is one of the most dramatic and influential events in the New Testament. It marked the transformation of Saul of Tarsus, a zealous Pharisee and persecutor of Christians, into Paul, an apostle of Jesus Christ. This conversion event is primarily recounted in the Book of Acts, chapters 9, 22, and 26, with Paul himself referring to it in his letters.

Here is a detailed examination of Paul's conversion, based on the account in Acts 9:1-19:

The Journey to Damascus (Acts 9:1-2):

Saul was fervently dedicated to his Jewish faith and saw the followers of Jesus as a threat to the Jewish tradition. He was not just passively against them; he actively pursued, arrested, and persecuted Christians. Saul had already been involved in the stoning of Stephen, the first Christian martyr (Acts 7:58). Now, he obtained letters from the high priest authorizing him to go to Damascus and arrest any followers of "the Way" (an early name for Christianity) and bring them back to Jerusalem.

The Encounter with Jesus (Acts 9:3-6):

As Saul was nearing Damascus, suddenly a light from heaven flashed around him. He fell to the ground and heard a voice saying to him, "Saul, Saul, why do you persecute me?" When Saul asked who was speaking, the voice replied, "I am Jesus, whom you are persecuting. Now get up and go into the city, and you will be told what you must do." This encounter was a direct revelation of Jesus Christ to Saul, not a vision or a dream, but a real objective encounter, as Paul later affirmed in his letters (1 Corinthians 9:1; 15:8).

Blindness and Ananias's Visit (Acts 9:7-19):

The men traveling with Saul stood speechless, hearing the voice but seeing no one. Saul got up from the ground, but when he opened his eyes, he could see nothing. So, they led him by the hand into Damascus. For three days he was blind and did not eat or drink anything.

In Damascus, a disciple named Ananias was instructed in a vision by the Lord to go to Saul. Despite his fear due to Saul's reputation, Ananias obeyed. He went to Saul, laid his hands on him, and said, "Brother Saul, the Lord—Jesus, who appeared to you on the road as you were coming here—has sent me so that you may see again and be filled with the Holy Spirit." Immediately, something like scales fell from Saul's eyes, and he could see again. He got up and was baptized.

This dramatic conversion experience led to a radical transformation in Saul's life. He began to preach about Jesus in the synagogues, arguing that Jesus is indeed the Son of God, to the astonishment of all who knew his previous fervent opposition to the followers of Jesus. Furthermore, he changed his name from Saul to Paul, signifying his new identity in Christ.

Paul's Understanding of Jesus: An Analysis of His Epistles

Understanding Paul's view of Jesus requires a deep dive into his letters, known as the Pauline Epistles. In total, 14 letters in the New Testament are traditionally attributed to Paul: Romans, 1 and 2 Corinthians, Galatians, Ephesians, Philippians, Colossians, 1 and 2 Thessalonians, 1 and 2 Timothy, Titus, Philemon, and Hebrews. Some of these letters are universally accepted as being written by Paul, while others have been disputed by some scholars.

Here are some key points to consider about Paul's understanding of Jesus based on his letters:

Jesus as the Crucified and Resurrected Messiah (1 Corinthians 15:3-4):

One of the most fundamental aspects of Paul's understanding of Jesus is as the crucified and resurrected Messiah. In 1 Corinthians 15:3-4, Paul writes, "For I delivered to you as of first importance what I also received: that Christ died for our sins in accordance with the Scriptures, that he was buried, that he was raised on the third day in accordance with the Scriptures."

Jesus as the Son of God (Romans 1:3-4):

Paul often refers to Jesus as the Son of God, highlighting his divine nature. In Romans 1:3-4, Paul writes about "his Son, who was descended from David according to the flesh and was declared to be the Son of God in power according to the Spirit of holiness by his resurrection from the dead, Jesus Christ our Lord."

Jesus as the Image of God and the Firstborn of Creation (Colossians 1:15-16):

In Colossians, Paul presents a high Christology, viewing Jesus as the visible image of the invisible God, and the firstborn of all creation. He writes, "He is the image of the invisible God, the firstborn of all creation. For by him all things were created, in heaven and on earth, visible and invisible, whether thrones or dominions or rulers or authorities—all things were created through him and for him."

Jesus as the Fulfillment of the Law (Romans 10:4):

Paul sees Jesus as the end of the law, the one who has fulfilled it and, in doing so, established a new way of righteousness based on faith. He states in Romans 10:4, "For Christ is the end of the law for righteousness to everyone who believes."

Jesus as the High Priest (Hebrews 4:14-16):

In the Epistle to the Hebrews, Paul describes Jesus as the great high priest who has passed through the heavens, sympathizes with our weaknesses, and was in all points tempted as we are, yet without sin. This high priestly role of Jesus is central to the theology of Hebrews.

Jesus as the Head of the Church (Ephesians 5:23):

Paul often speaks of Jesus as the head of the church, the body of which all believers are members. In Ephesians 5:23, he writes, "For the husband is the head of the wife even as Christ is the head of the church, his body, and is himself its Savior."

Jesus as the Coming Lord (1 Thessalonians 4:16-17):

Paul also emphasizes the future return of Jesus, a belief that significantly shaped early Christian eschatology. In 1 Thessalonians 4:16-17, he comforts the believers with the promise of Jesus' return: "For the Lord himself will descend from heaven with a cry of command, with the voice of an archangel, and with the sound of the trumpet of God. And the dead in Christ will rise first. Then we who are alive, who are left, will be caught up together with them in the clouds to meet the Lord in the air, and so we will always be with the Lord."

This passage is one of the key texts underlying Christian beliefs about the Second Coming of Christ, the Resurrection of the Dead, and the Rapture. Paul is affirming a future bodily resurrection and eternal life with Christ, which offers comfort and hope to believers.

In sum, Paul's understanding of Jesus in his epistles is multifaceted. He presents Jesus as the crucified and resurrected Messiah, the Son of God, the image of the invisible God, the fulfillment of the law, the High Priest, the head of the church, and the Lord who will return. His writings continue to significantly shape Christian understanding of Jesus.

The Influence of Jesus' Teachings on Paul's Writings

While Paul never met Jesus during his earthly ministry, his letters demonstrate a deep understanding and integration of Jesus' teachings. The impact of Jesus' teachings on Paul can be seen in several areas:

1. **Love and the Law**: Like Jesus, who taught that the greatest commandments are to love God and neighbor (Matthew 22:37-40), Paul emphasizes love as the fulfillment of the law. In Romans 13:8-10, he writes, "Owe no one anything, except to love each other, for the one who loves another has fulfilled the law."

2. **Humility and Selflessness**: Paul's exhortation in Philippians 2:3-8 echoes Jesus' teachings on humility and selflessness. Paul urges believers to "Do nothing from selfish ambition or conceit, but in humility count others more significant than yourselves." This is similar to Jesus' teachings in Mark 9:35, where He instructs His disciples that "If anyone wants to be first, he must be the very last, and the servant of all."

3. **Forgiveness**: Jesus' teachings on forgiveness are mirrored in Paul's writings. In Ephesians 4:32, Paul instructs, "Be kind to one another, tenderhearted, forgiving one another, as God in Christ forgave you." This echoes Jesus' teachings on forgiveness in Matthew 6:14-15.

4. **Kingdom of God**: Both Jesus and Paul preached about the Kingdom of God. Jesus' ministry was characterized by His proclamation of the Kingdom (Mark 1:15), and Paul also emphasized the Kingdom in his teachings (Acts 28:31).

5. **Faith and Justification**: Paul's central theme of justification by faith echoes Jesus' teachings on the primacy of faith. In Romans 3:28, Paul declares, "For we hold that one is justified by faith apart from works of the law." This aligns with Jesus' teachings, such as in John 3:16, where faith in the Son of God leads to eternal life.

These examples demonstrate the profound influence of Jesus' teachings on Paul's writings. Even though Paul did not directly learn from Jesus during His earthly ministry, his writings reflect a deep understanding and alignment with Jesus' teachings.

Paul's Interpretation of Jesus' Death and Resurrection

Paul's interpretation of Jesus' death and resurrection forms the cornerstone of his theology and message in his epistles. His understanding of these events deeply shaped his views on salvation, justification, and Christian living.

1. **Jesus' Death as Atonement for Sin**: Paul sees Jesus' death as a sacrificial offering that atones for human sin. In Romans 3:23-25, he writes, "For all have sinned and fall short of the glory of God, and are justified by his grace as a gift, through the redemption that is in Christ Jesus, whom God put forward as a propitiation by his blood, to be received by faith." Paul interprets Jesus' death as a sacrifice that satisfies God's justice, thereby enabling reconciliation between God and humanity.

2. **Jesus' Resurrection as Assurance of Salvation**: Paul views Jesus' resurrection as a confirmation of God's power over death and a guarantee of believers' resurrection. In 1 Corinthians 15:20-22, he declares, "But in fact Christ has been raised from the dead, the firstfruits of those who have fallen asleep. For as by a man came death, by a man has come also the resurrection of the dead. For as in Adam all die, so also in Christ shall all be made alive."

3. **Death and Resurrection as a Model for Christian Living**: Paul uses the metaphor of dying and rising with Christ to describe the transformative power of faith in the believer's life. In Romans 6:4, he writes, "We were therefore buried with him through baptism into death in order that, just as Christ was raised from the dead through the glory of the Father, we too may live a new life." For Paul, Jesus' death and resurrection is not just a historical event, but a spiritual reality that believers participate in, signifying the transition from the old life of sin to a new life in Christ.

4. **Jesus' Death and Resurrection as the Fulfillment of Scripture**: Paul often links the death and resurrection of Jesus to the fulfillment of Old Testament prophecies, underlining the continuity of God's plan of salvation. In 1 Corinthians 15:3-4, he writes, "For I delivered to you as of first importance

what I also received: that Christ died for our sins in accordance with the Scriptures, that he was buried, that he was raised on the third day in accordance with the Scriptures."

Thus, for Paul, Jesus' death and resurrection are pivotal events that provide the basis for salvation, inspire transformation in the believer's life, and fulfill God's redemptive plan as revealed in Scripture.

Jesus and Paul: Comparing Their Views on the Kingdom of God

The concept of the "Kingdom of God" (or "Kingdom of Heaven" in Matthew's Gospel) is central to both Jesus' and Paul's teachings, although each presents it from a slightly different perspective. These differences likely arise from their differing contexts and audiences, but they both see the Kingdom as a present reality and future hope, as a divine reign characterized by righteousness, peace, and joy.

Jesus' View on the Kingdom of God

Jesus' teachings about the Kingdom of God permeate the Gospels. He often spoke of it in parables, such as the Parable of the Mustard Seed (Matthew 13:31-32), the Parable of the Wheat and the Tares (Matthew 13:24-30), and the Parable of the Leaven (Luke 13:20-21). These parables often emphasize the Kingdom's mysterious growth and transformative power.

Furthermore, Jesus presents the Kingdom of God as both a present reality and a future hope. In Luke 17:21, He declares, "behold, the kingdom of God is in the midst of you," suggesting a present, spiritual reality. Yet, He also instructs His followers to pray for the Kingdom to come (Matthew 6:10) and speaks of it as a future inheritance (Matthew 25:34), indicating a future, physical reality.

Paul's View on the Kingdom of God

Paul's view of the Kingdom also carries this "already but not yet" tension. He sees believers as already belonging to the Kingdom (Colossians 1:13) while still awaiting its full revelation (2 Timothy 4:1).

In Romans 14:17, he describes the Kingdom of God as "righteousness and peace and joy in the Holy Spirit." This suggests that the Kingdom is not merely a geographical or political entity but a new order of life brought about by the Spirit, marked by restored relationships with God and others.

Paul also emphasizes the ethical implications of the Kingdom. He repeatedly warns that those who persist in unrighteous behavior will not inherit the Kingdom of God (1 Corinthians 6:9-10; Galatians 5:21; Ephesians 5:5). This reflects his view of the Kingdom as a transformative reality that should impact a believer's conduct.

Comparison

Both Jesus and Paul present the Kingdom of God as a central element of God's plan, a realm where God's will is done, and His rule acknowledged. They both see it as already present in some sense, yet fully realized in the future. They also both connect the Kingdom to ethical transformation: living under God's reign should produce righteousness, peace, and joy. However, while Jesus often uses parables to describe the Kingdom's nature and growth, Paul tends to focus more on its ethical implications and the role of the Spirit in bringing it about.

Jesus' Ethical Teachings and Paul's Moral Instructions

Jesus' ethical teachings and Paul's moral instructions both align with the broader moral framework of the Bible. They address the relationship between believers and God, as well as their relationships with each other and with the wider world. Both Jesus and Paul emphasize love, forgiveness, humility, and righteousness as key virtues for believers.

Jesus' Ethical Teachings

Jesus' ethical teachings can be seen throughout the Gospels. A central teaching is found in the Sermon on the Mount in Matthew 5-7. Here, Jesus provides a radical reinterpretation of the Law, focusing not just on outward actions but also on inward attitudes. For example, he teaches that anger is morally equivalent to murder (Matthew 5:21-22), and lust to adultery (Matthew 5:27-28).

Jesus also teaches the importance of love and forgiveness. In Matthew 22:37-40, he summarizes the Law and Prophets as loving God with all one's heart, soul, and mind, and loving one's neighbor as oneself. He teaches his disciples to forgive others as they have been forgiven (Matthew 6:14-15), and to love even their enemies (Matthew 5:44).

Paul's Moral Instructions

Paul's moral instructions are scattered throughout his epistles, often tailored to the specific situations of the communities he is writing to. Nevertheless, some common themes emerge.

Like Jesus, Paul emphasizes the primacy of love. In 1 Corinthians 13, he famously writes that love is the greatest virtue, more important than spiritual gifts or personal sacrifice. He also echoes Jesus' teaching on love fulfilling the Law, writing in Romans 13:8 that "he who loves his neighbor has fulfilled the law."

Paul also offers detailed moral instructions. In his letters to the Ephesians and Colossians, he gives instructions for Christian households (Ephesians 5:21-6:9, Colossians 3:18-4:1). In Romans 12-13, he gives a sweeping overview of Christian ethics, encouraging humility, patience, generosity, and respect for authorities. In 1 Corinthians 6:9-10 and Galatians 5:19-21, he warns against a variety of vices, including sexual immorality, idolatry, strife, and envy.

Comparison

Both Jesus and Paul teach that love is central to Christian ethics. They both see morality as more than just outward actions; it also involves the inner attitudes of the heart. They both emphasize humility, forgiveness, and love for others, including enemies. However, their teachings are not identical. Jesus often challenges the religious status quo and uses parables and hyperbole to push his listeners to deeper understanding. Paul, on the other hand, tends to give more practical instructions, often dealing with issues specific to the communities he is writing to.

The Role of the Holy Spirit in Jesus' and Paul's Teachings

Both Jesus and Paul emphasize the role of the Holy Spirit in the lives of believers, highlighting the Spirit as an essential aspect of the Christian faith. They address the Holy Spirit's work in empowering, guiding, and transforming the lives of those who follow Jesus.

Jesus' Teachings on the Holy Spirit

Jesus speaks about the Holy Spirit on multiple occasions throughout the Gospels. In John 14:16-17, Jesus promises to send the Holy Spirit, whom he calls the "Helper" or "Comforter," to be with his disciples after his departure. He says that the Spirit will abide with them forever and will dwell within them, guiding them in truth and helping them to remember Jesus' teachings (John 14:26).

In John 16:7-15, Jesus emphasizes the importance of the Holy Spirit's work, stating that it is better for him to go away so that the Spirit can come. He explains that the Spirit will convict the world of sin, righteousness, and judgment. Additionally, the Holy Spirit will guide the disciples in all truth and glorify Jesus by revealing things to come.

In the Synoptic Gospels, Jesus emphasizes the role of the Holy Spirit in empowering his followers for ministry. He tells his disciples that they will receive power when the Holy Spirit comes upon them, enabling them to be his witnesses (Acts 1:8). He also assures them that, when brought before authorities, the Holy Spirit will give them the words to speak (Matthew 10:19-20, Mark 13:11, Luke 12:11-12).

Paul's Teachings on the Holy Spirit

Paul also places great importance on the role of the Holy Spirit in the lives of believers. In Romans 8, he highlights the Holy Spirit's role in empowering believers to live righteous lives, stating that the Spirit enables them to fulfill the requirements of the law (Romans 8:4). He also asserts that the Holy Spirit dwells within believers and gives life to their mortal bodies (Romans 8:9-11).

Paul emphasizes the Holy Spirit's role in transforming believers, describing them as a "new creation" (2 Corinthians 5:17) and attributing this change to the work of the Spirit (2 Corinthians 3:18). He also mentions that the Holy Spirit produces fruit in the lives of believers, such as love, joy, peace, patience, kindness, goodness, faithfulness, gentleness, and self-control (Galatians 5:22-23).

Furthermore, Paul speaks about the Holy Spirit's role in uniting and equipping the Church. In 1 Corinthians 12, he discusses spiritual gifts, asserting that they are given by the Holy Spirit to build up the body of Christ. He teaches that all believers are baptized by the Holy Spirit into one body (1 Corinthians 12:13) and that the Spirit distributes gifts according to his will (1 Corinthians 12:11).

Comparison

Both Jesus and Paul emphasize the essential role of the Holy Spirit in the lives of believers. They describe the Spirit as a source of empowerment, guidance, transformation, and unity within the Christian community. While Jesus focuses on the Spirit's work in the context of his own departure and the continuation of his ministry through his followers, Paul expands upon the practical implications of the Spirit's presence in the lives of individual believers and the Church as a whole.

Jesus, Paul, and the Law: Similarities and Differences

The relationship between Jesus, Paul, and the Law (the Torah, or the first five books of the Old Testament) is a complex and highly studied aspect of Christian theology. Both Jesus and Paul affirmed the importance of the Law, but they also brought new perspectives on its role and function within the framework of the new covenant inaugurated through Jesus' life, death, and resurrection.

Jesus and the Law

In the Sermon on the Mount, Jesus clarifies his relationship with the Law: "Do not think that I have come to abolish the Law or the Prophets; I have not come to abolish them but to fulfill them" (Matthew 5:17). He goes on to stress the importance of the commandments and warns against breaking them (Matthew 5:19). However, throughout the Gospels, Jesus introduces a deeper understanding of the Law, focusing on its spirit rather than just its letter. For instance, he expands the commandment against murder to include anger (Matthew 5:21-22) and the commandment against adultery to include lust (Matthew 5:27-28).

Jesus also criticized the religious leaders of his time for their legalistic and hypocritical approach to the Law, accusing them of neglecting the "weightier matters of the law: justice and mercy and faithfulness" (Matthew 23:23). Furthermore, Jesus often prioritized mercy and human need over strict Sabbath observance, as seen in his healings on the Sabbath (Mark 3:1-6, Luke 13:10-17).

Paul and the Law

Paul, a former Pharisee, was deeply knowledgeable about the Law. His teachings on the Law are complex and nuanced, varying somewhat based on the context and audience of his letters.

On the one hand, Paul affirms the value of the Law, calling it "holy and righteous and good" (Romans 7:12). He also writes that the Law is not nullified by faith, but rather upheld (Romans 3:31).

On the other hand, Paul asserts that righteousness cannot be achieved through the Law. He states, "For by works of the law no human being will be justified in his sight" (Romans 3:20). He explains that the Law serves to reveal sin (Romans 7:7-13) and to lead people to Christ (Galatians 3:24).

Paul emphasizes that believers are freed from the Law through Christ, stating, "For Christ is the end of the law for righteousness to everyone who believes" (Romans 10:4). He teaches that Christians live under the "law of the Spirit" (Romans 8:2), and that the Spirit produces in them the righteous requirement of the Law (Romans 8:4).

Similarities and Differences

Both Jesus and Paul uphold the importance of the Law but also reorient its function in the light of the gospel. They both criticize legalistic or hypocritical applications of the Law and emphasize the spirit of the Law, including love, mercy, and justice.

However, there are also key differences. Jesus, living under the old covenant, observes and interprets the Law, while introducing a deeper, inward understanding of its commandments. Paul, on the other hand, writing after the death and resurrection of Jesus, emphasizes the new covenant reality that righteousness is through faith in Christ, not the works of the Law. He affirms the Law's goodness and its role in leading people to Christ but stresses that believers are now under the law of the Spirit.

The Concept of Love in the Teachings of Jesus and Paul

The concept of love features prominently in the teachings of both Jesus and Paul, and it serves as a foundational principle in their ethical and theological instructions.

Jesus and Love

Jesus' teachings about love were revolutionary and central to his message. In the Gospels, Jesus summarizes all the Law and the Prophets in the commandments to love God and love one's neighbor (Matthew 22:36-40). Love for God involves the whole being: heart, soul, and mind. Love for one's neighbor is likened to the love one has for oneself.

Furthermore, Jesus extends the definition of 'neighbor' to include even one's enemies, challenging his followers to love and pray for those who persecute them (Matthew 5:43-48). This radical commandment was a departure from the common "love your friend, hate your enemy" ethic of the time.

Jesus also demonstrates and commands love within his group of followers. At the Last Supper, he gives his disciples a new commandment: "Just as I have loved you, you also are to love one another. By this all people will know that you are my disciples, if you have love for one another" (John 13:34-35).

Paul and Love

Paul also emphasizes the central role of love in his teachings. In his letters, he often encourages the early Christian communities to love one another (Romans 13:8, 1 Thessalonians 4:9, 1 Peter 1:22). He echoes Jesus' teaching on love for enemies, urging believers not to repay evil for evil and to overcome evil with good (Romans 12:17-21).

In the famous "love chapter," 1 Corinthians 13, Paul extols the virtues of love, stating that without love, even the most impressive spiritual gifts are worthless. He describes love as patient, kind, not envious or boastful, not arrogant or rude, not insisting on its own way, not irritable or resentful, not rejoicing in wrongdoing, but rejoicing with the truth. Love, according to Paul, bears all things, believes all things, hopes all things, and endures all things. He concludes by saying, "So now faith, hope, and love abide, these three; but the greatest of these is love" (1 Corinthians 13:13).

Similarities and Differences

Both Jesus and Paul stress the paramount importance of love as the key ethical norm for the Christian community. They both expand the commandment to love one's neighbor to include even one's enemies and those outside the community. The love they speak of is not merely emotional affection but active goodwill and self-giving for the sake of others.

Differences in their teachings on love are more a matter of emphasis and context than fundamental disagreement. Jesus, in his earthly ministry, focuses on love as the fulfillment of the Law and the distinctive mark of his disciples. Paul, addressing specific issues in the early Christian communities, emphasizes love as the crowning virtue and the binding force in the body of Christ.

Christology: Paul's Perception of Jesus as the Christ

Paul's perception of Jesus as the Christ or Messiah is central to his teachings and forms the basis of his theology, often referred to as Pauline Christology.

Jesus as the Christ in Paul's Writings

Paul's writings in the New Testament frequently refer to Jesus as the Christ, which is the Greek equivalent of the Hebrew term "Messiah," both meaning "anointed one." He unequivocally identifies Jesus as the long-awaited Messiah, the savior of humanity.

In his letters, Paul often uses the title "Christ" almost as if it were part of Jesus' name, showing how deeply ingrained this understanding was in his theology. For instance, in Romans 1:1-4, Paul introduces himself as "a servant of Christ Jesus, called to be an apostle, set apart for the gospel of God, which he promised beforehand through his prophets in the holy Scriptures, concerning his Son, who was descended from David according to the flesh and was declared to be the Son of God in power according to the Spirit of holiness by his resurrection from the dead, Jesus Christ our Lord."

Jesus as the Son of God

Paul also affirms Jesus' divine nature, recognizing him as the Son of God. His understanding of Jesus as the Son of God is rooted in the resurrection. To Paul, the resurrection of Jesus is God's definitive act of raising Jesus to divine status, declaring him to be the Son of God with power (Romans 1:4).

Jesus as the Savior

Furthermore, Paul views Jesus as the Savior, the one who brings salvation to humanity. According to Paul, through Jesus' sacrificial death and resurrection, human beings are justified and reconciled to God (Romans 5:1-11). This is often referred to as the doctrine of "justification by faith," which asserts that faith in Christ, rather than adherence to the Law, is the means of salvation.

Jesus as the Lord

Additionally, Paul refers to Jesus as "Lord" (Kyrios), a title of respect and divinity in the Greek-speaking world. "Jesus as the Lord" is a common phrase used in Christian theology, which refers to the belief that Jesus Christ is not simply a human being or a prophet but is in fact divine. The term "Lord" is often used to describe Jesus in the New Testament, which emphasizes his divine status and authority. In particular, the Greek word Kyrios is frequently used to refer to Jesus, which carries the sense of "Lord" or "Master." In 1 Corinthians 8:6, Paul writes, "yet for us there is one God, the Father, from whom are all things and for whom we exist, and one Lord, Jesus Christ, through whom are all things and through whom we exist."

Jesus as the Image of God

Paul also presents Jesus as the "image of God" (2 Corinthians 4:4; Colossians 1:15). In Colossians, he describes Jesus as "the image of the invisible God, the firstborn of all creation." This suggests that Jesus is the perfect and ultimate revelation of God, showing us who God is.

In summary, Paul's perception of Jesus as the Christ is multifaceted, encompassing his identity as the Messiah, the Son of God, the Savior, the Lord, and the Image of God. His Christology profoundly shaped the development of early Christian doctrine and continues to influence Christian theology today.

Paul's Role in the Early Church: An Extension of Jesus' Mission

Paul's role in the early church can be seen as an extension of Jesus' mission. The Apostle Paul, once a persecutor of the early Christian community, experienced a dramatic conversion on the road to Damascus, as recounted in Acts 9. After his conversion, Paul became one of the most influential figures in the early Christian Church, and his missionary journeys, letters, and teachings significantly shaped the course of Christianity.

Paul as a Missionary

Paul is well known for his missionary journeys throughout the Eastern Mediterranean. In his capacity as a missionary, he established churches in key cities like Ephesus, Corinth, Philippi, and Thessalonica. His mission was not just to Jews but to Gentiles as well. This was a significant extension of Jesus' mission, as Jesus primarily preached to the Jews during his earthly ministry. Paul's outreach to the Gentiles was in line with Jesus' command to the apostles to spread the gospel to all nations (Matthew 28:19-20). Paul's commitment to this mission can be seen in his letter to the Romans, where he states, "I am under obligation both to Greeks and to barbarians, both to the wise and to the foolish. So I am eager to preach the gospel to you also who are in Rome." (Romans 1:14-15).

Paul as a Teacher

Paul's letters, or epistles, are a significant portion of the New Testament and form the backbone of much Christian theology. His teachings elucidate the implications of Jesus' life, death, and resurrection. He interpreted Jesus' teachings for the emerging Christian communities, guiding them on issues of faith, ethics, community life, and the nature of God, Christ, and salvation. His teaching role can be seen in his many letters where he instructs, admonishes, encourages, and prays for the various churches.

Paul as a Shepherd

Paul's pastoral care for the churches he founded is evident in his letters. He nurtured these communities, addressing their problems, correcting their errors, and guiding their growth in faith. His genuine concern for them is evident in passages like 2 Corinthians 11:28, where he says, "And, apart from other things, there is the daily pressure on me of my anxiety for all the churches."

Paul as a Sufferer for Christ

Paul's dedication to spreading the gospel often brought him into conflict with both Jewish and Roman authorities. He faced many hardships, including imprisonment, beatings, and shipwrecks. He considered his sufferings a participation in the sufferings of Christ and a testament to his commitment to Christ's mission (2 Corinthians 1:5, Philippians 3:10).

In conclusion, Paul's role in the early Church was a profound extension of Jesus' mission. He carried the message of Christ beyond the confines of Jerusalem to the Gentile world, established churches, provided teaching and pastoral care, and suffered for the sake of the gospel. His writings continue to provide instruction, encouragement, and inspiration for Christians today.

Debates and Controversies Surrounding the Jesus-Paul Relationship

The relationship between Jesus and Paul, particularly the nature of Paul's understanding and interpretation of Jesus' teachings, has been a subject of considerable debate among scholars and theologians. Several controversies and debates that have emerged surrounding the Jesus-Paul relationship include:

1. Paul's Conversion or Call?

One debate concerns whether Paul's Damascus Road experience (Acts 9:1-19) was a conversion from Judaism to Christianity or a call to apostleship within Judaism. Some scholars suggest that Paul did not convert but rather received a new revelation that expanded his understanding of his existing Jewish faith. They point to Philippians 3:4-6, where Paul argues that if anyone has reason to have confidence in the flesh, he has more, being circumcised on the eighth day, of the people of Israel, of the tribe of Benjamin, a Hebrew of Hebrews; as to the law, a Pharisee; as to zeal, a persecutor of the church; as to righteousness under the law, blameless.

2. Continuity or Discontinuity between Jesus and Paul?

A major controversy revolves around the continuity or discontinuity between Jesus' teachings and Paul's teachings. Some argue that Paul substantially altered Jesus' teachings to create a new religion, diverging from Jesus' original message. Others maintain that Paul faithfully interpreted and transmitted Jesus' teachings, and that apparent differences can be attributed to their different contexts and audiences. For example, Jesus' teachings were primarily directed to a Jewish audience during his earthly ministry, while Paul's mission was largely to the Gentiles.

3. Paul's Christology

Another area of debate is Paul's Christology, or understanding of Jesus as the Christ. Some argue that Paul's high Christology - seeing Jesus as preexistent and partaking in the divine nature (Philippians 2:5-11, Colossians 1:15-20) - is in sharp contrast with the synoptic gospels' presentation of Jesus. Others counter that the Gospel of John presents a similarly high Christology, and that Paul's writings are consistent with a development of early Christological understanding.

4. Paul's View on the Law

Paul's view on the Law is another contentious topic. Some claim that Paul negated the Torah, citing verses like Romans 6:14, "For sin will have no dominion over you, since you are not under law but under grace." Others argue that Paul's teachings about the Law are more nuanced, suggesting that the Law has a continued role, but it's no longer the basis for justification before God (Romans 3:21-31).

From a perspective that aligns with what the Bible teaches, the following responses could be given to these debates and controversies:

1. Paul's Conversion or Call?

Paul's Damascus Road experience is considered both a conversion and a calling. It marked a radical transformation in his life, from persecuting followers of Jesus to becoming one of the most zealous apostles. In Galatians 1:15-16, Paul himself says that God "set me apart before I was born, and who called me by his grace, was pleased to reveal his Son to me, in order that I might preach him among the Gentiles." This indicates that his encounter with Jesus was more than just a new understanding within Judaism; it was a transformative event that led him to embrace Jesus as the Messiah and to share this revelation with the Gentiles.

2. Continuity or Discontinuity between Jesus and Paul?

The Bible affirms the continuity between Jesus and Paul. The Holy Spirit inspired both the teachings of Jesus recorded in the Gospels and the writings of Paul, ensuring their theological coherence. Differences in emphasis or audience context do not imply contradiction or a substantial alteration of Jesus' original message. Instead, they reflect the different circumstances and purposes of Jesus' earthly ministry and Paul's apostolic mission.

3. Paul's Christology

The Bible affirms the deity of Jesus Christ, a belief clearly reflected in Paul's writings. For example, in Colossians 1:15-20, Paul describes Jesus as the image of the invisible God, the firstborn over all creation, and the one in whom all the fullness of

God was pleased to dwell. This high Christology is not seen as being in contrast with the synoptic gospels but rather as a more detailed exposition of the divine nature of Jesus, fully in line with the Gospel of John.

4. Paul's View on the Law

Paul's writings on the Law are understood to reflect the new covenant in Christ. The Law, in this perspective, is not negated but fulfilled in Christ (Matthew 5:17). Paul's teachings do not dismiss the Law but instead affirm that it is no longer the means of achieving righteousness before God. In Romans 3:21-31, Paul explains that righteousness comes through faith in Jesus Christ, a gift of grace, and not through the works of the Law.

These responses reflect the belief that the Bible, including the teachings of Jesus and the writings of Paul, presents a consistent, coherent message of God's redemptive plan for humanity through Jesus Christ. They assert that seeming tensions or controversies are reconciled when the entirety of Scripture is taken into account, interpreted in a way that is consistent with its overall message.

Paul's Influence on Christianity: A Jesus-Paul Synergy

Paul's influence on Christianity is far-reaching and significant, stemming from his writings in the New Testament, his missionary journeys, and his theological contributions. His relationship with Jesus, while not direct during Jesus' earthly ministry, is nevertheless profound and shaped by his transformative encounter with the risen Christ on the road to Damascus (Acts 9:1-19).

Paul's theological contributions are substantial and form a critical part of Christian doctrine. He developed some of the most foundational concepts of Christianity, including the understanding of Jesus as the Christ, the significance of the cross, the role of faith, the nature of the church, and the future hope of Christians.

1. **Understanding of Jesus as the Christ**: Paul's writings offer a rich Christology. He affirms the deity of Christ (Colossians 1:15-20), His role as the mediator between God and humanity (1 Timothy 2:5), and His resurrection as the cornerstone of Christian faith (1 Corinthians 15:14).

2. **Significance of the Cross**: Paul places a strong emphasis on the crucifixion of Jesus as the means through which sin was dealt with and salvation was achieved. In Romans 5:8, he writes: "But God demonstrates his own love for us in this: While we were still sinners, Christ died for us."

3. **The Role of Faith**: For Paul, faith is the means through which people receive the righteousness of God. In Romans 1:17, he writes, "For in the gospel the

righteousness of God is revealed—a righteousness that is by faith from first to last, just as it is written: 'The righteous will live by faith.'"

4. **Nature of the Church**: Paul uses the metaphor of the body to describe the church, emphasizing unity in diversity (1 Corinthians 12:12-31). He also develops the concept of the church as the "bride of Christ" (Ephesians 5:25-27).

5. **Future Hope**: Paul presents a clear eschatological perspective. He speaks of the return of Christ (1 Thessalonians 4:16-17), the resurrection of the dead (1 Corinthians 15:52), and the future inheritance of believers (Ephesians 1:13-14).

Paul's influence on Christianity, therefore, is not separate from Jesus but builds upon and expands the teachings and work of Christ. He was instrumental in spreading Christianity beyond the Jewish community to the Gentile world, broadening the understanding of Christianity as a universal faith. Through his writings, Paul helps to interpret the significance of Jesus, His teachings, and His work, solidifying key doctrines and practices that are foundational to Christianity.

CHAPTER 9 Pauline Forgeries: Myth or Reality?

The authorship of the Pauline epistles is a significant topic of scholarly debate amongst the liberal and moderate Bible scholars. While seven of the letters are generally accepted as being authentic, seven are disputed. The seven disputed letters, often referred to as the Deutero-Pauline letters, which some scholars suggest might be forgeries (written by Paul's followers after his death or by others using his name). What we will provide below is **(1)** paragraph written for with some Bible background, context, and proof for Pauline authorship. **(2)** The evidence presented in bullet points. **(3)** Lastly, the late world-renowned conservative evangelical Christian apologist, Norman L. Geisler with his evidence for Pauline authorship. These seven supposed forgeries include:

The Epistle of Paul to the Ephesians

Visualize yourself in prison, persecuted for your fervent dedication as a Christian missionary. Cut off from physically visiting and supporting the congregations you have established, what can you do? Can you not correspond with those who have embraced Christianity through your preaching? Are they not curious about your well-being and in need of encouragement? Indeed, they are! Thus, you follow in the footsteps of the apostle Paul, who composed letters while imprisoned in Rome for the first time around 59-61 C.E. Having appealed to Caesar, Paul enjoyed some freedom to engage in activities while awaiting trial. It was during this period that he penned the letter "To the Ephesians," most likely in 60 or 61 C.E., dispatching it with the assistance of Tychicus, accompanied by Onesimus. (Eph. 6:21; Col. 4:7-9)

From the very first word, Paul identifies himself as the author and refers to himself as "the prisoner in the Lord" four times throughout the letter. (Eph. 1:1; 3:1, 13; 4:1; 6:20) Despite arguments to the contrary, the authenticity of Paul's authorship remains unassailable. The Chester Beatty Papyrus No. 2 (P46), dated around 100-150 C.E., contains 86 leaves of a codex that includes Paul's epistles, among which is the Epistle to the Ephesians. This attests to its inclusion among Paul's writings at that time.

Early church writers also confirm Paul's authorship of the letter specifically addressed "To the Ephesians." For instance, Irenaeus, a second-century C.E. figure, quoted Ephesians 5:30, saying, "As the blessed Paul says in the epistle to the Ephesians, that we are members of his body." Clement of Alexandria, also from the same period, cited Ephesians 5:21, reporting, "Wherefore, also, in the epistle to the Ephesians he writes, Be subject one to another in the fear of God." Likewise, Origen, writing in the early third century C.E., quoted Ephesians 1:4, stating, "But also the apostle in the epistle to the Ephesians uses the same language when he says, Who chose us before the foundation of the world." Eusebius, a renowned authority on early Christian history (260-342 C.E.), included Ephesians in the canon of the Bible, while other early church writers consistently referred to Ephesians as part of the inspired Scriptures.

Regarding the destination of the letter, some manuscripts such as the Chester Beatty Papyrus, Vatican Manuscript No. 1209, and the Sinaitic Manuscript omit the words "in Ephesus" in chapter 1, verse 1, leaving the exact recipient uncertain. Furthermore, there is an absence of personal greetings to individuals in Ephesus, despite Paul's extended ministry there for three years. These factors have led to speculation that the letter might have been intended for another location or possibly served as a circular letter for the congregations in Asia Minor, including Ephesus. However, most other manuscripts include the words "in Ephesus," and as mentioned earlier, early church writers universally regarded it as a letter addressed to the Ephesians.

Understanding the historical background sheds light on the purpose of this epistle. In the first century C.E., Ephesus was renowned for its sorcery, magic, astrology, and the worship of the fertility goddess Artemis. A magnificent temple, considered one of the seven wonders of the ancient world, was erected in honor of the goddess, attracting tourists from all corners of the earth. The temple's platform measured approximately 240 feet wide and 418 feet long, with the temple itself spanning about 164 feet wide and 343 feet long. Adorned with 100 towering marble columns, each standing around 55 feet tall, the temple's roof boasted large white marble tiles. The craftsmanship was impeccable, with gold used instead of mortar to join the marble blocks. During festivals, the city would be flooded with hundreds of thousands of visitors, seeking to witness the splendor of the temple. The silversmiths of Ephesus profited greatly from selling small silver shrines of Artemis as cherished souvenirs to pilgrims.

During his second missionary journey, Paul briefly visited Ephesus, leaving Aquila and Priscilla behind to continue the work while he moved on. (Acts 18:18-21) However, on his third missionary journey, Paul returned to Ephesus and remained there for approximately three years, diligently proclaiming "The Way" and teaching many. (Acts 19:8-10; 20:31) Paul's tireless efforts in Ephesus included working diligently at his trade in the morning, teaching in the hall from 11 a.m. to 4 p.m., and engaging in evangelistic endeavors that extended into the late hours of the night. (Acts 20:34, 35, 20:20, 21, 31) Yet, his fearless denunciation of idolatry and the use of images in worship, which directly challenged the lucrative business of the silversmiths, sparked a violent uproar. Eventually, Paul was compelled to leave the city due to the ensuing turmoil. (Acts 19:23–20:1)

Now, confined in prison, Paul contemplates the challenges faced by the Ephesian congregation, surrounded by a sea of pagan worshipers and overshadowed by the awe-inspiring temple of Artemis. These born-again Christians undoubtedly required the profound illustration that Paul provides—an illustration of them constituting "a holy temple" where the Lord dwells through His Spirit. (Eph. 2:21) The revelation of "the mystery" to the Ephesians, pertaining to God's administration and His plan to restore unity and peace through Jesus Christ, surely served as a great source of inspiration and comfort to them. (1:9, 10) Paul emphasizes the unity of both Jews and Gentiles in Christ, urging them towards oneness and unity. Now, we can grasp the purpose, value, and unmistakable inspiration underlying this epistle.

Here is a summary of several pieces of evidence that prove Paul's authorship:

1. **Direct Claim**: The epistle itself begins with the claim of Pauline authorship. Ephesians 1:1 states: "Paul, an apostle of Christ Jesus by the will of God, To the saints who are in Ephesus, and are faithful in Christ Jesus."

2. **Writing Style and Vocabulary**: While some scholars argue that Ephesians has a unique style and vocabulary compared to other Pauline letters, it's important to note that the letter shares many similarities with the undisputed Pauline letters. For instance, it contains characteristic Pauline phrases and theological concepts.

3. **Theological Consistency**: The theological ideas presented in Ephesians align with those found in other letters attributed to Paul. Themes such as the unity of the church, the importance of love, the work of Christ, the role of the Spirit, and the hope of resurrection are consistent with Pauline theology.

4. **Comparison with Other Pauline Letters**: Ephesians shares a strong relationship with Colossians, another letter attributed to Paul, with some portions nearly identical. This suggests a common authorship.

5. **Early Christian Tradition**: Early church tradition attributed the letter to Paul. It was accepted as Pauline by Church Fathers like Irenaeus, Clement of Alexandria, and Tertullian. It's also included in the Chester Beatty Papyri (P46), a collection of Paul's letters from around 100-150 CE.

6. **Canonical Acceptance**: The epistle was universally accepted as part of the canon, indicating the early church's belief in its Pauline authorship.

On this the Late Dr. Norman L. Geisler wrote,

Who Wrote It?

Ephesians was written by Paul, the apostle to the Gentiles.

Internal Evidence

The internal evidence that the apostle Paul wrote this book is very strong. (1) There is the explicit claim in two places in the book that Paul is the author (1:1; 3:1). (2) The theology of the book is Pauline, stressing the exalted Christ, unity in the church, and the grace of God. (3) The vocabulary is Pauline, with minor deviations fitting the theme of the book. In fact the style is more Pauline than any imitators could have been. The use of a pseudonym was not practiced by early Christians. (4) Ephesians has close similarities to Colossians (see chapter 16), which also has strong evidence for Pauline authorship. Here again, the differences between the two books fits their respective themes.

External Evidence

The evidence from other sources also supports Paul's authorship. The earliest manuscripts of the book all bear Paul's name, indicating it was accepted into the canon of Scripture as a work of Paul. The early Fathers support Paul's authorship. Citations from this book with Paul's name on it are found in both Ignatius and Polycarp among the earliest Fathers and all the other main Fathers from Irenaeus to Augustine after them.[134]

The Epistle of Paul to the Colossians

Leaving Ephesus behind, two men embarked on a journey through Asia Minor, following the Maeander (Menderes) River. As they reached the Lycus tributary in Phrygia, they veered southeast, tracing the river through a picturesque valley adorned with lush green pastures and abundant flocks of sheep, which provided a vital source

---

[134] Norman L. Geisler, *A Popular Survey of the New Testament* (Grand Rapids, MI: Baker Books, 2014), 171–172.

of income for the region. On their right stood the prosperous city of Laodicea, serving as the administrative center for the district under Roman rule. To their left, across the river, they caught sight of Hierapolis, renowned for its temples and hot springs. Both cities housed Christian congregations, as did the smaller town of Colossae, located about ten miles further up the valley.

Their ultimate destination was Colossae, and both travelers were followers of Christ. One of them, named Onesimus, hailed from Colossae and was returning to his master, who was a member of the local congregation. Accompanying him was Tychicus, a fellow believer who was a free man. Both individuals served as envoys from the apostle Paul, entrusted with delivering a letter addressed to the "faithful brothers in Christ at Colossae." Although Paul himself never visited Colossae, the congregation, comprised mostly of Gentiles, was likely founded by Epaphras, who had labored among them and was currently with Paul in Rome. (Col. 1:2, 7; 4:12)

The apostle Paul explicitly identified himself as the author of this letter, as indicated in its opening and closing statements. (1:1; 4:18) He also stated that he wrote it while in prison. This corresponds to his initial imprisonment in Rome, which took place from 59 to 61 C.E., during which he composed various letters of encouragement, including the epistle to the Colossians, which was sent alongside the letter to Philemon. (Col. 4:7-9; Philem. 10, 23) Evidently, these letters were written around the same time, as they share numerous ideas and phrases.

There is no reason to doubt the authenticity of the letter to the Colossians. Its inclusion alongside other Pauline epistles in the Chester Beatty Papyrus No. 2 (P46), dating to around 100-150 C.E., demonstrates that early Christians recognized it as one of Paul's letters. The genuineness of this letter is attested to by the same early authorities who vouched for the authenticity of Paul's other epistles.

What prompted Paul to write this letter to the Colossians? Firstly, Onesimus was returning to Colossae, likely triggering Paul's desire to address the congregation. Additionally, Epaphras had recently joined Paul, and his report on the situation in Colossae likely provided further impetus for the letter. (Col. 1:7, 8; 4:12) The Christian congregation in Colossae faced a certain danger. The religious landscape of the time was undergoing significant changes, with existing religions crumbling and new ones constantly emerging through the amalgamation of various beliefs. The congregation encountered heathen philosophies that advocated asceticism, spiritism, and idolatrous superstitions. Moreover, the influence of Jewish practices, such as dietary restrictions and observance of specific days, may have affected some members. Though the exact nature of the problem is unclear, it was significant enough to compel Epaphras to undertake the arduous journey to Rome to seek Paul's counsel. However, Epaphras' report indicated that, as a whole, the congregation was not immediately at risk, as he praised their love and steadfastness. Upon hearing this report, Paul felt compelled to strongly defend the accuracy of knowledge and pure worship. He wrote this letter to the Colossian congregation, emphasizing the God-given supremacy of Christ in contrast to the prevalent heathen philosophy, angelic worship, and Jewish traditions.

Paul's letter to the Colossians served multiple purposes. Firstly, it aimed to reinforce the congregation's faith and counter any potential influence of false teachings and practices. The religious climate of the time was rife with syncretism, blending elements of different belief systems. Therefore, Paul stressed the preeminence of Christ, highlighting His role as the head of the congregation and emphasizing the completeness and sufficiency found in Him alone. (Col. 1:15-20)

Furthermore, Paul sought to address specific concerns within the Colossian congregation. The letter warns against deceptive philosophies that promoted self-imposed asceticism, the worship of angels, and rigid adherence to Jewish ceremonial laws. Paul emphasized that these practices held no spiritual value and were mere shadows compared to the substance found in Christ. Instead, he urged the Colossians to focus on their union with Christ, to cultivate virtues such as compassion, kindness, and forgiveness, and to devote themselves to prayer and thanksgiving. (Col. 2:8-23; 3:1-17)

In addition to combating false teachings, Paul sought to foster unity and harmony among believers. He encouraged the Colossians to exhibit mutual love, bearing with one another's weaknesses and striving for peace. He highlighted the importance of healthy relationships within the family, emphasizing the duties of husbands, wives, children, and servants. By addressing these practical aspects of Christian living, Paul aimed to strengthen the Colossian congregation and promote godly conduct in every sphere of life. (Col. 3:18-4:6)

The authenticity and importance of Paul's letter to the Colossians are evident in its inclusion among his other recognized writings. Its impact is also attested by the testimonies of early church authorities and its preservation in ancient manuscripts. The letter continues to serve as a valuable source of guidance and inspiration for believers, offering timeless truths about the supremacy of Christ, the dangers of false teachings, and the pursuit of godly living in the context of a diverse and challenging world.

The Epistle to the Colossians is traditionally attributed to the apostle Paul, based on several lines of evidence:

1. **Self-Attribution**: The letter itself claims Paul as its author. Colossians 1:1 states: "Paul, an apostle of Jesus Christ by the will of God, and Timothy our brother, To the saints and faithful brethren in Christ which are at Colosse."

2. **Pauline Themes and Vocabulary**: The letter contains typical Pauline themes such as the supremacy of Christ (Colossians 1:15-20), reconciliation through Christ (Colossians 1:22), and the importance of ethical conduct in response to Christ's work (Colossians 3:5-17). The vocabulary, while having some unique terms, still falls within the expected range for Paul.

3. **Historical Reference**: The references to Paul's circumstances in the letter align with what we know of his life. For example, he mentions being in prison (Colossians 4:3, 18), which aligns with the account of Paul's imprisonments in the book of Acts and his other letters.

4. **Coherence with Other Pauline Letters**: Colossians has significant parallels with Philemon, which is universally accepted as Pauline. Onesimus and Archippus, mentioned in Philemon, are also greeted in Colossians (Colossians 4:9, 17).

5. **Early Christian Tradition**: Early church tradition unanimously attributed the letter to Paul. It was accepted as Pauline by Church Fathers like Irenaeus, Clement of Alexandria, and Tertullian. The letter is also included in the Chester Beatty Papyri (P46), a collection of Paul's letters from around 200 AD.

6. **Canonical Acceptance**: The letter was universally accepted into the canon of the New Testament, reflecting the early church's belief in its Pauline authorship.

On this the Late Dr. Norman L. Geisler wrote,

Who Wrote It?

Colossians was written by Paul the apostle.

Internal Evidence

This epistle claims to be written by "Paul, an apostle of Jesus Christ" (1:1). The author repeats his name, saying "I, Paul" (v. 23). He repeats this claim at the end, saying, "This salutation by my own hand—Paul" (4:18). The companions mentioned support Paul's authorship, since many are known from elsewhere in the New Testament to be associates of Paul. They include Tychicus (4:7), Onesimus (v. 9), Aristarchus and Mark (v. 10), Justus (v. 11), Epaphras (v. 12), Luke and Demas (v. 14), and finally Archippus (v. 17). The character of the book is Pauline, as determined by the doctrinal emphasis, controversy, and approach to ministry. The style varies only as the content demands, since different opponents and topics demand some different words. The thirty-four new words, which do not appear in his other letters, fit the theme of the book and the thought of Paul. The content of the book is Pauline, manifesting his typical emphasis against heresy, disunity, and Judaistic influence in the Christian church.

External Evidence

The earliest manuscripts of the letter to the Colossians have Paul's name on them. Indeed, early Christian writers accepted it as Pauline, including Irenaeus, Clement of Alexandria, the Muratorian canon, and even the heretic Marcion. About half the verses are the same as in Ephesians (see chapter 14), which was written by Paul. There is also a close link to the book of Philemon, which is Paul's work. Both books have Timothy in the introduction (1:1); greetings are sent from the same people in both—Aristarchus, Mark, Epaphras, Luke, and Demas (4:10–14; Philem. 23–24); Archippus's ministry is mentioned in both (Col. 4:17; Philem. 2); Onesimus is referred to in both (Col. 4:9; Philem. 10).

Answering Critics

Some critics claim that Colossians is not Paul's work, since the vocabulary differs (thirty-four new words). However, all of Paul's letters have unique words. Words change with the topic. Some words are borrowed from the opposition to refute them.

Others insist that the style of Colossians differs, being more passive than Galatians. But Paul did not know the Galatians personally as he did the Colossians. And he is addressing an error in this letter that is different from the error addressed in Galatians. Further, Paul is older here and is writing under different conditions, namely, from prison.

Still others insist that the thought in this book differs from that in some of Paul's other books, since it contains nothing about justification or the Holy Spirit in our lives. Paul also adds new topics, like the cosmic significance of Christ. However, these charges are unjustified since Paul does affirm elsewhere that Christ is over the cosmos (1 Cor. 8:6; see Heb. 1:3), and justification by faith is not the issue here as it was in Romans and Galatians. Furthermore, Paul does speak here of love in the Holy Spirit (1:8), as well as growth (v. 6). Also it is noteworthy that this book is tied to Philemon (see above), the authorship of which is not doubted.[135]

The Second Epistle of Paul to the Thessalonians

The apostle Paul's second letter to the Thessalonians closely followed the first one. We know that it was written shortly after the initial letter, from the same city of Corinth, and once again, the brothers Silvanus and Timothy joined Paul in greeting the congregation in Thessalonica. These faithful servants of the early Christian congregation had been traveling together, although there is no record of their subsequent reunions after their time in Corinth. (2 Thess. 1:1; Acts 18:5, 18) The subject matter and urgency of the discussion indicate that Paul felt a pressing need to promptly address and correct a specific error that had arisen among the congregation.

The authenticity of this letter is as well established as that of the first letter to the Thessalonians. It is quoted by early writers such as Irenaeus (second century C.E.) and Justin Martyr (also of the second century), who appears to refer to 2 Thessalonians 2:3 when discussing "the man of lawlessness [sin]." The letter is included in the same early catalogues as the first letter. Although it is missing from the Chester Beatty Papyrus

---

[135] IBID, 188–189.

No. 2 (P46), it is highly likely that it was originally present in the first two of the seven missing leaves following the first letter.

What was the purpose of this letter? From the counsel provided by Paul to the Thessalonians, we learn that some individuals in the congregation were promoting the idea that the presence of the Lord was imminent. These speculators were actively preaching their theory and causing significant disturbance within the congregation. It appears that some were even using this belief as an excuse to neglect their responsibilities and not work for their own livelihood. (2 Thess. 3:11) In his first letter, Paul had made references to the Lord's presence, and it is likely that these speculators seized upon those statements and distorted their meaning. It is also possible that a letter falsely attributed to Paul had been misinterpreted as proclaiming that "the day of the Lord has come." (2:1, 2)

Paul, likely receiving a report on this situation, possibly from the person who delivered his first letter to the congregation, was deeply concerned about correcting the thinking of his beloved brothers. In the year 51 C.E., Paul, together with his companions, sent a letter from Corinth to the congregation in Thessalonica. Alongside addressing and correcting the erroneous viewpoint regarding Christ's presence, Paul provided warm encouragement to the Thessalonians, urging them to stand firm in the truth. He emphasized the need to remain steadfast in the face of challenges and tribulations, assuring them of God's justice and the eventual triumph of righteousness. (2 Thess. 2:15; 3:3-5) The letter served to strengthen the faith of the Thessalonians and provide them with the guidance they needed to navigate their Christian walk faithfully.

The Second Epistle to the Thessalonians, like most of the Pauline Epistles, identifies itself as having been written by the apostle Paul. Here is a summary of evidence supporting Pauline authorship:

1. **Self-Attribution**: The letter itself begins with "Paul, Silvanus, and Timothy, To the church of the Thessalonians" (2 Thessalonians 1:1). This self-attribution is a direct claim of Pauline authorship.

2. **Historical Reference**: The content of the letter matches what is known about Paul's missionary activities and the historical situation of the early church. For instance, the letter addresses the issue of the Day of the Lord and concerns about its immediate arrival, which is a topic Paul often dealt with in his other letters.

3. **Pauline Themes and Style**: The letter reflects Paul's distinctive theological ideas and writing style. For example, it emphasizes the return of Christ and the need for ethical conduct, both themes commonly found in Paul's undisputed letters.

4. **Early Christian Tradition**: Early church tradition supports Pauline authorship. The letter was accepted into the canon and is included in the earliest lists of New Testament books, such as the Muratorian Canon.

5. **Coherence with 1 Thessalonians**: The content and style of 2 Thessalonians have significant parallels with 1 Thessalonians, which is universally accepted as written by Paul.

6. **Canonical Acceptance**: The letter's inclusion in the New Testament canon suggests that early Christians accepted it as authentically Pauline.

On this the Late Dr. Norman L. Geisler wrote,

Who Wrote It?

Paul the apostle wrote 2 Thessalonians.

Internal Evidence

This Epistle claims to be written by Paul along with Silvanus (Silas) and Timothy (1:1). Indeed, it ends with "the salutation of Paul" (3:17). The greeting of "grace to you and peace" is Pauline (1:2). Likewise, the character of the book is Pauline, with a typical commendation of the congregation at the beginning (v. 3). In addition, the contents reflect the thought of Paul with his emphasis on the coming of Christ (1:7–10; 2:1), as in his first epistle (see chapter 17), and the condition of the church to whom Paul is writing is like that of the recipient of his first epistle (see 2:1–17).

External Evidence

The earliest manuscripts of 2 Thessalonians bear the name of Paul. Indeed, they contain the apostle's "trademark" salutation: "The salutation of Paul with my own hand, which is a sign in every epistle; so I write" (3:17). It is inconceivable that the early church would have accepted such a book if it were not Pauline. Likewise, the early Fathers accepted it as from the hand of the apostle, including Polycarp, Irenaeus, Justin Martyr, Clement of Alexandria, Tertullian, Origen, Cyril of Jerusalem, Eusebius, and St. Augustine. In addition, both the Muratorian canon and even Marcion's truncated canon contain 2 Thessalonians.

Answering the Critics

Some modern critics argue for several reasons that Paul did not write 2 Thessalonians.

1. They insist that Paul would not have written two letters so similar in such a short time. But the parallels are only about a third of the book and are easily explained by the repetition made for the sake of emphasis in this new context.

2. Some critics claim also that there are two conflicting views of Christ's coming. In 2 Thessalonians it is with signs, while in 1 Thessalonians it is without signs. However, this is not a contradiction, since these describe two different aspects of his

coming; first *for* his saints (which is without signs) and later *with* his saints (which has signs).

3. Nowhere else does Paul speak of "the lawless one" (2 Thess. 2:8), considered the Antichrist. But this only shows that Paul had no other occasion to speak of this evil personage of the last times. However, the apostle John did speak of him in 1 John 2:18 and Revelation 13:1–18.

4. Some critics claim that the tone of 1 Thessalonians and 2 Thessalonians is too different to have the same author. But conditions can change quickly. In 2 Corinthians Paul has two different tones in one book (chaps. 1–9 and chaps. 10–13).[136]

The First Epistle of Paul to Timothy

Luke's account of Paul's life in the book of Acts concludes with Paul in Rome, awaiting the outcome of his appeal to Caesar. During this time, Paul was residing in his own rented house, boldly proclaiming the Kingdom of God to all who came to him, unhindered. (Acts 28:30, 31) However, in his second letter to Timothy, Paul writes of his current situation, stating, "I am suffering, bound with chains as a criminal," and acknowledging the nearness of his impending death. (2 Tim. 2:9; 4:6-8) It is evident that a significant change had taken place between Luke's account in 61 C.E., marking the end of Paul's two years in Rome, and Paul's personal letter to Timothy, believed to have been written shortly before his death.

The challenge of reconciling the timeline of Paul's letters to Timothy and Titus with the events recorded in the book of Acts has led some biblical scholars to propose that Paul was released after his appeal to Caesar and experienced a period of freedom around 61 C.E. The New Westminster Dictionary of the Bible states, "The closing verse of Acts accords better with this view [of Paul's release after two years of confinement] than with the supposition that the imprisonment described ended in the apostle's condemnation and death. Luke emphasizes the fact that no one hindered his work, thus certainly giving the impression that the end of his activity was not near." Therefore, it is within the timeframe between Paul's release from his initial imprisonment in Rome and his subsequent final imprisonment, roughly spanning from 61 to 64 C.E., that the writing of First Timothy took place.

Upon his release, Paul likely resumed his missionary activities, partnering with Timothy and Titus. While it is uncertain whether Paul ever reached Spain, as some suggest, Clement of Rome (c. 95 C.E.) mentioned that Paul reached the "extreme limit of the West," which could include Spain.

Regarding the writing of the first letter to Timothy, it appears that Paul wrote it from Macedonia. First Timothy 1:3 indicates that Paul instructed Timothy to remain

---

[136] IBID, 206–207.

in Ephesus to address certain matters within the congregation while he continued his journey. It was from this location that Paul wrote the letter back to Timothy in Ephesus.

Both letters to Timothy have been accepted since early times as genuine Pauline writings and as part of the inspired Scriptures. Early Christian writers, including Polycarp, Ignatius, and Clement of Rome, all attest to their authenticity, and these letters are included in the catalogs of the early centuries as Paul's writings. The evidence from the early church provides strong support for their authorship.

Paul wrote the first letter to Timothy with the purpose of establishing clear organizational guidelines for the congregation. He also sought to warn Timothy about false teachings and to strengthen the brothers in their resistance against such erroneous knowledge. Given Ephesus's commercial nature, materialism and the love of money posed temptations that required timely advice. Timothy possessed a valuable background of experience and training for this work. He was born to a Greek father and a God-fearing Jewish mother. The exact timing of Timothy's initial encounter with Christianity is unclear. However, when Paul visited Lystra during his second missionary journey, likely in late 49 C.E. or early 50 C.E., Timothy, who was in his late teens or early twenties, was already highly regarded by the local believers. Paul arranged for Timothy to accompany him and Silas on their travels. Timothy is mentioned by name in eleven of Paul's fourteen letters, as well as in the book of Acts. Paul consistently showed paternal concern for Timothy and entrusted him with various responsibilities, indicating Timothy's effective service in the mission field and his qualification for significant responsibilities. Timothy's commendable reputation among the early Christian communities is evident in Paul's frequent mention of him and his reliance on Timothy's faithful support and assistance.

As Paul wrote the first letter to Timothy, he aimed to equip and empower his spiritual son for the challenges he would face as a leader in the congregation at Ephesus. Paul provided practical guidance on matters such as proper worship, the qualifications of overseers and deacons, and the appropriate behavior of men and women in the church. He urged Timothy to be vigilant in combating false teachings and to uphold the purity of doctrine, emphasizing the importance of love, faith, and sound instruction. (1 Tim. 4:12-16; 6:11-14)

Paul's letter to Timothy also addressed Timothy's personal well-being and spiritual development. He encouraged Timothy to remain steadfast in his faith, to persevere through challenges and opposition, and to take care of his health and spiritual nourishment. Paul reminded Timothy of his spiritual gifts and encouraged him to use them for the benefit of the congregation and the advancement of God's Kingdom. (1 Tim. 4:14-16; 6:20-21)

Throughout the letter, Paul's affectionate and fatherly tone shines through, reflecting his deep care and concern for Timothy's growth and success. Paul's own experiences, teachings, and example served as a source of inspiration and guidance for Timothy as he carried out his ministry.

The first letter to Timothy remains a valuable resource for understanding the organization and functioning of early Christian congregations. It provides timeless principles for effective leadership, sound doctrine, and the cultivation of a vibrant and faithful community. Its inclusion in the inspired Scriptures underscores its importance and enduring relevance for believers throughout the ages.

Here is a summary of the evidence supporting Pauline authorship for 1 Timothy:

1. **Self-Attribution**: The letter begins with "Paul, an apostle of Christ Jesus by command of God our Savior and of Christ Jesus our hope, To Timothy, my true child in the faith" (1 Timothy 1:1-2). This self-attribution is a direct claim of Pauline authorship.

2. **Content**: The letter addresses issues related to church organization, leadership, and doctrine, which would have been important during Paul's ministry.

3. **Language and Style**: Although there are some differences in vocabulary and style compared to the undisputed Pauline letters, portions of 1 Timothy show similarities to other letters attributed to Paul.

4. **Early Christian Tradition**: Early church tradition supports Pauline authorship. The letter was accepted into the canon and is included in the earliest lists of New Testament books, such as the Muratorian Canon. Church fathers, such as Irenaeus, Tertullian, and Clement of Alexandria, also attributed the letter to Paul.

5. **Historical Context**: The letter contains references to events and individuals that fit within the historical context of Paul's life and ministry. For example, Timothy is a well-known companion of Paul mentioned in several other Pauline letters.

On this the Late Dr. Norman L. Geisler wrote,

Who Wrote It?

The letter of 1 Timothy was written by Paul, the aged apostle.

Internal Evidence

This book claims to be written by Paul (1:1). Further, it mentions Paul's known companion twice (1:2; 6:20). What is more, the character of the polemical nature of the book is Pauline (compare Galatians and Colossians). Finally, the doctrinal content is Pauline, with its stress on sound doctrine (1:10).

External Evidence

This book was accepted in early biblical lists as Paul's (for example, in the Muratorian canon). Also, the earliest known manuscripts have Paul's name on them (1:1). What is more, it was cited by the earliest Fathers (for example, Clement of Rome, Ignatius, Polycarp, Irenaeus, Tertullian, Clement of Alexandria). It is also cited by the *Shepherd of Hermas* and the Didache. Likewise, the great Fathers to follow accepted the book with Paul's name on it as genuine, including Origen, Cyril of Jerusalem, Eusebius, Jerome, and St. Augustine.

Answering the Critics

Some modern critics have rejected the Pauline authorship of 1 Timothy. Two main arguments are set forth.

Fragmentary view. Some suggest that parts of the letter are Paul's (for example, 1 Tim. 1:13–15, 18; 2 Tim. 1:4–5; 3:14–15; 4:6–8). These fragments are said to have been incorporated by a later writer into his own material.

Response. In response, defenders of Pauline authorship have argued, first, that the claim of authorship in 1:1 stands for the whole book and would be false if the whole book were not from Paul. Further, the book forms a literary unity so that there is no need to attribute parts of it to others. In addition, if the fragments had been known to be Pauline, the writer could not have pawned them off as his own. And if they were not known as Pauline, there would have been no advantage in using them.

Fictional view. Other critics argue that a later writer used Paul's name to counter evils of his day and strengthen the Christian community. This is evidenced, they say, by a different (later) historical setting (2 Tim. 4:13, 20), different vocabulary from Paul's other writing (131 new words, one-third of the book), different church organization (with bishops and elders), lack of emphasis on gifts and working of the Spirit, no emphasis on Christ's return, and a doctrinal outlook that is different. These are serious charges and will be answered in order.

Response. None of these objections is telling and each is answerable. Hence, the internal and external evidence for the Pauline view stands.

1. The different (later) historical setting is explained by Paul's release from prison (Phil. 1:19; Philem. 22) and reimprisonment (2 Tim. 4:6–8). Paul had a desire to go to Spain, and Rome was on the way there (Rom. 15:28). Clement of Rome said he went to the "limits of the west" (1 Clement 5).

2. As for new vocabulary: (a) The vocabulary fits the new topic. (b) The sample is too limited to be determinative of authorship. (c) It begs the question by assuming the other epistles are Paul's style. (d) It overlooks the fact that Paul had different secretaries over the years. For example, Tertius helped with Romans (16:22), and Luke was with Paul when he wrote 2 Timothy (4:11). (e) Living authors express different styles in different books, depending on the topic and audience. One need only compare this author's *Philosophy of Religion* written for scholars and *Living Loud* penned

for teens. (f) Paul himself used different vocabulary in a book the critics accept. For example, Galatians, which critics accept, has thirty-five new words in it.

3. The church organization is not different. Elders (bishops) and deacons are found in early Acts (6:1–8; 14:23) and in an earlier epistle—Philippians (1:1), so there were bishops and elders at that time.

4. Gifts of the Spirit are mentioned (1 Tim. 1:18; 4:14). But sign gifts (2 Cor. 12:12; see 1 Cor. 14:22) may have ceased by that time, since they were needed by the apostles only to lay the foundation of the church (Eph. 2:19–20; see Acts 2, 10) and would die out with the apostles (Acts 1:22; 1 Cor. 9:1).

5. While Christ's return is not emphasized in Paul's Pastoral Epistles, it is mentioned. Titus is told to look for it expectantly (2:13). Paul looks forward to it in 2 Timothy 4:8 (see 2:12, 18) and exhorts believers in view of it in 1 Timothy 6:14–15. There are other possible allusions to it in 1 Timothy as well: 1:17; 3:9; 5:24–25; 6:7. It is understandable that it is not the chief emphasis here since Paul is concerned with church organization.

6. Finally, the doctrinal outlook in the Pastoral Epistles is Pauline. He stresses sound doctrine over and over (1 Tim. 1:3, 10; 4:6, 16; 6:3–4; 2 Tim. 1:13; 2:15; 3:10, 15–17; 4:2; Titus 1:9; 2:1). He writes of God, election (2 Tim. 1:8–10), sin (5:24; 2 Tim. 3:1–17), grace (Titus 2:11–13; 3:5–7), Christ (1 Tim. 3:16; 6:14–15), resurrection (2 Tim. 1:10; 2:18), and the second coming—all Pauline emphases.[137]

The Second Epistle of Paul to Timothy

Once again, Paul found himself imprisoned in Rome, but this time the circumstances were far more severe than his previous imprisonment. It was around 65 C.E., following a devastating fire that had engulfed Rome in July 64 C.E., causing widespread destruction in ten out of the city's fourteen regions. According to the Roman historian Tacitus, Emperor Nero, seeking to divert blame, falsely accused and unleashed brutal persecutions against a despised group known as Christians. Countless Christians were subjected to cruel tortures, including being covered in animal skins and torn apart by dogs, crucified, or burned alive to serve as gruesome nighttime illuminations in Nero's gardens. The atmosphere was one of fear and danger for anyone openly identifying as a Christian, with arrest and torture awaiting them.

In this dire context, Paul once again found himself imprisoned, this time in chains. He knew that release was unlikely, and he awaited his final judgment and execution. Visitors were scarce, as identifying oneself as a Christian meant risking arrest and death. Therefore, Paul expressed gratitude for Onesiphorus, a visitor from Ephesus, who fearlessly brought him comfort and support, diligently seeking him out in Rome.

---

[137] IBID, 213–215.

(2 Tim. 1:16, 17) Writing in the shadow of impending death, Paul identified himself as "an apostle of Christ Jesus by the will of God, according to the promise of the life that is in Christ Jesus." (1:1) He held firm to the hope of eternal life in union with Christ, fully aware of the course he had faithfully run, having preached in major cities from Jerusalem to Rome and possibly even reaching Spain. (Rom. 15:24, 28) Paul was prepared to finish his race faithfully to the end. (2 Tim. 4:6-8)

This letter, believed to have been written around 65 C.E., just before Paul's martyrdom, likely found Timothy still serving in Ephesus, as Paul had encouraged him to remain there previously. (1 Tim. 1:3) In this critical time, Paul urgently implored Timothy to come to him quickly and requested him to bring Mark, as well as Paul's cloak and scrolls that were left behind in Troas. (2 Tim. 4:9, 11, 13, 21) Written under such circumstances, this letter served as a powerful source of encouragement for Timothy, and its message has continued to provide solace and inspiration for genuine Christians throughout the ages.

The authenticity and canonicity of the book of Second Timothy are supported by the same reasons previously discussed regarding First Timothy. Early writers and commentators, including Polycarp in the second century C.E., recognized and utilized this letter, further affirming its place within the inspired Scriptures.

Below is a summary of some arguments supporting Pauline authorship for 2 Timothy:

1. **Self-Attribution**: The epistle begins with the verse, "Paul, an apostle of Christ Jesus by the will of God, in keeping with the promise of life that is in Christ Jesus, to Timothy, my dear son" (2 Timothy 1:1-2). This self-attribution is a clear claim of authorship by Paul.

2. **Content**: The letter contains personal details and emotions consistent with Paul's life and the narrative of his journeys in the book of Acts, lending credence to the idea that Paul was the author. For example, Paul makes references to his imprisonment (2 Timothy 1:8, 16-17; 2:9), which aligns with the historical account of Paul's life.

3. **Language and Style**: While there are differences in vocabulary and style between this letter and the undisputed Pauline letters, some scholars attribute this to the different context and audience of the Pastoral Epistles, or the potential use of a secretary (amanuensis) in their composition.

4. **Early Christian Tradition**: Early Church tradition generally accepts Pauline authorship. Church fathers such as Irenaeus, Clement of Alexandria, and Tertullian attributed the Pastoral Epistles to Paul. The epistle is also included in the earliest canonical lists like the Muratorian Canon.

5. **Historical Context**: The letter mentions characters such as Mark, Luke, and Alexander the metalworker, which are consistent with the historical context of Paul's life.

On this the Late Dr. Norman L. Geisler wrote,

Who Wrote It?

Paul, the departing apostle (1:1; see 4:6), wrote the epistle to Timothy. Luke may have served as secretary (4:11; see Rom. 16:22).

Internal Evidence

Despite some modern criticism, the evidence for Paul's authorship is strong. First, there is the clear claim of the book (1:1). Likewise, the companions mentioned—Mark and Luke—are Paul's (4:11–21). Also the content is Pauline, with its stress on sound doctrine and the Word of God (1:13; 2:15; 3:15–17; 4:2). The circumstances are clearly those of Paul, speaking of his imprisonment and imminent death (4:6–8).

External Evidence

External support for Paul's authorship is early and strong. The earliest known manuscripts bear his name. In addition, the early Fathers attribute it to Paul (Barnabas, Ignatius, *Shepherd of Hermas*, and Irenaeus). Also the great later Fathers, like Tertullian, Origen, Jerome, and Augustine, supported Pauline authorship. And the early Muratorian canon contained it. Finally, the objections of modern critics are based on specious arguments concerning alleged Pauline vocabulary (see the discussion of Paul's vocabulary in chapter 19).[138]

The Epistle of Paul to Titus

" Paul, a servant of God and an apostle of Jesus Christ . . . to Titus, my true child in a common faith." (Titus 1:1, 4) Thus begins Paul's epistle to his fellow worker and longtime companion Titus, whom he had entrusted with the task of organizing and strengthening the congregations on the island of Crete. Titus faced a formidable challenge in this endeavor. Crete, known as the dwelling place of the mighty "father of gods and men," had a reputation for deceitfulness, so much so that it had given rise to the saying, "to Crete a Cretan," implying the skill to outsmart a cunning person. The people of Crete were notorious for their falsehoods, being described even by their own prophet as "always liars, evil beasts, lazy gluttons." (1:12) In Paul's day, the Cretans were characterized as fickle, insincere, and quarrelsome, given to greed, immorality, falsehood, and excessive drinking. The presence of Jewish settlers among them had only exacerbated the immorality. Against this backdrop, the congregations of Crete had emerged, making it all the more vital for believers to renounce ungodliness and

---

[138] IBID, 226.

worldly desires, living instead with sound judgment, righteousness, and devotion to God, as Paul earnestly exhorted them. (2:12)

The Book of Titus provides limited details about the association between Paul and Titus. However, through references to Titus in Paul's other letters, we can gather valuable insights. Titus, a Greek, frequently accompanied Paul and even journeyed with him to Jerusalem on at least one occasion. (Gal. 2:1-5) Paul referred to him as a "partner and coworker." Following the writing of his first letter to the Corinthians from Ephesus, Paul dispatched Titus to Corinth. While in Corinth, Titus was involved in the collection of funds for the brothers in Jerusalem, and upon Paul's instruction, he returned to complete the collection. On his way back to Corinth from Macedonia, Titus was entrusted with carrying Paul's second letter to the Corinthians. (2 Cor. 8:16-24; 2:13; 7:5-7)

After Paul's release from his initial imprisonment in Rome, he once again collaborated with Timothy and Titus during the final years of his ministry. Their service together encompassed various regions, including Crete, Greece, and Macedonia. Eventually, Paul traveled to Nicopolis in northwest Greece, where he was likely arrested and taken to Rome for his final imprisonment and subsequent execution. It was during his visit to Crete that Paul left Titus behind to address and rectify any remaining issues within the congregations, appointing qualified elders in each city as instructed. Paul's letter to Titus was likely composed shortly after his departure from Crete, possibly while he was in Macedonia. (Titus 1:5; 3:12; 1 Tim. 1:3; 2 Tim. 4:13, 20) This letter aimed to encourage Titus in his work and provide him with authoritative support in fulfilling his responsibilities.

Paul is believed to have written this letter between his first and second imprisonments in Rome, approximately between 61 and 64 C.E. The evidence supporting the authenticity of the Epistle to Titus is as strong as that for the contemporary letters to Timothy, collectively known as Paul's "pastoral letters." The writing style exhibits similarities, and both Irenaeus and Origen quote from Titus, while numerous other ancient authorities attest to its canonicity. The Epistle to Titus is found in the Sinaitic and Alexandrine Manuscripts, two important ancient manuscripts of the Bible. Additionally, in the John Rylands Library, there exists a papyrus fragment, P32, dating back to the beginning of the second century (100-150) C.E., containing portions of Titus 1:11-15 and 2:3-8. These manuscript evidences further confirm the authenticity and inclusion of the book within the inspired Scriptures.

Without a doubt, the Epistle to Titus holds a significant place in the teachings of the early Christian church. Through Paul's letter, we gain insight into the challenges faced by the believers in Crete and the instructions given to Titus to address these issues. The letter serves as a valuable resource for guiding and encouraging church leaders in their responsibilities, emphasizing the importance of sound doctrine, good works, and the pursuit of godly living.

Thus, we can confidently affirm that the Epistle to Titus, like Paul's other letters, carries the weight of divine inspiration and provides timeless wisdom and guidance for believers throughout the ages. It stands as a testament to the enduring relevance of Scripture and its role in shaping the faith and conduct of the Christian community. The case for Paul's authorship of Titus is mainly built on the following points:

1. **Self-Attribution**: The letter begins with the statement, "Paul, a servant of God and an apostle of Jesus Christ" (Titus 1:1), which is a direct claim of authorship by Paul.

2. **Content and Historical Context**: The content of the letter and the historical circumstances it outlines are consistent with Paul's life and ministry. For instance, in Titus 1:5, Paul mentions that he left Titus in Crete to "put in order what was left unfinished," which aligns with the known missionary activity of Paul.

3. **Language and Style**: While some note differences in language and style between Titus and the undisputed Pauline letters, others attribute these differences to the different context, audience, and potentially the use of a secretary (amanuensis) in the composition of the letter.

4. **Early Christian Tradition**: Early Church tradition generally accepts Pauline authorship. Church fathers like Irenaeus, Clement of Alexandria, and Tertullian attributed the Pastoral Epistles to Paul. The letter is also included in the earliest canonical lists like the Muratorian Canon.

5. **Theological Continuity**: The letter contains key Pauline themes such as the grace of God (Titus 2:11), justification by faith (Titus 3:7), and the hope of eternal life (Titus 1:2, 3:7). These themes are consistent with the theology found in the undisputed Pauline letters.

On this the Late Dr. Norman L. Geisler wrote,

Who Wrote It?

Paul, the apostle, wrote Titus (1:1)[139]

The Epistle of Paul to the Hebrews

Paul, known as the apostle to the nations, had a ministry that extended beyond the non-Jews. Before his baptism and commissioning, Jesus himself declared that Paul was chosen to bear His name not only to the nations but also to kings and the sons of Israel. (Acts 9:15; Gal. 2:8, 9) Thus, the writing of the book of Hebrews aligns with Paul's commission to proclaim Jesus' name to the sons of Israel.

---

[139] IBID, 221.

However, some skeptics question Paul's authorship of Hebrews. One objection raised is the absence of Paul's name in the letter. However, this should not be seen as an obstacle since many canonical books do not explicitly name their authors, and the writers are often identified through internal evidence. It is also possible that Paul deliberately omitted his name when writing to Hebrew Christians in Judea, considering that his name had become a target of hatred among the local Jews. (Acts 21:28) The change in writing style from his other epistles is not a valid objection either. Whether addressing pagans, Jews, or Christians, Paul demonstrated his ability to adapt and relate to people from various backgrounds. In this case, he presented his reasoning in a manner that the Jewish audience could understand and appreciate, using arguments tailored to their perspective. (1 Cor. 9:22)

The internal evidence of the book supports Paul's authorship. The writer mentions being in Italy and having association with Timothy, which aligns with Paul's circumstances. (Heb. 13:23, 24) Furthermore, while the arguments in Hebrews are presented from a Jewish viewpoint to specifically appeal to the Hebrew congregation it was addressed to, the doctrine itself reflects Paul's teachings. The difference in style can be attributed to the intended audience's background, which differs from Paul's other letters.

The discovery of the Chester Beatty Papyrus No. 2 (P46) in 1930 provides additional evidence for Paul's authorship. This papyrus codex, written within 50 to 100 years after Paul's death, positions Hebrews immediately after Romans—an uncommon placement that indicates the early acceptance of its Pauline authorship. Scholarly opinions have strongly supported Paul as the author, with little substantial evidence favoring any other claimant.

Beyond the acceptance of Hebrews by early Christians, its contents bear the hallmarks of being "inspired of God." The letter consistently directs readers to the prophecies of the Hebrew Scriptures, citing numerous references to demonstrate how they were fulfilled in Jesus Christ. In the opening chapter alone, seven quotations from the Hebrew Scriptures are used to establish the superiority of the Son over the angels. The letter exalts the Word of the Lord and His name, emphasizing Jesus as the source of salvation and God's Kingdom through Christ as humanity's only hope.

Regarding the timing of its writing, it has been established that Paul wrote Hebrews while in Italy. In concluding the letter, Paul mentions that Timothy has been released and, if he arrives soon, Paul hopes to see the recipients. (Heb. 13:23) This suggests that Paul anticipated an imminent release from prison and desired to accompany Timothy, who had already been released. Thus, the final year of Paul's first imprisonment in Rome, around 61 C.E., is considered the likely date of writing.

At the close of the Jewish era of divine favor, the Hebrew Christians in Judea and particularly Jerusalem faced a time of severe testing. With the spread of the good news, animosity from the Jews intensified, reaching fanatical levels. Just a few years earlier,

Paul's presence in Jerusalem had sparked a riot, with enraged Jews demanding his removal and even taking an oath not to eat or drink until they had killed him.

In this hostile atmosphere of religious fanaticism and hatred towards Christians, the Hebrew congregation had to navigate their way, preach the Gospel, and remain steadfast in their faith. They needed a deep understanding of how Christ fulfilled the Law and to resist the temptation of reverting to Judaism with its rituals and animal sacrifices that were now obsolete.

Paul, who understood the pressure and persecution faced by Jewish Christians, was uniquely equipped to provide powerful arguments and refute Jewish traditions. As a former Pharisee, he drew on his extensive knowledge of the Mosaic Law, which he had learned under the renowned teacher Gamaliel. In Hebrews, Paul presented irrefutable evidence that Christ was the fulfillment of the Law, its ordinances, and sacrifices. He explained how these were now superseded by the new and superior realities brought about by Christ's work. His logical arguments were presented from a Jewish perspective, employing Hebrew Scriptures to convince even the most reasonable Jew.

With the letter to the Hebrew Christians, Paul provided them with a powerful weapon against their persecutors and a persuasive tool to convince honest Jews seeking God's truth. The letter demonstrated Paul's deep love for his fellow Hebrew Christians and his earnest desire to assist them practically during their time of great need.

In conclusion, while the authorship of Hebrews has been a subject of debate, the evidence strongly supports Paul as its writer. The absence of Paul's name does not diminish his authorship, as it is consistent with other canonical books. The internal evidence aligns with Paul's circumstances and his ability to adapt his writing style. Early Christian acceptance, the discovery of ancient manuscripts, and the contents of Hebrews all testify to its authenticity and divine inspiration. The letter served as a crucial source of encouragement and guidance for Hebrew Christians facing persecution, providing them with a firm foundation in the fulfillment of the Law through Jesus Christ.

The primary reasons for attribution to Paul were:

1. **Early Church Tradition**: Some segments of the early church, particularly in the East, ascribed Hebrews to Paul. This can be seen in the works of early church fathers such as Clement of Alexandria and Origen (though Origen also famously admitted, "who wrote the epistle, in truth, God knows"). The Western church was more hesitant to attribute it to Paul.

2. **Inclusion in Pauline Corpus**: The Epistle to the Hebrews is included in the collection of Paul's letters in the New Testament, suggesting that at least some early Christians believed it to be Paul's work.

3. **Theological Similarities**: Some of the theological themes in Hebrews are similar to those in Paul's undisputed letters. For example, both emphasize the supremacy of Christ and his priestly role, faith, and the New Covenant.

On this the Late Dr. Norman L. Geisler wrote,

Who Wrote It?

The author is unstated and unknown. There are several possibilities.

Internal Evidence

There are several possibilities as to who wrote Hebrews:

1. *Luke*. The evidence is: the polished Greek, his association with Timothy who is mentioned in 13:23, and the similarities with Paul's doctrine.

2. *Paul*. The evidence is: the Pauline doctrine, the early Fathers in the East attributed it to Paul, and the reference to Timothy (13:23), his trusted companion.

3. *Barnabas*. The evidence is: he was an associate of Timothy, some Fathers (for example, Tertullian) held this view, and he was a Levite (Acts 4:36), which fits with the emphasis in Hebrews.

4. *Apollos*. The evidence is: the style of Greek fits his training, the Old Testament quotes fit his emphasis, and its eloquence matches his oratorical skills (see Acts 18:24).

5. *Priscilla and Aquila*. Adolph Harnack held this view, but it lacks both positive internal and external evidence.

What Is Known about the Author?

Many things are known about the author of Hebrews: (1) He was not one of the twelve apostles (2:3–4). (2) He wrote before the destruction of Jerusalem (chaps. 7–8). (3) He was well versed in the Old Testament (ninety-eight citations). (4) He wrote in a more technical Greek than the other New Testament writers. (5) He was familiar with Platonic thought. (6) He emphasized Jesus's earthly ministry and high priestly ministry (chaps. 2, 7–10). (7) He was associated with Timothy (13:23). (8) He was in Italy when he wrote (v. 24). (9) He was known well enough to be accepted by the readers without mentioning his name.

Note: Paul, Luke, Apollos, and Barnabas all fit these characteristics, but Paul fits them best. However, those who reject Paul's authorship point out that many things are unlike Paul's other letters: his name is not given; the style is different; there is the common use of the name Jesus, the emphasis on Jesus's earthly ministry, and the stress on Jesus's high priestly ministry; all but one citation is from LXX; and greater warnings are given than Paul gave elsewhere. Those who support the Pauline authorship attempt to explain these by the special nature of the book, its message, and audience. They further note that doubts about Hebrews' canonicity in the West were overcome when they were convinced that it was the work of the apostle Paul. Origen's comment that only God knows for sure is apt.

External Evidence

Whoever the author was, the book was considered authentic from the time it was received by its first audience, who knew Paul's companion Timothy (see 13:23). It was cited in the first century by Clement of Rome. It is alluded to in *Shepherd of Hermas*. It was accepted by Irenaeus, Clement, Tertullian, Cyril of Jerusalem, Eusebius, Jerome, and Augustine. The West was slower to accept it because the author is not named and because the Montanist sect used chapter 6 to support their aberrant view that no second repentance is possible for those who slip away from the faith. But once the West was convinced of Hebrews' apostolic source, it was universally accepted. The many personal references (5:11–12; 6:10; 10:32–34; 12:4; 13:23–24) show the readers knew and accepted the author.[140]

---

[140] IBID, 234–235.

CHAPTER 10 Beyond the Canonical: A Look at Other Pseudo-Gospels

Introduction: Exploring Beyond the Canonical Gospels

The four Gospels included in the New Testament - Matthew, Mark, Luke, and John - are the only accounts of the life and ministry of Jesus Christ that are recognized as inspired and authoritative in mainstream Christianity, including most Protestant denominations. These Gospels were accepted into the canon because they were believed to have been written by apostles or close associates of apostles, and because their content was considered to be in line with the teachings of Jesus and the Apostles.

However, there were other writings about the life and teachings of Jesus that arose in the first few centuries after His death. These are often referred to as "pseudo-gospels" or "apocryphal gospels". These include texts like the Gospel of Thomas, the Gospel of Peter, the Gospel of Mary, and the Gospel of Judas, among others.

While these texts are of historical interest, it's important to understand why they are not included in the New Testament.

1. **Lack of Apostolic Authorship**: These texts are generally considered to have been written much later than the canonical Gospels, often in the 2nd or 3rd century CE. Unlike the canonical Gospels, which are traditionally attributed to

the apostles or their close associates, these pseudo-gospels were not believed to have been written by individuals who had direct contact with Jesus.

2. **Contradictory Teachings**: Many of the pseudo-gospels contain teachings that are significantly different from or even contradictory to the teachings found in the canonical Gospels and the rest of the New Testament. For example, the Gospel of Thomas contains Gnostic elements that are not found in the canonical Gospels.

3. **Lack of Early Church Acceptance**: The pseudo-gospels were not widely accepted by the early Christian church. While they may have been popular among certain groups, they did not have the widespread acceptance that the canonical Gospels had.

4. **Divine Inspiration**: The canonical Gospels are divinely inspired. This means that they were written under the guidance of the Holy Spirit. This is not the case with the pseudo-gospels.

In conclusion, while the pseudo-gospels provide a window into the diverse beliefs and interpretations of Jesus that existed in the early centuries of the Christian era, they are not considered to be authoritative or inspired accounts of the life and teachings of Jesus.

The Emergence of Other Gospels: Historical Context

Understanding the emergence of non-canonical, or pseudo-gospels, requires a bit of historical context. The time following Jesus' death, resurrection, and ascension was characterized by oral transmission of his teachings, deeds, and the significant events of his life. The canonical Gospels (Matthew, Mark, Luke, and John) were likely written during the latter half of the first century CE, drawing from these oral traditions as well as possibly other written sources.

However, Christianity was not a monolithic movement during these early years. There were varying interpretations of Jesus' teachings and the implications of his death and resurrection. As the movement spread beyond Jerusalem into different cultural contexts throughout the Roman Empire, these variations became more pronounced. This diversity, combined with ongoing persecution and a desire to preserve and promote particular understandings of Jesus' life and message, led to the creation of a variety of written texts about Jesus.

Many of these texts, which came to be known as pseudo-gospels or apocryphal gospels, were likely written in the 2nd and 3rd centuries CE. They emerged in different geographic and cultural contexts within the Roman Empire and often reflected the particular theological leanings of the groups that produced them.

For example, some groups emphasized knowledge (gnosis) as the path to salvation, resulting in what are now known as Gnostic gospels, like the Gospel of Thomas. Others may have wanted to fill in perceived gaps in the canonical accounts, resulting in infancy gospels like the Infancy Gospel of Thomas or the Protoevangelium of James that focus on Jesus' childhood.

However, it's essential to note that these non-canonical gospels were not accepted into the canon of the New Testament. Their teachings often deviated from what was recognized as the apostolic faith, and they lacked the apostolic authorship or endorsement that gave the canonical Gospels their authority. As such, while they can provide historical insight into the diverse beliefs of early Christian groups, they are not considered authoritative Scripture in mainstream Christianity.

The Gospel of Thomas: A False Collection of Jesus' Sayings

The Gospel of Thomas is one of the most well-known non-canonical texts. Unlike the canonical gospels, which include narrative accounts of Jesus' life, death, and resurrection, the Gospel of Thomas is a collection of 114 sayings of Jesus. Some of these sayings are similar to those found in the canonical gospels, while others are quite different and reflect a distinctly different theological perspective, often associated with Gnostic Christianity.

A key feature of Gnostic thought is the idea that salvation comes through special, hidden knowledge. This emphasis on knowledge is evident in the Gospel of Thomas. For example, in saying 1, the text begins with: "These are the hidden words that the living Jesus spoke. And Didymos Judas Thomas wrote them down." This introduction sets the tone for the rest of the text, which often presents Jesus' teachings as cryptic sayings that need interpretation.

Many of the sayings in the Gospel of Thomas are hard to reconcile with the teachings of Jesus as portrayed in the canonical gospels. Some of these sayings appear to devalue the material world, a common Gnostic theme, and some even present a very different view of gender and gender roles. For example, in saying 114, Simon Peter is quoted as saying that Mary should leave them because "females are not worthy of life." Jesus responds by saying, "Look, I will guide her to make her male, so that she too may become a living spirit resembling you males. For every female who makes herself male will enter the kingdom of Heaven." This saying is often seen as reflecting Gnostic attitudes towards the physical world and the body, but it's a stark contrast to the canonical gospels' teachings.

As the Gospel of Thomas post-dates the canonical Gospels and lacks their apostolic authorship or endorsement, it was not accepted into the New Testament canon. Its teachings, as exemplified by the sayings I've mentioned, often diverge significantly from the canonical accounts. As a result, while the Gospel of Thomas can provide valuable historical insight into the diversity of early Christian beliefs, it's not regarded as an authoritative or reliable source about Jesus' life and teachings within mainstream Christianity.

The texts often referred to as "apocryphal" or "pseudo-gospels" stand in stark contrast to the canonical Scriptures, which include the four Gospels in the New Testament. Composed around the mid-2nd century or later, these non-canonical texts arrived considerably after the Gospels of Matthew, Mark, Luke, and John. The portraits they paint of Jesus and the Christian faith often diverge dramatically from those found in the canonized Scriptures.

The Gospel of Thomas, a non-canonical text, attributes a variety of peculiar sayings to Jesus. One notable example is a statement suggesting that Mary would have to become a man to gain entry into the Kingdom of Heaven. This stands in contrast to the teachings of Jesus in the canonical Gospels, where He emphasizes faith, not gender, as the pathway to eternal life (John 3:16).

Additionally, the Infancy Gospel of Thomas presents an image of Jesus as a child that is unsettling and inconsistent with the canonical Scriptures. It depicts a young Jesus, between the ages of 5 and 12, performing a sequence of seemingly improbable miracles. Notably, this text portrays Jesus as a difficult and even vengeful child who uses His miraculous abilities to harm teachers, neighbors, and peers. This depiction contrasts sharply with the first miracle attributed to Jesus in the Gospel of John 2:11, where He changes water into wine at a wedding in Cana, a benevolent act that signifies the beginning of His public ministry.

Overall, these apocryphal writings present images of Jesus and the Christian faith that are quite distinct from the New Testament's teachings. Consequently, they are not recognized as authoritative or inspired Scripture within mainstream Christianity.

The Gospel of Peter: An Apocryphal False Passion Narrative

The Gospel of Peter is another non-canonical text, which offers a unique perspective on the crucifixion and resurrection of Jesus Christ. However, the account it provides does not align with the New Testament narratives, leading to its categorization as an apocryphal or pseudo-gospel.

This text aims to absolve Pontius Pilate of responsibility for the crucifixion, directly contradicting the Gospels of Matthew (27:24-26), Mark (15:15), Luke (23:24), and John (19:16), where Pilate is depicted as the one who gave the order for Jesus' execution. In addition, the Gospel of Peter describes the resurrection of Jesus in an extravagant manner, differing significantly from the more restrained accounts in the canonical Gospels (Matthew 28:1-10, Mark 16:1-8, Luke 24:1-12, John 20:1-10).

By the end of the 2nd century, the Gospel of Peter was found to be read publicly in some Christian congregations. However, due to its divergent content and the Church's commitment to preserving accurate apostolic teachings, it was declared to be false and was subsequently rejected. Eusebius, a renowned early Christian historian, records this in his Ecclesiastical History.

Therefore, like the Gospel of Thomas and other apocryphal writings, the Gospel of Peter does not hold canonical status within mainstream Christianity due to its incompatibility with the authoritative New Testament Scriptures.

The Gospel of Mary: A Gnostic Text

The Gospel of Mary, not to be confused with the canonical Gospel of Matthew, Mark, Luke, and John, is a non-canonical text believed to have been written in the 2nd century, attributed to Mary Magdalene. This text is part of a category of writings known as the Gnostic Gospels, which diverge significantly from the New Testament in their theological perspectives.

The Gospel of Mary presents a different narrative and perspective on Jesus and His teachings, particularly emphasizing the figure of Mary Magdalene. It asserts that she was a favored disciple and received special revelations and knowledge from Jesus, a view not supported by the canonical Gospels.

In the canonical Gospels, Mary Magdalene is a prominent figure as a follower of Jesus who witnessed His crucifixion and resurrection (Matthew 27:55-56, Mark 15:40-41, John 19:25). However, she is not singled out for receiving unique revelations. Moreover, the New Testament consistently holds that Jesus' teachings were publicly taught to all His followers, not selectively revealed to certain individuals (Matthew 5:1-2, Mark 4:1-2, Luke 6:17-20).

The Gospel of Mary also contains Gnostic elements, indicating a belief system that saw the material world as evil and spiritual knowledge as the path to salvation. This is not in line with the teachings of Jesus in the canonical Gospels, which emphasize faith in Him, repentance, and love as the path to eternal life (John 3:16, Luke 13:3, Matthew 22:37-40).

In conclusion, the Gospel of Mary, due to its late composition, Gnostic elements, and divergence from the New Testament narrative and theology, is not recognized as canonical by mainstream Christian traditions. Instead, it offers an insight into the diverse range of beliefs and practices that existed among various groups in the early centuries of Christianity.

The Infancy Gospels: False Narratives of Jesus' Early Life

The Infancy Gospels, which include texts such as the Infancy Gospel of Thomas and the Protoevangelium of James, are non-canonical texts that purport to describe the early life of Jesus. These texts, unlike the four canonical Gospels (Matthew, Mark, Luke, and John), focus on the childhood of Jesus and provide detailed, yet highly speculative and non-historical, accounts of His youth.

The Infancy Gospel of Thomas, for instance, portrays Jesus as a child performing various miracles, such as healing his playmates and turning clay birds into real ones. Some stories even depict Jesus in a less favorable light, using His divine powers to punish those who upset Him. These narratives sharply contrast with the depiction of Jesus in the New Testament, where He is portrayed as the embodiment of divine love, mercy, and righteousness (1 John 4:8, John 14:9).

The Protoevangelium of James, on the other hand, offers a narrative focusing on the early life of Mary, the mother of Jesus, and the miraculous birth of Jesus. However, it contains details that are not corroborated by the New Testament, such as the detailed description of Mary's upbringing in the temple.

The Infancy Gospels were likely written in the 2nd or 3rd century, well after the canonical Gospels, and they don't align with the theological and historical narratives in the New Testament. For example, the New Testament is silent on the details of Jesus' early life except for His birth and one incident at the age of twelve in the temple (Luke 2:41-52).

Due to their late authorship, historical inaccuracies, and theological inconsistencies with the New Testament, the Infancy Gospels are not considered part of the Christian canon. They are generally regarded as pseudepigraphal and apocryphal, created to satisfy curiosity about Jesus' early life rather than to provide accurate historical or theological information.

Gnostic Gospels: An Overview and Their Influence

The term "Gnostic Gospels" refers to a collection of early Christian texts that are not part of the New Testament canon. These texts are associated with Gnosticism, a diverse and complex movement that flourished during the first few centuries of the Common Era. The Gnostics held a variety of beliefs that diverged significantly from those of mainstream Christianity, including a distinct cosmology and a particular view of salvation.

Several Gnostic texts are styled as "gospels," such as the Gospel of Thomas, the Gospel of Mary, and the Gospel of Judas. However, these texts are vastly different from the canonical Gospels of Matthew, Mark, Luke, and John. The Gnostic Gospels often focus less on the historical actions of Jesus and more on revealing secret knowledge or wisdom, which is a central tenet of Gnosticism.

For example, the Gospel of Thomas is a compilation of sayings attributed to Jesus, some of which parallel the canonical Gospels, while others are strikingly different and align with Gnostic thought. The Gospel of Judas, on the other hand, paints a unique picture of Judas Iscariot, portraying him not as a betrayer but as someone who was acting on Jesus' instructions.

It's important to note that these texts were written later than the canonical Gospels—usually in the second to third centuries—and are not considered by most scholars to be reliable historical sources about Jesus or His teachings.

Despite being excluded from the canon, the Gnostic Gospels have exerted an influence on the study of early Christianity by providing insights into the diversity of beliefs and practices during this period. However, as they depart significantly from the teachings in the New Testament, they have often been viewed with suspicion or outright rejection by mainstream Christianity.

In the Bible, there are warnings against false teachings and doctrines that deviate from the apostolic faith (2 Timothy 4:3-4, 1 John 4:1-3, 2 Peter 2:1). These admonitions would be applicable to the teachings found in the Gnostic Gospels, which are in stark contrast to the theology presented in the New Testament. As such, from a Biblical perspective, the Gnostic Gospels are viewed as non-authoritative and their teachings as contradictory to the fundamental tenets of Christianity.

The Nag Hammadi Library: A Garbage Heap Trove of Gnostic Texts

The Nag Hammadi Library is a collection of ancient religious manuscripts that were discovered in 1945 near the town of Nag Hammadi, in Upper Egypt. This remarkable find consisted of 13 codices, or books, containing over 50 texts. Most of the texts are associated with Gnosticism, a religious movement that was widespread during the early centuries of Christianity.

These texts are written in the Coptic language, an ancient form of the Egyptian language written with the Greek alphabet. They are translations of earlier Greek documents, most of which have been lost. The codices themselves are thought to have been produced in the 4th century CE, but the texts they contain were likely written between the 2nd and 3rd centuries CE.

Among the Nag Hammadi texts, there are several that are called "gospels," including the Gospel of Thomas, the Gospel of Philip, and the Gospel of Truth. These texts differ significantly from the canonical gospels of the New Testament in both form and content. For instance, the Gospel of Thomas is a collection of sayings attributed to Jesus, without any narrative framework. Some of these sayings resemble those found in the New Testament, while others are distinctly Gnostic in character.

The Nag Hammadi Library also includes texts of other genres, such as dialogues, treatises, and apocalypses. They present a diverse range of religious ideas, many of which are at odds with mainstream Christian beliefs. For example, many of the Nag Hammadi texts espouse a dualistic cosmology, in which the material world is viewed as the creation of a flawed or evil deity, distinct from the supreme God.

While the Nag Hammadi Library is not considered authoritative in mainstream Christianity, it provides valuable insights into the diversity of beliefs that existed among early Christian and Christian-like communities. It's important to note, however, that these texts do not align with the teachings of the New Testament. The apostle Paul warned against false teachings in his letters (Galatians 1:6-9), and these admonitions would certainly apply to the divergent theologies found in the Nag Hammadi texts.

The Dating and Authorship of Non-Canonical Gospels

The dating and authorship of non-canonical gospels, often referred to as apocryphal gospels, pseudo-gospels, or gnostic gospels, are subjects of ongoing scholarly debate. These texts do not adhere to the orthodox Christian beliefs and traditions found in the canonical gospels of Matthew, Mark, Luke, and John.

1. **Dating**: Most non-canonical gospels are believed to have been written in the 2nd to 4th century CE, significantly later than the canonical gospels, which are generally dated to the late 1st century CE. This suggests that the non-canonical gospels were not based on firsthand accounts of Jesus' life and teachings.

2. **Authorship**: Unlike the canonical gospels, whose authors are traditionally linked to the apostles or their close associates, the non-canonical gospels are typically considered pseudonymous, meaning they were likely not written by the individuals whose names they bear. For instance, the Gospel of Thomas, the Gospel of Mary, and the Gospel of Judas are all named after figures from the New Testament, but there is no convincing evidence that these individuals were the actual authors of these texts.

It's important to note that the authorship and dating of these texts are significant factors in their exclusion from the Christian canon. The early church leaders who made decisions about the canon were concerned with apostolic authority and consistency with accepted Christian teaching. Texts that were written much later than the events they describe, or that show evidence of doctrinal deviation, were generally not considered reliable or authoritative.

In the New Testament, we see warnings against false teachings and doctrines that deviate from the message of Jesus and the apostles. For instance, in 2 Timothy 4:3-4, Paul writes: "For the time is coming when people will not endure sound teaching, but having itching ears they will accumulate for themselves teachers to suit their own passions and will turn away from listening to the truth and wander off into myths." This caution is applicable to the apocryphal gospels, which often present a different image of Jesus and his teachings than the one found in the canonical gospels.

Examining the Theological Differences: Orthodoxy vs Gnosticism

Examining the theological differences between orthodox Christianity and Gnosticism, as reflected in the canonical and non-canonical (or pseudo) gospels respectively, is crucial for understanding the diversity of early Christian thought.

1. **View of God and Creation**: In orthodox Christianity, God is the loving creator of the world and humanity, as expressed in Genesis 1:31: "God saw all that he had made, and it was very good." In contrast, Gnostic texts often depict the physical world as a corrupt, inferior creation of a lower deity, sometimes referred to as the demiurge.

2. **Understanding of Jesus**: The canonical gospels present Jesus as the Messiah, the Son of God, and the savior of humanity. His life, death, and resurrection are central to the redemption of human sin, as expressed in John 3:16: "For God so loved the world that he gave his one and only Son, that whoever believes in him shall not perish but have eternal life." In many Gnostic gospels, Jesus is portrayed primarily as a revealer of secret knowledge or gnosis, which leads to salvation. His physical suffering and death are often downplayed or reinterpreted.

3. **The Role of Knowledge and Faith**: Orthodox Christianity emphasizes faith in Christ as the means of salvation (Ephesians 2:8: "For it is by grace you have been saved, through faith—and this is not from yourselves, it is the gift of God"). Gnosticism, on the other hand, emphasizes personal enlightenment and the acquisition of secret knowledge for salvation.

4. **View of Humanity and Sin**: Orthodox Christianity understands humanity as inherently sinful due to the fall in the Garden of Eden (Romans 5:12: "Therefore, just as sin entered the world through one man, and death through sin, and in this way death came to all people, because all sinned"). In contrast, Gnosticism often sees humanity as divine sparks trapped in physical bodies, not inherently sinful but ignorant of their true divine nature.

These distinctions represent some of the fundamental theological differences between orthodox Christianity and Gnosticism, as reflected in the canonical and non-canonical gospels. These differences, among others, led to the rejection of the Gnostic texts from the Christian canon, and the affirmation of the four canonical gospels as authoritative for Christian faith and practice.

Assessing Historical Reliability: Canonical vs Non-Canonical Gospels

When assessing the historical reliability of the canonical versus non-canonical (or pseudo) gospels, several key factors come into play:

1. **Dating of the Texts**: The canonical gospels (Matthew, Mark, Luke, and John) were all written in the first century AD, within decades of Jesus' life. These gospels thus provide close temporal proximity to the events they describe. On the other hand, most non-canonical gospels were written much later, in the second century CE or beyond. This temporal gap reduces their reliability as historical sources.

2. **Authorship and Audience**: The canonical gospels were written by individuals who were either directly involved in the events (Matthew and John, traditionally considered apostles) or had access to eyewitness accounts (Mark and Luke). Moreover, these gospels were written for communities intimately connected with the early Jesus movement. Non-canonical gospels, in contrast, were often written by unknown authors and for specific groups with particular theological leanings, such as Gnostic communities.

3. **Consistency with Other Historical Documents**: The canonical gospels align more consistently with other historical documents from the time, including the writings of Paul and other New Testament letters, as well as some secular historical sources. Non-canonical gospels often contain teachings, stories, and concepts that are at odds with what is known from these other sources.

4. **Acceptance by Early Christian Communities**: The canonical gospels were widely accepted by diverse early Christian communities as authoritative and accurate accounts of Jesus' life, teachings, death, and resurrection. In contrast, non-canonical gospels were often contested and rejected by many early Christians, including influential church fathers.

5. **Theological Consistency**: The canonical gospels present a consistent theological view of Jesus, his mission, and his teachings. While they each offer a unique perspective, they all align in their basic depiction of Jesus as the Messiah and the Son of God. Non-canonical gospels, on the other hand, often present divergent and contradictory portrayals of Jesus and his message.

6. **The Criteria of Authenticity**: Scholars use various criteria to assess the authenticity of events or sayings in the gospels. These include the criterion of multiple attestation (is the event or saying reported in more than one independent source?), the criterion of embarrassment (does the event or saying present difficulties for the early Christian community?), and the criterion of coherence (does the event or saying fit with what is known about the historical context and the character of Jesus?). The canonical gospels tend to meet these criteria more often than the non-canonical gospels.

In light of these factors, the canonical gospels are generally seen as more historically reliable sources for understanding the life and teachings of Jesus than the non-canonical gospels.

The Criteria for Canonicity: Why Four Gospels?

The canon of the New Testament, including the four Gospels (Matthew, Mark, Luke, and John), was established over several centuries as the early Christian community sought to preserve and authenticate the apostolic teachings about Jesus. There were specific criteria used to determine which writings would be included in the canon. Here are those key criteria:

1. **Apostolic Origin**: For a book to be considered for the New Testament canon, it needed to have a connection to an apostle, either being written by an apostle themselves or by a follower or companion of an apostle. Matthew and John are traditionally attributed to the apostles of the same name, while Mark is associated with Peter, and Luke with Paul.

2. **Universal Acceptance**: Books that were widely recognized and used by the Christian community across different regions were more likely to be included in the canon. The four Gospels were universally accepted by the early church and were central to Christian worship and teaching.

3. **Liturgical Use**: If a book was read and used in early Christian worship, it was more likely to be considered canonical. The four Gospels, containing the life and teachings of Jesus, were integral to Christian liturgy.

4. **Consistent Message**: The book needed to be consistent with accepted Christian teaching and the other books that were already considered authoritative. The four Gospels provide a consistent message about Jesus, His life, His teachings, His death, and His resurrection.

5. **Inspiration**: The early church leaders believed that the books included in the canon were inspired by the Holy Spirit. This was often tied to the book's apostolic origin, its acceptance among the faithful, its use in worship, and its consistency with other accepted teachings.

The canon was not established by one person or even a single group of people at one time, but rather emerged as a consensus within the early Christian community over several centuries. The four Gospels in the New Testament canon were recognized as authoritative because they met these criteria and were seen as the most reliable and inspired accounts of Jesus' life and teachings.

Answering Objections: Why Not More Gospels?

The question of "Why not more Gospels?" arises from the existence of many other ancient texts which bear the title "gospel" but are not included in the New Testament canon. These texts, often referred to as the "apocryphal" or "non-canonical" gospels, include such writings as the Gospel of Thomas, Gospel of Peter, and Gospel of Mary, among others.

To answer this question, it is important to understand the criteria that were used by the early Church to discern which texts were divinely inspired and therefore should be included in the New Testament canon:

1. **Apostolic Origin**: The books of the New Testament were believed to have been written either by the apostles themselves or their close associates. The four canonical Gospels (Matthew, Mark, Luke, and John) have strong tradition and evidence linking them to the apostles or their immediate followers. Many of the non-canonical gospels, on the other hand, were written much later and lack a credible connection to the apostles.

2. **Universal Acceptance**: The canonical books were those that the majority of Christian communities across various regions recognized and used. The apocryphal texts were often confined to smaller groups and lacked this widespread acceptance.

3. **Consistency**: The accepted books had to be consistent with the teachings and doctrines that the apostles passed down. The non-canonical gospels often contain teachings that contradict those found in the canonical books, suggesting they were influenced by later theological developments rather than apostolic teaching.

4. **Divine Inspiration**: The canonical books were believed to be divinely inspired. This was determined through a combination of the book's apostolic origin, its acceptance by the Christian community, its use in liturgy, and its consistency with apostolic teaching.

Given these criteria, it becomes clear why the canonical Gospels were chosen and why other texts were not included. The four canonical Gospels provided the most reliable, authentic, and divinely inspired account of Jesus' life, teachings, death, and resurrection. The non-canonical gospels, despite bearing the name "gospel," did not meet these stringent requirements and therefore were not included in the canon of the New Testament.

The Significance of the Canonical Gospels in Christian Faith

The significance of the canonical Gospels - Matthew, Mark, Luke, and John - in Christian faith cannot be overstated. Each of these four books presents a unique perspective on the life, teachings, death, and resurrection of Jesus Christ, and together, they form the foundational narrative for Christian belief and practice.

1. Revelation of Jesus Christ: The canonical Gospels reveal Jesus Christ as the Son of God, the Messiah, and the Savior of the world. They recount His miracles, parables, and teachings, which reveal His divine nature and mission. Through His life and work, we see the character of God and His love for humanity. For example, John 1:1 states, "In the beginning was the Word, and the Word was with God, and the Word was God." This verse refers to Jesus, establishing His divinity.

2. Source of Christian Doctrine: The teachings of Jesus, as recorded in the Gospels, form the basis of Christian doctrine. Concepts such as love, forgiveness, faith, and the Kingdom of God are all derived from Jesus' words and actions. For instance, in the Sermon on the Mount (Matthew 5-7), Jesus lays out key elements of Christian ethics and spirituality.

3. Guide for Christian Living: The Gospels provide guidance for how Christians should live. Jesus' life is presented as a model of perfect obedience to God's will, and His teachings serve as a moral and ethical guide. In John 13:15, Jesus says, "I have set you an example that you should do as I have done for you."

4. Proclamation of Salvation: The canonical Gospels convey the central Christian message of salvation through faith in Jesus Christ. They chronicle His sacrificial death on the cross and His resurrection, affirming the hope of eternal life for those who believe in Him. John 3:16 encapsulates this message: "For God so loved the world that he gave his one and only Son, that whoever believes in him shall not perish but have eternal life."

5. Foundation for Worship: The Gospels are central to Christian worship. They are read and preached in churches, guiding worship and prayer. In liturgical traditions, the Gospel reading holds a special place in the service, signifying the presence of Christ in His word.

In essence, the canonical Gospels are indispensable to Christian faith. They affirm who Jesus is, what He taught, and what He accomplished through His death and resurrection. They guide Christian thought, life, and worship, and they provide the assurance of salvation through faith in Jesus Christ.

CHAPTER 11 Miracles in the New Testament: Fact or Fiction?

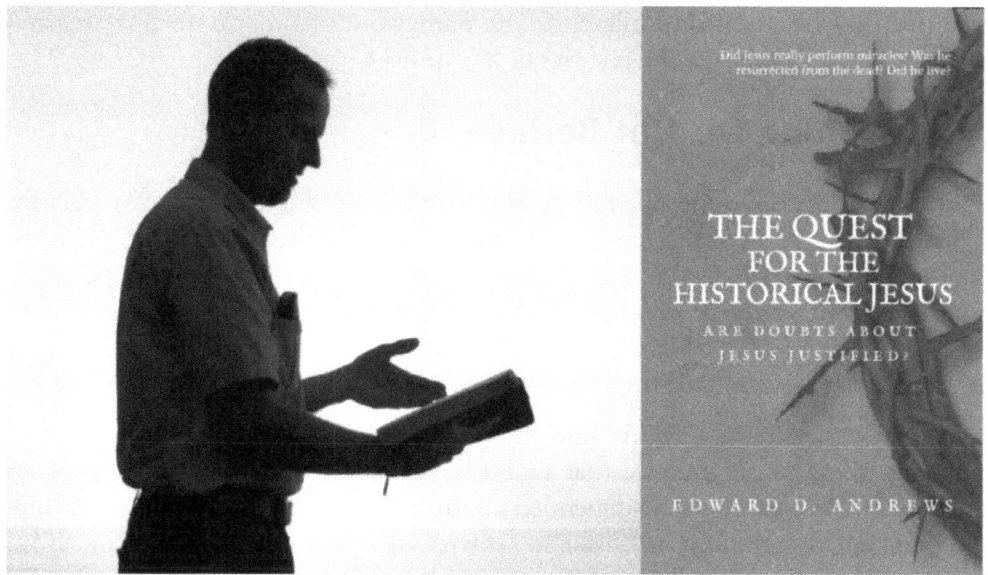

The Miracles—Did They Really Happen?

Luke 7:11-15 Updated American Standard Version (UASV)

[11] Soon afterward he went to a city called Nain, and his disciples and a large crowd went with him. [12] As he drew near to the gate of the town, look, a man who had died was being carried out, the only begotten son of his mother, and she was a widow, and a sizeable crowd from the town was with her. [13] And when the Lord saw her, he had compassion on her and said to her, "Do not weep." [14] Then he came up and touched the bier, and the bearers stood still. And he said, "Young man, I say to you, arise." [15] And the dead man sat up and began to speak, and Jesus gave him to his mother.

On a certain day in the year 31 CE, the narrative unfolds of Jesus and his disciples journeying to a city in northern Palestine known as Nain. As they neared the city's entrance, they encountered a mournful scene: a funeral procession. The deceased was a young man, the only son of his mother, who was herself a widow. Her loss was immense, leaving her utterly alone. The Biblical account tells us that Jesus felt a deep compassion for her, saying to her, "Do not weep." (Luke 7:13). He then walked forward, reaching out to touch the stretcher upon which the young man was laid. The bearers of the stretcher ceased their procession, and Jesus commanded the lifeless body, "Young man, I tell you, arise!" (Luke 7:14). The account concludes with the young man awakening from death, sitting up, and beginning to speak (Luke 7:15).

This narrative is undoubtedly heartening, yet some question its veracity. Many find it challenging to accept that such events truly transpired. However, the concept of miracles is deeply woven into the fabric of Biblical narrative. To believe in the Bible is to affirm the occurrence of miracles. The framework of Biblical truth is predicated on one paramount miracle: the resurrection of Jesus Christ.

Why Some Do Not Believe

Is your belief system open to the possibility of miracles? Or do you find, particularly in our age of scientific advancement, that the concept of miracles – extraordinary occurrences that suggest the intervention of a supernatural power – is an untenable proposition? If you find yourself in the latter camp, you are not alone. The Scottish philosopher David Hume, two centuries ago, held a similar stance, and perhaps your reasons mirror his.

Hume's skepticism towards miracles was primarily underpinned by three key arguments. Firstly, he contended that a miracle, by definition, is a violation of the laws of nature. Humans have always depended on these laws: understanding that a dropped object will fall, that the sun will rise and set with each passing day, and so on. It is an ingrained expectation that events will consistently conform to these patterns. Nothing will occur that contradicts these laws of nature. Hume proposed that this line of reasoning was as robust a counter-argument to the existence of miracles as any derived from empirical experience.

Secondly, Hume argued that human beings are innately susceptible to deception. Many are inclined to believe in the extraordinary, particularly when it pertains to religious phenomena, and history has shown that a multitude of proclaimed miracles have ultimately been exposed as fraudulent.

The third plank of Hume's argument was the assertion that reports of miracles predominantly originate from less enlightened times. He observed that as education and knowledge advance, the frequency of reported miracles diminishes. As Hume succinctly put it, "Such prodigious events never happen in our days." He interpreted this trend as evidence that miracles never genuinely occurred. The majority of contemporary arguments negating the existence of miracles closely align with Hume's original propositions. Therefore, it is worth delving into each of Hume's points in turn.

Is it a Violation of Natural Laws?

The argument that miracles are simply 'violations of the laws of nature,' hence impossible, may appear compelling at first glance. However, it's essential to scrutinize the underlying premise of this contention. Generally, a miracle is understood to be an event that transcends the ordinary laws of nature, an event so extraordinary that observers are persuaded of a divine hand at play. In essence, the argument being made here is essentially that 'miracles are impossible because they are miraculous.' Rather than making such a hasty judgment, shouldn't we first examine the evidence available?

In reality, the academically inclined individuals of today are less inclined than David Hume to assert that the universally recognized laws of nature are immutable and universally applicable. Contemporary scientists are open to hypotheses suggesting the existence of more than the three conventional dimensions of length, width, and height in the universe. They contemplate the existence of black holes, colossal stars that implode to a point of virtually infinite density. It is said that in the vicinity of such entities, space is so intensely warped that time comes to a standstill. Scientists have even entertained the idea that under certain circumstances, time could conceivably run in reverse!

Renowned physicist Stephen W. Hawking, Lucasian Professor of Mathematics at Cambridge University, once mentioned in a discussion about the origin of the universe that "In the classical theory of general relativity... the beginning of the universe has to be a singularity of infinite density and space-time curvature. Under such conditions, all the known laws of physics would break down." It is apparent then that modern scientists do not universally dismiss the possibility of phenomena that defy conventional natural laws. In extraordinary circumstances, extraordinary events can indeed transpire. If we hold faith in an omnipotent God, it is surely reasonable to accept that He possesses the capacity to orchestrate exceptional, miraculous events when they align with His grand design. As noted in Exodus 15:6-10 and Isaiah 40:13,15, God's power is beyond our comprehension.

What About Counterfeit Miracles?

It's undeniable that fraudulent miracles exist. For instance, numerous individuals have claimed the ability to miraculously heal the sick through faith healing. Medical doctor William A. Nolan took it upon himself to scrutinize such miraculous healings. He tracked numerous purported healings among both evangelical faith healers in the United States and alleged psychic surgeons in Asia. His findings? A litany of instances of disillusionment and deceit.

However, does the existence of such deceptions negate the occurrence of genuine miracles? Not necessarily. We often hear of counterfeit banknotes being circulated, but that doesn't render all currency counterfeit. Many sick individuals place immense faith in charlatans posing as doctors and willingly give them substantial amounts of money. However, this doesn't imply that all doctors are fraudsters. Some artists have proven adept at forging "old master" paintings. Yet, this doesn't mean all paintings are forgeries. Similarly, the fact that some miracles have been proven fraudulent doesn't mean that genuine miracles are impossible. As stated in 2 Thessalonians 2:9, "The coming of the lawless one is by the activity of Satan with all power and false signs and wonders." It is important to distinguish between false miracles and true miracles, which are expressions of divine power as shown in Exodus 14:21-22 when Moses parted the Red Sea.

Miracles Are Not a Contemporary Occurrence

The third contention encapsulates the notion: "Such extraordinary events never transpire in our times." Hume, having never witnessed a miracle, adamantly denied their feasibility. However, this line of reasoning is flawed. Any rational individual must concede that prior to Hume's era, "extraordinary events" transpired that were not replicated during his lifetime. What kind of events?

One example is the origin of life on Earth. Subsequently, certain life forms developed consciousness. Eventually, humans emerged, equipped with wisdom, creativity, the capacity for love, and the function of conscience. No scientist, relying on the currently operative laws of nature, can elucidate how these remarkable events transpired. Yet, we possess tangible proof that they indeed occurred.

What about the "extraordinary events" that have transpired since Hume's time? Suppose we were capable of time travel and could inform Hume about the contemporary world. Imagine the challenge of explaining to him that a businessman in Hamburg can converse with someone in Tokyo thousands of miles away without raising his voice; that a soccer game in Spain can be viewed globally in real-time; that vessels far larger than the oceanic ships of Hume's era can ascend from the Earth's surface and transport 500 individuals thousands of miles within a matter of hours. Can you envision his incredulous response? 'Impossible! Such extraordinary events never occur in our times!'

Yet, these 'extraordinary' events are a reality in our times. Why? Because humans, utilizing scientific principles unbeknownst to Hume, have learned to construct telephones, televisions, and airplanes. Consequently, is it so implausible to believe that God could have, using methods we still fail to comprehend, orchestrated events that appear miraculous to us in the past? As Jeremiah 32:27 says, "Behold, I am the LORD, the God of all flesh. Is anything too hard for me?"

The Question of Veracity: Can We Be Certain?

Just because miracles could have occurred doesn't necessarily imply that they did. In this contemporary age, how can we ascertain whether God truly performed authentic miracles through His servants in biblical times? What form of evidence should we anticipate for such phenomena? Picture a tribal man, extracted from his rural habitat and brought to a sprawling metropolis. Upon his return, how could he depict the marvels of modern civilization to his community? He lacks the capacity to articulate how a car operates or how music emits from a handheld radio. He can't construct a computer to authenticate its existence. His sole recourse is to recount what he witnessed.

We find ourselves in a comparable position to the fellow tribesmen of the man. If God truly executed miracles, the sole manner in which we can learn about them is through the accounts of eyewitnesses. These witnesses can't elucidate how the miracles transpired, nor can they replicate them. They can merely inform us of what they observed. Clearly, eyewitnesses can be deceived. They can also readily exaggerate or disseminate incorrect information. Therefore, if we are to accept their testimonies, we must be confident that these eyewitnesses are honest, credible, and have demonstrated noble motives, as highlighted in Proverbs 14:5: "A faithful witness does not lie, but a false witness breathes out lies."

The Most Evidenced Miracle

The most substantiated miracle recorded in the Bible is the resurrection of Jesus Christ. Let's examine this event as a prime example. First, let's evaluate the recounted facts: On the evening of Nisan 14, which aligns with our modern Thursday evening, Jesus was apprehended. He was brought before the Jewish leaders who charged him with blasphemy and determined that he should die. They presented Jesus to the Roman governor Pontius Pilate, who yielded to their insistence and consented to his execution. On Friday afternoon, still Nisan 14 according to the Jewish calendar, he was crucified, and within a few hours, he died (Mark 14:43-65; 15:1-39).

Following his death, a Roman soldier confirmed Jesus' demise by piercing his side with a spear. His body was then interred in a new tomb. The succeeding day, Nisan 15 (Friday/Saturday), was a Sabbath. However, on the morning of Nisan 16, which was a Sunday, some disciples visited the tomb only to discover it vacant. Not long after, accounts started spreading that Jesus had been sighted alive. The initial response to these stories was precisely what we would expect today - skepticism. Even the apostles initially refused to believe. Yet, when they personally encountered the living Jesus, they had no option but to accept that he had indeed been resurrected from the dead (John 19:31–20:29; Luke 24:11).

The Empty Tomb

Did the resurrection of Jesus occur, or is this all a mere myth? A pertinent question that individuals of that period might have posed is: Does Jesus' body remain in his tomb? If the opponents of Jesus' followers could have indicated his corpse still in its burial place, it would have been a significant hindrance, providing concrete proof that he had not been resurrected. However, there is no account indicating that they ever attempted this. Instead, as per the Bible, they bribed the soldiers tasked with guarding the tomb and instructed them to assert, "His disciples came during the night and stole him while we were asleep" (Matthew 28:11-13). We also have extra-biblical evidence supporting this action by the Jewish leaders.

Around a hundred years following Jesus' demise, Justin Martyr penned a piece named Dialogue With Trypho. In it, he stated, "You [the Jews] have dispatched chosen and ordained men throughout the entire world to announce that a godless and lawless heresy had arisen from one Jesus, a Galilean deceiver, whom we crucified, but his disciples stole him by night from the tomb, where he was laid."

Trypho was a Jew, and the Dialogue With Trypho was crafted to defend Christianity against Judaism. Hence, it is improbable that Justin Martyr would have made such a claim—that the Jews accused the Christians of absconding with Jesus' body from the tomb—unless the Jews had actually lodged such an accusation. If not, he would have exposed himself to a straightforwardly verifiable allegation of falsehood. Justin Martyr would have only made this claim if the Jews genuinely had dispatched such emissaries. And they would have done so only if the tomb was indeed vacant on Nisan 16, 33 C.E., and if they were unable to reference Jesus' body in the tomb as proof of his non-resurrection. Considering that the tomb was vacant, what had transpired? Had the disciples stolen the body, or was it supernaturally removed as evidence of Jesus' genuine resurrection?

The Verdict of Luke, the Doctor

One highly educated first-century individual who meticulously examined the evidence was Luke, a physician. (Colossians 4:14) Luke authored two books that are currently part of the Bible: one was a Gospel, or chronicle of Jesus' ministry, and the other, known as the Acts of the Apostles, was a record of Christianity's expansion in the years following Jesus' death.

In his Gospel's introduction, Luke references a plethora of evidence that was accessible to him but is no longer available to us. He mentions consulting written documents about Jesus' life. Additionally, he indicates having conversations with eyewitnesses to Jesus' life, death, and resurrection. Then, he states: "I have meticulously traced everything from the beginning." (Luke 1:1-3) Clearly, Luke's research was exhaustive. But was he a proficient historian?

Many have validated that he was. In 1913, Sir William Ramsay expressed in a lecture his thoughts on the historical credibility of Luke's works. His conclusion? "Luke is a first-rate historian; his statements of fact are not only trustworthy, but he also possesses the true historical sense." More recent researchers have arrived at the same conclusion. The Living Word Commentary, introducing its volumes on Luke, asserts: "Luke was both a historian (and an accurate one) and a theologian."

Dr. David Gooding, a former professor of Old Testament Greek in Northern Ireland, affirms that Luke was "an ancient historian in the tradition of the Old Testament historians and in the tradition of Thucydides [one of the most esteemed historians of the ancient world]. Like them, he would have taken great care in investigating his sources, selecting his material, and arranging that material. ... Thucydides combined this approach with a commitment to historical accuracy: there is no reason to think that Luke did less."

What was this highly skilled man's conclusion regarding the emptiness of Jesus' tomb on Nisan 16? Both in his Gospel and in the book of Acts, Luke asserts as a fact that Jesus was resurrected. (Luke 24:1-52; Acts 1:3) He harbored no doubt about it. Perhaps his belief in the miracle of the resurrection was fortified by his own experiences. While he was not an apparent eyewitness of the resurrection, he does report witnessing miracles executed by the Apostle Paul.—Acts 14:8-10; 20:7-12; 28:8, 9.

Witnesses of the Resurrected Jesus

Two of the Gospels are traditionally attributed to men who knew Jesus personally, witnessed his death, and asserted to have seen him after his resurrection. These are Matthew, the former tax collector turned apostle, and John, the beloved apostle of Jesus. Another Biblical author, Apostle Paul, also professed to have seen the risen Christ. Furthermore, Paul lists by name others who encountered Jesus alive post his death, and he mentions that at one point, Jesus appeared to "over five hundred brothers."—1 Corinthians 15:3-8.

Among those mentioned by Paul as eyewitnesses is James, Jesus' half-brother by birth, who would have known Jesus since their childhood. Another is Apostle Peter; historian Luke reports that Peter boldly testified about Jesus' resurrection just a few weeks after Jesus' death. (Acts 2:23, 24) Two epistles in the Bible are traditionally credited to Peter, and in the first of these, Peter demonstrates that his belief in the resurrection of Jesus remained a strong driving force even years after the event. He penned: "Blessed be the God and Father of our Lord Jesus Christ, for according to his great mercy he gave us a new birth to a living hope through the resurrection of Jesus Christ from the dead."—1 Peter 1:3.

So, much like Luke could converse with individuals who professed to have seen and spoken with Jesus after his death, we can read the words these people wrote. We can evaluate for ourselves whether these individuals were misled, whether they were attempting to deceive us, or whether they indeed witnessed the resurrected Christ. Frankly, they could not have been misled. Many of them were Jesus' close friends up until his death. Some bore witness to his suffering on the cross. They observed the blood and water gush out from the spear wound inflicted by the soldier. The soldier knew, and they knew, that Jesus was undeniably dead. Later, they claim, they saw Jesus alive and actually conversed with him. They could not have been deceived. So, were they attempting to deceive us by asserting that Jesus had been resurrected?—John 19:32-35; 21:4, 15-24.

To answer this, we simply need to ask: Did they truly believe what they were saying? Yes, unequivocally. For the Christians, including those who claimed to be eyewitnesses, the resurrection of Jesus was the bedrock of their faith. Apostle Paul stated: "If Christ has not been raised, our preaching is in vain and so is your faith ... If Christ has not been raised, your faith is futile." (1 Corinthians 15:14, 17) Do these sound like the words of a man lying about witnessing the resurrected Christ?

Reflect on what it entailed to be a Christian during that time. There were no gains in status, power, or wealth. Quite the opposite. Many early Christians 'joyfully accepted the confiscation of their property' because of their faith. (Hebrews 10:34) Christianity demanded a life of sacrifice and persecution that often culminated in martyrdom through a shameful, agonizing death.

Some Christians hailed from affluent families, like Apostle John, whose father presumably had a thriving fishing business in Galilee. Many had promising futures, like Paul who, upon embracing Christianity, had been a disciple of the renowned Rabbi Gamaliel and was starting to gain recognition among the Jewish leaders. (Acts 9:1, 2; 22:3; Galatians 1:14) Yet, all renounced worldly offerings to propagate a message grounded in the fact of Jesus' resurrection from the dead. (Colossians 1:23, 28) Why would they sacrifice so much to endure suffering for a cause they knew was based on a lie? The answer is, they wouldn't. Their willingness to suffer and even die for this cause signifies they were profoundly convinced of its truth. They were staking their lives on a cause they knew to be rooted in reality, not a fabricated tale. Their conviction offers compelling testament to the reality of Jesus' resurrection.

Miracles Really Happen

Indeed, the weight of testimonial evidence is overwhelmingly compelling. The resurrection of Jesus on Nisan 16, 33 C.E. truly took place. Given this event, all other miracles mentioned in the Bible also become possible—miracles for which we also have solid, first-hand accounts. The same Divine Power that resurrected Jesus also facilitated Jesus' ability to resurrect the son of the widow of Nain. This Power also allowed Jesus to perform the comparatively smaller yet still incredible miracles of healing. It was present during the miraculous feeding of the multitude, and enabled Jesus to walk on water. - Luke 7:11-15; Matthew 11:4-6; 14:14-21, 23-31.

Therefore, the presence of miracles in the Bible should not incite doubts about its veracity. Instead, the fact that miracles indeed occurred during biblical times serves as a robust testament to the Bible genuinely being the Word of God. However, another critique often levied against the Bible is the claim of internal contradictions, leading some to argue it cannot be the Word of God. Is this assertion valid? We discussed this at length back in Chapter 7.

CHAPTER 12 Historical Corroborations of the New Testament: Unveiling the Evidence

Introduction: The Importance of Historical Corroboration

Historical corroboration is a vital tool in assessing the reliability and authenticity of any ancient text, including the New Testament. It involves seeking external evidence, whether from other written accounts, archaeological findings, or historical records, that supports or confirms the events, persons, or places depicted in the text. In the case of the New Testament, such corroborations can offer significant insights into its historical context and shed light on its narratives.

The New Testament, as an ancient religious document, tells the story of Jesus Christ, his teachings, his disciples, and the early Christian community. It serves not only as a spiritual guide for Christians but also as a historical document providing a window into the society, culture, politics, and religious practices of the first-century Roman Empire. Therefore, historical corroboration is crucial for understanding the context and credibility of the New Testament.

1. **The Accuracy of Geographical and Political Details**

The New Testament offers detailed descriptions of geographical locations and political structures of the era. For instance, the Gospel of Luke mentions that Jesus was born in Bethlehem during the reign of Herod the Great (Luke 2:1-7) and started his ministry during the time John the Baptist was preaching in the wilderness (Luke 3:1-2). These details align with what we know from other historical sources about the time and place.

Corroboration from Non-Christian Sources

Various non-Christian sources, including Roman historians and Jewish texts, provide corroborating evidence for New Testament events and figures. For example, the Roman historian Tacitus (56-120 CE) wrote about Jesus' crucifixion under Pontius Pilate and the subsequent spread of Christianity in Rome (Annals 15.44). The Jewish historian Josephus (37-100 CE) also mentions Jesus, John the Baptist, and James the brother of Jesus in his Antiquities of the Jews.

Archaeological Evidence

Archaeological discoveries have provided physical evidence corroborating New Testament accounts. For instance, the Pilate Stone discovered in 1961 bears the name of Pontius Pilate, the Roman governor who presided over Jesus' trial as described in all four Gospels. The Caiaphas Ossuary, discovered in 1990, is believed to contain the bones of the high priest Caiaphas, who is mentioned in the New Testament as a key figure in the trial and crucifixion of Jesus (Matthew 26:57-68).

Early Christian Writings

Early Christian writings outside of the New Testament, such as the letters of Clement of Rome and Ignatius of Antioch, affirm many details about Jesus and early Christianity. These writings not only provide evidence for the existence of Jesus but also confirm the New Testament's portrayal of the beliefs and practices of the early Christian community.

In conclusion, historical corroboration is a powerful tool for understanding and affirming the historical context and reliability of the New Testament. The combination of geographical and political details, corroborations from non-Christian sources, archaeological evidence, and early Christian writings provides compelling evidence supporting the New Testament's historical authenticity. However, it's important to remember that historical corroboration, while valuable, is just one aspect of understanding and interpreting the New Testament. Other factors, such as textual criticism, literary analysis, and theological reflection, also play crucial roles.

The New Testament and Its Historical Context

The New Testament of the Bible is an anthology of 27 books written by various authors in the first century CE. These texts provide a chronicle of the life, teachings, death, and resurrection of Jesus Christ, and the subsequent spread of the Christian faith through his disciples and early believers. Understanding the historical context of the New Testament aids in comprehending its narratives, characters, and teachings.

The Roman Empire: The New Testament unfolds against the backdrop of the Roman Empire. At the time, the Romans ruled over a vast territory, including the regions where Jesus lived and taught, mainly Judea and Galilee. As the Gospel of Luke notes, Jesus was born during the reign of Caesar Augustus (Luke 2:1), the first Roman emperor, and his ministry began during the governorship of Pontius Pilate (Luke 3:1). This political landscape profoundly impacted the lives of the people, including their interactions and conflicts with the Roman authorities, often depicted in the New Testament.

Jewish Culture and Religion: The New Testament authors, as well as Jesus and most of his followers, were Jewish, living in a society deeply influenced by Jewish laws, customs, and religious beliefs. The Gospels frequently reference Jewish practices such as synagogue worship (Luke 4:16), observance of the Sabbath (Mark 2:23-28), and religious festivals like the Passover (Matthew 26:17-19). The Jewish religious leadership, including the Pharisees and Sadducees, also play significant roles in the New Testament narratives.

The Greco-Roman Culture: The New Testament also reflects the influence of the Greco-Roman culture, prevalent during the time. Greek was the lingua franca of the eastern Mediterranean, and the New Testament was written in Greek. Paul's letters to the early Christian communities in cities like Corinth, Ephesus, and Philippi highlight the challenges faced by these communities within their broader Greco-Roman cultural context (1 Corinthians 1:22-23, Ephesians 4:17-24, Philippians 1:27).

Prophecies and Messianic Expectations: The New Testament authors often draw on prophecies from the Hebrew Scriptures (Old Testament) to explain Jesus' life and mission. They present Jesus as the awaited Messiah, fulfilling prophecies about a savior or deliverer (Matthew 1:22-23, Luke 24:44-47). This messianic expectation played a crucial role in shaping the understanding and acceptance of Jesus' teachings among his followers and detractors alike.

The Early Christian Communities: The latter part of the New Testament, especially the Acts of the Apostles and the Epistles, depict the development of early Christian communities in the Mediterranean region. These texts illustrate the challenges, conflicts, and transformations within these communities as they navigated their faith in a diverse and often hostile environment (Acts 8:1-4, 1 Corinthians 1:10-13).

Understanding the historical context of the New Testament enables us to appreciate the complexity and richness of its narratives. It offers a broader perspective to interpret the events, characters, and teachings presented in these texts. However, it is essential to remember that while historical corroboration can provide valuable insights, it is only one aspect of understanding the New Testament. A comprehensive interpretation also requires considering theological, literary, and cultural dimensions of these texts.

Historical Evidence from Within the New Testament

The New Testament provides a wealth of historical evidence, both in its portrayal of first-century life and its references to specific people, places, and events.

Historical Figures: The New Testament includes numerous references to historical figures whose existence is corroborated by external sources. For instance, Pontius Pilate, the Roman governor who presided over Jesus' trial, is mentioned in all four Gospels (Matthew 27:1-2, Mark 15:1, Luke 23:1, John 18:29). His historical existence is also confirmed by inscriptions found at Caesarea Maritima and by Roman historian Tacitus. Similarly, the existence of Herod Antipas, the ruler of Galilee and Perea during Jesus' ministry, is affirmed both in the Gospels (Mark 6:14-29) and by Jewish historian Josephus.

Geographic Locations: The New Testament mentions numerous geographic locations, many of which have been verified through archaeological research. Jerusalem, Nazareth, Bethlehem, Capernaum, and other cities and towns where Jesus and his followers traveled are well-documented locations. The authors of the New Testament books also accurately depict various aspects of these locations, such as the layout of the Jerusalem Temple (Mark 11:11, John 10:23) or the topography around the Sea of Galilee (Matthew 4:18-22).

Events and Customs: The New Testament describes several historical events and social customs, providing insight into life in the first century. For example, the Gospels describe the process of Roman crucifixion in detail, as seen in the crucifixion of Jesus (John 19:16-30). The Gospels and Acts also depict various Jewish customs and practices of the time, such as the Passover meal (Luke 22:7-13) or the ritual of baptism (Acts 8:36-38).

Early Christian Communities: The letters of Paul and other New Testament writers provide valuable historical insight into the beliefs, practices, and struggles of early Christian communities in various cities around the Mediterranean, like Corinth, Ephesus, and Rome. These letters address specific issues faced by these communities, reflecting their historical and social contexts (1 Corinthians 1:10-17, Ephesians 2:11-22, Romans 1:8-17).

The Life and Ministry of Jesus: The Gospels provide a detailed account of Jesus' life, teachings, death, and resurrection. These include specific events, such as Jesus' birth in Bethlehem (Luke 2:1-7), his public ministry in Galilee (Mark 1:14-15), his trial and crucifixion in Jerusalem (Matthew 27:11-54), and his post-resurrection appearances to his followers (John 20:11-18). While these events have theological significance, they are also presented as historical realities.

Therefore, the New Testament provides valuable historical information, which is consistent with what we know from other historical and archaeological sources from the same period. While these internal evidences do not prove the theological claims of the New Testament, they do attest to the reliability of the New Testament as a historical document.

The Role of Archaeology in Corroborating the New Testament

Archaeology plays a significant role in corroborating the historical accuracy of the New Testament. Through the uncovering of ancient artifacts, inscriptions, and structures, archaeologists have been able to provide evidence supporting various aspects of the New Testament narrative.

Locations and Structures: Archaeological findings have affirmed the existence of many places mentioned in the New Testament, such as Jerusalem, Bethlehem, Nazareth, and Capernaum. In some instances, these excavations have even unearthed structures that correlate to New Testament accounts. For instance, the "House of Peter" in Capernaum, which some archaeologists believe to be the home of the apostle Peter, corresponds to accounts of Jesus' ministry in this town (Mark 1:29-31). Similarly, the Pool of Bethesda, where Jesus healed a paralyzed man (John 5:1-15), was discovered in Jerusalem in the 19th century, affirming the Gospel's accurate depiction of the city's geography.

Inscriptions: Archaeological discoveries have included inscriptions that affirm the existence of several New Testament figures. The Pontius Pilate inscription found at Caesarea Maritima affirms the existence of the Roman governor mentioned in the trial of Jesus (Matthew 27:1-2). Likewise, an ossuary bearing the inscription "James, son of Joseph, brother of Jesus" has been suggested as potential evidence of James, the brother of Jesus, mentioned in the New Testament (Galatians 1:19).

Artifacts: Various artifacts have been found that support the cultural and societal context of the New Testament. For instance, numerous crucifixion nails and heel bones pierced by such nails have been discovered, providing physical evidence of the Roman practice of crucifixion, as depicted in the Gospels (John 19:16-18).

Early Christian Writings: Archaeology has also unearthed early Christian writings that support the New Testament. For example, fragments of the Gospel of John discovered among the Dead Sea Scrolls indicate that this Gospel was already in circulation in the late first century or early second century, affirming the New Testament's timeline.

In conclusion, archaeological evidence provides a substantial amount of corroboration for the New Testament's historical accuracy. While archaeology alone cannot confirm the theological claims of the New Testament, it does lend credibility to the text as a reliable historical document. Through archaeological findings, we gain a clearer understanding of the world of the New Testament, affirming its historical context and adding depth to our reading of the biblical narrative.

Corroborations from Ancient Manuscripts and Inscriptions

Ancient manuscripts and inscriptions play a critical role in corroborating the historical claims of the New Testament. These historical records provide evidence for the existence of significant figures, events, and places mentioned in the biblical narratives, thereby contributing to its overall historical reliability.

Ancient Manuscripts: The New Testament has a rich manuscript tradition. Thousands of Greek manuscripts, along with numerous Latin, Coptic, and Syriac versions, contain portions or the entirety of the New Testament texts. This abundance of manuscripts, some dating as early as the second century, allows scholars to trace the transmission of the text over time, affirming its preservation and accuracy. One such manuscript, the Codex Sinaiticus, includes the entire New Testament and most of the Old Testament, demonstrating the early compilation of these texts.

The Septuagint: The Septuagint, a Greek translation of the Hebrew Scriptures completed in the third century BCE, often aligns with the Old Testament quotations found in the New Testament. This provides evidence that the New Testament authors were relying on existing, recognized Scripture (for instance, Matthew 1:23 quotes Isaiah 7:14 from the Septuagint).

Early Christian Writings: Writings from early Christian leaders, often called the Church Fathers, frequently quote and reference the New Testament, suggesting its widespread acceptance and use within the early Christian community. For example, Ignatius of Antioch, writing in the early second century, quotes from a range of New Testament books, including Matthew, Luke, Acts, Romans, and 1 Corinthians.

Inscriptions: Inscriptions provide further historical corroboration. For example, the Nazareth Inscription, a decree of Caesar found in Nazareth, indirectly supports the biblical account of Jesus' resurrection and the subsequent spread of Christianity (Matthew 28:2-7). The Pilate Stone found in Caesarea provides hard evidence of Pontius Pilate's existence, who is mentioned in the trial and crucifixion of Jesus (John 18:28-19:16).

Non-Christian Sources: Non-Christian sources, such as the writings of Josephus, Tacitus, and Pliny the Younger, reference Christians and occasionally Jesus

Himself, providing extrabiblical corroboration of the New Testament's historical context.

In sum, the wealth of ancient manuscripts and inscriptions, both Christian and non-Christian, provide substantial evidence supporting the New Testament's historical reliability. These documents attest to the existence of key figures and events, reinforce the cultural and societal context of the New Testament, and affirm the preservation of the New Testament text over time.

The Witness of Ancient Historians: Christianity's First to Third Centuries Non-Christian Witnesses for the Historicity of Jesus Christ

The Unshakable Historicity of Christ: Building Faith on Solid Ground

Christianity bears witness to its own truth, establishing a firm foundation for all believers. Through remarkable archaeological evidence, the historicity of Christ and Christianity remains unwavering and enduring. Christians do not rely solely on secular historians to strengthen their faith. However, as followers of Christ, we are called to make disciples of all nations (Matthew 28:19-20), engaging with unbelievers who may question the existence of Jesus. This includes atheists, agnostics, Bible critics, as well as liberal-moderate Bible scholars who propose circular reasoning in using the Bible and early Church writings to validate the historical reality of Jesus and early Christianity. As Christian apologists and evangelists, it is our duty to reason, explain, prove, persuade, and defend our faith. Therefore, we demonstrate the existence of Jesus Christ through sources beyond the Bible and the writings of the early Church Fathers. To those who doubt the authenticity of Christianity, the historicity of Jesus, and the authority of the New Testament, it is crucial to carefully examine the writings of secular historians and other authors. In doing so, one will discover that their accounts indeed align with the testimony presented in the Bible.

Christian believers should acquaint themselves with the testimonies of secular historians, as they reveal the significant impact Christianity had on the ancient Greco-Roman world nearly 1,980 years ago. When we consider the abundance of physical evidence, including archaeological discoveries of Bible manuscripts and early Church writings, alongside accounts and comments from non-Christian authors, we gain additional confirmation that the biblical narrative of Jesus Christ's life and ministry is not a mere fabrication or fictional tale. We can confidently affirm the historical reality of Jesus Christ and early Christianity as presented in the Bible. Their authenticity and historicity are firmly established, and even the disparaging remarks of contemporary critics cannot dismiss the evidence of these events.

It is important for Christians to recognize that Bible critics often argue with a default assumption that there is only one secular historical reference to Jesus Christ. However, this claim is made by individuals who either lack awareness or hope that Christians are uninformed. In truth, there exist twelve secular historical references to Jesus Christ. Once this fact is stated, the critic must retreat to their second default argument, which asserts that the number of references to Christ and Christianity in the existing writings of the first two centuries is relatively small. In response, it should be noted that, in ancient history, historians and writers predominantly focused on the wealthy, powerful, warriors, and politicians. Common people were rarely mentioned, and Jesus Christ, a carpenter from the humble town of Nazareth, was as ordinary as they come. In fact, the available references we have are quite remarkable. Even considering Jesus' role in founding Christianity and the apostles' efforts in growing it to include one million disciples by 130 CE, it is unlikely that many historians, particularly adversaries, would extensively document their activities. In a predominantly pagan world, early Christianity was regarded with profanity by various segments of society. They were viewed merely as a small faction emerging from the despised Jews, who had long been subjects of Roman hatred. Some even believed that their effective evangelism aimed to overthrow the Roman Empire and its prevalent idolatry of the time.

The Critical Handbook of the Greek New Testament, by Edward C. Mitchell, 1896, Chapter III.

> "There is, therefore, but little reason to expect that a heathen historian, writing of his own time, and having no personal interest in Christians, should make very frequent allusions to them, or be very minute or accurate in his description. And we should have still less reason to anticipate that literary men of the same period, whose themes are not necessarily related to Christianity, should go out of their way to make mention of it. Nevertheless, we shall find, upon examination, that a fair proportion of Pagan writers have in some way recognized the existence and spread of Christianity during the first two centuries."

The Greek historians Appian and Pausanias and the Latin historians ivy, Paterculus, Valerius, Justin, and Florus, all recorded their history before the reign of Tiberius (reigning from 14 to 37 CE), therefore, it is not unexpected that they would not mention Christ or Christianity. But we turn our attention to the Roman historian **Tacitus (56-120 CE)**, who stands high among all the secular historians of antiquity. He is believed to be accurate in his coverage and faithful in his judgments. In his Annals, Book 15, in describing how a rumor had been reported that it was, in reality, Emperor Nero, who was the one guilty of burning Rome,

Tacitus says in paragraph 44:

"To get rid of the report, Nero fastened the guilt and inflicted the most exquisite tortures on a class hated for their abominations, called Christians by the populace. Christus [Christ], from whom the name had its origin, suffered the extreme penalty during the reign of Tiberius at the hands of one of our procurators, Pontius Pilatus, and a most mischievous superstition, thus checked for the moment, again broke out not only in Judæa, the first source of the evil, but even in Rome, where all things hideous and shameful from every part of the world find their centre and become popular. Accordingly, an arrest was first made of all who pleaded guilty; then, upon their information, an immense multitude was convicted, not so much of the crime of firing the city, as of hatred against mankind. Mockery of every sort was added to their deaths. Covered with the skins of beasts, they were torn by dogs and perished, or were nailed to crosses, or were doomed to the flames and burnt, to serve as a nightly illumination, when daylight had expired."—Translated by A. J. Church and W. J. Brodribb.

Then we have the Roman satirist and poet, **Juvenal** (c. 60-140 CE), who was active in the late first and early second century. He made a reference to Tacitus' account of the persecution Christians had faced. (*Sat.* i. 155-157). There is the highly respected Roman Stoic philosopher, statesman, dramatist, **Seneca** (c. 4 B.C.- 65 CE), who became a tutor of Nero in 49 CE He made a passing reference to Christianity. (*Epist. xiv.*) So does the Greek orator, writer, philosopher, and historian **Dio Chrysostom** (c. 40-115 CE), the "golden mouthed." (*Orat. Corinthiac.* xxxvii. p. 463) Furthermore, **Arrian** (86/89 – c. after 146/160 CE), a Greek historian, public servant, military commander, and philosopher of the Roman period. (*Dissertat.* iv. 7. ¶ 5, 6) Moreover, we have **Suetonius** (c. 69 – 122 CE), the Roman historian who wrote during the early Imperial era of the Roman Empire, in depicting the life of Claudius Caesar. He says:

"[Claudius] expelled from Rome the Jews, who were continually exciting disturbances, at the *instigation of Chrestus* [Christ]." (Vit. *Claud.* cap. 25.) And again, in telling of the cruel persecution under Nero, Suetonius says: *"The Christians were punished,* a set of men of a *new* and mischievous superstition."—*Vit. Nero.* cap. 16.

Pliny the Younger (61 – c. 113 CE), who served as the governor of Bithynia, wrote a letter to Emperor Trajan seeking guidance on how to handle the early Christians. This correspondence took place around 110-112 CE, approximately 50 years after the martyrdom of the apostle Paul. Pliny, having not previously conducted a formal investigation into the Christians, sought Trajan's counsel to ensure his actions were appropriate. These preserved letters between Pliny and Trajan are valuable historical documents that provide early Roman references to the early Christians. They contribute to our confidence in the biblical account of Christ, confirming His existence, his profound teaching, and the presence of devoted disciples whose lives starkly contrasted with the pagan culture of the Roman Empire. It is this stark contrast that caught the attention of Roman authorities. These documents serve as a testament to the impact of Christianity during that time.

Pliny admitted in this letter that up unto the time of his writing, he had never personally attended the "trials concerning those who profess Christianity." he says:

> "The method I have observed toward those who have been denounced to me as Christians is this: I interrogated them whether they were Christians; if they confessed it I repeated the question twice again, adding the threat of capital punishment; if they still persevered, I ordered them to be executed.... Others ... at first confessed themselves Christians, and then denied it; true, they had been of that persuasion but they had quit it ... many years ... ago. They all worshipped your statue and the images of the gods, and cursed Christ (Ep. 10.96)." – Clinton E. Arnold, Zondervan Illustrated Bible Backgrounds Commentary: John, Acts., vol. 2 (Grand Rapids, MI: Zondervan, 2002), 148.

Still others, Pliny says, revealed that at one time they had been Christians and indeed had "addressed a form of prayer to Christ, as to a divinity", but they were no longer Christians, and had not been for some time.—*Harvard Classics,* vol. 9, pp. 425-428.

Pliny was making certain that Trajan supported these methods and tactics. Emperor Trajan replied to Pliny on how he had been handling the situation. "You have adopted the right course," Trajan wrote, "in investigating the charges against the Christians who were brought before you." Trajan was succeeded by his cousin Hadrian (117-138 CE), whom it is said that Trajan supposedly adopted on his deathbed. In writing to the proconsul of Asia concerning Christians, Hadrian declared: "If, therefore, in accusations of this sort, the people of the province can clearly affirm any thing *against the Christians,* so as to bring the case before the tribunal, to this only let them have recourse, and not to informal accusations and mere clamors."—Ap. Euseb. *Hist. Eccles.,* iv. 9.

Enemies of Christ and the Christians

Lucian (c. 125 – after 180 CE) was a Greek satirist and rhetorician who was born toward the end of Trajan's reign. He criticized the teachings of Christians and mocked their form of worship. Writing to Cronius (a celebrated Neopythagorean philosopher) concerning the death of Peregrinus Proteus (c. 95 – 165 CE), a famous Greek Cynic philosopher, Lucian says, among other things, that the Christians "spoke of him [Christ] as a god, and took him for a lawgiver, and honored him with the title of Master. They therefore still worship that great man who was crucified in Palestine, because he introduced into the world this new religion."

Origen (c. 185 – c. 254 CE), probably the most notable Church Father, has preserved the testimony of some additional non-Christians witnesses of ancient times for the historicity of Christ. For instance, there was a Greek philosopher named Numenius (mid-2nd century CE), of which, Origen says, "quotes a fragment from the history of Jesus Christ, of which he seeks the hidden interpretation." (McClintock & Strong, Cyclopedia, vol. 7, p. 225) Origen also speaks of Phlegon (2nd century CE), a Greek historian freedman of Emperor Hadrian, as mentioning the fulfillment of certain prophecies pertaining to Christ.—Contra. Cels. lib. ii., ¶ 14.

Celsus was a 2nd-century Greek philosopher and opponent of early Christianity, who lived about 130 years after the death of Jesus. He made numerous quotations from the Greek New Testament, explaining: "We take these things from your writings, to wound you with your own weapons." We do not have the original works of Celsus, but Origen in about 248 CE preserved nearly 80 of his quotations (Contra Celsum) from the Scriptures. Jesus, Celsus states, was portrayed as the Word of God; was called the Son of God; was from Nazareth, the son of a carpenter; declared to have had a miraculous conception. Celsus makes allusion to Jesus' being carried down to Egypt, to his baptism in the Jordan, to the voice declaring him to be God's son, to the temptations in the wilderness, to the choosing of the 12 apostles. He admits that Jesus performed great miracles: fed multitudes opened blind eyes, healed the lame, cured the sick, raised the dead. He also makes reference to many points of doctrine in the teachings of Christ. And in the end, he refers to the betrayal by Judas, Peter's denial, the scourging, crowning, and mockery heaped upon Jesus, as well as the darkness and earthquake that came at Jesus' death, and then the resurrection that followed. Thus this heathen writer unwittingly proved that such things were written down and were universally believed by Christians at that time.—Mitchell's *Critical Handbook of the Greek New Testament*.

Celsus addressed the miracles of Jesus, holding that "Jesus performed his miracles by sorcery (γοητεία)":

> O light and truth! he distinctly declares, with his own voice, as ye yourselves have recorded, that there will come to you even others, employing miracles of a similar kind, who are wicked men, and sorcerers; and Satan. So that Jesus himself does not deny that these works at least are not at all divine, but are the acts of wicked men; and being compelled by the force of truth, he at the same time not only laid open the doings of others, but convicted himself of the same acts. Is it not, then, a miserable inference, to conclude from the same works that the one is God and the other sorcerers? Why ought the others, because of these acts, to be accounted wicked rather than this man, seeing they have him as their witness against himself? For he has himself acknowledged that these are not the works of a divine nature, but the inventions of certain deceivers, and of thoroughly wicked men. – Ernest Cushing Richardson, Bernhard Pick (1905).

The Ante-Nicene fathers: translations of the writings of the fathers down to 325 CE, Volume 4. Scribner's. "But Celsus, wishing to assimilate the miracles of Jesus to the works of human sorcery, says in express terms as follows: "O light and truth! he distinctly declares, with his own voice, as ye yourselves have recorded, that there will come to you even others, employing miracles of a similar kind, who are wicked men, and sorcerers; and Satan. So that Jesus himself does not deny that these works at least are not at all divine, but are the acts of wicked men; and being compelled by the force of truth, he at the same time not only laid open the doings of others but convicted himself of the same acts. Is it not, then, a miserable inference, to conclude from the same works that the one is God and the other sorcerers? Why ought the others, because of these acts, to be accounted wicked rather than this man, seeing they have him as their witness against himself? For he has himself acknowledged that these are not the works of a divine nature, but the inventions of certain deceivers, and of thoroughly wicked men."

Turning to yet another non-Christian witness, the renowned Jewish historian, **Flavius Josephus** (37 – c. 100 CE), who was no friend of Christianity. A passage in his *Antiquities of the Jews* (Book XVIII, chapter iii, ¶3), though claimed to be, but not proved, spurious, reads: "Now there was about this time Jesus, a wise man, **if it be lawful to call him a man**; for he was a doer of wonderful works, a teacher of such men as receive the truth with pleasure. He drew over to him both many of the Jews and many of the Gentiles. **He was [the] Christ**. And when Pilate, at the suggestion of the principal men amongst us, had condemned him to the cross, those that loved him at the first did not forsake him; **for he appeared to them alive again the third day; as the divine prophets had foretold these and ten thousand other wonderful things concerning him**. And the tribe of Christians, so named from him, are not extinct at this day [about 93 CE]." Again, Josephus (Book XX, chapter ix., ¶1) tells how the high priest Ananus "assembled the Sanhedrin of judges, and brought before them the brother of Jesus, who was called Christ, whose name was James".— Translated by William Whiston.

The sections bolded in the above from Josephus are what is considered spurious, to have been added later by Christians in the church. Therefore, the Bible critic wanted to discount the entire writing. Of course, they would never do such a thing if it was referring to a secular person. They would simply remove what they knew to be a spurious interpolation and call the authentic portion historical evidence, as we should do here as well. When we remove what seems to be spurious, we still have a testimony from a Jewish historian who was no friend to the Christians, who still informs us about the historical Jesus Christ. Josephus has more to say about Jesus by way of talking about James, his half brother.

> "Ananus [who was a high priest], therefore, being of this character, and supposing that he had a favorable opportunity on account of the fact that Festus was dead, and Albinus was still on the way, called together the

Sanhedrim, and brought before them the brother of Jesus, the so-called Christ, James by name, together with some others, and accused them of violating the law, and condemned them to be stoned." – Eusebius of Caesaria, "The Church History of Eusebius," in Eusebius: Church History, Life of Constantine the Great, and Oration in Praise of Constantine, ed. Philip Schaff and Henry Wace, trans. Arthur Cushman McGiffert, vol. 1, A Select Library of the Nicene and Post-Nicene Fathers of the Christian Church, Second Series (New York: Christian Literature Company, 1890), 127.

So, we have two very early statements by Josephus, who lived 37-100 CE. Another Jewish source that refers to Jesus Christ as a historical person is the Talmud. One would think the Jewish Talmud would simply ignore any reference to Christ the founder of Christianity because that Christians and Jews were at odds with each other for almost 300 years at the time of compiling the Talmud in the fourth century.

Thus, we have given the reader a number of the testimonies of many non-Christian witnesses, who confirm the historicity of Christ and early Christianity, both being authentic and true. Let all non-believing Bible critics, therefore, who imagine that Christ has no historical support outside of the Bible, know that they simply have been taught false ideas and misconceptions, and they need to objectively investigate the historicity of Christ and the early Christians, accepting that the Word of God is truth. (John 17:17; Ps. 103:15; Isa. 40:8; 1 Pet. 1:25.) Stop feeding your skepticism, your unbelief, and be receptive to the idea that real historical evidence exists.

The writings of ancient historians offer valuable insights that can corroborate the historical accounts found in the New Testament. These accounts from ancient historians do not simply echo the New Testament. Instead, they provide independent attestations of the events and figures described within its pages. When considered alongside the New Testament, these historical accounts enhance our understanding of the life, death, and impact of Jesus Christ, as well as the early development of Christianity. This convergence of multiple sources bolsters the historical reliability of the New Testament.

Extra-Biblical Testimony About Jesus of Nazareth

1. Historians
   a. Josephus
   b. Tacitus
   c. Suetonius
   d. Thallus
   e. Phlegon
2. Government Officials
   a. Pliny the Younger
   b. Emperor Trajan
   c. Emperor Hadrian
3. Other Sources
   a. Jewish Talmud
   b. Lucian (Greek Satirist)
4. 15 Things We Can Know About Jesus
   a. He lived during the time of Tiberius Caesar
   b. He was from Nazareth
   c. He lived a virtuous life
   d. He was a wonder-worker
   e. He had a brother named James
   f. He was acclaimed to be the Messiah
   g. He was crucified under Pontius Pilate
   h. An eclipse and earthquake occurred when He died
   i. He was crucified on the eve of Passover
   j. He was considered a Jewish King
   k. His disciples believed He rose from the dead
   l. His disciples were willing to die for their belief
   m. Christianity spread rapidly as far as Rome
   n. His disciples denied Roman gods and worshipped Jesus as God
   o. His disciples took oaths to live morally as He taught them

Image by Shawn White

The New Testament and Jewish Sources: The Talmud and Midrash

Jewish historical and religious texts, such as the Talmud and Midrash, offer additional external corroboration of events and people found in the New Testament.

The Talmud: The Talmud is a central text of mainstream Judaism, consisting of the Mishnah and the Gemara. It is not a single book but a collection of tractates encompassing Jewish law, ethics, philosophy, customs, and history. Some passages in the Talmud refer to Yeshu, a figure that some scholars link with Jesus. The accounts depict Yeshu as a student of Jewish law who strayed into heresy, a picture differing significantly from the New Testament narrative. However, the references to his execution on the eve of Passover and the charges of sorcery and leading Israel astray appear to correlate with New Testament accounts of Jesus' trial and crucifixion (Matthew 26:57-68, Mark 14:53-65, Luke 22:63-71, John 18:12-24).

The Midrash: The Midrash is a method of interpreting biblical stories that goes beyond simple distillation of religious, legal, or moral teachings. It fills in gaps left in the biblical narrative regarding events and personalities that are only hinted at. Although the Midrash doesn't provide direct evidence about Jesus or early Christianity, its interpretations of messianic prophecies can help us understand the cultural and religious context in which Jesus and his followers lived. For example, the interpretation of Isaiah 53, a passage seen by Christians as prophetic of Jesus' suffering and death (Matthew 8:17, 1 Peter 2:24), varies significantly in Jewish tradition and provides insight into differing perceptions of the Messiah in the first century.

While these Jewish texts should be approached with caution as sources for Jesus' life and the early Christian movement, as they were compiled centuries after these events and often present a polemical or distorted view of Jesus, they nevertheless provide an external Jewish perspective on figures and events described in the New Testament. As such, they add another layer to the complex tapestry of historical evidence related to the New Testament.

The Crucifixion of Jesus: Historical Evidence

The crucifixion of Jesus is a central event in the Christian faith, and it's also a historical event that has been substantiated by various sources outside of the New Testament.

1. The New Testament Accounts: The Gospels of Matthew (27:32-56), Mark (15:21-41), Luke (23:26-49), and John (19:16-37) provide vivid and detailed accounts of Jesus' crucifixion. Each Gospel, while presenting unique details and perspectives, unanimously confirms that Jesus was crucified under the Roman governor Pontius Pilate. The crucifixion narrative also appears in the letters of Paul, notably in 1 Corinthians 1:23, 2:2, and Galatians 3:1, affirming the centrality of the event in the earliest Christian tradition.

2. **Roman Historians**: Tacitus, a Roman senator and historian, wrote in his Annals (circa 116 CE) about the execution of Jesus during the reign of Emperor Tiberius, under the governorship of Pontius Pilate. Though Tacitus shows contempt for Christians, his account affirms the crucifixion of Jesus as a historical event.

3. **Jewish Historian**: Flavius Josephus, in his "Antiquities of the Jews" (circa 93-94 CE), mentions Jesus' crucifixion by Pilate. Though the authenticity of some parts of the passage (Testimonium Flavianum) is contested, most scholars accept that Josephus did indeed write about Jesus' crucifixion.

4. **The Talmud**: As mentioned previously, the Babylonian Talmud includes passages referring to Yeshu's (possibly Jesus') execution on the eve of Passover, though the accounts differ significantly from the New Testament narrative.

The historical evidence corroborating the New Testament's account of Jesus' crucifixion is multi-sourced, coming from Christian, Roman, and Jewish perspectives. While the theological interpretations of the event vary, the basic historical fact of Jesus' crucifixion is widely affirmed.

Corroborations for the Apostolic Actions and Early Christian Persecution

The activities of the apostles and the persecution of early Christians are crucial themes within the New Testament, particularly in the Acts of the Apostles and several epistles. These accounts find support in historical and archaeological evidence, as well as in non-Christian sources.

Apostolic Actions: The missionary activities of the apostles, particularly Paul, are extensively recorded in the Book of Acts and in Paul's own epistles. Paul's travels to key cities such as Corinth (Acts 18:1-17; 1 Corinthians), Ephesus (Acts 19:1-41; Ephesians), and Rome (Acts 28:16-31; Romans) are confirmed by archaeological findings in these cities, including inscriptions and early Christian symbols. Similarly, Peter's ministry in Jerusalem (Acts 2:14-41) and possibly Rome (1 Peter 5:13) align with historical and traditional accounts of early Christian activity in these locations.

Early Christian Persecution: The New Testament describes several instances of persecution against early Christians (Acts 7:54-60; 8:1-3; 12:1-5; 2 Corinthians 11:23-27; Revelation 2:10). These accounts are corroborated by Roman historians such as Tacitus, who in his Annals, mentions the brutal persecution of Christians under Emperor Nero following the great fire of Rome in 64 AD. Similarly, the correspondence between Pliny the Younger, a Roman governor, and Emperor Trajan around 112 CE reveals the official Roman policy towards Christians, confirming the New Testament depiction of sporadic, localized persecutions.

The Martyrdom of Apostles: The martyrdom of apostles, including Peter and Paul, is not detailed in the New Testament but is affirmed by early Christian tradition and extrabiblical sources. For instance, Clement of Rome, in his letter to the Corinthians around 96 AD, refers to the martyrdom of Peter and Paul. The apocryphal Acts of Peter and Acts of Paul, although not historically reliable in all details, also attest to their martyrdom in Rome, consistent with early Christian tradition.

Therefore, the apostolic actions and early Christian persecution depicted in the New Testament are substantiated by a range of sources, including archaeological evidence, historical documents, and early Christian and non-Christian writings. These corroborations underscore the historical reliability of the New Testament's depiction of early Christian life and mission.

Paul and His Missionary Journeys: Archaeological and Historical Evidence

The Apostle Paul is a significant figure in the New Testament, known for his dramatic conversion and subsequent missionary journeys. These travels, as recorded in the Book of Acts and his epistles, spanned various regions of the Roman Empire and have been subject to extensive historical and archaeological scrutiny.

Paul's Conversion: Paul's transformation from a persecutor of Christians to a devoted apostle is recounted in Acts 9:1-19. While direct archaeological evidence for this event is absent, the narrative's historical plausibility is underlined by the fact that the road to Damascus, where the conversion occurred, was a well-traveled route in antiquity, linking key cities of the Roman Empire.

First Missionary Journey: Paul's first missionary journey (Acts 13:4-14:28) took him to Cyprus and then to the region of Galatia in Asia Minor. Archaeological findings in these areas, including inscriptions and ruins of ancient synagogues, affirm the presence of Jewish and Christian communities during Paul's time.

Second and Third Missionary Journeys: During his subsequent travels (Acts 15:36-21:17), Paul visited several key cities such as Philippi, Thessalonica, Corinth, and Ephesus. Archaeological discoveries in these cities, such as the "Gallio Inscription" in Corinth which helps to date Paul's visit, and the large theater in Ephesus where the riot against Paul occurred (Acts 19:23-41), provide tangible links to the biblical narrative.

Journey to Rome: Paul's voyage to Rome as a prisoner (Acts 27:1-28:31) includes specific details about the route, the ship, the storm, and the shipwreck on Malta. Many of these details are consistent with ancient seafaring practices and geographical markers, lending credibility to the account.

Paul's Letters: Paul's epistles provide additional historical evidence, as they mention specific individuals, locations, and events that coincide with the timeline and context of his journeys. The authenticity of many of these letters is widely accepted by scholars, further validating the historical reality of Paul's missions.

In conclusion, Paul's missionary journeys as portrayed in the New Testament are historically plausible and are supported by archaeological findings and historical research. This evidence reinforces the credibility of the New Testament as a valuable source of historical information about the spread of early Christianity.

Geographical and Topographical Accuracy in the New Testament

The New Testament consistently demonstrates a reliable grasp of geographical and topographical details, further establishing its credibility as a historical document. These geographical references span the regions of Palestine, Asia Minor, Greece, and Italy, and many of these locations have been confirmed through archaeological investigations and historical studies.

Palestine: The New Testament accurately references numerous locations in Palestine, such as Jerusalem, Bethany, Capernaum, and Nazareth. For instance, John 5:1-15 describes the Pool of Bethesda in Jerusalem with five roofed colonnades, a detail confirmed by archaeological excavations.

Asia Minor: The seven churches mentioned in Revelation (2:1-3:22) correspond to actual locations in Asia Minor (modern-day Turkey), including Ephesus, Smyrna, and Laodicea. Additionally, archaeological findings in these cities align with the descriptions and messages contained in John's letters.

Greece: The New Testament correctly identifies various cities and regions in Greece, including Athens, Corinth, and Thessalonica. Acts 17:22-31 describes Paul's speech at the Areopagus in Athens, a location that remains a significant archaeological site today.

Italy: The city of Rome is frequently mentioned in the New Testament, particularly in relation to Paul's imprisonment and trial (Acts 28:16-31). The narrative includes specific locations such as the Praetorian Guard where Paul was kept under house arrest (Philippians 1:13).

Travel Routes: The New Testament accurately portrays the travel routes and modes of transportation of the time. For example, Paul's missionary journeys (Acts 13-28) adhere to known travel routes of the Roman Empire, while his shipwreck off Malta (Acts 27:1-28:10) accurately reflects the hazards of ancient sea travel.

Topographical Details: The New Testament includes precise topographical details, such as the steep cliffs near the Sea of Galilee where the Gadarene swine plunged into the sea (Mark 5:1-20), and the location of Jacob's well near Sychar, where Jesus conversed with the Samaritan woman (John 4:5-26).

In conclusion, the New Testament's consistent accuracy in geographical and topographical details reinforces its reliability as a historical document. These details not only connect the biblical narrative to real-world locations but also provide a contextual backdrop for the events and teachings it records.

Linguistic and Cultural Consistencies in the New Testament

The New Testament, primarily composed in Koine Greek, displays remarkable consistency with the cultural and linguistic contexts of its time. This is evident in the use of language, idioms, and cultural customs that align with first-century Mediterranean society.

Language: The Greek of the New Testament corresponds with the common language of the Hellenistic world, known as Koine Greek. For instance, Paul's letters, the Gospels, and other New Testament texts use language and phrasing that align with known Greek writings of the time (1 Corinthians 2:13).

Idioms and Phrases: The New Testament also contains Semitic idioms and phrases, reflecting the Jewish context of many of its authors and characters. An example is the Aramaic phrase "Talitha cumi," which Jesus says to the daughter of Jairus in Mark 5:41, and is then translated into Greek in the same verse.

Cultural Customs: The New Testament accurately portrays various cultural customs of the time. This includes Jewish religious practices (Matthew 26:17-19, Luke 2:41-42), Roman legal procedures (Acts 25:11), and societal norms and structures (1 Corinthians 11:4-5, Philemon 1:10-16).

Jewish Scriptures: The authors of the New Testament frequently quote and allude to the Hebrew Scriptures, demonstrating their deep engagement with Jewish religious tradition (Matthew 4:4, Romans 3:10-18).

Greek and Roman Context: The New Testament also engages with the wider Greco-Roman cultural and philosophical context. For example, Paul's speech in Athens in Acts 17:22-31 displays familiarity with Greek philosophy and religious practices.

Diverse Social Contexts: The New Testament reflects the social diversity of the early Christian movement, including men and women, Jews and Gentiles, slaves and free people, all of whom played key roles in the emerging communities (Galatians 3:28).

In summary, the linguistic and cultural consistencies of the New Testament further corroborate its historical reliability. The text reflects the languages, idioms, and cultural customs of its time, further grounding the biblical narrative in its historical context.

The Historicity of Jesus: A Case Study in New Testament Corroboration

The historicity of Jesus is a significant area in the study of New Testament corroboration. Various elements within the New Testament, along with external sources, offer substantial evidence for Jesus as a historical figure.

Gospel Accounts: The four Gospels in the New Testament (Matthew, Mark, Luke, and John) are primary sources of information about Jesus' life, teachings, death, and resurrection. These documents, although having theological purposes, also contain historical data. For instance, Luke begins his Gospel by stating his aim to write an "orderly account" based on information handed down by "eyewitnesses and servants of the word" (Luke 1:1-4).

Letters of Paul: Paul's letters provide additional evidence for Jesus' historicity. They contain references to Jesus' life, teachings, death, and resurrection. For example, in 1 Corinthians 15:3-8, Paul recounts the tradition he received about Jesus' death and resurrection and his appearances to various individuals and groups.

External Corroboration: The New Testament accounts of Jesus are also corroborated by non-Christian sources. For example, Roman historian Tacitus (Annals 15.44) and Jewish historian Josephus (Antiquities 18.63-64) both make references to Jesus.

Archaeological Evidence: Archaeological findings provide further corroboration. For instance, the Pilate Stone, discovered in 1961, confirms the existence of Pontius Pilate, the Roman governor who presided over Jesus' trial (Matthew 27:1-2, 11-26).

Prophecy Fulfillment: The New Testament presents Jesus as fulfilling numerous Old Testament prophecies, adding another dimension to the historical corroboration. Examples include His birth in Bethlehem (Matthew 2:1-6, referencing Micah 5:2), His suffering and death (Mark 15, referencing Isaiah 53), and His resurrection (Luke 24:46, referencing Psalm 16:10).

Consistency of Details: The New Testament narratives display consistency in many details about Jesus' life, despite being written by different authors. This includes details about His ministry, miracles, teachings, crucifixion, and resurrection (Mark 6:30-56, John 6:1-21).

In summary, the New Testament, in conjunction with external sources and archaeological evidence, provides a multi-faceted case for the historicity of Jesus. This robust evidence contributes to the overall historical corroboration of the New Testament.

The Resurrection of Jesus: Examining the Historical Evidence

The resurrection of Jesus Christ is a cornerstone of Christian belief and is thoroughly documented within the New Testament. Several lines of evidence support this historical event.

Gospel Accounts: Each of the four Gospels provides a detailed account of Jesus' resurrection. They narrate the discovery of the empty tomb (Matthew 28:1-10; Mark 16:1-8; Luke 24:1-12; John 20:1-10), Jesus' post-resurrection appearances to His disciples (Matthew 28:16-20; Luke 24:36-49; John 20:19-29), and His ascension into heaven (Luke 24:50-53).

Paul's Testimony: Paul offers strong testimony to the resurrection. He identifies it as a central tenet of the faith (1 Corinthians 15:14) and recounts that Jesus appeared to him on the road to Damascus (Acts 9:3-6; 1 Corinthians 15:8). He also lists other eyewitnesses who saw the resurrected Christ, including the twelve apostles, more than five hundred brethren at once, James, and others (1 Corinthians 15:3-7).

Transformation of the Disciples: The dramatic transformation of Jesus' disciples provides further evidence. Before the resurrection, they were often fearful and uncertain (Mark 14:50; John 20:19). After witnessing the risen Christ, they became bold proclaimers of His resurrection, even facing persecution and death for their testimony (Acts 2:14-41; 4:1-20; 5:27-42).

Empty Tomb: The empty tomb is a crucial piece of evidence for the resurrection. Despite the Romans' and Jewish leaders' interest in quelling the new Christian movement, they were unable to produce Jesus' body (Matthew 28:11-15; John 20:1-10).

Early Christian Creed: Paul includes an early Christian creed in 1 Corinthians 15:3-7, attesting to the death, burial, and resurrection of Jesus. This creed is believed to have originated within a few years of Jesus' resurrection, indicating that the belief in His resurrection was not a later development.

The Origin of the Christian Church: The birth and rapid spread of the Christian Church, despite intense persecution, attest to the impact of the resurrection. The disciples and early Christians were willing to die for their belief in the resurrected Christ, a belief unlikely to have been maintained had the resurrection been a fabrication (Acts 4:1-22; 5:17-42; 7:54-60; 8:1-3).

In summary, the New Testament provides comprehensive historical evidence for the resurrection of Jesus. This event is attested by multiple independent sources within the New Testament, is supported by the transformation of Jesus' disciples, the existence and actions of the early Church, and is central to Christian belief and teaching.

The Historical Reliability of Acts: A Case Study

The Book of Acts, also known as the Acts of the Apostles, written by Luke, serves as a historical record of the early Christian Church, beginning with the ascension of Jesus and continuing through the missionary journeys of the Apostle Paul. There are several lines of evidence suggesting the historical reliability of Acts:

1. **Accuracy of Details**: The Acts of the Apostles presents precise and accurate details regarding places, titles, customs, and events that align with what historians and archaeologists know about the first-century Roman world. For instance, Acts 18:12 mentions Gallio as the proconsul of Achaia, a fact confirmed by an inscription discovered in Delphi.

2. **Consistency with Other Historical Documents**: The Book of Acts aligns with other historical documents of the time. For example, the account of the riot in Ephesus (Acts 19:23-41) corresponds with what is known about the city's devotion to the goddess Artemis and the importance of the silversmith trade there.

3. **External Corroboration**: Extra-biblical sources support events and circumstances described in Acts. The works of historians such as Josephus and Tacitus align with the broader socio-political context presented in Acts.

4. **Archaeological Evidence**: Archaeological findings have confirmed many details in Acts. For example, the existence of the "Bema Seat," where Paul was likely tried in Corinth (Acts 18:12-17), has been archaeologically validated.

5. **Internal Consistency**: Acts is consistent with the accounts provided in the Gospels and Paul's letters. For instance, Paul's conversion experience is narrated in Acts 9:1-19, and Paul refers to this experience in his letters (Galatians 1:13-17; 1 Corinthians 15:8-9).

6. **Prophecy Fulfillment**: Acts records the fulfillment of Jesus' prophecy about the spread of His Gospel: from Jerusalem, to all of Judea and Samaria, and to the ends of the earth (Acts 1:8). The historical progression of Christianity aligns with this prophecy.

In conclusion, the Book of Acts provides a historically reliable account of the early Christian Church. Its details align with external historical and archaeological evidence, and it is internally consistent with other New Testament documents.

Objections and Responses: Addressing Skeptical Claims

When it comes to historical verification of the New Testament, there are some objections that are commonly raised. However, these objections can be addressed by careful examination and study of the biblical text in conjunction with historical and archaeological findings.

1. **Objection**: The New Testament was written long after the events it describes, which casts doubt on its accuracy.

Response: The New Testament, particularly the Gospels, was written within the lifetime of the eyewitnesses to Jesus' life, death, and resurrection. For example, the Gospel of Mark is generally believed to have been written between 60-70 AD, just 30-40 years after Jesus' crucifixion. This period is not long enough for legends to develop and replace historical facts (1 Corinthians 15:3-8).

2. **Objection**: The New Testament contains supernatural events which are impossible and thus, its credibility is undermined.

Response: The belief in supernatural events is a matter of worldview. If one believes in a God who created the universe and intervenes in it, then miracles are not only possible but expected. The resurrection of Jesus, for example, is a central miraculous event that has significant historical support (1 Corinthians 15:14).

3. **Objection**: The New Testament authors were biased, so their accounts can't be trusted.

Response: Being a follower of Jesus does not automatically disqualify someone from accurately recording events. In fact, their close relationship with Jesus and the events of his life provided them with intimate, first-hand knowledge. Moreover, the apostles showed their commitment to the truth of their message by being willing to die for it (Acts 5:41).

4. **Objection**: The New Testament is inconsistent, with different accounts of the same events.

Response: Differences in accounts are common in historical reporting and do not necessarily indicate inaccuracies. They can reflect different perspectives or focuses of the authors. For example, the four Gospels emphasize different aspects of Jesus' life, teachings, death, and resurrection, but these differences are complementary rather than contradictory (John 20:31).

5. **Objection**: There are few external confirmations of the events in the New Testament.

Response: While it's true that we have limited external confirmations, it's important to note that we have some powerful ones, including writings of early Church Fathers, non-Christian historians like Tacitus and Josephus, and archaeological findings. Moreover, the lack of external confirmation is not surprising given the nature of historical records from the ancient world (Acts 17:28).

In conclusion, while skeptical claims are worth considering, careful study and analysis provide substantial responses that uphold the historical reliability of the New Testament.

Conclusion: The Trustworthiness of the New Testament in Light of Historical Evidence

The New Testament, while recognized as a spiritual text, has also proven to hold up remarkably well under the scrutiny of historical analysis. Its narratives align with the socio-political context of its era, from the reign of Roman rulers to the details of local Jewish customs. Archaeological findings have also confirmed many specific details mentioned in the New Testament, such as the Pool of Bethesda (John 5:1-9), the existence of Pontius Pilate (Luke 3:1), and the description of first-century Jerusalem.

The preservation of the New Testament text is also exceptional. The sheer number of ancient manuscripts, as well as their consistency, surpasses that of many other historical documents. The earliest of these manuscripts date back to the second century, not long after the original texts were written (2 Timothy 3:16-17).

External sources provide further corroboration. Historians such as Josephus and Tacitus make references that align with New Testament accounts, and even Jewish sources like the Talmud, while not agreeing with Christian beliefs, acknowledge the existence of Jesus and his execution.

The New Testament's portrayal of individuals, both of eminent status and lesser-known figures, is another compelling aspect. The apostle Paul, for example, is depicted with both strengths and flaws, a humanizing detail that lends credibility to the narrative (2 Corinthians 12:7-10). The willingness of the early Christians to endure persecution for their beliefs also attests to the sincerity of their convictions, which were grounded in the events described in the New Testament (Acts 5:41).

The resurrection of Jesus stands as the most significant event in the New Testament. It is not presented as a myth or allegory, but as a historical event, witnessed by individuals who subsequently dedicated their lives to proclaiming this truth (1 Corinthians 15:3-8). The transformation of these witnesses, most notably the apostle Paul, adds further weight to the authenticity of this event.

Thus, the New Testament, when examined in light of historical evidence, demonstrates a high level of trustworthiness. Its alignment with external historical sources, archaeological findings, consistency across numerous ancient manuscripts, and the depiction of its characters all attest to its reliability. This trustworthiness not only supports its spiritual teachings but also provides a robust foundation for faith in its message (John 20:30-31).

CHAPTER 13 Assessing the Trustworthiness of the New Testament: A Balanced Evaluation

Introduction: The Quest for Trustworthiness

The New Testament, as an integral part of the Bible, serves as a pivotal resource for spiritual guidance and faith. Its accounts, teachings, and prophetic messages have shaped the lives and beliefs of billions of people throughout history. However, the trustworthiness of the New Testament is not just grounded in faith alone, but also in its ability to withstand historical, textual, and logical scrutiny.

The New Testament is composed of 27 books and letters written by various authors during the first century CE. These texts contain an array of narratives, teachings, and prophecies, but they all share a common theme: the life, death, and resurrection of Jesus Christ and the subsequent growth of the early Christian Church.

The quest for trustworthiness in the New Testament begins with the scrutiny of its historical veracity. The Bible itself calls for testing and proving what is true (1 Thessalonians 5:21), and the New Testament withstands such examination.

The accounts in the New Testament do not exist in a vacuum. They are set in a well-documented historical period with a particular social, political, and cultural context, and they interact with these elements consistently. Many of the events, people, and places mentioned in the New Testament have been confirmed by archaeological evidence or corroborated by other historical sources.

Moreover, the preservation and transmission of the New Testament text over centuries is remarkable. The sheer quantity and quality of ancient manuscripts that have survived allow us to have confidence in the fidelity of the New Testament text that we have today.

The New Testament also exhibits a high degree of internal consistency. Despite the diverse authorship and wide range of topics covered, there is a consistent message and theology throughout the text.

The quest for trustworthiness, however, does not stop at confirming historical and textual reliability. It extends to assessing the coherence and applicability of the teachings and principles contained within the New Testament. Are the teachings and the moral code it espouses sound, beneficial, and applicable in various contexts throughout history and in the present day?

Ultimately, the trustworthiness of the New Testament is evaluated through a balanced consideration of these various factors, providing a foundation for belief that goes beyond blind faith to reasoned faith. As the writer of Hebrews notes, faith is the assurance of things hoped for, the conviction of things not seen (Hebrews 11:1), yet this faith is supported by a body of evidence that withstands rigorous scrutiny.

Understanding the Nature of the New Testament Documents

The New Testament consists of a compilation of 27 distinct documents, each with its own unique context, purpose, and genre. These documents were written by a variety of authors and can be classified into four main types: the Gospels, Acts of the Apostles, Epistles (letters), and the Apocalypse.

The Gospels - Matthew, Mark, Luke, and John - provide accounts of the life, teachings, death, and resurrection of Jesus Christ. Each Gospel offers a unique perspective and emphasis, and together they form a comprehensive picture of Jesus' life and mission. The Gospels are a blend of biography and theology, revealing not only the events of Jesus' life but also the significance of those events. The fact that they are grounded in historical reality can be confirmed by verses such as Luke 2:1-2, where the birth of Jesus is situated in a specific political context.

The Acts of the Apostles, written by Luke, is a historical account of the early Christian Church, starting from the ascension of Jesus and chronicling the missionary efforts of the apostles, especially Peter and Paul. Its historical accuracy is affirmed by its detailed descriptions of places, people, and events that align with other historical sources. For example, Acts 18:12 mentions Gallio as the proconsul of Achaia, a fact confirmed by an inscription found in Delphi.

The Epistles, or letters, make up the bulk of the New Testament and were written by several authors, including Paul, Peter, James, John, and Jude, to various Christian communities or individuals. They provide teachings, clarifications, exhortations, and sometimes rebukes, aimed at guiding the recipients in their faith and practice. They were written to address specific situations within the early Christian communities, as indicated, for example, by Paul's letter to the Corinthians addressing divisions within the church (1 Corinthians 1:10-11).

The book of Revelation, or the Apocalypse, is a highly symbolic and prophetic text written by John. It presents a series of visions related to the end times and the final triumph of God. Its nature and symbolism are rooted in the apocalyptic literature tradition, which was common in Jewish and Christian writings at the time.

Understanding the nature of these documents is crucial in assessing their trustworthiness. They were not written as detached, objective historical accounts, but as faith documents meant to convey theological truths and guide the early Christian communities. Yet, their historical grounding and the consistency of their message across different authors and contexts lend them a high degree of reliability and trustworthiness.

The Importance of Authorship: Apostolic Connections and Early Dates

The authorship of the New Testament documents plays a significant role in assessing their trustworthiness. It is widely accepted that these documents were written by individuals who either were apostles themselves or had strong connections to the apostles, thereby having access to firsthand accounts of the events and teachings they recorded.

The four Gospels, for instance, are traditionally attributed to Matthew, a disciple of Jesus; Mark, a companion of Peter; Luke, a companion of Paul; and John, a disciple of Jesus. The Gospel of John (John 21:24) indicates that it was written by "the disciple whom Jesus loved," traditionally understood to be John. Matthew's authorship is suggested by his intimate knowledge of tax practices (Matthew 9:9), reflecting his background as a tax collector.

The letters of Paul, Peter, John, James, and Jude are believed to be written by these apostles themselves or under their supervision. For example, several of Paul's letters begin with an explicit identification of him as the author (e.g., Romans 1:1, 1 Corinthians 1:1).

Moreover, the dating of these documents also contributes to their credibility. Most New Testament documents were written within the first century AD, within a few decades of Jesus' life, death, and resurrection. This close temporal proximity to the events they describe reduces the likelihood of legendary development or significant distortion of the facts. For instance, the consensus among scholars is that Paul's letters, which provide some of the earliest testimonies about Jesus, were written between 50 and 60 AD, only about two decades after Jesus' crucifixion.

Overall, the apostolic connections and the early dating of the New Testament documents strengthen the case for their historical reliability and trustworthiness. They suggest that these documents were written by individuals who had direct access to the events and teachings they wrote about, and that they were written when many other eyewitnesses were still alive to confirm or dispute their accounts.

Historical Accuracy: Corroborations and Consistencies

A crucial element to consider when evaluating the reliability of any historical document, including the New Testament, is the level of accuracy in the details. The New Testament, in numerous instances, aligns with known historical, geographical, and cultural facts of the era it represents.

One clear example of historical accuracy is Luke's account in the Book of Acts. Luke provides specific details regarding cities, islands, and governmental figures, many of which have been confirmed by archaeology and other historical sources. For instance, the inscriptions discovered at Delphi corroborate Luke's reference to Gallio as proconsul of Achaia (Acts 18:12).

In terms of geographical accuracy, the New Testament correctly identifies various locations, cities, and regions. For example, John's Gospel accurately describes the Pool of Bethesda with its five covered colonnades (John 5:2), a detail confirmed by archaeological excavations in Jerusalem.

Cultural practices and norms described in the New Testament also correspond with what we know of the first-century Mediterranean world. For instance, Paul's trial before the Sanhedrin aligns with the Jewish legal procedures of the time (Acts 22:30-23:10).

Furthermore, the consistency within the New Testament itself adds to its trustworthiness. For example, the independent accounts of Jesus' life, death, and resurrection found in the four Gospels present a coherent picture of these central events. Similarly, Paul's letters align with the narrative of Acts regarding his conversion and missionary activities (e.g., compare Acts 9:1-30 with Galatians 1:11-24).

In sum, the historical, geographical, and cultural accuracy, along with the internal consistency of the New Testament, supports its credibility as a reliable source of information about the life and teachings of Jesus and the early Christian movement.

The Transmission of the New Testament Texts: Fidelity Over Centuries

The process of transmitting ancient texts over centuries is an essential aspect to consider when assessing their reliability. In the case of the New Testament, the vast number of manuscripts available, their consistency, and the relatively short time gap between the original writings and the earliest copies, all attest to the fidelity of the transmission process.

Firstly, the sheer volume of New Testament manuscripts surpasses that of any other ancient document. There are approximately 5,800 Greek manuscripts, along with thousands of Latin Vulgate and other early versions, providing an immense wealth of material for comparison and study.

Secondly, these manuscripts exhibit a remarkable level of agreement. While there are minor variations due to copyists' errors or alterations, the central message and doctrine of the New Testament remain consistent across the manuscripts. As Paul stated, "Jesus Christ is the same yesterday and today and forever" (Hebrews 13:8).

The short interval between the composition of the New Testament books and the earliest existing copies also supports the fidelity of the text. For instance, fragments of the Gospel of John have been dated to around 125 CE, only a few decades after its composition. This short gap minimizes the possibility of significant alterations or embellishments to the text, strengthening the trustworthiness of the New Testament.

Finally, quotations from early church fathers, from the late first century onward, provide a kind of "chain of custody" for the New Testament. These early Christian writers extensively quoted the New Testament, and their writings match the text of our current New Testament. This affirms the fidelity of the New Testament's transmission over the centuries.

In conclusion, the process of the New Testament's textual transmission—considering the volume of manuscripts, their consistency, the time gap to the earliest copies, and the corroboration from early church fathers—provides compelling evidence of its reliability over the centuries.

The Canon of the New Testament: Criteria and Formation

The word "Bible," commonly used to refer to the inspired Scriptures, originates from the Greek word "bi·bli′a," meaning "little books." This term was derived from "bi′blos," which described the inner part of the papyrus plant used to create writing material in ancient times. The word "bi·bli′a" encompassed various written communications on this material, including scrolls, books, documents, scriptures, and library collections of little books.

Interestingly, the specific term "Bible" is generally not found within the text of English or other-language translations of the Holy Scriptures. However, by the second century B.C.E., the collection of inspired books in the Hebrew Scriptures was referred to as "ta bi·bli′a" in the Greek language. For instance, in Daniel 9:2, the prophet wrote, "I myself, Daniel, discerned by the books..." In this verse, the Septuagint uses the term "bi′blois," the dative plural form of "bi′blos." Additionally, in 2 Timothy 4:13, Paul wrote, "When you come, bring... the scrolls [Greek, bi·bli′a]." Throughout the Christian Greek Scriptures, the Greek words "bi·bli′on" and "bi′blos" appear in various grammatical forms, occurring over 40 times and often translated as "scroll(s)" or "book(s)." Over time, "bi·bli′a" was adopted as a singular word in Latin, and from Latin, the term "Bible" entered the English language.

The writers of the Bible testified to its being God's inspired Word in various ways. Here are a few examples:

1. **Direct Claims of Inspiration**: The biblical writers explicitly claimed to be writing under the inspiration of God. They attributed their words to divine revelation. For instance, the prophet Jeremiah declared, "The word of the Lord came to me" (Jeremiah 1:4), and the apostle Paul affirmed, "All Scripture is breathed out by God" (2 Timothy 3:16).

2. **Divine Commission**: Many biblical writers were chosen and commissioned by God to convey His messages to the people. They recognized their role as messengers of God's Word. For instance, the prophet Isaiah declared, "The Spirit of the Lord God is upon me because the Lord has anointed me to bring good news to the poor" (Isaiah 61:1), and Jesus Himself quoted this passage to affirm His divine mission (Luke 4:17-21).

3. **Fulfilled Prophecies**: The Bible contains numerous prophecies that were fulfilled in precise detail, often long after they were recorded. The fulfillment of these prophecies provides evidence of divine inspiration. For example, the prophecies concerning the birth, life, death, and resurrection of Jesus Christ serve as powerful testimonies to the authenticity and inspiration of the Scriptures.

4. **Unity of Message**: Despite being written by various authors over centuries, the Bible presents a unified and coherent message. The themes of redemption, salvation, and the nature of God are consistently woven throughout its pages. This consistency points to a divine authorship that guided and inspired the writers.

5. **Transformational Power**: The Bible has had a transformative impact on countless lives throughout history. Its teachings have brought about profound changes in individuals, societies, and cultures. The power of its message to change hearts and lives testifies to its divine inspiration.

6. **Confirmation by Jesus and the Apostles**: Jesus Christ and the apostles affirmed the divine authority and inspiration of the Scriptures. Jesus Himself frequently referred to the Old Testament scriptures, acknowledging them as God's Word. The apostles, guided by the Holy Spirit, wrote the New Testament books and affirmed their authority as inspired Scripture.

These testimonies, along with the internal consistency, historical accuracy, and the profound impact of the Bible, provide strong evidence for its divine inspiration. The collective witness of the biblical writers, the fulfillment of prophecies, and the transformative power of its message reinforce the belief that the Bible is God's inspired Word.

What man knows today as the Bible is, in fact, a collection of ancient divinely inspired documents. These writings were composed and compiled over a span of 16 centuries. Together, they form the Divine Library, known as the Bibliotheca Divina, as aptly described by Jerome in Latin. This library has an official catalog, a listing of publications that are authorized and pertain to its scope and specialization. Unauthorized books are excluded. Jehovah God, the Great Librarian, establishes the standard for inclusion, determining which writings should be part of this Divine Library. Thus, the Bible has a fixed catalog consisting of 66 books, all of which are products of God's guiding holy spirit.

The collection, or list, of books accepted as genuine and inspired Scripture is commonly referred to as the Bible canon. Originally, the Hebrew word "qa·neh'" denoted a reed used as a measuring rod when a piece of wood was not available. The apostle Paul also used the Greek word "ka·non'" to refer to a "rule of conduct" and the "territory" measured out as his assigned sphere of work (Galatians 6:16; 2 Corinthians 10:13). Therefore, canonical books are those that are true, inspired, and worthy to be used as a standard in determining the right faith, doctrine, and conduct. If we employ books that are not upright as a plumb line, our spiritual "building" will be flawed and will fail the test of the Master Surveyor.

The Bible's canon provides us with a reliable and trustworthy guide for our faith and practice. Through the guidance of the Holy Spirit, these books were carefully chosen and recognized as God's inspired Word. By adhering to the canon, we ensure that our beliefs and actions align with the divine standard established by Jehovah, the ultimate authority and source of truth.

Determining Canonicity. The canonicity of the 66 books of the Bible is determined by divine indications. These indications reveal that these documents deal with Jehovah's affairs in the earth, directing people to worship Him and fostering deep respect for His name and His work and purposes. They bear evidence of inspiration, being products of holy spirit (2 Peter 1:21). There is no appeal to superstition or creature worship, but rather an appeal to love and service of God. These writings must exhibit internal harmony and unity, supporting the one authorship of Jehovah God. They must also demonstrate accuracy, down to the smallest details. Each book's contents provide specific indications of inspiration and canonicity, which have been discussed in the introductory material to each of the Bible books.

Furthermore, special circumstances apply to the Hebrew Scriptures and others to the Greek New Testament, aiding in establishing the Bible canon. These circumstances provide additional support for the authenticity and divine inspiration of the included books.

By considering these divine indications, we can have confidence in the canonicity of the 66 books of the Bible. They have been recognized as God's inspired Word, guiding us in matters of faith, doctrine, and conduct. Through the careful selection and preservation of these writings, we have been provided with a reliable and authoritative source of truth, given to us by Jehovah Himself.

The Roman Catholic Church has claimed responsibility for deciding which books should be included in the Bible canon, citing the Council of Carthage in 397 C.E. as a significant event where a catalog of books was formulated. However, the truth is that the canon, including the list of books comprising the Christian Greek Scriptures, was already established by that time, not by the decree of any council, but by the guidance of God's holy spirit—the same spirit that inspired the writing of those books in the first place. The testimonies of later non-inspired catalogers are only valuable in acknowledging the Bible canon that had been authorized by God's spirit.

When we examine the evidence from early catalogs, we find that several fourth-century catalogs of the Christian Scriptures, predating the Council of Carthage, align precisely with our present canon. Some catalogs may omit only the book of Revelation. Even before the end of the second century, there was widespread acceptance of the four Gospels, Acts, and twelve of the apostle Paul's letters. Only a few of the smaller writings were subject to doubts in specific areas. This may have been due to factors such as limited initial circulation, which caused a longer process of acceptance as canonical.

The early catalogs and widespread acceptance of key books in the Bible canon demonstrate the recognition and acknowledgment of inspired Scripture. The unity and agreement among these catalogs, predating the Council of Carthage, underscore the divine guidance in establishing the canon of Scripture. It is evident that the canonicity of the Bible was not determined by the decisions of a particular council but by the work of God's Holy Spirit, ensuring the inclusion of the inspired writings that form the foundation of our faith.

One of the remarkable early catalogs is the fragment discovered by L.A. Muratori in the Ambrosian Library in Milan, Italy. This fragment, published by Muratori in 1740, provides valuable insights. Although the beginning of the fragment is missing, it references Luke as the third Gospel, indicating that it originally mentioned Matthew and Mark as well. The Muratorian Fragment, written in Latin, dates back to the latter part of the second century C.E. It is an intriguing document, and the following partial translation sheds light on its contents:

"[...] at which nevertheless he was present, and so he placed them in his narrative. The third book of the Gospel, that according to Luke. Luke, the well-known physician, after the ascension of Christ, when Paul had taken with him as one zealous for the law, composed it in his own name, according to general belief. Yet he himself had not seen the Lord in the flesh; and therefore, as he was able to ascertain events, so indeed he begins to tell the story from the birth of John."

This fragment attests to the early recognition and inclusion of the Gospels of Matthew, Mark, and Luke in the canon of Scripture. It highlights the authorship of Luke, the physician, who carefully investigated the events and composed his Gospel based on reliable testimony. The Muratorian Fragment provides us with a glimpse into the early acknowledgment and preservation of these essential books in the New Testament.

Such early catalogs, like the Muratorian Fragment, serve as valuable historical evidence, affirming the authenticity and canonicity of the biblical writings. They bear witness to the reverence and recognition given to these inspired books from the earliest centuries of Christianity, further solidifying our confidence in the divine inspiration and preservation of the Bible.

"The third book of the Gospel is that according to Luke. Luke, the well-known physician, wrote it in his own name . . . The fourth book of the Gospel is that of John, one of the disciples. . . . And so to the faith of believers there is no discord, even although different selections are given from the facts in the individual books of the Gospels, because in all [of them] under the one guiding Spirit all the things relative to his nativity, passion, resurrection, conversation with his disciples, and his twofold advent, the first in the humiliation arising from contempt, which took place, and the second in the glory of kingly power, which is yet to come, have been declared. What marvel is it, then, if John adduces so consistently in his epistles these several things, saying in person: 'what we have seen with our eyes, and heard with our ears, and our hands have handled, those things we have written.' For thus he professes to be not only an eyewitness but also a hearer and narrator of all the wonderful things of the Lord, in their order. Moreover, the acts of all the apostles are written in one book. Luke [so] comprised them for the most excellent Theophilus . . . Now the epistles of Paul, what they are, whence or for what reason they were sent, they themselves make clear to him who will understand. First of all he wrote at length to the Corinthians to prohibit the schism of heresy, then to the Galatians [against] circumcision, and to the

Romans on the order of the Scriptures, intimating also that Christ is the chief matter in them—each of which it is necessary for us to discuss, seeing that the blessed Apostle Paul himself, following the example of his predecessor John, writes to no more than seven churches by name in the following order: to the Corinthians (first), to the Ephesians (second), to the Philippians (third), to the Colossians (fourth), to the Galatians (fifth), to the Thessalonians (sixth), to the Romans (seventh). But though he writes twice for the sake of correction to the Corinthians and the Thessalonians, that there is one church diffused throughout the whole earth is shown [?i.e., by this sevenfold writing]; and John also in the Apocalypse, though he writes to seven churches, yet speaks to all. But [he wrote] out of affection and love one to Philemon, and one to Titus, and two to Timothy; [and these] are held sacred in the honorable esteem of the Church. . . . Further, an epistle of Jude and two bearing the name of John are counted . . . We receive the apocalypses of John and Peter only, which [latter] some of us do not wish to be read in church."—*The New Schaff-Herzog Encyclopedia of Religious Knowledge,* 1956, Vol. VIII, page 56.

In the latter part of the Muratorian Fragment, it is worth noting that only two of John's epistles are mentioned. However, an encyclopedia cited on page 55 explains that these two epistles can be identified as the second and third epistles of John, where the writer refers to himself as "the elder." The author of the fragment had already addressed the first epistle incidentally in connection with the Fourth Gospel, affirming his firm belief in its Johannine origin. Therefore, the author chose to focus specifically on the two smaller letters in this context.

Regarding the apparent absence of any mention of Peter's first epistle, the same source continues to explain that it is likely due to the loss of a few words or perhaps a line in which the first epistle of Peter and the Apocalypse of John were named as accepted. The encyclopedia further concludes on page 56, based on the Muratorian Fragment, that the New Testament is considered to consist definitively of the four Gospels, the Acts, thirteen epistles of Paul, the Apocalypse of John, probably three of his epistles, Jude, and probably the first epistle of Peter. However, opposition to another writing attributed to Peter had not yet been completely silenced at that time.

These observations from the Muratorian Fragment, along with the insights provided by the encyclopedia, shed light on the understanding and acceptance of specific books in the New Testament canon. While the fragment does not mention all the books we now recognize as part of the canon, it reveals the recognition and inclusion of key writings and offers valuable historical evidence regarding the formation of the New Testament.

Around the year 230 C.E., Origen accepted the books of Hebrews and James as part of the inspired Scriptures, even though they were not mentioned in the Muratorian Fragment. While Origen acknowledged that some doubted the canonicity of these books, it demonstrates that by that time, most of the Greek Scriptures were accepted as canonical, with only a few doubts regarding some lesser-known epistles.

Subsequently, figures such as Athanasius, Jerome, and Augustine confirmed the earlier lists and defined the canon as consisting of the same 27 books we have today.

The majority of the catalogs in the chart provide specific lists of accepted canonical books. The lists from Irenaeus, Clement of Alexandria, Tertullian, and Origen are compiled based on the quotations they made in their writings, which reveal their regard for the referenced writings. These lists are further supplemented by the records of the early historian Eusebius. However, the absence of certain canonical writings in their references does not undermine their canonicity. It simply means that these writers did not happen to mention them in their specific works, either by choice or due to the subjects they were addressing. But why do we not find precise lists of the canon earlier than the Muratorian Fragment?

The need for such lists arose in the middle of the second century C.E. when critics like Marcion emerged, raising questions about which books should be accepted by Christians. Marcion constructed his own canon to align with his doctrines, selectively choosing certain letters of the apostle Paul and an edited version of the Gospel of Luke. The emergence of Marcion's canon, along with the proliferation of apocryphal literature during that time, prompted catalogers to explicitly state which books they accepted as canonical. This response was necessary to safeguard the true canon from various distorted and unauthorized writings that were circulating at that time.

The writers of the Greek New Testament had close associations with the original leaders of the Christian church, including the apostles chosen by Jesus, such as Peter and John. Matthew, John, and Peter were part of the original twelve apostles, while Paul was later chosen as an apostle but not counted among the twelve. While Paul was not present at the special outpouring of the Holy Spirit at Pentecost, Matthew, John, and Peter were present, along with James, Jude, and possibly Mark (Acts 1:14). Peter even includes the letters of Paul in the category of "the rest of the Scriptures" (2 Pet. 3:15-16). Mark and Luke, who were close associates and traveling companions of Paul and Peter, were also intimately connected to the original Christian leaders (Acts 12:25; 1 Pet. 5:13; Col. 4:14; 2 Tim. 4:11).

All these writers were granted miraculous abilities through the Holy Spirit. Some received special outpourings of the Spirit, as seen during Pentecost and Paul's conversion (Acts 9:17-18), while others likely received the Spirit through the laying on of the apostles' hands, as in the case of Luke (Acts 8:14-17). The writing of the Greek New Testament was completed during a time when these special spiritual gifts were active.

Our faith in the almighty God, who inspired and preserves His Word, gives us confidence that He guided the compilation of its various parts. Therefore, we wholeheartedly accept the 27 books of the Greek New Testament, along with the 39 books of the Hebrew Scriptures, as the unified Bible authored by Jehovah God. We recognize that His Word, in its 66 books, is our trustworthy guide, and its harmonious and balanced message testifies to its completeness. Let us give praise and honor to Jehovah God, the Creator of this unparalleled book! It equips us thoroughly and guides us on the path of life. May we use it wisely in every opportunity we have.

Assessing Alleged Contradictions: Contextual Interpretation and Harmonization

"The entirety of Your word is truth," proclaims the Bible. (Psalm 119:160) If God cannot lie, how then can His book contain apparent contradictions and discrepancies and still be considered His inspired Word? It cannot. But why do these discrepancies exist?

Over the centuries, as the Bible was meticulously copied by hand and translated into different languages, some variations and errors may have crept in. However, none of these variations are significant enough to cast doubt on the overall inspiration and authority of the Bible. Through careful examination, apparent contradictions can be resolved. Often, those who claim that the Bible contradicts itself have not conducted a thorough investigation but have accepted the opinions of those who do not wish to believe or submit to the Bible. The Bible wisely advises, "The one who gives an answer before he listens—it is foolishness and a humiliation to him." (Proverbs 18:13)

At times, people object to differences among Bible writers regarding figures, the order of events, wording of quotations, and other matters. But consider this: If you were to ask several eyewitnesses of an event to write down what they saw, would their accounts coincide word-for-word and detail-by-detail? If they did, wouldn't you be suspicious of collusion? In the same way, Bible writers were allowed to maintain their own styles and language, while God ensured that His ideas and essential facts were accurately conveyed.

Quotations from earlier writings might be slightly modified by the new writer to suit their purpose, while still preserving the intended meaning. Similarly, the arrangement of events could differ depending on the writer's focus or association with ideas. Omissions would also be based on the writer's perspective and the need for concise accounts. For example, Matthew mentions two blind men being healed by Jesus, whereas Mark and Luke mention only one. (Matthew 20:29-34; Mark 10:46; Luke 18:35) Matthew's account is not contradictory; he simply provides more specific details about the number of individuals, while Mark and Luke highlight the conversation directed towards one man.

Furthermore, different methods of calculating time existed. The Jewish nation used two calendars—the sacred calendar and the secular or agricultural calendar—each starting at a different time of the year. Therefore, writers who mention different months and days for the same event may simply be using different calendars. Additionally, Oriental writers rarely used fractions, so parts of a year were often rounded off to the nearest whole number. This can be observed, for instance, in the genealogical records found in Genesis chapter 5.

While there may be apparent discrepancies and variations in the Bible, a careful and thorough examination reveals that these do not undermine its overall integrity and accuracy. The Bible remains a reliable and inspired source of truth, reflecting the nature of its infallible Author, Jehovah God.

Harmonizing Seeming Contradictions

Critics of the Bible often point out passages that seem to contradict each other. However, a closer examination reveals that these apparent contradictions can be harmonized. Let's consider a few examples that have been raised:

In John 3:22, it is stated that Jesus "did baptizing," while John 4:2 states that "Jesus himself did no baptizing." Upon closer inspection, we find that Jesus' disciples performed the baptisms under his direction and authority. This is similar to a scenario where a businessman and his secretary can both be credited with writing a particular letter.

Another example is found in Genesis 2:2, which states that God rested "from all his work," while in John 5:17, Jesus says that God "has kept working until now." The context clarifies that the rest mentioned in Genesis refers specifically to God's work of material creation, whereas Jesus was referring to God's ongoing work of divine guidance and care for humanity.

A seeming contradiction arises when comparing Exodus 34:7 with Ezekiel 18:20. Exodus states that God would bring punishment for the sins of fathers upon their sons and grandsons, while Ezekiel states that a son will not bear the guilt of his father's sins. However, when examined in context, it becomes clear that Exodus refers to the collective punishment that would befall the nation of Israel if they sinned against God and were taken into captivity. Ezekiel, on the other hand, emphasizes individual accountability for one's own actions.

Differences can also be found in the accounts of Jesus' birth as recorded in Matthew 1:18-25 and Luke 1:26-38. However, these differences do not indicate contradictions. Just like reading two biographies about the same person, variations can arise due to the writer's perspective, sources used, emphasis on specific details, and target audience.

These examples demonstrate that apparent contradictions in the Bible can often be resolved through careful analysis, considering the writer's viewpoint and the context. Many people dismiss the Bible as contradictory without putting in the necessary effort to understand and reconcile these passages. By engaging in thorough research and study, we can harmonize seemingly conflicting passages and appreciate the cohesive message of the Scriptures.

Deserving of Our Confidence

The Holy Spirit allowed Bible writers much leeway in writing their reports. Acts 3:21 states, "Heaven must receive him until the time comes for God to restore everything, as he promised long ago through his holy prophets." Thus, they were able to vividly and faithfully depict what they witnessed. The differences in their accounts, far from casting doubt, actually reinforce their credibility and honesty. 2 Peter 1:16-21 affirms their reliability, saying, "We did not follow cleverly devised stories when we told you about the coming of our Lord Jesus Christ in power, but we were eyewitnesses of his majesty."

While writers may have used different styles and perspectives, they all conveyed the same message with a unified purpose: to reveal God's plan for mankind's happiness and to guide individuals in obtaining His approval. Proverbs 2:3-6, 9 emphasizes the importance of seeking wisdom and understanding from Jehovah.

The Bible is a book that engages our reasoning faculties. It maintains harmony throughout and does not contradict itself. With its 66 books, consisting of 1,189 chapters and 31,173 verses, it deserves our unwavering confidence. Indeed, the Bible is trustworthy!

If you come across a perceived "contradiction" in the Bible, consider the following possibilities:

- You may lack knowledge of specific historical facts or ancient customs that provide context.
- You might have overlooked the surrounding verses or passages that clarify the intended meaning.
- The writer's unique viewpoint or literary style may account for apparent differences.
- It is possible that you are trying to reconcile mistaken religious ideas with what the Bible actually teaches.
- Using an inaccurate or outdated Bible translation could lead to misunderstandings.

By carefully examining these factors and approaching the Scriptures with an open mind, you can resolve potential contradictions and gain a deeper understanding of God's message.

The Jesus of the Gospels: Consistency of Character and Message

The figure of Jesus as presented in the four Gospels is another critical aspect when assessing the trustworthiness of the New Testament. The consistency of His character and message across all four accounts is an essential indicator of the New Testament's reliability.

In the Gospels of Matthew, Mark, Luke, and John, we see a uniform depiction of Jesus. His character, teachings, and actions remain consistent, revealing a compassionate healer, a profound teacher, and a selfless leader. Despite the different authors and audiences, Jesus' core message of love, forgiveness, and the kingdom of God remains the same.

For instance, Jesus' commandment to love God and others is a central theme echoed across the Gospels. Matthew records Jesus saying, "You shall love the Lord your God with all your heart, with all your soul, and with all your mind. This is the first and great commandment. And the second is like it: 'You shall love your neighbor as yourself.'" (Matthew 22:37-39). The same command is also found in Mark (Mark 12:30-31) and Luke (Luke 10:27).

Jesus' miracles, parables, and interactions with various individuals are consistently presented across the Gospels. The miracles, like the feeding of the five thousand (Matthew 14:13-21, Mark 6:31-44, Luke 9:12-17, John 6:1-14), and parables, like the parable of the sower (Matthew 13:3-9, Mark 4:3-9, Luke 8:5-8), are shared with minor variations, but the essential message remains the same.

Furthermore, Jesus' passion, crucifixion, and resurrection are fundamental events recorded in all four Gospels. Despite variations in details, the core narrative of Jesus' sacrificial death and triumphant resurrection is uniform, underscoring the central Christian belief in Christ's redemptive work.

In summary, the Jesus depicted in the Gospels exhibits a consistent character and message. This consistency, despite different authors and audiences, provides a strong argument for the trustworthiness of the New Testament's portrayal of Jesus.

Pauline Authorship: Responding to Claims of Forgeries

Paul's authorship of the letters traditionally attributed to him in the New Testament is a crucial topic when evaluating the trustworthiness of these documents. There have been claims suggesting that some of these epistles were forgeries, but there are compelling arguments to counter these claims.

Of the 27 books in the New Testament, 14 were written by Paul. These include Romans, 1 and 2 Corinthians, Galatians, Ephesians, Philippians, Colossians, 1 and 2 Thessalonians, 1 and 2 Timothy, Titus, Philemon and Hebrews. However, scholars have questioned the authorship of Ephesians, Colossians, 2 Thessalonians, 1 and 2 Timothy, and Titus, terming them as the disputed letters.

One argument supporting the genuineness of Pauline authorship is the consistency of theological themes across both the undisputed and disputed letters. For example, the theme of justification by faith is a central tenet in Romans (Romans 3:28), an undisputed letter, and also appears in Titus (Titus 3:7), a disputed letter.

Furthermore, the letters reflect a deep understanding of the Old Testament scriptures and Jewish customs, consistent with Paul's background as a Pharisee. For instance, in 1 Timothy (a disputed letter), Paul refers to the Law, highlighting his deep understanding of it (1 Timothy 1:7-8).

Claims of forgery often stem from perceived differences in style and vocabulary between the undisputed and disputed letters. However, it's important to consider factors such as the use of scribes, the diversity of recipients, and the different contexts and purposes of each letter, all of which could contribute to these variations.

Moreover, Paul's letters, including the disputed ones, were accepted into the canon of the New Testament by the early Church, a process that involved rigorous examination and widespread agreement among early Christian communities.

In conclusion, while there are scholarly debates regarding the authorship of some of Paul's letters, there is substantial evidence supporting the fact that Paul wrote all the letters traditionally attributed to him as we have shown in this book. The consistency in theological themes, the reflection of Paul's background, and the early Church's acceptance of these letters, all support the authenticity of Pauline authorship.

The Role of Miracles: Supernatural Events within a Historical Framework

Some claim that miracles are impossible because they violate the laws of nature. Our understanding of the laws of nature is based on what scientists have observed happening in the natural world around us. However, those laws are similar to the grammar rules for a language—there may be some exceptions to the rule. Our understanding of these "rules" may, in fact, be very limited. Job 38:4 reminds us, "Where were you when I laid the foundation of the earth? Tell me, if you have understanding."

A dedicated scientist may have spent a lifetime studying a certain law of nature. But all it takes is one "exception" for him to have to reevaluate his understanding of that law. As the saying goes, "Just one black swan undoes the theory that all swans are white." Even in everyday life, we encounter phenomena that defy our understanding.

A humorous story related by John Locke illustrates how easy it is to form an opinion based on incomplete facts. The Dutch ambassador, when describing his country to the king of Siam, mentioned that at times it was possible for an elephant to walk on water. The king, lacking personal experience of such a phenomenon, dismissed it as a lie. Unbeknownst to the king, the freezing of water into ice allows it to support the weight of an elephant. The king's skepticism stemmed from a lack of complete information.

When we consider the remarkable advancements achieved in recent decades, it becomes evident that what was once considered impossible can now be accomplished:

1. **Air Travel**: The ability to board an airplane and travel across the world in a matter of hours would have been unimaginable in the 1800s. People would have been astonished by the speed and convenience of air travel.

2. **Internet and Smartphones**: The seamless connectivity and instant access to information through the internet and smartphones would have been seen as pure magic. The idea of carrying a device in your pocket that allows you to communicate with anyone, access a vast amount of knowledge, and even navigate through unknown places would have been mind-boggling.

3. **Electric Lighting**: In the 1800s, gas lamps and candles were the primary sources of artificial light. The widespread availability of electric lighting, illuminating entire cities and homes with a simple flick of a switch, would have been seen as a miraculous advancement.

4. **Medical Advancements**: The progress made in medical science since the 1800s would be nothing short of miraculous to people of that era. Concepts such as antibiotics, vaccines, organ transplants, and advanced surgical procedures would have been inconceivable and life-saving breakthroughs.

5. **Instant Communication**: The ability to communicate instantaneously across long distances through telephone calls, text messages, and video chats would have been seen as incredible. Waiting weeks or months for a letter to arrive by mail was the norm, so the idea of real-time conversations would have been awe-inspiring.

What logical conclusion can we draw from these examples? It is this: If human ingenuity and progress can achieve feats that were once deemed impossible, then surely the God who created the universe and all its wonders can perform amazing acts that surpass our current understanding. As Genesis 18:14 and Matthew 19:26 remind us, "Is anything too hard for the Lord?" and "With man this is impossible, but with God all things are possible."

Some claim that the Bible relies on miracles to make people believe. The Bible does not tell us to believe all miracles. In fact, the opposite is true. The Bible warns us to be very careful when it comes to trusting miracles and powerful signs. Notice this clear warning: "The coming of the lawless one will be in accordance with the work of Satan displayed in all kinds of counterfeit miracles, signs and wonders, and in every sort of evil that deceives."—2 Thessalonians 2:9, 10, New International Version.

Jesus Christ also warned that many would claim to follow him but would not be his genuine followers. Some would even say to him: "Lord, Lord, did we not prophesy in your name, and in your name drive out demons and perform many miracles?" (Matthew 7:22) But Jesus said that he would not accept those people as his followers. (Matthew 7:23) Obviously, then, Jesus did not teach that all miracles are from God.

God does not tell his worshipers to base their faith simply on miracles. Rather, their faith should be firmly established on facts.—Hebrews 11:1.

Let us consider, for example, one of the well-known miracles recorded in the Bible, the resurrection of Jesus Christ. Years after that event, some Christians in Corinth started to question whether Jesus had been resurrected. How did the apostle Paul help those Christians? Did he simply say, "Have more faith"? No. Notice how he reminded them of established facts. He stated that Jesus "was buried, yes, . . . he has been raised up the third day according to the Scriptures; and that he appeared to Cephas, then to the twelve. After that he appeared to upward of five hundred brothers at one time, the most of whom remain to the present."—1 Corinthians 15:4-8.

Did it matter whether those Christians believed in that miracle? Paul goes on to say: "If Christ has not been raised up, our preaching is certainly in vain, and our faith is in vain." (1 Corinthians 15:14) Paul did not take the matter lightly. Either the miracle of the resurrection of Jesus was true or it was not! And Paul knew that it was true because of the hundreds of eyewitness accounts of people who were still living at that time. In fact, those eyewitnesses were willing to die rather than deny what they had seen.—1 Corinthians 15:17-19.

Some claim that miracles are just natural phenomena that are misunderstood by uneducated people. Some scholars try to explain the miracles in the Bible as merely natural events that occurred without divine intervention. They feel that this makes the Biblical accounts more believable. While it is true that natural phenomena may have been associated with some miracles—such things as earthquakes, plagues, and landslides—these explanations have one thing in common. They disregard the timing of the miracle as explained in the Scriptures.

For example, some have argued that the first plague brought upon Egypt, the turning of the Nile River into blood, was actually the result of red soil that had been washed down the Nile, along with reddish organisms called flagellates. However, the Bible account says that the river was turned into blood, not red mud. A careful reading of Exodus 7:14-21 shows that this miracle occurred at the time that Aaron, at Moses' direction, struck the Nile River with his rod. Even if the transformation of the river were caused by a natural occurrence, the timing of Aaron's striking the river was in itself miraculous!

As another example of the importance of the timing of a miracle, consider what happened when the nation of Israel was poised to enter the Promised Land. Their way was blocked by the Jordan River at flood stage. The Bible account tells us what happened next: "At the instant that the carriers of the Ark came as far as the Jordan and the feet of the priests carrying the Ark were dipped in the edge of the waters . . . , then the waters descending from above began to stand still. They rose up as one dam very far away at Adam." (Joshua 3:15, 16) Was this the result of an earthquake or a landslide? The account does not say. But the timing of this event was miraculous. It occurred exactly at the time Jehovah had said that it would.—Joshua 3:7, 8, 13.

So, then, are there such things as miracles? The Bible says that there are. According to what it tells us, these are not just natural phenomena. Really, then, is it logical to say that it is impossible for them to happen just because they do not occur every day?

Miracles in the Bible: A Reasoned Belief

The credibility of a narrative often relies heavily on the trustworthiness of its narrator. An individual with a consistent record of truth-telling would likely inspire belief in their accounts. This principle also applies to the miraculous events documented in the Bible. While none of us were present to witness these miracles, we can evaluate the Bible's credibility through various factors that lend authenticity to these accounts.

Many of the biblical miracles were public events, witnessed by thousands or even millions of people (Exodus 14:21-31; 19:16-19). They weren't shrouded in secrecy, but rather occurred in broad daylight, in full view of the public.

The simplicity of these miracles further adds to their credibility. There were no elaborate displays, special effects, or manipulation of lighting. Many of them were spontaneous, happening as a response to encounters or individual requests (Mark 5:25-29; Luke 7:11-16). This spontaneity makes it unlikely that these events were staged.

The motives behind performing these miracles were not self-centered. Instead of seeking personal fame, glory, or wealth, these miracles were performed to glorify God (John 11:1-4, 15, 40). Any attempts to profit from such miraculous powers were strictly condemned (2 Kings 5:15, 16, 20, 25-27; Acts 8:18-23).

The variety of miracles depicted in the Bible suggests a divine hand at work. Miracles such as calming the sea and wind, turning water into wine, initiating and stopping rain, healing the sick, and restoring sight to the blind could not have been mere human feats (1 Kings 17:1-7; 18:41-45; Matthew 8:24-27; Luke 17:11-19; John 2:1-11; 9:1-7).

Even those who opposed Jesus and his followers did not dispute the occurrence of these miracles. For instance, when Lazarus was resurrected, the religious adversaries of Jesus didn't deny that Lazarus had been dead; they merely questioned the source of Jesus' miraculous power (John 11:45-48; 12:9-11; Acts 4:1-13).

The authenticity of the Bible's accounts of miracles is further reinforced by its attention to historical detail, including time, place, and the people involved. Critics have often been astounded by the historical accuracy of the Bible. Moreover, the Bible has consistently provided invaluable advice for nurturing happy human relationships.

The prophecies about the birth, life, and death of Jesus Christ, recorded in the Old Testament and fulfilled in the New Testament, further attest to the Bible's reliability (Micah 5:2; Isaiah 7:14; 35:5-6; 53:3; 53:12; Psalm 22:18). In addition, its teachings, such as the Golden Rule (Matthew 7:12) and the command to love one another (John 13:34), have had profound impacts on human societies over the centuries.

The belief in the Bible's miracles necessitates faith, described by Paul as "the assurance of things hoped for, the conviction of things not seen." (Hebrews 11:1). This faith isn't blind but is a reasoned trust based on the evidence presented. The Bible's consistency, credibility, and the fulfillment of prophecies provide a strong foundation for such faith.

The Resurrection: The Foundation of New Testament Reliability

The resurrection of Jesus Christ is at the core of the Christian faith and is a central theme in the New Testament. The reliability of the New Testament hinges significantly on the credibility of the resurrection accounts. This event is cited as a demonstration of God's power and the validation of Jesus' claims, teachings, and His divine nature.

The resurrection is primarily recorded in the four Gospels - Matthew (Matthew 28:1-20), Mark (Mark 16:1-8), Luke (Luke 24:1-53), and John (John 20:1-21:25). Each account provides a different perspective, but they all converge on the fundamental fact: the tomb, where Jesus was laid after His crucifixion, was found empty, and He appeared alive to His disciples and others.

In 1 Corinthians 15:3-8, the Apostle Paul provides an early creedal statement about the resurrection: "For what I received I passed on to you as of first importance: that Christ died for our sins according to the Scriptures, that he was buried, that he was raised on the third day according to the Scriptures, and that he appeared to Cephas, and then to the Twelve. After that, he appeared to more than five hundred of the brothers and sisters at the same time, most of whom are still living, though some have fallen asleep. Then he appeared to James, then to all the apostles, and last of all he appeared to me also, as to one abnormally born."

This passage shows that the belief in Jesus' death and resurrection was not a later development but was a foundational belief from the earliest days of the Christian faith. It also provides the eyewitness testimony of those who saw the resurrected Christ, including a group of over 500 people at once. This wide range of witnesses, including skeptics like James and persecutors like Paul, attests to the transformative power of the resurrection event.

In Romans 1:4, Paul states that Jesus "was declared to be the Son of God in power according to the Spirit of holiness by his resurrection from the dead." This highlights the resurrection as a divine validation of Jesus' claims and His role as the Messiah. If the resurrection did not occur, then the foundational claims of the New Testament would be undermined.

The apostle Peter, in his sermon recorded in Acts 2:22-36, used the resurrection as the central argument for Jesus being the promised Messiah. He cites Psalm 16:10, stating that David, being a prophet, foresaw the resurrection of Christ.

In conclusion, the resurrection is not just an isolated miracle within the New Testament. It serves as a linchpin that holds together the teachings, the miracles, the sacrificial death, and the promised return of Jesus. The historical and testimonial evidences of the resurrection offer a robust foundation for the reliability of the New Testament. However, it should be noted that accepting the resurrection as a historical event also requires faith, as is true with many aspects of religious belief.

The New Testament and Archaeology: Unearthing Historical Support

Archaeological findings have been instrumental in corroborating many of the geographical, cultural, and historical details mentioned in the New Testament. These evidences serve to support the historical accuracy of the New Testament and its reliability as a source of ancient history.

Geographical Accuracy: The New Testament refers to specific cities, regions, and landmarks, many of which have been confirmed through archaeological excavations. For instance, Luke's descriptions of Thessalonica, Philippi, Athens, and Corinth in Acts 17 align with archaeological discoveries.

Inscriptions and Monuments: Numerous inscriptions and monuments corroborate the existence of figures mentioned in the New Testament. For instance, an inscription found in Caesarea Maritima, known as the "Pilate Stone", affirms the historical existence of Pontius Pilate, the Roman governor who presided over the trial of Jesus (Matthew 27:2; Luke 3:1).

The Pool of Bethesda: In John 5:1-15, there's an account of Jesus healing a man at the Pool of Bethesda. John provides a detailed description of this pool, stating that it had five covered colonnades. For a long time, there was no evidence of such a place, leading some to question John's accuracy. However, in the 19th century, archaeologists discovered a pool fitting John's description in the northeast quarter of Jerusalem's Old City, affirming the historical accuracy of the Gospel account.

The Crucifixion and Burial of Jesus: The details of Jesus' crucifixion and burial align with archaeological findings related to Roman crucifixion methods and burial customs. The discovery of the ossuary (bone box) of Caiaphas, the high priest who was involved in the trial of Jesus (Matthew 26:57), provides additional archaeological support.

Corinthian Gallio Inscription: An inscription discovered in Delphi, Greece, mentions Gallio, the proconsul of Achaia who dismissed charges against the apostle Paul (Acts 18:12-17). This inscription provides an external confirmation of Gallio's existence and his position, supporting the historical reliability of Acts.

While archaeology does not prove the spiritual truth claims of the New Testament, it does provide external evidence that supports the New Testament's historical accuracy. Archaeological findings affirm that the New Testament writers accurately depicted the world in which they lived, lending credibility to their accounts.

Non-Canonical Gospels: Understanding Their Place and Purpose

The term "non-canonical Gospels" refers to early Christian writings that tell about the life and teachings of Jesus but are not included in the New Testament canon. These include texts such as the Gospel of Thomas, the Gospel of Peter, the Gospel of Mary, and others. Though these texts are historically interesting, it's essential to understand their place and purpose in relation to the canonical Gospels—Matthew, Mark, Luke, and John.

Date of Composition: Non-canonical Gospels are generally believed to have been written later than the canonical Gospels. The Gospels of Matthew, Mark, Luke, and John are thought to have been composed in the first century AD, within a generation or two of Jesus' life. In contrast, most non-canonical Gospels are believed to have been written in the second century CE or later, at a greater remove from the events they describe.

Apostolic Tradition: The canonical Gospels are believed to be closely linked to the apostolic tradition—that is, they were either written by apostles (Matthew and John), or by their close associates (Mark, a companion of Peter, and Luke, a companion of Paul). This close connection to the apostles lends them credibility. On the other hand, the non-canonical Gospels are not directly linked to the apostles and are often attributed to later figures.

Doctrinal Consistency: The canonical Gospels present a consistent picture of Jesus and his teachings. This coherence is demonstrated in their depiction of Jesus' life, death, and resurrection, and the significance of these events for faith and salvation. Non-canonical Gospels, on the other hand, often present views of Jesus that are significantly different from those found in the canonical Gospels, reflecting different theological perspectives and concerns.

The Role of the Holy Spirit: In John 14:26, Jesus promises that the Holy Spirit will teach the disciples all things and remind them of everything He said. This suggests that the canonical Gospels, which were accepted by the early church under the guidance of the Holy Spirit, are trustworthy records of Jesus' life and teachings. Non-canonical Gospels, which were not recognized by the early church in this way, do not have this same assurance of divine guidance.

In conclusion, while the non-canonical Gospels provide interesting insights into the diverse ways in which early Christians understood Jesus, they do not carry the same weight as the canonical Gospels in terms of historical credibility, apostolic authority, doctrinal consistency, and divine inspiration.

The Impact of the New Testament: Its Transformative Power as Evidence

The New Testament's transformative power is often seen as a form of evidence attesting to its trustworthiness. This transformative power is evident in the lives of individuals, communities, and societies that have been profoundly changed by its teachings.

Transformation of Individuals: The New Testament presents stories of individuals whose lives were drastically changed after encountering Jesus and his teachings. For example, the apostle Paul, originally named Saul, was a zealous persecutor of the early Christian church (Acts 8:1). However, after a dramatic encounter with Jesus on the road to Damascus, he became one of the most influential apostles, spreading the gospel across the Roman Empire (Acts 9:1-31). This radical transformation, from persecutor to proclaimer, is a testament to the transformative power of the New Testament message.

Transformation of Communities: The New Testament also depicts the transformative effect of the gospel on entire communities. In the book of Acts, we see the birth and growth of the early Christian community, which despite persecution, grew rapidly and spread throughout the Roman Empire (Acts 2:41-47). These early Christian communities were known for their love, unity, and generosity, living out the teachings of Jesus in a practical and tangible way.

Societal Transformation: Over centuries, the New Testament has profoundly shaped societies and cultures around the world. Its teachings have inspired social reforms, influenced laws and ethical norms, and motivated acts of charity and compassion. For instance, Jesus' commandment to "love your neighbor as yourself" (Mark 12:31) has been a foundational principle inspiring countless humanitarian efforts.

Inner Transformation: The New Testament speaks of a spiritual transformation that occurs through faith in Jesus Christ. In 2 Corinthians 5:17, Paul writes, "Therefore, if anyone is in Christ, he is a new creation. The old has passed away; behold, the new has come." This internal transformation, resulting in a change of character and behavior, is a powerful testament to the transformative power of the New Testament.

The Endurance of the New Testament: The fact that the New Testament has endured over two millennia, in spite of various cultural, political, and intellectual challenges, also speaks to its transformative power. As the writer of Hebrews declares, "Jesus Christ is the same yesterday and today and forever" (Hebrews 13:8). The enduring relevance and impact of the New Testament suggest a timeless and universal truth that continues to transform lives.

In sum, the transformative power of the New Testament serves as evidence of its trustworthiness. Its ability to change individuals, shape communities, influence societies, and endure through time testifies to the power and truth of its message.

The Testimony of Early Church Fathers: Affirmation of New Testament Texts

The early Church Fathers' writings provide affirmation of the New Testament texts, offering significant insight into how early Christians understood and interpreted these texts. Their writings, which include letters, treatises, and commentaries, often quote or allude to the New Testament, helping to confirm its early and widespread usage and acceptance.

Clement of Rome: Clement, writing around 95 CE, shows familiarity with several New Testament texts. His letter to the Corinthians quotes from or alludes to several books, including Romans (1 Clement 32:2 with Romans 1:32), Corinthians (1 Clement 47:1 with 1 Corinthians 1:12-13), and Hebrews (1 Clement 36:2-5 with Hebrews 1:3-7).

Ignatius of Antioch: Ignatius, in his seven letters written around 107 CE, provides evidence for several New Testament texts. He quotes from Matthew (Ignatius to the Smyrnaeans 1:1 with Matthew 3:15), Romans (Ignatius to the Ephesians 5:3 with Romans 1:3), and 1 Corinthians (Ignatius to the Ephesians 18:2 with 1 Corinthians 15:53), among others.

Polycarp of Smyrna: Polycarp's letter to the Philippians (around 110-140 CE) contains numerous references to New Testament texts. For instance, he quotes Ephesians (Polycarp to the Philippians 12:1 with Ephesians 4:26), Philippians (Polycarp to the Philippians 3:1 with Philippians 2:10), and 1 John (Polycarp to the Philippians 7:1 with 1 John 4:3).

Irenaeus of Lyons: Irenaeus, writing around 180 CE, shows extensive knowledge of the New Testament. In his work "Against Heresies," he confirms the four Gospels (Matthew, Mark, Luke, and John) as authoritative Scripture (Against Heresies 3.1.1).

Justin Martyr: Justin, in his "First Apology" written around 155-157 CE, refers to the Gospels as the "memoirs of the apostles" (First Apology 66.3).

Tatian's Diatessaron: A student of Justin Martyr, Tatian compiled a harmony of the four Gospels known as the Diatessaron around 170 CE, which further attests to the early acceptance of these Gospels.

The testimony of the early Church Fathers, through their quotations and allusions, provides compelling evidence for the early existence and widespread acceptance of the New Testament texts. Their writings affirm the continuity of Christian teaching from the apostolic age through the early church period, reinforcing the trustworthiness of the New Testament.

Dealing with Difficult Passages: Trustworthiness Amidst Complexity

Understanding and interpreting difficult passages in the New Testament can be challenging, but these complexities do not necessarily undermine its overall trustworthiness. Here are a few strategies, grounded in scripture, to approach these tricky texts:

Context is key: When faced with a complex or difficult passage, it's crucial to consider its immediate context within the passage, the broader context within the book, and the overall context of the Bible as a whole. For instance, in Matthew 16:28, Jesus says, "Truly I tell you, some who are standing here will not taste death before they see the Son of Man coming in his kingdom." This might seem confusing at first glance, but when read in context with the Transfiguration in the next chapter (Matthew 17:1-9), it becomes clear that Jesus was referring to this event, not His Second Coming.

Understand genre and literary devices: The New Testament contains different genres, including Gospels, letters, and apocalyptic literature. Recognizing the genre can help understand the author's intent. For instance, in the parables of Jesus (Mark 4:2-34), we understand that these are not historical accounts but stories with a moral or spiritual lesson.

Consider cultural and historical background: Understanding the culture and historical context in which the New Testament was written can provide valuable insight. For example, Paul's instructions on head coverings in 1 Corinthians 11:2-16 make more sense when we understand that in the Corinthian culture, a woman's uncovered head was often associated with sexual impropriety.

Harmonizing with clear passages: If a passage is unclear, it can often be interpreted in light of other, clearer passages that address the same topic. For example, the concept of faith and works in James 2:14-26 can seem contradictory to Paul's emphasis on faith in Romans 3:28. However, when read together, it becomes clear that both authors agree that faith and works are inseparable - Paul argues that faith leads to justification, while James emphasizes that genuine faith results in good works.

Consult reliable commentaries and scholars: When wrestling with a difficult passage, it can be helpful to consult reliable commentaries, Bible dictionaries, and scholarly articles. These resources often provide valuable insights and different perspectives.

Prayer and humility: Finally, approaching the scripture with humility and prayer is vital. As James 1:5 says, "If any of you lacks wisdom, you should ask God, who gives generously to all without finding fault, and it will be given to you."

While the New Testament does contain some challenging and complex passages, it's important to remember that the central message of the Gospel – the life, death, and resurrection of Jesus Christ for the salvation of mankind – is clear and consistent throughout. These difficult passages invite deeper study and engagement with the text, leading to a richer understanding and appreciation of the Bible's message.

Responding to Modern Criticisms: An Apologetic Approach

In responding to modern criticisms of the New Testament, it's important to remember that an apologetic approach does not mean being defensive or argumentative, but rather presenting a reasoned case for faith. Here are several strategies, grounded in scripture, to address common criticisms:

Alleged Contradictions: Critics often point out perceived contradictions within the New Testament. However, many of these can be resolved through careful study and understanding the context. For example, the Gospel accounts of the resurrection might seem to conflict at first glance, but when read closely, they can be harmonized as different perspectives of the same event. It's important to keep in mind 2 Timothy 3:16, which states, "All Scripture is God-breathed and is useful for teaching, rebuking, correcting and training in righteousness."

Historical Accuracy: The New Testament is sometimes criticized for its historical accuracy. However, Luke 1:1-4 demonstrates the careful historical approach taken by the authors: "Many have undertaken to draw up an account of the things that have been fulfilled among us, just as they were handed down to us by those who from the first were eyewitnesses and servants of the word." The New Testament has also been supported by various archaeological findings and external historical writings.

Exclusivity of Salvation: Critics often question the exclusivity of salvation in Christianity. John 14:6 presents Jesus' claim: "I am the way and the truth and the life. No one comes to the Father except through me." While this claim may seem exclusive, it's important to remember that Christianity also teaches the inclusivity of the offer of salvation - it is open to all who would believe (John 3:16).

Miracles and Supernatural Events: Some people struggle with the miracles and supernatural events recorded in the New Testament. However, these miracles serve to confirm the message and the messenger. For instance, in Acts 2:22, Peter refers to Jesus as "a man attested to you by God with miracles and wonders and signs that God did through him in your midst."

Problem of Suffering: Critics may question how a good and powerful God could allow suffering. While the New Testament doesn't provide a full answer to this question, it does show God's response to suffering: in Jesus, God enters into human suffering and ultimately overcomes it through the resurrection (Romans 8:18-39).

Textual Variations: Critics may also point to variations in the New Testament manuscripts. However, none of these variations impact any core doctrine of the Christian faith. The New Testament is the most well-attested document from antiquity, and as stated in 1 Peter 1:24-25, "All people are like grass, and all their glory is like the flowers of the field; the grass withers and the flowers fall, but the word of the Lord endures forever." Moreover, it must be understood that many dozens of world renowned New Testament textual scholars over the past 500 years have restored the original words that were in the original documents to a 99.99% reflection of the originals.

In responding to these criticisms, it's important to approach discussions with gentleness and respect, as 1 Peter 3:15 advises: "But in your hearts revere Christ as Lord. Always be prepared to give an answer to everyone who asks you to give the reason for the hope that you have. But do this with gentleness and respect."

Conclusion: The Trustworthiness of the New Testament—A Balanced Evaluation

In concluding a balanced evaluation of the trustworthiness of the New Testament, we can assess the multitude of dimensions that affirm its credibility. This involves not only the historical and textual accuracy but also the consistency of its message, the fulfillment of prophecies, and the transformative impact it has had throughout centuries.

Historical and Textual Accuracy

The New Testament presents historical events within specific geographical and cultural contexts. For example, Luke's account begins by placing the birth of John the

Baptist and Jesus in the reigns of Herod the Great, Caesar Augustus, and other historical figures (Luke 1:5, Luke 2:1-2). Archaeology and other historical records have consistently affirmed the New Testament's historical claims.

In terms of textual reliability, the New Testament's preservation is unparalleled among ancient documents. Despite minor variations, the central teachings of the New Testament remain unaffected. As Revelation 22:18-19 warns, altering the words of the text is a grave offense, indicating the high regard for textual fidelity in the early Christian community.

Consistency of Message

Despite being written by various authors in diverse contexts, the New Testament consistently centers on the life, death, and resurrection of Jesus Christ, and the implications of these events for humanity's relationship with God. In Hebrews 1:1-2, the author writes, "In the past God spoke to our ancestors through the prophets at many times and in various ways, but in these last days he has spoken to us by his Son."

Fulfillment of Prophecies

The New Testament documents the fulfillment of numerous Old Testament prophecies. The life, death, and resurrection of Jesus align with prophecies in the books of Isaiah, Micah, Psalms, and others. For instance, Jesus cites Isaiah 61:1-2 in Luke 4:18-21, asserting that He is the fulfillment of this prophecy.

Transformative Impact

The transformative power of the New Testament is evident in the lives of individuals and societies throughout history. The teachings of Jesus and the apostles have shaped ethical norms, legal codes, and cultural values in numerous societies. As Paul writes in Romans 12:2, believers are "transformed by the renewing of [their] mind."

In conclusion, the trustworthiness of the New Testament can be affirmed through a balanced evaluation of its historical and textual accuracy, consistency of message, fulfillment of prophecies, and transformative impact. The Bible itself encourages such scrutiny, as Acts 17:11 commends the Berean Jews, who "examined the Scriptures every day to see if what Paul said was true." Such an examination can strengthen confidence in the New Testament as a reliable source of spiritual truth.

CHAPTER 14 Overcoming Modern Skepticism: A Response to Contemporary Challenges

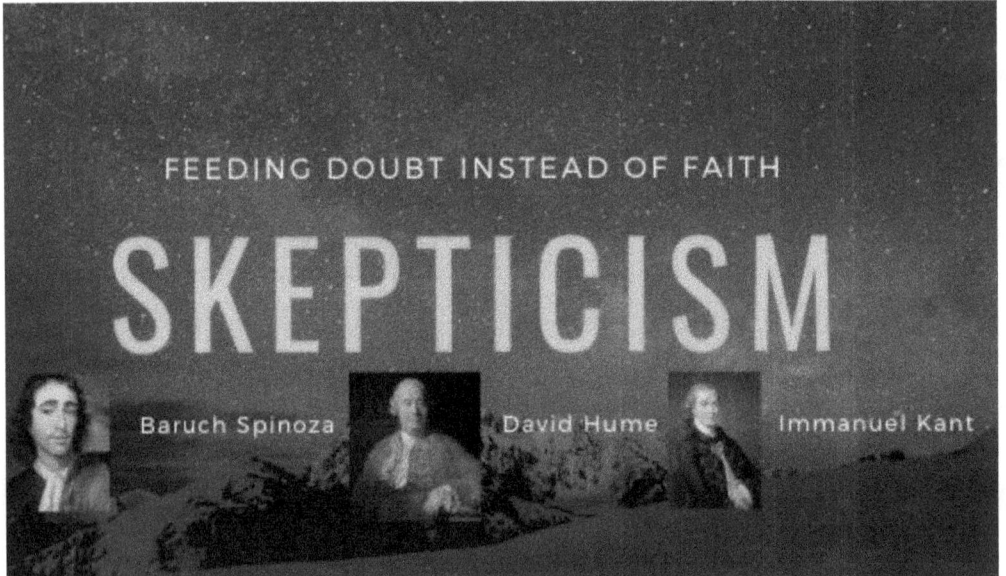

Introduction: The Rise of Modern Skepticism

In the modern era, there has been a rise in skepticism towards religious beliefs and institutions, including skepticism towards the Bible. This is often influenced by factors such as increased secularism, the questioning of religious authority, and the influence of scientific and philosophical ideas that challenge traditional religious beliefs.

The Bible itself acknowledges the presence of skepticism and doubt. For example, in the Gospel of Matthew, when some of the disciples see the resurrected Jesus, they worship him, "but some doubted" (Matthew 28:17). In the Gospel of John, Thomas initially refuses to believe in the resurrection of Jesus without direct physical evidence, earning him the nickname "Doubting Thomas" (John 20:24-29).

The Apostle Paul encountered skepticism during his missionary journeys. When he was in Athens, a city known for its philosophical debates, he preached about Jesus and the resurrection. Some Athenians dismissed him as a "babbler," while others were intrigued and wanted to hear more (Acts 17:16-21).

Even in the face of skepticism, the New Testament emphasizes the importance of faith. Hebrews 11:1 defines faith as "the assurance of things hoped for, the conviction of things not seen." Yet this faith is not blind—it is often based on evidence, testimony, and personal experience.

The New Testament also emphasizes the importance of engaging with skepticism in a respectful and thoughtful manner. In 1 Peter 3:15, believers are advised to "always be prepared to give an answer to everyone who asks you to give the reason for the hope that you have. But do this with gentleness and respect."

So, while modern skepticism presents challenges, it also offers opportunities for dialogue and deeper understanding. The New Testament provides a foundation for engaging with skepticism—acknowledging doubts, providing reasoned answers, and maintaining a posture of respect and gentleness.

Identifying the Common Objections: A Catalogue of Contemporary Challenges

Modern skepticism towards the Bible often revolves around a few common objections, many of which are informed by scientific, philosophical, historical, and ethical considerations. Let's explore these objections and provide responses that are rooted in biblical texts.

1. **Science and the Bible**: Some people argue that the Bible is incompatible with modern scientific understanding. For instance, the creation accounts in Genesis 1-2 are often contrasted with the theory of evolution and the Big Bang theory.

However, many biblical scholars argue that Genesis was not intended to provide a scientific account of creation. Instead, it uses the cultural and symbolic language of the ancient Near East to convey theological truths about God as the creator and sustainer of the universe (Genesis 1:1, "In the beginning God created the heavens and the earth.").

2. **Historical Accuracy**: Skeptics often question the historical accuracy of the Bible, citing supposed contradictions between biblical accounts and archaeological or historical evidence.

However, there are numerous instances where the Bible's historical narratives align with external evidence. For example, the existence of historical figures mentioned in the New Testament, like Pontius Pilate (Luke 3:1), has been confirmed by archaeological evidence.

3. **Ethical Objections**: Some skeptics object to the ethics presented in the Bible, pointing to instances of violence, patriarchy, or intolerance.

While these concerns must be taken seriously, it's important to understand the Bible in its historical and cultural context. The Bible contains a diverse collection of texts written over many centuries, reflecting different cultural norms and ethical perspectives. Yet, it consistently emphasizes love, justice, and mercy as core ethical principles (Micah 6:8, "He has shown you, O mortal, what is good. And what does the LORD require of you? To act justly and to love mercy and to walk humbly with your God.").

4. **Miracles**: Skeptics often find it difficult to accept the Bible's accounts of miraculous events, arguing that they violate the laws of nature.

While miracles do transcend our usual experience of the natural world, they are presented in the Bible as signs of God's power and love. For instance, Jesus' miracles are portrayed as signs of the coming of God's kingdom (Luke 7:22, "Go back and report to John what you have seen and heard: The blind receive sight, the lame walk, those who have leprosy are cleansed, the deaf hear, the dead are raised, and the good news is proclaimed to the poor.").

5. **The Problem of Evil**: Skeptics often question how a good and powerful God could allow suffering and evil in the world.

The Bible acknowledges this problem and wrestles with it in texts like the book of Job. In the New Testament, the crucifixion of Jesus is presented as God's response to human suffering and evil—God enters into human suffering and ultimately overcomes it through the resurrection (Romans 8:18, "I consider that our present sufferings are not worth comparing with the glory that will be revealed in us.").

Engaging with these objections requires both a deep understanding of the Bible and a willingness to enter into thoughtful and respectful dialogue with skeptics.

The Problem of Miracles: Responding to Philosophical Naturalism

Philosophical naturalism is the worldview that all phenomena can and should be explained by natural causes and laws, and it rejects the existence of supernatural events like miracles. This perspective can pose a challenge to biblical accounts, which frequently involve miraculous events, from the parting of the Red Sea in Exodus (Exodus 14:21-22) to Jesus feeding the five thousand (Matthew 14:13-21), to his own resurrection from the dead (Luke 24:1-7).

However, one can respond to philosophical naturalism by examining the nature of miracles and the assumptions underlying naturalism.

Understanding Miracles: Miracles, as depicted in the Bible, are not arbitrary or random occurrences. Instead, they serve specific purposes in the narratives where they occur. They often signify God's involvement in the world and affirm the messages of prophets and apostles. For example, when Jesus turns water into wine in John 2:1-11, it's not just an impressive feat; it's a sign that reveals his divine authority.

Challenging Naturalism's Assumptions: Philosophical naturalism assumes that the material universe, governed by consistent laws, is all that exists. This assumption, however, is not self-evident or unquestionable. The Bible presents a different perspective: a universe created and sustained by God, where the natural and supernatural aren't separate domains but part of a unified, divinely-governed reality. For instance, Colossians 1:16-17 says of Christ, "For by him all things were created, in heaven and on earth, visible and invisible... And he is before all things, and in him all things hold together."

The Role of Faith: Belief in miracles doesn't mean rejecting reason or science. Instead, it acknowledges that our understanding of the universe may have limits and that there may be realities beyond what we can empirically observe or comprehend. This is where faith comes into play, as Hebrews 11:1 states, "Now faith is confidence in what we hope for and assurance about what we do not see."

Miracles and Testimony: Many miracles in the Bible were witnessed by multiple people, suggesting they were not merely subjective experiences or mythological tales. For instance, 1 Corinthians 15:3-8 refers to the post-resurrection appearances of Christ, which were witnessed by hundreds of people.

In conclusion, while philosophical naturalism presents a challenge to the biblical accounts of miracles, this challenge can be met by understanding the nature and purpose of miracles, questioning the assumptions underlying naturalism, and acknowledging the role of faith and testimony in affirming miraculous events.

Alleged Contradictions: A Closer Look at the Text

When faced with claims of contradictions within the Bible, it's essential to approach the text with a careful and discerning eye. Recognizing the literary, cultural, and historical context of the scriptures can often resolve apparent discrepancies. Here are a few principles and examples:

Different Perspectives: Different authors may provide different perspectives on the same event without necessarily contradicting each other. The four Gospels, for instance, contain different details and emphasis in their accounts of Jesus' life, death, and resurrection. Matthew (Matthew 28:1-10), Mark (Mark 16:1-8), Luke (Luke 24:1-12), and John (John 20:1-10) each provide unique details about the discovery of the empty tomb, but these accounts can be harmonized rather than seen as contradictory.

Cultural and Literary Context: Understanding the cultural and literary context of biblical writings can resolve apparent contradictions. For example, in Proverbs 26:4-5, the advice "Do not answer a fool according to his folly" is immediately followed by "Answer a fool according to his folly". This apparent contradiction can be resolved by understanding the nature of ancient Hebrew wisdom literature, which often presents two sides of a complex issue.

Chronological Ordering: Not all biblical accounts are in strict chronological order, which can sometimes lead to perceived contradictions. For example, in Matthew 4:5-11 and Luke 4:5-13, the order of Jesus' temptations in the wilderness differs. However, neither author specifies that the temptations happened in the exact order presented, suggesting that the differences could simply reflect thematic rather than chronological ordering.

Paraphrasing and Summarizing: Sometimes, biblical authors paraphrase or summarize speeches or events, which can result in different wordings of the same account. For instance, the wording of the Ten Commandments varies between Exodus 20:1-17 and Deuteronomy 5:4-21, reflecting Moses' summarizing and elaborating on God's laws for the Israelites.

Figurative Language: Biblical authors often use figurative language to convey truths. For example, the Psalms describe God as a shepherd (Psalm 23:1), a rock (Psalm 18:2), and a shield (Psalm 28:7). These are not contradictions but metaphors expressing different aspects of God's character.

Therefore, when examining alleged contradictions in the Bible, it's crucial to remember the diverse literary styles, cultural contexts, and theological purposes of the biblical texts. Often, what seem like contradictions at first glance can be reconciled with a deeper understanding of the text.

Questioning the Historical Jesus: An Apologetic Response

The question of the historical Jesus is a topic of considerable debate among scholars. However, an analysis of the New Testament and other historical records provides compelling evidence for the existence and deeds of Jesus. It's important to note that examining the historical Jesus doesn't inherently contradict faith; instead, it can deepen one's understanding of the person and work of Jesus.

New Testament Evidence: The New Testament provides the most comprehensive accounts of Jesus' life, teachings, death, and resurrection. These texts, written by Jesus' contemporaries or their immediate successors, present a consistent picture of Jesus. For instance, the Gospels depict Jesus as a powerful teacher and miracle-worker who claimed to be the Messiah (Matthew 16:16-17), was crucified under Pontius Pilate (Mark 15:15), and rose from the dead (Luke 24:1-7). Meanwhile, Paul's letters affirm Jesus' divine nature (Philippians 2:5-11), His crucifixion (1 Corinthians 15:3), and resurrection (1 Corinthians 15:4).

Early Christian Writings: Early Christian writings outside of the New Testament, such as the letters of Ignatius of Antioch and the writings of Justin Martyr, provide further affirmation of Jesus' life and teachings.

Non-Christian Sources: Non-Christian sources from the first century also corroborate the existence of Jesus. The Roman historian Tacitus, for instance, referred to Jesus' execution under Pontius Pilate (Annals 15.44). Jewish sources like the Talmud also acknowledge Jesus, albeit unfavorably.

Archaeological Evidence: Archaeology also supports the historical Jesus. For example, the Pilate Stone discovered in Caesarea Maritima confirms Pontius Pilate's role as the Roman governor of Judaea, consistent with the New Testament's account of Jesus' crucifixion under Pilate.

The Impact of Jesus: The transformative impact of Jesus on His followers offers indirect but powerful evidence of His historical reality. His followers were willing to endure persecution and death for their belief in Jesus' resurrection, a commitment that's difficult to explain if Jesus was not a real, historical figure (Acts 4:18-20).

In sum, the historical Jesus is not just a figure of faith but also a figure rooted in history. Though some aspects of Jesus' life and teachings remain a subject of ongoing research and debate, the core claims about Jesus in the New Testament—His teachings, His crucifixion, His resurrection—are well-supported by historical evidence and scholarly consensus.

The Trustworthiness of the Gospels: Overcoming the Myth Theory

The "myth theory" is a term generally used to refer to the view that the events described in the Gospels are not historical events but rather are symbolic or allegorical narratives. Those who ascribe to the myth theory argue that the miracles, teachings, and even the resurrection of Jesus are not meant to be understood literally but are allegories that convey spiritual truths.

However, several reasons suggest that the Gospels should be seen as trustworthy historical documents rather than collections of myths:

The Gospels Are Based on Eyewitness Accounts: The Gospels are based on the firsthand experiences of Jesus' followers. The Gospel of John, for instance, claims to be based on the testimony of the "disciple whom Jesus loved" (John 21:24). In 2 Peter 1:16, the apostle Peter explicitly states that the disciples were not following "cleverly devised myths" but were eyewitnesses of Jesus' majesty.

Early Date of the Gospels: Most scholars date the writing of the Gospels to the first century CE, within a few decades of Jesus' life. This means that the Gospels were written while many of those who had known Jesus were still alive and could corroborate or contradict the accounts.

Consistency of the Accounts: Despite variations in perspective and emphasis, the four Gospels present a consistent picture of Jesus' life, teachings, death, and resurrection. This suggests that they were working from a common historical reality, rather than creating myths independently.

The Gospels Present Difficult Teachings and Events: If the Gospels were merely mythological, it would be strange for the authors to include teachings and events that were difficult or embarrassing for the early Christian community. For instance, the crucifixion of Jesus was a scandalous event, for "cursed is everyone who is hanged on a tree" (Galatians 3:13, quoting Deuteronomy 21:23). Yet the Gospel writers reported it because it was a historical fact, not a mythical invention.

The Gospels Are Rooted in Historical and Geographical Reality: The Gospels are full of specific references to real people (like Pontius Pilate and Herod Antipas), places (like Jerusalem and Capernaum), and events (like the census of Quirinius in Luke 2:2). This is not typical of mythological literature, which tends to occur in vague or non-specific settings.

In conclusion, while the Gospels do convey deep spiritual truths, they do so through the medium of historical events. The evidence suggests that they are not myths but trustworthy accounts of the life, teachings, death, and resurrection of Jesus.

The Resurrection: Addressing Skepticism About the Central Event

The Resurrection of Jesus Christ is the central event in Christianity. The apostle Paul, in 1 Corinthians 15:14, writes, "And if Christ has not been raised, then our preaching is in vain and your faith is in vain." If the Resurrection did not happen, then the basis for Christian faith crumbles. However, there are reasons based on the New Testament that argue for its historical reliability.

The Empty Tomb: In the four Gospels, we find that the tomb where Jesus was buried was found empty on the third day after his crucifixion (Matthew 28:1-10, Mark 16:1-8, Luke 24:1-12, John 20:1-10). The fact that the tomb was empty is significant because it suggests that Jesus' body was not there. This is difficult to explain unless the Resurrection occurred.

The Post-Resurrection Appearances: The New Testament records multiple instances of Jesus appearing to his disciples after his death (1 Corinthians 15:3-8). These appearances were not to just one person but to different groups of people, in different locations, and at different times. These accounts are hard to dismiss as hallucinations or fabrications, especially considering the transformations these experiences sparked in the disciples.

The Transformation of the Disciples: The disciples went from hiding in fear after Jesus' crucifixion (John 20:19) to boldly proclaiming the Resurrection in the face of persecution (Acts 4:1-22). This radical change is inexplicable unless they had encountered the risen Christ.

The Origin of the Christian Church: The Christian Church grew rapidly after the death of Jesus, and its central message was the Resurrection (Acts 2:24, 31-32). The best explanation for the origin and growth of the Church is that Jesus did indeed rise from the dead.

The Willingness to Die for Belief in the Resurrection: Many of the early Christians, including the apostles, were willing to die for their belief in the Resurrection (Acts 7:54-60, 2 Timothy 4:6-8). While people may die for what they believe to be true, it is unlikely they would willingly die for something they know to be a lie.

The Change in Worship: Early Christians, who were mostly Jews, started worshipping on Sunday, the day of the week on which Jesus rose from the dead (Acts 20:7, 1 Corinthians 16:2). This significant change is best explained by a historical event as transformative as the Resurrection.

Skepticism about the Resurrection is understandable, given its supernatural nature. However, when considering the evidence provided in the New Testament, the most reasonable conclusion is that the Resurrection is a historical event. The Resurrection was the catalyst for the rapid growth and transformative power of the early Christian Church, changing lives then and continuing to do so today.

The Reliability of Paul's Letters: Countering Claims of Pseudepigraphy

The Pauline epistles are a crucial part of the New Testament, contributing significantly to Christian theology. While the authorship of some of these letters is widely accepted (like Romans, 1 & 2 Corinthians, Galatians, Philippians, 1 Thessalonians, and Philemon), others are often questioned by modern skeptics. These disputed letters include Ephesians, Colossians, 2 Thessalonians, and the Pastoral Epistles (1 & 2 Timothy, Titus). These skeptics suggest pseudepigraphy, meaning they were not actually written by Paul but by someone else using his name. However, there are solid reasons, grounded in the text itself, to trust in their Pauline authorship.

Consistency in Theological Themes: Despite some stylistic and vocabulary differences, which can be attributed to different scribes or the different circumstances and audiences of the letters, there is a consistent theological theme running through all of Paul's letters, including the disputed ones. This includes the theme of justification by faith (Romans 3:28, Galatians 2:16, Titus 3:7), the centrality of the Resurrection (1 Corinthians 15:17, 2 Timothy 2:8), and the idea of the Church as the body of Christ (1 Corinthians 12:27, Ephesians 4:12).

Personal Claims of Authorship: In the disputed letters, Paul explicitly claims authorship (Ephesians 1:1, Colossians 1:1, 2 Thessalonians 1:1, 1 Timothy 1:1, 2 Timothy 1:1, Titus 1:1). While it's possible for someone to falsely claim authorship, the early church was rigorous in its acceptance of canonical books, and it's unlikely that such a deception would have passed unnoticed.

Early Church Tradition: Early Church fathers like Irenaeus, Clement of Rome, and Polycarp accepted the Pauline authorship of these letters. They were closer to the time of the letters' writing and had access to information and traditions that we do not.

The Personal Touch in the Letters: The disputed letters contain personal greetings, specific advice, and details about Paul's life that are consistent with his other letters and the book of Acts. For example, compare the personal remarks in Philemon 1:4-22 with those in 2 Timothy 4:9-21.

The Difficulty of Pseudonymous Writing: Writing a letter in the name of a well-known figure like Paul without detection would have been a formidable task. The early Christian community had mechanisms to verify the authenticity of letters, and false letters were often detected and rejected (2 Thessalonians 2:2).

While it's crucial to approach the authorship question with intellectual honesty, these points provide strong support for the Pauline authorship of all 13 letters traditionally attributed to him in the New Testament. The continuity in theology, personal claims of authorship, acceptance by the early church, personal details, and the difficulty of successful pseudonymous writing all argue in favor of Paul's authorship.

The Formation of the Canon: Responding to Claims of Arbitrary Selection

The formation of the New Testament Canon, or the selection and recognition of the books that comprise the New Testament, has been the subject of much discussion and debate. Skeptics often claim that this process was arbitrary, perhaps politically motivated, or even manipulative. However, the evidence suggests a thoughtful, careful process guided by clear criteria. The church did not create the canon; rather, it recognized the books that were already accepted as authoritative and inspired.

Apostolic Authority: One of the main criteria used in recognizing the books of the New Testament was apostolic authority. The books were written by an apostle or by someone closely associated with an apostle. For example, the Gospel of Matthew is attributed to Matthew the Apostle, while the Gospel of Luke is believed to have been written by Luke, a close associate of the Apostle Paul (Colossians 4:14).

Consistency of Message: Another important criterion was the consistency of the message with what was already known of Jesus' teaching and the apostles' doctrine. The New Testament books had to be in harmony with the established faith. A text like the Gospel of John, which begins with an affirmation of Jesus' divine nature (John 1:1), was clearly in line with the Church's understanding of Christ.

Universal Acceptance: The books of the New Testament were those that had been universally accepted and used by the Christian community across different regions. A letter like Romans, for example, was circulated and accepted as authoritative early on, as indicated by its references in the writings of early Church fathers like Ignatius and Polycarp.

Spiritual Edification: The books that were recognized as part of the New Testament were those that had proven useful for instruction, reproof, correction, and training in righteousness (2 Timothy 3:16). They were the texts that had nourished the Church's faith and life.

Evidence of Divine Inspiration: The Church also sought evidence of divine inspiration, believing that the Holy Spirit guided the process. The Apostle Peter, for instance, acknowledged Paul's letters as Scripture (2 Peter 3:15-16).

Rejection of Gnostic Texts: Many texts, often associated with Gnosticism (a belief system that diverged significantly from early Christian teaching), were rejected from the canon. These texts, like the Gospel of Thomas, often lacked apostolic authority, were not universally accepted, and contained teachings inconsistent with the apostolic faith.

In conclusion, the formation of the New Testament canon was not an arbitrary process. It was a careful recognition and collection of the authoritative and inspired texts that had been acknowledged and used by the Christian community since the time of the apostles. These texts were in line with the apostolic faith, were universally accepted, and had proven spiritually edifying. The canon was not so much created as it was recognized and confirmed by the early Church.

Non-Canonical Gospels: Why They Don't Threaten the Canonical Four

The non-canonical Gospels, often referred to as the "Gnostic Gospels," include texts such as the Gospel of Thomas, the Gospel of Mary, and the Gospel of Judas, among others. These documents, discovered mainly in the 19th and 20th centuries, are not included in the New Testament canon. There are several reasons why these texts do not threaten the reliability and authority of the four canonical Gospels: Matthew, Mark, Luke, and John.

Later Authorship: The non-canonical gospels were written later than the canonical ones. The four New Testament Gospels were all written in the first century AD, within the lifetime of the apostles and those who knew Jesus. In contrast, most of the non-canonical gospels were written in the second century CE or later. For example, the Gospel of Thomas is generally dated to the mid-2nd century CE. This means the canonical Gospels are closer to the events they describe and are more likely to be accurate.

Lack of Apostolic Authority: The canonical Gospels are linked to the apostles either directly (Matthew and John) or indirectly (Mark is associated with Peter; Luke with Paul). This gives them apostolic authority. On the other hand, non-canonical gospels, despite bearing the names of apostles or other figures from the New Testament, do not have demonstrable connections to these individuals. They are considered pseudepigraphal – falsely attributed works, texts whose claimed author is not the true author.

Inconsistency with Apostolic Teaching: The non-canonical gospels often contain teachings that are inconsistent with the teachings found in the New Testament. Many of them reflect Gnostic thought, a philosophy that was considered heretical by the early Church. For example, the Gospel of Thomas advocates for a secret knowledge necessary for salvation, a view not found in the canonical Gospels which emphasize faith in Jesus Christ (John 3:16; Ephesians 2:8).

Rejection by the Early Church: The early Church did not accept the non-canonical gospels as authoritative. They were not widely circulated or quoted by the Church Fathers. In contrast, the four Gospels were universally recognized and used in the liturgy and teaching of the Church from the earliest times.

Lack of Historical Reliability: The non-canonical gospels often lack historical detail and credibility. They tend not to situate Jesus in a specific historical and geographical context, unlike the canonical Gospels which contain numerous references to places, people, and events that have been confirmed by archaeology and other historical sources. For example, Luke's Gospel is notable for its historical precision (Luke 3:1-2).

In summary, while the non-canonical gospels provide interesting insights into the diverse beliefs of early Christian and Gnostic communities, they do not pose a threat to the canonical Gospels. The four New Testament Gospels – Matthew, Mark, Luke, and John – maintain their unique position due to their early authorship, apostolic authority, consistency with apostolic teaching, acceptance by the early Church, and historical reliability. These factors contribute to their recognition as the authoritative accounts of the life, death, and resurrection of Jesus Christ.

The Role of the Early Church: Countering the Conspiracy Theory

The early Church plays a vital role in understanding the formation and preservation of the New Testament. Some modern skeptics propose a conspiracy theory that the early Church leaders manipulated or forged documents to consolidate their power and suppress dissenting views. However, an examination of the historical context, the nature of the New Testament writings, and the statements of early Church leaders presents a different picture.

Historical Context: The early Church was a persecuted minority, not a powerful institution with the capability to enforce a uniform belief system or to manipulate texts. Early Christians were frequently persecuted by both Jewish and Roman authorities, as stated in several biblical passages (Acts 8:1, Acts 12:1-3, Revelation 2:13).

Nature of the New Testament Writings: The New Testament writings themselves show no signs of being part of a conspiracy. They are composed in various genres (letters, historical narratives, apocalyptic literature) and address a wide range of real-life situations in multiple geographical locations. They show diversity in their emphasis and perspectives, yet they also display a remarkable unity in their central message: Jesus Christ, his life, death, and resurrection. Their emphasis on truth, both in content (John 14:6, John 8:32) and in the ethics of communication (Ephesians 4:25, Colossians 3:9), argues against the idea of a conspiracy.

Statements of Early Church Leaders: The early Church leaders, also known as the Church Fathers, were adamant about the importance of truth and the dangers of heresy. They took great pains to preserve and transmit the teachings they had received. For example, Irenaeus, the bishop of Lyons in the late 2nd century, wrote extensively against Gnostic teachings in his work "Against Heresies," emphasizing the apostolic tradition that he and other orthodox leaders were preserving. The early Church leaders' concern for truth and their willingness to suffer for their beliefs makes the idea of a conspiracy unlikely.

Canon Formation: The formation of the New Testament canon (the list of books recognized as authoritative Scripture) was a complex process that took several centuries to finalize. However, it was not an arbitrary process or one controlled by a small group of powerful individuals. Instead, it was a communal process involving the whole Church, with criteria such as apostolicity (link to an apostle), orthodoxy (consistency with the rule of faith), catholicity (widespread use among various churches), and antiquity (written in the apostolic era) guiding the selection. This process further argues against the idea of a conspiracy.

In conclusion, the role of the early Church in preserving and transmitting the New Testament writings, as well as in defending the apostolic faith against heresies, argues against the idea of a conspiracy. Instead, it testifies to the early Christians' commitment to truth, even in the face of persecution, and their desire to preserve faithfully the teachings they had received about Jesus Christ.

The Challenge of Science and Faith: Compatibility, Not Conflict

The relationship between science and faith has been a topic of intense discussion and debate for centuries. Some view these two disciplines as being in conflict, but a close examination of the principles of both reveals not conflict, but compatibility.

Both Science and Faith Seek Truth: Both science and faith are engaged in the pursuit of truth. Science seeks to understand the natural world and its principles, while faith seeks to understand spiritual truths and divine realities. These two quests are not necessarily in conflict but rather can complement each other. The Bible upholds the value of truth in numerous passages such as Psalm 119:160: "The sum of your word is truth, and every one of your righteous rules endures forever."

God as the Creator: The belief that God is the Creator of the universe is foundational to Christian faith (Genesis 1:1, John 1:3). This belief does not preclude the exploration and understanding of the natural world through scientific investigation. In fact, it can motivate such exploration. The more we learn about the complexity and beauty of the natural world, the more we can appreciate the wisdom and power of its Creator. As Romans 1:20 says, "For his invisible attributes, namely, his eternal power and divine nature, have been clearly perceived, ever since the creation of the world, in the things that have been made."

Faith and Reason: Faith, according to the Bible, is not contrary to reason. Hebrews 11:1 describes faith as "the assurance of things hoped for, the conviction of things not seen." This does not mean that faith is blind or irrational, but that it goes beyond what can be perceived by the senses or known by human reason alone. It does not mean that faith is against evidence but rather that it interprets and understands evidence in the light of a broader, spiritual perspective.

Miracles: Miracles, as recorded in the Bible, are not violations of natural laws but are divine interventions that go beyond the regular patterns of nature. They are not meant to contradict or negate science but demonstrate God's sovereignty over His creation (John 2:11, Acts 2:22).

Evolution and Faith: The theory of evolution, one of the most contentious issues in the science-faith debate, does not necessarily negate the belief in a Creator. Some Christians interpret the biblical account of creation in a literal way, believing in a young earth and six 24-hour days of creation, while others interpret it in a more metaphorical or allegorical way, compatible with theistic evolution. These differing interpretations demonstrate the complexity of the issue and the possibility of harmonizing scientific understanding with faith convictions.

In conclusion, science and faith need not be in conflict. Both can coexist and complement each other, providing a fuller and deeper understanding of reality. As Proverbs 25:2 says, "It is the glory of God to conceal things, but the glory of kings is to search things out." This can be applied to both the spiritual quest of faith and the empirical quest of science.

The Problem of Evil: A Christian Response

The problem of evil is one of the most difficult questions faced by believers. It asks, "If God is good and all-powerful, why is there so much suffering and evil in the world?" The Bible, while not providing a comprehensive answer, does offer insights that can help us grapple with this question.

1. **The Origin of Evil**: According to the Bible, evil and suffering are not part of God's original creation. In Genesis 1:31, after God finished His creation, He declared it "very good." However, evil entered the world through human disobedience. In Genesis 3, Adam and Eve chose to disobey God, which led to sin and its consequences, including suffering and death.

2. **God's Sovereignty and Human Free Will**: The Bible upholds both God's sovereignty and human free will. This means that while God is in control of everything (Psalm 115:3), He allows humans to make choices, even choices that lead to evil and suffering (Deuteronomy 30:19). This does not mean God causes evil or approves of it, but that He allows it for reasons known fully only to Him (Isaiah 55:8-9).

3. **God's Response to Evil**: God does not remain indifferent to evil and suffering. In the Bible, He is consistently described as a compassionate and just God (Psalm 86:15). He acts to judge evil (Psalm 94:1-2), comforts those who suffer (2 Corinthians 1:3-4), and ultimately promises to eliminate all evil and suffering (Revelation 21:4).

4. **The Cross**: The cross of Jesus Christ is central to the Christian response to the problem of evil. In the crucifixion, God Himself experienced immense suffering and evil. Jesus' death and resurrection show that God is not distant from human suffering but enters into it and ultimately overcomes it (John 16:33).

5. **The Promise of Redemption**: The Bible promises a future time when evil will be fully defeated and suffering will be no more (Revelation 21:4). This does not negate or minimize the reality of suffering now, but it provides a hope that sustains believers in the midst of suffering (Romans 8:18).

6. **The Role of Suffering**: The Bible also suggests that God can use suffering to achieve good purposes. For example, suffering can produce character and

hope (Romans 5:3-5), discipline us for our good (Hebrews 12:7-11) and make us more reliant on God's grace (2 Corinthians 12:9-10).

In conclusion, while the problem of evil is a profound challenge, the Christian faith offers a nuanced and hopeful perspective on suffering and evil. These biblical insights do not provide an exhaustive answer to every question about evil, but they frame a perspective in which trust in God's goodness, wisdom, and justice is maintained, even in the midst of suffering.

Ethical Objections: Slavery, Women's Roles, and Homosexuality in the New Testament

This topic requires a nuanced and careful examination of the Bible, as it involves highly sensitive and controversial subjects. The Bible was written in a cultural and historical context that is different from the modern era, which affects how its teachings on certain ethical issues are understood. Here are biblical perspectives on the mentioned subjects:

Slavery: The New Testament mentions slavery because it was a common practice in the ancient world. The apostle Paul, for instance, instructs slaves to obey their earthly masters (Ephesians 6:5), and also implores masters to treat their slaves justly and fairly (Colossians 4:1). However, it's important to note that the Bible's discussion of slavery does not mean it endorses the practice. For example, Paul's letter to Philemon encourages him to welcome his runaway slave Onesimus "no longer as a slave, but better than a slave, as a dear brother" (Philemon 1:16). This was a radical idea in a culture where slaves were often dehumanized.

In the context of the Roman Empire where slavery was prevalent, first-century Christians were instructed to respect the legal rights of slave owners and to conduct themselves in a manner that reflected their faith. The apostle Paul, in his letter to Philemon, exemplified this by sending back the runaway slave Onesimus, who had become a Christian. By doing so, Paul demonstrated the principle of respecting the authority of slave owners, even when they were fellow believers. (Philemon 10-17)

Paul further emphasized the need for Christian slaves to maintain proper conduct and not take advantage of their relationship with believing masters. He urged them not to look down on their masters, but rather to serve them willingly and diligently, recognizing the bond of brotherhood in Christ. (1 Timothy 6:2) Paul also encouraged slaves to exhibit good fidelity, even in the face of injustice, following the example of Jesus Christ who endured suffering for righteousness' sake. (1 Peter 2:18-25)

The apostle Paul advised Christian slaves to be obedient to their masters, not merely to please men, but with sincerity of heart, as if working for Jehovah. Their whole-souled effort in their work would bring honor to God and prevent Christianity from being criticized due to the laziness or misconduct of slaves. (Colossians 3:22-23; Ephesians 6:5-8; 1 Timothy 6:1)

However, it is important to note that a slave's obedience should not extend to disobeying God's commandments. Their Christian conscience and commitment to God's law would guide their actions. They were to adorn the teachings of their Savior and God by living in accordance with the principles of righteousness and integrity. (Titus 2:10)

Within the Christian congregation, all individuals, regardless of their social status, were equal in standing before God. The anointing of the Holy Spirit united them as members of one body, and they shared the same hope. (1 Corinthians 12:12-13; Galatians 3:28; Colossians 3:11) Although the opportunities for spreading the good news might be limited for a Christian slave, they were encouraged to seize any opportunity for freedom, which would enable them to further contribute to the work of the Christian community. (1 Corinthians 7:21-23)

In summary, first-century Christians respected the legal rights of slave owners, conducted themselves with integrity, and obediently served their masters. They maintained their Christian identity while being mindful of their responsibilities as slaves. Despite their circumstances, they understood that their true freedom came from their relationship with God and their hope in Christ.

Women's Roles: The New Testament includes passages that suggest women should be submissive, such as Ephesians 5:22 ("Wives, submit to your own husbands, as to the Lord"). In discussing the gifts given by Christ to the church, it is important to note that the specific roles mentioned, such as apostles, prophets, evangelizers, shepherds, and teachers, are described in the masculine gender. (Ephesians 4:8, 11) This is evident in the original language and the rendering of these terms in translations. For example, the American Translation renders Ephesians 4:11 as "And he has given us some men as apostles, some as prophets, some as missionaries, some as pastors and teachers." (Psalm 68:18)

Furthermore, when the apostle Paul wrote to Timothy regarding the qualifications for the service positions of overseers (episkopoi) and servants (diakonoi) in the church, he specifically states that they must be men. If they were married, they should be "the husband of one wife." There is no discussion or mention of the office of "deaconess" by any of the apostles. (1 Timothy 3:1-13; Titus 1:5-9; Acts 20:17, 28; Philippians 1:1)

While Phoebe is mentioned in Romans 16:1 as a "minister" (diakonos) without the Greek definite article, it is clear that she was not an appointed female servant in the church. The Scriptures do not provide for such a position. The apostle Paul does not instruct the church to receive instructions from her, but rather to receive her well and assist her in any matter where she might need their help. Paul's reference to Phoebe as a minister likely pertains to her activity in spreading the good news, and he speaks of her as a female minister associated with the church in Cenchreae. (Acts 2:17, 18)

In the context of the home, the Scriptures describe the woman as "a weaker vessel, the feminine one." She is to be treated accordingly by her husband, with respect and consideration. (1 Peter 3:7) The woman has important privileges, such as participating in teaching the children and managing the internal affairs of the household under her husband's guidance and approval. (1 Timothy 5:14; 1 Peter 3:1, 2; Proverbs 1:8; 6:20; Proverbs 31) She has the duty of submission to her husband and fulfilling her marital obligations. (Ephesians 5:22-24; 1 Corinthians 7:3-5)

Homosexuality: The Scriptures provide specific guidance on the topic of homosexuality. According to the Bible, "men who engage in passive homosexual acts, or men who engage in active homosexual acts... will not inherit God's Kingdom" (1 Corinthians 6:9, 10). This principle also extends to women, as mentioned in Romans 1:26.

The Holy Book stipulates that sexual relations should only be between a man and a woman who are joined in matrimony (Genesis 1:27, 28; Proverbs 5:18, 19). However, it's important to note that while the Bible speaks against homosexual behavior, it does not advocate for discrimination, hostility, or any form of mistreatment towards those who identify as homosexual (Romans 12:18).

Many conservative Christians view the Bible's moral teachings as the optimal guide for leading a virtuous life, adhering to its decrees (Isaiah 48:17). Consequently, they denounce all forms of sexual misconduct, which includes homosexuality, according to their interpretation of 1 Corinthians 6:18. This adherence to biblical teachings is a lifestyle choice that conservative Christians have the right to uphold.

In the first century, individuals from diverse backgrounds and lifestyles sought to become Christians, often necessitating significant changes in their way of living. The Bible mentions, "neither fornicators, nor idolaters, nor adulterers, nor men engaged in passive or active homosexual acts, ... will inherit the kingdom of God," and it continues, "That is what some of you were" (1 Corinthians 6:9-11).

The Greek terms used in these passages refer to men who partake in passive and active roles in consensual homosexual activities - "neither men who engage in passive homosexual acts [μαλακοὶ], nor men who engage in active homosexual acts [ἀρσενοκοῖται]."

The exact influence of nature versus nurture on same-sex attraction remains a subject of scientific debate. However, the Bible makes it clear that all humans are prone to erroneous thinking and tendencies (Romans 3:23).

If you're grappling with same-sex attraction or bisexuality, it can be a challenging experience. Some may advise you to accept your sexuality and publicly identify as bisexual. It's important to remember that for many, same-sex attraction can be a transient phase during their development. However, even if your feelings are deeply rooted, the Bible offers a reachable goal: the choice to refrain from acting on incorrect desires. Consider this parallel: some psychologists propose the existence of sex addiction, where an individual feels compelled to engage in sexual relations with numerous partners. From a biblical perspective, we would counsel that individual to gain control over their desires, rather than dismiss biblical teachings on fornication and adultery due to their struggle with addiction.

The Exclusivity of Salvation: Responding to Religious Pluralism

The question of the exclusivity of salvation, in context of religious pluralism, is a significant one. The New Testament presents Jesus as the unique and exclusive means of salvation. The apostle Peter asserts in Acts 4:12, "Salvation is found in no one else, for there is no other name under heaven given to mankind by which we must be saved." This view is further supported by Jesus' statement in John 14:6, "I am the way and the truth and the life. No one comes to the Father except through me."

However, this exclusivity is often viewed as problematic in our modern, pluralistic society where many different religions exist. To respond to this, Christians may emphasize the uniqueness of Christ's life, death, and resurrection. According to Christian belief, the incarnation (God becoming human in Jesus), crucifixion (Jesus' death for humanity's sins), and resurrection (Jesus' victory over death) are unique historical events that provide the only means of reconciliation between humanity and God. This is exemplified in passages such as 1 Corinthians 15:3-4, "Christ died for our sins according to the Scriptures, that he was buried, that he was raised on the third day according to the Scriptures."

Yet, the New Testament also acknowledges the religious sincerity and piety of non-Christians, such as in Acts 10, where Cornelius, a Roman centurion, is recognized for his faith before he knows about Christ. This suggests that while salvation is through Christ, God's grace and mercy might be broader than human understanding. In Romans 2:14-15, Paul also acknowledges that Gentiles who don't know the Jewish law but follow its principles demonstrate that the law is "written on their hearts."

In summary, while the New Testament presents Christ as the unique means of salvation, it also shows an awareness of and respect for non-Christian religiosity. Christians are called to respect and love people of all faiths, even while believing in the unique salvation offered through Christ.

Biblical Prophecy: An Antidote to Skepticism

Biblical prophecy holds a unique place in Christian belief as it is seen as a form of divine foreknowledge and a testament to the reliability of the scriptures. Prophecies in the Bible can serve as a counterbalance to skepticism, because their fulfillment provides tangible evidence of the Bible's authenticity and divine inspiration.

One of the most compelling aspects of biblical prophecy is its occurrence in the Old Testament, prophesying events in the New Testament. For instance, the life, death, and resurrection of Jesus Christ were prophesied centuries before they happened. These prophecies include:

Jesus' birthplace in Bethlehem, foretold in Micah 5:2: "But you, Bethlehem Ephrathah, though you are small among the clans of Judah, out of you will come for me one who will be ruler over Israel, whose origins are from of old, from ancient times."

His betrayal for thirty pieces of silver, predicted in Zechariah 11:12-13: "So they paid me thirty pieces of silver. And the Lord said to me, 'Throw it to the potter'—the handsome price at which they valued me! So I took the thirty pieces of silver and threw them to the potter at the house of the Lord."

His crucifixion, described in Psalms 22:16-18: "Dogs surround me, a pack of villains encircles me; they pierce my hands and my feet. All my bones are on display; people stare and gloat over me. They divide my clothes among them and cast lots for my garment."

These are just a few examples among many others. Each fulfilled prophecy builds the case for the trustworthiness of the Bible and provides a basis for belief in its message.

In addition to prophesying events in the life of Christ, the Bible also contains prophecies about the future of nations, the end times (Book of Revelation), and moral and societal trends (2 Timothy 3:1-5), many of which Christians believe are coming true or have already come to pass.

Prophecy in the Bible serves as a testament to the Bible's divine inspiration and its ability to accurately predict future events. It serves as an antidote to skepticism by offering concrete evidence of the Bible's trustworthiness and accuracy.

The Power of Testimony: Personal Experiences and the Case for Faith

The power of personal testimony is often emphasized in the New Testament, with numerous instances of individuals sharing their experiences of encountering Jesus or witnessing his miracles. These personal narratives serve as evidence of the transformative power of faith and the authenticity of the Christian message.

In the Gospel of John, for instance, we find the story of the woman at the well (John 4:1-42). After her encounter with Jesus, the woman becomes a witness to the people in her city, declaring, "Come, see a man who told me everything I ever did.

Could this be the Messiah?" (John 4:29). Her personal testimony leads many in the city to believe in Jesus.

Paul's conversion on the road to Damascus is another powerful personal testimony found in Acts 9:1-19. Paul (Saul at that time), a zealous persecutor of Christians, encounters the risen Christ and undergoes a dramatic transformation. He later shares his testimony repeatedly, such as in Acts 22:6-21 and Acts 26:12-23, as a proof of the transformative power of Jesus.

Peter, one of Jesus' apostles, also emphasizes the importance of personal testimony. In 2 Peter 1:16, he writes, "For we did not follow cleverly devised stories when we told you about the coming of our Lord Jesus Christ in power, but we were eyewitnesses of his majesty."

These accounts underscore the value of personal experience and testimony in the Christian faith. They serve as a testament to the transformative power of Jesus, provide an example for believers to follow, and offer a compelling case for faith.

It is also worth noting that the power of personal testimony extends beyond the pages of the New Testament. Countless believers throughout history and in contemporary times share their experiences of faith, transformation, and encounter with God, further reinforcing the relevance and impact of the Christian message. In 1 Peter 3:15, believers are encouraged to always be prepared "to give an answer to everyone who asks you to give the reason for the hope that you have."

While personal testimony cannot be empirically verified in the same way as physical evidence, it remains a significant aspect of the Christian faith, offering a form of experiential evidence that can be deeply persuasive to both believers and non-believers alike.

Equipping for Engagement: Tools for Effective Apologetics

Engaging effectively in apologetics, or the defense of the Christian faith, requires a variety of tools. These include knowledge of the scriptures, an understanding of common objections and how to respond to them, and the ability to communicate with kindness, respect, and clarity.

1. Knowledge of the Scriptures: The Bible is the foundation of Christian belief, and a thorough understanding of it is crucial for effective apologetics.

- "Study to shew thyself approved unto God, a workman that needeth not to be ashamed, rightly dividing the word of truth." (2 Timothy 2:15, KJV)

2. Understanding of Common Objections: Being aware of the challenges and objections often raised against Christianity can help one prepare thoughtful, informed responses.

- "Be wise as serpents and innocent as doves." (Matthew 10:16, ESV)

3. Ability to Communicate with Kindness, Respect, and Clarity: How one communicates is as important as what one communicates. The Bible emphasizes the importance of speaking with love, gentleness, and respect.

- "But in your hearts revere Christ as Lord. Always be prepared to give an answer to everyone who asks you to give the reason for the hope that you have. But do this with gentleness and respect," (1 Peter 3:15, NIV)
- "Rather, speaking the truth in love, we are to grow up in every way into him who is the head, into Christ," (Ephesians 4:15, ESV)

4. Dependence on the Holy Spirit: The Holy Spirit plays a crucial role in equipping believers for the task of apologetics. This includes illuminating understanding, providing wisdom, and guiding conversations.

- "But the Helper, the Holy Spirit, whom the Father will send in my name, he will teach you all things and bring to your remembrance all that I have said to you." (John 14:26, ESV)

5. Living a Life that Reflects Christ: Finally, the most compelling apologetic is a life well-lived. Believers are called to live in a manner consistent with their faith, providing a compelling witness to the truth of the gospel.

- "In the same way, let your light shine before others, so that they may see your good works and give glory to your Father who is in heaven." (Matthew 5:16, ESV)

In sum, the Bible provides numerous tools and principles that can equip believers for effective engagement in apologetics. These include a deep understanding of the scriptures, an awareness of common objections, the ability to communicate effectively, reliance on the Holy Spirit, and a life lived in conformity with the teachings of Christ.

CHAPTER 15 The New Testament and Archaeology: Digging into Historical Context

Introduction: The Interplay of Archaeology and the New Testament

The interplay between archaeology and the New Testament is a fascinating and important area of study. Archaeology can provide invaluable context to the stories and teachings found in the New Testament, offering insights into the culture, politics, and daily life of the time.

1. **Contextualizing Biblical Narratives:** Archaeological findings can help us better understand the world in which the New Testament was written. For example, the discovery of first-century homes in Capernaum and Nazareth provides a glimpse into the type of living conditions Jesus and his disciples may have experienced.

    - "And when he returned to Capernaum after some days, it was reported that he was at home." (Mark 2:1, ESV)

2. **Corroboration of Biblical Accounts:** Archaeology can also offer external evidence that supports the historicity of the New Testament. For instance, the discovery of the Pool of Bethesda with its five porticoes, as described in John 5:1-15, adds credibility to this biblical account.

- "Now there is in Jerusalem by the Sheep Gate a pool, in Aramaic called Bethesda, which has five roofed colonnades." (John 5:2, ESV)

3. **Insights into Societal and Cultural Backgrounds:** Archaeological findings can provide insights into the societal and cultural contexts of the New Testament. The Dead Sea Scrolls, for example, shed light on Jewish religious thought and practices at the time of Jesus.

- "Beware of the scribes, who like to walk around in long robes, and love greetings in the marketplaces and the best seats in the synagogues and the places of honor at feasts," (Luke 20:46, ESV)

4. **Understanding Biblical Imagery:** Lastly, archaeology can help clarify the meaning of certain biblical images or metaphors by revealing their cultural context. The importance of agricultural metaphors, for instance, becomes clearer when we understand the agricultural society of the time.

- "I am the true vine, and my Father is the vinedresser." (John 15:1, ESV)

In conclusion, archaeology plays a crucial role in our understanding of the New Testament. It helps contextualize biblical narratives, corroborates biblical accounts, provides insights into societal and cultural backgrounds, and aids in understanding biblical imagery. These aspects contribute to a more nuanced and informed understanding of the New Testament.

The Nature and Role of Biblical Archaeology

Biblical archaeology is a sub-discipline of archaeology focused on the ancient civilizations of the Near East, including Israel, Jordan, Egypt, and surrounding areas from roughly 2000 B.C. to 600 A.D. This time period spans both the Old and New Testament eras, making biblical archaeology highly relevant to understanding the historical context of the Bible.

1. **Understanding the Nature of Biblical Archaeology:**

Biblical archaeology involves the excavation and study of artifacts, inscriptions, and structures that can shed light on the historical and cultural context of the biblical narrative.

- "Is not my word like fire, declares the LORD, and like a hammer that breaks the rock in pieces?" (Jeremiah 23:29, ESV)

In this verse, we see the metaphorical use of a hammer breaking rock, which can be seen as a reflection of the archaeological process - careful, methodical work that slowly reveals the truth hidden within.

2. **Providing Historical Context:**

Archaeology can provide valuable insights into the daily life, customs, political structures, and religious practices of the people and times described in the Bible.

- "And on the Sabbath day we went outside the gate to the riverside, where we supposed there was a place of prayer, and we sat down and spoke to the women who had come together." (Acts 16:13, ESV)

In this verse from Acts, we see the practice of gathering by the river for prayer, which reflects the cultural and religious practices of the time.

3. **Corroborating Biblical Accounts:**

Biblical archaeology can provide external evidence that supports the events, places, and people described in the Bible.

- "And the high priest said, 'Are these things so?' And Stephen said: 'Brothers and fathers, hear me. The God of glory appeared to our father Abraham when he was in Mesopotamia, before he lived in Haran,'" (Acts 7:1-2, ESV)

The mention of Mesopotamia and Haran in Acts relates to geographical locations that can be explored and studied through archaeology.

4. **Understanding Biblical Language and Imagery:**

Archaeology can help us understand the original language, metaphors, and images used in the Bible by uncovering the cultural and historical backdrop to these elements.

- "The stone that the builders rejected has become the cornerstone." (Psalm 118:22, ESV)

The metaphor of a cornerstone is deeply rooted in the construction practices of the time, something that archaeology can help us understand more fully.

In conclusion, the nature and role of biblical archaeology is to provide historical context, corroborate biblical accounts, and help us understand the language and imagery of the Bible. By doing so, it brings us closer to the world of the biblical authors and the people they wrote about.

Archaeological Evidence for New Testament Cities: Jerusalem, Capernaum, and More

Archaeology has provided valuable insights into the cities and regions mentioned in the New Testament, including Jerusalem, Capernaum, and others. Let's examine some of these cities in light of biblical references:

1. **Jerusalem:** This city is central to the New Testament narrative, particularly in the life, death, and resurrection of Jesus.

- "As he approached Jerusalem and saw the city, he wept over it and said, 'If you, even you, had only known on this day what would bring you peace—but now it is hidden from your eyes.'" (Luke 19:41-42, NIV)

Excavations in Jerusalem have uncovered parts of the city from the time of Jesus, including the Pool of Bethesda where Jesus healed a paralytic (John 5:1-15), and the likely location of the high priest Caiaphas' house, where Jesus was brought for trial (Matthew 26:57).

2. **Capernaum:** This was the base of Jesus' Galilean ministry and the home of several of his disciples.

- "And leaving Nazareth, he came and dwelt in Capernaum, which is upon the sea coast, in the borders of Zabulon and Nephthalim." (Matthew 4:13, KJV)

Archaeological excavations in Capernaum have revealed a synagogue from around the 4th or 5th century, built on the foundations of an earlier synagogue where Jesus likely taught (Mark 1:21-28). A house identified as Peter's house by an ancient inscription has also been found, which matches the biblical description (Mark 1:29-31).

3. **Bethsaida:** This was the hometown of Peter, Andrew, and Philip.

- "Philip, like Andrew and Peter, was from the town of Bethsaida." (John 1:44, NIV)

Archaeologists have found a city they believe to be Bethsaida, where artifacts and structures from the first century have been uncovered, providing context for understanding the lives of some of Jesus' earliest followers.

4. **Corinth:** Paul visited this city and wrote two letters to the Christian community here.

- "After this, Paul left Athens and went to Corinth." (Acts 18:1, NIV)

The city of Corinth has been extensively excavated, revealing marketplaces, temples, and a judgment seat ('bema') where Paul may have been tried (Acts 18:12-17).

These archaeological findings, among others, provide valuable historical and cultural context for the New Testament narrative, corroborating the biblical accounts and helping us to visualize the places where these events occurred.

The World of Jesus: Archaeology and the Gospels

The Gospels present a vivid picture of Jesus' life and ministry, set against the backdrop of first-century Palestine. Archaeology has greatly enhanced our understanding of this period and the settings of the Gospel narratives. Let's examine some key archaeological findings in relation to the Gospels:

Bethlehem: The birthplace of Jesus, as stated in Matthew 2:1 and Luke 2:4-6. Archaeological evidence corroborates the historical existence of this town in the first century, with artifacts and structures from the period found in and around modern-day Bethlehem.

Nazareth: The hometown of Jesus, as mentioned in Matthew 2:23 and Luke 1:26. Archaeological excavations in Nazareth have uncovered first-century homes and artifacts, providing insights into the modest, agricultural lifestyle of its inhabitants, as suggested by Mark 6:3, where Jesus is referred to as a carpenter.

Sea of Galilee and Surrounding Areas: Much of Jesus' ministry took place around the Sea of Galilee, including towns like Capernaum and Bethsaida. Archaeological finds, such as ancient boats and harbors, provide context for Gospel narratives involving fishing and seafaring (Mark 1:16-20, Matthew 8:23-27).

Jerusalem: The city where Jesus was crucified and resurrected. Archaeology has provided insights into key places associated with Jesus' final days, such as the Pool of Bethesda and the Pool of Siloam, both of which are mentioned in John's Gospel (John 5:2-9, John 9:1-11).

Crucifixion and Burial Practices: Archaeological evidence of first-century crucifixion and burial practices provide valuable context for the accounts of Jesus' death and resurrection. For example, the discovery of the ossuary (bone box) of a crucified man named Yehohanan in the 1960s gave us direct evidence of Roman crucifixion methods. Similarly, the uncovering of first-century Jewish tombs has given us insights into burial customs, consistent with the Gospel accounts of Jesus' burial (Matthew 27:57-61, Mark 15:42-47, Luke 23:50-56, John 19:38-42).

Inscriptions: The Pilate Stone, discovered in Caesarea Maritima, confirms the existence of Pontius Pilate, the Roman prefect who presided over Jesus' trial (Matthew 27:11-26). The 'James Ossuary', if authentic, may provide archaeological evidence for James, the brother of Jesus (Matthew 13:55, Galatians 1:19).

Through such findings, archaeology offers a tangible connection to the world of Jesus as presented in the Gospels, reinforcing the narratives with physical evidence from the period.

Archaeological Insights into the Life and Times of Jesus

The archaeological findings of the first-century world in which Jesus lived offer us unique insights into His life and times, enhancing our understanding of the Gospel narratives. Here are a few key examples:

Synagogues and Religious Life: The discovery of synagogues from the first century, such as the one in Capernaum (Matthew 4:13), provides insight into Jewish religious life and practices during Jesus' time. These were places where Jesus often taught (Mark 1:21, Luke 4:16-30).

First-Century Homes: Excavations in Nazareth and Capernaum reveal typical first-century homes, often with rooms surrounding a courtyard. These homes give us a glimpse into Jesus' familial and social context (Mark 2:1-12).

The Temple in Jerusalem: The Temple was central to Jewish religious life during Jesus' time. Archaeological finds, like the remnants of the Western Wall, provide context for events like Jesus' teachings and disputes with religious leaders (Matthew 21:23-27, Luke 19:45-48).

Crucifixion: Archaeological evidence of first-century crucifixion, such as the heel bone of a crucified man named Yehohanan, discovered in a family tomb in Jerusalem, offers insights into the brutal form of execution that Jesus underwent (Matthew 27:32-56, Mark 15:21-41, Luke 23:26-49, John 19:16-37).

Coins and Inscriptions: Coins and inscriptions from the era give us additional context for the socio-political environment in which Jesus lived. For example, the tribute penny mentioned in Matthew 22:19-21, and inscriptions mentioning Pontius Pilate (Matthew 27:2) and Caesar Augustus (Luke 2:1) all connect the biblical narrative with its historical context.

Tombs and Burial Customs: The discovery of first-century tombs, such as the Garden Tomb and the Talpiot Tomb, along with ossuaries (boxes for holding bones), shed light on the burial customs described in the Gospel accounts of Jesus' burial (Matthew 27:57-60, John 19:38-42).

The Dead Sea Scrolls: While not directly related to Jesus, the Dead Sea Scrolls have offered valuable insights into Jewish religious thought and the diversity of beliefs during the Second Temple period. This context aids in understanding the religious milieu in which Jesus and the early Christian movement emerged.

In essence, archaeology provides us with a window into the life and times of Jesus, enabling us to visualize the social, religious, and political environment depicted in the Gospels, and lending further credibility to the New Testament narratives.

Pontius Pilate and the Trial of Jesus: Archaeological Corroboration

The trial of Jesus and the role of Pontius Pilate, the Roman governor of Judaea, are key events in the New Testament narratives, primarily detailed in the Gospels (Matthew 27:11-26, Mark 15:1-15, Luke 23:1-25, John 18:28-19:16). Archaeological findings have provided significant corroboration of Pilate's existence and his involvement in these events.

The "Pilate Stone": One of the most important archaeological findings concerning Pontius Pilate is a limestone block discovered in 1961 at the site of ancient Caesarea Maritima, the Roman capital of Judaea. This block, known as the "Pilate Stone", bears an inscription in Latin that translates to "Pontius Pilate, Prefect of Judaea." This inscription provides direct archaeological evidence of Pilate's existence and his role as the Roman governor during the time of Jesus, aligning with the New Testament's depiction of him.

The Trial of Jesus: The Gospel accounts of Jesus' trial before Pilate detail a reluctant governor, pressured by the Jewish leaders and the crowd to crucify Jesus. While there are no direct archaeological findings related to the trial, the discovery of the Antonia Fortress in Jerusalem, where the trial likely took place, provides a setting for these events.

Release of Barabbas: The Gospels tell us that Pilate offered to release a prisoner in honor of the Passover feast, and the crowd chose Barabbas over Jesus (Mark 15:6-15). This practice of releasing a prisoner during festivals is not documented in other historical sources but does fit with what we know about Roman efforts to maintain peace and order, particularly during potentially volatile times like Jewish festivals.

Crucifixion: The Gospels state that Pilate sentenced Jesus to death by crucifixion. The practice of crucifixion is well-attested in Roman history and archaeological evidence. The discovery of the heel bone of a crucified man named Yehohanan in a family tomb in Jerusalem provides tangible evidence of this form of execution in the first century.

In conclusion, archaeological evidence corroborates the New Testament's depiction of Pontius Pilate and provides context for the trial and crucifixion of Jesus. These findings anchor the Gospel narratives in real historical events and locations, enhancing our understanding of these key episodes in the New Testament.

The Crucifixion and the Tomb of Jesus: Archaeology and the Easter Story

The crucifixion and resurrection of Jesus are key tenets of Christian faith, and their accounts are found in the Gospels (Matthew 27:32-28:10, Mark 15:21-16:8, Luke 23:26-24:12, John 19:16-20:18). These narratives describe the events around the crucifixion, burial, and resurrection of Jesus, and while there is no direct archaeological evidence confirming these specific events, several archaeological findings provide context and corroborate the plausibility of these accounts.

Crucifixion: The Gospels describe in detail the crucifixion of Jesus at a place called Golgotha, which means "place of a skull" (Mark 15:22). Archaeological and historical evidence confirms that crucifixion was a common method of execution employed by the Romans during Jesus' time. The discovery of the heel bone of a crucified man named Yehohanan, as mentioned earlier, provides tangible evidence of this form of execution in the first century.

The Tomb of Jesus: According to the Gospels, Jesus was buried in a new tomb owned by a man named Joseph of Arimathea (Matthew 27:57-60). The Gospels describe this as a rock-hewn tomb, which aligns with known practices of wealthy Jews in the first century. In Jerusalem, many such tombs have been discovered, adding credibility to this aspect of the Gospel accounts. The Church of the Holy Sepulchre in Jerusalem is traditionally considered the site of Jesus' crucifixion and burial, although the exact location is a matter of faith and tradition rather than verifiable archaeological evidence.

The Stone and the Seal: The Gospels state that a large stone was rolled against the entrance of the tomb, and the tomb was sealed and guarded by Roman soldiers (Matthew 27:66). Sealing and guarding a tomb would be consistent with Roman practices for ensuring that a grave was not disturbed, providing historical context for these details in the Gospel accounts.

The Empty Tomb: On the third day after Jesus' crucifixion, the Gospels record that women followers of Jesus found the tomb empty (Luke 24:1-12). The concept of an empty tomb is central to the Christian belief in the resurrection of Jesus. While there is no archaeological evidence for the event of the resurrection itself - as it is, by nature, a miraculous event beyond the realm of archaeology - the persistent early Christian tradition of an empty tomb suggests that this was a significant aspect of early Christian belief.

In conclusion, while archaeology can't confirm the specific events of Jesus' crucifixion, burial, and resurrection, it does affirm the plausibility of the Gospel narratives and provides valuable historical and cultural context. The archaeological findings align with the practices of the time and place as described in the New Testament, thereby supporting the historical grounding of these central Christian beliefs.

The Book of Acts in the Light of Archaeology

The Book of Acts in the New Testament, authored by Luke, provides a historical account of the early Christian Church, starting with the ascension of Jesus and continuing through the spread of the Church and the works of the apostles, primarily Peter and Paul.

Archaeology provides a rich backdrop that supports various elements in the Book of Acts, adding to the historical reliability of the account. This doesn't prove the veracity of every detail in Acts, but it does lend credibility to the narrative by confirming its historical and geographical accuracy in many respects.

Here are some key archaeological findings related to the Book of Acts:

Cities and Locations: Acts describes Paul's missionary journeys throughout the Roman Empire, including cities such as Jerusalem, Antioch, Philippi, Corinth, Ephesus, and Rome. Archaeological discoveries and historical records confirm the existence and significance of these cities during the first century AD. Furthermore, the specific details about these cities' customs, landmarks, and languages align with what we know from archaeological and historical studies.

The 'Politarchs' in Thessalonica: In Acts 17:6, Luke refers to the city officials in Thessalonica as "politarchs", a term not used in any other contemporary literature. For a time, this led to accusations that Luke had erred or fabricated the term. However, inscriptions using the term 'politarch' have since been found in archaeological digs in Thessalonica, vindicating Luke's unique usage.

Sergius Paulus Inscription: In Acts 13:6-12, Sergius Paulus is described as the proconsul of Cyprus. An inscription was found near Paphos, Cyprus, bearing the name of Sergius Paulus, providing external evidence for this New Testament character.

Gallio Inscription: Acts 18:12-17 describes an incident involving Paul and Gallio, the proconsul of Achaia. An inscription found at Delphi in Greece refers to Gallio and dates his proconsulship to around 51-52 CE, which aligns with the timeline in Acts.

The Ephesian Artemis: Acts 19:23-41 gives an account of a riot in Ephesus over the threat that Paul's preaching posed to the worship of Artemis and the trade of her silver shrines. Archaeologists have discovered numerous miniature silver shrines and statues of Artemis, confirming this lucrative trade in Ephesus.

These archaeological findings, among others, provide external corroboration for many of the geographical and historical details in the Book of Acts, suggesting that the narrative is grounded in actual first-century events and circumstances.

It should be noted, though, that while archaeology can support the historical framework of the biblical account, it cannot prove the supernatural events or theological teachings contained within the text. The interpretation of these elements remains a matter of personal belief and faith.

Unearthing Evidence for Paul's Missionary Journeys

The New Testament's Book of Acts, primarily chapters 13-28, details the missionary journeys of the apostle Paul. These journeys take him through various regions of the Roman Empire, including Asia Minor, Macedonia, Greece, and eventually Rome. Throughout these travels, Paul is depicted as preaching the Gospel, establishing churches, and encountering both acceptance and intense opposition.

Archaeology and historical research have provided considerable support for the authenticity of the places and some events described in these journeys. While these fields cannot verify every detail or the supernatural elements of the accounts, they do offer a valuable backdrop that aligns with the New Testament narrative.

Here are some key archaeological findings and historical confirmations related to Paul's missionary journeys:

Cities and Locations: Paul's journeys, as described in Acts, took him through many cities and regions that are well-attested in other historical sources and archaeological findings. These include Syrian Antioch, Cyprus, cities in Asia Minor like Iconium, Lystra, Derbe, Ephesus, and regions like Galatia and Phrygia. He also traveled to Philippi, Thessalonica, Athens, and Corinth in Greece, and eventually to Rome. The existence and importance of these cities during the first century CE is well-documented.

Social and Cultural Details: In Acts, we see Paul engaging with different cultural and religious contexts, from Jewish synagogues to Greek philosophical forums (like the Areopagus in Athens, Acts 17:22-34). Archaeological findings and historical research confirm these diverse cultural settings in the cities Paul visited.

Ephesian Artemis: Acts 19:23-41 describes a riot in Ephesus instigated by silversmiths who felt their business of making silver shrines of Artemis (also known as Diana) was threatened by Paul's preaching. Archaeologists have found numerous small shrines and statues of Artemis in Ephesus, confirming the existence of this trade.

Inscriptions and Official Titles: Archaeology has validated Luke's accurate use of official titles in different regions. For instance, "politarchs" were city officials in Thessalonica (Acts 17:6), and "proconsul" was the correct title for Sergius Paulus in Cyprus (Acts 13:7-12) and Gallio in Corinth (Acts 18:12-17).

The Bema Seat in Corinth: In Acts 18:12-17, Paul is brought before the judgment seat, or "bema," in Corinth. The bema has been discovered and can be visited today in the ruins of ancient Corinth.

These and other archaeological findings correspond with the New Testament narrative, suggesting that the Book of Acts accurately reflects the historical and geographical context of the first-century Roman Empire. Again, it's important to note that while these findings support the historical context of Paul's journeys, they don't prove the spiritual and theological claims made in these accounts. The interpretation of these aspects is a matter of personal faith and belief.

The Seven Churches of Revelation: What Archaeology Reveals

The Book of Revelation, the last book in the New Testament, starts with letters to seven churches in Asia Minor (modern-day Turkey). These letters, addressed to the churches in Ephesus, Smyrna, Pergamum, Thyatira, Sardis, Philadelphia, and Laodicea, contain both praises and criticisms for the congregations, as well as prophetic messages. Archaeology has contributed to our understanding of these churches' historical and cultural contexts, reinforcing the letters' specific messages. Here are some key archaeological findings and historical confirmations related to the seven churches:

Ephesus (Revelation 2:1-7): The letter to Ephesus commends the church for their deeds and hard work, but criticizes them for forsaking their first love (Rev 2:4). Archaeological excavations have unearthed Ephesus as a significant city in the Roman Empire, known for its grand architecture, including the Temple of Artemis, one of the Seven Wonders of the Ancient World. This vibrant, cosmopolitan setting may have presented challenges and distractions for the early Christians, aligning with the warnings in the letter.

Smyrna (Revelation 2:8-11): The letter to Smyrna speaks of suffering and poverty but declares that they are rich. It encourages them to be faithful, even to the point of death. Smyrna (modern Izmir) was a prominent and wealthy city, but Christians there likely faced persecution, aligning with the message of the letter.

Pergamum (Revelation 2:12-17): Pergamum is described as a place where Satan has his throne, likely referring to the city's strong pagan cults, including a grand altar to Zeus. Archaeological evidence attests to the city's reputation as a significant religious center.

Thyatira (Revelation 2:18-29): The letter to Thyatira criticizes them for tolerating a false prophetess. Historical records indicate that Thyatira was known for its trade guilds, which often had associated gods and goddesses, possibly leading to the syncretism criticized in the letter.

Sardis (Revelation 3:1-6): The letter to Sardis suggests that the church had a reputation for being alive, but it was dead. Sardis was a wealthy city but had a history of being easily conquered due to complacency, mirroring the spiritual condition of the church as described in Revelation.

Philadelphia (Revelation 3:7-13): The letter to Philadelphia contains no rebuke, only commendation and encouragement to endure patiently. Archaeological evidence shows that Philadelphia (modern Alasehir) was a city prone to earthquakes, making the promise of a "pillar in the temple of my God" (Rev 3:12) particularly poignant.

Laodicea (Revelation 3:14-22): The Laodicean church is rebuked for being lukewarm. Laodicea was known for its lukewarm water supply, unlike the nearby hot springs at Hierapolis and cold water in Colossae. This physical reality served as a metaphor for their spiritual condition.

In each case, the messages to the churches in Revelation correspond well with what we know about these cities from archaeological and historical research. These findings help us to better understand the real-life situations of these early Christian communities and the specific challenges they faced.

Archaeology and the Persecution of the Early Church

The New Testament, particularly in the Book of Acts and the Epistles, provides numerous accounts of the persecution faced by the early Christian church. Archaeology, along with historical documents, provides corroborative evidence that supports these biblical accounts. Here are some key instances where archaeological findings correspond with the New Testament's depiction of early Christian persecution:

Jerusalem and Stephen's Martyrdom: The first Christian martyr, Stephen, was stoned to death in Jerusalem as depicted in Acts 7:54-60. While archaeological evidence doesn't directly confirm this event, it does affirm that stoning was a form of capital punishment used by Jewish authorities, as evidenced by other archaeological findings of stoning from this period.

The Persecution under Nero: In Rome, the Emperor Nero is known to have persecuted Christians after the great fire in 64 CE, blaming them for the disaster. Tacitus, a Roman historian, recorded this event, providing extra-biblical confirmation. Additionally, archaeological excavations in Rome have unearthed evidence of vast catacombs, where Christians are believed to have sometimes gathered for worship, perhaps in response to periods of intense persecution.

Paul's Imprisonments: The Apostle Paul was imprisoned several times, as he himself attests in his letters (e.g., Philippians 1:12-14). The Mamertine Prison, traditionally believed to have held Paul, can still be visited in Rome today. Additionally, the Book of Acts recounts Paul's arrest in Jerusalem and his trials before Roman officials such as Felix and Festus, in Caesarea (Acts 23-26). The archaeological remains of the praetorium in Caesarea Maritima, where these trials likely took place, are a tangible link to these events.

Persecution under Domitian: Domitian, the Roman emperor who reigned from 81-96 CE, is traditionally believed to have persecuted Christians, though the historical evidence is somewhat debated. The Book of Revelation may have been written during his reign, and its vivid imagery of persecution and martyrdom could reflect the experiences of Christians during this time. The ruins of the imperial palace on the Palatine Hill in Rome, where Domitian resided, serve as a reminder of his rule.

Persecution under Trajan: Pliny the Younger, a Roman governor, wrote a letter to Emperor Trajan (reign 98-117 CE) asking for guidance on how to handle Christians, who were deemed illegal but were "guilty" only of being Christians. Trajan's response, advocating a kind of "don't ask, don't tell" policy, confirms the existence of Christians in the empire and suggests a degree of state-sanctioned persecution.

These archaeological and historical elements, while not providing direct evidence of specific biblical events, do corroborate the overall New Testament depiction of an early church that often faced persecution for its faith.

Archaeological Discoveries and the Reliability of New Testament Texts

Archaeological discoveries have shed light on various aspects of the New Testament, providing additional context and support for its reliability. While archaeology does not directly confirm or verify specific theological claims, it does offer evidence that supports the historical and cultural accuracy of the New Testament texts. Archaeological discoveries have repeatedly affirmed the historical reliability of the New Testament texts. Again, while archaeology cannot prove the theological truths of the New Testament, it can and does provide tangible evidence that corroborates the historical and cultural context, and many specific details found within the New Testament. Here are some examples:

Manuscripts: The discovery of numerous early New Testament manuscripts has helped to confirm the accuracy and consistency of the text we have today. Examples include the Dead Sea Scrolls, which include fragments of every book of the Old Testament (except for Esther) and provide valuable insight into the textual transmission of the Hebrew Bible, and the John Rylands Papyrus (P52), which contains a small portion of the Gospel of John and dates to around 100-150 CE, demonstrating the early circulation of John's Gospel.

Cities and locations: Archaeological excavations have confirmed the existence of many cities and locations mentioned in the New Testament, such as Jerusalem, Capernaum, Caesarea Philippi, and Ephesus. These findings provide historical context for the events described in the Gospels and the Book of Acts.

Inscriptions: Inscriptions discovered through archaeology have confirmed some names and titles of individuals mentioned in the New Testament. For example, the Pilate Stone, found in Caesarea Maritima, bears the name and title of Pontius Pilate, the Roman governor who presided over Jesus' trial (Matthew 27:11-26). Similarly, the Gallio Inscription, found in Delphi, Greece, mentions Gallio, the proconsul of Achaia mentioned in Acts 18:12-17.

Cultural practices: Archaeological evidence has provided insight into various cultural practices of the time, helping to contextualize certain passages in the New Testament. For example, archaeologists have discovered stone vessels and ritual baths in Jewish homes from the first century, which help to illustrate the importance of ritual purity in Jewish culture, as mentioned in the Gospels (e.g., Mark 7:1-5). Archaeological findings have helped illustrate cultural practices and societal norms mentioned in the New Testament. Examples include the commonality of tax collection in the 1st century (Matthew 9:9-13), the prevalence of slavery (Philemon 1:10-16), and the significance of hospitality (Luke 10:38-42). Understanding these cultural norms can provide insights into the societal contexts in which the New Testament events took place.

Cities, Regions, and Landmarks: The existence and location of many cities, regions, and landmarks mentioned in the New Testament have been confirmed through archaeology. For instance, the Pool of Bethesda (John 5:1-15), the Pool of Siloam (John 9:1-7), the city of Capernaum (Mark 2:1), and the city of Ephesus (Acts 19:1) have all been excavated.

Coins and Inscriptions: Coins and inscriptions provide some of the most direct archaeological evidence relating to the New Testament. For example, an inscription found in Caesarea Maritima confirms Pontius Pilate as the Roman Prefect during the time of Jesus' crucifixion, as recorded in all four gospels (Matthew 27:2, Mark 15:1, Luke 23:1, John 18:29).

Rituals and Traditions: Archaeological findings have also shed light on religious rituals and traditions. For example, remains of ritual baths, or mikvehs, and stone vessels, found in numerous Jewish homes from this period, highlight the importance of ritual purity in Jewish culture, a theme that is echoed in the New Testament (Mark 7:1-23).

Economic Systems: Archaeological studies on coins, inscriptions, and structures have given us a better understanding of the economic systems of the Roman Empire during the time of the New Testament. For instance, Jesus' parable of the talents (Matthew 25:14-30) makes more sense when we understand the economic value of a talent in the 1st-century Greco-Roman world.

Political Landscape: Inscriptions and monuments reveal the political landscape of the Roman Empire, providing context for the political figures and events mentioned in the New Testament. For example, the Pilate Stone, found in Caesarea, confirms the existence and position of Pontius Pilate, the Roman governor who presided over the trial of Jesus (Matthew 27:11-26).

Architectural Structures: Discoveries of architectural structures, such as synagogues, Roman governmental buildings, homes, and marketplaces, help us understand the spaces where New Testament events occurred. For example, the discovery of a synagogue in Capernaum (Mark 1:21-28) helps contextualize the account of Jesus teaching and performing miracles there.

Ossuaries: The discovery of ossuaries, or bone boxes, from the first century has shed light on Jewish burial practices during the time of Jesus, helping to contextualize the accounts of Jesus' burial in the Gospels (e.g., Matthew 27:57-61; John 19:38-42).

Synagogues: The remains of first-century synagogues, such as those found in Capernaum and Magdala, provide context for Jesus' teaching ministry in the Gospels (e.g., Mark 1:21-28; Luke 4:31-37).

The Temple in Jerusalem: Archaeological remains of the Temple in Jerusalem, such as the Temple Mount and the Western Wall, provide context for events that took place there, as described in the New Testament (e.g., Jesus' cleansing of the Temple, as recounted in Matthew 21:12-13 and John 2:13-22).

These archaeological discoveries, among others, contribute to the overall reliability of the New Testament texts by confirming various historical, cultural, and geographical details. While they do not prove the truth of the theological claims made in the New Testament, they do provide valuable context and support for the accuracy of the text. Through these findings, archaeology helps to contextualize the New Testament, providing us with a clearer understanding of the historical, cultural, and societal backdrop against which these events took place. While archaeological evidence does not prove the theological truths in the New Testament, it supports the historical accuracy of the text, further solidifying its reliability.

Responding to Skepticism: Archaeology as an Apologetic Tool

Archaeology can serve as an apologetic tool by providing physical evidence that corroborates the historical narratives presented in the New Testament. While it doesn't directly prove religious or theological beliefs, archaeological findings can support the veracity of the Bible as a historical document.

Affirmation of Historical Details: Luke, for example, is noted for his detailed accounts of locations and people. In Acts 18:12, he mentions Gallio, the proconsul of Achaia, before whom Paul was brought. An inscription discovered at Delphi in Greece, known as the Gallio Inscription, confirms Gallio's position, validating Luke's account.

Corroboration of Events: The crucifixion and burial of Jesus are central events in the New Testament. Archaeological discoveries, such as the remains of crucified individuals, lend credence to the descriptions of crucifixion in the Gospels (Matthew 27:32-56, Mark 15:21-41, Luke 23:26-49, John 19:17-37). Moreover, the discovery of Jewish ossuaries, or bone boxes, from the time of Jesus align with the Gospel accounts of Jesus' burial (Matthew 27:57-61, Mark 15:42-47, Luke 23:50-56, John 19:38-42).

Validation of People and Places: The discovery of the Pool of Bethesda (John 5:1-15) and the Pool of Siloam (John 9:1-11), where Jesus performed miracles, and the Pilate Stone, which mentions Pontius Pilate, the Roman governor who sentenced Jesus to crucifixion (Matthew 27:11-26), all provide archaeological support for the existence of these places and people mentioned in the New Testament.

Clarification of Cultural Context: Understanding the cultural context of the New Testament helps us to interpret it accurately. Archaeology can illuminate this context. For instance, the discovery of numerous ritual baths (mikvehs) and stone vessels in ancient Jewish homes sheds light on the Jewish practices of ritual purity, which Jesus discusses in the Gospels (Mark 7:1-23).

Countering Skepticism: Skeptics often argue that the New Testament is not reliable due to alleged historical inaccuracies. However, as we've seen, many details in the New Testament have been confirmed by archaeological findings. While archaeology cannot confirm every detail (nor can it disprove them), the substantial number of corroborations lends credibility to the New Testament and can be a valuable tool in discussions with skeptics.

In conclusion, archaeological evidence can serve as a powerful apologetic tool by supporting the historical reliability of the New Testament. It aids in our understanding of the text and provides external validation for many of its details, reinforcing the New Testament's credibility in the face of modern skepticism.

The Limits and Strengths of Archaeology in New Testament Study

When using archaeology to study the New Testament, it is important to recognize both its limitations and strengths.

Limitations of Archaeology in New Testament Study

Incomplete Record: Archaeology can't confirm every detail mentioned in the New Testament because not all artifacts or structures from the first century have survived or been discovered. For instance, no archaeological evidence has been found to date specifically confirming the existence of particular individuals such as the apostle Peter or Judas Iscariot.

Interpretation Required: Archaeological findings often require interpretation. Two scholars might interpret the same evidence in different ways. For example, the nature of the "Jesus Family Tomb" discovered in Jerusalem has been the subject of much debate.

Absence of Evidence is not Evidence of Absence: The lack of archaeological evidence for a particular person, place, or event mentioned in the New Testament doesn't necessarily mean that it didn't exist or occur. Many first-century structures were destroyed or built over in subsequent centuries.

Strengths of Archaeology in New Testament Study

Confirmation of New Testament Details: Archaeology can provide physical evidence that supports the historical narratives of the New Testament. For example, the discovery of an ossuary (a box for storing bones) bearing the inscription "James, son of Joseph, brother of Jesus" provides potential archaeological evidence for figures mentioned in the New Testament (Matthew 13:55).

Cultural Context: Archaeology provides insights into the culture, customs, and living conditions of the people and places mentioned in the New Testament. For instance, understanding Roman crucifixion practices, informed by archaeological findings, adds depth to our understanding of Jesus' crucifixion (Matthew 27:32-56, Mark 15:21-41, Luke 23:26-49, John 19:17-37).

Validation of Biblical Texts: Archaeological discoveries have validated the accuracy of many New Testament texts. The discovery of the Pool of Bethesda and the Pool of Siloam, mentioned in John's Gospel (John 5:1-15, John 9:1-11), confirm the Gospel's accurate depiction of Jerusalem's geography.

In conclusion, while archaeology has its limitations, it is a powerful tool in the study of the New Testament. Its findings can confirm historical details, provide context, and validate biblical texts, thereby supporting the New Testament's reliability and enriching our understanding of its message.

Archaeology, Faith, and the New Testament: An Integrated Approach

Archaeology, faith, and the New Testament can be integrated in a way that allows each to enrich our understanding of the others.

Archaeology and the New Testament

Archaeology helps us understand the historical and cultural context of the New Testament. It provides tangible evidence that affirms the historical accuracy of many details found in the New Testament. For example, the discovery of the Pool of Siloam mentioned in John 9:1-7, where Jesus healed a man born blind, confirms the accuracy of the geographical details in John's Gospel.

Faith and the New Testament

Faith is central to the message of the New Testament. Passages such as John 3:16 emphasize the importance of belief in Jesus for eternal life, while Hebrews 11:1 defines faith as "confidence in what we hope for and assurance about what we do not see." The New Testament presents faith not as blind belief, but as trust in the character and promises of God, informed by His actions throughout history, as recorded in the scriptures.

Archaeology and Faith

While archaeology can provide historical corroboration for some aspects of the New Testament, it is not the basis of faith. Rather, it can bolster faith by confirming the reliability of the scriptures. However, faith ultimately rests on the person and work of Jesus Christ, as revealed in the scriptures and experienced in personal relationship with Him.

An Integrated Approach

An integrated approach recognizes that archaeology, faith, and the New Testament each have their unique contributions. Archaeology provides historical and cultural context, the New Testament provides the theological framework, and faith provides the personal commitment and trust in God.

This integrated approach is reflected in the Bereans' response to Paul's message in Acts 17:11: "Now the Berean Jews were of more noble character than those in Thessalonica, for they received the message with great eagerness and examined the Scriptures every day to see if what Paul said was true." They eagerly received the message (faith), but also examined the Scriptures (New Testament) to confirm its truthfulness (akin to the archaeological/historical investigation).

In conclusion, an integrated approach to archaeology, faith, and the New Testament allows each to enrich our understanding of the others, leading to a fuller and more nuanced understanding of the Christian faith.

CHAPTER 16 New Testament Textual Criticism: The Quest for the Original Text

Introduction: The Purpose and Importance of Textual Criticism

Textual criticism is a discipline that plays a key role in understanding and interpreting the Bible, including the New Testament. This process aims to uncover the original wording of the biblical text, taking into account the various manuscripts and sources that have come down to us through the centuries.

The Purpose of Textual Criticism

The primary purpose of textual criticism is to try to recover, as far as possible, the original wording of the biblical text. This is important because, over the centuries, the text has been copied and recopied countless times, and in the process, scribes have sometimes introduced changes—either accidentally (through simple human error) or intentionally (for clarification or harmonization purposes).

2 Timothy 3:16-17 states, "All Scripture is God-breathed and is useful for teaching, rebuking, correcting and training in righteousness, so that the servant of God may be thoroughly equipped for every good work." If we accept this premise, then it becomes crucial to determine the original wording of the Scripture as accurately as possible, so we can confidently use it for these purposes.

The Importance of Textual Criticism

The importance of textual criticism lies in its contribution to the reliability, understanding, and interpretation of the New Testament text.

By examining the thousands of New Testament manuscripts and fragments in the original Greek and other languages, textual critics can identify variations and work to discern which rendering is most likely the original. It's important to note that the vast majority of these variations are minor and don't impact key Christian doctrines.

An example can be seen in the ending of the Gospel of Mark. The earliest and most reliable manuscripts end at Mark 16:8, while later manuscripts include additional verses (Mark 16:9-20). Textual criticism helps us acknowledge and understand these differences, leading to more informed interpretations of the text.

Textual criticism, therefore, is a valuable tool for ensuring that the text of the New Testament we have today is as close as possible to the original writings. This is significant for both academic study and personal faith, as it bolsters confidence in the New Testament as a reliable source of knowledge about Jesus and His teachings.

The Transmission of the New Testament Text: From Original to Copies

Understanding the transmission of the New Testament text is critical to the practice of textual criticism. From the initial autographs to the numerous copies that have reached us today, the text has undergone a fascinating journey.

The Original Autographs and the Early Copies

The original autographs of the New Testament writings, penned by the biblical authors themselves, are believed to have been written in the first century CE. For instance, Paul's letters (like 1 Corinthians which is referenced in 1 Corinthians 16:21, "I, Paul, write this greeting in my own hand") are considered some of the earliest New Testament writings. However, none of these autographs have survived to the present day.

Instead, we have copies of these original writings, and copies of copies, dating from the second century CE onwards. These were often written on papyrus and later on parchment. Despite the nonexistence of the original autographs, the sheer number of these early copies and their relative closeness in time to the originals give us confidence in the reliability of the New Testament text.

The Process of Copying

In the early centuries of Christianity, the copying process was largely a manual one. This meant that scribes would write out each word by hand, a process prone to human error. Some of these errors were simple mistakes, such as a missed word or a duplicated line. Others were intentional alterations made by a scribe who thought the text could be improved or clarified.

This is seen in the Comma Johanneum (1 John 5:7-8), which is included in the King James Version: "For there are three that bear record in heaven, the Father, the Word, and the Holy Ghost: and these three are one. And there are three that bear witness in earth, the Spirit, and the water, and the blood: and these three agree in one." However, this passage is not found in the earliest and most reliable Greek manuscripts and is generally considered a later addition.

Variants and their Significance

The differences in the texts, known as variants, can provide insight into the transmission process. Most of these are minor, such as spelling differences or word order changes, and they do not affect the fundamental teachings of the New Testament.

However, some variants are more significant and require careful analysis to determine the most probable original reading. This is where textual criticism comes in. For instance, the story of the woman caught in adultery (John 7:53-8:11) is a beloved passage but is absent from the earliest and most reliable manuscripts. Textual criticism helps us understand these issues and assess their impact on our understanding of the text.

In conclusion, the transmission of the New Testament text from the original autographs to the copies we have today is a complex process that has resulted in some variations. However, with the tools of textual criticism and the wealth of manuscripts available, we can have confidence in the reliability of the New Testament text.

Understanding the Manuscript Evidence: Papyri, Uncials, Minuscules, and Lectionaries

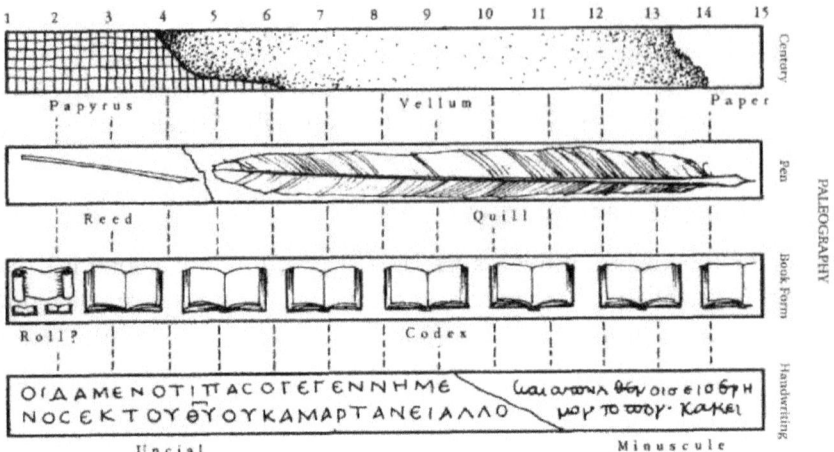

The New Testament has been preserved in a variety of manuscript forms. These include papyri, uncials, minuscules, and lectionaries. The differences among these types of manuscripts lie in the material used, the style of writing, and their purpose.

Papyri:

Papyrus was a common writing material in the ancient world. It was made from the papyrus plant, which was abundant in the Nile Delta. Papyrus was relatively cheap and easy to produce, making it a popular choice for scribes.

The earliest existing copies of the New Testament are found on papyrus manuscripts. These papyri provide some of our most valuable insights into the earliest forms of the New Testament text. For example, P52, a small fragment from the Gospel of John (John 18:31-33, 37-38), is generally dated to the first half of the second century, making it one of the oldest known fragments of the New Testament.

Uncials:

Uncials are Greek manuscripts written in a distinct style of large, uppercase letters. These manuscripts were typically written on parchment or vellum and were in use from the 3rd to the 10th centuries.

Important uncial manuscripts include Codex Sinaiticus and Codex Vaticanus, both from the 4th century. These are among our earliest complete (or nearly complete) copies of the New Testament and are crucial in the work of textual criticism.

Minuscules:

In contrast to the large, uppercase letters of uncials, minuscules were written in a smaller, lowercase script. This style came into use around the 9th century and became the most common form of writing in later centuries.

Minuscule manuscripts are numerous and often contain the complete New Testament. While they are generally later than the papyri and uncials, they still provide valuable evidence for the text of the New Testament.

Lectionaries:

Lectionaries were books that contained sections of the Gospels and Epistles arranged according to the church calendar for reading in public worship. They were widely used in the Eastern Orthodox Church and offer a different kind of textual evidence.

The lectionary tradition shows us how the New Testament was used in the life of the early church and how the text was transmitted in this context. It is another piece of the puzzle in reconstructing the original text of the New Testament.

In conclusion, understanding the manuscript evidence, including papyri, uncials, minuscules, and lectionaries, is crucial in the task of textual criticism. Each type of manuscript contributes to our understanding of the New Testament text and its transmission over time. Despite the variations found among the manuscripts, the overall consistency across these diverse sources attests to the remarkable preservation of the New Testament text.

The Multitude of Manuscripts: An Embarrassment of Riches

The New Testament is preserved in more manuscripts than any other ancient work, leading some scholars to refer to it as an "embarrassment of riches." This term is used to highlight the sheer number of New Testament manuscripts and the challenges and opportunities this presents for textual criticism.

As of 2023, there were over 5,800 known Greek manuscripts of the New Testament, along with tens of thousands of Latin Vulgate and earlier versions in various languages, including Coptic, Syriac, and Armenian. These manuscripts range from small fragments to complete New Testaments and date from the 2nd century to the Middle Ages.

The advantage of having such a multitude of manuscripts is that it provides a wealth of evidence for the text of the New Testament. Each manuscript is a witness to the text as it existed at the time and place of its creation. By comparing these witnesses, textual critics can identify variations and work towards reconstructing the original text.

For example, in 2 Timothy 3:16, the Greek text reads, "πᾶσα γραφὴ θεόπνευστος καὶ ὠφέλιμος πρὸς διδασκαλίαν, πρὸς ἐλεγμόν, πρὸς ἐπανόρθωσιν, πρὸς παιδείαν τὴν ἐν δικαιοσύνῃ," which translates to "All Scripture is God-breathed and is useful for teaching, rebuking, correcting and training in righteousness." If a manuscript were found where a word was missing or different, scholars could compare it with other manuscripts to determine the most likely original wording. It is the weightiness of the evidence both internal and external that will determine the original reading.

However, the number of manuscripts also presents challenges. Because no two manuscripts are exactly alike, there are many variations to sort through. Some of these variations are significant, but most are minor differences in spelling, word order, or grammar that do not affect the meaning of the text.

In conclusion, the multitude of New Testament manuscripts is both a challenge and an opportunity. It presents textual critics with a complex task, but it also provides a robust foundation for confidence in the reliability of the New Testament text. Despite the variations among the manuscripts, the overall message of the New Testament remains consistent across the manuscript tradition, affirming the essential truths of the Christian faith.

The Early Translations and the Church Fathers: Additional Witnesses to the Text

Beyond the Greek manuscripts of the New Testament, there are also thousands of early translations of the New Testament in languages such as Latin, Syriac, Coptic, Armenian, and others. These translations, also known as versions, are valuable witnesses to the text of the New Testament, as they represent how the text was understood by different communities and at different times.

For instance, the Latin Vulgate, translated by Jerome in the late 4th century, was widely used in the Western Church and provides valuable insight into the state of the Greek text at that time. Similarly, the Peshitta, a Syriac version of the New Testament, helps scholars understand how the text was interpreted in the Syriac-speaking communities of the East.

In addition to the versions, the writings of the early church fathers are another crucial source of evidence for the New Testament text. These church fathers frequently quoted and interpreted the New Testament in their own writings, providing us with many citations of the New Testament text.

In 1 Corinthians 15:3-7, for example, Paul writes, "For I delivered to you as of first importance what I also received: that Christ died for our sins in accordance with the Scriptures, that he was buried, that he was raised on the third day in accordance with the Scriptures, and that he appeared to Cephas, then to the twelve. Then he appeared to more than five hundred brothers at one time, most of whom are still alive, though some have fallen asleep. Then he appeared to James, then to all the apostles."

This passage, which is central to the Christian message, is quoted or alluded to by numerous church fathers, including Clement of Rome, Polycarp, and Irenaeus. By comparing these citations with the Greek text and the versions, scholars can gain a better understanding of how this passage was transmitted and understood in the early church.

In summary, the early translations of the New Testament and the writings of the church fathers provide valuable additional witnesses to the text of the New Testament. By comparing these witnesses with the Greek manuscripts, scholars can work towards a more accurate reconstruction of the original text. Despite the challenges, the vast number of witnesses to the New Testament text - in Greek, in other languages, and in the writings of the church fathers - provides a robust foundation for confidence in the text's reliability.

The Variants in the Text: Nature, Types, and Significance

In the process of transmitting the New Testament text, various kinds of variants or differences in the wording of the text arose. These variants came about for a variety of reasons: scribes made unintentional errors, they attempted to correct what they thought were errors, or they made changes to clarify the meaning of the text.

Understanding these variants and their significance is an essential part of textual criticism. It's important to note from the outset, however, that the vast majority of these variants do not affect the core teachings of the New Testament.

1. **Spelling and Grammar Variants:** These are the most common type of variants, representing about 75% of all differences. They include differences in spelling, word order, and grammatical constructions. For example, in Matthew 1:7-8, some manuscripts spell the name of the king Asa as "Asaph," a name that is otherwise associated with a psalmist.

2. **Minor Changes:** These include changes that do not significantly affect the meaning of the text. An example can be found in 1 Thessalonians 2:7. Some manuscripts have Paul saying, "But we were gentle among you," while others have, "But we were infants among you."

3. **Meaningful Variants:** These are changes that have an impact on the interpretation of the text. An example is in Revelation 13:18, where some manuscripts give the number of the beast as 666, while others give it as 616.

4. **Major Variants:** These are the fewest in number and include differences that affect a substantial portion of the text. An example is the ending of the Gospel of Mark (Mark 16:9-20), which is absent in some of the earliest and most reliable manuscripts.

It's important to recognize that even though there are thousands of variants in the New Testament manuscripts, most of them are minor and do not affect the core teachings of the New Testament. The variants that do have a significant impact on the interpretation of the text are the subject of ongoing scholarly debate, but they represent a small percentage of the text.

In conclusion, while the presence of variants in the New Testament manuscripts may initially seem concerning, a closer examination reveals that the text of the New Testament is remarkably stable and reliable. Even Bart Ehrman, a noted critic of the New Testament, admits that most of these variants are insignificant and that no essential belief is in jeopardy due to them. Thus, despite the variants, we can have confidence that the text of the New Testament we have today accurately represents the original writings.

Hebrews 2:7

TR: You have made him a little lower than the angels; You have crowned him with glory and honor, And set him over the works of Your hands.

MT/CT: You have made him a little lower than the angels; You have crowned him with glory and honor.

New Testament Textual Criticism, often referred to as lower criticism, is the study of the copies of any written document whose original is unknown or non-extant, with the purpose of determining the original text. This process is essential for the New Testament, which was originally written in Greek, because we don't have the original manuscripts (autographs). Instead, we have thousands of copies, none of which are identical.

The Textus Receptus (TR) and the Majority Text/ Critical Text (MT/CT) are different types of Greek texts used as a basis for New Testament translations. Textus Receptus, or "received text," was the Greek text used for many of the earliest translations of the New Testament into vernacular languages. The Majority Text, also known as the Byzantine text-type, represents the text of a majority of Greek manuscripts, while the Critical Text is the outcome of textual criticism, incorporating readings from a broader range of manuscripts, including the older ones.

Hebrews 2:7, in the above, is an interesting example of a variant between the Textus Receptus and the Majority/Critical Text. Here's how textual criticism might approach this:

1. **Manuscript Evidence**: The first step is to examine the available manuscripts. The MT/CT is based on the earliest and most reliable manuscripts available. The TR is based on a smaller number of later manuscripts. The version in the TR includes an additional clause ("And set him over the works of Your hands") that is not present in the MT/CT.

2. **Internal Evidence**: Textual critics then consider what the author might have originally written by evaluating the style and vocabulary of the entire document. In this case, the writer of Hebrews often quotes the Old Testament, particularly the Septuagint (Greek Old Testament). The quote in Hebrews 2:7 is from Psalm 8:5-6. The additional clause in the TR version matches the Septuagint of Psalm 8:6, but the writer of Hebrews may not have intended to quote the entire verse.

3. **External Evidence**: This involves looking at the writings of early Church Fathers, early translations, and lectionaries. If an early Church Father quoted this verse, their quote might support one reading over the other.

4. **Principle of the harder reading**: Textual critics often favor the "harder reading," the version that is more difficult to understand why a scribe would have changed it. In this case, the "harder reading" would be the shorter version in the MT/CT, as scribes were more likely to add clarifying phrases rather than remove them.

5. **Coherence with the immediate context**: Sometimes the context can help decide between variants. Here, the context doesn't strongly favor one reading over the other.

Here, we see a difference between the Nestle-Aland/UBS text (NU) and the variant reading found in the Textus Receptus (TR) and Westcott-Hort text (WH). The NU represents what is typically used in most modern translations, while the TR is the basis for the King James Version and the New King James Version.

The NU text, supported by the earliest manuscripts (P46 B) and the majority of manuscripts, reads, "with glory and honor you crowned him." This is found in modern translations such as the NKJV (marginal note), RSV, NRSV, ESV, NASB (marginal note), NIV, TNIV, NEB, REB, NJB, NAB, NLT, HCSB, and NET.

The variant/TR WH text adds the clause, "and you set him over the works of your hands." This is found in the KJV, NKJV, RSV (marginal note), NRSV (marginal note), ESV (marginal note), NASB, NLT (marginal note), HCSB (marginal note), and NET (marginal note).

This discrepancy likely arose either from a transcriptional mistake (the shorter text) or scribal expansion (the longer text). Textual critics typically use a principle of preferring the "harder reading," and in this case, the shorter reading would be considered "harder" because it's less likely a scribe would intentionally leave out a portion of a biblical quotation.

Paul in the book of Hebrews often quotes from the Septuagint (the Greek translation of the Old Testament), and in this instance, the quote comes from Psalm 8:6. However, Paul doesn't necessarily replicate the Septuagint verbatim. The writer's purpose isn't to provide an exact quote, but to make a theological point about the status of humanity in relation to angels and the created order. The point can be made without the full quote, which could be why the shorter reading exists.

Thus, given the evidence and applying the principles of textual criticism, many scholars conclude that the shorter reading in the NU text may represent the original wording of Hebrews 2:7. The longer reading in the TR/WH could be a scribal addition to bring the quotation in line with the full verse from the Septuagint version of Psalm 8:6.

Acts 15:34

TR: However, it seemed good to Silas to remain there.

MT/CT: Spurious interpolation verse omitted because early weighty manuscripts do not contain this

As for the verse you've pointed out, Acts 15:34, there is a discrepancy between the Textus Receptus (TR) and the Majority Text/Critical Text (MT/CT). The TR includes the verse, while in the MT/CT, it is considered a spurious interpolation and is omitted. Here's how we might analyze this:

1. **Manuscript Evidence**: A key principle of textual criticism is that the reading found in the earliest and most diverse array of manuscripts is likely to be original. In the case of Acts 15:34, the verse is not found in some of the earliest and most reliable manuscripts such as Codex Sinaiticus (א) and Codex Vaticanus (B).

2. **Internal Evidence**: In addition to manuscript evidence, scholars will also consider the author's style and vocabulary. In this case, Luke, as the author of Acts, often proceeds quickly from one narrative to another, and the statement about Silas staying behind might be viewed as unnecessary for his narrative flow.

3. **External Evidence**: The writings of early Church Fathers, early translations, and lectionaries are considered. If they quote this verse or show awareness of its existence, it could be an argument for its originality. However, there's not substantial external evidence to support the inclusion of Acts 15:34.

4. **Principle of the shorter reading**: Textual critics often favor the shorter reading, assuming that scribes were more likely to add to a text to explain or

expand it than to take away from it. In this case, the shorter reading (without Acts 15:34) is in the MT/CT.

5. **Coherence with the immediate context**: The coherence principle evaluates whether a reading fits with the immediate literary and historical context. In this case, the omission of verse 34 does not affect the overall narrative of the Jerusalem Council and its aftermath.

Acts 15:34 does not appear in many modern translations because it is missing from the Westcott-Hort and Nestle-Aland/UBS texts (WH NU). The Textus Receptus (TR), the Greek text underlying the King James Version and other Reformation-era translations, includes the verse in a couple of forms.

1. The WH NU text, supported by some of the earliest and most reliable manuscripts (P74, ℵ, A, B, E, Ψ), along with the majority of manuscripts (Maj), the Syriac (syrp), and Coptic (copbo) versions, omits the verse entirely.

2. The variant/TR text includes the verse in two forms:

(1) "But it seemed good to Silas to remain there." This is supported by manuscript C, 33, 614, 1739, Syriac (syr**), and Coptic (copsa).

(2) "But it seemed good to Silas to remain with them, so Judas traveled alone." This form is found in manuscript D and the Old Latin (it,w).

The verse seems to contradict Acts 15:33, which states that both Silas and Judas were sent away from Antioch to Jerusalem. Yet, later in Acts 15:40, Silas is described as being in Antioch. This discrepancy may have prompted a scribe to add verse 34 to explain why Silas was still in Antioch.

Erasmus, who compiled the Greek text that later became the Textus Receptus, included this verse despite its absence in the Byzantine text (Maj). He found it in the margin of the Greek manuscripts he was using and also likely knew of its inclusion in the Latin Vulgate. He may have supposed that it was omitted in the Greek manuscripts due to a scribal error. From Erasmus's text, it was included in the Textus Receptus and translated in the King James Version.

Most modern versions, out of deference to the KJV tradition, note the omission. The New American Standard Bible (NASB) retains the verse but includes a note stating that early manuscripts do not contain it.

Given the evidence, many textual critics conclude that Acts 15:34 is likely a later addition to the text to resolve the apparent contradiction between Acts 15:33 and 15:40. Its absence in the earliest and most reliable manuscripts supports this conclusion.

The Science and Art of Textual Criticism: Principles and Methods

Textual criticism is a discipline that seeks to determine the original wording of any documents whose original copies have been lost but have survived in various later copies. For the New Testament, this involves analyzing the vast body of manuscript evidence to determine the most likely original wording of the text.

The process of textual criticism involves both science and art. The science involves rigorous examination of the manuscript evidence, while the art involves making educated judgments based on that evidence.

Here are some principles and methods used in textual criticism:

1. **External Evidence:** This involves the examination of the manuscripts themselves. Factors considered include the age of the manuscript, the geographical distribution of the manuscripts that contain a particular reading, and the quality of the manuscripts.

2. **Internal Evidence:** This involves the examination of the text itself. Factors considered include the style and vocabulary of the author, the immediate context of the passage, and the consistency with the rest of the document.

3. **The Principle of the Hardest Reading:** This principle posits that the more difficult reading is likely the original one. Scribes were more likely to simplify and clarify the text rather than make it more difficult. For example, in Mark 1:2, some manuscripts read "in the prophets" while others read "in Isaiah the prophet". The latter is a more difficult reading since the quotation that follows is not from Isaiah alone but a combination of Malachi 3:1 and Isaiah 40:3. Thus, the difficult reading "in Isaiah the prophet" is likely the original.

4. **The Principle of the Shortest Reading:** This principle suggests that the shorter reading is more likely to be original. Scribes were more likely to add to the text for clarification or out of piety, rather than subtract from it. For instance, in Luke 24:3, some manuscripts include "of the Lord Jesus" after "the body", while others do not. Given the principle of the shortest reading, it's likely that "the body" is the original reading.

5. **Coherence with the Author's Style and Context:** This principle suggests that a variant reading should not contradict the known style and context of the author. For example, Paul often uses the phrase "brothers and sisters" in his letters (e.g., 1 Corinthians 1:10; 2 Corinthians 1:8; Galatians 1:2; Philippians 1:12). So, a variant reading that included a different address would be suspect.

Textual criticism is a meticulous and challenging task, but it is essential for ensuring that the New Testament we read today reflects as closely as possible the original text. Despite the thousands of variants, the overall message of the New Testament remains clear and consistent, confirming the reliability of the Scriptures.

Major Textual Issues in the New Testament: Case Studies

While the vast majority of textual variants in the New Testament are minor and do not affect the overall meaning of the text, there are a few significant variants that have drawn considerable attention. Here are a few of these major textual issues, discussed using a balanced evaluation and citing relevant Bible verses:

1. **The Ending of Mark (Mark 16:9-20):** The earliest manuscripts and some other ancient witnesses do not have Mark 16:9-20. These verses include appearances of the resurrected Jesus and his commissioning of the disciples, which are not found in the earliest and most reliable manuscripts. Many scholars believe that this was a later addition, intended to provide a more satisfying conclusion to the Gospel of Mark. While these verses are not found in the earliest manuscripts, the events they describe are consistent with other New Testament accounts.

2. **The Woman Caught in Adultery (John 7:53-8:11):** This passage, also known as the Pericope Adulterae, is a famous story about Jesus and the woman caught in adultery. However, it is not found in many of the earliest manuscripts of John's Gospel. It also seems to interrupt the flow of the text around it. This has led many scholars to view it as a later insertion. Nevertheless, while its place in the original text of John's Gospel is uncertain, the story aligns well with Jesus' teaching on mercy and judgment elsewhere in the Gospels.

3. **The Comma Johanneum (1 John 5:7-8):** In the King James Version, these verses read, "For there are three that bear record in heaven, the Father, the Word, and the Holy Ghost: and these three are one. And there are three that bear witness in earth..." However, the phrase "in heaven, the Father, the Word, and the Holy Ghost: and these three are one. And there are three that bear witness in earth" is not found in any Greek manuscript before the 14th century and is believed to be a later addition, probably reflecting Trinitarian theology.

4. **The Longer Ending of Romans (Romans 16:25-27):** Some early manuscripts place this doxology after Romans 14:23, while others include it after both chapters 15 and 16. Still, others don't include it at all. The placement and inclusion of this passage vary among the manuscripts, suggesting it may have been a marginal note that was later incorporated into the text.

These textual issues, while interesting and important for understanding the transmission of the text, do not undermine the core teachings of the New Testament.

They are also evidence of the rigorous work of textual critics in examining the manuscript evidence and seeking to determine the original text of the New Testament.

The Role of Conjectural Emendation in Textual Criticism

Conjectural emendation is an advanced method of textual criticism that involves the proposal of a possible correction to a corrupted or unclear text in order to restore its original reading. In other words, when an ancient manuscript or text is damaged, missing, contradictory, or contains errors, textual critics may make a conjectural emendation, which is a proposed solution to the problem based on scholarly analysis and knowledge of the language, culture, and context in which the text was written. Conjectural emendation is a contested and debated practice among textual critics, as it involves a degree of speculation and subjectivity, and it may not always be possible to discern the original reading of a text.

This is a contentious practice, highly debated in certain circles. It is derived from the principle that when a reading is exceedingly difficult, to the point of impossibility, it should be rejected. Typically, the alternative is to choose an easier reading. However, in rare cases, some scholars may conclude that there is no acceptable alternative reading. In such instances, they may propose another reading, based on conjecture (a well-informed "guess"), which is not found in any existing manuscript. In defense of this practice, it can be argued that many early manuscripts have been lost over time, and this method has been routinely employed to restore other ancient Greek texts. I can personally attest to this, as I (Wilkins) have witnessed at least one instance where a speculative interpretation of a classical text proved to be correct. Nevertheless, there are significant distinctions between classical and biblical manuscripts. One notable difference is that we possess a far greater number of biblical manuscripts, which arguably renders this practice unnecessary. Furthermore, there is a theological consideration of divine preservation (a point where proponents of the Textus Receptus and textual critics surprisingly find common ground). Most faith-oriented textual critics hold a de facto position that God has preserved the New Testament text in existing Greek manuscripts. Supporters of speculative interpretation can argue, akin to advocates of the Masoretic Text or the Textus Receptus, that the resulting text from any of these critics does not exist in any extant manuscript (and never will). The counterargument lies in the reality of mixture (or contamination) found in all existing manuscripts: we are striving to reconstruct the original text; if the result were in agreement with any extant manuscript, it would either be a failure, or we would have the astonishing outcome that the resulting Greek text is both the original and that the agreeing manuscript is a copy of the original.

Addressing Allegations of Corruption and Conspiracy

Allegations of corruption and conspiracy in the transmission of the New Testament text often arise from misunderstandings about the nature of the transmission process and the wealth of manuscript evidence. It's essential to remember that textual variants do not mean the text has been corrupted beyond recognition, nor do they indicate a conspiracy to alter Christian doctrine.

1. The Nature of Textual Variants: Most textual variants involve minor issues like spelling, word order, or the inclusion or exclusion of a definite article, none of which affect the overall meaning of the text. For instance, in 1 Thessalonians 2:7, some manuscripts describe Paul and his companions as being "gentle among you," while others use the term "infants among you." Both readings can make sense in the context, and they do not significantly alter the message of the passage.

2. The Quantity of Textual Variants: The large number of variants is often due to the vast number of New Testament manuscripts. With over 5,800 Greek manuscripts, we can compare and contrast these documents to identify where variants occur. The sheer quantity of these documents is a testament to the text's overall reliability, not a cause for suspicion. As the saying goes among textual critics, "We have 100 times more New Testament Greek manuscripts than any other ancient writing, and the New Testament's textual accuracy is more certain than that of any other ancient documents."

3. The Impact of Textual Variants: No Christian doctrine hangs on a disputed reading. Even when considering significant variants like the ending of Mark's Gospel or the story of the woman caught in adultery in John, these passages do not introduce new doctrines not found elsewhere in the New Testament.

4. The Transparency of the Process: Modern Bible translations are open about significant textual variants, often noting them in the footnotes. This transparency shows there is no conspiracy to hide these issues from readers.

In conclusion, as Paul says in 2 Timothy 3:16, "All Scripture is God-breathed and is useful for teaching, rebuking, correcting and training in righteousness." The rigorous process of textual criticism helps us get as close as possible to the original writings, confirming the overall integrity and reliability of the New Testament text.

The Reliability of the Text: Comparisons with Other Ancient Documents

The reliability of the New Testament text, when compared to other ancient documents, is often highlighted due to the wealth of manuscript evidence and the relatively short time gap between the original writings and the earliest copies. These factors contribute significantly to the credibility of the New Testament as a historical document.

1. Wealth of Manuscript Evidence: The New Testament is preserved in over 5,800 Greek manuscripts, along with tens of thousands of Latin Vulgate manuscripts and other early versions. This is an unparalleled amount of evidence when compared to other historical works. For instance, the 'Histories' of Herodotus, a critical source for our understanding of ancient Greek history, survives in only a handful of manuscripts, the earliest of which dates from the 10th century AD, over a millennium after Herodotus' death.

2. Short Time Gap: The earliest copies of the New Testament books date within a few decades to a couple of centuries after their original composition. This is a remarkably short interval when compared to other ancient documents. The earliest copies of works by classical authors like Homer, Herodotus, or Plato date many centuries after their original composition. Yet, historians generally consider these works to be reliable representations of the original texts.

3. Consistency Across Manuscripts: Despite the many thousands of manuscripts and the inevitable textual variants that occur in the transmission process, the New Testament texts are remarkably consistent. Most variants are minor, such as differences in spelling or word order, and do not affect the overall message or doctrine of the text. This consistency across so many manuscripts is evidence of the text's reliability.

4. Confirmation from Outside Sources: The New Testament writings are also confirmed by quotations in the writings of early Church Fathers and non-Christian historians like Josephus and Tacitus. These external sources corroborate key details and events described in the New Testament.

These factors make the New Testament the best-attested document of the ancient world. As stated in 1 Peter 1:24-25, "All people are like grass, and all their glory is like the flowers of the field; the grass withers and the flowers fall, but the word of the Lord endures forever." This truth is seen in the remarkable preservation of the New Testament text over the centuries.

The Implications of Textual Variants for Doctrinal Integrity

Textual variants in the New Testament manuscripts have been a subject of extensive study in the field of textual criticism. It's important to note that while there are numerous variants due to the extensive number of manuscripts available, the vast majority of these variants do not impact the overall message or doctrine of the New Testament. In fact, they serve to confirm the integrity of the text as they help us understand the accuracy and reliability of the transmission process over centuries.

1. Nature of the Variants: Most of the variants in the New Testament manuscripts are minor, such as differences in spelling, word order, or the inclusion/exclusion of a definite article. These variants do not change the overall meaning of the text. For example, in some manuscripts of Revelation 1:4, the phrase is "from him who is, and who was, and who is to come," while in others, it is "from him who is, and was, and is to come." The slight difference does not change the fundamental truth being conveyed about God's eternal nature.

2. Variants and Doctrine: No essential Christian doctrine is impacted by any textual variant. Even when considering significant variants like the longer ending of Mark (Mark 16:9-20) or the story of the woman caught in adultery (John 7:53-8:11), these passages do not introduce new doctrines but rather reiterate teachings found elsewhere in Scripture. Therefore, the integrity of Christian doctrine remains sound even when these passages are scrutinized.

3. Confirmation of Core Truths: Despite the variants, the core truths of the Christian faith are affirmed in multiple passages throughout the New Testament. For instance, the deity of Christ is not only affirmed in John 1:1 ("In the beginning was the Word, and the Word was with God, and the Word was God"), but is also echoed in other passages like Philippians 2:6-11, Colossians 1:15-20, and Hebrews 1:1-3. Similarly, the doctrine of salvation by faith is articulated in numerous passages (Ephesians 2:8-9, Romans 3:23-24, John 3:16), demonstrating that key doctrines are not based on isolated verses but are the consistent message of the New Testament.

4. Transparency of the Variants: The presence of textual variants is openly acknowledged in most modern Bible translations, often in the form of footnotes indicating where certain manuscripts differ. This transparency is a testament to the rigorous scholarly work in the field of textual criticism and the commitment to presenting the most accurate text possible.

As Paul reminds us in 2 Timothy 3:16, "All Scripture is God-breathed and is useful for teaching, rebuking, correcting and training in righteousness." This confidence in the inspiration and utility of Scripture extends to our understanding of its transmission and preservation and reinforces the doctrinal integrity of the New Testament despite the presence of textual variants.

Textual Criticism and Bible Translation: An Interconnected Process

The process of Bible translation is intricately connected with the field of textual criticism. Textual criticism aims to determine the most original form of a text, and in the case of the New Testament, it involves studying the thousands of Greek manuscripts and fragments that have been preserved over centuries. Bible translation, on the other hand, is the process of rendering the original languages of the Bible (Hebrew, Aramaic, and Greek) into various other languages.

Here's a detailed explanation of how these two processes work together:

1. Establishing the Base Text: Before a translation can begin, scholars need to establish the base text. This involves comparing the numerous available manuscripts to ascertain the most likely original wording. For example, in 1 John 5:7-8, some later manuscripts include a passage known as the Comma Johanneum, which explicitly mentions the Trinity. However, this passage is absent in the earliest and most reliable Greek manuscripts. As a result, most modern Bible translations do not include this passage in the main text but may note it in a footnote.

2. Dealing with Variants: Textual critics categorize and evaluate the textual variants in the New Testament manuscripts based on several criteria, including the date of the manuscript, the geographical spread of the reading, and the context of the passage. The goal is to determine which variant has the highest likelihood of being original. For instance, in Mark 1:41, there is a variant where Jesus is said to be "moved with compassion" (in most Greek manuscripts) or "moved with anger" (in a few early manuscripts). Translators must weigh this evidence and make a decision based on the best available data.

3. Incorporating Scholarly Updates: The field of textual criticism is continually evolving as new manuscripts are discovered and as our understanding of ancient languages and cultures deepens. Translations must take these updates into account to ensure the most accurate representation of the original text. For example, the discovery of the Dead Sea Scrolls in the mid-20th century shed new light on the text of the Old Testament, and many Bible translations have since been updated to reflect this new information.

4. Rendering the Text in the Target Language: Once the base text is established, translators then work to render the text in the target language. This is a complex process that must balance the need for accuracy with readability. Translators often need to make choices about how to best convey the meaning of the original text in a way that is understandable in the target language.

5. Footnotes and Marginal Notes: Because of the nature of textual variants, many Bible translations include footnotes or marginal notes to indicate where significant variants occur. This provides transparency about the translation process and allows readers to understand the manuscript evidence behind the translation.

In all these steps, the ultimate aim is to convey the original message of the New Testament as accurately as possible. As 2 Timothy 2:15 exhorts, "Do your best to present yourself to God as one approved, a worker who does not need to be ashamed and who correctly handles the word of truth." Both textual criticism and Bible translation are essential parts of this work of handling the word of truth correctly.

Modern Developments in Textual Criticism: The Role of Technology

The role of technology in the field of New Testament textual criticism has been transformative. It has not only improved the accuracy and speed of textual analysis, but it has also democratized access to primary sources and scholarly discussions. Below is a detailed discussion on how technology impacts this field:

1. Digital Archiving and Accessibility:

One of the significant contributions of technology to textual criticism is the digitization of manuscripts. This has made texts, which were previously accessible to only a few scholars, readily available for study worldwide. The Codex Sinaiticus, one of the most important biblical manuscripts dating back to the 4th century, is a great example of this. It has been digitized and made available online for anyone to study. This is in line with the Biblical principle found in Deuteronomy 31:12: "Assemble the people—men, women and children, and the foreigners residing in your towns—so they can listen and learn to fear the LORD your God and follow carefully all the words of this law."

2. Advanced Analytical Tools:

Computer software has revolutionized the way textual critics analyze manuscripts. Software can compare thousands of variants across numerous manuscripts quickly, a task that would be daunting for human scholars. For example, the Coherence-Based Genealogical Method (CBGM) is a computer-based method that has been used to analyze the textual history of the New Testament. It helps in visualizing the relationships among the different manuscripts, aiding in the identification of the most likely original reading.

3. Imaging Technology:

Modern imaging technologies like multi-spectral imaging and 3D scanning have allowed scholars to read damaged and faded texts that were previously illegible. This is reminiscent of the story of the discovery of the book of the law in 2 Kings 22:8, where a previously lost text was found and its message was once again made clear to the people.

4. Collaborative Platforms:

The internet has enabled scholars from around the world to collaborate and share their findings. Online databases, forums, and academic social networks have become platforms for scholarly discussion and peer review. This allows for a more robust analysis of the text and echoes the communal aspect of the early church in Acts 2:42: "They devoted themselves to the apostles' teaching and to fellowship, to the breaking of bread and to prayer."

5. Virtual Reality (VR) and Augmented Reality (AR):

While still emerging, these technologies hold potential in offering immersive experiences of the historical and geographical context of the biblical text. This could provide scholars with a more profound understanding of the cultural and linguistic nuances of the New Testament.

All these technologies embody the principle found in Proverbs 18:15: "The heart of the discerning acquires knowledge, for the ears of the wise seek it out." They are tools that help textual critics in their quest to seek out the most accurate form of the New Testament text.

Responding to Skepticism about Textual Integrity

Skepticism about the textual integrity of the New Testament is often expressed in the form of questioning the accuracy of the transmission process or highlighting the existence of textual variants. Here's how these concerns might be addressed using Biblical passages and principles:

1. The Accuracy of Transmission:

The transmission of the New Testament text from the original autographs to the copies we have today was a process carried out by many scribes over centuries. While human error inevitably crept in, the sheer number of extant manuscripts allows scholars to cross-check readings and reconstruct the most likely original wording.

A relevant Bible passage here is Proverbs 11:14: "Where there is no guidance, a people falls, but in an abundance of counselors there is safety." In the context of textual criticism, the "abundance of counselors" could be seen as the multitude of manuscripts, each serving as a witness to the text, and providing a safety net against significant distortions of the original message.

2. Textual Variants:

Textual variants, which are differences in wording among the manuscripts, are often brought up in discussions about textual integrity. However, it's important to note that the vast majority of these variants are minor, such as spelling differences, and do not affect the meaning of the text.

Matthew 5:18 provides an apt verse for this: "For truly, I say to you, until heaven and earth pass away, not an iota, not a dot, will pass from the Law until all is accomplished." Jesus' words here affirm the enduring nature of God's Word, even down to the smallest details, which could be seen as a reassurance that minor variants do not undermine the core message of the New Testament.

3. Doctrinal Consistency:

Despite the existence of textual variants, no central Christian doctrine is jeopardized by any of them. The essential teachings about Jesus, salvation, and the nature of God remain consistent across the manuscripts.

In 2 Timothy 3:16, we read: "All Scripture is breathed out by God and profitable for teaching, for reproof, for correction, and for training in righteousness." This verse suggests that all Scripture, in its entirety, is inspired by God and serves a purpose. Even if there are minor differences between manuscripts, the overall teachings remain profitable for Christian faith and practice.

4. The Reliability Compared to Other Ancient Texts:

When compared to other ancient texts, the New Testament has far more extant manuscripts, with a shorter time gap between the original writing and the earliest copies. This increases confidence in the reliability of its text.

Isaiah 40:8 proclaims: "The grass withers, the flower fades, but the word of our God will stand forever." This verse could be seen as a reminder of the enduring nature of God's Word, which has been preserved through the centuries despite various challenges.

In conclusion, while skepticism about the New Testament's textual integrity is understandable, a careful study of the manuscript evidence and an understanding of the transmission process can provide solid grounds for confidence in the New Testament's reliability.

CHAPTER 17 Understanding the New Testament Authors: Their Lives and Times

Introduction: Unraveling the Lives Behind the Words

Understanding the authors of the New Testament, their backgrounds, and the contexts in which they wrote can provide us with a richer understanding of their writings. Here's an overview of the authors and their contexts, using relevant Bible verses:

1. Matthew the Tax Collector:

Matthew, formerly a tax collector, is traditionally held to be the author of the Gospel of Matthew. His background as a tax collector would have given him a unique perspective on both the Jewish society and the Roman authorities. Matthew's calling is described in Matthew 9:9, "As Jesus passed on from there, he saw a man called Matthew sitting at the tax booth, and he said to him, 'Follow me.' And he rose and followed him."

2. Mark the Companion of Peter:

Traditionally, the author of the Gospel of Mark is believed to be John Mark, a companion of both Paul and Peter. His close association with these key figures of the early Church would have provided him with firsthand knowledge of their teachings and experiences. Acts 12:12 refers to Mark's mother's house as a meeting place for early Christians, indicating Mark's close ties to the early Church.

3. Luke the Physician and Historian:

Luke, the author of the Gospel of Luke and the book of Acts, is described as a physician in Colossians 4:14: "Luke, the beloved physician, greets you, as does Demas." His careful attention to detail, as seen in his writings, reflects his background as a physician and historian.

4. John the Beloved Disciple:

John, the son of Zebedee, is traditionally held to be the author of the Gospel of John, the three letters of John, and the book of Revelation. Known as the disciple whom Jesus loved (John 13:23), John's writings reveal a deep, intimate understanding of Jesus' teachings.

5. Paul the Apostle to the Gentiles:

Paul, formerly Saul of Tarsus, is the author of 14 letters in the New Testament. His dramatic conversion experience on the road to Damascus is described in Acts 9. As an apostle to the Gentiles, Paul's writings reveal his deep understanding of both Jewish and Gentile cultures, as well as his theological insights into the meaning of Jesus' life, death, and resurrection.

6. Other New Testament Authors:

Other New Testament authors include Peter, James, and Jude, who each wrote a letter bearing their name, with Peter penning two letters. Each of these authors wrote in their own unique contexts, addressing specific issues and audiences.

In understanding these authors and their contexts, we can better appreciate the diversity and richness of the New Testament writings. As 2 Peter 1:21 reminds us, "For no prophecy was ever produced by the will of man, but men spoke from God as they were carried along by the Holy Spirit." Recognizing the human authors behind these divine words can help us to more fully understand and apply their teachings.

The Apostles: Witnesses to the Life of Jesus

The apostles held a special role as the immediate disciples of Jesus Christ, witnessing His life, miracles, death, and resurrection. Their experiences had a significant influence on their writings in the New Testament. Here's an overview of some of the apostles' roles and experiences, supported by references from the Bible:

1. Peter:

Peter, originally known as Simon, was one of the first disciples Jesus called. He was part of Jesus' inner circle and was present at significant events like the

Transfiguration (Matthew 17:1-9). Peter is the author of two epistles in the New Testament and was a prominent leader in the early Christian community. He famously denied Jesus three times before the crucifixion (Matthew 26:69-75) but was restored after the resurrection (John 21:15-19), showing his deep personal experience of grace.

2. John:

John, the son of Zebedee, is traditionally believed to be the author of the Gospel of John, three epistles, and the book of Revelation. Known as "the disciple whom Jesus loved," John had a close relationship with Jesus and was the only one of the twelve apostles present at the crucifixion (John 19:26). He was also the first disciple to reach the empty tomb after Jesus' resurrection (John 20:4).

3. James:

James, also the son of Zebedee and brother of John, was part of Jesus' inner circle of disciples along with Peter and John. He was present at the Transfiguration (Matthew 17:1-2) and in the Garden of Gethsemane (Matthew 26:36-37). James was the first apostle to be martyred, as recorded in Acts 12:2, demonstrating his commitment to the gospel message.

4. Matthew:

Matthew, also known as Levi, was a tax collector before he was called by Jesus to be a disciple (Matthew 9:9). His background likely made him particularly aware of the radical inclusivity of Jesus' message. He is traditionally believed to be the author of the Gospel of Matthew, which includes many teachings of Jesus not found in the other Gospels.

5. Thomas:

Thomas, often called "Doubting Thomas," famously questioned the resurrection of Jesus until he saw Jesus and touched his wounds (John 20:24-29). His doubt and subsequent belief represent a very human response to the incredible news of Jesus' resurrection.

6. Judas:

Judas Iscariot, the disciple who betrayed Jesus, serves as a sobering example of the potential for human failure and betrayal, even among those who are close to Jesus (Matthew 26:14-16). His actions led to Jesus' arrest and subsequent crucifixion.

The apostles' experiences with Jesus and their roles in the early Church significantly shaped their writings and teachings in the New Testament. By understanding these authors and their experiences, we can gain a deeper understanding of their writings and the life and teachings of Jesus.

Matthew: A Tax Collector Turned Gospel Writer

Matthew, also known as Levi, was a tax collector before he became one of Jesus's disciples. His life and conversion are described in the New Testament, and he is traditionally attributed as the author of the Gospel of Matthew.

Matthew's Call:

Matthew's calling is described in Matthew 9:9, "As Jesus went on from there, he saw a man named Matthew sitting at the tax collector's booth. 'Follow me,' he told him, and Matthew got up and followed him." Tax collectors were generally disliked in Jewish society as they were seen as collaborators with the Roman Empire and often accused of extortion. However, Jesus's call to Matthew signified a radical acceptance of people regardless of their social standing or past.

Matthew's Feast:

After his calling, Matthew hosted a feast for Jesus at his house, inviting other tax collectors and "sinners" to dine with them (Matthew 9:10-13). This event led to criticism from the Pharisees who questioned why Jesus ate with sinners. Jesus replied, "It is not the healthy who need a doctor, but the sick... For I have not come to call the righteous, but sinners."

Matthew's Gospel:

The Gospel of Matthew is traditionally attributed to Matthew the tax collector. This Gospel uniquely combines a firm understanding of Jewish tradition and law, likely from Matthew's Jewish background, with a clear assertion of Jesus's universal message for all people. For example, Matthew's Gospel begins with a genealogy of Jesus (Matthew 1:1-17), rooting Jesus in Jewish history, yet it ends with the Great Commission (Matthew 28:19-20), Jesus's command to make disciples of "all nations."

Significance of Matthew's Conversion:

Matthew's conversion from a tax collector to a disciple of Jesus shows the transformative power of Jesus's call. Matthew left behind a lucrative career to follow Jesus, illustrating the profound impact of Jesus's ministry. Matthew's life and Gospel emphasize the inclusive nature of Jesus's message, showing that all people, regardless of their background or previous life, are invited to follow Jesus.

Mark: The Interpreter of Peter

John Mark, often simply known as Mark, is traditionally believed to be the author of the Gospel of Mark. He is often identified with the Mark mentioned in various New Testament books (Acts 12:12, 25; 15:37, 39; Col. 4:10; 2 Tim. 4:11; Philemon 24; 1 Peter 5:13).

Mark and Peter's Connection:

Mark is often considered to be a close associate of Peter. This is primarily based on 1 Peter 5:13, where Peter sends greetings from "my son Mark," indicating a close, possibly spiritual, relationship.

Church tradition, particularly from the 2nd-century Church historian Papias, holds that Mark wrote his Gospel based on Peter's teachings and reminiscences, serving as Peter's "interpreter". This view is often supported by the vivid and detailed narrative found in Mark's Gospel, especially in recounting events where Peter was present.

Mark's Role in the New Testament:

Mark's significance is also noted in the book of Acts. In Acts 12:12, after Peter's miraculous release from prison, he went to the house of Mary, the mother of John also called Mark, where people were praying for him.

Mark also accompanied Paul and Barnabas (Mark's cousin according to Colossians 4:10) on their first missionary journey (Acts 12:25; 13:5). However, Mark left them and returned to Jerusalem (Acts 13:13), which later led to a sharp dispute between Paul and Barnabas, resulting in their separation (Acts 15:37-39).

Much later, however, Mark became useful to Paul's ministry and was with him during his first imprisonment (Colossians 4:10; Philemon 24). Paul even requested Mark's presence during his final imprisonment (2 Timothy 4:11).

The Gospel of Mark:

The Gospel of Mark is the shortest of the four Gospels and is often characterized by its fast-paced, straightforward narrative style – "immediately" is a frequently used term.

While the Gospel doesn't begin with a genealogy or birth narrative as Matthew and Luke do, it starts with the proclamation of John the Baptist and quickly proceeds to Jesus's public ministry, focusing on his deeds more than his discourses.

The Gospel of Mark ends with the discovery of Jesus's empty tomb and the women's fear and silence (Mark 16:1-8). The longer ending (Mark 16:9-20), found in some later manuscripts, includes post-resurrection appearances of Jesus and the Great Commission. However, internal evidence and manuscripts are quite clear that Mark 16:9-20 were not in the original.

Overall, Mark's life and his Gospel's portrayal of Jesus emphasize the actions and servanthood of Christ, often encapsulated in Mark 10:45, "For even the Son of Man did not come to be served, but to serve, and to give his life as a ransom for many."

Luke: The Physician and Detailed Historian and Companion of Paul

Luke, often referred to as "Luke the Beloved Physician" (Colossians 4:14), is the attributed author of both the Gospel of Luke and the Acts of the Apostles, which together make up a significant portion of the New Testament. Luke is unique among New Testament authors in that he was likely a Gentile, or at least a Hellenistic Jew, and he was not one of the original twelve apostles.

Luke's Background and Profession:

Not much is known about Luke's early life. The reference to him as a physician in Colossians indicates that he probably had a good education, as medical training in the ancient world required substantial learning.

Luke's Connection to Paul:

Luke is most well-known for his close companionship with the Apostle Paul. He is mentioned as a fellow worker in Philemon 1:24. Luke's presence with Paul is seen during the latter's imprisonment, where in Colossians 4:14, Paul sends greetings to the Colossians from Luke, the beloved physician, and in 2 Timothy 4:11, Paul mentions that only Luke is with him.

Luke as a Historian:

Luke's writings show that he was an excellent historian. His Gospel begins with a prologue (Luke 1:1-4) stating his desire to provide an "orderly account" of the events of Jesus' life, suggesting a careful compilation of information and interviews from those who were eyewitnesses of the events. This detail-oriented nature is also evident in the book of Acts, where Luke provides a meticulous account of the early Christian community and the spread of the Gospel.

His writings also show familiarity with the geographical and social landscape of the regions he mentions. He correctly titles various officials and accurately describes various locations. His account in Acts of Paul's sea journey to Rome and the subsequent shipwreck has been lauded for its nautical accuracy.

Luke's Gospel and Acts:

Luke's Gospel is the longest of the four Gospels and has a particular emphasis on the marginalized, the poor, women, and social outcasts. It is also the only Gospel that contains certain famous parables, such as the Good Samaritan and the Prodigal Son.

The book of Acts, serving as a sequel to his Gospel, tells the story of the early Christian church, focusing on the ministries of Peter and Paul, and the spread of the Gospel from Jerusalem to Rome.

Luke's overarching theme in both his Gospel and Acts is the universality of the Gospel message, highlighting that salvation through Jesus is for all people, Jews and Gentiles alike, as seen in Luke 2:32 and Acts 10:34-35.

John: The Beloved Disciple and His Unique Perspective

John, often referred to as "John the Beloved Disciple" or "John the Apostle," is traditionally considered the author of the Gospel of John, the three Epistles of John (1 John, 2 John, and 3 John), and the book of Revelation. The Gospel of John is known for its unique perspective on the life and teachings of Jesus, different from the synoptic gospels (Matthew, Mark, and Luke).

John's Relationship with Jesus:

John was one of the twelve apostles and is often identified as one of Jesus' closest followers. He, along with Peter and James (his brother), formed the inner circle of Jesus' disciples, as they were present at key moments in Jesus' ministry, such as the Transfiguration (Matthew 17:1-9) and the Garden of Gethsemane (Matthew 26:36-46).

In his gospel, John refers to himself as "the disciple whom Jesus loved" (John 13:23, 19:26, 20:2, 21:7, 21:20), reflecting a close, intimate relationship with Jesus. It's also worth noting that during Jesus' crucifixion, Jesus entrusted the care of His mother Mary to John (John 19:26-27), which further emphasizes the special relationship between them.

John's Gospel:

John's gospel differs significantly from the synoptic gospels. While the synoptics focus more on Jesus' deeds and sayings, John's gospel focuses on the identity of Jesus, presenting Him as the divine Word (Logos) who became flesh (John 1:1-14). The "I AM" statements of Jesus (e.g., "I am the bread of life" - John 6:35, "I am the way, the truth, and the life" - John 14:6) are unique to John's gospel, emphasizing Jesus' divine identity and mission.

The Gospel of John also contains certain events not recorded in the synoptic gospels, such as the wedding at Cana (John 2:1-11), the raising of Lazarus (John 11:1-44), and Jesus' meeting with Nicodemus (John 3:1-21).

John's Epistles and Revelation:

The three letters attributed to John in the New Testament focus on love and truth, reinforcing the themes of his gospel. They are written to provide assurance of salvation to believers (1 John 5:13) and to warn against false teachers and teachings (1 John 4:1-6, 2 John 7-11).

The book of Revelation, also traditionally attributed to John, is a highly symbolic work that provides visions of the end times and the return of Jesus. It offers encouragement and hope to believers in the face of persecution and challenges, promising that God will ultimately triumph over evil.

In summary, John's writings provide a unique and profound perspective on Jesus' identity as the divine Son of God, the importance of belief in Him for eternal life (John 20:31), and the power of love and truth in the life of believers.

Paul: From Persecutor to Proclaimer of the Gospel and Author of Fourteen Letters

Paul, originally known as Saul, is one of the most prominent figures in the New Testament and is traditionally considered the author of 14 letters (Romans, 1 & 2 Corinthians, Galatians, Ephesians, Philippians, Colossians, 1 & 2 Thessalonians, 1 & 2 Timothy, Titus, Philemon, and Hebrews).

Paul's Early Life and Conversion:

Paul was a Pharisee, a strict Jewish sect known for its commitment to the Mosaic Law. He was a zealous persecutor of the early Christian movement, as he believed it to be a blasphemous sect that threatened Judaism (Acts 8:1-3, Philippians 3:5-6). His dramatic conversion occurred on the road to Damascus, where he encountered the risen Jesus and was struck blind. His sight was later restored by Ananias, a disciple of Jesus, and Paul was baptized (Acts 9:1-19). This experience transformed Paul from a persecutor of Christians to one of the most passionate proclaimers of the Gospel.

Paul's Missionary Journeys:

Paul undertook three main missionary journeys (Acts 13-14, Acts 15:36-18:22, Acts 18:23-21:17) and a journey to Rome (Acts 27-28). These journeys took him across the Roman Empire, establishing and strengthening Christian communities. He preached to both Jews and Gentiles, emphasizing the universal message of the Gospel.

Paul's Letters:

Paul's letters, or epistles, form a significant part of the New Testament. They were written to provide instruction, encouragement, and correction to various churches and individuals.

His letters often discuss theological concepts such as justification by faith (Romans 3:21-26, Galatians 2:15-16), the role of the Law (Romans 7:1-6, Galatians 3:23-25), the nature of the Church as the body of Christ (1 Corinthians 12:12-27, Ephesians 4:11-16), and the return of Christ (1 Thessalonians 4:13-18).

Paul's Imprisonment and Death:

Paul was often met with opposition and persecution. He was imprisoned multiple times, and some of his letters were written from prison (Philippians, Ephesians, Colossians, Philemon). According to tradition, Paul was eventually martyred in Rome under Emperor Nero.

In summary, Paul's life and writings have had a profound impact on Christianity. His transformation from a persecutor to a follower of Christ, his missionary efforts, and his deep theological insights have shaped Christian understanding and practice throughout history.

James: The Brother of Jesus and Leader of the Jerusalem Church

James, often referred to as James the Just, is a key figure in the New Testament. He's identified as the brother (or close relative, as the Greek word "adelphos" can also mean) of Jesus (Matthew 13:55, Mark 6:3, Galatians 1:19) and played a critical role in the early church.

James' Relationship with Jesus:

During Jesus' ministry, it seems that his family, including James, were skeptical about his messianic claims. John 7:5 states, "For even His own brothers did not believe in Him." However, according to 1 Corinthians 15:7, the resurrected Jesus appeared to James, which presumably led to his conversion.

James' Role in the Early Church:

James quickly rose to prominence in the Jerusalem church after Jesus' ascension. Acts 15 details a council at Jerusalem, where the apostles and elders met to discuss the issue of whether Gentile converts needed to follow the Law of Moses. James played a key role in this council, suggesting that Gentiles should be welcomed into the fellowship without being burdened by the full Jewish law, marking a significant turning point for the inclusion of Gentiles in the church (Acts 15:13-21).

The Epistle of James:

The Epistle of James in the New Testament is traditionally attributed to James the brother of Jesus. This letter is noted for its practical wisdom and ethical teachings. James 1:22 advises, "Do not merely listen to the word, and so deceive yourselves. Do what it says." He also emphasizes the importance of faith accompanied by works in James 2:14-26.

Death of James:

There's no biblical account of James' death, but the Jewish historian Josephus recorded that James was stoned to death in Jerusalem around 62 CE. His death was ordered by the high priest Ananus, a Sadducee, who took advantage of a gap between Roman governors to condemn James for breaking the law.

In summary, James played a vital role in the early Christian Church. From initial skepticism during Jesus' ministry to becoming a leader in the Jerusalem Church, James' journey demonstrates a significant transformation. His teachings, particularly in the Epistle of James, continue to guide Christian ethical behavior and understanding of faith.

Peter: Passionate Fisherman Turned Apostle

Peter, whose original name was Simon, is one of the most prominent figures in the New Testament. His life is characterized by a journey from being a humble fisherman to a leading apostle and influential figure in the early Christian church.

Peter's Early Life and Calling:

The Gospels tell us that Peter was a fisherman by profession, working in the Sea of Galilee. This was where Jesus first encountered Peter and his brother Andrew. According to Matthew 4:18-20, Jesus called them to leave their nets and follow Him, promising that He would make them "fishers of men."

Peter's Relationship with Jesus:

Peter was part of Jesus' inner circle, along with James and John. He was present at significant events such as the Transfiguration (Matthew 17:1-9) and Jesus' prayer in the Garden of Gethsemane (Mark 14:32-42).

Matthew 16:13-20 records a significant exchange between Jesus and Peter. When Jesus asked His disciples, "Who do you say I am?" Peter boldly confessed, "You are the Messiah, the Son of the living God." Jesus commended Peter for this revelation, saying that this truth was revealed to him by God. However, contrary to some interpretations, when Jesus said "on this rock I will build my church," the rock here refers to the truth of Peter's confession—that Jesus is the Christ—not Peter himself, as indicated by 1 Corinthians 10:4 where Christ is referred to as the spiritual rock.

Peter's Denial and Restoration:

Despite his close relationship with Jesus, Peter also had moments of weakness. The most notable is his denial of Jesus during the latter's trial, as predicted by Jesus (Matthew 26:31-35, 69-75). Yet, after the resurrection, Jesus graciously restored Peter in John 21:15-19, asking him three times if he loved Him, mirroring Peter's threefold denial.

Peter's Role in the Early Church:

After Jesus' ascension, Peter assumed a leadership role in the early church. On the day of Pentecost, he preached a powerful sermon that led to about 3,000 people becoming believers (Acts 2:14-41). Throughout the book of Acts, Peter is seen actively spreading the gospel and performing miracles.

Peter's Letters:

Two letters in the New Testament—1 Peter and 2 Peter—are traditionally attributed to Peter. These letters provide spiritual guidance, encouragement amidst suffering, and warnings about false teachers.

In summary, Peter's life is a testament to transformative power of faith in Jesus. Despite his shortcomings and mistakes, his unwavering faith and commitment to the gospel played a pivotal role in the establishment and growth of the early church.

Jude: A Servant of Jesus Christ and Brother of James

Jude, also known as Judas or Thaddaeus, is one of the lesser-known figures in the New Testament. Despite having only one book to his name in the Bible, his letter carries valuable insight and instruction for believers. He identifies himself as "a servant of Jesus Christ and brother of James" (Jude 1:1).

Relationship to Jesus and James:

Jude's self-identification as a servant of Jesus Christ and brother of James suggests his familial relationship to Jesus. According to Matthew 13:55 and Mark 6:3, Jesus had brothers named James and Judas (Jude), making Jude a likely candidate for being Jesus' biological brother. It's important to note that during Jesus' ministry, His brothers were initially skeptical of His messianic claims (John 7:5). However, the post-resurrection appearances of Jesus changed this, as Acts 1:14 reports that Jesus' brothers were among the believers gathered in the upper room after Jesus' ascension.

The Letter of Jude:

Jude's letter is a brief but forceful call to contend for the faith against certain individuals who had crept into the church and were perverting the grace of God. He warns the readers about these false teachers, and provides examples from the Old Testament, and Jewish tradition, to illustrate the judgment that awaits them (Jude 1:5-16).

Despite the stern warnings, Jude's letter is not without hope. He encourages believers to build themselves up in the faith, pray in the Holy Spirit, keep themselves in the love of God, and wait for the mercy of Jesus that leads to eternal life (Jude 1:20-21). He also instructs them to show mercy to those who doubt and save others by snatching them out of the fire of condemnation (Jude 1:22-23).

Jude's Humility:

Interestingly, Jude does not boast of his biological relationship to Jesus, but rather identifies himself as a servant, or slave, of Jesus Christ. This title signifies his commitment and obedience to Jesus as Lord. His humility is also seen in his reference to himself as the brother of James, indicating that he recognized his brother's prominent role in the early church (Acts 15, Galatians 2:9).

In conclusion, although Jude's presence in the New Testament is brief, his letter provides a powerful testament to his faith, humility, and his commitment to uphold the truth of the gospel against false teachings.

The Social, Political, and Religious Context of the New Testament Authors

The New Testament, as the inspired Word of God, transcends the human authors who penned it. However, in His divine wisdom, God chose to inspire these authors within their specific social, political, and religious contexts. Recognizing this does not detract from the divine authorship of the Bible but rather illuminates the profound way in which God communicates His eternal truths.

The authors of the New Testament lived in a time that was politically complex and religiously diverse. God, in His infinite knowledge and understanding, used these contexts to bring about His Word in a manner that was relevant to the people of that era, and which remains applicable to us today.

For instance, when Paul addresses issues concerning Roman law or Jewish customs in his letters, it's not that these earthly matters influenced the Word of God. Instead, it was God who, through the Holy Spirit, guided Paul to address these issues as part of His eternal message.

When we discuss the social, political, and religious context of the New Testament authors, it's not to suggest that these human factors influenced God or changed His message. Rather, it's to recognize that God, in His wisdom, chose to inspire human authors who lived in specific historical and cultural contexts. The Holy Spirit guided these authors to write God's truth in a way that their contemporaries could understand and relate to, and that remains meaningful and relevant for us today.

The Apostle Peter, in 2 Peter 1:21, explains this beautifully: "For no prophecy was ever produced by the will of man, but men spoke from God as they were carried along by the Holy Spirit." The "carrying along" by the Holy Spirit implies that the authors were actively involved in the writing process, but the ultimate source and direction of their writings was God Himself.

So, while the New Testament reflects the first-century Jewish and Greco-Roman contexts in which it was written, these reflections are part of God's inspired and infallible Word. God used these contexts as a vessel to convey His timeless truths, ensuring His message would be understood by the people of that time and continue to be understood by people today.

The Writings of the New Testament That Touched on Jewish and Greco-Roman Culture

The New Testament is rich with references to both Jewish and Greco-Roman cultures. The authors were living in a world where these two cultures coexisted and often intersected, and their writings naturally reflect this reality.

Jewish Culture in the New Testament

Jewish culture is reflected extensively in the New Testament, as all its authors were Jewish or deeply acquainted with Jewish culture and religion.

1. **Jewish Religious Practices**: The Gospel accounts frequently mention Jewish practices such as Sabbath observance (Mark 2:23-28), dietary laws (Mark 7:1-23), and feasts like the Passover (Matthew 26:17-19).

2. **Jewish Scriptures**: The New Testament authors consistently quote from and allude to the Jewish Scriptures (Old Testament). For example, Matthew's Gospel frequently cites Old Testament prophecies to show their fulfillment in Jesus (Matthew 1:22-23, 2:15, 2:17-18, etc.).

3. **Jewish Expectations of Messiah**: The Jewish expectation of a coming Messiah is a significant theme. Jesus is presented as fulfilling these expectations, though often in unexpected ways (Luke 24:25-27).

Greco-Roman Culture in the New Testament

The influence of Greco-Roman culture is also evident in the New Testament, reflecting the broader cultural context of the Roman Empire.

1. **Greek Language and Thought**: The New Testament was written in Greek, the lingua franca of the eastern Mediterranean at the time. Paul, in his letters, often engages with Greek philosophical ideas. For instance, in Acts 17:28, he quotes Greek poets while speaking to the Athenians.

2. **Roman Government**: The New Testament frequently mentions the Roman government and officials, reflecting the political reality of the time. For example, the trial and crucifixion of Jesus involve Roman officials like Pontius Pilate (John 18:28-19:16).

3. **Greco-Roman Social Practices**: Greco-Roman social norms and practices are often the backdrop for New Testament teachings. For instance, Paul's

instructions on household codes in Ephesians 5:22-6:9 reflect typical Greco-Roman household structures.

4. **Greek and Roman Religions**: The New Testament reflects a world where many gods were worshipped. For example, in 1 Corinthians 8, Paul addresses the issue of eating food offered to idols, a common practice in Greco-Roman religion.

In summary, the New Testament writings are embedded in and interact with both Jewish and Greco-Roman cultures, reflecting the complex cultural world of the first-century Mediterranean.

Understanding the Language, Genre, and Style of the New Testament Authors

The New Testament was primarily written in Koine Greek, the common language of the eastern Mediterranean from the 4th century BC to the 4th century AD. This widespread language was used by the Holy Spirit to reach a broad audience with the Gospel message.

The variety of genres in the New Testament, from historical narrative (Gospels, Acts), to letters/epistles (Pauline and General Epistles), to apocalyptic literature (Revelation), testifies to the diversity of God's revelation. He chose to convey His truths in ways that would resonate with different people and in various contexts.

The apostle Paul, for example, often used legal and athletic metaphors, reflecting both his Pharisaic background and the Hellenistic culture of his readers. In 1 Corinthians 9:24-27, Paul uses an athletic metaphor to describe the Christian life, "Do you not know that in a race all the runners run, but only one receives the prize? So run that you may obtain it."

Similarly, Luke's Gospel and the Acts of the Apostles, known for their detailed historical and geographical references, reflect Luke's background as a physician and careful historian (Colossians 4:14).

The apostle John's writings, including his Gospel, three letters, and the Book of Revelation, are marked by profound theological insights presented in a simple, yet profound language. His unique style is evident in passages such as John 1:1, "In the beginning was the Word, and the Word was with God, and the Word was God."

While God divinely inspired the writing of the New Testament, He did not override the personalities and writing styles of the human authors. Instead, He worked through their individual styles and backgrounds to produce a text that was both divine and human, much like the person of Christ Himself.

In this way, the language, genre, and style of the New Testament authors both reflect their unique contexts and testify to the divine inspiration of the Scripture as affirmed in 1 Thessalonians 2:13, " And we also thank God constantly for this, that when you **received the word of God**, which you heard from us, you accepted it not as the word of men but as what it really is, **the word of God**, which is at work in you believers. "

Responding to Claims of Pseudonymity and Forgery in New Testament Writings

The claims of pseudonymity and forgery often center around the New Testament epistles, particularly those attributed to Paul (Ephesians, Colossians, 2 Thessalonians, 1 & 2 Timothy, and Titus) as well as the Petrine epistles and others. Critics argue that these letters were written by followers of the apostles, using their names to lend authority to their words.

However, it is essential to understand the New Testament's claims for itself. For instance, in 2 Peter 1:16-21, Peter asserts the eyewitness and divine origin of his message: "For we did not follow cleverly devised stories when we told you about the coming of our Lord Jesus Christ in power, but we were eyewitnesses of his majesty... Above all, you must understand that no prophecy of Scripture came about by the prophet's own interpretation of things. For prophecy never had its origin in the human will, but prophets, though human, spoke from God as they were carried along by the Holy Spirit."

Paul also affirms his own authorship in many of his letters. In Galatians 1:1, Paul states, "Paul, an apostle—not from men nor through man, but through Jesus Christ and God the Father, who raised him from the dead."

From a biblical perspective, the New Testament writings were not just human compositions but were divinely inspired, as Paul stated in 2 Timothy 3:16, "All Scripture is breathed out by God..."

Moreover, there is no historical or biblical evidence that the New Testament authors were deceptive about their identities. In fact, the New Testament authors often faced severe persecution, even death, for their testimony (Acts 12:2; 2 Timothy 4:6-8), which indicates their deep conviction in the truth of their writings.

The early church was also rigorous in its canonization process, accepting only writings that were apostolic and orthodox in their teachings. The letters questioned by modern critics were accepted as authentic by early church leaders like Irenaeus, Clement of Alexandria, and Tertullian.

Therefore, while questions of pseudonymity and forgery are important to address, there is strong biblical and historical evidence affirming the authenticity and divine inspiration of the New Testament writings.

Conclusion: The New Testament Authors and the Message They Proclaimed

The New Testament authors, coming from diverse backgrounds and living in different social, political, and religious contexts, were moved by the Holy Spirit to convey God's message through their writings (2 Peter 1:21). Their experiences and perspectives not only enriched the New Testament text but also demonstrated how God's grace and truth transcended cultural and personal barriers.

The central message proclaimed by the New Testament authors is the life, death, and resurrection of Jesus Christ (1 Corinthians 15:3-4). Through Jesus, God offered humanity salvation and reconciliation (John 3:16; Romans 5:8). These authors testified to the transformative power of the gospel, not just in their own lives but also in the lives of those who received their message (Acts 4:13).

In their writings, the New Testament authors emphasized the importance of faith in Jesus Christ (Ephesians 2:8-9), love for God and others (Matthew 22:37-40), and the hope of eternal life (John 14:1-3). They encouraged believers to stand firm in their faith (Ephesians 6:10-18), to grow in spiritual maturity (Colossians 1:28), and to be prepared for Christ's return (1 Thessalonians 5:1-11).

By examining the lives and times of the New Testament authors, believers can better appreciate the richness and depth of their writings. This understanding, combined with a reliance on the Holy Spirit for guidance and wisdom (John 16:13), will enable believers to more effectively live out the message these authors proclaimed and, in doing so, glorify God and advance His kingdom on earth (Matthew 28:18-20).

CHAPTER 18 The New Testament's Impact: How Trustworthy Texts Shaped History

Introduction: The New Testament's Profound Influence on History

From its inception, the New Testament has had a profound influence on the course of human history. As the cornerstone of Christian faith, it has shaped the lives of individuals and societies alike, guiding moral principles, inspiring art and literature, and instigating social and political change.

In 2 Timothy 3:16-17, the apostle Paul writes, "All Scripture is God-breathed and is useful for teaching, rebuking, correcting and training in righteousness, so that the servant of God may be thoroughly equipped for every good work." This verse encapsulates the New Testament's purpose and influence, underscoring its role as a guide for moral and spiritual instruction.

A tangible example of its impact is seen in the formation of the early Christian communities. Acts 2:42-47 records the transformative power of the Gospel message, leading to the creation of a community marked by unity, generosity, and the shared commitment to the teachings of the apostles.

In a broader historical context, the New Testament's teachings on love, forgiveness, and the intrinsic value of every human life have fostered a sense of equality and justice, influencing legal systems, human rights, and social welfare. For instance, the principle of love and respect for all, as taught by Jesus in Matthew 22:39 ("...Love your neighbor as yourself."), has been foundational in the development of ethical norms and humanitarian efforts.

The New Testament's impact also extends to the intellectual and cultural sphere. It has inspired countless works of art, literature, and music, from the grandeur of Michelangelo's Sistine Chapel ceiling to the soul-stirring verses of John Milton's "Paradise Lost."

Therefore, the New Testament's influence on history is pervasive and profound, shaping not just personal faith but also the moral, social, and cultural fabric of societies. As the trustworthy Word of God, it continues to guide, inspire, and transform lives, echoing Hebrews 4:12, "For the word of God is alive and active. Sharper than any double-edged sword, it penetrates even to dividing soul and spirit, joints and marrow; it judges the thoughts and attitudes of the heart."

The Early Church: The Formation and Growth of Christianity

The formation and growth of early Christianity can be traced back to the teachings of the New Testament. The events, teachings, and principles outlined in these texts served as the foundation upon which the early Christian Church was built.

In Acts 2:41-47, the immediate aftermath of the Pentecost is described, marking the formation of the first Christian community. The passage records, "Those who accepted his message were baptized, and about three thousand were added to their number that day. They devoted themselves to the apostles' teaching and to fellowship, to the breaking of bread and to prayer... And the Lord added to their number daily those who were being saved."

This passage demonstrates the rapid growth of the early Church, grounded in the teachings of the apostles, communal fellowship, shared meals (which likely included the Lord's Supper), and prayer. The message of salvation through faith in Jesus Christ, central to the New Testament, was the driving force behind this growth.

Furthermore, the New Testament epistles (letters) give insight into the establishment and guidance of various early Christian communities. For instance, Paul's letters to the Corinthians, Ephesians, and Philippians, among others, address specific issues faced by these communities, providing teachings and counsel that would shape the development of Christian doctrine and practices.

These texts underscore the value of love, unity, humility, and service, as in Philippians 2:3-4, "Do nothing out of selfish ambition or vain conceit. Rather, in humility value others above yourselves, not looking to your own interests but each of you to the interests of the others." Principles such as these guided the ethos and behavior of early Christian communities, setting them apart in the Roman world and attracting others to the faith.

Thus, the New Testament played a crucial role in the formation and growth of early Christianity, providing theological teachings, moral guidance, and a model for communal life that fostered the rapid expansion of the faith.

The Persecution of Christians and the Triumph of the Faith

Persecution is a recurring theme in the New Testament, beginning with the persecution of Jesus Himself and extending to His followers. Jesus forewarned His disciples about this in John 15:20, stating, "Remember what I told you: 'A servant is not greater than his master.' If they persecuted me, they will persecute you also."

Following the death and resurrection of Jesus, the early Christians faced severe persecution, as detailed in the Book of Acts and the Epistles. The stoning of Stephen (Acts 7:54-60), the imprisonment of Peter (Acts 12:1-17), and the numerous hardships endured by Paul (2 Corinthians 11:23-27) illustrate the hostile environment in which the early Church grew.

Despite this, the New Testament consistently conveys a message of hope and perseverance in the face of persecution. Romans 8:35-39 affirms that no hardship can separate believers from the love of God, while 2 Timothy 3:12 reminds readers that those who live a godly life will face persecution. This understanding of suffering as an aspect of Christian life provided the early Church with the resilience to endure and even grow amidst persecution.

The resilience of the early Christians and the power of their message ultimately led to the 'triumph' of Christianity, as it spread throughout the Roman Empire and beyond, despite the attempts to suppress it. In the face of death, Christians held fast to their faith, exemplifying Paul's words in Philippians 1:21, "For to me, to live is Christ and to die is gain."

The New Testament texts, therefore, not only document the persecution faced by the early Christians but also provide the spiritual resources that enabled them to endure and overcome these trials. Their steadfast faith in the face of persecution served as a powerful witness, contributing to the growth and eventual acceptance of Christianity within the Roman Empire.

The Development of Christian Doctrine: Creeds, Councils, and Controversies

The New Testament itself does not chronicle the development of Christian doctrine in the centuries following the apostolic era, but its texts serve as the foundational basis for these developments. As controversies and heresies arose, the early Church looked to the teachings of Jesus and the apostles in the New Testament to clarify and articulate its beliefs.

The Creeds: The Apostle's Creed and Nicene Creed, developed in the early centuries of the Church, summarize key Christian beliefs in the Trinity and the person of Christ. They echo the teachings of the New Testament. For instance, the Apostle's Creed's assertion "I believe in Jesus Christ, God's only Son, our Lord" aligns with John 3:16, "For God so loved the world that he gave his one and only Son, that whoever believes in him shall not perish but have eternal life."

Councils: Major councils of the Church, such as the Council of Nicaea (325 AD) and Council of Chalcedon (451 CE), were convened to settle major doctrinal disputes. For instance, the Council of Nicaea dealt with Arianism, a heresy that denied the full divinity of Christ. The council affirmed the New Testament teaching that Jesus is fully divine, as stated in verses like John 1:1, "In the beginning was the Word, and the Word was with God, and the Word was God."

Controversies: Various controversies throughout history have necessitated a return to the New Testament texts to affirm orthodox Christian beliefs. For instance, the New Testament's teachings on grace and faith became central during the Protestant Reformation. Ephesians 2:8-9 says, "For it is by grace you have been saved, through faith—and this is not from yourselves, it is the gift of God—not by works, so that no one can boast." This verse became a key scriptural basis for the doctrine of justification by faith alone.

Thus, the New Testament has played a crucial role in the development of Christian doctrine. Through creeds, councils, and controversies, the early Church used the New Testament as the authoritative source for defining and defending the core tenets of the Christian faith.

The Role of the New Testament in Shaping Christian Worship and Liturgy

The New Testament provides the core principles and practices that have shaped Christian worship and liturgy throughout history.

Worship: Worship in the New Testament is primarily focused on glorifying God through Jesus Christ. Colossians 3:16-17 emphasizes this, "Let the word of Christ dwell in you richly, teaching and admonishing one another in all wisdom, singing psalms and hymns and spiritual songs, with thankfulness in your hearts to God. And whatever you do, in word or deed, do everything in the name of the Lord Jesus, giving thanks to God the Father through him." This focus on Christ-centered worship is a defining feature of Christian liturgy.

The Lord's Supper (Eucharist): One of the key practices in Christian worship is the celebration of the Lord's Supper, also known as Communion or the Eucharist. This practice is based on the Last Supper, as Jesus instructed in 1 Corinthians 11:24-25, "And when he had given thanks, he broke it, and said, 'This is my body which is for you. Do this in remembrance of me.' In the same way also he took the cup, after supper, saying, 'This cup is the new covenant in my blood. Do this, as often as you drink it, in remembrance of me.'"

Baptism: Baptism is another significant aspect of Christian worship, marking the initiation of a believer into the faith. The practice is rooted in the Great Commission in Matthew 28:19, where Jesus instructs, "Go therefore and make disciples of all nations, baptizing them in the name of the Father and of the Son and of the Holy Spirit."

Prayer: The New Testament provides numerous examples and instructions on prayer, shaping the prayer life of Christian communities. In Philippians 4:6, Paul writes, "Do not be anxious about anything, but in everything by prayer and supplication with thanksgiving let your requests be made known to God."

Reading and Preaching of the Word: The public reading of Scripture, followed by preaching, is a key component of Christian liturgy, as indicated in 1 Timothy 4:13, "Until I come, devote yourself to the public reading of Scripture, to exhortation, to teaching."

Hence, the New Testament has fundamentally shaped Christian worship and liturgy, providing the basis for key practices such as the Lord's Supper, baptism, prayer, and the reading and preaching of God's Word. These practices have helped Christians throughout history to focus their worship on God, remember the work of Christ, express their faith, and learn from the teachings of Scripture.

The New Testament's Impact on Art, Architecture, and Music

The influence of the New Testament on art, architecture, and music has been profound and pervasive throughout history, with countless works of art, architectural designs, and musical compositions rooted in its teachings and narratives.

Art: Many iconic works of art derive their themes and subjects directly from the New Testament. For instance, Leonardo da Vinci's "The Last Supper," depicts the scene from John 13 where Jesus has His final meal with His disciples before His crucifixion. Another example is Rembrandt's "The Prodigal Son," inspired by the parable in Luke 15:11-32. In these and countless other works, artists have used their craft to visualize and interpret New Testament stories and themes.

Architecture: Christian architecture, too, has been heavily influenced by the New Testament. Churches and cathedrals around the world are designed to facilitate practices and observances mentioned in the New Testament. For example, the presence of baptismal fonts or immersion pools in many churches reflects the importance of baptism, a practice that originates from the Great Commission in Matthew 28:19. The architectural design of the altar area in many churches references the Last Supper (1 Corinthians 11:24-26).

Music: The New Testament's influence is also evident in music, particularly in hymnody and choral music. Many hymns and songs are based on the Psalms, but also on specific New Testament passages. For example, the famous hymn "Amazing Grace" reflects the themes of redemption and grace that are central to the New Testament, particularly in books like Romans and Ephesians. In the realm of classical music, Handel's "Messiah" is a prime example of the New Testament's impact, as it sets passages directly from the King James Bible, including many from the New Testament, to music.

Thus, the New Testament has had a significant impact on art, architecture, and music, providing inspiration and thematic material for artists, architects, and composers throughout history. This impact reflects the New Testament's central role in Christian thought and culture and underscores the enduring relevance of its teachings and narratives.

The Bible and the Founding of Educational Institutions: From Monasteries to Universities

The New Testament, as part of the larger Christian Bible, has played an influential role in the founding and operation of educational institutions throughout history, from monastic schools to universities.

Monasteries: Monastic orders, which were largely inspired by New Testament principles, played a crucial role in education during the Middle Ages. Monks devoted themselves to a life of prayer, study, and work, echoing the teachings of Paul in 1 Thessalonians 4:11, "Make it your ambition to lead a quiet life: You should mind your own business and work with your hands." As part of their work, many monks copied manuscripts, preserving not only religious texts but also many classical Greek and Roman works. Monasteries often ran schools to educate young boys, many of whom would later become monks themselves.

Universities: The New Testament also played a significant role in the founding and curriculum of many of the world's earliest universities. Universities such as

Oxford, Cambridge, and the University of Paris were originally Christian institutions, where theology was a primary subject of study. The New Testament, as a foundational Christian text, was central to these studies. The encouragement to seek wisdom found throughout the New Testament, such as in James 1:5, "If any of you lacks wisdom, you should ask God, who gives generously to all without finding fault, and it will be given to you," inspired many early academics in their pursuit of knowledge.

Curriculum: The New Testament itself has often been a subject of study in these institutions. Scholars have studied it in its original languages for centuries, seeking to understand its message and implications for life and faith. The emphasis on teaching found in the New Testament, such as in Matthew 28:19-20, "Therefore go and make disciples of all nations, baptizing them in the name of the Father and of the Son and of the Holy Spirit, and teaching them to obey everything I have commanded you," has inspired the mission of countless Christian educational institutions.

Overall, the principles and teachings of the New Testament have significantly shaped the development of educational institutions throughout history, from the monastic schools of the Middle Ages to modern universities. The New Testament has not only been a subject of study but also a guiding influence on the values and goals of these institutions.

The New Testament and the Moral Transformation of Society

The New Testament has played a pivotal role in the moral transformation of societies across history, impacting a wide range of areas from human rights to law and ethics.

Human Rights and Dignity: The New Testament's teachings on the intrinsic value and worth of every individual, regardless of status, have profoundly shaped societal understandings of human rights. In Galatians 3:28, Paul writes, "There is neither Jew nor Gentile, neither slave nor free, nor is there male and female, for you are all one in Christ Jesus." This declaration of universal equality has inspired movements for social justice and human rights throughout history.

Law and Ethics: New Testament principles have also influenced the development of legal systems and ethical codes. Jesus' command to "So in everything, do to others what you would have them do to you, for this sums up the Law and the Prophets" (Matthew 7:12), often referred to as the Golden Rule, has been foundational in constructing ethical standards that value respect, empathy, and justice.

Compassion and Charity: The New Testament's emphasis on compassion and charity has led to the establishment of countless humanitarian organizations and initiatives. Jesus' Parable of the Good Samaritan (Luke 10:25-37) underscores the importance of helping those in need, regardless of their identity or circumstances. This has been a driving force behind efforts to alleviate poverty, combat disease, and provide relief in times of disaster.

Peace and Reconciliation: The New Testament's teachings on forgiveness, reconciliation, and peace have likewise been instrumental in efforts to resolve conflicts and heal divisions within societies. Jesus' Sermon on the Mount (Matthew 5-7), where He said, "Blessed are the peacemakers, for they will be called children of God" (Matthew 5:9), has inspired countless individuals and movements working toward peace and reconciliation.

Sanctity of Life: The New Testament's affirmation of the sanctity of life, as expressed in passages such as John 10:10, "The thief comes only to steal and kill and destroy; I have come that they may have life, and have it to the full," has influenced societal views on issues such as abortion, euthanasia, and capital punishment.

In conclusion, the New Testament has played a vital role in shaping societal norms and values, promoting a moral transformation that values human dignity, justice, compassion, peace, and the sanctity of life. The influence of the New Testament on moral transformation is a testament to its enduring power and relevance throughout history.

The Reformation: Sola Scriptura and the Return to the New Testament

The Protestant Reformation, which occurred in the 16th century, marked a significant turning point in the history of Christianity. One of the core principles that emerged from this period was "Sola Scriptura," a Latin phrase meaning "Scripture Alone." This principle asserted that the Bible, and particularly the New Testament, is the ultimate authority for Christian faith and practice.

The Authority of Scripture: The concept of Sola Scriptura is anchored in verses like 2 Timothy 3:16-17, "All Scripture is God-breathed and is useful for teaching, rebuking, correcting and training in righteousness, so that the servant of God may be thoroughly equipped for every good work." This passage was used by Reformers to underscore the sufficiency and authority of Scripture.

Justification by Faith Alone: The doctrine of justification by faith alone, or "Sola Fide," is a key New Testament teaching that was reclaimed during the Reformation. This belief is grounded in verses like Romans 3:28, where Paul states, "For we maintain that a person is justified by faith apart from the works of the law."

Priesthood of All Believers: The Reformation also emphasized the "priesthood of all believers," a concept based on verses like 1 Peter 2:9, "But you are a chosen people, a royal priesthood, a holy nation, God's special possession, that you may declare the praises of him who called you out of darkness into his wonderful light."

This principle highlighted the accessibility of God's grace to all believers and undermined the hierarchical structure that had previously dominated the church.

The Centrality of Christ: The Reformation re-emphasized the centrality of Christ in Christian faith, grounded in verses like John 14:6, "Jesus answered, 'I am the way and the truth and the life. No one comes to the Father except through me.'" This led to a renewed focus on the person and work of Jesus Christ as depicted in the New Testament.

In conclusion, the Reformation represented a return to the New Testament's teachings, restoring principles such as the authority of Scripture, justification by faith alone, the priesthood of all believers, and the centrality of Christ. The impact of these reforms continues to shape Christian theology and practice today.

The Missionary Movement: Taking the Gospel to the Ends of the Earth

The missionary movement has been a key part of Christian history and the expansion of the faith worldwide. This endeavor is rooted in the commands and examples given in the New Testament, particularly in the ministry of the Apostle Paul and Jesus's Great Commission.

The Great Commission: In Matthew 28:19-20, Jesus commands His followers, "Go therefore and make disciples of all nations, baptizing them in the name of the Father and of the Son and of the Holy Spirit, teaching them to observe all that I have commanded you." This directive has served as a key impetus for the missionary movement throughout history, prompting Christians to spread their faith across the globe.

The Apostle Paul: The Apostle Paul's missionary journeys, as recorded in the book of Acts, also serve as a critical example for the missionary movement. Paul, once a persecutor of Christians, became one of the most prolific missionaries in the early church, taking the Gospel message to numerous cities throughout the Roman Empire (Acts 13-28). His writings continue to guide missionary work today.

The Power of the Gospel: Romans 1:16, where Paul declares, "For I am not ashamed of the gospel, for it is the power of God for salvation to everyone who believes," underscores the motivation behind missionary work. The belief in the transformative power of the Gospel drives the missionary movement, encouraging believers to share this message of salvation.

The Scope of the Mission: The call to reach all nations is also echoed in Revelation 7:9, which envisions a multitude from "every nation, from all tribes and peoples and languages" standing before God's throne. This passage illustrates the universal scope of the Christian message and the goal of the missionary movement.

In conclusion, the missionary movement, inspired and directed by the New Testament, has had a profound impact on the course of Christian history. Through the commitment and dedication of countless individuals and organizations, the Gospel message has been carried to virtually every corner of the globe.

The New Testament's Influence on Social Reforms and Human Rights Movements

The principles and teachings found in the New Testament have played a significant role in inspiring and guiding various social reforms and human rights movements. These movements, motivated by the concepts of love, justice, and equality presented in the scriptures, seek to improve the lives of individuals and communities.

Love and Compassion: The New Testament is filled with exhortations to love and care for others. Jesus Himself declared the second greatest commandment to be "Love your neighbor as yourself" (Mark 12:31). He also shared the parable of the Good Samaritan (Luke 10:25-37), demonstrating that our "neighbor" includes everyone, even those different from us.

Equality and Justice: The principle of equality is emphasized in scriptures such as Galatians 3:28, which states, "There is neither Jew nor Greek, there is neither slave nor free, there is no male and female, for you are all one in Christ Jesus." Also, in James 2:1-9, favoritism and discrimination are condemned, and fair treatment of all, regardless of their status, is encouraged.

Care for the Poor: While the New Testament encourages personal responsibility, it also strongly advocates for caring for the needy. Passages such as James 1:27, which says "Religion that God our Father accepts as pure and faultless is this: to look after orphans and widows in their distress," show a call to action to assist those in need, providing a "hand up" rather than a "hand out."

Freedom and Dignity: The New Testament also values human dignity and freedom. For instance, Paul writes in Galatians 5:1, "For freedom Christ has set us free; stand firm therefore, and do not submit again to a yoke of slavery."

These principles have inspired many to champion social reforms and human rights movements. However, it is crucial to differentiate between advocating for justice and dignity for all people, and supporting ideologies that may contradict the Bible's teachings. The New Testament calls for transformation of individuals and societies, but this transformation is to be in line with God's standards, not those of the world.

Edward D. Andrews

The Role of the New Testament in Shaping Political Thought and Government

The New Testament teachings have had a profound impact on political thought and the structure of government over the centuries, both directly and indirectly. Here are a few examples:

The principle of human dignity and equality: In Galatians 3:28, Paul writes, "There is neither Jew nor Greek, there is neither slave nor free, there is no male and female, for you are all one in Christ Jesus." This principle has been influential in shaping political ideologies and systems that emphasize human rights, equality, and justice.

The separation of spiritual and temporal authority: When confronted about paying taxes to the Roman Emperor, Jesus said, "Render to Caesar the things that are Caesar's, and to God the things that are God's" (Mark 12:17). This statement has often been interpreted as an endorsement of the separation of church and state, leading to the development of political systems that allow religious freedom and limit the interference of the state in religious affairs.

The concept of servant leadership: Jesus taught His disciples, "You know that the rulers of the Gentiles lord it over them, and their high officials exercise authority over them. Not so with you. Instead, whoever wants to become great among you must be your servant" (Matthew 20:25-26). This teaching has influenced political philosophies that emphasize the role of leaders as servants of the people, rather than rulers over them.

The notion of law and order: In Romans 13:1-7, Paul instructs Christians to submit to governing authorities, as they are instituted by God for maintaining order and justice. This passage has been influential in shaping political systems that uphold law and order, and respect for authority.

The value of peace: The New Testament repeatedly emphasizes the value of peace. Jesus said, "Blessed are the peacemakers, for they will be called children of God" (Matthew 5:9). This teaching has influenced political efforts towards peace and reconciliation, both within nations and in the international community.

Voting and Democratic Participation: The New Testament encourages believers to pray for their leaders and to live peaceably within their societies. In 1 Timothy 2:1-2, Paul writes, "First of all, then, I urge that supplications, prayers, intercessions, and thanksgivings be made for all people, for kings and all who are in high positions, that we may lead a peaceful and quiet life, godly and dignified in every way." This instruction implies an engagement with the political process and the leaders who govern. By extension, it can be understood to suggest that Christians should actively participate in selecting their leaders through voting, always seeking those who would uphold principles of religious freedom and Christian values, thereby facilitating a peaceful environment for evangelism and the practice of the Christian faith. However, it's important to note that the New Testament does not explicitly discuss voting or democratic processes, as these were not common political practices during the time the texts were written.

In all these ways, the New Testament has shaped political thought and government over the centuries. However, it's important to note that the Bible's teachings are often interpreted and applied differently in different political contexts. It's also important to recognize that while the Bible can influence political thought, it is primarily a guide for personal faith and conduct, not a manual for political governance.

The New Testament and the Development of Modern Science

While the New Testament is not a scientific document, its teachings and underlying worldview have indirectly contributed to the development of modern science. Here are some of the ways:

1. **The belief in a rational and orderly universe**: The New Testament, like the Old, presents a view of the universe as the creation of a rational God. This belief in an orderly cosmos, governed by consistent laws, provided a philosophical foundation for the scientific method. Hebrews 1:3 states that Christ "upholds the universe by the word of His power," suggesting a stable, orderly universe maintained by God's continual activity.

2. **The value of human life and the physical world**: The New Testament affirms the goodness and value of physical life and the material world, which motivated many early scientists to study the natural world in order to benefit humanity. For example, in Matthew 10:31, Jesus says, "Fear not, therefore; you are of more value than many sparrows," affirming the intrinsic value of human life.

3. **The principle of humility and the pursuit of truth**: The New Testament emphasizes humility and the pursuit of truth. In 1 Corinthians 8:2, Paul notes that "if anyone imagines that he knows something, he does not yet know as he ought to know." This humility and openness to new truth can be seen as parallel to the scientific method, which is based on the idea that our understanding of the world is always growing and changing, and that we must be open to new evidence and ideas.

4. **The compatibility of faith and reason**: The New Testament presents faith and reason as compatible, not contradictory. This can be seen in passages like Luke 1:1-4, where Luke explains that he has "carefully investigated everything

from the beginning" in order to write an "orderly account" of the events of Jesus' life. This suggests a compatibility between faith and careful, rational investigation – a principle that has been important in the development of science.

It's important to note that while the New Testament has indirectly influenced the development of science, it is not a scientific textbook. Its primary purpose is to reveal God and His redemptive work in Christ, not to provide a detailed explanation of natural phenomena. Nevertheless, the worldview it presents has been instrumental in fostering a context in which scientific exploration could flourish.

The New Testament's Impact on Language, Literature, and Popular Culture

The New Testament has undeniably had a profound influence on language, literature, and popular culture. Many common phrases and expressions in English and other languages are derived from the New Testament. For example, the phrase "the blind leading the blind" comes from Jesus' teaching in Matthew 15:14, "Let them alone: they be blind leaders of the blind. And if the blind lead the blind, both shall fall into the ditch."

In the realm of literature, countless works have been influenced by the themes, characters, and stories found in the New Testament. For instance, the parables of Jesus have been retold and reinterpreted in many forms of literature and drama. Similarly, the themes of redemption, sacrifice, and forgiveness in the New Testament have provided inspiration for countless novels, plays, and poems.

In popular culture, the New Testament has influenced film, music, visual art, and more. The life of Jesus has been depicted in numerous films, and the themes of the New Testament have been explored in countless songs across a variety of genres. The influence of the New Testament can also be seen in the visual arts, from Renaissance paintings to modern graphic novels.

Finally, the moral teachings of the New Testament have shaped societal norms and customs. Concepts such as the Golden Rule ("Do unto others as you would have them do unto you," Matthew 7:12), have been integrated into the moral fabric of many societies.

The New Testament's influence on language, literature, and popular culture testifies to its enduring relevance and its power to speak to all areas of human life.

Responding to Criticisms and Misconceptions about the New Testament's Influence

There have been criticisms and misconceptions about the New Testament's influence throughout history. Some of these criticisms are based on misinterpretations of its teachings, while others come from a misunderstanding of historical events or the actions of certain individuals or groups who claimed to be acting in the name of Christianity.

One common criticism is that the New Testament teachings have been used to justify violence and oppression. While it is true that individuals and groups have misused the New Testament in this way, it is important to note that such actions are contrary to the central teachings of Jesus. In Matthew 22:37-39, Jesus taught the two greatest commandments: "Love the Lord your God with all your heart and with all your soul and with all your mind. This is the first and greatest commandment. And the second is like it: Love your neighbor as yourself." Violence and oppression clearly violate these commandments.

Another misconception is that the New Testament promotes intolerance or exclusivity. In response to this, one can point to the teachings of Paul in Galatians 3:28, "There is neither Jew nor Gentile, neither slave nor free, nor is there male and female, for you are all one in Christ Jesus." This verse emphasizes the inclusivity of the Gospel and the equal value of all people in the sight of God.

Some critics also argue that the New Testament has been used to suppress scientific progress. However, this view overlooks the many Christian thinkers who have contributed significantly to the sciences and the fact that many foundational principles of scientific inquiry are compatible with Christian belief. In Romans 1:20, Paul wrote: "For since the creation of the world God's invisible qualities—his eternal power and divine nature—have been clearly seen, being understood from what has been made, so that people are without excuse." This verse suggests that studying the natural world can lead to a greater understanding of God's character, supporting the pursuit of scientific knowledge.

In responding to criticisms and misconceptions, it is essential to differentiate between the teachings of the New Testament itself and the ways those teachings have been interpreted and applied throughout history. While it is undeniable that there have been instances of misuse and misinterpretation, these do not diminish the profound positive impact of the New Testament's teachings when understood and applied correctly.

Conclusion: The Trustworthiness of the New Testament and Its Lasting Legacy

The New Testament's lasting legacy is a testament to its trustworthiness and the profound truths it carries. From the formation of the early church to the shaping of modern society, its influence is evident in nearly every aspect of human history and culture.

The New Testament presents the life, death, and resurrection of Jesus Christ, and the teachings He and His apostles provided for humanity. These messages have touched billions of people throughout the centuries, transforming individual lives and societies.

The central message of the New Testament is the Gospel of Jesus Christ, a message of salvation and hope for all people. This is perhaps best summarized by John 3:16: "For God so loved the world, that he gave his only Son, that whoever believes in him should not perish but have eternal life." This transformative message has offered hope and purpose to countless individuals throughout history.

The apostle Paul, writing to his protégé Timothy, emphasized the trustworthiness of the Scripture in 2 Timothy 3:16-17: "All Scripture is God-breathed and is useful for teaching, rebuking, correcting and training in righteousness, so that the servant of God may be thoroughly equipped for every good work." This verse underscores the conviction that the New Testament, as part of the Holy Scripture, is not a mere human product, but rather, it is inspired by God Himself and serves as a reliable guide for faith and practice.

The influence of the New Testament has not been confined to religious settings. It has played a critical role in the development of legal and educational systems, inspired countless works of art and literature, shaped political philosophies, and underpinned significant advances in science and technology.

In the face of criticisms and challenges, the New Testament has proven its resilience and relevance. Its teachings continue to provide guidance and solace in a rapidly changing world, and its principles remain foundational to the pursuit of justice, peace, and love.

The trustworthiness of the New Testament and its lasting legacy are evidence of its divine origin. As the Word of God, it carries a timeless message that continues to resonate with humanity and shape the course of history.

APPENDIX A What Are Textual Variants and How Many Are There?

The first part of this chapter will cover the gist of what is most often discussed in New Testament textual criticism today. After that, we will discuss what should be the primary focus of NTTC (New Testament Textual Criticism). It would seem that Bart D. Ehrman and other Bible critics of his persuasion have sent many textual scholars on a quest. These scholars have become obsessed with discussing how many variants there are, how to count the textual variants, and whether they are significant or insignificant. Below, we will cover what is being said about variants and whether some are more significant than others, and then close the chapter with what actually is the most important mission in NTTC.

Some Bible critics seem, to begin with, the belief that if God inspired the originals and they were fully inerrant, the subsequent copies must continue to be inerrant for the inerrancy of the originals to have value. They seem to be asking, "If only the originals were inspired, and the copies were not inspired, and we do not have the originals, how are we to be certain of any passage in Scripture?" In other words, God would never allow the inspired, inerrant Word to suffer copying errors. Why would he perform the miracle of inspiring the message to be fully inerrant and not continue with the miracle of inspiring the copyists throughout the centuries to keep it inerrant? First, we must acknowledge that God has not given us the specifics of every decision he has made in reference to humans. If we begin asking, "Why did God not do this or do that," where would it end? For example, why didn't God just produce the books himself and miraculously deliver them to people as he gave the commandments to Moses? Instead of using humans, why did he not use angelic messengers to pen the message, or produce the message miraculously? God has chosen not to tell us why he did not move the copyists along with the Holy Spirit, so as to have perfect copies, and it remains an unknown. However, it should be noted that if we can restore the text to its original wording through the science of textual criticism, i.e. to an exact representation thereof, we have, in essence, the originals.

We do know that the Jewish copyists and later Christian copyists were not infallible as were the original writers. The Holy Spirit inspired the original writers, while the most that can be said about the copyists is that the Holy Spirit **guided** them. However, do we not have a treasure-load of evidence from centuries of copies, unlike ancient secular literature? Regardless of the recopying, do we not have the Bible in a reliable critical text and trustworthy translations, with both improving all the time? It was only inevitable that imperfect copyists, who were not under inspiration, would cause errors to creep into the text. However, the thousands of copies that we have enable textual scholars to identify and reject these errors. How? For one thing, different copyists made different errors. Therefore, the textual scholar compares the work of different copyists. He is then able to identify their mistakes.

A Simple Example

Suppose 100 people were invited or hired to make a handwritten copy of Matthew's Gospel, with 18,345 words. Further, suppose that these people fit in one of four categories as writers: **(1)** struggle to write and have no experience as a document maker; **(2)** skilled document makers (recorders of events, wills, business, certificates, etc.); **(3)** trained copyists of literature; and **(4)** the professional copyists. There is little doubt that these copyists would make some copying errors, even the professionals. However, it would be impossible that they would all make the same errors. Suppose a trained textual scholar with many years of religious education, including textual studies and decades of experience, was to compare the 100 documents carefully. In that case, he could identify the errors and restore the text to its original form, even if he had never seen that original.

The textual scholars of the last 250 years, especially the last 70 years, have had 5,000+ and now over 5,898 Greek manuscripts at their disposal. A number of the manuscripts are portions dating to the second and third centuries C.E. Moreover, more manuscripts are always becoming known; technology is ever advancing, and improvements are always being made.

Hundreds of scholars throughout the last three centuries have produced what we might call a master text through lifetimes of hard work and careful study. Are there places where we are not certain of the reading? Yes, of course. However, we are considering very infrequent places in the Greek NT text containing about 138,020 words, which would be considered difficult to arrive at what the original reading was. In all these places, the alternative readings are provided in the apparatus. Bible critics who exaggerate the extent of errors are misleading the public on several fronts. First, some copies are almost error-free and negate the critics, who claim, "We have only error-ridden copies."[141] Second, the vast majority of the Greek New Testament has no scribal errors. Third, textual scholarship can easily identify and correct the majority of the scribal errors. In addition, of the remaining errors, we can still say most are solved with satisfaction. Of the small number of scribal errors remaining, we can say that most are solved with some difficulty, and there remain very few errors of which textual scholarship continues to be uncertain about the original reading at this time.

400,000 to 500,000 Supposed Variants in the Manuscripts

With this abundance of evidence, what can we say about the total number of variants known today? Scholars differ significantly in their estimates—some say there are 200,000 variants known, some say 300,000, some say **400,000 or more!** We do not know for sure because, despite impressive developments in computer technology, no one has yet been able to count them all. Perhaps, as I indicated earlier, it is best simply to leave the matter in comparative terms. There are more variations among our manuscripts than there are words in the New Testament.[142]

Bart D. Ehrman has some favorite, unprofessional ways of describing the problems, which he stresses without qualification, in every interview he has for a lay audience or seminary students. Below are several, the first two from the quotation above:

- Scholars differ significantly in their estimates—some say there are 200,000 variants known, some say 300,000, some say **400,000 or more**!

- There are **more variations** among our manuscripts **than there are words** in the New Testament.

- We have only **error-ridden copies**, and the vast majority of these are centuries removed from the originals and different from them, evidently, in thousands of ways. (*Whose Word is It*, 7)

- We don't even have copies of the copies of the originals, or **copies of the copies of the copies of the originals**. (*Misquoting Jesus*, 10)

- **In the early Christian centuries, scribes were amateurs** and as such were more inclined to alter the texts they copied. (*Misquoting Jesus*, 98)

---

[141] (Bart D. Ehrman, Misquoting Jesus: The Story Behind Who Changed the Bible and Why 2005, 7)
[142] Ibid., 89-90

- **We could go on nearly forever** talking about specific places in which the texts of the New Testament came to be changed, either accidentally or intentionally. (*Misquoting Jesus*, 98)
- The Bible began to appear to me as a very **human book**. (*Misquoting Jesus*, 11)

Each of the bullet points above claimed by Ehrman can be categorized as an exaggeration, misinformation, misleading, or just a failure to be truthful. Many laypersons-churchgoers have been spiritually shipwrecked in their faith by such unexplained hype. What the uninformed person hears is that we can never get back to the originals or even close, that there are hundreds of thousands of significant variants that have so scarred the text, we no longer have the Word of God, and it is merely the word of man. How such a knowledgeable man cannot know the impact his words are having is beyond this author.

Miscounting Textual Variants

In 1963, Neil R. Lightfoot penned a book that has served to help over a million readers, *How We Got the Bible*. It has been revised two times since 1963, once in 1988, and again in 2003. There is a "miscalculation" in the book which has contributed to a misunderstanding in how textual variants are counted. In fact, there are several other books repeating it. A leading textual scholar, Daniel B. Wallace, has brought this to our attention in an article entitled, *The Number of Textual Variants an Evangelical Miscalculation*.[143] World-renowned Bible apologist Norman L. Geisler has commented on it as well.

Lightfoot wrote,

> From one point of view, it may be said that there are 200,000 scribal errors in the manuscripts. Indeed, the number may well considerably exceed this and obviously will grow, as more and more manuscripts become known. However, it is wholly misleading and untrue to say that there are 200,000 errors in the text of the New Testament. (Actually, textual critics consciously avoid the word "error;" they prefer to speak of "textual variants.") This large number is gained by counting all the variations in all of the manuscripts (5,898). This means that if, for example, one word is misspelled in 4,000 different manuscripts, and it amounts to 4,000 "errors." Actually, in a case of this kind, only one slight error has been made, and it has been copied 4,000 times. But this is the procedure which is followed in arriving at the large number of 200,000 "errors."[144]

Wallace makes this observation in his article:

---

[143] http://bible.org/article/number-textual-variants-evangelical-miscalculation
[144] *How We Got the Bible* (Grand Rapids: Baker, 2003; p). Lightfoot says (53-54)

In other words, Lightfoot was claiming that textual variants are counted by the number of manuscripts that support such variants, rather than by the wording of the variants. This book has been widely influential in evangelical circles. I believe over a million copies of it have been sold. And this particular definition of textual variants has found its way into countless apologetic works." He goes on to clarify just what a textual variant is, "The problem is, the definition is wrong. Terribly wrong. A textual variant is simply any difference from a standard text (e.g., a printed text, a particular manuscript, etc.) that involves spelling, word order, omission, addition, substitution, or a total rewrite of the text. No textual critic defines a textual variant the way that Lightfoot and those who have followed him have done.

Geisler writes,

Some have estimated there are about 200,000 of them. First of all, these are not "errors" but variant readings, the vast majority of which are strictly grammatical. Second, these readings are spread throughout more than 5300 manuscripts, so that a variant spelling of one letter of one word in one verse in 2000 manuscripts is counted as 2000 "errors."[145]

Lightfoot evidently was thought to have erred by counting manuscripts rather than the variants in the text. In fairness to Lightfoot, it should be pointed out that he deplored the system of counting "errors" by the number of manuscripts, as the quotation above reveals. He was simply saying that critics were doing this, not that it was proper. It is difficult to see why Wallace would attribute responsibility for the system to Lightfoot. Also, Wallace cited Lightfoot's 1963 edition that did not include the distinction between "error" and "textual variant."

Let me offer the reader an example for our purposes. First, we should underscore a few important points raised: 1) we have so many variants because we have so many manuscripts. 2) We do *not* count the manuscripts; we count the variants. 3) A variant is any portion of the text that exhibits variations in its reading between two or more different manuscripts. This is more precisely called a **variation unit**. It is important to distinguish variation units from variant readings. Variation units are the places in the text where manuscripts disagree, and each variation unit has at least two variant readings. Setting the limits and range of a variation unit is sometimes difficult or even controversial because some variant readings affect others nearby. Such variations may be considered individually or as elements of a longer single reading.

We should also note that the terms "manuscript" and "witness" may appear to be used interchangeably in this context. Strictly speaking, "witness" (see below) only refers to the content of a given manuscript or fragment, so the witness predates the physical manuscript on which it is written to a greater or lesser extent. However, the

---

[145] *Baker Encyclopedia of Christian Apologetics*, by Norm Geisler (Grand Rapids: Baker, 1998; p. 532)

only way to reference the "witness" is by referring to the manuscript or fragment that contains it. In this book, we have sometimes used the terminology "witness *of* x or y manuscript" to distinguish the content in this way.

We begin by choosing our "base" or "standard text." We are primarily using the *standard text* (critical or master text), **N**estle-Aland (NA) Greek Text (28th edition), and the **U**nited Bible Society (UBS) Greek Text (5th edition). These two critical texts are the same. However, we also include the 1881 **W**estcott and **H**ort (WH) critical text. Therefore,

Note: When the acronym **NU** is used, **N** stands for **N**estle-Aland, the **U** for United Bible Societies, since the texts are the same. The apparatuses are different, and the UBS version is designed primarily for translators (more on this below). The acronym **WH** is for Westcott and Hort Greek text. Here is another opportunity to emphasize the documentary approach in making textual decisions, which is shown in the fact that about 155 variant decisions were made by the editors of the NU text when the preferred reading is found in the WH text. When we consider the WH NU texts, we can argue that we have a critical text that is a 99.99% reflection of the original.

In this writer's opinion, the critical WH NU texts are as close as we can get to what the original would have been like.[146] Therefore, we can use the reading in the critical text as the original reading, and anything outside of that in the manuscript history is a variant: spelling, word order, omission, addition, substitution, or a total rewrite of the text. Any difference in two different manuscripts is a variant, technically speaking.

Before going to our example, I want to emphasize that Bible critics, who grumble and repeat over and over again how there are 400,000+ variants in the text of the New Testament, have only one agenda: they want to discredit the Word of God. They use the issue of variants as a misrepresented excuse for their having lost their faith, having shipwrecked their faith, or having had no faith from the start. These Bible critics are no different from the religious leaders Jesus dealt with in the first century. Jesus said of them, "Blind guides! You strain out a gnat yet gulp down a camel!" (Matt. 23:24). They thrust aside 99.99 percent because 0.01 of one percent is not absolutely certain! Now let's turn to our example, which comes from the Apostle Paul's letter to the Colossians.

---

[146] It is true that some scholars, such as Philip Comfort, argue that the NU could be improved upon because in many cases it is too dependent on internal evidence, when the documentary evidence should be more of a consideration in choosing readings. It should be pointed out, however, that this is in only a relative handful of places, when one considers 138,020 words in the Greek New Testament, and it is hardly consequential. I would also mention that this writer would agree with Comfort in the matter of giving more weight to documentary evidence.

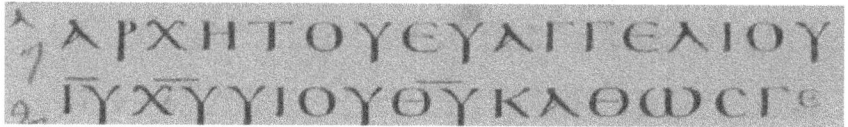

Nomina Sacra Mark 1.1_ Codex Vaticanus

Example of a Textual Variant

Colossians 2:2 Updated American Standard Version (UASV)

² that their hearts may be comforted, having been knit together in love, and into all riches of the full assurance of understanding, and that they may have a complete knowledge[147] of the mystery **of God**, namely **Christ**, [τοῦ θεοῦ Χριστοῦ; tou theou Christou]

See the chart below.

---

[147] *Epignosis* is a strengthened or intensified form of *gnosis* (*epi*, meaning "additional"), meaning, "true," "real," "full," "complete" or "accurate," depending upon the context. Paul and Peter alone use *epignosis*.

Variants	Variant	MSS or Versions
NU[148]	of the God of Christ	Standard Text
1	of the God	10 MSS[149]
2	of the Christ	1 MS
3	of the God who is Christ	4 MSS
4	of the God who is concerning Christ	2 MSS
5	Of the God in the Christ	2 MSS
6	of the God in the Christ Jesus	1 MS
7	of the God and Christ	1 MS
8	Of God the father Christ	4 MSS
9	Of God the father of Christ	5 MSS
10	Of God and Father of Christ	2 MSS
11	Of God father and of Christ	4 MSS
12	Of God father and of Christ Jesus	3 MSS
13	Of God father and of Lord of us Christ Jesus	2 MSS
14	Of God and father and of Christ	38 MSS
Total 14	14 Variants in 79 MSS	79 MSS

These variants are found in 79 MSS. Thus, we have 14 variants in 79 manuscripts, not 79 variants. We do not count manuscripts, as most textual scholars know. In trying to paint a picture about the trustworthiness of the text, this author does not think talking about variants is really helpful, and it can confuse the layperson. The churchgoer needs to know what a variant is and the general extent of the variants, but in the long run, it is the places in the text that are affected by variants that most matter and what we have as our text in the end.

The United Bible Society's "A" "B" "C" and "D" ratings are fine, and the definitions by UBS, i.e., [A] **certain**, [B] **almost certain**, [C] **difficulty in deciding**, and [D] **great difficulty in arriving at**, are helpful but should be better qualified, with some numbers of what percentage of the text fall under each area.

All Variant Units (Places)

What we need to talk about is how many **places** there are where we find variants. What percentage is this of the entire New Testament text?

---

[148] Recall that NU is an acronym for two critical manuscripts: (1) Nestle-Aland Greek Text (28th ed.) and (2) United Bible Societies Greek Text (5th ed.)

[149] This is only a partial list of the manuscripts, as we are just offering an example, to see how we count the variants.

We can then discuss:

- What percentage of the text is untouched by variants?
- Of the percentage affected, how much can we say or surmise to be given an "A" rating, a "B" Rating, a "C," or "D" rating?

Variant Reading and Variation Unit

This section is based in large part on the work by Eldon Jay Epp and Gordon D. Fee, *Studies in the Theory and Method of New Testament Textual Criticism* (Grand Rapids, MI: Eerdmans, 1993), wherein Eldon J. Epp expands on the brief 1964 article of Ernest C. Colwell (1901–74) and Ernest W. Tune on "Variant Readings: Classification and Use."

Again, we need to discuss how many variation units (places) there are where we find variations. Before doing so, let us define some terms.

SIGNIFICANT AND INSIGNIFICANT READINGS AND OR VARIANTS: Below, we have what are commonly described as significant and insignificant variants. *Significant* would mean any reading that has an impact on the transmission history of a variant unit. For example, it would apply to how we determine the relationship of the manuscripts to one another, such as where a particular manuscript would fall in the history and transmission of the manuscripts. It would also be impactful if the reading could help the textual scholar establish the original. Therefore, *insignificant* would mean just the opposite, referring to a reading with very little to no impact in *many* aspects of a transmission history. We stop at "many" aspects here because all readings in a manuscript play a role in some aspects of the transmission history, such as the characteristics of the manuscript it is in and the scribal activity within that individual manuscript.

Insignificant—Nonsense Reading: As Epp points out, a nonsense reading is "a reading that fails to make sense because it cannot be construed grammatically, either in terms of grammatical/lexical form or in terms of grammatical structure, or because in some other way it lacks a recognizable meaning. Since authors and scribes do not produce nonsense intentionally, it is to be assumed (1) that nonsense readings resulted from errors in transmission, (2) that they, therefore, cannot represent either the original text or the intended text of any MS or alert scribe, and (3) that they do not aid in the process of discerning the relationships among MSS."[150] It should also be stated that the original did not contain any nonsense readings, as the Holy Spirit led the writers. Before

---

[150] Eldon Jay Epp and Gordon D. Fee, *Studies in the Theory and Method of New Testament Textual Criticism* (Grand Rapids, MI: Eerdmans, 1993), 58.

publication, the inspired author would have corrected any error by a scribe such as Tertius or Silvanus.

Insignificant—Certainty of Scribal Errors: while these errors "can be construed grammatically and make sense," there is a certainty on the part of textual scholars that these are scribal errors. These are not nonsense readings but rather readings that make sense, which are scribal errors beyond all reasonable doubt. These would "be certain instances of haplography and dittography, cases of harmonization with similar contexts, hearing errors producing a similar-sounding word, and the transposition of letters or words with a resultant change in meaning."[151] The problem that we sometimes encounter here is that what may be listed as a *certainty* of the scribal error to one scholar may instead be an *almost certainty* to another, and even less so to another. The key element here in determining a reading that is understandable as insignificant is that it can be "demonstrated" so by the scholar making such a claim.

Insignificant—Incorrect Orthography (Greek for "correct writing"): this term is used loosely to refer to the spelling of words, which (for Greek) can include breathing and accent marks. Thus, one can refer to variations in the orthography of a word or even to incorrect orthography. When a variation in orthography is due merely to dialectical or historical changes in spelling for variant readings, the variations are often ignored in the decision process because the reading in question is identical to another reading, once the orthographical differences are factored in (*mutatis mutandis*). Epp writes, "Mere orthographic differences, particularly itacisms and nu-movables (as well as abbreviations) are 'insignificant' as here defined; they cannot be utilized in any decisive way for establishing manuscript relationships, and they are not substantive in the search for the original text. Again, the exception might be the work of a slavish scribe, whose scrupulousness might be considered useful in tracing manuscript descent, but the pervasive character of itacism, for example, over wide areas and time-spans precludes the 'significance' of orthographic differences for this important text-critical task."[152]

Insignificant—Singular Readings: a singular reading is technically a variant reading that occurs only once in only one Greek manuscript and is therefore immediately suspect. There is some quibbling over this because critics who reject the Westcott and Hort position on the combination of 01 (Sinaiticus) and 03 (Vaticanus) might call a reading "nearly singular" if it has only the support of these two manuscripts. Moreover, it is understood that not all manuscripts are comparable. Thus, for example, one would comfortably reject a reading found only in a single late manuscript, while many critics would not find it so easy to reject a reading supported uniquely by 03. Some also give more credit to singular readings that have additional support from versions. Singular

---

[151] Ibid. 58.

[152] Ibid. 58.

readings that are insignificant would be nonsense readings, transcriptional errors, meaningless transpositions, and itacisms.

Significant Variants: a *significant* reading/variant is any reading that has an impact on any major facet of the transmission history of a variant unit. One approach to identifying these is to remove the insignificant variants first: nonsense readings, determined (without doubt) scribal errors, incorrect orthography, and singular readings. Those readings that cannot be ruled out in this process are probably significant.

Number of Variants, Significant and Insignificant Variants vs. Level of Certainty

It would seem that some scholars have lost sight of the most important goal of textual criticism, namely, reconstructing the original. There is little doubt that agnostic Bible scholar Dr. Bart D. Ehrman has led the conversation on how many textual variants exist. The author of this publication is focusing their attention on the initial goal of textual criticism, returning to the original. We believe that even now, the Greek New Testament is entirely reliable. However, some 2,000 textual places within the New Testament need to be dealt with because the witnesses and internal evidence require consideration and deliberation.

Level of Certainty

The level of certainty charts below is generated from A TEXTUAL COMMENTARY ON THE GREEK NEW TESTAMENT (Second Edition), A Companion Volume to the UNITED BIBLE SOCIETIES' GREEK NEW TESTAMENT (Fourth Revised Edition) by Bruce M. Metzger.

The letter {A} signifies that the text is certain.

The letter {B} indicates that the text is almost certain.

The letter {C} indicates that the Committee had difficulty in deciding which variant to place in the text.

The letter {D}, which occurs only rarely, indicates that the Committee had great difficulty in arriving at a decision. In fact, among the {D} decisions sometimes none of the variant readings commended itself as original, and therefore the only recourse was to print the least unsatisfactory reading.

The Greek-English New Testament Interlinear (GENTI), Produced by Christian Publishing House, Cambridge, Ohio seeks to make a notable addition to the Greek-English Interlinear family by providing a text of the Greek New Testament that is based on the most recent research and is grounded in the earliest manuscript witnesses, to ascertain the original wording of the original texts.

TERMS AS TO HOW WE SHOULD OBJECTIVELY VIEW THE DEGREE OF CERTAINTY FOR THE READING ACCEPTED AS THE ORIGINAL by GENTI[153]

The modal verbs are **might** have been (30%), **may** have been (40%), **could** have been (55%), **would** have been (80%)**, must** have been (95%), which are used to show that we believe the originality of a reading is certain, probable or possible.

The letter **[WP]** stands for **Weak Possibility (30%)**, which indicates that this is low-level proof that the reading *might have been* original in that it is enough evidence to accept that the variant *might have been possible*, but it is improbable. We can say the reading **might** have been original, as there is *some evidence* that is derived from manuscripts that carry very little weight, early versions, or patristic quotations.

The letter **[P]** stands for **Plausible (40%)**, which indicates that this is low-level proof that the reading *may have been* original in that it is enough to accept a variant to be original, and we have enough evidence for our belief. The reading **may have** been original but is probably not so.

The letter **[PE]** stands for **Preponderance of Evidence (55%)**, which indicates that this is a higher-level proof that the reading *could have been* original in that it is enough to accept as such *unless another reading emerges as more probable*.

The letter **[CE]** stands for **Convincing Evidence (80%)**, which indicates that the evidence is an even higher-level proof that the reading *surely* was the original in that the evidence is enough to accept it as substantially *certain* unless proven otherwise.

The letter **[BRD]** stands for **Beyond Reasonable Doubt (95%)**, which indicates that this is the highest level of proof: the reading **must have been** original in that *there is no reason to doubt it*. It must be understood that feeling as though we *have no reason to doubt* is not the same as one hundred percent absolute certainty.

NOTE: This system is borrowed from the criminal just legal terms of the United States of America, the level of certainty involved in the use of modal verbs, and Bruce Metzger in his A Textual Commentary on the Greek New Testament (London; New York: United Bible Societies, 1994), who borrowed his system from Johann Albrecht Bengel in his edition of the Greek New Testament (Tübingen, 1734). **In addition**, the percentages are in no way attempting to be explicit, but instead, they are nothing more than a tool to give the non-textual scholar a sense of the degree of certainty. However, this does not mean the percentages are not reflective of the certainty.

---

[153] https://christianpublishinghouse.co/greek-english-interlinear/

The word count below is taken from the Nestle-Aland Novum Testamentum Graece using Logos Bible Software.[154] While this author has compiled the numbers regarding the level of certainty of readings from Metzger's Textual Commentary, he has not gone to the point of counting the letters or words at each variant place. We will just offer the reader the general statement that almost all textual variants in the commentary were based on a letter or a few letters in a Greek word, to two-three words. Seldom was it an entire sentence or verse, very rarely several verses like the long ending of Mark. Therefore, we have chosen three words as the average to multiply the total number of variants so that the reader can see the truly small number of variants that are even worthy of consideration instead of the total number of words in the New Testament. For example, Matthew has 18,346 words with a mere 153 places where we find variants selected for the GNT, affecting about 459 words.

We need to add and emphasize that the GNT editors selected all of the variants counted as relevant for translation, and the total does not include other variant units that were not considered relevant for that purpose. A good number of these additional variants can be found in the NA apparatus, but only with considerable difficulty in many cases because the same variants are frequently handled differently in the GNT and NA apparatuses. The author of this book does consider all variant units relevant even if a good number of them are difficult or virtually impossible to represent in translation (depending on the target language). We recommend that the reader adjust the figures offered below by multiplying the numbers of variants by a factor of two, which should compensate for any variants that are not reported in the GNT text. We see no reason to assume a significantly different outcome in the ratings that might have been assigned to these variants if they had been included in the GNT, except possibly where no decisions might be possible in the cases of competing readings that were fully acceptable (rather than difficult).

For readers who have a working knowledge of NT Greek, it may be informative simply to select a few random pages of corresponding text from the GNT and NA and compare the apparatuses to see what is missing from the GNT relative to the NA apparatus. We believe that our suggestion of multiplying the variant figures below by a factor of two will appear more than reasonable; however, even using a factor of three or four will still leave a relatively minute percentage of "C" and "D" readings, as revealed below.

So then, if we look at Matthew and first multiply the GNT variant units by three for an average of three words a variant, we have 459 words. Of the 153 variant units found in Matthew, we are certain of about 32 of them, almost certain about 70, have a little difficulty deciding on 50, and great difficulty deciding on only one variant unit. When we say that we have difficulty deciding, this does not mean that we cannot

---

[154] Word Counts for Every Book of the Bible ..., http://overviewbible.com/word-counts-books-of-bible/ (accessed April 20, 2017).

decide as we can. Moreover, a good translation will list the alternative reading in a footnote. So, in the entirety of the Gospel of Matthew, there is only one variant place (Matt 23:26) which we would count as about three out of 18,346 words, where there was great difficulty in deciding the original. As it turns out, in this case, the GNT apparatus handles it as a variant of eight words, while NA breaks it into two variants, thus illustrating our point about the difficulty of comparing the two apparatuses. Some translations have incorporated the variant (ESV, NASB, NIV, TNIV, NJB, and the NLT), viewing it as the original, while other translations (NRSV, NEB, REB, NAB, CSB, and the UASV) see the variant as an addition taken from the previous verse.

Matthew 23:26 Blind Pharisee, cleanse first the inside of the cup,[155] so that the outside of it may also become clean. (UASV)

NU has καθάρισον πρῶτον τὸ ἐντὸς τοῦ ποτηρίου, ἵνα γένηται καὶ τὸ ἐκτὸς αὐτοῦ καθαρόν "first cleanse the **inside of the cup, that the outside** of it may also become clean," which is supported by D Θ f¹ it^(a,c) syr^s (bold mine).

Variant/Byz WH καθαρισον πρωτον το εντος του ποτηριου και της παροψιδος ινα γενηται και το εκτος αυτων καθαρον have "first cleanse the **inside of the cup [and the dish], that the outside** of them may also become clean," which is supported by ℵ (B²) C L W 0102 0281 Maj.

Looking at the above support alone, it would seem that the witnesses for the longer reading ("and the dish") are weightier, making the longer reading the likely original. Then, when we consider the presence of a few manuscripts (B* f¹³ 28 *al*) that are not listed for the shorter reading because they have the longer reading ("and the dish"), the weight shifts over to the shorter reading's being the original. Why? Because these few manuscripts have the singular αυτου instead of αὐτῶν, even though they have the longer reading. This tells us that the archetype text was the shorter reading. Clearly, the copyist added ("and the dish") from the previous verse, Matthew 23:25, which reads, "Woe to you, scribes and Pharisees, hypocrites! because you cleanse **the outside of the cup and of the dish**, but inside they are full of greediness and self-indulgence."

Below, we will look at all of the numbers, the total words in the Greek New Testament, the number of A, B, C, and D variants in each book as they were selected by the GNT committee, followed by the total number of variants listed in Metzger's textual commentary.

---

[155] The NU (D Θ f¹ it^(a,c) syr^s) has the above reading. A variant, WH and Byz (ℵ (B²) C L W 0102 0281 Maj) add "and of the dish." The variant is an addition taken from the previous verse.

The Entire New Testament (138,020 Words)

{A-D}	New Testament
{A}	505
{B}	523
{C}	354
{D}	10
Total Var.	1,392
Words	138,020

The Gospels (64,767 Words)

{A-D}	Matt	Mark	Luke	John
{A}	32	45	44	44
{B}	70	49	73	62
{C}	50	45	44	41
{D}	1	1	0	2
Total Var.	153	140	161	149
Words	18,346	11,304	19,482	15,635

The Acts of the Apostles (18,450 Words)

{A-D}	Acts
{A}	74
{B}	82
{C}	40

{D}	1
Total Var.	197
Words	18,450

Paul's Fourteen Epistles (37,361 Words)

{A-D}	Rom	1 Cor	2 Cor	Gal.	Eph.	Php	Col.
{A}	39	21	12	16	16	10	8
{B}	19	22	17	3	11	7	12
{C}	20	15	10	8	7	3	8
{D}	1	1	0	0	0	0	0
Total Var.	79	59	39	27	34	20	28
WORDS	7,111	6,830	4,477	2,230	2,422	1,629	1,582

{A-D}	1 Th	2 Th	1 Tim	2 Tim	Tit	Phm.	Heb.
{A}	9	3	15	2	2	2	20
{B}	2	3	2	6	1	3	11
{C}	3	2	2	1	1	0	12
{D}	0	0	0	0	0	0	0
Total Var.	14	8	19	9	4	5	43
WORDS	1,481	823	1,591	1,238	659	335	4,953

The General Epistles (7,591 Words)

{A-D}	Jam	1 Pet	2 Pet	1 Jn	2 Jn	3 Jn	Jude
{A}	7	21	8	18	4	1	9
{B}	12	9	7	7	1	1	0
{C}	4	7	6	4	0	0	3
{D}	0	0	1	0	0	0	1
Total Var.	23	37	22	29	5	2	13
WORDS	1,742	1,684	1,099	2,141	245	219	461

The Book of Revelation (9,851 Words)

{A-D}	Revelation
{A}	23
{B}	31
{C}	18

{D}	1
Total Var.	73
Words	9,851

As noted above, the author of this publication maintains that all variation units or places where variations occur are significant because we are dealing with the Word of God, and reconstructing the original wording is of the utmost importance. Recall Lightfoot once more. "What about the significance of these variations? Are these variations immaterial, or are they important? What bearing do they have on the New Testament message and on faith? To respond to these questions, it will be helpful to introduce three types of textual variations, classified in relation to their significance for our present New Testament text. 1. Trivial variations which are of no consequence to the text. 2. Substantial variations which are of no consequence to the text. 3. Substantial variations that have a bearing on the text."**156**

Whether we are talking about the addition or omission of such words as "for," "and," and "the," or different forms of similar Greek words, differences in spelling, or the addition of a whole verse or even several verses, the importance lies **not with the significance of the impact** on the meaning of the text but rather **the certainty of the wording in the original**. What we want to focus on is the certainty level of reconstructing every single word that Matthew, Mark, Luke, John, Paul, Peter, James, and Jude penned.

We will use Lightfoot's example of Matthew 11:10-23, that is, fourteen verses of 231 words; we have eleven variants in verses 10, 15, 16, 17, 18, 19(2), 20, 21, and 23(2). This may seem worrisome to the churchgoer or someone new to textual criticism. However, while all variants are found in the NA28 critical apparatus (2012), pp. 31–32,**157** the following sources below only covered seven of them because four are not even an issue. Why are they not an issue? We know what the original reading is with absolute certainty. The seven that have some uncertainty are mentioned in the textual commentaries below.

- Comfort *New Testament Text and Translation* covers verses 15 and 19

- Comfort *Commentary on the Manuscripts* and *Text of the New Testament* covers verses 12 and 19

- Metzger's *Textual Commentary on the Greek New Testament* covers 15, 17, 19, and 23.

---

[156] *How We Got the Bibles*, by Neil R. Lightfoot (Grand Rapids: Baker, 1998; p. 95-103)

[157] Eberhard Nestle and Erwin Nestle, *Nestle-Aland: NTG Apparatus Criticus*, ed. Barbara Aland et al., 28. revidierte Auflage. (Stuttgart: Deutsche Bibelgesellschaft, 2012), 31–32.

Immediately we need to note that verse 12 is absolutely certain as to the original words as well. Verse 19a is mentioned in Comfort's textual commentary because he is drawing attention to the "Son of Man" being written as a nomen sacrum ("sacred name" that is abbreviated) in two early manuscripts (א W), as well as in L. Therefore, verse 19a is absolutely certain as well. We are now down to five variants. The original readings of verses 15, 17, 19a and the two in verse 23 where variants occur are almost certain. The committee's textual scholars for four leading semi-literal and literal translations (ESV, LEB, CSB, and the NASB) agree on ten of the eleven variants. There is disagreement on **Matthew 11:15**. Even so, the reader has access to the original and alternatives in the footnote.

"He who has ears to hear, let him hear." (ESV, NASB, UASV)

The variant is ο εχων ωτα ακουειν ακουετω "the one having ears to hear let him hear," which is supported by א C L W Z Θ f[1,13] 33 Maj syr[c,h,p] cop

"The one who has ears to hear, let him hear!" (LEB, cf. CSB)

WH and NU have ὁ ἔχων ὦτα ἀκουέτω "the one having ears let him hear," which is supported by B D 700 it[k] syr[s]

As is usually the case in more difficult decisions, the variant readings are divided in their support between the leading Alexandrian manuscripts. One reading has 01 (Sinaiticus) on its side, the other has 03 (Vaticanus). This tends to cancel out the weight of documentary evidence.

Now, we return to the charts above. There are 138,020 words in the New Testament. Just 1,392 textual variants deemed relevant for translation have enough of an issue to even be considered in the textual commentary. Again, if we average three words per variant, this amounts only to about 3.026 percent of the 138,020 words, or about 6 percent when we compensate for variant units ignored by the GNT editors. We can also remove the 505 {A} ratings because they are certain. Then, we really have no concerns about the {B} ratings because they are almost certain as well. This means that out of 138,020 words in the Greek New Testament, we only have 364 variants (1,092 words by our average) with which we have difficulty, a mere 10 of which involve great difficulty in deciding which reading to put in the text. Our average would make these variants 0.791 percent of the text without accounting for any difficult variants not included because they were considered irrelevant for translation.

We need not be disturbed or distracted by worries of how many variants there are, or whether they are significant or insignificant. We need only to deal with the certainty of each variation unit, endeavoring to determine the original reading. We should also be concerned with the role textual criticism plays in apologetics. There is no possibility of apologetics if we do not have an authoritative and true Word of God. J. Harold Greenlee was correct when he wrote, "Textual criticism is the basic study for the accurate knowledge of any text. New Testament textual criticism, therefore, is the basic biblical study, a prerequisite to all other biblical and theological work. Interpretation, systemization, and application of the teachings of the NT cannot be done until textual criticism has done at least some of its work."[158] We would add apologetics to that list for which textual criticism is a prerequisite. How are we to defend the Word of God as inspired, inerrant, true, and authoritative if we do not know whether we even have the Word of God? Therefore, when Bible critics try to muddy the waters of truth with misinformation, it is up to the textual scholar to correct the Bible critic's misinformation.

Again, it is true that Lightfoot erred if he was counting the manuscripts instead of the variants. However, we need not count variants either but rather variation units, namely, the places where there are variations. The above Colossians 2:2 example of variations that are found in 79 manuscripts was seen to have 14 variants in 79 manuscripts, not 79 variants. While this is true, it is also true that this is simply one variation unit, i.e., one place, where a variation occurs. This may sound as though we are trying to rationalize a major problem of hundreds of thousands of variants. However, it is actually the other way around. The Bible critic is misrepresenting the facts, trying to talk about an issue without giving the reader or listener all of the facts. We need to consider Benjamin Disraeli's words on statistics: "There are three types of lies: lies, damn lies, and statistics."

The Certainty of the Original Words of the Original Authors

Virgil (70-19 B.C.E.) wrote the *Aeneid* between 29 and 19 B.C.E. for which only five manuscripts are dating to the fourth and fifth centuries C.E.[159] Jewish historian Josephus (37-100 C.E.) wrote *The Jewish Wars* about 75 C.E., for which we have nine complete manuscripts, seven of major importance dating from the tenth to the twelfth centuries C.E.[160] Tacitus (59-129 C.E.) wrote *Annals of Imperial Rome* sometime before 116 C.E., a work considered vital to understanding the history of the Roman Empire during the first century, and we have only thirty-three manuscripts, two of the earliest that date 850 and 1050 C.E. Julius Caesar (100-44 B.C.E.) wrote his Gallic Wars between 51-46 B.C.E.,[161] which is a firsthand account in a third-person narrative of

---

[158] *Introduction to New Testament Textual Criticism*, by J. Harold Greenlee (Peabody: Hendrickson Publishers, 1995; p. 7)

[159] Preface | Dickinson College Commentaries. (April 25, 2017) http://dcc.dickinson.edu/vergil-aeneid/manuscripts

[160] Honora Howell Chapman (Editor), Zuleika Rodgers (Editor), 2016, A *Companion to Josephus* (Blackwell Companions to the Ancient World), Wiley-Blackwell: p. 307.

[161] Carolyn Hammond, 1996, Introduction to *The Gallic War*, Oxford University Press: p. xxxii.

Max Radin, 1918, The date of composition of Caesar's Gallic War, *Classical Philology* XIII: 283–300.

the war, of which we have 251 manuscripts dating between the ninth and fifteenth centuries.[162]

On the other hand, New Testament textual scholars have over 5,898 Greek manuscripts, not to mention ancient versions such as Latin, Coptic, Syriac, Armenian, Georgian, and Gothic, which number into the tens of thousands. We have many early and reliable manuscripts in Greek and the versions, a good number that cover almost the entire New Testament dating within 100 years of the originals. Therefore, reconstructing the original Greek New Testament is a realistic goal for Bible scholars. This belief and goal that we could anticipate a time when we would recover the original wording of the Greek New Testament had its greatest advocates in the nineteenth century, in Samuel Tregelles (1813-75), B. F. Westcott (1825-1901), and F. J. A. Hort (1828-92). While they acknowledged that we would never recover every word with absolute certainty, they knew that it was always the primary goal to come extremely close to the original. When we entered the twentieth century, there were two textual scholars who have since stood above all others, Kurt Aland and Bruce Metzger. These two men carried the same purpose with them, as they were instrumental in bringing us the Nestle-Aland and the United Bible Societies' critical editions, which are at the foundation of almost all modern translations.

From the days of Johann Jacob Griesbach (1745-1812) to Constantin Von Tischendorf (1815-1874), to Samuel Prideaux Tregelles (1813-1875), to Fenton John Anthony Hort (1828-1892), to Kurt Aland (1915-1994), to Bruce M. Metzger (1914-2007),[163] we have been blessed with extraordinary textual scholars. These scholars have devoted their entire lives to providing us with the transmission of the New Testament text and the methodologies by which we can recover the original words of the New Testament authors. They did not construct these histories and methodologies from textbooks or in university classrooms. No, they spent decades upon decades working with manuscripts and putting their methods of textual criticism into practice, as they provided us with one improved critical edition after another. As their knowledge grew, the number of manuscripts they had to work with fortunately grew.

---

[162] O. Seel, 1961, *Bellum Gallicum*. (Bibl. Teubneriana.) Teubner, Leipzig.

W. Hering, 1987, *C. Iulii Caesaris commentarii rerum gestarum, Vol. I: Bellum Gallicum*.(Bibl. Teubneriana.) Teubner, Leipzig.

Virginia Brown, 1972, *The Textual Transmission of Caesar's Civil War*, Brill.

Caesar's Gallic war - Tim Mitchell. (April 25, 2017) http://www.timmitchell.fr/blog/2012/04/12/gallic-war/

[163] These textual scholars provided us with histories of the transmission of the New Testament text and methodologies. However, we have had dozens of textual scholars who have given their lives to the text of the New Testament. To mention just a few, we have Brian Walton (1600-1661), John Fell (1625-1686), John Mill (1645-1707), Edward Wells (1667-1727), Richard Bentley (1662-1742), Johann Albert Bengel (1687-1752), Johann Jacob Wettstein (1693-1754), Johann Salomo Semler (1725-1791), Johann Leonard Hug (1765-1846), Johann Martin Augustinus Scholz (1794-1852), Karl Lachmann (1793-1851), Erwin Nestle (1883-1972), Allen Wikgren (1906-1998), Matthew Black, (1908-1994), Barbara Aland (1937-present), and Carlo Maria Martini (1927-2012).

Samuel Tregelles stated that his purpose was to restore the Greek New Testament text "as nearly as can be done on existing evidence."[164] B. F. Westcott and F. J. A. Hort declared that their goal was "to present exactly the original words of the New Testament, so far as they can now be determined from surviving documents."[165] Metzger said that the goal of textual criticism is "to ascertain from the divergent copies which form of the text should be regarded as most nearly conforming to the original."[166] Sadly, after centuries, textual criticism is losing its way, as new textual scholars have begun to set aside the goal of recovering and establishing the original wording of the Greek New Testament. They have little concern for the certainty of a reading as to whether it is the original.

In speaking of the positions of agnostic Bart D. Ehrman (author of *The Orthodox Corruption of Scripture*) and David Parker (author of *The Living Text of the Gospels*), Elliott overserved, "Both emphasize the living and therefore changing text of the New Testament and the needlessness and inappropriateness of trying to establish one immutable original text. The changeable text in all its variety is what we textual critics should be displaying."[167] Elliott then reflects further on his goals within textual criticism: "Despite my own published work in trying to prove the originality of the text in selected areas of textual variation … I agree that the task of trying to establish the original words of the original authors with 100% certainty is impossible. More dominant in text critics' thinking now is the need to plot the changes in the history of the text. That certainly seemed to be the consensus at one of the sessions of the 1998 SBL conference in Orlando, where the question of whether the original text was an achievable goal received generally negative responses."[168]

We strongly disagree. The goal of textual criticism had been and still should be **to restore** the New Testament Greek text **in every word that the New Testament authors originally penned** in a critical edition. Suppose we are aiming only "to plot the changes in the history of the text," as Elliott put it. In that case, we are unable to do so precisely at the time when we have the greatest need to see what happened, i.e., soon after the NT books were first published, if we actually deny and rob ourselves of any chance to recover the original. Then we must admit either that we can never have the complete word of God (the new position), or that any and potentially every quality Greek witness must be considered the word of God. The latter might even be said of a quality version, or at least of readings clearly inferred from such a version. In reality, however, any manuscript that departs from the original in its witness is more or less damaged goods.

---

[164] Tregelles, *An Account of the Printed Text of the Greek New Testament*, 174.

[165] Westcott and Hort, *Introduction to the New Testament in the Original Greek*, 1.

[166] Metzger, *The Text of the New Testament*, v.

[167] J. K. Elliott, *New Testament Textual Criticism: The Application of Thoroughgoing Principles: Essays on Manuscripts and Textual Variation*, 592.

[168] Ibid. 592.

We obviously do not think such pessimism is the necessary or inevitable response. In looking at the numbers above as to the certainty level of the restoration of the original Greek New Testament, we have come a long way since John Fell (1625-1686). A spot comparison of changes in ratings between GNT5 and previous GNT editions indicates that the level of certainty is increasing in most cases, and when it does not, the preference tends toward the earliest and most reliable manuscripts.[169] To set aside the primary goal of textual criticism now would be an insult to the lives of many textual scholars who preceded us, not to mention to the authors who penned the New Testament books and the Almighty God who inspired them.

---

[169] Sample comparisons of the General Epistles in GNT5 with previous GNT editions led to this conclusion. When the level of certainty decreased–which was infrequent compared to the reverse–the trend seemed to be that more weight was being given to 03 and/or 01 in opposition to internal factors. It is also expected that certainty levels will increase with the use of the CBGM.

APPENDIX B Papyrus 52 (P52) - A Small Fragment of John 18:31-33, 18:37-38, Dating from Around 100-150 CE

INTRODUCTION: Papyrus 52, also known as P52 or the Rylands Library Papyrus P52, is one of the most important early New Testament manuscripts. Comprising a small fragment of the Gospel of John (18:31–33, 37–38), it provides key evidence for the dating of this Gospel's original text.

CONTENTS: The contents of P52 consist of portions of seven verses from the 18th chapter of the Gospel of John (John 18:31–33, 37–38), written in Greek. The fragment contains parts of Pilate's dialogue with Jesus during his trial. The front (recto) holds John 18:31-33 and the back (verso) contains John 18:37-38.

DATE: The date of P52 has been subject to significant debate, with most scholars agreeing it originates from the early second century (ca. 100–150). This estimation is based on paleographic analysis, a method that compares the handwriting on the papyrus with other dated documents.

HOUSING LOCATION: P52 is currently housed in the John Rylands University Library in Manchester, England, where it is catalogued as Gr. P. 457.

PHYSICAL FEATURES: P52 is a single leaf papyrus fragment measuring approximately 18 cm x 22 cm, with 18 lines per page. It is written in a reformed documentary hand, a style that bridges the gap between formal book-hand and a more casual, cursive style.

TEXT TYPE: The text type of P52 is considered to be "Alexandrian" or what Kurt Aland and Barbara Aland termed as "normal". The Alexandrian text-type is one of several text types used in textual criticism to describe and group the textual character of biblical manuscripts.

TEXTUAL CHARACTER: Though the fragment is too small for a comprehensive textual analysis, the existing text aligns well with the standard text of the Gospel of John, indicating an early, accurate transmission of the text.

COMMENTS FROM KURT ALAND: While Kurt Aland did not specifically comment on P52, his work on the categorization of New Testament manuscripts informed the classification of P52 as a "normal" text type. This classification suggests that the text of P52 was not heavily influenced by the editorial work of later scribes and remains close to the original.

COMMENTS FROM BRUCE M. METZGER: Bruce M. Metzger, a renowned New Testament scholar, referred to the text of P52 as "Alexandrian." This implies that the scribe who wrote P52 likely worked in or near Alexandria, Egypt, where this precise, scholarly style of copying was practiced.

COMMENTS FROM PHILIP W. COMFORT: Philip W. Comfort, a noted scholar in the field of papyrology and textual criticism, has affirmed the early dating of P52. He suggests that this manuscript may be only 20 years removed from the original, given the consensus dating of the Gospel of John's composition around 80-85 AD. This underlines the remarkable significance of P52, testifying to the rapid spread and circulation of the Gospel of John within the early Christian communities.

In conclusion, P52 serves as a crucial piece of historical evidence for the early composition and transmission of the Gospel of John. Despite its size, the fragment's early date, the precision of its text, and its geographic origin in Egypt—far from the Gospel's traditional place of composition in Ephesus—contribute significantly to our understanding of the New Testament's early textual history.

The P52 Project

In the realm of religious studies, particularly in the study of the Bible, individuals such as parishioners, Bible college enrollees, and seminary scholars may find themselves at a crossroads when faced with diverging interpretations from various Bible scholars. This is often exemplified in the case of P52, a fragment of the Greek New Testament, where scholars propose different dates of creation. To clarify, P52 refers to a manuscript written on sheets of papyrus paper, derived from an Egyptian plant known as papyrus, with the number 52 denoting its catalogued discovery.

This uncertainty can be particularly disconcerting for those not deeply immersed in the field, only equipped with a fundamental knowledge base. With multiple scholars offering differing viewpoints, it raises the question - how can one discern the truth? Even more so, it can lead to awkward moments on social media platforms for Christians, such as when an atheist challenges the widely accepted dating of P52 to 100-150 C.E., countering with recent research suggesting a later date of 200 C.E. or beyond. How can a Christian respond to this?

The approach we will utilize in THE P52 PROJECT can serve as a useful tool for Christians confronted with such scholarly disagreements. Guided by God-given wisdom, we will evaluate the evidence from all sides, applying logic and reasoning. THE P52 PROJECT will be approached as if we were in a court of law, with P52 itself on trial. Through this method, we aim to reach a resolution that respects the evidence and upholds the truth.

World-Renowned Paleographers and Textual Scholars Date P52 Early

- 100-150 C.H. Roberts
- 100-150 Sir Frederic G. Kenyon
- 100-150 W. Schubart
- 100-150 Sir Harold I. Bell
- 100-150 Adolf Deissmann
- 100-150 E. G. Turner
- 100-150 Ulrich Wilken
- 100-150 W. H. P. Hatch
- 125-175 Kurt and Barbara Aland
- 100-150: Philip W. Comfort
- 100-150 Bruce M. Metzger
- 100-150 Daniel B. Wallace
- 125-175 Pasquale Orsini
- 125-175 Willy Clarysse

The New Uncertain and Ambiguous Minded Textual Scholars Date P52

- 175-225 Brent Nongbri
- 200-300 Michael Gronewald

In New Testament textual studies, there are but two ways to make a name for oneself as a textual scholar. **(1)** The person would have to make a discovery that overwhelms the scholarly world in the extreme. **(2)** The person has to take a view or a position on something and then go out and find evidence that changes that view or position. Brent Nongbri seems to be trying **(2)** in his efforts to have his place within the history of New Testament Textual Studies. In 2120, scholars can look back at who changed the dates of the early papyri.

ESTABLISHING THE DATE OF P52

The significance of P52 is twofold; it lies in its proposed early dating and its geographic distribution from the supposed location of authorship, traditionally believed to be Ephesus. Since the fragment isn't the original but a copy, the Gospel of John's authorship must have occurred a few years before P52 was written, whenever that was. The fragment's discovery in Egypt adds to this time frame, accounting for the documents' spread from the place of authorship and transmission to the place of finding.

The Gospel of John is possibly referenced by Justin Martyr, making it plausible that it was written before approximately 160 CE. However, 20th-century New Testament scholars, notably Kurt Aland and Bruce Metzger, using the proposed early dating of P52, have suggested that the Gospel's latest possible composition date should be recalibrated to the early parts of the second century. Some scholars even posit that the discovery of P52 suggests a composition date for the Gospel no later than the traditionally accepted date of around 90 CE, or even earlier.

Doubts about using P52 to date the Gospel of John (not questioning the fragment's authenticity) stem from two main issues. Firstly, the papyrus's age has been determined solely based on the handwriting, without the corroboration of dated textual references or related archaeology. Secondly, like all other surviving early Gospel manuscripts, this fragment is from a codex, not a scroll. If it indeed dates from the first half of the second century, this fragment would be among the earliest surviving examples of a literary codex. (In approximately 90 CE, Martial introduced his poems in parchment codex form, claiming this to be a new innovation.)

In the year preceding the publication of P52, the British Museum library acquired papyrus fragments of the Egerton Gospel (P.Egerton 2), which also came from a codex, and these were published in 1935 by H. Idris Bell and T.C. Skeat. Since P52's text is from a canonical gospel, the Gospel of John, and the Egerton Gospel's text isn't, there was significant curiosity among biblical scholars about whether P52 could be dated as the earlier of the two papyri.

Colin Roberts' Analysis

P52 is a literary text and, like almost all such papyri, lacks an explicit date marker. Consequently, determining its age required comparison with texts that have dates, usually found in documentary hands (contracts, petitions, letters). Nonetheless,

Roberts identified two undated literary papyri as most comparable to P52: P. Berol. 6845 (a fragment of an Iliad scroll kept in Berlin and paleographically dated to around the end of the first century), and P.Egerton 2, which was then approximated to date around 150 CE. Roberts argued that, except for the alpha letter, P. Berol. 6845 is "the closest parallel to our text," a view supported by Frederic Kenyon, an authority in the field. He also stated that in the Egerton Gospel, "most of the characteristics of our hand are to be found, though in a less accentuated form."

Roberts' establishment of the Berlin Iliad P. Berol 6845 as a reference was crucial in suggesting an early 2nd century date for P52. The Berlin papyrus had been dated to the end of the first century by Wilhelm Schubart, whose papyrological study illustrated its hand's resemblance to that of P. Fayum 110, a personal letter penned by a professional scribe in a "literary type" hand and explicitly dated 94 CE. Skeat and Bell, in assigning a mid-second-century date to P. Egerton 2, also relied on comparison with P.Fayum 110.

Roberts proposed two additional dated papyri in documentary hands as comparators for P52: P. London 2078, a private letter written during Domitian's reign (81–96 CE), and P. Oslo 22, a petition dated 127 CE. He noted the particular similarity of P. Oslo 22 in some of the more distinctive letter forms, such as eta, mu, and iota. Roberts shared his analysis with Frederic G. Kenyon, Wilhelm Schubart, and H. I. Bell, all of whom agreed with his dating of P52 to the first half of the 2nd century.

In 1935, Roberts' date assessment was supported by A. Deissmann, who suggested a date in the reigns of Hadrian (117–138) or even Trajan (98–117), although without providing actual evidence. In 1936, Ulrich Wilcken supported the dating based on a comparison between the hand of P52 and those of papyri in the extensive Apollonius archive, which are dated 113–120.

Philip Comfort's Analysis

Later, other comparative literary papyri were proposed, notably P. Oxy. XXXI 2533, which contains a second-century literary text in a hand very similar to P52. This text was written on the back of a reused document in a late first-century business hand. Also, three biblical papyrus codices were proposed as comparators: P. Oxy. LX 4009 (an apocryphal gospel fragment, paleographically dated to the early/mid-second century), and P. Oxy. L 3523 (P90) and P. Oxy. LXIV 4404 (P104), both paleographically dated to the later second century. The discovery of other papyrus codices with second-century hands, like the Yale Genesis Fragment (P. Yale 1), suggested that this book form was more common for literary texts at this date than previously assumed.

Thus, until the 1990s, the inclination among New Testament commentators, supported by several paleographers like Philip W. Comfort, was to propose a date for P52 towards the earlier half of the range suggested by Roberts and his correspondents.

However, the discovery that a papyrus fragment in Cologne is part of the Egerton Gospel raised caution. In this fragment, the letters gamma and kappa are separated by a hooked apostrophe, a feature infrequent in dated second-century papyri. To the newer papyrologists this feature implies a date for the Egerton Gospel closer to 200 CE and underscores the difficulties in dating a papyrus text of which only a small part of two pages survives.

Brent Nongbri's Critique

The early date for P52, favored by many New Testament scholars, was questioned by Andreas Schmidt, who suggests a date around 170 CE, give or take twenty-five years. He bases this on a comparison with Chester Beatty Papyri X and III and the re-dated Egerton Gospel. Brent Nongbri has criticized both Comfort's early dating of P52 and Schmidt's late dating. He disputes all attempts to establish a date for undated papyri within narrow ranges based purely on paleographic grounds, along with any inference from the paleographic dating of P52 to a precise terminus ad quem for the composition of the Fourth Gospel.

Nongbri notes that both Comfort and Schmidt propose their respective revisions of Roberts's dating solely based on paleographic comparisons with papyri that had themselves been paleographically dated. In response to these tendencies, Nongbri collected and published images of all explicitly dated comparator manuscripts to P52. He demonstrated that although Roberts's assessment of similarities with a succession of dated late first to mid-second-century papyri could be confirmed, two later dated papyri, both petitions, also showed strong similarities. These papyri include P. Mich. inv. 5336, dated around 152 CE, and P.Amh. 2.78, an example first suggested by Eric Turner, that dates to 184 CE.

Nongbri suggests that older styles of handwriting might persist much longer than some scholars had assumed, and that a wider range of possible dates for the papyrus must be considered. He criticizes the way scholars of the New Testament have used and potentially misused papyrological evidence. He emphasizes that paleography is not the most effective method for dating texts, particularly those written in a literary hand, and argues that P52 cannot be used to silence other debates about the existence of the Gospel of John in the first half of the second century.

While Nongbri does not provide his own opinion on the date of P52, he seems to agree with the relatively cautious terminology of Roberts's dating and his speculations on the possible implications for the date of John's gospel. Some commentators have interpreted Nongbri's accumulation of later dated comparators as undermining Roberts's proposed dating; however, this fails to consider the essential similarity of Roberts's and Nongbri's main findings. Nongbri extends the range of dated primary reference comparators both earlier and later than in Roberts's work, suggesting that the actual date of P52 could conceivably be later (or earlier) still. He emphasizes that a late second (or early third) century date for P52 cannot be discounted based solely on paleographic evidence. His chief criticism is directed at those who have tended to take the midpoint of Roberts's proposed range of dates, treat it as the latest limit for a possible date for this papyrus, and then infer that the Gospel of John cannot have been written later than around 100 CE.

Stanley Porter's Perspective

Stanley E. Porter has delved deeper into the relationship between P52 and P.Egerton 2. He brings into the discussion two more early biblical papyri for both texts, P. Oxy IV 656 (a fragment of Genesis) and P.Vindob. G. 2325 (another apocryphal gospel, the Fayum Fragment). Porter presents a comprehensive overview of the history and spectrum of opinion among papyrologists regarding the dating of P52 and P.Egerton 2. He presents arguments supporting Robert's assertion that the two are close parallels, likely written around the same time, and that P52 is probably the earlier of the two.

Porter points out that P.Egerton 2 is written in a "less heavy hand with more formal rounded characteristics, but with what the original editors called 'cursive affinities.'" He adds, "Both manuscripts were apparently written before the development of a more formal Biblical majuscule style, which began to develop in the late second and early third centuries." Porter also acknowledges that the hooked apostrophe form found in the Cologne fragment of P.Egerton 2 is rare in the second century, but he identifies at least one example in a papyrus dated to 101 CE and three others from the mid or late second century. His findings place the two manuscripts somewhere in the middle of the second century, perhaps leaning towards the early part.

Stanley Porter also questions Nongbri's claim that valid comparisons can be made between P52 and documentary papyri from the later second and early third centuries. He cites Eric Turner's cautionary note that comparing book hands with dated documentary hands can be unreliable due to the different intentions of the scribes. In this regard, Porter warns against what he sees as Nongbri's 'overly skeptical' disregard for comparators without an explicit date, which forces comparisons for literary texts to be limited to purely documentary hands. Porter argues that Nongbri's proposed late second and third century comparators are, in several cases, quite different from P52, compelling a focus on detailed letter forms without consideration of the overall formation, trajectory, and style of the script.

If typological letter comparisons are applied using published series of dated representative script alphabets instead of document by document comparisons, then, Porter asserts, both P52 and P.Egerton 2 "fit comfortably within the second century. There are of course some letters that are similar to those in the third century (as there are some in the first century) but the letters that tend to be given the most individualization, such as alpha, mu and even sigma, appear to be second century."

Both Porter and Nongbri acknowledge that Eric Turner, despite his proposal of P.Amh. 2.78 as a parallel for P52, continued to believe that "The Rylands papyrus may therefore be accepted as of the first half of the second century". However, Nongbri has since pointed out the limited usefulness of Porter's study as it makes no reference to manuscripts with secure dates, rendering it circular (several undated manuscripts are used to provide a date for another undated manuscript).

John Rylands Library's Perspective

The John Rylands Library provides a perspective on the dating of the fragment. The initial editor placed the fragment in the first half of the second century (between 100-150 AD), based on paleographic estimation. This process involved comparing the handwriting with that of other manuscripts.

Importance for Textual Criticism and History

The discovery of early Christian papyri from Egypt provides the earliest solid physical evidence for Christianity and the Gospels. There is considerable overlap in the proposed dating for these papyri, so it's not definitive whether 𝔓52 is older than other New Testament fragments thought to be from the 2nd century, such as P90 (100-150 CE), P104 (100-125 CE), and 𝔓64+67 (150-175 CE). This also applies to some early non-canonical texts like P. Egerton. 2, P.Oxy. LX 4009. Additionally, there are several Greek fragments of Old Testament books (mainly Psalms) dated to the 2nd century, whose characteristics suggest a Christian rather than Jewish or pagan origin. All these papyri have been dated paleographically, and P52 is often recognized as having earlier characteristics.

Despite its small size, the text that remains in P52 provides an early witness to several historical aspects of Jesus's life. Even though Jesus isn't named, the verses indicate a man tried before the Roman authorities during Pontius Pilate's governorship, at a specific location (the Praetorium in Jerusalem), sentenced to a specific punishment (crucifixion), all orchestrated by the Jewish Temple authorities.

Assuming P52 indeed dates back to the early 2nd century, its codex form (rather than a scroll) implies an early adoption of this writing style among Christians, contrasting with the common Jewish practice of the time. An analysis of the length of missing text between the front and back sides aligns with the corresponding Gospel of John, suggesting no significant additions or deletions in this part. Except for two iotacisms and the likely omission of a phrase, P52 generally agrees with the Alexandrian text base.

Despite its small size, it is presumed that the original text was nearly full gospel length to justify the effort of writing in codex form. However, considering the large size and format of the P52 codex pages, it's improbable that it initially contained all four canonical gospels.

Although P52 is small and its coverage of the Gospel of John is necessarily limited, it has sparked some debate about whether the name 'Jesus' was originally written as a sacred name, or nomen sacrum, contracted to 'ΙΣ' or 'ΙΗΣ' as per Christian practice in other early Gospel manuscripts. The verses included in P52 are also found in the Bodmer Papyrus P66 – dated 100-150 CE – and there is some overlap with P90 from 100 to 150 CE. Kurt Aland described it as a "Normal text," and due to its age, categorized it in Category I.

The P52 papyrus, also known as the Rylands Library Papyrus P52, is of significant interest to scholars for a few key reasons:

Age and Physical Evidence: The P52 papyrus is one of the earliest known fragments of the New Testament, making it an invaluable resource for scholars studying the historical development of the New Testament and early Christianity.

Textual Evidence: Despite its small size, P52 provides insights into the text of the Gospel of John. While there has been some debate about whether the name 'Jesus' was originally written as a sacred name, the presence of certain verses in P52 corresponds with other early copies of the Gospel of John, suggesting a level of consistency in the transmission of the text.

Adoption of the Codex: If P52 indeed dates back to the early 2nd century, its form as a codex (a type of book) rather than a scroll suggests an early adoption of this writing style among Christians, providing insights into the technological and cultural shifts of the time.

APPENDIX C Papyrus 66 (P66) - A Manuscript of John 1:1–6:11, 6:35b–14:26, 29–30; 15:2–26; 16:2–4, 6–7; 16:10–20:20, 22–23; 20:25–21:9, 12, 17, Dating from Around 100-150 CE

INTRODUCTION: Papyrus 66 (P66) is an important early Christian papyrus codex, named for its location in the Bodmer collection of Swiss libraries. It contains a large portion of the Gospel of John and is one of the oldest known New Testament manuscripts. It is a significant resource for textual critics, historians, and biblical scholars due to its age and relatively high-quality preservation.

CONTENTS: P66 includes most of the Gospel of John, specifically 1:1–6:11; 6:35–14:26, 29–30; 15:2–26; 16:2–4, 6–7; 16:10–20:20, 22–23; 20:25–21:9, 12, 17. Notably, it does not contain the pericope of the adulteress (John 7:53–8:11), making it the earliest manuscript not to include this passage, often considered a later addition to the text.

DATE: The date of P66 is a matter of some debate, but it is generally agreed to have been written in the middle of the second century (around 150 AD), making it one of the earliest substantial New Testament manuscripts. The dating is based on paleographical analysis, comparing the handwriting style to other known dated texts.

HOUSING LOCATION: P66 is currently housed in the Bibliotheca Bodmeriana in Cologny-Geneva, Switzerland (P. Bodmer II), with one leaf located in the Institut für Altertumskunde der Universität zu Köln in Cologne, Germany (inv. nr. 4274/4298).

PHYSICAL FEATURES: P66 comprises 39 folios, equivalent to 78 leaves or 156 pages, each measuring 14.2 cm x 16.2 cm. The writing contains 15–25 lines per page, with page numbers ranging from 1 to 156. The manuscript's handwriting suggests it was likely created by a professional scribe.

TEXT TYPE: The text of P66 is a Greek text of the New Testament, specifically the Gospel of John. It is part of the Alexandrian text-type, a group of early New Testament manuscripts associated with Alexandria, Egypt.

TEXTUAL CHARACTER: Studies by Berner and Comfort suggest that P66 likely reflects the work of three individuals: the original scribe, a thorough corrector (or diorthōtēs), and a minor corrector. The original scribe's work is characterized by a free interaction with the text, including several singular readings, suggesting an active interpretation of the text. The diorthōtēs made many substantial corrections, likely adjusting the copy according to a different exemplar.

COMMENTS FROM KURT ALAND: Kurt Aland, a renowned New Testament scholar, categorizes P66 as Category I in his classification system, indicating that it is a manuscript of very special quality. He recognizes its textual independence and its significant contribution to our understanding of the early text of the New Testament.

COMMENTS FROM BRUCE M. METZGER: Bruce M. Metzger, another prominent New Testament scholar, also acknowledges the importance of P66. He notes its early date, its substantial content, and its significance for textual criticism, particularly its value in demonstrating the fluidity of the New Testament text in the second century.

COMMENTS FROM PHILIP W. COMFORT: Philip W. Comfort, a scholar specializing in papyrology and New Testament text criticism, has extensively analyzed P66. He emphasizes the textual character of the manuscript, highlighting its distinctiveness and independence. Comfort considers the scribe of P66 as competent and the manuscript reliable, despite some peculiarities and mistakes. Furthermore, Comfort discusses the role of the correctors in the manuscript's transmission, arguing that their work reflects careful and thoughtful engagement with the text.

In conclusion, Papyrus 66 is an essential piece of early Christian literature, providing valuable insights into the early text of the New Testament and its transmission. Its study continues to contribute significantly to our understanding of the early Christian world.

APPENDIX D v Papyrus 75 (P75) - A Manuscript of Luke 3:18-24:53; John 1-15, Dating from Around 175-225 CE

INTRODUCTION: Papyrus 75, also known as P. Bodmer XIV and XV, is an important early New Testament papyrus manuscript containing portions of the Gospel of Luke and the Gospel of John. The manuscript is highly valued by textual scholars due to its textual reliability and early date. It provides significant insights into the early text of the New Testament and sheds light on the development of the Alexandrian text type.

CONTENTS: P75 contains Luke 3:18–22; 3:33–4:2; 4:34–5:10; 5:37–6:4; 6:10–7:32, 35–39, 41–43; 7:46–9:2; 9:4–17:15; 17:19–18:18; 22:4–24:53; and John 1:1–11:45, 48–57; 12:3–13:1, 8–10; 14:8–29; 15:7–8. It does not include John 7:53–8:11, making it the second earliest witness not to include this spurious passage.

DATE: P75 is dated to the late second or possibly early third century, based on its comparability with other papyri from the same period.

HOUSING LOCATION: The manuscript is housed at the Bibliotheca Bodmeriana in Cologny-Geneva, Switzerland.

PHYSICAL FEATURES: P75 consists of 36 folios (72 leaves, 144 pages), measuring 13 cm x 26 cm. It has 38–45 lines per page and was written by a professional scribe.

TEXT TYPE: Textual scholars classify P75 as an early example of the Alexandrian text type. It has been described as "proto-Alexandrian" by Bruce M. Metzger and having a "strict text" by Kurt Aland and Barbara Aland.

TEXTUAL CHARACTER: P75 is considered a reliable and accurate copy of the New Testament text. Its scribe demonstrated discipline and care in producing an exact copy, with no evidence of revision or systematic correction. However, the scribe did make several corrections (116 in Luke and John) and had a tendency to shorten the text, particularly by dropping pronouns. Despite these flaws, P75 is highly regarded for its textual reliability.

COMMENTS FROM KURT ALAND: Kurt Aland, a leading New Testament textual scholar, initially believed that the second and third-century manuscripts exhibited a text in flux or a "mixed" text. However, after the discovery of P75, Aland changed his perspective, stating that P75 shows such a close affinity with Codex Vaticanus that the supposition of a recension of the text at Alexandria in the fourth century can no longer be held.

COMMENTS FROM BRUCE M. METZGER: Bruce M. Metzger, another prominent New Testament textual scholar, referred to P75 as "proto-Alexandrian," indicating its early representation of the Alexandrian text type. Metzger recognized P75 as an important witness to the New Testament text and its development.

COMMENTS FROM PHILIP W. COMFORT: Philip W. Comfort, a scholar specializing in papyrology and New Testament text criticism, has studied P75 extensively. He agrees with the dating of P75 to the late second century, possibly early third century. Comfort emphasizes the textual character of P75, highlighting its reliability and the scribe's discipline in producing an accurate copy. He also discusses the connection between P75 and Codex Vaticanus, noting that while the two texts share a close affinity, it's unlikely that the scribe of Codex Vaticanus directly used P75 as his exemplar. This is due to the difference in line length between the two texts: the scribe of Vaticanus appears to have copied from a manuscript with an average line length of 12-14 letters, while P75 has an average line length of about 29-32 letters. As such, Comfort suggests that the scribe of Vaticanus likely used a manuscript similar to P75, but not P75 itself.

This conclusion emphasizes the existence of a highly accurate, 'Alexandrian' type text that predates Codex Vaticanus, challenging previous theories that proposed the Alexandrian text was the culmination of a recension, or revision process, occurring in the fourth century. Instead, the evidence from P75 suggests that the 'Alexandrian' or 'neutral' text already existed in a relatively pure form by the late second century.

APPENDIX E Papyrus 104 (P104) - A Manuscript of Matt. 21:34-37, 43, 45(?), Dating from Around 100-150 CE

INTRODUCTION: Papyrus 104, often referred to as P104, is a small fragment of a papyrus manuscript of the New Testament. Its discovery and subsequent analysis have provided valuable insight into the early transmission of the New Testament text.

CONTENTS: P104 contains a portion of the Gospel according to Matthew, specifically Matthew 21:34-37 and 43, with the possibility of verse 45. Notably, it does not include Matthew 21:44, making it the earliest manuscript witness to the exclusion of this verse.

DATE: The dating of P104 is a topic of scholarly discussion. The manuscript's editor, J. D. Thomas, places it in the late second century. However, other scholars, including Philip W. Comfort, have suggested an earlier date. Comfort points to the manuscript's handwriting style, which is reminiscent of the Roman uncial script commonly seen in the Ptolemaic period, suggesting that P104 could potentially date back to the late first or early second century. If this earlier date is accepted, P104 could be considered one of the earliest New Testament manuscripts in existence.

HOUSING LOCATION: P104 is currently housed in the Ashmolean Museum in Oxford, England.

PHYSICAL FEATURES: P104 consists of a single leaf, measuring approximately 14 cm x 25 cm. The lettering is clearly visible on one side, and barely visible on the other, suggesting that the text was written on both sides of the papyrus. The manuscript originally contained 31 lines per page.

TEXT TYPE: While the small size of P104 makes a definitive categorization challenging, the text is in agreement with the UBS4/NA27, a widely accepted scholarly edition of the Greek New Testament, save for the exclusion of Matthew 21:44. This alignment suggests an early 'Alexandrian' text type, a category of manuscripts known for their accuracy and reliability.

TEXTUAL CHARACTER: Despite its small size, P104 is considered an important witness to the New Testament text. Its exclusion of Matthew 21:44, a verse found in many later manuscripts, provides valuable evidence concerning early textual variants.

COMMENTS FROM KURT ALAND: While there is no specific commentary from Kurt Aland on P104 available, his work on categorizing New Testament manuscripts would likely place P104 within Category I, which he reserves for manuscripts of the Alexandrian text type that are typically dated before the fourth century.

COMMENTS FROM BRUCE M. METZGER: Bruce M. Metzger, another influential New Testament scholar, did not specifically comment on P104. However, his work on the textual commentary of the Greek New Testament may have classified P104 as an important witness to the exclusion of Matthew 21:44.

COMMENTS FROM PHILIP W. COMFORT: Philip W. Comfort, a scholar specializing in papyrology, suggests that P104 may date back to the late first or early second century. He highlights the manuscript's similarity to other texts from this period, including P. Oxy. 4301 and PSI 1213. According to Comfort, these similarities could potentially make P104 the earliest New Testament manuscript or at least one of the earliest. Comfort's analysis of P104 emphasizes the significance of this small fragment in understanding the early transmission of the New Testament text.

Edward D. Andrews

APPENDIX F Papyrus 45 (P45) - A Manuscript of the Gospels and Acts, Dating from Around 175-225 CE

INTRODUCTION: Papyrus 45 (P45) is one of the most important early New Testament manuscripts, known for its substantial content and unique textual character. It is one of the Chester Beatty Papyri, a group of early Christian manuscript codices (bound books) from the 2nd to the 4th centuries. P45 is the first of this collection, also known as P. Chester Beatty I.

CONTENTS: P45 contains portions of the four canonical Gospels (Matthew, Mark, Luke, and John) and the Acts of the Apostles. The portions of the text preserved show a range of passages from each book, with numerous gaps due to the damaged and fragmentary state of the manuscript.

DATE: The manuscript is generally dated to the early third century. This dating is based on the handwriting style, comparison with other texts, and the educated judgments of various scholars such as Frederic Kenyon, W. Schubart, and H. I. Bell.

HOUSING LOCATION: P45 is currently housed in the Chester Beatty Library in Dublin, Ireland. It was purchased by Chester Beatty, a wealthy American collector living in Ireland, in 1931.

PHYSICAL FEATURES: The original codex of P45 is estimated to have had 224 pages, with the extant pages numbering 193 and 199. The surviving portions measure approximately 20 cm wide by 25 cm high. Each page contains an average of 36-37 lines of text. The first and last pages were blank, probably serving as a protective cover for the manuscript. The handwriting of P45 displays a reformed documentary hand, a style typical of the period.

TEXT TYPE: The text type of P45 varies with each book. In Mark, it shows affinities with the so-called Caesarean text type, while in Matthew, Luke, and John, it stands somewhere between the Alexandrian and Western text types. In Acts, P45 aligns most closely with the Alexandrian text type.

TEXTUAL CHARACTER: The scribe of P45 is known for his "free" style, often seen as more of an exegete and paraphraser than a strict copyist. He seemed to work phrase by phrase, often abbreviating, harmonizing, and smoothing out the text, resulting in a very readable, though not always strictly accurate, rendering of his exemplars.

COMMENTS FROM KURT ALAND: Kurt Aland, a notable New Testament scholar, has not directly commented on P45. However, he classified it as Category I (strict text) for the Gospels and Category II (good, normal text) for Acts in his standard work "The Text of the New Testament," indicating the high quality and importance of the manuscript.

COMMENTS FROM BRUCE M. METZGER: Bruce Metzger, another leading scholar of New Testament textual criticism, noted in his works the unique character of P45's text. He emphasized the freedom and creativity of the scribe in shaping the text, making it one of the distinctive early witnesses to the New Testament.

COMMENTS FROM PHILIP W. COMFORT: Philip W. Comfort, a scholar specializing in papyrological and textual studies, has done extensive work on P45. He has highlighted the scribe's intelligent engagement with the text and the ways in which the scribe made the text more concise and readable. Comfort has also argued for the high quality of the manuscript and its importance for understanding the early history of the New Testament text.

Edward D. Andrews

APPENDIX G Papyrus 90 (P90) - A Manuscript of John 18:36–19:7, Dating from Around 100-150 CE

INTRODUCTION: Papyrus 90, often referred to as P90, is a small fragment of the New Testament in Greek, containing portions of the Gospel of John 18:36–19:7. Designated by the Gregory-Aland numbering system, this fragment is recognized for its valuable contributions to the textual criticism of the New Testament. Its provenance is traced back to Oxyrhynchus, Egypt, a significant location known for yielding numerous papyrus documents of historical importance.

CONTENTS: The contents of P90 are limited but significant, containing a portion of the Gospel of John (18:36–19:7). This passage encompasses the final parts of Jesus' trial before Pilate, with a dialogue between Jesus and Pilate concerning the nature of Jesus' kingdom, concluding with Pilate's statement to the Jewish leaders, "I find no basis for a charge against him."

DATE: The fragment is dated palaeographically to the period between 100 and 150 CE. Paleography is the study of ancient writing, and the dating is estimated based on the script style and other material characteristics. This places P90 in the early 2nd century, making it one of the oldest extant fragments of the New Testament.

HOUSING LOCATION: P90 is currently housed in the Ashmolean Museum in Oxford, England, specifically in the Sackler Library's Papyrology Rooms (P. Oxy. 3523). The Ashmolean Museum is renowned for its extensive collection of historical artifacts, including numerous papyrus fragments.

PHYSICAL FEATURES: The fragment, originally measuring 12 cm by 16 cm, is written on a single leaf and contains 24 lines per page. The script is a reformed documentary hand, which is a style of handwriting used in formal or official documents during the Hellenistic period. The hand is decorated and rounded, showing similarities with the Egerton Gospel and P. Oxy. 656 (Genesis), both from the 2nd century.

TEXT TYPE: The Greek text of P90 is a representative of the Alexandrian text-type. The Alexandrian text-type is one of several text types used in textual criticism for categorizing New Testament manuscripts. Alexandrian manuscripts are known for their scrupulous adherence to the text, suggesting a careful copying process from an early stage in their transmission.

TEXTUAL CHARACTER: P90 shows a strong textual affinity with P66, another early Greek manuscript of John's Gospel, but it does not concur with P66 in its entirety. Additionally, it has some textual affinity with Codex Sinaiticus, designated by the Hebrew letter Aleph (א). This suggests that these documents may have been part of a similar textual tradition or may have had a common ancestor.

COMMENTS FROM KURT ALAND: Kurt Aland, a prominent New Testament scholar and co-founder of the Institute for New Testament Textual Research, classified P90 in Category I in his system of categorization. This category is reserved for manuscripts of the New Testament that are at least from the 3rd century and earlier, and which provide a careful and precise text, often aligned with the Alexandrian text type.

COMMENTS FROM BRUCE M. METZGER: Bruce M. Metzger, a well-respected biblical scholar and textual critic, recognized the value of P90 as an early witness to the text of John's Gospel. Although specific comments from Metzger regarding P90 are not provided, his work in New Testament textual criticism often underscored the importance of such early papyrus fragments in understanding the transmission and variants of the New Testament text.

COMMENTS FROM PHILIP W. COMFORT: Philip W. Comfort, a scholar known for his work in New Testament textual criticism, particularly papyrological studies, has noted P90's close textual affinity with P66 and some connection with Codex Sinaiticus (א). Comfort's work emphasizes the significance of these early papyrus fragments, like P90, in shedding light on the early text of the New Testament and its transmission. His recognition of the textual relationships between these manuscripts contributes to a broader understanding of the historical development and reliability of the New Testament text.

Edward D. Andrews

APPENDIX H Papyrus 115 (P115) - A Manuscript of Rev. 2-3; 5-6; 8-15; Dating from Around 225-275 CE

INTRODUCTION: Papyrus 115 (P. Oxy. 4499), often referred to as P115, is a fragmented manuscript of the New Testament written in Greek on papyrus. This papyrus is part of the Oxyrhynchus Papyri collection, discovered by the scholars Bernard Pyne Grenfell and Arthur Hunt in Oxyrhynchus, Egypt. P115 is identified with the Gregory-Aland numbering as 𝔓115 and contains various parts of the Book of Revelation.

CONTENTS: The surviving text of P115 includes passages from the Book of Revelation: 2:1–3, 13–15, 27–29; 3:10–12; 5:8–9; 6:5–6; 8:3–8, 11–13; 9:1–5, 7–16, 18–21; 10:1–4, 8–11; 11:1–5, 8–15, 18–19; 12:1–5, 8–10, 12–17; 13:1–3, 6–16, 18; 14:1–3, 5–7, 10–11, 14–15, 18–20; 15:1, 4–7. There is also evidence of nomina sacra, abbreviations for certain divine names, used in the manuscript.

DATE: The manuscript is dated through paleographical analysis to the middle to late third century (225-275 CE). The handwriting style of P115 resembles two manuscripts from the Heroninos Archive, P. Flor. 108 and P. Flor. 259, which predates 256 CE. It also bears resemblance to P. Oxy. 1016, which predates 234 CE according to a land register on the other side.

HOUSING LOCATION: P115 is currently housed in the Ashmolean Museum in Oxford, England. The Ashmolean Museum is one of the most renowned museums worldwide, boasting an extensive collection of historical artifacts, including the valuable Oxyrhynchus Papyri.

PHYSICAL FEATURES: The manuscript consists of 26 fragments of a codex, likely containing only the Book of Revelation. The original codex was about 15.5 cm by 23.5 cm, with 33–36 lines per page. The document appears to have been written in a codex that was already bound before the scribe began his work, as the width of writing on pages with binding to the right-hand side (even-numbered pages) tends to be narrower than those with binding to the left-hand side (odd-numbered pages).

TEXT TYPE: P115 is a witness to the Alexandrian text-type, aligning with the text of Codex Alexandrinus (A) and Codex Ephraemi Rescriptus (C). This text-type is one of several categories used in textual criticism of the New Testament to group manuscripts based on their shared textual characteristics.

TEXTUAL CHARACTER: One of the notable aspects of P115 is its textual alignment with Codex Alexandrinus (A) and Codex Ephraemi Rescriptus (C), which are generally regarded as providing superior testimony to the original text of Revelation. This makes P115's textual witness significant in the study of the Book of Revelation.

A unique element of P115 is that it gives the number of the beast in Revelation 13:18 as 616 (chi, iota, stigma (XIϚ)), rather than the majority reading of 666 (chi, xi, stigma (XΞϚ)), as does Codex Ephraemi Rescriptus.

COMMENTS FROM KURT ALAND: Kurt Aland, a German theologian and biblical scholar, recognized the importance of papyrus manuscripts like P115 in illuminating the early text of the New Testament. He did not comment directly on P115, but his significant work on categorizing New Testament manuscripts by content, date, and text-type provides a contextual framework for understanding P115's contribution to New Testament textual criticism.

COMMENTS FROM BRUCE M. METZGER: Bruce M. Metzger, a renowned American biblical scholar, has not directly commented on P115, as it was published after his death. However, his extensive work on New Testament textual criticism provides valuable context for interpreting P115. His work emphasizes the importance of early papyri in providing the earliest possible text of the New Testament and helping to clarify textual variants.

COMMENTS FROM PHILIP W. COMFORT: Philip W. Comfort is known for his work in New Testament textual criticism, particularly in papyrological studies. While his direct comments on P115 may not be available, his recognition of the textual relationships between early papyri contributes to a broader understanding of the historical development and reliability of the New Testament text. Comfort's work highlights the significance of these early papyrus fragments, like P115, in shedding light on the early text of the New Testament and its transmission.

Edward D. Andrews

APPENDIX I Papyrus 46 (P46) - A Manuscript of the Pauline Epistles, Dating from Around 100-150 CE

INTRODUCTION: Papyrus 46 (P46) is an ancient Greek manuscript of the New Testament, an early witness to the texts of Pauline Epistles. The papyrus is named after Chester Beatty, a mining engineer who purchased it, and it's often referred to as P. Chester Beatty II.

CONTENTS: The contents of P46 primarily consist of most of Paul's Epistles. It includes substantial parts of Romans, Hebrews, 1 Corinthians, 2 Corinthians, Ephesians, Galatians, Philippians, Colossians, and 1 Thessalonians, with varying levels of completeness. The Pastoral Epistles (1-2 Timothy and Titus) are notably absent.

DATE: The date of P46 is a matter of scholarly debate. Sir Frederic Kenyon originally dated the codex to the early third century, largely based on the handwriting of the stichometrical notes at the end of several epistles. However, other scholars, such as Ulrich Wilcken and Hans Gerstinger, argue that it belongs to the second century, around 200 CE. A later proposal by Young Kyu Kim even suggested a date in the reign of Domitian (81–96 CE). However, a more accepted consensus places P46 in the middle of the second century, allowing time for the formation of the Pauline corpus and its circulation in Egypt.

HOUSING LOCATION: P46 is housed in two locations. Thirty leaves are located at the University of Michigan, Special Collections Library, while fifty-six leaves are part of the Chester Beatty Collection in Dublin, Ireland.

PHYSICAL FEATURES: P46 is composed of papyrus leaves, and its handwriting is considered an upright, informal uncial, reflecting an early style, manifesting sometimes a running hand, while maintaining the upper line. The manuscript has suffered from wear and tear, with many pages damaged or fragmented.

TEXT TYPE: P46 is a representative of the Alexandrian text-type, one of the earliest and most respected text types of New Testament manuscripts.

TEXTUAL CHARACTER: The text of P46 shows a strong affinity with Codex Vaticanus (B), Codex Sinaiticus (ℵ), and the 10th-century Alexandrian manuscript 1739. The manuscript has been corrected by multiple hands, implying that it was well-used, perhaps by various members of a church or monastery. The text exhibits various idiosyncrasies, including the rearrangement of the Pauline Epistles, and placing the Letter to the Hebrews between Romans and 1 Corinthians.

COMMENTS FROM KURT ALAND: Kurt Aland, a renowned New Testament scholar, categorized P46 as Category I, indicating that it is of a very high quality and represents the Alexandrian text-type very well.

COMMENTS FROM BRUCE M. METZGER: Bruce M. Metzger, another leading biblical scholar, acknowledged the significance of P46 as one of the oldest and most extensive witnesses to the Pauline corpus. He also noted the peculiar order of the Epistles in P46, which differs from the canonical order and from most manuscripts.

COMMENTS FROM PHILIP W. COMFORT: Philip W. Comfort, a scholar specializing in textual criticism of the New Testament, opined that P46 likely belongs to the middle of the second century, which allows time for the formation and circulation of the Pauline corpus. He also pointed out that the manuscript was professionally produced and used extensively by various readers, as evidenced by multiple corrections and lectoral marks.

Edward D. Andrews

APPENDIX J Papyrus 47 (P47) - A Manuscript of Revelation 9:10-17:2, Dating from Around 200-225 CE

INTRODUCTION: Papyrus 47 (P47), also referred to as P. Chester Beatty III, is an early Greek New Testament manuscript inscribed on papyrus. The document is of significant value in biblical studies due to its antiquity and the content it carries. Its existence helps scholars analyze variations and similarities in the text of the New Testament, contributing to a more comprehensive understanding of the historical and textual development of biblical writings.

CONTENTS: The contents of P47 include text from the Book of Revelation, specifically chapters 9:10-11:3; 11:5-16:15; and 16:17-17:2. However, due to fragmentation, the manuscript does not provide a complete record of these chapters. The absence of complete text is not unusual in the world of ancient manuscripts where deterioration and damage over centuries can result in partial losses.

DATE: Based on paleographic analysis, which involves the examination and comparison of writing styles, P47 is dated to the beginning of the third century (200-225 CE). Its provenance is believed to be either from the Fayum of Egypt or perhaps the ruins of a church or monastery near Atfih, ancient Aphroditopolis.

HOUSING LOCATION: The manuscript is currently housed in the Chester Beatty Collection in Dublin, Ireland.

PHYSICAL FEATURES: Physically, P47 consists of thirty leaves, measuring approximately 14 cm x 24 cm, with 26-28 lines written per page in a documentary hand. The consistent abbreviation of numerals suggests that the scribe was practiced at making documents. A second corrector (c2) made some additional corrections and darkened many letters, providing further insight into the manuscript's production and later interventions.

TEXTUAL CHARACTER: Textually, the character of P47 is deemed closest to Codex Sinaiticus (represented by the symbol ℵ), making them witnesses for one type of the early textual forms of the Book of Revelation. The text of this manuscript is classified as a representative of the Alexandrian text-type, one of the primary textual families along with Western and Byzantine, which is characterized by specific or generally related readings differing from other groups.

COMMENTS FROM KURT ALAND: Notably, biblical scholar Kurt Aland categorized P47 as a Normal text and placed it in Category I, referring to manuscripts of the New Testament in the original Greek language, of which the character of the text is considered particularly significant.

The commentary provided by scholars offers additional insights into P47's historical and textual significance. For instance, Frederic G. Kenyon, who first examined P47, initially stated that the manuscript was on the whole closest to ℵ and Codex Ephraemi Rescriptus (C), with a bit more distance from Codex Alexandrinus (A). However, further analysis suggested that P47 and ℵ are more closely allied, with A, C, and Papyrus 115 (P115) forming a distinct textual group for Revelation.

COMMENTS FROM BRUCE M. METZGER: Bruce M. Metzger, another esteemed biblical scholar, noted the importance of P47 in understanding textual variance and agreement within the manuscripts of Revelation. Despite the observable differences, Metzger underscored the manuscript's value as an early witness to the text of Revelation.

COMMENTS FROM PHILIP W. COMFORT: Philip W. Comfort, known for his extensive work on New Testament texts, also contributed to the discourse surrounding P47. Like other scholars, Comfort recognized the manuscript's textual character as closest to Codex Sinaiticus and emphasized its contribution to our understanding of the Book of Revelation's textual history.

In conclusion, Papyrus 47 provides a precious glimpse into the textual history of the New Testament, specifically the Book of Revelation. It aids in tracing the evolution and transmission of biblical texts over the centuries. Despite its fragmentary state, P47 continues to be a subject of ongoing study and analysis, offering scholars valuable information about the New Testament's historical and textual development.

Edward D. Andrews

APPENDIX K Papyrus 72 (P72) - A Manuscript of Jude, 1 Peter, 2 Peter, Dating from Around 200-250 CE

INTRODUCTION: Papyrus 72 (P72), also known as P. Bodmer VII and VIII, is an early Greek New Testament manuscript written on papyrus, serving as a valuable historical and academic resource. It contains text from the first and second epistles of Peter and the epistle of Jude, shedding light on the evolution and dissemination of these texts in the early Christian era.

CONTENTS: The contents of P72 include 1 Peter 1:1–5:14; 2 Peter 1:1–3:18; Jude 1–25. In addition to these canonical texts, the document also carries non-canonical writings such as the Nativity of Mary, the apocryphal correspondence of Paul to the Corinthians, the eleventh ode of Solomon, Melito's Homily on the Passover, a fragment of a hymn, the Apology of Phileas, and Psalms 33 and 34.

DATE: Based on paleographic analysis, P72 is dated to the early to middle third century (ca. 200-250). The manuscript is considered part of the Jabal Abu Mana Manuscripts, though it likely comes from a later find in the same vicinity.

HOUSING LOCATION: The codex is currently housed in the Bibliotheca Bodmeriana in Cologny-Geneva, Switzerland, while 1 and 2 Peter are kept in the Biblioteca Vaticana.

PHYSICAL FEATURES: Physically, P72 consists of three parts of a 72-page codex, measuring approximately 14.5 cm x 16 cm, with 16-20 lines written per page. The text of 1 and 2 Peter is paginated from 1 to 36, while Jude is paginated from 62 to 68. The manuscript exhibits a documentary hand and features several marginal topical descriptors beginning with περὶ (concerning).

TEXTUAL CHARACTER: P72's textual character displays a free and often careless transcription of a fairly reliable exemplar. Its text represents the Alexandrian text-type, one of the main textual families along with Western and Byzantine.

COMMENTS FROM KURT ALAND: According to biblical scholar Kurt Aland, 1-2 Peter exhibit a normal text in P72, while Jude displays a free text, each with unique peculiarities. Aland categorizes P72 into Category I, reflecting the significance of its textual character.

Biblical scholars have contributed to our understanding of P72. Michel Testuz, who extensively studied the Bodmer Papyri, underlines the significance of P72 in the study of the epistles of Peter and Jude. Additionally, Carlo M. Martini provided a new transcription for 1 and 2 Peter, enhancing the accuracy of scholarly investigations.

COMMENTS FROM BRUCE M. METZGER: Bruce M. Metzger, another esteemed biblical scholar, recognized the value of P72 as an early witness to the text of these epistles. Despite the observed textual peculiarities and the somewhat uncontrolled text in parts, he highlighted the codex's contribution to textual studies.

COMMENTS FROM PHILIP W. COMFORT: Philip W. Comfort, renowned for his work on New Testament texts, highlighted the manuscript's uniqueness. Comfort noted that while 1 Peter showed clear Alexandrian affinities, especially with Codex Vaticanus (B) and then with Codex Alexandrinus (A), the text of 2 Peter and especially Jude exhibited more of an uncontrolled type, usually associated with the "Western" text. Comfort also noted that P72 is thought to have been produced by four scribes for private use, not for church meetings.

It's worth noting that P72 is the earliest known manuscript of the epistles of Peter and Jude, underscoring its significance for biblical scholarship. It shares a scribe with P. Bodmer X and XI, and it includes the usual nomina sacra, special abbreviated forms used in New Testament manuscripts for several words of significance, along with a few non-standard ones.

To summarize, Papyrus 72, despite its textual peculiarities and the presence of non-canonical writings, offers a unique glimpse into the textual history of the New Testament, particularly the epistles of Peter and Jude. Its combination of canonical and non-canonical texts and its distinctive transcription style make it an important object of study for understanding the dissemination and evolution of Christian texts in the early centuries.

Edward D. Andrews

APPENDIX L Papyrus 137 (P137) The Earliest Fragment of Mark 1:7-9; 1:16-18, Dating from Around 100-125 CE

INTRODUCTION: Papyrus 137 (P137), part of the Oxyrhynchus Papyri, is an early Greek New Testament manuscript written on papyrus that contains a small fragment from the Gospel of Mark. Despite its minimal size, P137 is of significant interest to scholars due to its early date and its contribution to the study of the textual transmission of the Gospel of Mark.

CONTENTS: The contents of P137 include Mark 1:7-8 and Mark 1:16-18, constituting only a small fragment of the larger Gospel. Based on paleographic analysis, the manuscript is dated to the early to middle second century, making it the earliest extant manuscript fragment of the Gospel of Mark.

The provenance of P137 is Oxyrhynchus, Egypt, a location known for its wealth of papyrus findings, making a significant contribution to our understanding of ancient writings and everyday life.

HOUSING LOCATION: Today, this precious artifact is housed in the Ashmolean Museum, located in Oxford, England.

PHYSICAL FEATURES: The physical features of P137 are modest. The fragment preserves parts of the bottom five lines of a leaf, both recto and verso. The fragment may have come from the first page of a single-quire codex, with a proposed original page layout of 25 lines per page and a written area of 9.4cm x 12 cm. Interestingly, on the recto side, the papyrus strips are laid vertically, while on the verso side, they are laid horizontally. Regrettably, the letters on the recto are seriously abraded, affecting legibility.

Due to its small size, the textual character of P137 is challenging to determine definitively. However, the surviving handwriting is noted to be in a formal bookhand, described by the manuscript's editors as having the characteristics of the "Formal Mixed" hand, found in dateable documents from the later second and third centuries.

From the perspective of textual scholar Philip W. Comfort, he would acknowledge the inherent limitations of working with such a small fragment. Even so, they would agree on its historical significance given its early date and status as the earliest known fragment of Mark's Gospel.

The readings of P137 are noteworthy. The term "Holy Spirit" at verse 8 on the recto is abbreviated as a nomen sacrum. Additionally, the dative preposition εν ('in') is not found in P137 either before 'water' or before 'Holy Spirit'. This omission is in contrast to the standard text of Mark in Novum Testamentum Graece (NA28), which includes the dative preposition before 'Holy Spirit'. The omission of 'in' before 'water' and 'Holy Spirit' is in agreement with the reading in the Codex Vaticanus and in editions of the Nestle-Aland Novum Testamentum Graece up to NA25.

In summary, Papyrus 137, despite its small size and fragmentary state, is an essential artifact for understanding the early textual transmission of the Gospel of Mark. Its early date, the unique textual features it presents, and its connection to the important archaeological site of Oxyrhynchus all contribute to its importance in New Testament studies.

APPENDIX M Codex Vaticanus (B or 03): Dating from 300-330 CE

Codex Vaticanus

Codex Vaticanus (also known as Vaticanus B or Codex B) is one of the oldest and most important extant Greek manuscripts of the Bible, dating back to the 4th century CE. It holds immense significance in the field of biblical studies and textual criticism, as it provides critical information for understanding the development and transmission of the biblical text. The codex is housed in the Vatican Library, where it has been since at least the 15th century.

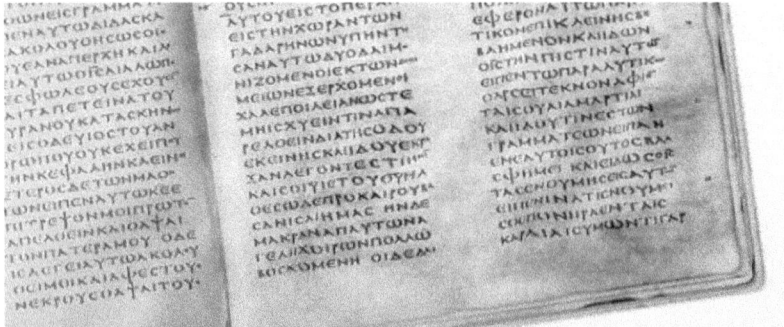

1. **Description and Contents**: Codex Vaticanus is a large parchment codex, consisting of 759 leaves and measuring approximately 27 x 27 cm. It is written in Greek uncial script, which features large, distinct, and rounded letters, with three columns per page. The manuscript originally contained the entire Old Testament, including the Septuagint (the Greek translation of the Hebrew Bible), as well as the New Testament and some early Christian writings, such as the Epistle of Barnabas and portions of the Shepherd of Hermas. However, parts of the manuscript have been lost or damaged over time, and some books are incomplete.

2. **Textual Features**: Codex Vaticanus is considered one of the best witnesses to the Alexandrian text-type, which is characterized by its relative accuracy, brevity, and polished style compared to other text-types. It is particularly valuable for its early and reliable representation of the Septuagint, and it is a key source for reconstructing the original text of the New Testament. The manuscript exhibits numerous corrections and revisions made by different scribes over the centuries, providing insight into the textual history and the scribal practices of the time.

3. **Discovery and Study**: Although Codex Vaticanus has been in the Vatican Library for centuries, its significance was not widely recognized until the 19th century. The renowned German scholar Constantin von Tischendorf was granted access to the codex in the mid-19th century and published its text, bringing its importance to the attention of biblical scholars worldwide. Since then, Codex Vaticanus has become a cornerstone for modern critical editions of the Greek Bible, such as the Nestle-Aland Novum Testamentum Graece and the United Bible Societies' Greek New Testament.

4. **Relationship to Other Manuscripts**: Codex Vaticanus, along with Codex Sinaiticus and Codex Alexandrinus, is part of the group of the three earliest and most significant biblical manuscripts. Codex Sinaiticus, also a 4th-century manuscript, is especially important for its complete New Testament text, while Codex Alexandrinus, from the 5th century, contains the entire Bible with some additional early Christian writings. Together, these three manuscripts provide essential information for the study of the early text of the Bible and the history of its transmission.

In conclusion, Codex Vaticanus is a critically important Greek manuscript of the Bible that has significantly contributed to our understanding of the biblical text's early history and transmission. As one of the oldest extant witnesses to the Alexandrian text-type, it has played a crucial role in shaping modern critical editions of the Greek Bible and remains an invaluable resource for biblical scholars and textual critics.

APPENDIX N Codex Sinaiticus (א or 01): Dating from 330-360 CE

Codex Sinaiticus

Codex Sinaiticus, also known as א or Aleph, is one of the most significant and oldest extant manuscripts of the Greek Bible, dating to the mid-4th century CE. It is an invaluable source for biblical scholars and textual critics, as it provides critical information on the early transmission and development of the biblical text. The codex is currently preserved in various institutions, with the majority of the manuscript held at the British Library in London.

1. **Description and Contents**: Codex Sinaiticus is a parchment codex comprising 400 leaves, each measuring approximately 38 x 34.5 cm. It is written in Greek uncial script, characterized by large, distinct, and rounded letters, with four columns per page. The manuscript originally contained the entire Old Testament, including the Septuagint (the Greek translation of the Hebrew Bible), as well as the complete New Testament, and some early Christian writings, such as the Epistle of Barnabas and the Shepherd of Hermas. Over time, some portions of the manuscript have been lost or damaged, resulting in gaps within certain books.

2. **Textual Features**: Codex Sinaiticus is considered an important witness to the Alexandrian text-type, which is characterized by its relative accuracy, brevity, and polished style compared to other text-types. It is particularly valuable for its early and reliable representation of the Septuagint, and it is a key source for reconstructing the original text of the New Testament. The manuscript displays numerous corrections and revisions made by different scribes over the centuries, providing insight into the textual history and scribal practices of the time.

3. **Discovery and Study**: The story of Codex Sinaiticus's discovery is intriguing. It was found by the German scholar Constantin von Tischendorf during his visits to Saint Catherine's Monastery on Mount Sinai in the 19th century. In 1844, Tischendorf discovered 43 leaves of the codex and later returned in 1859 to find the majority of the remaining manuscript. The codex was subsequently presented to Tsar Alexander II of Russia, who sponsored its publication. In 1933, the Soviet government sold the manuscript to the British Library, where it is now held.

The publication and study of Codex Sinaiticus have significantly impacted the field of biblical studies, particularly textual criticism. The manuscript has been extensively analyzed, and its text has served as a basis for modern critical editions of the Greek Bible, such as the Nestle-Aland Novum Testamentum Graece and the United Bible Societies' Greek New Testament.

4. **Relationship to Other Manuscripts**: Codex Sinaiticus, along with Codex Vaticanus and Codex Alexandrinus, is part of the group of the three earliest and most significant biblical manuscripts. Codex Vaticanus, also a 4th-century manuscript, is especially important for its representation of the Septuagint, while Codex Alexandrinus, from the 5th century, contains the entire Bible with some additional early Christian writings. Together, these three manuscripts provide essential information for the study of the early text of the Bible and the history of its transmission.

In conclusion, Codex Sinaiticus is an indispensable Greek manuscript of the Bible that has considerably contributed to our understanding of the early history and transmission of the biblical text. As one of the oldest and most complete extant witnesses to the Alexandrian text-type, it has played a crucial role in shaping modern critical editions of the Greek Bible and remains an invaluable resource for biblical scholars and textual critics.

APPENDIX P Codex Alexandrinus (A or 02): A 5th-century manuscript

Codex Alexandrinus

Codex Alexandrinus, designated as "A" or "02," is a highly significant and relatively complete manuscript of the Greek Bible, dating to the early 5th century CE. It is an essential resource for biblical scholars and textual critics, providing crucial insights into the early transmission and development of the biblical text. The codex is currently housed in the British Library in London.

1. **Description and Contents**: Codex Alexandrinus is a parchment codex containing 773 leaves, each measuring approximately 32 x 26 cm. It is written in Greek uncial script, characterized by large, distinct, and rounded letters, with two columns per page. The manuscript originally contained the complete Old Testament, including the Septuagint (the Greek translation of the Hebrew Bible), as well as the New Testament, and several early Christian writings, such as the First and Second Epistles of Clement. Over time, some portions of the manuscript have been lost or damaged, resulting in gaps within certain books.

2. **Textual Features**: Codex Alexandrinus is considered an important witness to the Byzantine text-type, characterized by its tendency for expansion and harmonization of parallel passages. However, in some sections, especially the Gospels, the text exhibits mixed characteristics with Alexandrian and Western readings. The manuscript is particularly valuable for its early and relatively complete representation of the Septuagint, and it is an important source for reconstructing the original text of the New Testament.

3. **History and Study**: The exact origins of Codex Alexandrinus remain uncertain, but it is believed to have been produced in Alexandria, Egypt, or its surrounding region. The manuscript was brought to Constantinople in the early 17th century and later presented to King Charles I of England by the Orthodox Patriarch Cyril Lucar in 1627. After the British Museum was established in 1753, the codex was transferred to its manuscript collection, and it is now held in the British Library.

The publication and study of Codex Alexandrinus have significantly impacted the field of biblical studies, particularly textual criticism. The manuscript has been extensively analyzed, and its text has been considered in the preparation of modern critical editions of the Greek Bible, such as the Nestle-Aland Novum Testamentum Graece and the United Bible Societies' Greek New Testament.

4. **Relationship to Other Manuscripts**: Codex Alexandrinus, together with Codex Vaticanus and Codex Sinaiticus, forms the group of the three earliest and most significant biblical manuscripts. Codex Vaticanus, a 4th-century manuscript, is especially important for its representation of the Septuagint, while Codex Sinaiticus, also from the 4th century, contains the entire Bible and some additional early Christian writings. These three manuscripts provide essential information for the study of the early text of the Bible and the history of its transmission.

In conclusion, Codex Alexandrinus is a vital Greek manuscript of the Bible that has contributed greatly to our understanding of the early history and transmission of the biblical text. As one of the oldest and relatively complete extant witnesses to the Byzantine text-type with mixed characteristics, it plays a critical role in shaping modern critical editions of the Greek Bible and remains an invaluable resource for biblical scholars and textual critics.

APPENDIX P Codex Ephraemi Rescriptus (C or 04): A 5th-century Greek manuscript of the Bible

Codex Ephraemi Rescriptus

Codex Ephraemi Rescriptus (C or 04) is a 5th-century Greek manuscript of the Bible that is of significant importance in biblical studies due to its antiquity and the textual variants it contains. Named after Ephraem the Syrian, whose works were written over the biblical text, this codex is a palimpsest, a manuscript in which the original writing has been scraped off and overwritten with a later text.

Introduction

Codex Ephraemi Rescriptus is one of the oldest surviving manuscripts of the Greek Bible. It is designated as 'C' in the Gregory-Aland numbering system and '04' in the von Soden system. The manuscript is written on vellum and contains partial texts of the Old and New Testaments. It is notable for being a palimpsest, a manuscript that has been overwritten on an erased older work.

Contents

Originally, the manuscript likely contained the whole Bible. However, due to its state as a palimpsest, many sections have been lost. Today, it contains 64 leaves of the Old Testament and 145 leaves of the New Testament. The Old Testament portions include sections of the Septuagint version of the Prophets and the Wisdom books. The New Testament sections contain portions of every book except Second Thessalonians and Second John.

Date

Codex Ephraemi Rescriptus is typically dated to the 5th century CE. This dating is based on an analysis of the handwriting, or paleography, of the manuscript.

Housing Location

The codex is currently housed in the National Library of France (Bibliothèque nationale de France) in Paris.

Physical Features

The codex is written on vellum, a type of fine parchment made from animal skin. The pages are approximately 31.4 cm by 26.2 cm. The text is written in one column per page and in scriptio continua, meaning there are no spaces between words. The ink used for the original text is brown, while the Ephraemi text is written in a darker ink. The writing of the original text is in a literary uncial hand, with the newer text in a later minuscule hand.

Text Type

The text type of Codex Ephraemi Rescriptus is mostly Alexandrian, one of the major text types used to classify and group New Testament manuscripts. However, in the Book of Acts and the Pauline epistles, it has a more Western type of text. The text type influences the variant readings found in the codex.

Textual Character

The textual character of the codex is significant due to the unique readings and textual variants it contains. For instance, in Matthew 1:11, it includes the name Amos in the genealogy of Jesus, a reading only shared with a few other manuscripts. In Acts, it contains additional text for Acts 20:32 and lacks text in Acts 8:39, compared to other manuscripts.

APPENDIX Q Codex Bezae (D or 05): A 5th-century manuscript containing most of the four Gospels and Acts, and a small part of III John in Greek and Latin texts

Codex Bezae

Codex Bezae, also known as Codex Cantabrigiensis or designated as "D" or "05," is a distinctive and significant ancient manuscript of the Greek New Testament and the Old Latin version. The manuscript, dating to the 5th century CE, contains the Gospels and Acts of the Apostles in both Greek and Latin, with the two languages presented side by side in parallel columns. Codex Bezae is housed at the Cambridge University Library in England.

1. **Description and Contents**: Codex Bezae is a parchment codex containing 406 extant leaves, each measuring approximately 26 x 21.5 cm. It is written in Greek uncial script and Latin script, with one column per page for each language. The manuscript originally contained the complete text of the four Gospels and Acts of the Apostles, as well as the General Epistle of James and the Third Epistle of John. However, portions of the text have been lost over time, and the surviving leaves are incomplete.

2. **Textual Features**: Codex Bezae is known for its unique textual characteristics, representing the Western text-type, which is marked by extensive additions, omissions, and variations from the standard text. The manuscript is particularly famous for its unusual readings, including some that are not found in any other extant manuscript. The text is often characterized as "free" or "wild," reflecting the scribe's apparent willingness to alter the text, either intentionally or unintentionally. This makes Codex Bezae a crucial resource for understanding the diversity of early Christian textual traditions.

3. **History and Study**: The origin and provenance of Codex Bezae are uncertain, although it is generally believed to have been produced in either southern France or western North Africa. The manuscript was acquired by the French humanist and biblical scholar Theodore Beza in the 16th century, and he later donated it to the University of Cambridge in 1581. Since then, it has been the subject of extensive study and analysis by scholars seeking to understand its unique textual features and the broader history of the New Testament text.

4. **Relationship to Other Manuscripts**: Codex Bezae is one of several important early witnesses to the Western text-type, which includes other Greek, Latin, and Syriac manuscripts. Among these, Codex Bezae is considered one of the most significant due to its bilingual nature and the extent of its textual variations. Other notable manuscripts representing the Western text-type include Codex Washingtonianus, Codex Claromontanus, and the Old Latin versions of the New Testament.

5. **Impact on Biblical Scholarship**: The study of Codex Bezae has had a considerable impact on the field of biblical scholarship, particularly in the area of textual criticism. Its unique textual features have led scholars to reconsider assumptions about the transmission and development of the New Testament text and to explore the complex relationships between various textual traditions. The manuscript has also been influential in the development of theories about the role of scribes and the processes of textual change in the early Christian period.

In conclusion, Codex Bezae is an invaluable manuscript that offers a unique perspective on the textual history of the New Testament. Its distinctive textual features, bilingual nature, and historical significance make it an essential resource for understanding the development and diversity of early Christian textual traditions, as well as the broader history of the New Testament text.

Edward D. Andrews

APPENDIX R Codex Washingtonianus (W or 032): A 4th or 5th-century manuscript of the Gospels

Codex Washingtonianus

Codex Washingtonianus (W or 032) is a 4th or 5th-century Greek manuscript of the Gospels, a valuable artifact for biblical studies due to its age and the unique characteristics of its text. Also known as the Washington Codex, it's one of the oldest known copies of the Gospels and contains several intriguing textual variants and unique readings.

Introduction

Codex Washingtonianus is an ancient manuscript containing the four Gospels of the New Testament. It's also known as Codex Washingtonensis or the Washington Codex due to its current location. In the Gregory-Aland numbering system, it's designated as 'W' or '032'.

Contents

The codex contains the four canonical Gospels in the order of Matthew, John, Luke, and Mark. This sequence is unusual and distinctive, departing from the more commonly observed order in most manuscripts. It also includes a unique and lengthy textual variant known as the "Freer Logion," a post-Resurrection dialogue between Jesus and his disciples, which appears after Mark 16:14.

Date

The dating of Codex Washingtonianus is a matter of scholarly debate. It is typically assigned to the 4th or 5th century CE based on paleographical analysis - the study of its handwriting style.

Housing Location

The codex resides in the Freer Gallery of Art, part of the Smithsonian Institution in Washington, D.C., USA. It was bought in Egypt by Charles Lang Freer, an American industrialist and art collector, and subsequently became a part of his extensive collection donated to the nation.

Physical Features

Codex Washingtonianus is written on parchment, and the manuscript's dimensions are approximately 21 cm by 16 cm. The text is presented in one column per page, with the lines written in a continuously flowing script without breaks between words, a style known as scriptio continua. It includes the Eusebian Canons – an early system of Gospel cross-references – and has several illuminations, an aspect that separates it from most other biblical manuscripts of this age.

Text Type

The text type of the Washington Codex is predominantly Byzantine, the text type found in the majority of later Greek New Testament manuscripts. However, the Gospel of Mark, especially Mark 1-5, exhibits a more 'Western' type of text, which features more substantial variations from the Byzantine text.

Textual Character

The textual character of the Washington Codex is particularly noteworthy because of the unique readings it offers, such as the "Freer Logion" in Mark 16. In general, the textual character is mixed but largely consistent with the Byzantine tradition, with notable exceptions in the early chapters of Mark.

Edward D. Andrews

APPENDIX T Codex Claromontanus (D or 06): A 5th or 6th-century Greek and Latin diglot manuscript of the Pauline Epistles

Codex Claromontanus (D or 06), dating to the 5th or 6th century, is a Greek and Latin diglot manuscript that houses the Pauline Epistles. It is significant for its detailed historical information about the Bible canon, and its text offers unique insights into the evolution of the New Testament.

Introduction

Codex Claromontanus is an ancient Greek and Latin diglot, or bilingual, manuscript of the New Testament. It is designated by 'D' or '06' in the Gregory-Aland numbering system and is named after the Clermont library in France where it was stored in the 18th century.

Contents

The Codex Claromontanus contains the Pauline Epistles, including Hebrews, which was traditionally attributed to Paul in the Western church, though this is generally not accepted in modern scholarship. At the end of the Epistle to Philemon, it has a unique stichometric catalogue (a list with the line numbers of each book) of the Old and New Testaments, which provides valuable historical information about the early Christian canon.

Date

The Codex Claromontanus is typically dated to the 5th or 6th century based on paleographical analysis, the study of its handwriting style.

Housing Location

Currently, the manuscript is held at the Bibliothèque Nationale in Paris, France.

Physical Features

The Codex is written on parchment in uncial letters. It's a bilingual manuscript, with Greek text on the left-hand pages and Latin text on the right-hand pages. The codex has 533 leaves, 26.5 cm by 21.5 cm, with the text written in a single column per page.

Text Type

The Greek text of Codex Claromontanus is of the Alexandrian text-type, which is characterized by a rigorous, academic approach to the copying of texts, with fewer additions and alterations than other text types. The Latin text is of the Western text-type, which is known for more paraphrastic renderings and additional explanatory material.

Textual Character

The textual character of Codex Claromontanus is particularly valued for its stichometric catalogue. The catalogue includes several New Testament apocryphal books and omits some canonical ones, offering a unique perspective on the development of the New Testament canon in the early church.

APPENDIX U Codex Basilensis (E or 07): A 8th-century Greek manuscript of the Gospels

Codex Basilensis (E or 07), an 8th-century Greek manuscript, houses the Gospels and contributes essential insights into the history and evolution of the New Testament text.

Introduction

Codex Basilensis, denoted as 'E' or '07' under the Gregory-Aland numbering system, is an 8th-century Greek manuscript of the New Testament, preserving the text of the four Gospels. The codex is named after the city of Basel, Switzerland, where it currently resides.

Contents

The Codex Basilensis contains the four canonical Gospels of the New Testament: Matthew, Mark, Luke, and John. However, some sections are missing, including Matthew 1:1-25; Mark 1:1-32; Luke 24:46-53; and John 1:1-20.

Date

Paleographical analysis, which examines the manuscript's handwriting style, attributes Codex Basilensis to the 8th century.

Housing Location

The manuscript is currently held at the University Library of Basel, Switzerland.

Physical Features

Codex Basilensis is written on parchment leaves, in the form of a codex. The manuscript measures approximately 27 cm by 21.5 cm. It contains the text of the Gospels written in one column per page, in 23 lines per page. The writing is in Greek uncial script, a majuscule script (written entirely in capital letters) commonly used from the 3rd to 8th centuries CE.

Text Type

The Greek text of Codex Basilensis is of the Byzantine text-type, which is characterized by later, more harmonized readings that may smooth out difficulties and apparent discrepancies in the text.

Textual Character

The textual character of Codex Basilensis is largely Byzantine. However, it exhibits some minor readings that are shared with the earlier Alexandrian text-type. The combination of text-types demonstrates the mixed textual nature of this manuscript and its value in text-critical studies.

APPENDIX V Codex Seidelianus I (H or 013): A 9th-century Greek uncial manuscript containing the text of the four Gospels

Codex Seidelianus I (H or 013), a 9th-century Greek uncial manuscript, provides invaluable insights into the text of the four Gospels and its transmission.

Introduction

Codex Seidelianus I, also known as Codex Mutinensis, is referenced as 'H' or '013' under the Gregory-Aland numbering system. This Greek uncial manuscript of the New Testament dates back to the 9th century and contains the text of the four Gospels.

Contents

The Codex Seidelianus I carries the four canonical Gospels of the New Testament: Matthew, Mark, Luke, and John. It should be noted, however, that some parts are missing or have been supplemented from other manuscripts due to damage or loss over time.

Date

Based on the paleographical analysis of the manuscript, which examines handwriting style, Codex Seidelianus I is generally dated to the 9th century.

Housing Location

Currently, the manuscript is kept at the Biblioteca Estense in Modena, Italy, under the shelfmark 'Greek 71'.

Physical Features

The Codex Seidelianus I is written on parchment leaves and is in the codex form. The text is written in Greek uncial letters (majuscule script) in one column per page, and typically 21 lines per page. The manuscript measures approximately 29.5 cm by 22 cm. It is notable for its clear, careful, and competent scribe's hand.

Text Type

The Greek text of Codex Seidelianus I represents the Byzantine text-type, which is later and more harmonized than other text types, such as the Alexandrian. It is also part of the family 1 in the Gospels, a group of New Testament manuscripts that display a consistent pattern of variant readings.

Textual Character

The text of Codex Seidelianus I is primarily Byzantine, but it belongs to the so-called 'Caesarean text-type', which some scholars suggest is an early offshoot from the Alexandrian text. It presents certain peculiar readings, which add value to its text-critical significance.

APPENDIX W Codex Regius (L or 019): An 8th-century uncial manuscript containing the text of the four Gospels

Codex Regius (L or 019), an 8th-century uncial manuscript, is one of the important textual witnesses to the Greek New Testament, specifically the four Gospels.

Introduction

The Codex Regius, also known as Codex Lectionarius 97, is a Greek uncial manuscript of the New Testament. Designated by the siglum 'L' or '019' in the Gregory-Aland numbering, this manuscript has great historical significance in the study of the New Testament.

Contents

The Codex Regius contains the complete text of the four canonical Gospels in the New Testament: Matthew, Mark, Luke, and John. The order of the Gospels in the codex is Matthew, John, Luke, and Mark.

Date

The Codex Regius is dated to the 8th century, as determined by the script's palaeographic analysis and comparative manuscript studies.

Housing Location

The Codex Regius is currently housed at the Bibliothèque Nationale in Paris, France, with the shelf mark 'Gr. 62'.

Physical Features

The Codex Regius is composed of parchment, written in an uncial script (Greek capital letters), with one column per page and typically 20 lines per page. It measures approximately 26 cm by 21.5 cm. It includes lectionary markings and incipits (initial words of a text) in the margin for liturgical reading.

Text Type

The Greek text of the Codex Regius represents the Alexandrian text-type, also known as the "Neutral Text" tradition. This text-type is typically considered to contain the earliest form of the New Testament text and is characterized by a high degree of purity and consistency.

Textual Character

The Codex Regius is characterized by textual variants aligning with the Alexandrian text tradition, and its readings are often found to be in agreement with other major Alexandrian texts such as the Codex Vaticanus and the Codex Sinaiticus. It does have some Byzantine readings as well, making it a critical witness to the textual history of the Gospels.

Bibliography

Aland, K. a. (1987). *The Text of the New Testament.* Grand Rapids: Eerdmans.

Andrews, E. (2020). *FROM SPOKEN WORDS TO SACRED TEXTS: Introduction-Intermediate New Testament Textual Studies.* Cambridge: Christian Publishing House.

Andrews, E. D. (2023). *ARCHAEOLOGY & THE NEW TESTAMENT.* Cambridge, Ohio: Christian publishing House.

Andrews, E. D. (2023). *GOD'S OUTLAW: William Tyndale and the English Bible.* Cambridge, Ohio: Christian Publishing House.

Andrews, E. D. (2023). *HOW WE GOT THE BIBLE.* Cambridge, OH: Christian Publishing House.

Andrews, E. D. (2023). *THE SCRIBE AND THE TEXT OF THE NEW TESTAMENT: Scribal Activities in the Transmission of the Text of the New Testament.* Cambridge, Ohio: Christian Publishing House.

Bagnall, R. S. (2009). *The Oxford Handbook of Papyrology (Oxford Handbooks).* Oxford, NY: Oxford University Press.

Comfort, P. W. (2005). *ENCOUNTERING THE MANUSCRIPTS: An Introduction to New Testament Paleography and Textual Criticism.* Nashville, TN: Broadman & Holman.

Comfort, P., & Barret, D. (2019). *THE TEXT OF THE EARLIEST NEW TESTAMENT MANUSCRIPTS: Papyri 1-72, Vol. 1 .* Grand Rapids, MI: Kregel Academic.

Comfort, P., & Barret, D. (2019). *THE TEXT OF THE EARLIEST NEW TESTAMENT MANUSCRIPTS: Papyri 75-139 and Uncials, Vol. 2.* Grand Rapids, MI: Kregel Academic.

Elwell, W. A., & Comfort, P. W. (2001). *Tyndale Bible Dictionary.* Wheaton: Tyndale House Publishers.

Gamble, H. Y. (1997). *Books and Readers in the Early Church: A History of Early Christian Texts.* New Haven and London: Yale University Press.

Greenlee, J. H. (1995). *Introduction to New Testament Textual Criticism.* Peabody: Hendrickson.

Hixon, E. G. (2019). *MYTHS AND MISTAKES iN NEW TESTAMENT TEXTUAL CRITICISM.* Downer Groves: InterVarsity Press.

Holmes, M. W. (2007). *"The Apostolic Fathers: Greek Texts and English Translations"*. Grand Rapids, MI: Baker Books.

Hurtado, L. W. (2019). *TEXTS AND ARTIFACTS: Selected Essays on Textual Criticism ans Early Christian Manuscripts.* New York, NY: T & T Clark.

Kenyon Sr., F. G. (1896). *Our Bible and the Ancient Manuscripts: Being a History of the Text and Its Translations.* London: Eyre & Spottiswood.

Metzger, B. (2001). *The Bible in Translation: Ancient and English Versions.* Grand Rapids: Baker Academic.

Metzger, B. M. (1964, 1968, 1992). *The Text of the New Testament: Its Transmission, Corruption, and Transmission.* New York: Oxford University Press.

Metzger, B. M. (1994). *A Textual Commentary on the Greek New Testament.* New York: United Bible Society.

Metzger, B. M., & Ehrman, B. D. (2005). *The Text of the New Testament: Its Transmission, Corruption, and Restoration (4th Edition).* New York: Oxford University Press.

Omanson, R. L., & Metzger, B. M. (2006). *A Textual Guide to the Greek New Testament: An Adaptation of Bruce M. Metzger's Textual Commentary for the Needs of Translators.* Stuttgart: Deutsche Bibelgesellschaft.

Porter, S. E. (2013). *HOW WE GOT THE NEW TESTAMENT: Text, Transmission, Translation.* Grand Tapids, MI: Baker Academic.

Royse, J. R. (1981). *Scribal Habits in Early Greek New Testament Papyri (Ph.D. diss.,).* Berkeley, CA: Graduate Theological Union.

Wegner, P. D. (2006). *A Student's Guide to Textual Criticism of the Bible: Its History Methods & Results.* Downers Grove: InterVarsity Press.

www.ingramcontent.com/pod-product-compliance
Lightning Source LLC
Chambersburg PA
CBHW080910170426
43201CB00017B/2275